world trade policies

the changing panorama, 1920-1953

a series of contemporary periodic surveys by

WORLD TRADE POLICIES

HENRY CHALMERS

Foreword by J. B. Condliffe

UNIVERSITY OF CALIFORNIA PRESS
BERKELEY AND LOS ANGELES 1953

UNIVERSITY OF CALIFORNIA PRESS
BERKELEY AND LOS ANGELES, CALIFORNIA
CAMBRIDGE UNIVERSITY PRESS
LONDON, ENGLAND

LIBRARY OF CONGRESS CATALOG CARD NUMBER: 53-11236

To

SALLIE

who has shared in this venture from the very beginning

FOREWORD

The regulations by which governments control trading transactions across their frontiers do not make inspiring reading. They are detailed, technical, voluminous, and dull. Economists must try to fathom their implications. Customs officers must enforce, and traders must conform to them. But they have few other readers. In recent years they have issued from government printing offices in a never-ceasing stream of legalistic jargon, schedules, and definitions, repulsive to all but the initiated. In times of strain the stream of regulations flows out like a cataract. This mass of orders, regulations, schedules, and interpretations, for the most part written in "gobbledygook," piles up in customhouse files and defies analysis by all but the most patient specialists. It has often been used to illustrate and justify Thomas Carlyle's definition of political economy as "the dismal science."

By Carlyle's test, however, all science is dismal. The wonder-working formulae of the experimental scientists are not arrived at simply by a glamorous process of creative and imaginative thought. They are not facile and cloudy generalizations derived by the intuition of supermen from scraps of evidence and personal prejudices. Behind them lies the patient drudgery of experiment, drudgery that is shared by great numbers of trained experimenters upon whose detailed results, as well as upon the imaginative insight of the men who contribute the final synthesis, all scientific discovery rests. In his laboratory, the scientist works with materials that are generally minute and mostly dull in themselves. Sometimes, indeed, they are repulsive—

> . . . the flaccid tissues of long-dead issues,
> Offensive to God and mankind.

Out of this unpromising material, the scientist, by patient and laborious research, slowly gleans an understanding of mechanisms and processes. He is often confused, uncertain, baffled, and frustrated. But ultimately his understanding builds up into tested scientific knowledge.

In many respects, the raw material from which an economist must wring an understanding of the mechanisms and processes by which the work of the world goes on is more complicated than the materials with which the chemists and physicists and even the biologists work. Economic data are derived from the actions and motivations of men, individually and in organized groups. They can never be arrested for closer observation, repeated, or even dissected into their elements. Life is a unity in constant process of change.

It is all the more desirable, therefore, that important aspects of the changing scene shall be accurately recorded for historical analysis. This is what Henry Chalmers has done in regard to commercial policy. The method by which he has worked is scientific in the true sense of that word, as meaning organized knowledge. From a mass of material he has distilled an account of events which is coherent and has meaning. His detailed sources were the dull technicalities of specific actions by governments all over the world. In his hands these sources become not only meaningful but of lively interest, since they throw a flood of light upon the disintegration of the economic system by which men and nations had coöperated for more than a century, and upon the complexities that confront any effort to build a new system of world trade.

Once governments embark upon the regulation of trade, there is no escape from complex technical detail. Trade across national boundaries is protean. The enterprise of traders offers scope for infinite ingenuity. The variety of commodities traded in, and the more subtle variety of payments, ramify in more complex fashion than do the circulatory and nervous systems of the human body, with which they have often been compared. Trade is in truth the lifeblood of the economic system and there is much evidence that many in government offices who began to regulate it were unaware of the intricate nature of its operations. Hence the continuing stream of edicts, rising to a flood in every crisis.

The collection of this material is beyond the capacity of any private individual. As many economists have discovered, to their consternation, it pours in from every country till it becomes almost unmanageable and incomprehensible in its detail. Mr. Chalmers has had at his command the most far-flung agency of collection in the world—the reporting services of United States missions and consulates all over the world. In these days, when the foreign service of our country is subject to carping criticism based upon notions of diplomacy that are naïve, the faithful service of those who year in and year out have striven to report facts from abroad, pleasant and unpleasant, which bear upon our prosperity and security, deserves a word of recognition. We can never understand the world we live in, or frame intelligent policies to cope with its frustrations, unless this material continues to be reported honestly and fully.

But more is necessary than the mere accumulation of the crude facts. By their sheer bulk, to say nothing of their technicality, they cannot be used by those who must frame policy. The nonspecialist certainly cannot gain from them any clear notion of what has been happening. They must be sorted, classified, and analyzed before their meaning becomes evident. This is the task that Mr. Chalmers has performed now for well over a quarter of a century. Part of his work, a laborious part, might be likened to that performed by the ingenious mechanical contrivances into which punched cards are fed, to be sorted and counted. Only those who have wrestled at first hand with the labor of bringing some sort of order out of the heterogeneous bulk of trading and payments regulations can fully appreciate the endurance, patience, and skill he has brought to this task. In all research, mechanical drudgery is inescapable. The really productive research worker knows that, whatever mechanical or human assistance he may be able to command, his insight into the material he is working on depends upon mastering this material in detail by his own effort. In fact, like most significant scientific workers, Mr. Chalmers has, in all but the collection of material, plowed a lonely furrow. Consultation and criticism have been available, but the essential labor has been his own.

Consultation and criticism, moreover, are most effective at the stage of analysis that involves interpretation after the data have been classified and analyzed. Preliminary formulation of hypotheses which offer a consistent explanation of the facts that have been analyzed is always an uncertain process. At this stage, the researcher must submit his hypotheses to the rigorous criticism of his fellow workers. Angles and emphases of interpretation that have escaped him are brought to his attention, judgments are checked, and any tendency to the riding of hobbyhorses is eliminated. All this is a familiar process in research. Where experiment is possible as in chemistry, physics, and biology, there are objective tests to be applied. In social studies, the only substitute for such objective tests is the critical judgment of informed specialists in the field.

The annual reports that Mr. Chalmers has made for the United States Department of Commerce since 1928 have gone through these processes of assembling, classifying, and analyzing the measures of trade regulation adopted by governments all over the world. It is no small feat to compress thousands of pages of data into the compass of a single short article. That this feat was successfully accomplished is indicated by the fact that these annual articles can now be reprinted without alteration. They are technical, but they are written in the American language, without technical jargon. Read continuously, they recall in vivid, reportorial style, the events of recent years. The effect is almost like that produced by the staccato realism of a stream-of-consciousness novel. They are shot through with judgments and observations, the validity of which have been attested by later developments. Thus, in 1931, before exchange control systems had emerged from the experimental stage of devices for debt collection, Mr. Chalmers foresaw that they would become the central agencies of trade regulation. In 1943, at the height of their seeming triumph, he could observe the weakening of the Axis powers and of Japan through their failure to organize well trade with the areas they had overrun. It is a significant fact that after Japan had in its grasp "all the wealth of the Indies," it could not make use of its conquest, and therefore was weakened rather than strengthened by its military successes. The realistic insight of these annual surveys was further demonstrated when, as early as 1947, Mr. Chalmers pointed out that the dollar shortage was the result, rather than the cause, of the inability of certain European countries to pay for all the imports they desired. In subsequent years much was made of this concept of the dollar gap, but in his closing chapter, Mr. Chalmers reports that by 1952 it was being realized that the causes of dollar shortage were to be found mainly abroad rather than in the United States.

The story these pages reveal is first of all the story of the disintegration of the trading system, based on Western Europe, by which the world had lived and expanded throughout the nineteenth century. Too evident is the extension of nationalism into the economic sphere. No moral is drawn. The facts are merely recorded. But there can be no misconception of their meaning. The subheadings, chapter by chapter, are illuminating. They are much concerned with "short-run measures to meet shifting situations," with "commercial shifts resulting from military developments," with the "failure of hopes of collective action" which prompted "more drastic national measures." This is the record of a breakdown in the central regulatory mechanisms and their replacement by decentralized, *ad hoc* expedients.

It is interesting to see the reflection of this breakdown in the difference between the two postwar periods that are covered. The first paragraph of the book, introducing a survey of commercial policies in the years 1920–1923, is optimistic. The movement for extremely high tariffs and restrictive trade measures appeared to have spent its force. Europe was moving toward reconciliation and reconstruction. It would not be long before a hopeful, but vain, attempt would be made to restore the international gold standard that had worked so well in the past. There is no parallel optimism after World War II. The gold standard, restored in 1925, never worked effectively in the changed conditions after World War I. It limped along for six years, but broke down in 1931. In the eight years that have now elapsed since the end of World War II, there has never been any real hope of its revival. Faith in the drastic discipline of national adaptation to an international monetary standard has revived very slowly. Nationalism was too strongly entrenched.

What is of even greater interest, however, is the concluding chapter in which Mr. Chalmers summarizes the international economic outlook as he saw it in the summer of 1953. The views of one whose working life has been spent in mastering the detailed complexities of international economic relations are worth pondering. It would be presumptuous to attempt in a few sentences to summarize what is already severely summarized as the considered conclusions of a lifetime. With certain aspects of those conclusions, however, it seems impossible to disagree. The basic problems must be solved nationally. World trade must be rebuilt from the ground up. The present equilibrium between the nations is precarious. Even a mild depression might destroy it. Those countries that have brought their own economies into a situation where uncontrolled inflation is no longer a menace have progressed furthest toward equilibrium in their international payments. Once the national economies have been brought into healthier economic condition, the best hope of restoring a freely working and expanding system of world trade lies in "concerted rather than collective action." To this end the *General Agreement on Tariffs and Trade* offers a vehicle of gradual but sure improvement in trade relations. Such conclusions, here somewhat boldly and freely interpreted, reflect the wisdom that comes only from complete objective understanding and insight.

In all this the United States has a part to play, but only a part. It is a great part since we are now the most productive community in the world, the largest potential source of capital, and the greatest trading market. What applies to other peoples applies to us. The greatest contribution we can make to economic order in the world is to maintain a strong, free, and stable economy at home. In some respects these are not entirely compatible objectives of policy. A free economy is a developing economy, liable to short-term interruptions of stability; but stability ought not to be regarded as synonymous with rigidity. Indeed, biology teaches us that flexibility within a narrow range is an essential element of organic stability.

Such an economy in the United States cannot be maintained for long, if it continues to be exploited by minority groups whose interests are protected at the expense of the general welfare. Whether we like it or not, we are a part, indeed the dynamic, dominant part, of what remains of the free world community, as dependent upon the rest of that community as it is dependent on us. As the years pass, our dependence increases, for markets, for raw materials, for capital outlets, and ultimately for allies. We cannot strengthen our security and surround ourselves by dependable allies if we do not allow friendly peoples to earn their way by trading with us. This has been said very often, but despite reiteration it is the least understood and most neglected economic truism of our time.

Mr. Chalmers deals with the central international economic question of the day. He has contributed heavily over many years to our understanding of this question. Like everyone interested in this field, so vital to our progress and prosperity, I have learned much from him. It is an honor and a privilege to be allowed to introduce the fruits of his labor to a wider audience.

J. B. Condliffe

PREFACE

The distinctive character of this volume is derived from two facts. It brings together a series of periodic surveys of current events in the broad field of commercial policy over the past generation; and it represents the appraisal of those events by the same objective observer, surveying the scene from the same vantage point, year after year.

These successive panoramic sketches have been collected in response to the urging of a number of students in the field that there would thus become available a unique continuous account of an important aspect of recent economic history. It is not a retrospect over the course of foreign trade policies since World War I as it might be appraised today, with the benefit of hindsight. In fact, to retain the current atmosphere of each period and the judgment of events as they appeared to a contemporaneous observer, it was felt that the articles should be reprinted substantially as they originally appeared. No attempt has therefore been made to retouch, in the light of subsequent events, the judgments expressed at the time. The changes that have been made are essentially editorial in nature, such as revision of titles and subheads, recasting of footnotes, and occasional transfer or consolidation of passages for compactness.

However, since each article picks up where the preceding one left off, there is an inherent continuity in the material itself. Reading them in succession, one can easily follow the broad general shifts in the commercial policies of the nations from year to year, as well as the major regional currents and cross currents, as influenced by the changing pressures in the world climate during this tumultuous period.[1] To emphasize this continuity, each chapter has been given a title that characterizes the dominant feature or mood of its period. This is then amplified by subheads which highlight, in predominantly narrative form, the principal developments within the period. These subheads are reproduced in the table of contents, to bring together the salient events that build up to the general characterization of each period, and at the same time to serve as a rough index to the volume.

A few words on how the initial article came about will indicate the method and viewpoint which guided the preparation of the whole series. That appraisal of how the countries of Europe were readjusting their foreign trade relations during the first few years after the War of 1914–1918,[2] made at the close of 1923, was based upon two years' observation of events from Washington, with the aid of the constant inflow of Foreign Service reports and foreign publications, supplemented by several months' first-hand study of the situation in the principal countries of Western and Central Europe. The impulse for its preparation came from the fact that no comprehensive account was available of the many and unusual trade control measures to which the European countries were resorting during that critical period of postwar readjustment. Moreover, it seemed important not only to bring together the facts, but also to go behind them to motives and objectives, to see whether the events followed any general patterns and whether they added up to definite trends.

About three years later, the request of *Current History Magazine* for an article on the significance of certain new turns in European commercial relations—particularly the first postwar trade rapprochement between France and Germany—afforded the occasion for a review of the general developments in foreign trade policies since the first article. The practice of annually preparing similar reviews and appraisals was begun in 1928 and continued without interruption until 1952. Written at first for the *American Year Book,* these articles soon found their regular place in the official organ of the Department of Commerce (*Commerce Reports,* and its

[1] Since most of the articles constituting the chapters of this book originally appeared at intervals of about a year, and sometimes in sections printed weeks apart, each needed to be self-contained. The reader of successive chapters may therefore find a certain amount of repetition, in the way of background information or definitions of terms and common practices. For such unavoidable repetition, the author begs tolerance.

[2] In the chapters dealing with the 1920's and 1930's, any mention of "the war" or the "World War" is to be understood to refer to the War of 1914–1918, known only later as World War I.

successor, *Foreign Commerce Weekly*), appearing shortly after the close of each year.

The annual series is uniform in scope. Each article endeavored to bring together and analyze the outstanding developments and emerging trends in the commercial policies of the principal countries during the year just ended, appraising them against the background of the general international scene at the time. The reviews have varied somewhat in length and detail, mainly in accordance with the varying complexity and significance of the events of particular years. However, they have been consistent in their coverage and viewpoint, and based throughout on the same exceptional body of information and interpretation that was available to the author in connection with his daily work.

Since the author's official function has been primarily to follow the tariffs and commercial policy of foreign countries, the reviews for the early years made little direct mention of actions by the United States. Since the depression years, however, it has become generally recognized that the commerical policy measures of the United States counted heavily in the world complex, and important expressions of American policy naturally found their place in the annual reviews of current trade relations between the nations.

To round off the volume, a brief closing chapter has now been added, which attempts to appraise the prospect in general international trade policy in the summer of 1953, three years after the outbreak of hostilities in Korea.

The author wishes to acknowledge his basic indebtedness to the Department of Commerce, his connection with which afforded him access to the large body of original information on which these studies were mainly based; to the far-flung corps of Commercial Attachés and other Foreign Service Officers of the United States, whose dispatches have constituted the major part of the basic material used; and finally, to his colleagues in the Department of Commerce for the data and comment they have generously afforded him. To *Current History Magazine* and *The American Year Book,* thanks are extended for permitting the use of certain material originally prepared for them.

To Professor Arthur W. Cole of Harvard University, Chairman of the Committee for Research in Economic History, the author is indebted for originally suggesting the idea that these studies be brought together into a collected volume; to Dr. James T. Shotwell, President Emeritus of the Carnegie Foundation for International Peace, go warm thanks for his help in advancing the project; and to Professor John B. Condliffe of the University of California, appreciation for his invaluable assistance in bringing it to fruition.

Henry Chalmers

Washington, D. C.
September, 1953

CONTENTS

1920–1923

Extreme Postwar Trade Restrictions Moderated As Disorganization Diminishes 1

Postwar European Upheaval in Foreign Trade Controls — *Dominance of strong nationalistic sentiments* — *Complications of unstable prices and currencies* — General Movement for Tariff Revision Upward — *Piecemeal revisions by administrative action* — *New states seek economic self-sufficiency* — Import and Export Restrictions and Licensing Systems — *Trade restrictions induced by depreciated currencies* — Anti-dumping Duties and Related Abnormal Exchange Measures — *Spread of multiple tariffs and customs surtaxes* — Postwar Movements for Revision of Commercial Treaties — *Weakening of most-favored-nation balance wheel* — *Tendency toward preferential tariff concessions* — Signs of Moderation of Restrictive Trade Policies — *Tempering of tariffs and restrictions by treaties* — *Growing stabilization of market levels and currencies* — *Assertive trade nationalism becoming less marked* — Revival of Most-favored-nation Treaty Arrangements — *Revised United States commercial treaty policy* — Significance of the Geneva Customs Conference

1924–1926

Trade Policies Move Toward Less Restrictive and More Stable Basis 23

European Restrictionist Attitudes Softening — Tariff Revisions and Administrative Controls Widespread — Prevalence of Import and Export Restrictions in Europe — Germany Extreme Example of Postwar Tightening and Relaxation — Some Special Situations Still Bring New Restrictions — Treaty Negotiations Mark the Settling Down Process — Restoration of Germany to Status of Trade Equality — Progress in United States Commercial Treaty Program

1927

Moderating Tendencies Evolve Into Programs Through Treaties and Conferences 32

Europe — *Increased import duties moderated by negotiations* — *Proposed convention for abolition of trade restrictions* — Latin America — *Upward tariff revisions, mostly for revenue* — British Empire — *Canada and West Indies exchange tariff preferences* — The Orient — *Persia, Siam, and China seek tariff autonomy* — Economic Rapprochement — *Moves toward closer trade relations among groups of European countries* — International Conferences — *Series of meetings seek agreement upon more liberal trade practices*

1928

Distinct Progress Toward Tariff Stability and Moderation of Trade Restrictions 39

Slowing up in Tariff Revisions and License Restrictions — Europe — *Duty reductions and license removals more frequent* — *More liberal provisions being embodied in treaties* — Latin America — *Tariff overhaulings less frequent* — *Duty exemptions for productive equipment more common* — British Empire — *Tariff preferences slowly expanding* — *Malaya and Ceylon terminate crude rubber restrictions* — The Orient — *China and Persia announce autonomous tariffs*

1929

Relative Lull Follows Trade Policy Readjustments of First Postwar Decade 46

Few Important Markets Institute Major Tariff Changes — Exceptional Control Measures Experimented with for Farm Relief — Principal Countries Effecting or Considering Tariff Revisions — European Countries Negotiate Many Trade-stabilizing Treaties — International Conferences — *Agreement for free exportation of hides and bones effective — Convention to end general license restrictions in doubt — Briand's proposal for a "United States of Europe" — American Republics move toward simpler customs regulations*

1930

General Economic Depression Becomes Dominant Influence on Commercial Policies 53

Economic Nationalism Intensified by the Depression — Protection of Home Market and Prices Prime European Aim — Low World Prices and Reduced Exports Worry Latin and British Areas — Continental Europe — *Emergency measures reflect special concern for farm producers — Various proposals for joint remedial action, all unpromising* — British Empire — *Widespread trade control changes in overseas areas — Action postponed on proposals for enlarged Empire preferences* — Latin America — *Many export control changes to stimulate foreign buying* — Near and Far East — *Chinese tariff revised upward — Egypt installs autonomous tariff with differentiated rates*

1931

Market Shrinkages and Financial Crises Prompt Drastic Trade Control Measures 67

National Emergency Measures Threaten Further to Contract World Trade — Concern for Financial Solvency and Currency Values Bring Exchange Controls — Restrictive Measures by

One Country Provoke Defensive Action by Others — Resort to Unusual Methods of Export Stimulation to Move Surpluses — Continental Europe — *Great diversity of trade control objectives and measures — Required mixing of certain domestic with imported products — Revival of import quotas, for trade balance and protection — Efforts to facilitate trade by special treaties, bilateral and regional — Exchange restrictions prompted by financial crises become trade controllers* — British Empire — *Britain abandons the gold standard and traditional limited-tariff policy — Various Empire areas tighten up on imports by administrative action* — Latin America — *Revenue and trade balance chief objectives of the many trade control changes — Much discussion of economic agreements, regional and overseas* — Asia and Africa — *Much changing of tariffs for diverse purposes — Persian foreign trade made a state monopoly — International agreements for export control of tin and sugar*

1932

Economic Difficulties Under Deepening Depression Shape Course of Trade Policies 91

Trade Barriers Increased in More Than Half of the Important Markets — Efforts to Reduce Imports to Lowered Level of Exports — Current Hopes Rest upon Coming World Economic Conference — Continental Europe — *Spread of import quota or license restrictions — Exchange restrictions, often discriminatory, become dominant control — Efforts to temper restrictions by bilateral clearing agreements — Proposed special trade arrangements to aid Danubian states — North European plans for prior consultations and progressive reductions* — British Empire — *Britain adopts general tariff system, mainly on non-Empire products — Ottawa Conference results in wide extension of Empire preferences — Significance of general trade commitments at Ottawa — Preferences effected mainly by additional handicaps on non-Empire goods — New British tariff made basis for bargaining with foreign countries — Depreciated currencies operate as additional barrier to imports from outside* — Latin America — *Reduced purchasing power prime limitation upon imports — Relative absence of quotas and similar import restrictions — Treaty negotiations active, with tendency toward special concessions*

1933

Failure of Hopes for Collective Action Prompts More Drastic National Measures 113

London Economic Conference Fails — General Return to National Expedients only Worsens Situation — Continental Europe — *Import quotas and exchange controls become trade bargaining weapons — Period marked by short-run measures to meet shifting situations* — British Empire — *Program for trade integration of the Empire areas spreads — Import quotas and guarantees prominent in Britain's new pacts — International agreements for export control of wheat, tea, and tin* — Latin America — *Availability of exchange still the prime trade determinant — Contrast between British and United States trade offers to Latin America*

1934

Great Activity in Trade Controls Nets Little Easement in Over-all Restrictions 121

Revival of Foreign Trade Lagging Behind Internal Recovery — Reciprocal Agreements Often Trade Diverting Instead of Enlarging — Bilateral Balancing Idea Hampering World Trade Recovery — New United States Trade Agreement Program Aims at Trade Expansion — Continental Europe — *Quantitative controls become chief method of regulating trade — Quota bargaining frequent feature of European trade pacts — Growth of centralized import controls over foods or materials — Financial pressures prompt efforts at bilateral trade balancing — Unsatisfactory operation of clearing and compensation agreements* — Latin America — *Unlike Europe, import duties remain prime trade control measures — Better raw material prices allow freer exchange operations — Important differences in types of recent trade agreements* — British Empire — *Duties continue dominant, with Empire preferences growing — Treaty negotiations of diverse types and purposes — International agreements for export control of tin and rubber*

1935

Domestic Economic Recovery Brings Some Relaxation of Foreign Trade Barriers 136

Continental Europe — *Many trade control changes but no clear policies or consistent programs — Quantitative controls continue dominant — Trade pacts deal mainly with quotas, usually on exclusive balanced basis — Evidences of reaction against trade-contricting policies — Beginnings toward more liberal trade controls — War in Ethiopia prompts limitations on trading with Italy* — British Empire — *British fostering of home agriculture and stop-loss trade agreements — Canada and United States exchange tariff concessions, reversing recent policies — Australia revises tariff downward; South Africa sets penalty duties — Differing experiences of international export controls on rubber and tin* — Latin America — *"Correcting" bilateral balances by raising duties or restricting exchange — Recovery in exports and prices allow some relaxation of import controls — Readiness for concessions in trade-easing agreements — Stiffer attitude in pacts with countries pressing for trade balancing — Further reciprocal trade easements between South American neighbors — Wide resort to subsidies and other aids to staple exports*

1936

Trade Recovery Favored by Improving Conditions Held Back by Uncertainties 154

Year Marked by Two Opposing Types of Developments — German Program Extreme Example of Subsidies and Tied Sales — Reviving Economic Activity Stimulates Freer Flow of Commerce — United States Trade Agreements Give Lead to Liberalization — Gold Bloc Countries Devalue and Ease Trade Controls — Progress in Trade Liberalization Deterred by Uncertainties

1937

Easement of Depression Tensions Encourages Relaxation of Emergency Measures 160

Year Sees Net Progress in Checking Depression-born Restrictions — Japan, Germany, and Italy Move Toward Greater Restrictiveness — More Typical Are the Moves Toward Trade Barrier Moderation — "Oslo Powers" Begin Joint Action for Reducing Trade Restrictions — Proposed United Kingdom–United States Trade Negotiations Raise High Expectations — Improvement in Demand, Prices, and Financial Stability Favorable Factors — Some Doubts as to Stability of Recovery Counsel Caution — Trade Expansion Stimulated by Rearmament Regarded Dubiously — Closed-economy Programs of Totalitarian States Cause Concern

1938

Incipient Trade Liberalizing Moves Checked by Recession and Political Tensions 168

Late Upturn in American Economy Reverses Earlier Trade Slump — Political Apprehensions over German Program Create Uneasiness — United States, United Kingdom, and France Protest Japan's Trade Violations in China — Moves Toward Trade Barrier Liberalizations — *United States agreements with United Kingdom and others important impulse to freer trade — Unilateral tariff reductions and restriction easements encouraging* — Moves Toward Greater Trade Restrictions — *Bountiful harvests bring reversal of 1937 easings of grain trade — "Oslo Powers" give up joint effort for trade control relaxations — Declines in exports and prices prompt primary producers again to restrict imports — Drastic state control of Japanese economy extends to foreign trade* — Examination of Spread of Barter Trade and the Reactions to It — *Germany and Italy intensify tightly controlled compensation deals — Special concern over German deals with the Balkans and Latin America — Analysis of trade results finds German relative gains quite limited — Over 70 per cent of world trade still on open competitive basis — United Kingdom and United States take steps to offset barter trade and stiffen resistance*

1939

Outbreak of War Brings Wide Resort to Precautionary Trade Controls and Deals 181

PREWAR PERIOD (BEFORE SEPTEMBER 1)

Europe — *Wide adoption of precautionary trade measures against possible emergencies — Basic trade control changes following territorial occupations* — British Empire — *United Kingdom and United States arrange bulk exchange of rubber for cotton as war reserves — The other British areas proceed with more normal trade programs* — Latin America — *Early months relatively uneventful in trade controls* — Far East — *Japan tightens hold on China; United States denounces treaty with Japan*

WARTIME PERIOD

Europe — *General move for centralized controls over all economic life — Trade control machinery of neutrals primarily precautionary — Belligerents' contraband controls prime restriction on commerce with neutrals — Destination control prime object of export-licensing systems — Britain and France restrict imports to conserve exchange and shipping — Close Anglo-French economic collaboration includes trade and currencies — British and French imports of American goods selective, to conserve dollars — Neutrals negotiate to maintain normal trade against opposing pressures — Strenuous rivalry of belligerents for products of the Balkans* — British Empire — *Wartime controls advance commercial integration of sterling areas — Dominions apply their administrative trade controls lightly — British purchase or price undertakings for staple Empire exports* — Latin America — *Obtaining supplies and conserving stocks objects of trade control measures — French and British engage for Argentine staples under tied sales*

1940

Spread of the War Causes Sharp Shifts in World Trade and Controls 201

Increased Demands for War Supplies Offset Drop in Normal United States Exports — Continental Europe — *Spread of war and contraband controls determine trade possibilities — Areas annexed militarily usually lose customs identity — Germany directs economies and trade of "independent" occupied areas — Progressive shrinkage of areas accessible to overseas trade — Neutrals centralize regulation of foreign as well as domestic transactions — Negotiations between reachable areas center on obtaining supplies — Germany intervenes in arrangements between neutral and occupied areas — Germany tries to adjust arbitrarily terms of trade with other Europeans — Trade arrangements of European overseas territories vary greatly — Britain promises to maintain economies of Free French Africa and Belgian Congo — Netherlands Indies treated like sterling bloc by eastern British areas* — British Empire — *Desire to maintain normal trade gives way to needs of war effort — Britain seeks imports, officially selected, and preferably from Empire sources — Pressure to curtail civilian purchases and to conserve shipping — Credit balances from British imports made usable only for sterling products — Empire trade oriented to Britain's needs and restricted with others — Many Empire staples purchased by Britain or used as "exchange arsenals"* — Far East — *Trading conditions restricted with Japan and occupied China* — Latin America — *Loss of continental European markets the dominant problem — Increase in replacement purchases from United States greater than in sales — South American exchange shortages prompt more import restrictions — Arrangements with United Kingdom and United States for disposal of surpluses — Local crop supports by official purchases or required mixing — Financial aid from United States for immediate needs and long-term development — Plans for intensifying economic relations of American Republics*

1941

Year of Commercial Deterioration Climaxed by Pearl Harbor and World-wide War 229

Far East — *Japanese attacks close off already shrunken Far East trade — Japan aims at self-sufficient regional economic bloc under her direction — German invasion of Russia plus British blockade cut Japan's trade routes — United States, British Empire, and Netherlands Indies apply economic sanctions to Japan — Japanese program exemplified by commercial subordination of Indo-China* — British Empire — *United States Lend-Lease Act allows Britain to ease export drive — Volume of goods supplied Britain under Lend-Lease far exceeds normal trade — Empire areas tighten import controls in support of war program — Canada and United States coördinate production programs to aid democracies — British extend support undertakings for Empire staples* — Latin America — *Increased United States purchases and support programs avert economic crises — General financial improvement allows relaxation of import controls — United States undertakes to facilitate supplying essential import needs of Latin America — Interlocking hemispheric controls to prevent undesired reëxportations — United States allocates scarce products on basis of joint requirements surveys — United States makes bulk purchase agreements for Latin American strategic products — Local support of undisposable surpluses and diversification of production — Long-term moves for closer inter-American economic relations* — Continental Europe — *Conquests progressively cut off continent from overseas trade — British blockade plus all-American export license controls restrict external supplies — Further German steps toward commercial absorption of conquered areas — German exploitation of occupied areas through one-sided trade transactions — German rigid supervision of external trade of occupied areas — German pressure on neutrals through trade, credit, and price arrangements — Trade arrangements between Italy and other European countries — Required trade settlements through Berlin presage "New European Order"*

1942

As War Becomes Global, Normal Trade Relations Eclipsed by Emergency Arrangements 259

FORCES CONTROLLING TRADE WITHIN THE AXIS AND THE NON-AXIS WORLDS

The Two Axis-dominated Regions Blockaded and Separated — Trade Routes to Most Other Areas Kept Open by Allied Navies — War Demands on Commodities and Shipping Curtail Civilian Commerce — Differences Between the Axis and Allied Pooling of Resources — Cash and Private Trade Not Displaced by Intergovernmental Shipments — Trade Determined More by Controls of Exporting than of Importing Country — Axis Intensifies Efforts for Commercial Absorption of Controlled Areas

ECONOMIC POOLING AND LEND-LEASE OPERATIONS AMONG THE ALLIES

Unprecedented Movements Superimposed on Traditional Trade Patterns — Moves for Concerted Economic Action Broadened Since Pearl Harbor — British-American Combined Boards Act for All Friendly Nations — Joint Plans for Supplying Needs of Special Areas and for Preclusive Buying — Suspension of Usual Duties and Controls on Products for Official Use — Spread of Lend-Lease Principle Among the Allied Nations — *Operation of United States Lend-Lease program: volume, composition, and destinations — Lend-Lease operations of United Kingdom, Canada, and other United Nations — Increasing reciprocal Lend-Lease aid to United States forces abroad — Bearing of Mutual Aid arrangements on postwar trade policy*

1943

Trade Conditions Worsen in Axis Regions While Improving Among Allies 281

COMMERCIAL SHIFTS RESULTING FROM MILITARY DEVELOPMENTS

Access to Mediterranean Basin Curtailed for Axis; Enlarged for Allies — Smaller Shifts in Pacific Region, Also to Allies' Advantage

TRADE TRENDS OUTSIDE THE AXIS REGIONS

General Features of Current Limitations on Civilian Trade — Improvements in Allied Shipping Allows Freer Flow of Many Products — Expansion of United States–Canadian Output Allows More Goods for Civilian Trade

TRADE TRENDS WITHIN THE AXIS REGIONS

Conditions of Trading for the German-controlled Territories — Shortages of Supplies Plus Bombing Damage to Plants and Transport — Mounting Complaints over Uncompensated Exports to Germany — Stiffening Attitude of Neutrals Against Further Credits to Germany — Limited Outside Trade Contacts of European Neutrals — Sinkings Cut Down German-Japanese Exchanges of Scarce Products — Japan Unable to Utilize Products or Supply Needs of "Southern Regions" — Southern Reports of Economic Distress, Forced Loans, and Crop Diversions — Plan for Self-sufficient "Inner Zone" of Japan and Near-by Areas

1944

Prospect of War's End Brings Plans for More Normal Trading Conditions 299

COMMERCIAL SHIFTS RESULTING FROM MILITARY DEVELOPMENTS

Sharp Shrinkage in European Areas Within Trade Reach of Axis — Neutrals Begin to Divert Their Trade Toward the Allies — Efforts Toward Resumption of Trading with Liberated Areas — *In the Pacific* — *In Africa and other colonial areas* — *In Western Europe (Italy, France, Belgium, and the Netherlands)* — *In Eastern Europe*

STEPS TOWARD RELAXATION OF WARTIME EXPORT CONTROLS

Procedures Simplified on United States Exports to Large Part of World — United States Discourages Foreign Bulk Buying Through Purchasing Missions — Revival of British Exports Planned, but Controls Only Slightly Eased — Canada Waives Export Permits for Many Products, but Guardedly — Small but Definite Increase in Commercial Trade Among Non-Axis Countries

REACTIONS OF IMPORTING COUNTRIES TO PROSPECTIVE SUPPLY EASEMENTS

Canada, India, and Australia Relax Restrictions on Non-sterling Goods — Diverse Reactions Among Latin American Countries — *Some loosen import controls to reduce living costs — Others adopt measures potentially restrictive but lightly applied — Several set import conditions designed to advance industrialization* — Concern Over Indefinite Continuation of Wartime Expedients — *Potentially arbitrary use of broad import license systems — Fear of British and French preferential licensing continuing — Concern over official bulk buying becoming regular import method* — United States Curtails Bulk Procurement and Centralized Control of Imports

1945

War's End Brings Only Limited Progress Toward Demobilization of Controls 328

GENERAL SURVEY OF POSTWAR READJUSTMENTS AND PROSPECTS

Progress Toward Return to Normal Uneven in the Different Regions — Prospects for More Normal Trade Policies and Collective Action in 1946 — *Bretton Woods agreements promise wide collaboration in financial relations — United States loan to Britain expected to hasten trade liberalization — High hopes for program of collective action on tariffs and trade principles*

READJUSTMENT MEASURES BY UNITED STATES, BRITISH EMPIRE, AND LATIN AMERICA

Wartime Joint Controls Taper Off as Supply Situation Improves — United States — *Controls on civilian production and commerce promptly relaxed — End of Lend-Lease followed by large credits for foreign rehabilitation* — British Empire — *Canada relaxes most export and import controls and extends foreign credits — Exchange shortage forces sterling areas to restrict dollar imports — United Kingdom gives priority to exports at cost of domestic austerity* — Latin America — *Trend to firmer import controls after United States re-*

laxes export control — Direct import controls, lightly applied, have several purposes — Foreign bulk purchase contracts for strategic materials taper off

EFFORTS TOWARD TRADE RESUMPTION WITH FORMER SECLUDED AREAS

Former European Neutrals — *Operating without special controls, seek broader trade range — Sweden and Switzerland assist liberated areas with goods and credits* — Western Europe — *Under prevailing disorganization, imports arranged by governments — Revival of exports hampered by shortages and commercial derangement — Import duties often suspended to reduce cost of essential supplies — Trade negotiations center on exchanges of goods each desires — United States helps revive trade by unfreezing funds and extending credits—Most buying in United States handled or coördinated by official agencies* — Eastern Europe — *Imports from the West mainly relief supplies — Impoverished and disorganized, oriented to Russia, trade resumption meager — Governmental control of economies dims prospect for private foreign trade — United States eases reëstablishment of commercial channels with Eastern Europe* — Far East — *Liberation incomplete; abnormal conditions hold back trade resumption — Only Philippines and China able to begin restoration of overseas commerce — Rehabilitation of economies of Southeast Asia in governmental hands*

1946

Acute Needs of the Recently War-involved Areas Are the Dominant Trade Forces 365

PRINCIPAL TRADE PROBLEMS AND EFFORTS TO DEAL WITH THEM

Shortage of Goods and Inability to Pay Are the Chief Limitations — Credit and Relief Offered Meet Financial Needs Only Partly — Governmental Trade Controls Important Mainly on the Export Side — Most Purchasing Missions Giving Way to Controlled Private Trade — Bilateral Supply Agreements Make Possible Limited Trade Resumption — Limited Exchanges with Occupied Areas Handled by Governmental Bodies — Prospects for Concerted Action Toward Liberal Trade Policies — *Setting up of exchange parities a step toward currency stability — Large goals set for prospective international trade conference*

SALIENT DEVELOPMENTS IN CONTROLS ON EXPORTS

Joint International Controls Terminating, Except on Farm Products — Operations of UNRRA to End Early in 1947 — United States and Most British Areas Relax Export Controls as Supplies Improve — Latin America Widens Export Controls on Foods and Materials — Western Europe Uses Export Controls in Bargaining for Supplies — Special Situations in India and China — Efforts in Southeast Asia to Shift Trade Out of Governmental Hands

SALIENT DEVELOPMENTS IN CONTROLS ON IMPORTS

United States Ends Most Administrative Controls and Official Procurement — Exchange Shortage of Sterling Area Holds Back Outside Purchases — Latin America Eager for Imports but Concerned Over Exchange Reserves — Beyond Basic Needs, Western European Imports Moving Into Private Hands — Eastern European Trade Closely Controlled and Oriented Toward Russia — China Still Disordered; Other Asian Trade Moving Into Private Channels

1947

Increased Importations Beyond Earnings Bring Renewed Tightening of Controls 384

Slow European Recovery and Overbuying Cause Wide Restrictive Reaction — Summary of Salient Developments in the Different Regions — Prime Aim of Restrictions to Readjust Buying Programs to Ability to Pay — Is Dollar Shortage or Production Shortage Prime Cause of Trade Imbalances? — Shrinkage in Means of Covering Trade Deficits Forces Drain on Reserves — Normal Trade with War-disrupted Areas Awaits Aid in Rehabilitation — Marshall Plan Proposes Reinforcing European Efforts Toward Recovery — Geneva Agreements for

Tariff Concessions Significant for the Future — Western Europe — *Principal causes of European trade difficulties — General resort to restricting imports of less essential goods — Imports of dollar goods especially limited to essentials — Drive to increase exports handicapped by overvalued currencies — Despite operating difficulties, bilaterally balanced agreements continued — Benelux and other Western European customs union projects* — Eastern Europe — *Refusing Marshall Plan, Russia makes long-run agreements with satellites — Satellites seek pacts also with the West and increase trade with them* — Trading with the Occupied Ex-enemy Countries — *Private trade with Germany being resumed, mainly in exports —Beginning of private trade with Japan, curtailing official operations* — British Empire — *Drain upon sterling-area dollar resources causes financial crisis — As corrective, British countries cut imports, notably of dollar goods — Unusable European balances force Canada to cut dollar imports* — Latin America — *Heavy buying surge drains war-accumulated exchange reserves — General resort to selective import license and exchange priorities — More protection for local producers through tariffs and license restrictions — Efforts to increase exchange receipts by official assistance to exports* — Far East — *India and Pakistan, now independent, develop separate trade regimes — Chinese trade corrective efforts hampered by civil war and yuan depreciation — Many Netherlands Indies exports and some imports revert to private hands — Indo-China and Siam ease trade barriers; Burma tightens them*

1948

Substantial Improvement Fails to Materialize and the Marshall Plan Is Launched 420

United States Marshall Plan Aid Materially Alleviates World Dollar Shortage — Inconvertibility and Unreal Exchange Rates Hinder Freer Goods Exchanges — Partial or Selective Depreciation Widely Tried as Trade Balance Corrective — Giving Production for Export Priority over Domestic Needs Another Device — Summary of Salient Developments in the Principal Regions — *Western Europe — Eastern Europe —*

British Commonwealth — Latin America — Asia — The occupied areas — Western Europe the Scene of Exceptional Developments in Trade Relations — *Marshall Plan aid part of larger program for recovery and collaboration — Still unable to afford all imports desired, selective restrictions continued — Dollar resources reserved for essentials; other purchases diverted elsewhere — Insistence on bilateral balance retards intra-European trade recovery — Trade often scaled down to avoid gold payments or unusable credits — Resistance to "nonessentials" reacts against each country's exports — Artificial exchange rates cause trade distortion and irregular deals — Secondary importance of import duty revisions and suspensions — Special arrangements to loosen up intra-European trade and payments*

1949

First Broad Efforts to "Loosen up the Log Jam" of Trade and Currencies 442

Summary of Salient Developments in the Different Regions — Basic Structure of Foreign Trade Controls Unchanged and Even Tightened — Current Status of Foreign Import License and Exchange Control Systems — Influence of Domestic Inflationary Pressures on Excessive Import Demand — United States Financial Aid to Europe and Japan a Bolster to General World Trade — Protectionist Element in Import Restrictions, Emergency or Otherwise — Western Europe — *Despite recovery, high demand for dollar goods keeps restrictions on — Trade still limited by bilateralism and resistance to "nonessentials" — Devaluation by Britain and Western Europe a step to reduce dollar deficits — Move to loosen intra-European trade by gradual lifting of import quotas — Decision on proposed intra-European currency clearing plan postponed — Little progress on plans for trade liberalization among smaller groups* — Eastern Europe — *No perceptible difference after Soviet bloc sets up Economic Council — Yugoslavia turns West for trade after Soviet bloc suspends relations — Limitation on goods to offer prevents larger exchanges with the West* — British Commonwealth — *Aggravated dollar deficit prompts fur-*

ther import cut and devaluation — Drive to increase dollar sales, partly by diversion from sterling markets — Most sterling areas follow British action on currency and import cuts — Bulk-purchase program curtailed for materials, continued for foods — Latin America — *Prevalence of direct import controls and bilateral-balancing agreements — Frequency of exchange manipulations to curb imports and aid exports — Foreign exchange budgeting helps clear up debts and regulate imports — Sharp shifts in prices of export staples reflected in trade controls* — Major Asiatic Areas — *Exceptional influence of political developments on trade potentials — Japanese yen stabilized and private trade conditions simplified — Depleted Philippine reserves, from overbuying, forces drastic import cuts — Indonesian independence promising for trade but dollar imports restricted — Political and currency differences cause India-Pakistan trade impasse — India announces wider range of imports; Pakistan tightens controls*

1950

Trade Approaches Normalization Until Korea Brings Scramble for Supplies 473

Recuperative Forces Checked by Emergency Pressures After Midyear — Continuation of Easy Trading and High Level of Exchanges Uncertain — Sharp Reduction of Dollar Gap by Combination of Factors Eases World Trade — *Influence of larger United States purchases at high prices and of decline in exports* — Uneven Narrowing of Dollar Gap Reflected in Degree of Trade Easement — *Canada abolishes all import restrictions; South Africa moderates them — Most sterling areas do not feel warranted in easing dollar-goods curbs — South Americans substantially relax import controls after midyear — Intra-European trade enlarged by quota liftings and payment clearances — Western Europe still confines dollar purchases to more essential products — Varying attitudes observed in Near East and Africa — India-Pakistan trade still blocked; overseas imports liberalized — Chinese buying from the West active despite state-controlled trading — Security restrictions imposed by United States and others on exports to China — Greater part of trade with Japan returns to private channels — Further drastic cuts in Philippine imports to restore balance of payments — Indonesian exchange measures stimulate exports and restrict imports* — Tariff Revisions and Other Changes in Costs of Imports — *Secondary importance of duty changes during period of direct controls — Significance of third round of simultaneous tariff negotiations at Torquay — Several unilateral tariff revisions in Latin America, mostly upward — Cost of imports into many countries increased by exchange manipulations* — Tighter Export Controls and Higher Export Taxes — *Controls on exports tighten again as unusual demand for goods mounts — Increasing destinational control of exports on security grounds — Price rises of primary products prompt imposition of high export taxes — International action urged for equitable allocation of scarce products* — Trading With and Within the Soviet Sphere — *Communist countries less responsive to general world trade currents — Russia presses satellites to intensify trade within the Soviet bloc — Poor results of efforts for larger East-West trade commitments — Soviet bloc tries to tie in trade of East Germany and Communist China*

1951

Subsidence of Post-Korean Trade Boom Brings Price Drops and Renewed Import Curbs 500

HIGHLIGHTS OF THE TWO PHASES IN POST-KOREAN TRADE DEVELOPMENTS

Early Upsurge in Demand and Prices for Materials Checked in 1951 — Differing Impact on Primary-producing and on Industrial Countries — Desire for Increased Imports Prompts Most Countries to Loosen Controls — Import Relaxations by Primary Producers Substantial; Moderate Elsewhere — Heavy Imports Beyond Current Earnings Bring Restrictive Reaction — Post-Korean Developments Create Acute Situation for Britain and France — Despite Inward Facing of Soviet Bloc, Wider Outside Trade Invited — Strong Demand for Materials and Equipment Brings Wide Controls on Exports — *Prospective supply shortages overestimated; consumers' goods ample — Increasing curbs on strategic shipments or diversions to Soviet bloc* — Purposes and Effects of High Export Taxes on Primary Products — International Collaboration in Allocating Raw Materials Steadies Markets

POST-KOREAN TRADE EXPERIENCE OF PRINCIPAL PRIMARY-PRODUCING COUNTRIES

More Conservative Buying Plus Revived Controls Bring Stabilizing Period — Primary Producers in Net Improved Position Even After Boom Subsides — Special Features of Recent Experiences of Primary-producing Countries — *South and Southeast Asia* — *Latin America* — *Overseas sterling area* — *Near East*

POST-KOREAN TRADE EXPERIENCE OF WEST EUROPEAN INDUSTRIAL COUNTRIES

Increased Rearmament Imports and Poor "Terms of Trade" Create Problems — Intra-European Trade Increases Under Import Quota Liberalization — National Trade Deficits or Surpluses Strain European Payments Union — Larger Essential Purchases from Dollar Sources Again Widen Dollar Gap — Bearing of Mutual Security Program Upon Trade Programs and Controls — Proposed European Curtailments and Diversions of Dollar Purchases — Sterling Area Over-all Trade Deficit and Plans for Its Correction — Import Cuts by Most Sterling Countries a Short-run Measure

1952–1953

Looking Ahead in World Trade Policies 528

SHORT-TERM TRENDS

Settling Down to an Indefinite Period of Uneasy Peace — Efforts to Adjust Trade Balances, Mainly by Curbing Imports — Factors Favoring and Retarding Greater Stability in Trade Controls — Little Trade Relaxation Except Among Western European Countries — Export Controls on Short Supply Grounds Being Relaxed — Post-Korean Resort to High Export Taxes Being Reversed — Currency Convertibility Depends on Balance-of-payments Stability

LONGER-TERM PROSPECTS

Recognitions of Responsibility Improve Prospect for Correction — Relative Responsibilities of Creditor and Debtor

Countries — External Deficits a Reflection of Overspending and Overexpansion — Importance to External Balance of Internal Economic Measures — Commonwealth Economic Plan Exemplifies New Line of Approach — Gap in World Payments Hitherto Bridged by Unusual Means — Present Balance Precarious and Dependent on Continued Restrictionism — Trade Policy Goals Call for More Basic Measures and Joint Programs — Inward Orientation of Soviet Bloc Unpromising of Trade Expansion — Recent Import Curbs by Free World Nations Probably Temporary Regression — Inconsistencies and Domestic Political Pressures May Require Tolerance — Further Spread of State Trading in Free-economy Countries Unlikely — Progress Toward Customs Unions or International Commodity Agreements Difficult — Greater Likelihood of Progress Through Concerted than Collective Action — GATT System of Multilateral Trade Engagements a Definite Advance — New Standards for Official Trade Practices Growing in Prestige — Serious Retreat by GATT Nations from Liberal Trade Goals Unlikely

1920–1923

EXTREME POSTWAR TRADE RESTRICTIONS MODERATED AS DISORGANIZATION DIMINISHES

The movement for extremely high tariffs and restrictive trade measures, which has marked the commercial policy of most European nations since the war, appears largely to have spent its force, and there are indications that a distinct reaction is underway. This is the outstanding impression from a recent first-hand study of the tariff situation and trend of commercial policies in the principal countries of Western and Central Europe.

Postwar European Upheaval in Foreign Trade Controls

The Great War and its aftermath had so considerably changed the economic map of Europe and so shaken up the commercial relations between its various parts that a corresponding upheaval in tariff legislation and in the general policy toward foreign trade on the part of both the old and the new nations was well-nigh unavoidable. As a result, there appears to have been ushered in, in the wake of the war, a new era of intensified protectionism and of strong governmental control of the currents of trade through devices new and old, which substantially may be expected to prevail for some time to come.

The major causes underlying this radical and widespread movement are clear and understandable. The shifting of political boundaries following the war has involved, not only the realignment of the shifted districts with the larger areas to which they were being joined, but a reconsideration of the general economic and tariff policy of the major countries affected by the shift, in the light of the resources or industries which were being separated from one economic entity and grafted onto another.

Dominance of strong nationalistic sentiments.—The creation of new political entities out of the territories of the former Russian and Austro-Hungarian empires, and the erection of customs frontiers between areas hitherto forming an unrestricted economic whole, presented an entirely new series of tariff problems. Under such conditions any new tariffs or measures of trade control adopted by these countries were necessarily experiments and subject to frequent changes as actual operation showed their inadequacy to national interests as then conceived. At the same time the wrenching of the old sectional division of labor, and the creation of barriers to the long-established channels of trade exchanges, which had grown up within the customs boundaries of the old political body, called for the most delicate adjustments. And, unfortunately, the strong separatist feelings between the various peoples involved were not calculated to make these adjustments easy.

On the other hand, the widely unequal division of resources among the new states, with varying degrees of dependence upon other countries for foods and materials, as well as for markets, made it especially necessary to control the movement of goods and money across the national boundaries, if anything like a balance of foreign trade was to be maintained and the exchange value of the depreciated national currency kept from too great fluctuation. The elaborate systems of restrictions upon imports and exports, marking the regime of so many European countries in recent years, have often been dictated as much by exigencies of national finance as by strictly commercial considerations.

Among the older established countries the immediate dominant motives of tariff revisions were somewhat different. During the abnormal wartime years certain industries had been severely dislocated, if not crippled, as in the case of the invaded areas of France, Belgium, Italy, and Poland; while others had been stimulated to rapid development in order to supply from within what could not well be obtained from abroad. Moreover, the effects of the protective wall of the wartime blockade, and of the abnormal demand for goods that continued into the years immediately following the war, were felt in the neutral countries, such as Holland and Spain, as well as in the combatant nations, giving stimulus to industrial revival or expansion in a range of lines to a degree otherwise hardly possible.

With the return of more normal conditions of competitive trade, most governments felt called upon to impose additional tariffs or other restrictions on imports for a twofold purpose: first, to protect reviving domestic industries against the too ready importation of foreign competitive products; and second, to nurture the industries born or expanded during the abornmal period that they might become permanent gains to the national industrial structure. This twofold motive was greatly reinforced by the strong nationalistic sentiment everywhere engendered by the war, which favored the encouragement of all efforts to make each nation economically self-dependent to the fullest extent possible.

It hardly needs to be added that the desire to increase the national income was a prominent auxiliary motive in almost every country. The heavy burden of governmental expenditure and debts incurred during the war, and the largely increased need for funds to carry the postwar obligations and projects, added impetus to the desirability of tariff revision upward as a ready and fairly certain means of increasing the national revenue.

Furthermore, the abrogation by the war of all the treaties between the Central Powers and Allied countries cut some of the main strands in that network of commercial treaties that had kept the European trade structure in balance. It was apparent, moreover, that it would be but a short time before most nations would seek to relieve themselves of prewar treaty obligations, in order to be free to reshape their commercial relations with individual countries on terms more advantageous to their changed national interests as they now viewed them. The revision of the basic tariff would, of course, be the first step, and following the traditional European procedure, the countries with multiple tariffs might be expected to set their new duties higher than actually necessary, in order to afford a good basis for the inevitable concessions in the new treaty negotiations that were to follow.

Complications of unstable prices and currencies.—Such were some of the salient considerations in the postwar tariff problems of the European countries. The actual working out of the measures in particular cases was considerably complicated by a number of factors, particularly the unequal degree of depreciation of the currencies of the various countries and the unsettled state of costs and market prices. As a result, the early measures had to be largely experimental and temporary in many cases, subject to alteration at almost any time.

Under these circumstances, it is hardly surprising to find that in many of the countries of Europe tariff making—usually regarded as the prerogative of legislative bodies, or at least calling for their approval—had during recent years been largely delegated to ministerial or administrative officials, usually with full authority to change tariff rates up or down and to impose or remove restrictions on imports or exports of particular commodities as they saw fit. Obviously, only the great instability of conditions of trade would induce legislatures to waive their direct legislative control over important fiscal and trade measures, and to substitute a regime involving the uncertainty in the practical conduct of trade that is unavoidable when important changes can be brought about simply by administrative order.

However, the fact that many countries have found it desirable to lodge in an administrative body, for a period of several years, the power to modify the country's tariff upon its own initiative, as a practical means of effecting not only quick adjustments to changing market conditions, but even selective tariff revision in accordance with economic needs, affords an interesting contribution to this difficult problem of flexible tariff adjustment so much discussed in the United States during recent years.

Broadly considered, four types of measures may be distinguished as having characterized the commercial policy of the European countries since the war:

1. Tariff revisions, usually upward, of more or less general scope.

2. Import and export restrictions, in the form of total prohibitions, contingents, or governmental licensing systems.

3. Antidumping duties, depreciated currency surtaxes, and similar measures to meet abnormal exchange conditions.

4. Revisions of basic treaty relations.

Observation of the way in which particular countries have been working out their major tariff problems helps to a more concrete understanding of the general postwar situation.

General Movement for Tariff Revision Upward

Almost every country of Europe has revised its tariff in a more or less general way in the last three years. The differences have been mainly in the extent and form of the revision. Some countries carried through a thorough overhauling of the old tariff and a reappraisement of the proper duty on every class of goods, similar to that worked out a year ago last September in the United States. Thus, in the middle of 1921, Italy put into effect a considerable advance in duties over practically the whole schedule of imported products, excepting only those rates which because of existing treaties could not then be changed. The new Italian tariff was frankly an upward revision, intended both to yield increased revenue to the government, and to afford increased protection to domestic industries during the difficult period of postwar reconstruction and readjustment. It has also been alleged that the Italian scaling up of all import duties indicated a desire, if not to retaliate against, at least to counteract the advances in the import duties put into effect by a number of countries following the war which hurt the sale of Italian products in their markets.

Piecemeal revisions by administrative action.—The history of the French tariff from 1919 to 1923 illustrates another method of revision distinctive of the postwar period, namely, the coefficient system. This consists of leaving the basic rate unchanged and simply announcing a coefficient of 2, or 3.5, or 6, by which that basic rate is to be multiplied until further notice. It should be kept in mind that France, as most European countries, uses mainly specific tariff rates. A coefficient of 2 thus doubles the original duty, or advances it 100 per cent; a coefficient of 6 raises the duty 500 per cent, and so on—always, however, in the terms of the depreciated French franc.

The interministerial commission which was charged with administering this system, ordered what amounted to partial revisions of the French tariff, often as frequently as once a month, by announcing the imposition or change of coefficient on lists of particular commodities. This method was well adapted to several purposes. It served well the declared primary purpose of the French Government in adopting it, namely, of maintaining, under the changing level of prices and exchange values, about the same level of protection to domestic industries as prior to the war. Incidentally, it served to keep up the volume of actual government income from customs receipts which had naturally fallen off with the depreciation of the franc. At the same time the coefficient system lent itself admirably to use as a flexible method of effecting actual changes, from time to time, in the tariff treatment of particular commodities, in accordance with changes in industrial conditions or economic needs as they became apparent, without making necessary a thoroughgoing overhauling of the entire tariff schedule such as the United States has recently gone through.

Quite a number of European countries, in addition to France, had recourse to the coefficient system in some form, including Belgium, Italy, Czechoslovakia, Poland, and Turkey. In certain cases, notably in Czechoslovakia, the coefficient system has been used as a definite instrument of piecemeal tariff revision and adjustment to changing commercial needs. Also, tariff concessions in the course of treaty negotiations were sometimes effected through offering a lower coefficient on particular articles than those in effect at the time. But whatever the form, the general direction of practically all European tariff revisions since the war, whether partial or total, has been distinctly upward, varying only in the degree of advance and the particular commodities affected.

Even England, long the stanch exponent of relatively free trade, could not entirely resist the general movement toward protectionism. Since October, 1921, there has been imposed, under the Safeguarding of Industries Act, a duty of 33⅓ per cent upon the admission of foreign-made products affecting so-called British key industries. The list of commodities so dutiable is not very extensive, comprising mainly optical and chemical glassware and porcelain, scientific instruments, hosiery, needles, tungsten and rare earth metals, and synthetic organic chemicals (other than dyestuffs, which are under special license control). The character of the dutiable list was determined by the fact that the immediate impulse to this action was the recognition of the close relation between industrial and military preparedness, and the desire to avoid the possible recurrence of the wartime situation, when the British found themselves unable to obtain sufficient supplies of these essential commodities, most of which had for years been imported and mainly from Germany.

It is not fair to say, however, that England has become definitely committed to the protectionist policy. The Safeguarding of Industries Act is definitely to expire late in 1924, with considerable doubt as to whether public sentiment will support an extension of even these "key industry duties." This unlikelihood is confirmed by the events in England during the past few months. At the Imperial Economic Conference held in London last October, for the purpose of working out means of closer trade relations within the Empire, the utmost that the British Government felt able to offer the Dominions in the way of tariff advantages was an additional measure of preference on a number of secondary commodities, comprising mainly dried and preserved fruits, tobacco, canned fish, raw apples, fruit juices, and honey. The expressed desire of the leading Dominions for a duty to be imposed by England on the general importation of foods and certain raw materials—the lines making up the bulk of their shipments to the mother country—which would then be rebated by a preference to products originating within the Empire, had to go unsatisfied. In the election later precipitated by Prime Minister Baldwin, on the clear issue of the adoption of a protective tariff as the remedy for the widespread unemployment, the country expressed itself so emphatically in the negative as to leave little doubt that the rank and file of the British people still believe in free trade as the most desirable policy for the nation.[1]

New states seek economic self-sufficiency.—In the case of some of the newer countries of Central Europe, such as Czechoslovakia, the setting up of high tariffs against imports had been the expression of the desire for economic self-sufficiency to the highest degree, which appears to have followed in their minds as a corollary to the newly liberated spirit of nationalism. The wisdom of such a policy has been seriously called into question. For however just the tardy recognition of the right of the newly created nations to political independence, the economic interdependence that had grown up during the long years of the Austro-Hungarian Empire obviously could not be gainsaid, or immediately removed, simply by the partition of the Empire into a number of separate political entities. Yet the early policies of a number of the Austrian Succession States in setting up trade barriers against each other indicated a desire to do away as quickly as possible with all economic as well as political ties which formerly bound them together.

Under the sectional division of labor that had grown up within the old customs area, most of the products of each of the states of the Austro-Hungarian Empire found their markets in the neighboring states of the Empire, and with the same ease with which Massachusetts exchanges products with Georgia and Ohio with California. After the partition of the Empire, serious hindrances began to impede this normal movement of goods from passing over the new political frontiers. Barriers were set up in the form of high customs duties, supplemented often by the even more restrictive method of forbidding the importation or exportation of many classes of goods, except under government license for each individual shipment.

Import and Export Restrictions and Licensing Systems

This second type of trade control measure, that is, import and export restrictions, is closely allied to the movement for upward revision of tariffs, having much the same practical effect on trade as prohibitive

[1] News has recently been received from London that the budget submitted by the Labour Government on April 29, 1924, proposes important reductions in the British tariff. The duties on tea, coffee, cocoa, and chickory are to be cut in half, the duty on sugar to be reduced by somewhat more than half, and the duty on dried fruit to lapse on August 1. More significant, perhaps, is the abolition of the so-called "McKenna duties" of 33⅓ per cent on pleasure cars and accessories, motorcycles, watches and clocks, musical instruments, and motion-picture films. These duties were temporarily imposed during the war but had been renewed each year since and had become, in effect, protective measures.

duties. Originally called into being by the wartime necessities of conserving tonnage and devoting national resources to the most essential uses, the policy of maintaining prohibitions, or restrictions through governmental licenses, upon the importation or exportation of broad classes of commodities has been gradually relaxed in most countries of Western Europe as wartime conditions have passed.

Such restrictions are still an important feature, however, of the postwar trade regime of the countries of Central and Eastern Europe. Their motive for continuing these restrictions on foreign trade are, in principle, reasonable. The restrictions on imports have been intended to check the importation of luxuries or dispensables until the country was sufficiently supplied with necessities; or to keep down the importation of competitive goods which could at all be supplied by domestic industries. These motives have been enforced by the need for keeping the balance of foreign trade more nearly even, lest the already depreciated currency sink to still lower levels. The primary object of the licensing of exports has been to restrict the sending out of native foodstuffs or raw materials to those neighboring countries which, because of the generally higher level of prices or superior strength of currency values, are able to outbid domestic purchasers for commodities particularly needed within the country. Most of the countries of Central and Eastern Europe are still struggling with the difficult problems of postwar economic readjustments, and the present control of foreign trade may be expected to continue to some extent so long as the conditions giving rise to them persist.

There has been a strong feeling that these restrictions have in many cases been carried quite too far, to the point of so damming up natural currents of trade as to work injury not only upon the neighboring states but even upon the legislating country itself. The impossibility of maintaining such restrictions upon foreign trade in their full rigor led, before long, to partial relaxations in the form of "contingent agreements," whereby two contracting states promised to allow as between themselves the importation or exportation of fixed quantities of specified classes of commodities during a given period, the quotas and commodities being subject to revision at the end of six months or a year. These contingent agreements have become so superimposed upon the trade regime of certain Central European countries that, even in the negotiation of more permanent treaties with distant countries, it has been found difficult to come to terms without embodying contingents as a measure of the extent to which the country was willing to moderate its restrictions upon foreign trade.

Trade restrictions induced by depreciated currencies.—In a class almost by themselves stood the licensing systems which until quite recently governed the movement of goods out of Germany and Austria. With a currency depreciating in the international foreign exchange market more rapidly than the rate of advance in internal wages and prices, restrictions upon exportation of domestic products and manufactured articles have been almost inevitable on the part of these countries, in order to prevent what has come to be termed "Ausverkauf"—literally, the "selling out" of domestic supplies to foreigners with a currency of higher purchasing power and the denuding of the local shops and home markets to the point of inadequacy for domestic needs.

The German workman, clerk, or professional man, for instance, whose advance in wages or salary lagged considerably behind the advance in prices which followed each step in the depreciation of the exchange value of his country's currency, had for some time been finding the mark diminishing in value while in his hands and unable to secure for him his supplies of household necessities in face of the advance in prices. Could he fairly be blamed for feeling unkindly toward the foreigner, who with his "strong" dollars, francs, or lire could outbid him in his own market and thus force up prices and make scarce his own country's products? Multiply this individual resentment by the large numbers in a population so affected, and there is lacking but the official decree or order to crystallize that resentment into an effective national policy of export restriction.

The worst problems of the depreciating currency period, including the dangers of "Ausverkauf," appear to be mostly over. However, the recent temporary revival by France of export restrictions on a range of commodities, following the sudden drop in the exchange value of the franc early in 1924, illustrates rather pointedly that flarebacks of direct government control of trade are not to be unexpected, even in the countries of Western Europe, when conditions become for a time highly disturbed.

Antidumping Duties and Related Abnormal Exchange Measures

A third type of measure, which has been prominent in the commercial regime of most of the European countries since the war, has been brought into being almost entirely by the unusual situation with regard to currency depreciation. It has taken two forms: on the part of the high-currency nations, "antidumping measures" to check the too ready influx of goods from the depreciated-currency countries; and, on the part of the low-currency nations, what might be termed "depreciated-currency surtaxes" to compensate for what otherwise would become an almost negligible import tariff.

Antidumping legislation of the type now prevailing in Europe had hardly been known prior to the war. Dumping, in the strict technical sense of selling in a foreign market at a price below that asked in the home market, has long been considered an unfair practice in international trade, although only during recent years has the movement grown for the establishment of means to detect the instances of such dumping and for penalizing shippers engaged in that practice.

Part II of the American emergency tariff act of May, 1921, carried over under the permanent tariff act of September, 1922, typifies the straight antidumping measure. It provides that where the purchase price or exporter's sale price on shipments to the United States is proven to be less than the foreign market value (or, in the absence of such value, than the cost of production), there shall be paid on such imports, in addition to the regular duties, a special dumping duty in an amount equal to such difference.

Under stress of postwar competition, however, and forced at times by fear for the continuance of a war-born or recently established domestic industry, the term "antidumping" has been applied more broadly, to include also measures intended to meet intensified competition from countries possessing an advantage in depreciated currency and consequently lower production costs.

Perhaps the most striking instance of such legislation is that embodied as Part II of the British Safeguarding of Industries Act. It provides that an antidumping duty of 33⅓ per cent may be imposed upon the imports of such products as were being offered for sale in the United Kingdom at prices which, by reason of the depreciation of the currency of the country of manufacture, were below the prices at which similar goods could be profitably manufactured in the United Kingdom.

The check provided against the possible abuse of this means of emergency relief is characteristic of the temper of British legislation generally. Before such an antidumping duty is ordered, the committees set up by the British Board of Trade must be satisfied on two points: first, that by reason of the continued imports of the particular product, employment in any industry in the United Kingdom is being or is likely to be seriously affected; and that production in the industry manufacturing similar goods in the United Kingdom is being carried on with reasonable efficiency and economy.

The first two years' results of the actual operation of the plan have been interesting. The committees reported favorably upon the imposition of an antidumping duty of 33⅓ per cent on fabric gloves, glove fabric, glassware for domestic use, illuminating glassware, and domestic hollow ware, if manufactured in Germany; their recommendation became effective for a period of two years from August, 1922. In the case of a number of other commodities, such as toys, gold leaf, and enameled bathtubs, the proposals were definitely dropped upon the adverse reports of the committees that those cases did not fulfill the conditions of the act cited above. The products rendered dutiable under the original "key industries" portion of the act, as well as its antidumping provisions, are largely of German origin.[2]

Spread of multiple tariffs and customs surtaxes.—Differing from the British only in form, has been the legislation adopted by a number of continental countries, principally Belgium, France, and Spain. By the Belgian emergency tariff act of November, 1921, increases of from 100 to 300 per cent of the usual duties were imposed upon certain classes of German manufactured goods entering into direct competition with Belgian industries. Textile, chemical, and mechanical products were the principal classes of goods affected.

Earlier in 1921 France added to its general and minimum tariff system a new scale of duties, providing for rates often double and higher than the previous upper level, and in general averaging about four times as high as the minimum rates of the French tariff, which are those enjoyed by most European countries. This new scale of duties has been applicable mainly to the products of Germany and Austria, which had lost their treaty status with France as a result of the war. As in the case of Belgium, these maximum duties were officially declared to have for their purpose the protection of French industries against severe competition from countries with depreciated currencies.

That the same object can be achieved in any one of several ways is further illustrated by the antidumping device adopted by Spain. While the manner of assessment has been modified since first imposed in June, 1921, essentially, the Spanish method has consisted of a surcharge upon the products from countries with depreciated currencies, the amount of the surtax on particular shipments varying with the degree of depreciation of the currency of the country of origin as measured by the quotations on the Madrid Bourse during the preceding month.

[2] It has since been intimated by the President of the Board of Trade that the antidumping duties imposed under Part II of the Safeguarding of Industries Act will be allowed to lapse in August, 1924, without request for their renewal.

The prevalence and apparent effectiveness of these antidumping measures lends point to that rather neglected phase of the recommendations of the committee of experts who reported in 1922 on the economic condition of Germany: namely, that in any economic readjustment Germany be assured, on the part of the other European countries, most-favored-nation treatment in the matter of import duties.

On the part of many low-currency countries the exchange depreciation had the effect at first of making the duties almost nominal, paid as they were in the terms of the old currency, with the consequent loss of most of the revenue as well as the protection which the original duties were intended to afford. This situation reached an extreme stage in Germany, Austria, and many of the newer states whose currencies were severely depreciated and sinking, although a number of countries with a relatively moderate measure of depreciation, such as Spain, Italy, and Greece, also felt its effects.

Resort was soon had to one of two devices intended to compensate for the abnormal currency situation. In the case of Italy and Greece, for instance, the basic duties were declared to mean gold duties, and periodically an official rate of conversion was announced between gold and paper lira or drachma. Thus, for some time past the official Italian conversion rate (locally known as coefficient of increase) has been about 3½, which means that an article listed in the tariff as liable to a duty of 100 lire per hundred kilos, actually pays, in the paper currency of the country, an additional 350, or a total of 450 paper lire.

Other European countries, such as Austria and Poland, adopted a corrective device which amounted to the same thing but was usually given the more specific term of "agio" or "paper surtax." Here again the basic gold rates were allowed to stand but, when paid in the actual paper currency of the country, were to be multiplied by a figure intended to compensate, in a measure, for the current degree of depreciation in its exchange value. This system had one important difference from that described for Italy, in that the paper surtax was not uniform for all classes of goods, being set lowest on imports of necessary materials, somewhat higher on ordinary merchandise of convenience, and highest of all on what were deemed luxury goods. In some cases the attempt was made to advance the "agio" so as to keep the actual amount of duty collected, at least on the luxuries, fully up to the original value of the gold duties. Only rarely, however, in the case of the very low currency countries, have these surtaxes actually resulted in the collection of duties on an effective gold basis.

Post War Movement for Revision of Commercial Treaties

Probably most important, because of its far-reaching effects, is that fourth and last tendency which has marked European commercial policy since the war, that is, the widespread movement for the revision of the basic treaties which have for many years governed the trading relations between the various European countries, and, in many cases, also their relations with the principal countries overseas, such as the United States and Japan.

The prewar state of commercial relations in Europe has been aptly described as "protectionism tempered by treaties." For had the basic or general tariffs of the various European countries been actually applied against all foreign goods, the exchange of products with other nations would have in many instances been well-nigh impossible. High tariff barriers would have meant stagnation to many industries and even ruin to certain producing areas.

Most countries of Europe had, however, long ago adopted the multiple tariff system, with the highest or "general" scale of duties constituting the "asking price," which most countries expected would be considerably reduced by concessions through the process of "higgling" in the international treaty market. Through this process of bargaining, reciprocal concessions were made from the original "general" tariff schedule, until the actual "selling prices"—the duties at which good actually moved from one country into another—consisted in most cases rather of a series of "conventional" or "minimum" rates, usually much below the original general or "asking prices."

By virtue of its strong and growing economic position in Europe, and enforced by its scientifically constructed and highly specialized tariff system, Germany had for several decades taken the lead in the shaping of the commercial policy of Europe. Its present reduced economic position, joined with the limitations placed upon it by the Treaty of Versailles, render it impossible for Germany to continue this role, and no other country of Europe has thus far shown signs of being able successfully to take it up.

Weakening of most-favored-nation balance wheel.—The balance wheel in the whole treaty system was the most-favored-nation clause, which formed an important feature of most of the treaties between European countries. Following, moreover, the traditional European interpretation of the most-favored-nation clause, whereby all privileges which one nation granted to another were to be automatically extended also to all others enjoying most-favored-nation status—irrespective of whether such privileges were freely given or in consideration for reciprocal favors—there was brought about, in effect, a condition of equality of treatment in matters of customs duties which placed almost any two European countries in the same favorable position in competing for the trade of any third country.

With the abrogation by the war of all the treaties between the Central and the Allied Powers, and the tremendous changes wrought by war in general European economic conditions, it seemed but a matter of time before that whole network of treaties would be unraveled, in order that it might give way to a newer one, rewoven at least partly out of the old materials, but designed to bring about something like a new pattern in the postwar commercial texture of Europe. Even before the war was over France announced its intention of terminating all commercial treaties containing the most-favored-nation clause. One after another, as their particular situation allowed, various governments of Europe gave notice of an intention to terminate their prewar treaty obligations, and invited the negotiation of new treaties, to be built in the light of the changed economic interests and commercial relations of the nations involved.

The negotiating nations often found it difficult to accept each other's terms for a new commercial arrangement, when first presented. In some cases the situation was deadlocked, and a solution came only after a "tariff war"—in which each country imposed its maximum and most difficult conditions upon the admission of the other's products into its territory—showed that the commercial need of the two nations for each other was stronger than the desire of each to carry through its will, and ultimately a formula of agreement was found. In most cases, however, the old favorable tariff relations between the various treaty countries are being temporarily maintained by means of a short-time "modus vivendi," renewable successively, until new permanent arrangements can be negotiated.

When the period of active treaty negotiation set in there was appreciable cause for gratification, for it represented the rebuilding stage, and the conclusion of each new commercial treaty, bringing as it necessarily does assurance of stable if not more liberal conditions of trading between the contracting countries, wove another strand into the fabric of European commercial relations which had been so badly torn by the war and what followed in its wake. However, judging from the early results of the treaty-revision period, it seemed for a time as if that great prewar moderator in international tariff relations, the most-favored-nation clause, was to be considerably restricted in its application if not abandoned altogether by certain nations.

Tendency toward preferential tariff concessions.—The lead in this direction was early taken by two prominent countries of Western Europe, France and Spain, who found themselves in much the same economic situation and endeavored to give prevalence to a new type of treaty relation. Both countries were eager to afford increased protection against foreign competition to certain of their own industries which had expanded during the abnormal years; at the same time they wanted to keep open foreign markets for their characteristic export products on the most favorable terms. France and, subsequently, Spain therefore set out upon a policy of special and restrictive tariff bargaining.

Starting by advancing considerably the general or highest scale of import duties, these countries then offered to grant reductions on particular commodities to such countries as would concede, in return, special tariff advantages to their distinctive export products. The character and extent of the concessions exchanged differed in each case, and, usually, a striking feature of these arrangements was the lack of a general promise that the present contracting nation would have the benefit of any further moderations in duties which might later be made by virtue of a treaty with a third nation. The great activity of the two nations insistent upon limited concessional arrangements soon resulted in such a number of these treaties coming into operation as to forecast a possible general state of unequal tariff relations in Europe. That would give the producers of one country special preferential treatment in a given market, while those of a neighboring and competing country might be subject to a distinct handicap in the same trade.

It may fairly be recognized that, under the abnormal relations between certain nations after the war, the denial of the most-favored-nation tariff treatment may not always have been entirely inequitable. But for such a system of preferential and discriminatory duties to come into general practice as the permanent principle of tariff relations between nations would have meant the ushering in of so radical and upsetting a departure from the prewar situation, of practically equal commercial opportunity all around, as to give considerable concern to those who believed that the principle of the competitive open door held out the best assurance of peaceful and fair development of national industries and international commerce.

Joined with the other restrictive tendencies indicated, it seemed for a time as if the preponderance of forces in the European postwar situation was making for a long period of national exclusiveness and unequal commercial relations that did not bode well for the recovery or the stability of normal trading relations either among the family of European nations themselves or with the trading countries overseas.

Signs of Moderation of Restrictive Trade Policies

During the past year, however, events have multiplied which tend to indicate that the movement for extremely restrictive trade measures on the part of the European nations has largely spent its force and that a distinct reaction is under way. This impression was confirmed in the course of a personal visit last fall to the principal countries of Western and Central Europe for the purpose of studying their tariff situations on the ground.

It would be too much to expect that a moving up of the tariff rates in this or that particular case may not still be carried out, for certain European countries have been modifying their tariff only piecemeal and have still to put through an ultimate thoroughgoing revision. In general, however, the present duties of many countries which have put new tariffs into operation since the war are materially lower than those originally enacted. Whether or not individual rates were originally placed high purposely as a basis for negotiation with other countries, the total effect of the actual treaty negotiations of the past two years or so has been to effect material reduction on a broad range of products in the tariffs of many European countries. By virtue of our most-favored-nation status, the United States has, in most but not all cases, obtained the benefit of these concessions.

Tempering of tariffs and restrictions by treaties.—Moreover, the multitude of prohibitions and licensing controls on imports or exports, which has been so marked a feature of the conditions of doing business with many countries of Europe as to have made the tariff duties themselves in some cases of secondary consequence, have been considerably moderated during the past year. In a number of Central European countries officials have declared that further moderation of trading restrictions were now under consideration, and in some of the countries that had devoted themselves more earnestly to the problem of economic readjustments the whole structure of licensing control is on its way to substantial withdrawal. This is coming about partly by the negotiation of treaties in which the liberalization of the licensing regime is made a bargaining point, but in good measure also because of the fact that the legislating countries themselves appear to have become doubtful of the wisdom of the continued maintenance of such restrictive policies, with all the difficulties and abuses attendant upon them. This feeling is one upon which they can now act the more freely, because the most acute conditions which prompted their imposition are to a considerable extent passing away.

Growing stabilization of market levels and currencies.—The internal economy of individual countries has become better organized during the years since the armistice and more nearly adjusted to the major shifts in the economic structure of Europe under which the nations will apparently need to carry on for some time ahead. There is now much less fear of severe competition from the products of low-currency countries than there was a year or two ago; and on the other hand, there is not as much danger of wholesale "selling out" for export of a country's products by foreigners with currencies of "strong" exchange value, as there was in Austria during the chaotic days of 1920 and later in Germany, for internal wages and production costs have so nearly caught up with the degree of exchange depreciation as to bring the prices of staple commodities in most low-currency countries close up to general world market prices.

No one who has visited Germany within recent months could fail to be impressed with the fact that general prices had not only reached the world level, but in many cases gone considerably above them. This fact readily explains the practical abolition, last September, of the German export-licensing system. So definite appears the feeling that it will not be necessary to reinstate such control that most of the "Aussenhandelsstellen," through which the control over exports was exercised, have been definitely liquidated.[8]

Earnest efforts are being made in a number of European countries that experienced great fluctuations in exchange after the war to bring about and to maintain—by heroic measures in some cases—a state of sufficient stability in their currency to allow the nation as well as its merchants to plan long-gauged undertakings with security. In Italy, Austria, and Czechoslovakia, for instance, one is impressed with the fact that the country's currency appears to have about found its level and that business plans do not involve, as they did only a few years ago, gambling on the future of the exchange. Even in Germany prices are now practically on a gold basis, with a fairly well-sustained official conversion rate of one billion paper marks to the gold mark, and with the gold mark at the old prewar ratio of 4.2 to the dollar.

Of course, with the major problem of Germany's external obligations

[8] It is significant that, in its recent report on measures for the financial reconstruction of Hungary, the finance committee of the League of Nations declared it essential that all direct obstacles in the way of exports should be abolished immediately, and, in the case of imports into Hungary, advised a rapid reduction of restrictions and prohibitions.

still unsettled, it would be too much to expect definite stability in her currency at the present time. And, unfortunately, a number of the countries of Central and Southeastern Europe have not yet reached that stage in their financial readjustment—such as has been attained by Czechoslovakia, for instance—that allows of judgment as to the level on which their currencies are likely to find relative stability. Sufficient progress has, however, been made in the direction of currency stabilization to warrant the moderation of many of the special measures of trade control called into being by the abnormal exchange relations of recent years.

Assertive trade nationalism becoming less marked.—There are also encouraging indications that the first postwar burst of assertive nationalism among the newer nations, which sought to emphasize political independence through tariff barriers and restrictions against neighboring countries, has been considerably moderated. Many leaders are coming to recognize, even if their people are slow to do so, that the nations of Europe are too greatly bound up with one another, through the intensified sectional specialization of labor and long-established channels of commodity exchanges, to be able to escape that vital dependency simply by the creation of new political entities and the shifting of tariff frontiers.

In the two particular sections of Europe where the need was most urgent for reweaving the network of commercial relations destroyed by the political partition of territories, that is, the Succession States to the old Russian and Austrian empires, hopeful signs are appearing. After a series of conferences, Latvia and Esthonia have recently agreed to take steps toward removing the tariff wall between them, so as to make the two countries substantially one economic area.[4] This action is probably a forerunner of similar steps toward tying up more closely the former parts of the Russian Empire, although the unsettled trading status of Soviet Russia makes the ultimate adjustment in this region difficult to anticipate.

In the case of the seven countries among whom the territories of the former Austro-Hungarian Empire were divided, the difficulties in the way of bringing about more liberal trade relations have been particularly great. Ground was broken, however, at the Porto Rosa conference of November, 1921, where the representatives of these nations recognized frankly the severely dislocated economic relations that had followed the dismemberment of the old Austrian Empire. While it could hardly be expected that the ambitious program recommended by the Porto Rosa conference would be carried through directly by the various nations, the progress made in

[4] Lithuania is also reported to be studying the arrangement with a view possibly to joining the customs union.

that direction in the two years since is of considerable significance for the future. Arrangements have been made for facilitating the movement and exchange of railway cars across each other's boundaries, and at least a dozen commercial treaties have been concluded between various sets of these states during the past two years, each bringing about more liberal trading relations between the contracting states, and in almost every case embodying an exchange of promises for the unconditional most-favored-nation treatment in the matter of tariffs.

Revival of Most-Favored-Nation Treaty Arrangements

During the past year there has also taken place in Europe a general reassertion of the old most-favored-nation provision, which now seems likely to retain its role as the guiding principle of commercial relations between the nations. With a few marked exceptions, the great majority of the treaties or other commercial arrangements entered into by the various European nations during the year just closed—ranging from Switzerland to Finland—have embodied as their central feature the undertaking, on the part of each contracting nation involved, to accord to the other country, particularly in all matters affecting commerce, the same privileges as may be granted to the most-favored nation. It is also significant that this promise is, in most cases, not made conditional upon the granting of equivalent or reciprocal favors in order to obtain any benefits later granted to a third nation.

Even among a number of countries which had hitherto negotiated arrangements on the reciprocal concession basis, there is apparently growing the feeling that stability in their own tariff and an adequate measure of protection to their industries cannot allow further special concessions to be granted in each treaty negotiated. Instead, there is a tendency to consolidate the concessions made in the various treaties already negotiated into a single conventional schedule, and to offer that schedule of reduced rates in the new negotiations, under a generalized most-favored-nation clause.

Treaties embodying promises of most-favored-nation treatment have, in some cases, carried also provisions for specific concessions in duties on one or both sides. Such concessional arrangements do not appear, however, to be inconsistent with the general spirit and purpose of favored-nation treaties, provided the concessions are generalized to all other countries on a similar status. The fact that many of these new treaties are for relatively short duration is symptomatic of the instability of the times, but the basis upon which they are being built is significant.

In the treaties of the Baltic countries and the states that have succeeded to various parts of the old Austro-Hungarian Empire reservation is often made for such special privileges as they have or may accord to certain of their neighbors. Reservations of this sort are recognized as proper and quite natural, in view of the specially close economic bonds still tying these areas, and in view of the possible later measures to bring about less hampered trade relations between former parts of the Russian or Austrian Empire.

One disturbing factor has recently appeared in this connection: namely, the interpretation assumed by certain Central European states that their obligations under a most-favored-nation treaty do not extend to partial relaxations of import or export restrictions in the form of contingents or annual quotas. It is obvious that, if persisted in, such an interpretation might nullify the effect of most-favored-nation treaties entered into by these countries; for a promise of lowest duties is of little account if the importation of commodities is subject to restrictions, and licenses are granted in varying quotas to some nations which are not extended equally to other nations on a most-favored-nation status.

These contingent arrangements are, however, by their very nature, temporary and may be expected to pass with more stable economic conditions in Central Europe. In fact, the officials of more than one of these countries have declared that they would be quite ready to see abolished most of these license restrictions as well as the contingent arrangements under them, if they could be assured that the other countries of Central Europe would do the same.

Revised United States commercial treaty policy.—This movement for the reassertion of the principle of full most-favored-nation treatment in international tariff relations has been reinforced by the recent declaration of treaty policy on the part of the United States. In the thoroughly revised American tariff act, brought into operation in September, 1922, was embodied an authorization to the government to take defensive measures against discriminatory treatment of American commerce by other countries, through the granting of power to the President to impose new or additional import duties upon the products of countries which in any way "place the commerce of the United States at a disadvantage compared with the commerce of any foreign country." The government has since given positive form and expression to this attitude by active efforts to rebuild its treaty relations with other countries on the policy of "fair field, no favor," or, in other words, the exchange of unconditional most-favored-nation treatment.

Treaties embodying the most-favored-nation clause as the basic principle have been offered by the United States within the last six months to some ten or eleven countries of Europe and six of Latin America. Naturally, negotiations were first taken up with those nations with whom prior treaty relations had been severed or terminated and with the newer countries of Central Europe with whom no formal commercial arrangements yet existed. The State Department has also indicated, in a recent published letter, that it contemplates extending its treaty activities and would be ready to undertake the negotiation of new treaties, or the modification of existing arrangements, in order to bring its general commercial relations into harmony with this principle of offering and expecting unconditional most-favored-nation treatment in customs matters.

In view of the special conditions in certain countries which prefer the concessional method of treaty arrangement or still maintain the license and contingent method of foreign trade control, the full outcome of the treaty overtures on the part of the United States cannot yet be anticipated. It is indicative, however, of the general success of this policy that thus far three definite commercial agreements have been concluded on this basis, subject to the usual ratification, and that two other temporary arrangements have been made substantially assuring American commerce most-favored-nation treatment.

Significance of the Geneva Customs Conference

Finally, if there is any single event of the recent past which more than another has impressed the writer with the fact that the current in commercial policy is now running in the direction of moderation of too restrictive measures on the conduct of trade between nations, it was the International Customs Conference which held an intensive three weeks' session at Geneva last fall.

There were assembled the responsible representatives of some thirty-odd nations, comprising practically all the countries of Europe, those of the Far East, and several of Latin America. The United States was represented by observers, the writer among them. An earnest effort was made to examine the various phases of customs formalities through which the countries' commercial policies are carried out, to see to what extent the restrictions and limitations now hampering the conduct of their international trade could be removed. An agreement was reached upon a convention, embodying a long series of articles intended to standardize international practices on a clearer and simpler basis.

If the actions of their representatives at Geneva are ratified by so much as half the nations participating, considerable progress will have been made in the direction of clarifying customs formalities, and of liberalizing the intimate conditions of moving goods from one country into another.

1924–1926

TRADE POLICIES MOVE TOWARD LESS RESTRICTIVE AND MORE STABLE BASIS

If these sober years of settlement after the World War have brought home any one predominant idea, it has been the essentially economic nature of international difficulties. The basic causes of the war are now clearly seen to have been economic pressure and international trade rivalries, and it was not until the economic consequences of the peace were fully realized that any real basis of settlement was reached for the problems that the war left in its wake.

European Restrictionist Attitudes Softening

So viewed, the developments of the recent past in the measures of control adopted by the various European countries to govern their import and export trade furnish a very significant and hopeful barometer. They bespeak both a growing stabilization in economic conditions within most of the countries and a greater readiness of individual governments to remove artificial restrictions that have hampered trade exchanges since the war, and to accommodate their measures of trade control to each other's needs. While nationalistic motives and high tariff policies are still dominant, the general direction of developments during the past three years has, for the most part, been toward a less restrictive and more stable basis for the conduct of trade both among the European countries and between those nations and the United States.

The general trend of tariff revisions during the past few years has, in most countries, been toward higher new levels of duties on imports, at least immediately following enactment. These revisions have, however, often been accompanied by a modification, if not a complete removal, of licensing systems and similar artificial restrictions on imports and exports, which have dominated the trade regime of many European countries since the war. Further, they have usually been followed by a series of treaties with various trading countries, in the course of which tariff concessions were exchanged. As a result, the rates of duty under which many lines of goods now actually move into these countries are often appreciably lower than the duties carried by the tariff bills as originally enacted.

The extension to the products of other countries of duty concessions granted in the course of individual treaty negotiations has been quickened by the marked general revival of the unconditional most-favored-nation clause. This time-honored prewar principle has formed the basis of the great majority of the new commercial treaties of the last few years, whereby nations are renewing their trade relations broken or disturbed by the war and its aftermath.

Outside Europe and the United States, recent years have been relatively quiet in the field of trade control, at least as affecting imports. In the matter of export control, however, which is of most concern to the countries in Latin America and the Orient that produce raw materials, there have been certain important developments of quite a different character.

Tariff Revisions and Administrative Controls Widespread

Between 1924 and early 1927, over forty countries have announced more or less comprehensive revisions of their import tariffs, or general changes in their duties. Geographically distributed, they may be grouped as follows:

In Europe.—Austria, Belgium, Bulgaria, Cyprus, Denmark, Estonia, Finland, France, Germany, Greece, Hungary, Iceland, Irish Free State, Italy, Lithuania, Netherlands, Norway, Poland, Portugal, Rumania, United Kingdom, and Yugoslavia.

In America.—British Guiana, Canada, Cuba, Ecuador, Haiti, Mexico, Newfoundland, Panama, Paraguay, Peru, Uruguay, and Venezuela.

In the rest of the world.—Australia, British India, China, Dutch East Indies, Gambia, Mauritius, New Caledonia, Siam, Syria, and the Union of South Africa.

The extent and nature of the revisions have varied with the individual country. Thus, in the case of Austria, the revision was thoroughgoing and generally upward; in the case of South Africa the revision affected only selected groups of commodities, with the changes sometimes upward and sometimes downward; while in Cuba the revision consisted of adding to most existing duties a small percentage of increase on ordinary merchandise and a higher surtax on luxuries.

Broadly viewed, certain general tendencies stand out. The motive of protection to established or nascent domestic industries was strongly marked in most of the tariff revisions of countries that are at all industrialized. Desire for increased revenue was a prominent motive in almost all cases, and particularly in the nonmanufacturing countries and those depending upon customs collections for a substantial part of their governmental income. In a number of the newer countries of Europe, such as Poland, the object of the tariff changes has been to curtail the importation of goods which to them might be considered luxuries, for the purpose of rectifying the general trade balance and improving the exchange value of the nation's currency.

In addition to the more or less comprehensive revisions, changes in the duties on individual commodities or groups of commodities have taken place during recent years in almost all countries, to a greater or less extent, as developments in a particular line appeared to call for a readjustment of the conditions of admission of foreign goods.

Prevalence of Import and Export Restrictions in Europe

The revisions of import duties, especially in the countries of Europe, do not convey the full picture of recent developments in foreign trade control unless viewed in conjunction with the changes that have taken place in the various official restrictions upon import and export trade. Under the exigencies of the World War, the movement of goods into and out of most countries of Europe was made subject to governmental restriction of various types. With modifications or extensions they were continued into the years after the war, and in various forms, such as: requirements for import or export licenses for each individual transaction, or exchange restriction upon the funds obtainable for settlement of foreign obligations, or an absolute prohibition of import or export on certain classes of goods.

In most countries of Western Europe these governmental restrictions were gradually relaxed within a few years after the war. In Central and Eastern Europe, however, where the older countries had suffered partition of territory or general economic dislocation, and where a number of new national entities had been created, there were the additional problems of working out a balanced economic structure adapted to the new boundary lines and resources, and of developing some degree of stability in national budgets and in the value of national currencies. All these complicated the situation immensely and postponed the time when artificial and fluctuating controls upon the exchange of goods with other countries could well be relaxed.

The year 1925 witnessed considerable progress toward the relaxation of artificial and unsettling measures of trade control, and may, in fact, be regarded as distinctly ushering in, at least as regards most countries in Europe, a period when international transactions can be planned with assurance of relative freedom from administrative and unpredictable restrictions beyond those definitely set down in the customs tariffs, high as they may be. Perhaps the most striking development of this type during the year was the almost complete abolition of the import-licensing regime of Germany, which since the war had been so prominent a feature of the conditions of doing business with that country as to have made tariff duties in most cases of secondary consequence.

Germany Extreme Example of Postwar Tightening and Relaxation

Although extreme in their intensity, the developments in Germany well illustrate the general movement. Since 1917 the importation and exportation of most classes of goods into and out of Germany could be accomplished only upon applying for a governmental license for each transaction. Whether or not the particular transaction would be permitted depended upon a number of considerations. Decision often hinged upon the ability of domestic producers to supply the article begin sought for importation, or upon the adequacy to the requirements of the domestic market of the supplies of the particular commodity sought for export. These basic questions were complicated by the current state of German exchange as compared with that of the other country, the status of the general balance of trade at the time, the reasonableness of the price of the particular goods in view of the general or international market prices, and the like. To these considerations was added the question of the other country involved in the transaction, since more or less definite quotas, or varying attitudes of liberality in the granting of licenses, came to be adopted as regards different countries. The attitude toward transactions with the nationals of a given country varied with treaty obligations, relative balance of trade between the two countries, general friendly relations, and similar factors.

The uncertainties of trading under these conditions, and the considerable number of formalities and delays and abuses to which business was subject, were recognized as artificial and temporary methods of trade control which could not be expected to endure. As the more acute conditions immediately following the war moderated and as German currency approached stability in exchange value, the restrictions on export of goods were gradually withdrawn during 1923 and 1924. However, the very strength of the efforts to stabilize the value of the mark resulted in such an elevation of price levels and of costs of production in Germany as to have made even more necessary the maintenance, at least for a time, of the restrictions on the importation of foreign goods.

The German Government found it necessary during 1924 and far into 1925 to restrict more severely the granting of import licenses and quotas, both in order to prevent excessive importations which could not be balanced by exportations of German goods, and to afford domestic producers an opportunity to adjust themselves to the new conditions while the domestic market was secure for them.

The counterpressure from traders and consumers for less restricted access to foreign goods led to a compromise, whereby a provisional upward revision of the German import tariff was worked out and brought into effect on October 1, 1925, almost simultaneously with the fairly complete abolition of the whole license regime. Although the new tariff often meant the reimposition of duties that had been waived for years, or the considerable advancement of the duties hitherto in effect, the change appears to have been hailed as a decided improvement, since merchants could now make their plans for a period ahead with a certain knowledge that the trade was unburdened by restrictions other than those definitely set down.

This experience of Germany has been paralleled during the last few years in about half a dozen other countries of Europe, notably Austria, Czechoslovakia, and Hungary. Some modifications and limitations were necessitated by the peculiar conditions in the individual country.

Some Special Situations Still Bring New Restrictions

In certain European countries the developments during the past year have been in the opposite direction of new and increased restrictions on import and export trade. Owing to the differences with Germany over the amounts of coal from Polish Silesia that could be shipped into German territory, the Polish Government declared a substantial prohibition in June, 1925, upon the importation of a large range of products, particularly manufactured articles, when coming from countries restricting the admission of Polish products. Germany adopted a similar measure against Polish goods. The aggravated unsettlement of the whole Polish trade balance resulting from this difficulty led to the extension of the import restrictions by Poland to similar goods from all countries, tempered only by contingents of specified goods, which could be admitted from individual countries and only upon the obtaining of a license in each case. Early 1927 saw this situation still unchanged.

Prompted by a somewhat similar need for reducing the adverse balance of trade, the Greek Government placed a practical prohibition in August, 1925, upon a long list of luxury articles, only part of which has since been withdrawn. From somewhat different motives the Greek Government found it necessary to restrict the olive oil that might be exported, to particular grades least in demand within the country, and later to declare a total prohibition upon the exportation of all olive oil.

Few countries outside of Europe have built up restrictions on imports of ordinary merchandise, other than the regular duties, so that elsewhere the past three years brought few changes in such measures.

Treaty Negotiations Mark the Settling Down Process

The recent past has been marked by particular activity for the negotiation of commercial treaties. The fact that about fifty sets of nations took up or concluded arrangements to govern the trade relations between their nationals marked considerable progress in the settling down process to postwar conditions. It also indicated a greater readiness among nations to consider the mutual accommodation of their individual policies of trade control to the needs of commercial intercourse with other nations, so far as they were consistent with the internal interests of each contracting country. The number as well as the necessity of such treaties was naturally increased by the new national entities who need to work out a definite basis for trading, both with the older countries and among themselves.

It is significant that the great majority of the recent treaties have been built on the basic principle of reciprocal promises that each country would treat the other as well as the most-favored nation. In many cases these treaties also carried provisions for specific concessions in duties, or other privileges, on one or both sides. It was exceptional, however, for a treaty not to carry assurances that if either of the contracting parties later established new concessions, or more favorable conditions, for the goods of any third country, the same privileges would be automatically extended to the other nation concerned, without further negotiations or requiring further compensation. The movement for the restoration of equality of trade through commercial treaties has by no means been completed, and certain countries still appear to hold out for limited and exclusive arrangements, but the year 1925 witnessed the most important progress in the direction of such equality since the war.

The most important single recent development of this character was the termination on January 10, 1925, of the five-year period during which Germany was obliged to accord most-favored-nation treatment in tariff and related matters to all the Allied and associated powers, without any similar obligation on the part of those powers toward the products of Germany. Handicaps in various forms had in the meantime been established by the former Allied countries on the admission of German goods into their territories. In part, these were no doubt induced by the fear of severe German competition during the period of disordered exchanges and abnormally low production costs in Germany. However, the severity of these maximum duties, import prohibitions, and other devices for keeping out German goods was so great even after the German mark was stabilized, and production costs advanced in Germany, that the recovery of Germany as an exporting nation of consequence in the markets of Europe seemed almost impossible so long as that array of barriers was maintained.

These handicaps obviously could not be maintained after the expiration of the five-year period of the peace treaty and the restoration of Germany to full tariff autonomy, without inviting retaliation. The various nations promptly initiated negotiations for the conclusion of commercial treaties, to adjust their trading relations with Germany under the changed conditions, and on a more mutual basis. It is interesting to note that after the war the United States, unlike most of the Allied and associated powers, imposed on German goods no special restrictions that did not apply equally to similar products from other countries, and that the United States was the first to offer to Germany a full-bodied commercial treaty on favorable terms, and as far back as more than a year before the expiration of the five-year obligatory period under the Treaty of Versailles.

Restoration of Germany to Status of Trade Equality

The essential German objective during these treaty negotiations has been to bring about the removal of any special restrictions upon the admission of German goods, as against those of competitive origin, into other countries, and also upon the operation of German nationals in foreign countries. Considerable progress in this direction has been made. Thus far, Germany has been successful in securing assurance of such most-favored-nation treatment by treaties with the United States, the United Kingdom, Italy, Greece, and substantially that with Belgium. Similar arrangements have also been concluded with a number of non-Ally countries, including the Netherlands, Switzerland, Austria, Hungary, Turkey, and Portugal. The commercial agreements with Spain and with Russia have been of an exceptional nature, but in both cases the field for German commercial enterprise with and in those countries has been broadened.

The series of complex problems outstanding between France and Germany have naturally been the most difficult to adjust, and negotiations have been proceeding almost continuously for over a year. A temporary commerical agreement was finally signed on February 12, 1926, which now awaits ratification. While the negotiators of France and Germany have not yet reached the stage in their rapprochement where they can assure each other's products treatment equal to that of the most-favored nation, the tariff concessions exchanged by the temporary agreement represent a considerable advance, particularly in comparison with the handicapped position of the products of Germany in the French market during the years since the war. After so long a period of economic estrangement, a halfway arrangement for the transitional period is quite understandable, but the ground appears to have been laid for an ultimate permanent treaty that will probably restore much of the stability and reciprocal character natural to the trade relations between these two highly interdependent European countries.

Progress in United States Commercial Treaty Program

The United States has made substantial progress during the past few years toward harmonizing its treaty relations with foreign countries, on the general basis of its new policy of unconditional most-favored-nation exchanges in commercial matters. The first thoroughgoing trade treaty of this type—that with Germany—was concluded on December 8, 1923, ratified by the United States Senate on February 10, 1925, and made definitely effective from October 14, 1925. Temporary commercial agreements have been concluded, on substantially the most-favored-nation basis, by exchanges of notes with the following European countries: Czechoslovakia, Estonia, Finland, Greece, Latvia, Lithuania, Poland, Rumania, Spain, and Turkey; and with the following countries in Latin America: Brazil, Dominican Republic, Guatemala, Haiti, and Nicaragua.

Negotiations were first taken up with those new or reconstructed countries of Europe with whom formal commercial understandings were naturally most necessary, and with those countries where there existed a handicap of preferential duties denied American products which needed to be removed. Ultimately these temporary arrangements are planned to be replaced by permanent commercial treaties, adapted to the particular problems in the relations with the individual country, as soon as they can be worked out. Such permanent treaties have already been concluded with Estonia, Hungary, Turkey, and El Salvador, and negotiations to the same end with a number of other countries are actively under way.

There are, indeed, a number of important tariff revisions yet to be worked out; trade restrictions of minor consequence still linger in some countries; and a goodly number of difficult international trade relations which yet await the healing influence of commercial treaties. The day has not yet returned when international business can proceed with full confidence in the stability of tariffs and the related conditions of foreign trading, and with the assurance that no artificial and unexpected restrictions will be encountered. The seasons may yet make their rounds several times before there is reached sufficient stabilization of internal conditions and harmonization of conflicting trade interests between nations, to allow that restoration of conditions of substantial equality of treatment in commercial relations which will place almost any two competing countries in the same favorable position for participating in the trade with any third country. Viewed in the perspective of the past decade, however, international trade relations appear to have made an important turn in the road, and progress in the new direction goes on at a stride.

1927

MODERATING TENDENCIES EVOLVE INTO PROGRAMS THROUGH TREATIES AND CONFERENCES

In the main, 1927 was marked by a continued working out of the policies and tendencies in the control of foreign trade which have governed the actions of nations in recent years. However, the year has shown signs of planning for more stable and permanent conditions in international trade relations, and the emergence, through the various international conferences, of new and advanced principles in measures of trade control which, in time, are expected to find realization in a generally more favorable attitude toward international commerce.

The principal events in this field characterizing the year will be discussed separately for Europe, Latin America, the British Empire, and the Orient.

Europe

Increased import duties moderated by negotiations.—Ten of the twenty-six countries of continental Europe put into operation during 1927 more or less comprehensive revisions of their import tariffs, and a number of additional countries have initiated investigations looking to tariff revision within the next year or so. In the majority of cases the general direction of tariff revision has been distinctly upward, evincing the continued strength of the motive of protection to established or new domestic industries. Increased attention has been given to the tariff needs of agricultural producers. In addition to protective duties, the efforts during the past year to aid domestic producers took the form in a number of European countries of reductions or waivers of import duty on industrial machinery or materials, assurance of exemptions from local taxation, or other special privileges. In only a few cases have the tariff changes been downward, and then limited to selected commodities.

To a certain extent the initial increases in duties were later moderated through the negotiation of commercial treaties between different European countries, the majority of which involved material concessions in duties on the part of one or both contracting parties. Practically all of the commercial treaties concluded during the year, with the exception of those to which France was a party, also carried an exchange of assurances that each country would treat the commerce of the other as well as that of the most-favored nation. The return of the nations to an almost general acceptance of the most-favored-nation principle, as the proper governor of trade relations, whether with or without exchange of particular tariff concessions, has had the effect of generalizing fairly widely the reductions established in connection with individual treaties, so that the great bulk of the trade actually moves on the basis of the conventional rather than the original general duties.

Proposed convention for abolition of trade restrictions.—Evidence of growing stabilization is afforded by the fact that, with nine countries of Europe making material changes during the year in their system of restriction upon exports or imports, the majority of the changes have been distinctly in the direction of moderation of the restrictions formerly imposed. Even more gratifying progress in this direction was made at the International Conference held at Geneva in October, which resulted in a multilateral convention, whereby the contracting parties agreed to the abolition of import and export restrictions within six months after the convention should come into effect, with exception only for restrictions of a sanitary or similar character, which are generally recognized, and certain special restrictions which various countries are permitted to maintain temporarily. While this convention was international in scope, the participants and signers including a number of countries outside of Europe, the effect of the agreement will be felt particularly in the countries of Europe, where the device of controlling trade by restrictions and licenses has been most commonly resorted to since the War of 1914–1918.

Latin America

Upward tariff revisions, mostly for revenue.—Twelve of the twenty republics of Latin America put into operation during 1927 complete tariff revisions or substantial changes in their import duties, with proposals for thoroughgoing revisions either being worked on or before the legislatures in five other countries. While the revisions took different forms in the various countries, the general direction of the tariff changes has been, with few exceptions, distinctly upward. Unlike the situation in Europe, however, the protective motive figured prominently in only two or three countries, the need for increased national revenue appearing as the dominant motive for the upward duty revisions in Latin America.

The dependence of Latin American countries upon customs and similar collections for the greater part of their governmental revenue is further indicated by the increase in the consular fees ordered by four of them during the past year. There has been much criticism of the substantial size of the fees required by various of these countries for the consular legalization of shipping documents. It is urged that such fees be recognized as a service charge rather than an additional duty, and either reduced in amount or collected at destination. This subject figures on the program for the Sixth Pan American Conference opening at Havana in January, 1928.

Alongside of the general trend toward upward revision of duties on general merchandise, there has appeared in Latin America a growing tendency to reduce or remove duties on imports of machinery, industrial materials, and in some cases, foodstuffs, for the purpose of encouraging the economic development of the country or keeping down living costs. The negotiation of commercial treaties has been much less common than among the countries of Europe. Most republics of the American continent maintain but single schedules of duties and do not follow the European practice of negotiating for reductions in each other's duties. Such treaties as have been concluded by Latin American countries during the past year have been mainly with their European connections, and practically always of a simple most-favored-nation type.

British Empire

The strong motive toward protection of domestic industries evidenced in Europe and some Latin American countries has also been noticeable in the British areas during 1927. Great Britain has added several products to its dutiable list under the "Safeguarding of Industries" scheme, while several of the British areas, notably Australia and New Zealand, effected broad revisions of their tariffs, generally upward.

Canada and West Indies exchange tariff preferences.—More distinctive have been the efforts to tie the various parts of the British Empire into closer trade relations through new or increased preferences in the duties on each other's products. A notable instance of this type during 1927 was the bringing into operation of tariff concessions exchanged between Canada and the British West Indies by their agreement of 1925.

The British areas illustrate most markedly the growing tendency toward the establishment of tariff commissions or similar bodies for the consistent study of a country's tariff needs and problems, and of regularly making any legislative action dependent upon the report of such investigating body.

The Orient

Persia, Siam, and China seek tariff autonomy.—The most significant general development in international trade control in the Orient during 1927 has been the series of bold steps on the part of Persia, Siam, and China to throw off the limitations hitherto imposed by the Powers upon their national tariff autonomy. That system of control upon the tariff policy of less developed areas appears to be definitely on the wane. Turkey, which had long been under the capitulations regime, had asserted its tariff autonomy in 1921, following the victorious campaigns of its Nationalist leaders.

Persia denounced during the year its existing commercial treaties with the various Powers, which had been based on the capitulations regime similar to that of Turkey. This action was tantamount to general notice that Persia too meant to assume autonomous control of its tariff policy. Already Persia has a number of new treaties, built on a reciprocal basis, under negotiation.

Siam completed in 1927 the series of treaties with various of the Powers whereby general consent was secured for the recognition of the tariff autonomy of that country, and put into effect its first national customs tariff.

Although the control of China has been divided among the various contending groups, the keen desire for the termination of the so-called "unequal treaties" and the attainment of tariff autonomy has been a cardinal feature of the program of all the factions. Only the protests from many directions prevented the actual enforcement of the entirely new autonomous tariff announced by the Nanking Nationalist authorities, with a scale of duties ranging up to 57½ per cent. There are, however, being enforced practically throughout China the ordinary and luxury surtaxes contemplated by the Washington Conference of 1922, which were to have been imposed only after agreement with the Powers, but which the Peking Government on its own authority ordered to be collected early in 1927. In addition, the local authorities in a number of provinces or regions are levying special surtaxes of varying amounts.

Economic Rapprochement

Moves toward closer trade relations among groups of European countries.—The year was marked by steps toward tariff and, to some extent, general economic rapprochement between several groups of neighboring countries standing in close economic relation to each other.

The movement for a customs union between Latvia and Estonia, both formerly parts of the Russian Empire, culminated in an agreement, ratified by both countries during 1927, which contemplates the coördination of their customs tariffs within the year, and of their internal taxes, railway tariffs, and banking policies within three years, when the proposed customs union is actually to come into effect.

The final conclusion of the commercial treaty between France and Germany, after negotiations of over two years, is regarded as a most important step toward the mutually beneficial adjustment of the economic interests and trade relations of the two principal contending countries in the late War. For the five years prior to 1925, Germany was required under the Peace Treaty to accord most-favored-nation treatment to all the Allies, without any corresponding obligations on their part; France imposed on German products during that period duties several times as high as those levied on products from more favored sources. The Franco-German Commercial Treaty of 1927 ushers in a regime of a decidedly more mutually advantageous character. After an exchange of reciprocal duty concessions, the Germans from their current tariff and the French from their proposed new tariff, each country granted to the principal export products of the other practically the most favorable duties of its tariff, with a condition of complete, unconditional most-favored-nation treatment between them to be achieved by December, 1928.

Among the Austrian Succession States, where the need has been keenly felt for less obstructive trade policies between what had for years formed parts of a single economic area, the year marked progress. The various schemes for a Danubian Confederation are coming to be recognized, under the present state of nationalist sentiments, as a possible ideal rather than a practical objective. Adjustment of relations has rather been sought through the negotiation of carefully worked out commercial treaties between various sets of these states, embodying reciprocal moderations of the present duties and trade restrictions on commodities of particular interest to each other, so as to allow easier trading relations between the producing and consuming elements in each other's territories.

International Conferences

Series of meetings seek agreement upon more liberal trade practices.—The year was notable for its good resolutions on the part of the nations in the matter of control of foreign trade. It was marked by a number of international conferences where various problems in the regulation of commerce were subjected to fresh examination, and from which emerged a series of principles and standards which it was agreed should govern the nations in their policies and practices. These conferences were notable not only as occasions for a discussion of problems and overhauling of standards with a thoroughness never before shown, but also for the concrete manifestation of the growing recognition that the prosperity and general welfare of all countries would be advanced by the adoption of simpler and more liberal measures to govern the flow of trade between them, and that there was much to be gained from common standards and practices.

Outstanding was the World Economic Conference held at Geneva in May, under the auspices of the League of Nations.[1] This was followed by the Stockholm meeting of the International Chamber of Commerce where, with some modifications, the resolutions of the Geneva conference received the endorsement of the representatives of the busniess world, who pledged themselves to efforts within their respective countries toward the realization of those standards.

At Washington there was convened the Third Pan American Commercial Conference, made up of representative businessmen from the twenty-one American Republics. It gave prominent place on its program to the subject of barriers to inter-American trade, particularly the need for simpler and more uniform consular procedures and customs regulations. One of the concrete results of this Conference was the creation of the Pan American Commission on Consular Procedure, made up of technically competent official representatives of the member republics. At its sessions, held during October, there was developed a series of advanced standards with regard to the preparation and handling of shipping documents, and consular regulations and practices which, as they become built into the actual regime of the individual countries, are expected to mark considerable advance and appreciable relief from the present situation. The recommendations of this

[1] A first-hand account of this little-known first World Economic Conference, in which the writer participated as adviser on the United States Delegation, will be found in *The American Year Book* for 1927. Unfortunately, the implementation of its constructive recommendations in the fields of commerce, industry, and agriculture had barely begun before they were swamped by the outbreak of the great depression of 1929.

Commission on Consular Procedure now go before the Sixth International Conference of American States at Havana for endorsement by the plenipotentiary representatives of the member countries and final reference to the respective governments for action.

One of the first fruits of the World Economic Conference, which was made up of unofficial representatives of the fifty countries participating—whose opinions were therefore not binding upon their governments—was the "diplomatic" conference held at Geneva in the fall, made up of authorized governmental representatives, for the purpose of working out a convention for the abolition of import and export restrictions. This convention, earlier referred to, has already been signed by eighteen important countries. When it has been ratified by those and any additional countries, an important step will have been taken toward the stabilization and liberalization of international trade, through the condemnation of restrictions and prohibitions as regular devices of trade control, and through the removal of the great majority of restrictions which for some years have handicapped the normal flow of trade.

1928

DISTINCT PROGRESS TOWARD TARIFF STABILITY AND MODERATION OF TRADE RESTRICTIONS

Slowing Up in Tariff Revisions and License Restrictions

In general, 1928 was marked by a slowing up in the number of general revisions or comprehensive changes in the import tariffs of foreign countries, accompanied by some indications of a tendency toward moderation of tariffs and other restrictions on the movement of goods from one country into another. The large number of commercial treaties negotiated during the year between various sets of countries suggests a closer approach to a state of stability in the conditions of trading between nations, particularly in view of the definite adoption almost universally of the unconditional most-favored-nation principle.

While still far from receiving general adoption, the recommendations of the World Economic Conference of 1927 are beginning to show their influence in a limited way, in the movement observed toward moderation and stabilization of tariffs and trade relations. The various conferences and international studies centering at Geneva are coming to play an appreciable part in the formulation of world principles in matters of trade control, and in facilitating international agreement on more liberal and more uniform standards of practice. The most important concrete step in this field during 1928 was the final conclusion of the convention for the abolition of import and export prohibitions and restrictions, which has already been signed by the representatives of twenty-seven countries and now awaits ratification.

While not particularly motivated by the Geneva discussions, along the same direction has been the termination, on November 1, 1928, of the export restrictions on crude rubber maintained for several years past in British Malaya and Ceylon, which constituted perhaps the most noteworthy case of restriction upon quasi-monopolized raw materials in recent years.

On the other hand, the year saw an accentuation of the tendency for tying up of certain European countries with their overseas dominions or colonies, through preferential tariffs or other measures for closer relations, with some consequent disadvantage to outside countries. The announcement by the Nationalist Government of China, toward the close of the year, of the first autonomous tariff for that country, to be effective provisionally from February 1, 1929, represents a notable instance of advance in existing tariff levels.

Viewed from the commodity standpoint, the principal classes of goods that appear to have been the subject of particularly widespread change in tariffs or trade control during the past year have been: wheat and other cereal products, mineral oil, motion-picture films, pharmaceutical preparations, and what might be termed luxury goods. Machinery and industrial materials became subject to more liberal tariff treatment in an additional number of countries during the past year, as a means of aiding the development of local industries.

The events in this field characterizing the year are here discussed separately for Europe, Latin America, the British Empire, and the Orient.

Europe

Duty reductions and license removals more frequent.—Five of the twenty-six countries of continental Europe (France, Poland, Latvia, Norway, and Finland) put into operation during 1928 more or less comprehensive revisions of their import tariffs. Compared with the ten tariff revisions during 1927, this constitutes a significant indication of the progress in the settling down process in European tariffs. In addition, a number of European countries made changes in their import duties on a limited number of commodities at various times during the past year. The majority of these duty modifications have indeed been upward; but it is noteworthy that a much larger proportion of the European tariff changes during 1928 were downward than in earlier years. The reductions in duties were in many cases brought about in the course of treaty negotiations involving duty concessions by one or both countries on selected lists of articles. However, a number of downward changes have been autonomous, resulting from the voluntary decision of particular governments. In the most notable case, that of Germany, the reductions were partly in accordance with a definite program contemplated during the last general revision for the later or gradual reduction in the initial duties on particular commodities.

Perhaps the most noteworthy modification in European trade control during the past year has been in the matter of restrictions on imports and exports, a system which has marked the trade control regime of many countries of Europe since the war. In about ten European countries the year 1928 saw moderation or removal in varying degrees of the licensing controls or other restrictions that had hitherto governed importation or exportation, with the result that the restriction system of controlling trade has almost disappeared in Western Europe, and has been considerably limited in its scope in the countries of Central and Eastern Europe. In part, these actions are a reflection of the greater stabilization in economic conditions which makes such arbitrary controls on foreign trade less necessary. In part such actions have also been stimulated by the growing general recognition, emphasized at international conferences, that restrictions have proved arbitrary, inequitable, and, in the long run, unprofitable as a regular means of controlling the movement of goods in and out of a country.

More liberal provisions being embodied in treaties.—The progress during 1928 in the subsidence of the unsettled state of trade relations of the past decade is further seen in the particularly large number of commercial treaties or agreements concluded by European countries during the year among themselves and with their trading countries across the seas. The practice of exchanging reciprocal duty concessions in the course of many of these treaties has already been noted. The most significant feature in this field, however, has been the apparently definite reëstablishment of the unconditional most-favored-nation clause as the essential governing principle in international trade relations, even Spain and France, who for a time pursued the special-concession policy, having announced their intention during the past year of going over to the unconditional most-favored-nation policy. There is thus being restored the assurance, which was fairly general before the war, that treaty countries will be on a basis of equality in competing for the supplying of the import requirements of each other, the benefit of any later concessions in duty to third countries being extended to each other automatically and without additional compensation.

It is of further significance that the commercial treaties negotiated during the last year or so contain, with increasing frequency, provisions granting broader assurance than had hitherto been common, with regard to liberal treatment of each other's trade. Particularly noteworthy have been the undertakings to grant most-favored-nation treatment in the matter of import or export restrictions, and in an increasing number of treaties a definite exchange of promises not to impede the trade between the two countries through the imposition of any prohibitions or special restrictions upon their imports or exports beyond those for purposes of public safety, health, or protection of plants or animals, and the like, which are generally excepted. The propriety of indirect trade was further recognized in a number of treaties, either through promises to accord goods coming through the territory of the other country the same treatment as direct shipments, or through assurances that goods of that other country arriving indirectly through a third country will be granted as favorable customs treatment as if they had come directly.

Latin America

Tariff overhaulings less frequent.—Among the countries of Latin America, as of Europe, 1928 witnessed a slowing up in the frequency of tariff changes. Only five of the American Republics can be said to have put into operation during 1928 thoroughgoing or at all large-scale revisions of their import duties, as compared with about twelve such revisions during 1927. Of the five indicated, three countries (Chile, Haiti, Peru) actually put through general overhaulings of their tariffs during the year; a fourth (Uruguay) continued its program of gradual revision by issuing new official valuations for duty purposes covering a number of its tariff schedules; and the fifth country (Mexico) ordered so many individual changes both in import and export duties during the course of the year as to materially change the complexion of its tariff although without a general overhauling. In addition, an appreciable number of duty changes on individual commodities were ordered during 1928 by the governments of the countries of Latin America, as they have been for some years past, but the number of such tariff changes was noticeably smaller than in earlier years.

The method of tariff making in the countries of Latin America has, however, seen no appreciable change. The regime of many of these countries is marked by the fact that the executive, or a particular cabinet minister, is vested with authority to order changes in the duties on individual commodities or in other measures of trade control at almost any time, and without requiring legislative approval or prior notice. In fact, the prevalence of this practice was accentuated during 1928 by the tariff authority vested in the president of Chile in the course of the general revision of the tariff of that country.

Duty exemptions for productive equipment more common.—In five of the Latin American countries (Bolivia, Costa Rica, Ecuador, Guatemala, and Haiti) additional measures were taken during the past year to reduce, if not completely to waive, the import duties on specified classes of machinery, equipment, or materials for use in production or construction. These represent extensions of the policy followed by many of these countries of encouraging the economic development of the country, whether in agriculture, mining, or industry, through the granting of privileges in connection with the admission of the necessary machinery and materials, or the waiver of local taxes. Peru appears to have been following a regular policy of granting reduced rates of duty on importations of specified industrial materials in shipments of a given minimum quantity.

A considerable number of countries of Latin America appear to have taken up for reconsideration their regulations on the admission of pharmaceutical or medicinal preparations, with the revised regulations commonly requiring that such a product may not be sold in the country unless it has been previously submitted for registration, and, in some cases, also for analysis.

British Empire

The only British countries to put into operation during 1928 a sufficiently broad modification of their import-duty schedules to warrant the term "revision" were Australia and possibly Canada, although quite a number of these areas made changes in duties on selected classes of commodities and several of the smaller colonies resorted to the addition of uniform customs surtaxes, apparently as a means of effecting an increase in revenue. While the majority of the changes have been upward, material reductions in duties appear among the changes made in several of the Dominions and a number of British colonial areas.

Tariff preferences slowly expanding.—In general, the tide of tariff preference keeps advancing in the British Empire. This year, for the first time, preferential duties for the products of Great Britain were introduced in British Borneo, and a Canada-Newfoundland agreement was concluded, exchanging tariff concessions. In quite a number of additional British areas existing preferential duties were extended in scope or amount. In fact, the tariff revisions consummated during the past year in Canada, Austrialia, and Mauritius were marked largely by increasing margins of preference for the products of Great Britain and certain other British areas, thus correspondingly increasing the handicaps on importations of products from other countries. On the other hand, the Union of South Africa, in a treaty concluded with Germany, undertook that any future concessions to the products of British areas will be automatically extended to similar German products.

Malaya and Ceylon terminate crude rubber restrictions.—In the matter of restrictions, the most significant event in British areas during the past year was the abolition of the restriction on the exports of crude rubber from Malaya and Ceylon, following reductions in the export duties effected earlier in the year. As one of the most important efforts in recent times to control the supply of an important raw material for which the particular areas were the source of a majority of the supplies, its eventual abandonment after six years of experience, and the reasons prompting that action, are of particular significance in the field of commercial policy. Another type of restriction introduced or discussed in England and several of the British areas, during 1928, has been the requirement that a given quota of the motion-picture films which may be licensed for exhibition in the country must be of British origin, with that term strictly defined.

The Orient

China and Persia announce autonomous tariffs.—The developments in the Chinese tariff situation during 1928 were undoubtedly among the outstanding events of the year in the field of trade control. Following the military unification of the country under the control of the Nationalist or Nanking authorities, notice was given to various powers of the denunciation of the old so-called "unequal treaties" which, among other things, had for years limited the height of the Chinese tariff, with an invitation for negotiation of new treaties on the basis of equality. The United States was the first country definitely to recognize Chinese autonomy in tariff matters and to negotiate a treaty on that basis (July, 1928), asking for American trade no more than assurances of equal treatment in China with that accorded the commerce or citizens of any third country. By the end of the year, a number of additional countries had taken definite steps toward the similar recognition of Chinese tariff autonomy, and in early December, 1928, the Nanking Government announced the first autonomous tariff for

China, to be brought into operation for one year from February 1, 1929. The proposed new schedule replaces the former uniform treaty rate of 5 per cent, which had been increased by various surtaxes in the different provinces, by a highly differentiated schedule with the rates of duty ranging from 5 per cent to 27½ per cent.

The new tariff schedule put into operation during 1928 by Persia, another of the oriental countries recently to have attained autonomy in tariff matters, carries important upward and downward changes in duties, according to the relation of the various classes of goods to the economic interests of the country. Notable are the duty exemptions for motor vehicles, aircraft, telephone and telegraph instruments, and typewriters. Industrial and agricultural machinery had already been admitted duty-free for several years, as part of the plan to encourage the modernization of the country. Following the denunciation of the old treaties which expired during 1927, about ten countries have thus far concluded new commercial arrangements with Persia, practically all of them—with the notable exception of the Russian treaty—providing simply for an exchange of most-favored-nation treatment.

Perhaps the only other noteworthy development in trade control in the Orient during the past year was the action of Japan in designating thirty-seven varieties of domestically produced manufactures which were to receive preferences over foreign articles in government purchases, with the intimation that a considerable number of still other products are planned for addition to this list, including textile machinery, metals, chemical products, and electrical appliances.

1929

RELATIVE LULL FOLLOWS TRADE POLICY READJUSTMENTS OF FIRST POSTWAR DECADE

Few Important Markets Institute Major Tariff Changes

Compared with the extreme unsettlement in the conditions of international trading during the first decade following the close of the World War, the year 1929 witnessed something of a lull. Fewer countries put into effect during the year general revisions of their customs tariffs than in preceding years, and these included very few of the major markets. However, tariff revisions are in various stages of preparation in quite a number of countries of Europe and of Latin America, indicating that the process of readjustment to the more or less settled postwar conditions is not yet over, and that the stage of relative stability in tariffs and other conditions of trading between nations is still to be attained.

Changes in the duties on selected commodities, amounting in some cases to partial readjustments of the tariff schedule, occurred during the year in many countries, although these have usually been limited in the number of commodities affected. The limited nature of the tariff changes during 1929 was somewhat offset in a number of countries by the practice of bringing changes into operation frequently with little or no notice to the trade, with the consequent continuance of the state of commercial uncertainty.

The trend in recent years for tariff changes to be predominantly upward has in the main continued during 1929—in most European countries and some of the British Dominions, primarily for protection; in Latin America and in the British colonies and China, primarly for revenue. However, the year has not been without a considerable number of duty changes downward, perhaps more frequently than has been the case in the years immediately preceding. Agricultural products have most often figured among the duty increases of the year; industrial products have been more prominent among the commodities upon which reductions of duty were made. Machinery, producers' equipment, and materials have been with striking frequency the subject of duty reductions or even total exemptions, evidencing the desire of many governments to facilitate the expansion of domestic production in their countries, in agriculture as well as in manufacturing and occasionally in mining or construction.

Exceptional Control Measures Experimented With for Farm Relief

Farm products have been particularly prominent in the trade control legislation of many countries during the past year, especially those of Europe, reflecting the widespread condition of agricultural overproduction, and the earnest concern that is felt by many governments over the relatively disadvantageous position of their agricultural producers. The efforts to ameliorate the situation have taken various forms in the different countries, and a variety of exceptional devices for the control and stimulation of trade in agricultural products are being tried out. Aside from the usual first resort to increased duties against similar imports, the measures of relief being experimented with include: a government monopoly on grain; insistence upon domestic flour containing a given proportion of domestic wheat; sliding-scale tariffs on sugar and other agricultural products; and a system of import certificates issued upon the exportation of grains and certain other farm products.

Principal Countries Effecting or Considering Tariff Revisions

Among the European countries, thoroughgoing tariff overhaulings were effected only in Rumania and Turkey, the first mainly downward and the second upward. The so-called revision of the Swedish tariff was largely one of form, and the Finnish revision consisted only of the annual group of selective changes. General revisions are reported in process or under consideration in Finland, Germany, Greece, Poland, Portugal, Spain, and Yugoslavia.

In accordance with the customs in many British areas of introducing tariff changes once a year in connection with the annual budget, quite a number of Dominions and colonies effected limited changes in their import tariffs during 1929. The broad upward revision of import duties by Australia represents probably the only comprehensive tariff revision in the Empire. Important tariff changes are in prospect in two major British areas: in Great Britain, where the new Labour Government has declared for fewer protective duties, and in Canada, where extensive hearings are being held before the Tariff Advisory Board. There were some small steps taken during the year, and larger projects agitated, for bringing about closer trade relations between the various parts of the British Empire and curtailing imports from foreign sources.

Guatemala was the only country of Latin America that put into operation during 1929 an actual comprehensive tariff revision, with changes both upward and downward. The new Mexican tariff is essentially a readjustment of the present schedule so as to consolidate with the duties the consular fee and the customs surcharge hitherto collected separately. Projects for general tariff revision have been prepared and are reported under way in Brazil, Colombia, and Peru. In the matter of duties or controls on exports, an important feature in buying from many countries of Latin America, the year was marked by numerous changes, particularly in Mexico, Guatemala, and Argentina. The establishment of an exclusive selling agency for the handling of the sugar crop by the Cuban Government was a feature of the year.

The first autonomous tariff of China, distinctly upward, was the outstanding revision of the year in the Orient. Japan made some changes, mostly downward, and has a general revision in prospect before long. In the Near East, a considerable revision of the Palestine customs tariff was noted, while Egypt announced an autonomous tariff to be effective as soon as the last of the present limiting treaties with the Powers expires in 1930.

European Countries Negotiate Many Trade-stabilizing Treaties

Well over one hundred commercial treaties or agreements were negotiated or made effective during 1929. While counterbalanced by a rather considerable number of treaties denounced or terminated, the year saw a substantial net addition to the arrangements by various sets of countries for the stabilizing and regularizing of the conditions of trading between their nationals. The majority of these treaties involved the various countries of Europe. This is natural in view of the great prevalence of differential tariffs on the Continent, necessitating definite arrangements in order to secure minimum rates of duty or the most favorable conditions of admission.

However, the process of the reduction or binding ("conventionalization") of duties among the countries of Europe has been going on for a number of years, and it is not unlikely that the original tariff schedules have in most cases been brought to the level that the governments consider approximately their indispensable minimum. Whether for this reason, or because of the increasingly universal adoption of the broad most-favored-nation or tariff-equality principle—or whatever the explanation—it is notable that the granting of tariff concessions in the course of commercial treaties has been less frequent recently than in earlier years.

The great majority of treaties of the year provide essentially for an exchange of most-favored-nation treatment in customs and related matters, with tariff adjustments downward as well as upward appearing to be made most often by autonomous action on the part of the individual governments. As a notable but rather isolated exception to the most-favored-nation principle, there appeared toward the end of the year the Swiss treaties with France and Belgium, reserving duty reductions made in the course of multilateral agreements of a certain specified type, an innovation obviously related to the current discussion of a possible European agreement for collective tariff reductions. The undertakings which were noted in a number of the commercial treaties of 1928, not to impede the trade with the other contracting country through the imposition of any prohibitions or restrictions on their imports or exports (beyond the usually recognized exceptions), have appeared with increasing frequency as a feature of the commercial treaties negotiated during the past year.

International Conferences

Agreement for free exportation of hides and bones effective.—The year was marked by active discussions and increasing efforts for the collective handling of trade control problems, through simultaneous action by a number of countries along the lines worked out at international conferences. On October 1, 1929, there were brought into operation as between seventeen countries of Europe the Geneva agreements for the abolition of restrictions on the exportation of hides and skins and of bones. An exceptional feature of these agreements is the undertaking for the removal or limitation of export duties on these products. This is the more exceptional because of the failure thus far of all proposals to carry the plan of collective action into the field of reductions of import duties on specific commodities.

Convention to end general license restrictions in doubt.—The major Convention for the Abolition of Import and Export Prohibitions and Restrictions, worked out at the two Geneva conferences of 1927 and 1928, to which the agreements on hides and bones are subsidiary agreements, had been planned to be brought into permanent operation January 1, 1930. Under this convention, the participating countries are obligated to abolish as between each other all restrictions or prohibitions of an economic character on imports or exports, other than those specifically recognized or excepted in the convention, within a period of six months from the date of its coming into force. The restrictions of this character still maintained in the various countries affect a wide range of producers, from growers of prunes to manufacturers of automobiles. It is clearly understood that the convention does not affect the tariff systems or the treaty-making methods of any of the contracting countries.

More than the necessary eighteen ratifications had been secured, but a number of them made their ratification conditional upon similar action by certain other governments, not all of whom have thus far ratified. The failure of Czechoclovakia and Poland to ratify, for various reasons, appeared the main difficulty. At a special Paris conference in December, agreement was reached between the representatives of the nineteen ratifying countries, including the United States, upon temporarily designating January 1, 1930, as the effective date of the convention.

Because of the difficulty mentioned, January 1 is designated as only a provisionally effective date, in that any of the countries may withdraw from the convention on June 30, 1930, if the two nonadhering countries named have not ratified by the end of May. The hope was, however, expressed by the leaders of the conference that either the two particular countries would ratify within the period, or that the others would waive their right to withdraw and continue the convention indefinitely in operation. When finally operative, the convention is expected to result in a material liberation of international trading from what has come to be recognized as one of the worst forms of artificial trade barriers. Its value lies not only in the abolition of the various economic restrictions in the form of special licensing, quota, or other controls on foreign trade still existing in any of the contracting countries, but in the assurance it carries against the reimposition by them of what is being thus condemned as a disapproved device for the purpose of control of commerce.

Briand's proposal for a "United States of Europe."—A project of far-reaching significance, hitherto mainly of theoretic interest, was brought closer into the realm of practical consideration by the declarations of M. Briand and others at the 1929 League of Nations Assembly urging the desirability of an economic federation among the European states. The objective of what is sometimes loosely referred to as a proposal for a "United States of Europe" is the gradual removal or scaling down of the many customs barriers now dividing the European continent, and the establishment of as nearly as possible one large and unobstructed economic area.

The leaders of the movement regard this program as essential to the economic health and progress of Europe as a whole, under the changed conditions of modern competition. They declare the scaling down of European tariff walls the indispensable condition for the effective development of large-scale production in Europe, pointing out its dependence upon having a large consuming population within the producers' assured market area, with goods originating in any part of the area moving with considerable freedom from tariff hindrance over the whole of it. The objective as well as the organization envisaged seem distinctly patterned on the lines which are regarded as having been largely responsible for the remarkable economic progress and prosperity of the United States.

The political as well as the economic difficulties in the way of consummation of such a scheme have become apparent in the course of study that has since been made of the projects to that end, and its actual attainment is coming to be generally recognized as at best an ultimate possibility. The only practical proposal that has thus far been put forward to the various governments has been the invitation of the League of Nations to an international conference early in 1930, to consider an agreement for a "tariff truce" among as large a number of countries as possible for a period of several years, during which time plans for future steps toward the mutual moderation of tariff barriers may be worked out.

American Republics move toward simpler customs regulations.—On the American continent, the recent effort toward simpler and more liberal conditions for the movement of trade between countries has been mainly in the field of customs and port administration, and in the procedures in connection with the documentation and actual movement of goods between them. Considerable progress has been made in this direction during the last few years. Several of the Latin American countries have consolidated with the basic schedule of import duties the various customs surcharges, so much a feature of the tariffs of these countries. Others have transferred the collection of the consular fee for the legalization of shipping documents, which often is assessed as a percentage of the shipment's value, from the foreign exporter to the domestic importer, thus giving it its proper place as an additional customs charge.

During 1929, six of these countries announced revised consular and customs regulations or codes, and all but one were efforts in the direction of greater simplicity and expedition of trade. The recommendations of the experts of the American Republics who participated in the Pan American Conference on Customs Procedure and Port Formalities at Washington in November, 1929, are expected to give impetus to this tendency for simpler and more uniform requirements and practices in these matters, irrespective of the degree to which the draft convention recommended by that conference receives wide acceptance, as a whole, by the American governments. This expectation arises partly from the evidence already apparent of the influence of the recommendations of the similar Pan American Conference on Consular Procedure of 1927 upon the builders of the revised consular regulations which have since been issued by various of the American countries.

1930

GENERAL ECONOMIC DEPRESSION BECOMES DOMINANT INFLUENCE ON COMMERCIAL POLICY MEASURES

Economic Nationalism Intensified by the Depression

The economic depression that affected almost the entire world during 1930 has been a dominant influence in the trend of the commercial policy of most foreign countries in the past year. The sense of common distress led several groups of countries to come together during the year to consider various plans for closer economic coöperation, either by moderating the barriers to exchanges of goods or by common action in the marketing of surplus products. Up to the end of 1930, however, these various efforts at concerted action had shown little result. The majority of tariff changes and other measures for control of international trade actually adopted during the year by the various foreign countries seem, rather, the expression of a sense of an increased tension in international competition and of a sharper spirit of economic nationalism.

Whatever may be the final judgment as to the basic causes of the current world depression, most of the measures taken by the various countries during 1930 to control imports or to stimulate exports appear to have been directed primarily at the immediate difficulties experienced in each particular country, in the hope of relieving the domestic situation, at least temporarily. Various long-time projects and plans looking to basic remedies have indeed been widely discussed, but it remains for the future to see to what extent these will be brought into practical operation. The events of 1930 in the field of commercial policy may mark a permanent trend, or may prove a temporary phase. Judging by the majority of actual events and measures put into operation, however, the year has seen a distinct drift toward intensified protection and restrictive nationalism.

The character of the measures for control of foreign trade taken during 1930 under the influence of the depression has naturally varied in different parts of the world, and among various countries, in accordance with the particular domestic problems giving the most concern.

Protection of Home Market and Prices Prime European Aim

Thus, in the countries of Europe, the increasing industrial unemployment and the falling off in trade gave urgency in many cases to measures designed to reserve the home market more exclusively to domestic manufacturers, by means of higher duties or other restrictions against the importation of similar foreign goods. In a few cases, the danger of budgetary deficit because of reduced governmental income, partly resulting from the depression, has led to increased duties for revenue purposes. However, with the depression having been most prolonged and most marked among the agricultural producers, arising largely out of overproduction of food staples and the low prices at which competitive products were being offered from overseas countries and from Russia, the majority of European foreign trade control measures during 1930 have been aimed at ameliorating their agricultural situations.

The farm surplus-producing countries of Eastern Europe examined every means for individual and joint aid in the disposal of their crops abroad, even to urging that the food-importing countries of Middle and Western Europe afford them preferential duties or other means of assuring the preferred purchase of their products, in return for improved markets in their territories for the industrial products of Western Europe. However, the similar distress of the agrarian elements in these food-importing countries has thus far rather prompted them to give first consideration to their own producers and, by increased duties or other means, to attempt to hold up home market prices. The appearance of quantities of Russian products on various European markets, during the latter months of the year, at prices that were regarded as foreshadowing a program of dumping, increased the tension of the situation.

The common depression gave considerable poignancy to the discussions of a United States of Europe and other proposals for concerted economic action, but little resulted beyond the crystallization of a number of possible regional agreements among various groups of European countries. These various developments will be discussed in some detail later.

Low World Prices and Reduced Exports Worry Latin and British Areas

In most of the countries of Latin America, the nature of the pressures prompting changes in tariffs and similar measures were somewhat different from those observed in Europe. Here the outstanding fact was the sharp decline in world market prices and curtailed demand for their staple raw materials and foods, the profitable exportation of which constitute both the barometer of national prosperity and the principal source of governmental income. Also, anxiety over their foreign exchange situation led a number of these countries to a policy of curtailing imports as one of the means of supporting their falling currencies.

Two types of measures were observed during 1930 in these areas. Tariff revisions of more or less broad scope were resorted to in many of the Latin American countries, primarily as a means of affording additional revenues from imports of noncompetitive manufactures and luxury articles, although the effort to foster secondary industries and to keep imports more nearly balanced with exports also figured in a number of cases. With regard to outgoing trade, the influence of the depression was very strongly manifested among the countries of Latin America in the measures taken for the control or stimulation of their staple export products.

The various British Dominions and colonies found their principal difficulties much the same as those of Latin American countries, namely, depressed prices and lowered demand for their export staples, which are produced primarily for world markets. In a number of these areas, moreover, the situation was aggravated by considerable industrial unemployment and by disturbed financial situations and budgetary difficulties arising partly out of the depressed state of exports and unusual relief expenditures.

Among the British areas, the efforts at relieving the depression through foreign trade control measures took two forms. In the principal Dominions, drastic upward tariff revisions were resorted to, sometimes enforced by restrictive customs regulations or licensing controls on imports. These revisions aimed primarily at curtailing imports of products which could be at all supplied domestically, or in some cases from British or Empire sources. The motive in at least one case was, frankly, to curtail the volume of importation of dispensable goods, in an effort to right the trade balance and improve the exchange position. Among the British colonies, the protective motive for their smaller range of products was often the less urgent cause for tariff changes than was the need for increased governmental revenue, which they derive largely from the customs.

In addition, relief was sought for the trade depression among the British areas through the active consideration of the possibility of greater reciprocal tariff preferences between various parts of the Empire, with a view to reserving each other's necessary purchases more largely to suppliers within the Empire, and thus reducing dependence upon outside countries both as markets and suppliers. Thus far, these plans made little headway, in view of the inability of the present English Government to agree to a more general tariff system for England, which was put forward as essential to the larger plan contemplated. The possibilities of greater imperial tariff preference are, however, to be further explored during 1931.

Among the countries of the Orient the immediately depressing factors were apparently not such as to suggest material relief through changes in tariffs and similar measures. The most aggravating factor in the Japanese situation—namely, the sharp drop in the price of raw silk, owing to the reduced demands from the depressed Western countries—is a case in point. The disturbed political conditions and the drop in the price of silver being the chief depressants of the Chinese situation, the principal impulse for tariff change there was the need for additional revenues, and a mainly upward revision for that purpose was announced toward the end of the year.

A more detailed summary of the nature and extent of the measures for control of foreign trade adopted or prominently discussed during 1930, in each of the various groups of countries, follows.

Continental Europe

Unlike the case in previous years, the mere number of revisions of import tariffs and related measures during 1930 is not an adequate reflection of the year's developments in the field of foreign trade control on the continent of Europe. With the general business recession that developed late in 1929 aggravating the disturbed situation arising from the already existing European agricultural depression, it is not surprising that the year 1930 was one of increased tension in international competition and of considerable tightening up in commercial policy. In addition, it was marked by experimentation with new devices and agitation for new arrangements in the field of foreign trade control.

There were, indeed, six general or extensive tariff revisions on the part of that many European countries during 1930, with the general trend of the rates upward. More significant, however, was the state of unsettlement that led all but two of the governments of continental Europe to make some changes in their tariffs during the year, often affecting fairly important groups of commodities, with several countries making two or more series of limited changes during the twelve-month period. While the tariff changes during 1930 were, indeed, practically all downward in the case of three countries, and several made selective revisions that provided for decreases as well as increases, the great majority of the new European duties are higher than the old.

Emergency measures reflect special concern for farm producers.—In about half of the European countries that increased their import tariffs during the year, various groups of manufactured commodities were affected, either for the purpose of protecting the market for home industries that were particularly depressed, or as a means of increasing national revenues or improving the trade balance. In all but five of the twenty-four countries making tariff changes, however, agricultural products figured prominently, reflecting the widespread concern of governments over the need for relief to the particularly depressed agrarian elements in their populations. In fact, the year was marked by extension of old schemes and a burst of new measures on the part of many of the countries of Europe, either to reserve the home markets or check the decline in prices for their domestic agricultural producers, by various forms of restriction on imports, or to assist in the disposal in other markets of surpluses with which they were burdened. The latter plans not infrequently involved exporting at prices below those of the home market and, in some cases, under stimulus of arrangements amounting to export bounties.

The majority of grain-importing countries on continental Europe increased their duties on wheat or flour or both, during 1930, and several of them more than once. A third country was added to the two which already made the importation of cereals subject to restriction or license. Five European countries enforced their protective duties by requiring that given proportions of domestic wheat or flour be mixed with the imported. Several countries resorted to governmental monopolies or state controls of trade in one or more grains—a device that had come and gone in earlier years. To insure quickly adjustable controls on imports, authority to change duties on cereals and other foods was, in a few countries, vested in the Minister of Finance or of Commerce. In a number of cases, the restrictive measures on cereals were extended also to hogs and meat products, while the idea of aiding domestic producers by requiring the mixing of a given proportion of domestic with foreign products was applied also to other commodities—principally the mixture of domestic alcohol with imported gasoline.

Prominent among the measures to aid exportation of food surpluses was the more active use, and at increased values, of certificates issued on exportation and acceptable in the payment of import duties on the same or related commodities. Among the other arrangements were: the reduction or waiver of export duties; in one case, drawback arrangements distinctly stimulating exportation of domestic grain; and, in at least two countries, the payment of direct premiums on the exportation of cereals and hog products. Mention has already been made of the plan advanced by the agricultural countries of Eastern Europe, although thus far without success, calling for preferential treatment of their surpluses in other parts of Europe.

In addition to the autonomous changes in duties and other trade control measures, 1930 saw considerable activity in the way of negotiations or amendments of commercial treaties by the European countries, mainly with other countries of that Continent. For the most part, the tariff provisions of the new treaties consisted of the exchange of minimum rates and the promise of most-favored-nation treatment, with a view to regularizing trade relations between the countries concerned on a basis of equality with other competitors. However, over twenty of these treaties of the past year involved tariff concessions on one or both sides.

It is notable that about half of the European bargaining treaties or amendments of 1930 were negotiated for the purpose of allowing one or both of the contracting parties freedom of action with regard to the duties on which they were hitherto bound and which they now desired to increase. Many of the new or amended treaties granting duty concessions were, therefore, in the nature of compensation treaties, the new concessions replacing other conventional duties withdrawn.

Moreover, a number of European commercial treaties denounced have not been permanently replaced, owing to disagreement over the restrictive duties and measures adopted by one or both of the parties concerned during the past year or so. The differences between Hungary and Czechoslovakia, over each other's duties and agricultural measures, constituted a notable case of a break between neighboring states that has left a difficult situation unbridged by treaty.

Of particular interest to American exporters was the frequency with which the proposal was discussed in various European countries during 1930 for putting import duties on particular commodities on a contingent basis, whereby the existing or reduced rates were to apply only up to a given quantity, with imports from any country above that amount to be subject to much higher duties. The major proposals of this character affected automobiles and did not materialize, although such duty contingents were embodied in a number of inter-European treaties affecting certain secondary farm products.

Various proposals for joint remedial action, all unpromising.—More prominent than the actions of individual countries, and possibly more momentous for the future, were the various proposals discussed among the European countries during 1930, looking toward concerted economic action, particularly in matters of trade control. These efforts toward concerted action are significant, not for the little that was accomplished during the year, but for the growing recognition of the desirability of greater European economic solidarity, and for the replacement of vague expressions of generous sentiment by the exposing of the actual positions, as well as the desires and limitations, of the various countries with regard to the vital problem of the control of their trade exchanges.

As indicated, 1930 saw a record of many attempts at European concerted action and, thus far, little practical result. The so-called Tariff Truce Conference early in the year—which it was originally hoped would result in a general agreement not to change tariffs further for a period of several years, preparatory to a movement for concerted tariff reductions—could agree on little more than tentative promises to stabilize duties contained in existing treaties for a period of one year. Moreover, with only nine countries ratifying by the original date set, there is only the hope that the postponement of that date to April 1, 1931, may give the agreement formal validity, even for its limited scope.[1]

The International Convention for the Abolition of Import and Export Restrictions and Prohibitions, which had been worked out at earlier Geneva conferences and ratified by about twenty countries (including the United States), gave promise of marking an important further step through the early removal of one of the worst forms of trade barrier. However, it failed of coming into operation in July, 1930, as planned, through the

[1] Up to March, 1931, thirteen countries had ratified, but these did not include at least two of the countries upon whose ratification a number of others had made theirs contingent. The convention was, therefore, suspended, with the way left open for its being brought into operation at some later date.

inability of one important country to ratify. As a result, the majority of countries which had already ratified, but contingent upon similar action by others, withdrew their ratifications, leaving only seven countries unconditionally adhering. The trend of the past year in European commercial policy renders doubtful the likelihood of this agreement being revived and extended at an early date.

The large scheme for a European Federal Union (popularly referred to as the United States of Europe), which had been launched by M. Briand of France at the League Assembly of 1929 and amplified this past year, attracted a great deal of attention during 1930. The early reactions from various European countries showed fairly general enthusiasm for its broad purposes, and the psychological mood bred of the common depression rendered particularly attractive the prospect of larger unobstructed markets on the continent of Europe that were envisaged by the scheme. The more careful later replies by the various governments, however, and the discussions at the 1930 Assembly soon revealed the remoteness of practical progress on this plan. While the major objections appear to arise from the political assumptions and complications of the Briand scheme, there were obvious indications of the unreadiness or inability of most of the European countries, in the present unequal stage of economic advancement, to make the sacrifices of existing or prospective economic activities necessary to anything approaching a European customs union. After much discussion, the general problem was referred to a Commission of Enquiry for European Union for further exploration, while special League committees or conferences were asked to work out solutions for certain specific immediate problems such as the wheat-surplus question.[2]

The thoroughgoing discussion of the subject of a European union has had the interesting reaction, however, of bringing to a head the sentiment among various smaller groups of countries on the European continent that it would serve their common interests to enter into regional agreements, either regarding common tariff action or for concerted organization in production and marketing. Most important and most prominent of these groups was that of the agricultural countries of Eastern Europe, whose successive meetings at Sinaia, Bucharest, and Warsaw developed the now well-known proposal for tariff preferences to their food products in the more western countries of Europe. Without despairing over their failure thus far to obtain such tariff or other preferences for their products in

[2] Up to the end of March, 1931, no definite progress has been made by the meetings either of the European commission or of the special conferences held at Geneva and Paris.

European markets, despite several meetings on the subject with other European governments, five of these eastern countries (Poland, Hungary, Rumania, Yugoslavia, and Bulgaria) are endeavoring to proceed with an autonomous program worked out at the Belgrade conference in November, 1930, limited to the centralized planning of the production and exportation of their grain surpluses.

Somewhat overlapping and of secondary importance was the smaller movement launched at the Athens conference, of unofficial representatives from the Balkan states, urging upon their governments closer coöperation in political and cultural as well as economic relations, with particular stress upon closer tariff relations and coöperation in the marketing of the export products of the Balkans.

Of a different character, and yet growing out of the same unpromising discussions at Geneva of continent-wide European concerted action, is the regional agreement signed at Oslo as the year closed, among five northern European states (Norway, Sweden, Denmark, Belgium, and Holland). The signatories obligate themselves to refrain from increasing their customs tariffs, except upon due notice; and, in a protocol regarding future negotiations, declare themselves willing to support any further international efforts to diminish obstacles to commercial intercourse and improve conditions for exchange of commodities. They also agree to investigate the possibilities of extending the principle of this agreement to other matters affecting their mutual economic interests.

The current commercial policy measures and proposals in Europe have special significance for non-European countries. Most of the plans for regional or continental tariff agreements between various countries of Europe, as well as a number of the measures adopted or considered by individual countries, almost necessarily involve evasion or partial abandonment of the most-favored-nation principle. After a postwar period of confusion and discriminatory practices, this principle has been reëstablished in recent years, with the strong indorsement of the World Economic Conference, as the fairest governor of commercial relations between nations, eliminating discrimination in the official conditions of trading and assuring equality of treatment to competitive suppliers.

During the past year or so, however, there has been heard in Europe considerable criticism and chafing at the most-favored-nation obligation now built into most existing treaties. This has often been carried to the point of declaring that it constituted an obstacle to the moderation of tariffs and trade barriers between European countries, since the declared objective would be largely defeated if the concessions exchanged had to be extended also to overseas countries or to nonparticipating nations of Europe. Similarly, the very purpose of duty contingents, government purchasing boards, and similar measures now prominently discussed, could hardly be attained if the administration of these schemes were limited by the necessity of equal curtailment of normal imports from each country involved, or of equal opportunity to competitive suppliers in all countries.

However, such individual measures involving evasion of the most-favored-nation objective have not yet been carried very far and the regional plans are all still in the proposal stage. The very careful safeguards set at the November Conference for Concerted Economic Action upon any plan for preferential treatment of Eastern European grain, indicate that the majority of European countries still attach great importance to the most-favored-nation principle as a safeguard and governor of international trade, and are not ready to consent to any measures that would materially weaken its effectiveness.

British Empire

Widespread trade control changes in overseas areas.—The year was marked by important tariff revisions in the four principal Dominions and less extensive changes in most of the British colonies. Particularly notable were: the further marked increases in the Australian duties, enforced by restrictions or prohibitions on certain commodities, in the effort to help the trade balance and financial position of the country, as well as to foster the development of secondary or manufacturing industries; the somewhat less extensive upward revision in New Zealand, marked by increases in the margin of British preference; and the two revisions of the tariff and customs law in Canada, the first (by the Liberal Government) designed to foster greater Empire trading, as well as domestic industries, and the second (by the Conservative Government) for the distinct purpose of giving every aid to the lines of production already established in Canada and to invite others. By contrast, the limited tariff changes made by Newfoundland were almost all downward.

Great Britain was almost the only British area making no appreciable changes in its tariff during 1930, beyond allowing the so-called safeguarding duties on a group of commodities to lapse at the end of their term. There has been considerable sentiment for protection within England, although thus far this has been resisted by some leaders in the Labour Government. Practically all other British areas made some change in their duties during the year, including many areas not following the practice of an annual tariff bill. In the great majority of cases, the duty changes during 1930 were upward, and appear to fall roughly into two categories. Many of the areas producing sugar, flour, or butter, increased the import duties on these products for the protection of the home market; while others apparently sought increased revenues by raising their duties on commodities they regarded as luxuries, principally tobacco, matches, liquor, automobiles, tires, and gasoline.

Action postponed on proposals for enlarged Empire preferences.—The possibilities of getting together the various British areas into a more self-sufficient economic empire, through the exchange of greater tariff preferences to encourage buying from each other rather than from outside countries, was the subject of exceptionally active discussion throughout the British Empire during the year. The discussions came to a focus at the Imperial Conference assembled at London in October, where the Dominions offered larger measures of preference in their import duties to English manufactured products, in return for the mother country adopting a more general tariff system, particularly on foodstuffs, which duties could then be rebated or waived to the products of the Empire.

This program was not acceptable to the MacDonald Government, which felt it was against the best interests of England to adopt a general tariff, particularly on foods for its people and raw materials for its industries. Nor was the English offer of import boards for the bulk purchase of foodstuffs, with quota preferences to Empire producers, accepted by the Dominion Prime Ministers. The subject goes over to the Ottawa Conference in 1931, with the possibility of a changed position on the part of England by then, should the Conservative party—committed to a broader protective program for England, with larger Empire preferences—return to power as the result of a general election. In the meantime, Canada and Australia are attempting to work out an additional preferential arrangement for diverting trade to each other; and similar negotiations between other sets of British areas are reported in contemplation.

Latin America

The changes in import duties during 1930 in at least five of the Latin American Republics were sufficiently extensive or important to be regarded as general tariff revisions. In two of these countries, the overhauling resulted in an appreciable number of decreases in duties, but the great majority of the changes were substantially upward. In addition, six other countries effected changes in their tariffs of less extensive scope. Three general tariff revisions are reported to be in preparation.

The prime object of the duty increases in most of the Latin American countries has usually been larger governmental revenues, although there are growing indications that several of these governments are working on programs of more or less selective protection to aid existing lines of production—including some industries thus far existing only on a very small scale—and to encourage diversification into new lines of production, agricultural as well as industrial. In several of these countries an important motive for duty increases during 1930 was to help right the trade balance and improve the value of the national currency.

The variety of objectives is illustrated by the fact that the tariff increases in one country might be on a group of manufactured articles apparently regarded locally as luxuries, including notably automobiles, tires, and petroleum products, whereas another or the same country might introduce decreases in duties on machinery or materials for production or construction. Two countries definitely enlarged the list of machinery and productive equipment which are admitted entirely duty-free. On the other hand, duties were imposed or increased by several Latin American countries during 1930 on selected commodities in order to stimulate larger domestic production of those lines or assure a better domestic price. Directed to the same end was the action of Peru in ordering flour millers to use 30 per cent domestic wheat, and of Bolivia in introducing an ascending scale of duties on wheat, looking to ultimate independence of imports.

The general need for increased governmental revenues on the part of many Latin American countries was also evidenced during 1930 in a number of increases in the consular fees, which are often collected as a percentage of the value of the shipment being legalized; in general advances in the rate of customs surtaxes in a few countries; and in the adoption or consideration by several governments of monopolies on petroleum and matches.

Many export control changes to stimulate foreign buying.—Possibly the most important among the long-run measures in Latin America during 1930 were the numerous changes in the taxes, controls, and other conditions on the exportation of staple raw materials and foods, so basic to the economy of these countries. Facing an accumulation of stocks, with sharp declines in foreign demand and market prices, Brazil arranged for the gradual liquidation of the coffee valorization plan maintained for some years; Chile abolished the export tax on nitrates and iodine, which was replaced by agreements with producing interests that are to yield certain revenues to the government; while Cuban-American sugar interests, backed by the Cuban Government, worked out an agreement with the cane producers of Java and with the principal European sugar-beet countries for concerted restriction of the exportation of sugar over a period of five years.

In the effort to stimulate foreign buying, half a dozen other Latin American countries reduced or abolished their export taxes on various products, particularly coffee, hides, and cereals. Uruguay continued the export bounty on wheat, and proposed a bounty to grape growers. Chile has authorized the payment of bounties on agricultural exports.

Two sets of Central American countries concluded agreements for the reciprocal free admission of certain natural products of the other, namely, Guatemala and El Salvador, Honduras and Nicaragua.

The establishment of arrangement for parcel post service between the United States and Cuba, while of secondary importance, was an event of the year of particular interest to many American exporting firms.

Near and Far East

Chinese tariff revised upward.—The Chinese tariff situation was the only one of particular activity in the Far East during the year. Aside from the conversion of the duties to a gold basis, as a measure of stabilizing customs revenues under the shifting values of the silver tael, the principal development was the announcement of a materially upward revision of the Chinese import tariff, effective January 1, 1931. The need for increased national revenue is the declared motive for the revision. It is also proposed that the long-standing internal taxes known as "likin" be replaced by other internal levies, less burdensome upon trade. While Chinese autonomy in tariff matters has been recognized by practically all the Powers, the treaty with Japan still limits the duties that China may impose upon cotton goods, flour, sugar, and certain other commodities produced domestically.

Despite considerable investigation and recommendation for tariff changes on selected commodities, no action was taken by the Japanese Diet during the year, either on the tariff revision or on the proposal that had been made to delegate tariff authority to the Minister of Finance for a year as an emergency measure, in view of the disturbance caused by the recent removal of the gold embargo.

The Netherlands East Indies made effective a uniform 10 per cent increase of the existing duties.

Egypt installs autonomous tariff with differentiated rates.—With the lapse of the treaties limiting Egypt to a uniform levy of 8 per cent, and with the agreement of the Powers, Egypt put a revised autonomous tariff into operation early in 1930, carrying differentiated schedules of duties, partly for the declared purpose of fostering articles produced or believed producible in Egypt. The general agricultural depression affected the country toward the end of the year to the extent of bringing additional increases in the import duties on cereals, sugar, and other foods.

Among the other countries in the Near East, the tariff changes in Palestine and Syria also included increased duties on wheat, flour, and sugar, and selected manufactured products, notably automobiles. Iraq (Mesopotamia) ordered a general advance of existing duties by one-tenth to one-fifth.

Persia introduced a stringent system of importation under permit upon a considerable range of manufactured goods during 1930, as a means of improving the trade balance through drastic curtailment of foreign purchases.

[The broad upward revision of the United States import duties enacted in June, 1930, commonly referred to as the Hawley-Smoot tariff, has been the subject of such wide public discussion as to require no more than mention in this survey, which is concerned primarily with the trade control measures of foreign countries.]

1931

MARKET SHRINKAGES AND FINANCIAL CRISES PROMPT DRASTIC TRADE CONTROL MEASURES

The cumulative effect of the world economic depression, as it continued into its second year, led many foreign countries to a further tightening up of their markets during the year 1931, by higher tariffs and by a variety of other drastic trade control measures. The influence of the depression in this direction was accentuated by the general shrinkage of exports, resulting in part from the increased tariffs and other restrictive measures adopted by many countries during 1930, and was aggravated by the financial difficulties of governments, which spread rapidly after midsummer of 1931.

Under these exceptional conditions, the usually dominant protective motive for the curtailment of imports has been often overshadowed during the past year by the need for increasing governmental revenues, correcting adverse trade balances, protecting currency values, or maintaining the government's financial solvency altogether. To attain these ends, the trade control measures taken during 1931 have included, not only increases in duties, but quota limitations, restrictions on imports in other forms, exchange controls, and even gold embargoes, with all their consequences. On the other hand, among the official measures to stimulate exports or improve export price have been special tariff treaties, export subsidies, and governmental monopolies or control of trade in particular commodities.

National Emergency Measures Threaten Further to Contract World Trade

The measures in process and the plans in prospect in various countries early in 1932 foreshadow still greater contraction of international trade during the year ahead, including many markets of primary interest to American exports. In a number of foreign countries, evidences are indeed apparent of growing restiveness on the part of commercial interests over the effects of drastic trade control measures—those adopted by their own governments as well as by others. However, the likelihood of definite action during 1932 by foreign countries in the reverse direction, of moderation of trade barriers, appears to depend largely upon the early resolving of the financial crisis and upon the appearance of substantial signs of recovery from the general economic depression—the dominant forces now prompting these measures of extreme nationalism and apprehensive trade restriction.

With overcapacity, if not actual overproduction, shrinking markets, falling prices, increased unemployment, unbalanced budgets, frozen credits, and general financial uncertainty afflicting practically every country; with an increasing number of countries finding themselves during the past year facing also heavily adverse trade balances and slipping currencies; and with the difficulties of one country rapidly involving others through reciprocal reaction, many governments have resorted to whatever trade control measures suggested themselves that promised at least to alleviate their particular immediate difficulties.

Among the obvious first-aid measures widely resorted to by foreign countries during 1931 have been further increases in import duties for the usual purpose of reserving the home market more largely to home producers. This tendency was particularly noticeable among certain parts of the British Empire and of Latin America, and was the type of measure more common during the first half than in the last half of the year. During 1931 as a whole, however, tariff revision for protective purposes was less common than during 1930, notably among the countries of continental Europe. Particularly during the latter months of the year did the trade control measures taken by many governments in all parts of the world appear to have been prompted by other motives than protection, and to have taken a variety of other forms.

In many countries of Latin America, certain countries of Europe, and a few Oriental areas, duty advances, often horizontal in character, were widely resorted to during 1931, as a means of obtaining larger governmental revenues. The immediate urge was the necessity of meeting increasing domestic expenditures and fixed foreign obligations during the very period when the diminished imports and lowered domestic business activity were yielding lower revenues than normal, both from customs and from internal taxes. Many countries, particularly in Latin America and Europe, adopted drastic measures aimed at the sheer curtailment of the volume of imports, either to keep them in balance with, or below, the shrinking volume of exports, or as a means of conserving foreign exchange and protecting currency values.

The year was characterized by a marked revival, particularly on the continent of Europe, of methods of controlling foreign trade that had been common during the years following the World War, namely, by license restrictions or quota limitations upon the importation of specified lists of commodities. On a few products, notably wheat, a favorite European device of the past few years has been the limitation of imports to given percentages of the purchases of similar or substitutive domestic products. Since the early fall of 1931, however, the resort to import quotas and restrictions has grown rapidly and spread to other commodities.

By January, 1932, the use of one or the other had been either adopted or authorized by at least a dozen European countries, with prospects of their more intensive use during 1932. Incidentally, it is significant that, in the case of several countries, import restrictions have been authorized primarily for the purpose of offsetting earlier restrictive measures on the part of other countries. But whatever the immediate motive, the revival of such quota and license controls has already had an unsettling, if not constricting, effect upon foreign trade. Evidence has also appeared of the difficulty of preventing the operation of quota systems from curtailing unequally the normal course of imports from different countries, and from weakening the governing value of fixed duties or carefully worked-out existing treaties.

Concern for Financial Solvency and Currency Values Bring Exchange Controls

The financial difficulties that became prominent in early summer, and aggravated during the latter months of the year, introduced a seriously complicating element in international trade. This was particularly true after the suspension of the gold standard by England, which was followed by most of the far-flung British areas, by Scandinavia, and later by Japan. That strained the finances and currencies of many European countries, involving a rapid shifting of reserves and freezing of credits. The repercussions of the financial derangements of these countries, in turn, accentuated the problems arising from the already depreciated currencies and financial stringencies of most countries of Latin America.

Toward the end of the year the effort to maintain financial solvency or currency values abroad, in the face of fixed foreign obligations, led to the adoption of foreign exchange controls by the majority of the countries of continental Europe and by almost all of Latin America, although not everywhere with the same severity. In effect, these exchange controls are operating as additional restrictive measures upon international trade, and in some countries are reported to be more important than prices or import duties in determining whether particular commercial transactions shall be attempted.

The growing number of arrangements between governments, notably in Central Europe, for the bilateral clearance of exchange transactions between their nationals, represents an effort to moderate the trade-constricting effect of exchange controls, although these are apparently premised upon the unusual expectation that the value of the trade between each pair of countries should balance.

Restrictive Measures by One Country Provoke Defensive Action by Others

Under the highly interdependent world economic system of today, the repercussions of the trade control measures or financial dislocations of any important country are so widespread as to lead to similar or defensive reactions on the part of other countries. They have taken the form either of additional trade restrictive measures or of enlarged authority to some branch of the government to increase duties or limit importations. These delegations of authority were expected to furnish prompt means of meeting new international situations or of offsetting the effects of commercial or financial measures of other nations, actual or anticipated. The extent of the reaction varied widely among the different countries, depending upon the previous intensity of their domestic depression, the degree of economic or financial stability, and the measure of dependence upon world markets or foreign financial centers, as well as upon the mental state of apprehension over future prospects.

With the agricultural depression the more prolonged and pronounced in most countries, the majority of the ordinary tariff changes and trade control measures adopted by foreign countries during 1931, on both imports and exports, have involved agricultural or raw products. Tariff adjustments, however, have been made with various purposes in view. As already indicated, revenue, trade balance, and financial considerations have been more prominently in mind than in earlier years. In a great many cases, therefore, the trade control measures taken for various purposes have curtailed the market opportunity for foreign goods of all kinds, whether manufactured or agricultural, and have often borne most severely upon those foreign products regarded as luxuries or those most easily dispensable.

Resort to Unusual Methods of Export Stimulation to Move Surpluses

In the effort to dispose of surpluses in glutted or timid world markets, and with depressed prices; to overcome the newer foreign import barriers; to improve the country's general competitive position in foreign markets; or to assure better world prices for particular products; experiments were made during 1931 with a variety of devices to stimulate or control exports, in addition to those familiar from earlier years.

Most notable were the special arrangements to facilitate trade exchanges between several sets of neighboring countries or areas which are members of the same political family. Such arrangements were worked out in Central Europe, among the Baltic countries, between certain British Dominions, and between the areas around the River Plate. The plan for unified control of the export surpluses of grain, agreed to by representatives of the Danubian countries at the Belgrade conference late in 1930, apparently was not acceptable to the governments; their efforts during 1931 were directed mainly toward bilateral agreements with grain-importing countries of Europe for preferential outlets in their markets. In the case of the Scandinavian countries and Japan, the pressure to maintain the country's competitive place in its principal markets, whose currencies had depreciated, is reported to have influenced those governments in their decision to suspend the gold standard, with the consequent depreciation of their own currencies in varying degree.

The year also saw some extensions of the methods of export stimulation already in operation in some countries. Probably the most notable instances were: the Chilean fund from which bounties were paid to foster certain agricultural exports, the steps by the Union of South Africa toward an export subsidy upon primary products, and the bounties upon coal and wheat initiated by Canada. Recourse to the familiar device of governmentally controlled wheat monopolies was taken by three countries of Europe.

In the direction of export control rather than stimulation, in an effort to improve the general world price of sugar and of tin, international agreements were put into operation during 1931 between the principal exporting countries in each case, to restrict the quantities of these commodities to be exported by national quotas.

Many of the drastic measures restricting import trade taken by foreign countries during 1931 are obviously temporary and may be expected to pass as the conditions creating them ease off. Many of the measures are of an indefinite term, however, and by their nature are not readily withdrawable. Such a step as the British abandonment of the traditional limited tariff policy, in favor of a program of more general and substantial tariff protection, is probably the most striking illustration of the year of a more or less permanent character.

The curb upon foreign trade through exchange control carries a certain amount of internal self-correction by the inherent difficulties and handicaps of their operation. Moreover, since the operation of import quota systems as well as of the foreign exchange controls are within the discretion of the governmental administrators or financial authorities, they can more readily be relaxed or tapered off as conditions prompting them improve. On the other hand, advances in duties, whether horizontal for revenue purposes or selective for protection, are less readily withdrawn or reduced. Similarly, special tariff arrangements between various sets of countries have their course to run, and they may create new trade orientations likely to persist.

However, as earlier intimated, the likelihood of a material easing up of the trade barriers of foreign countries during 1932 appears to depend largely upon the early resolving of the financial crisis and upon the appearance of substantial signs of general economic recovery.

The character of the tariff changes or other trade control measures taken during 1931 under the influence of the general depression or more special factors have naturally varied in different parts of the world and among various countries in accordance with the particular domestic problems giving the most concern. These will be examined more closely by broad world regions.

Continental Europe

With the continuation and deepening of the economic depression during 1931, bringing further decline in export trade, so important to the prosperity of most countries of Europe, and with the situation aggravated by increasing anxiety of governments over budget deficits and financial uncertainties as the year went on, the international trade problems of most of the countries of continental Europe during the past year were most abnormal. As a consequence, the majority of the tariff and trade control measures of these countries during 1931 were not in the nature of ordinary tariff adjustments to changing conditions of production and competition.

Most of the countries of the Continent did make some selective changes in their import duties during 1931 on particular groups of commodities, most often in connection with the commercial treaties with other European countries. A few decided upon horizontal advances of customs duties for revenue purposes, and several of the smaller (Baltic) countries made more extensive changes. However, no major country of continental Europe made any general overhauling of its tariff during the past year. The important tariff shift in England will be discussed later in connection with the British Empire.

To a certain extent, the predominately fixed form of the tariff rates of the European countries—expressed, for example, by a specific number of francs per 100 kilos—automatically increases the burden on importations during a period of sharply falling prices, and affords domestic producers some additional protection against foreign goods. But under the rapidly changing conditions of the last year, the usual recourse to tariff revision as a means of meeting new or difficult situations was apparently found unsuited to the times. This probably accounts for the more general resort to other forms of controlling import trade, which were more immediately responsive, if more drastic. Particularly since the late spring of 1931, when financial difficulties came into prominence and reacted upon other countries as soon as they affected one, have the trade relations with many of the European countries been subject to new and special obstacles.

Great diversity of trade control objectives and measures.—The year 1931 may be said to have been marked on the continent of Europe by the diversity of measures to control foreign trade, with various ends in view and by special devices and arrangements, many of which were of an obviously emergency or shifting nature. In a summary fashion, the various objectives and the methods adopted to attain them might be brought together briefly before they are discussed in detail:

1. To stimulate greater consumption of domestic products (by quota limitations, occasional license restrictions, mixing requirements, as well as by increased duties);

2. To afford governments additional revenues (by horizontal advances

in duties, in sales or excise taxes, etc., or by substantial increases in the duties on products locally regarded as luxuries);

3. To improve an unfavorable trade balance by cutting down the volume of imports, sometimes accompanied by efforts to facilitate exports (the former, by import restrictions or quota limitations, by exchange controls operated to discourage importation of less essential commodities; the latter, by reciprocal trade agreements, by stimulated exportation, particularly of farm staples, by control of foreign exchange dealings, and, in the case of the Scandinavian countries, by the sympathetic suspension of the gold standard following the British action);

4. Toward the latter part of the year, primarily to maintain the financial solvency or currency exchange value of the country (by intensive application of one or more of the methods indicated above); or,

5. To offset actual or prospective intensified competition or trade restrictive measures on the part of other countries (by vesting in the governments emergency authority to control foreign trade, either by provisional tariff adjustments, or, more often, by the right to set import quotas or otherwise to restrict importations of particular commodities).

The only extensive or comprehensive duty changes of the year, which, as already indicated, were limited to the Baltic countries (Estonia, Finland, Latvia, and Lithuania), took place mostly during the first part of the year. They seemed to have the character of the tariff adjustments made in the normal course of events as in years past and included decreases as well as increases. However, the tariff changes made by these same countries during the latter months of the year were distinctly upward, and the commodities included indicated that the prime objective had changed somewhat, and was directed primarily either to produce greater revenue from the customs, or to check the outflow of currency by the curtailment of imports.

More limited autonomous changes in duties were effected during 1931 in about ten other continental countries, some downward but mostly upward, and principally affecting agricultural products.

The majority of the tariff changes on the part of the countries of Europe during the past year were brought about in the course of numerous commercial treaties or agreements between various sets of governments, the prominent feature of which was generally the exchange of tariff advantages on products of special interest to each other, either through reductions of the duties then operative, or by "consolidations," that is, assurances that the existing duties would not be changed during the life of the agreement. In some cases, the object of the treaty negotiations was primarily to release one or both countries from earlier agreements not to increase particular duties, when freedom of action seemed particularly desirable to the governments involved. In such cases, the revised agreements often carried higher duties on the same commodities than did the original agreements, but those were frequently offset by duty concessions on different products or other advantages.

The financial disturbances and exchange controls that developed toward the end of the year seriously complicated matters and, for the time being, partly nullified the benefits of these trade agreements. Broadly viewed, however, the duties of a number of the countries of Central and Eastern Europe at the close of the year, in themselves, probably presented less hindrance to the movement of the principal products normally exchanging between them than did the duties in force at the beginning of 1931. The provisions of some of the special treaty arrangements will be touched upon later.

As intimated, tariff revision for protective purposes was less common in the countries of Europe last year than for fiscal purposes. Probably the most striking tariff advance of the year among the major continental countries of Europe was the Italian imposition of an additional 15 per cent ad valorem surtax on most commodities, whether dutiable or free (unless Italy was bound by treaties to maintain the existing treatment), for the declared purpose of obtaining additional governmental revenue. More moderate measures, for the same purpose of offsetting declining customs revenues as trade fell off, were the increase by one-fourth of the existing duties into the Netherlands (which have been generally 8 per cent ad valorem), as an emergency fiscal measure to expire in three years; and the bill now before the French Parliament proposing a general increase in the present 2 per cent turnover tax on imports to 4 per cent for semifinished and 6 per cent for finished products.

The pressing need for increased revenues on the part of many European countries found expression also in the advances of the general sales and luxury taxes on the part of Belgium, Germany, Hungary, and Italy; of the excise taxes on motor fuel in Austria, Belgium, Czechoslovakia, Denmark, Estonia, Italy, Norway, and Sweden; and of the excise taxes on tobacco in Finland, Greece, Latvia, and Norway.

Required mixing of certain domestic with imported products.—As indicated, material changes in protective duties among the major countries of Europe were less frequent in 1931 than in previous years, and those involved mainly staple agricultural products, where the pressure of overproduction and the low prices had been most prolonged and most general.

As another means of assuring larger consumption of domestic cereals without materially increasing prices to domestic consumers, about ten European countries established or continued the requirement for the mixing of a specified percentage of domestic wheat or other grain with the imported product, or of requiring the purchase of a given proportion of the domestic product as a condition of admission of the foreign. This mixing percentage varied among the different countries and fluctuated within particular areas, the domestic proportion of such mixtures ranging from 10 up to 97 per cent of the flour produced.

The ratio method of insuring a market for domestic products extended in some cases to meats, in other cases to mixing with domestic substitutes, such as rye with potatoes, and, in one case, domestic butter with imported margarine. Three additional European countries adopted during 1931 another method of accomplishing the same general purpose, through the familiar device of a governmental or governmentally controlled monopoly of the grain trade, tried out by other countries in the past. The requirement that imported gasoline be mixed in certain proportion with domestic alcohol, already operative with varying success in a number of countries, was proposed in three additional European areas.

Revival of import quotas, for trade balance and protection.—The device of controlling foreign trade by license regimes and quota systems, which had so prominently marked the postwar period but had been gradually tapering away for some years, was actively revived during 1931. It came into particular prominence during the latter months of the year, as governments grew more concerned over trade balances, currency exchange values, or possible abnormally large importations from countries whose export trade was being stimulated—at least temporarily—by depreciated currencies, governmental fostering of exports, the need to sell at any price, or other influences.

Thus, early in the fall, France introduced a series of import quotas, limiting the quantities of lumber, meats, dairy products, fish, sugar, and other products that might be admitted during given periods from the various foreign countries. These quotas were based on the average shipments during a period of years preceding.[1] For the double purpose of curtailing exchange demands and protecting domestic producers, Latvia

[1] During the first six weeks of 1932 the rationing of imports into France was extended to radio equipment, certain steel sheets, farm tools, electrical apparatus, and leathers, with similar import restrictions reported as in preparation for a considerable list of additional commodities.

announced quotas on several lists of products, fixed at a fraction of the imports during 1930, to continue for one year. Turkey, primarily concerned over an unbalanced trade and its financial implications, took the drastic measure of limiting the importation of over a thousand commodities to specified quotas, fixed by quarters and to be drawn on in order of arrival. Poland continued the allocation of import quotas for different commodities from various countries, as for several years past, and expanded it at the close of the year by temporary import restrictions on a broad range of agricultural and manufactured goods.

The authorities vested in the governments of several of the countries during December, 1931, to ration foreign trade by administrative order foreshadowed similar action in other countries. The Netherlands Government was authorized, for a period of three years, to impose import quotas whenever deemed necessary to keep imports within normal bounds.[2] Declaring itself motivated by the obstacles which various countries had established against Spanish exports, and impressed by Spain's unbalanced trade exchanges with various countries, the Spanish Minister of Commerce has been authorized to fix import quotas on a list of commodities (subject to amplification), and to distribute such quotas among the exporting countries "according to the necessities of Spanish economy." The Swiss Federal Council has received authority, for one year, to limit the importation of any class of goods, to safeguard national production, whenever vital interests appear to be threatened, and to reduce unemployment; any such action to be submitted to the Federal Assembly at its next session for decision as to its continuance or modification.[3]

This device of import control by contingents reappeared during the year with increasing frequency also in the treaty arrangements between particular countries. Thus, in treaties with neighboring states, Austria agreed to allow contingents of their agricultural products to come in at reduced rates; Czechoslovakia fixed the amount of German coal that may come in, in return for a German quota on Czech lignite; France, in the treaty with Greece, limited the reduced duty on Greek wines to a given annual quantity; and an amendment to the Franco-German treaty fixed the amount of German brandy that may come in.

[2] Under this authority, import quotas into the Netherlands were established, early in 1932, on meats, footwear, and certain textile products.

[3] The day after the expiration of the treaty with Germany, on February 4, 1932, Switzerland inaugurated import duty contingents on 38 products from thirteen designated countries, all imports in excess of the contingents to pay much higher duties. For the United States, such duty contingents were set for only two products, motorcycles and softwood boards.

Restrictions on import trade, by requiring a license, to be applied for in advance, for each transaction in particular foreign commodities, without the establishment of definite quotas, was also revived in about ten European countries during 1931, although in most of them the license system was applied to a very limited list of products. Wheat, coal, and nitrogenous fertilizers were most commonly made subject to license, the last following the termination of the international nitrogen agreement.

Czechoslovakia successively extended its license system to include, by the end of 1931, a substantial list of products. Iceland ordered that a considerable list of products might be imported only under special license. Toward the end of the year, the importation of a broad range of staple products was placed under centralized control in Estonia, and the operation of the license system was delegated to selected private firms. In the establishment of the quota limitations upon the majority of the products imported into Turkey, that government announced that products for which no quotas were fixed were to be prohibited altogether. The restrictions upon import trade imposed by various countries of Europe in connection with the operation of their controls of foreign exchange—amounting on many commodities to prohibitions—will be discussed later.

Efforts to facilitate trade by special treaties, bilateral and regional.—Particularly noteworthy developments during the year were the special treaties worked out or proposed by the countries of Central and Eastern Europe (the Austro-Hungarian Succession States and the Baltic States) with each other and with other continental countries. They were of two main types: the first, to meet the immediate problem of special facilities for the disposal of the Eastern European grain surpluses, and the second to bring certain neighboring areas, highly interdependent economically, into a position of permanently closer trade relations.

The various meetings of League of Nations commissions and committees, as well as the special wheat conferences, having resulted in no feasible collective plan for the control of the grain trade to afford relief for the surplus of the supplying countries of Eastern Europe, bilateral treaties were then resorted to. Thus, in return for certain reductions in Hungarian industrial duties, to be generalized to other treaty countries, Germany undertook to accord Hungarian wheat special concessions in duty, subject to agreement of the other countries having most-favored-nation rights; in a similar arrangement with Rumania, Germany offered special duty concessions on Rumanian corn and fodder barley. Austria made a similar arrangement with Yugoslavia, and the reduction in the Austrian duty on

Yugoslav wheat was likewise made conditional upon the agreement of other countries with most-favored-nation rights.

France concluded treaties with Hungary, Rumania, and Yugoslavia, promising to refund to those governments, for the benefit of their wheat exporters, sums not exceeding 30 per cent of the regular duties paid upon their shipments of wheat into France up to specified proportions of the total French import requirements. In return, it is reported that in these treaties, not yet ratified, Hungary, Rumania, and Yugoslavia established reduced conventional duties, applicable to all treaty countries, on a list of distinctive French products.

With regard to the German-Rumanian and German-Hungarian agreements, owing to the objections raised by certain treaty countries to the exclusive German concessions to Eastern European grain, those provisions were not put into operation when the treaties were made effective.

Among the arrangements designed to establish closer trade relations of a more permanent character between neighboring European countries, the most notable of the year was the proposal for a customs union between Austria and Germany. Its short-lived history is well known. It was announced in March, as a step in the general program of closer continental trade relations, and put forward as the nucleus for a European customs union of larger scope. It was withdrawn by both countries in September, after serious objection was brought to bear from a number of other European governments.

About the same time, a more limited degree of economic rapprochement was embodied in a treaty worked out between Austria and Hungary whereby the usual reductions or consolidations of duties on each side were accompanied by special arrangements to facilitate the exchange of goods between the two countries. This is to be accomplished by special facilities with regard to freight rates and credit, to be administered by special organizations established "to grant legal and financial privileges to such trade," with the respective governments undertaking to provide these organizations with the necessary means. It is reported that a similar treaty has been concluded between Austria and Italy.[4]

Going further along the same direction was the action during 1931 of

[4] The Austro-Hungarian treaty also provided for premiums to be paid on the exportation of agreed-upon quantities of specified merchandise from each country to the other country, in the form of refunds by each government of the duties paid to the customs of the other, subject to a financial balancing between the two countries at the end of the year. It is also reported that these measures of approach to preferential regional agreements have been so drafted as to minimize the technical grounds for objection on the part of other countries having most-favored-nation treaty rights.

the four Baltic countries, Estonia, Latvia, Lithuania, and Finland. They concluded a series of treaties with each other providing for special reciprocal concessions in the duties of each on lists of products that the others were particularly able to supply, thus restoring a measure of the freedom with which trade moved between these areas when they were all part of the old Russian Empire. The distinctive feature of these arrangements was that the concessions exchanged were exclusive and not to be extended to outside countries, this exception having been fairly generally recognized by other nations through the embodiment in many treaties of the so-called "Baltic clause" reservation.

Exchange restrictions prompted by financial crises become trade controllers.—While not strictly a form of trade control in the sense of being enforced at the customs, a prominent feature of the current European trade situation is the centralized control of foreign exchange resorted to by many continental countries during late 1931, as a means of protecting their currencies and of insuring a sufficient supply of foreign exchange to cover fixed obligations abroad, or for indispensable foreign purchases. The larger part of continental Europe is now in the grip of a financial crisis, precipitated first by the financial difficulties of the Central Powers in early summer, and then by the suspension of the gold standard by England and a number of other European countries largely dependent upon the pound sterling or upon the British market. In many countries, a schedule of exchange priorities among the different categories of commodities has been established (though seldom published); and, in some cases, the importation of particular lines of goods has been practically prohibited by the authorities controlling exchange. In fact, it is reported that in a number of countries of Central and Eastern Europe, as well as of Scandinavia, foreign trade at the beginning of 1932 depended more upon the operation of this exchange control than upon prices, import duties, or other usual considerations.

The central banks, or other bodies charged with the control of foreign exchange for their countries, naturally grant the means of paying for foreign goods more readily in the case of necessities or industrial materials than for more dispensable classes of commodities. Also, they may find themselves more readily able to furnish exchange for imports from countries in which larger exchange balances are being created, through purchases from the controlling country. In fact, the arrangements between certain Central European governments for the bilateral clearance of all exchange transactions between their nationals appear to be aimed at attaining an approximate balance of trade (or of international payments) between each pair of countries, as the desirable state of affairs.

Under the circumstances, complaints have been heard that the regulation of foreign trade through exchange control has been operating to curtail, with unequal severity, the trade from countries whose products fall into the less essential categories, or whose trade balance with the particular controlling country happens to be unfavorable to that country.

Indicative of the tense and apprehensive state of mind over future trade developments, or the possible injurious effects of the actions of other countries, are the surprisingly large number of European countries where the governments have been vested with authority to order prompt defensive trade control measures if circumstances should warrant. The action of the governments of France, Estonia, Latvia, Poland, and Turkey in regulating imports by restrictions or quotas have already been mentioned, as well as the authority to the Dutch, Spanish, and Swiss governments to limit imports by quotas. In addition, the Austrian and Hungarian governments have been authorized to make imports from nontreaty countries subject to permits. Late in December, a group of Italian ministries were jointly authorized to establish lists of products the importation of which may be prohibited in the public interest, with provision for the lifting of any embargo so established for nations who will give "reciprocal treatment" to Italian goods.

On December 1, President Hindenburg granted Prime Minister Brüning blanket authority to modify import duties and make commercial treaties, as an emergency measure, until the German Reichstag reassembles in February, 1932. A similar blanket authority, in the absence of Parliament, was granted to the President of Finland. The ministries of Yugoslavia were authorized to increase, reduce, or abolish import or export duties on any article, any such action later to be presented to Parliament for approval.

The fact that the laws of many of these countries now carry no authority for antidumping duties, or that there is no clear common understanding as to what constitutes dumping, may account for some of these new authorizations being regarded necessary. This is clearly indicated in the Dutch legislation, stated to be intended to protect Dutch industry from "artificial foreign competition."

The measures taken or considered to offset intensified competition from countries whose exporters were at least temporarily benefiting from depreciating currencies constitute a special phase of the tendency toward measures of defense against uncertain prospects. While this motive may have figured in a number of the general delegations of trade control authority to executive officials, who could act with greater promptness, the only actual instance in 1931 of duty surtaxes being levied against imports from countries with depreciated currencies appears in France.[5] While initiated only in mid-November, the French action has already brought protests from other countries, on the grounds of violation of treaty obligations, and of failing to take account of price advances in the depreciated-currency countries that have in some measure offset the drop in exchange values. In fact, the Spanish Government has been authorized to impose surcharges on merchandise from countries which levy increased duties on Spanish goods because of the depreciation of the peseta.

British Empire

The year 1931 was marked in the British Empire by an abnormally widespread tendency for the increase or extension of duties or other restrictive measures on imports, including even Great Britain, as well as practically all of the Dominions and a great many of the colonies. In the partial upward revisions made by some of the areas—notably Canada and South Africa—the protective motive appeared to predominate, as it did in the measures initiated by England toward the end of the year. Most of the 1931 tariff changes in the British areas, however, appear to reflect primarily the growing acuteness of the financial situation of the various countries and the problems arising from shrinking exports and unfavorable trade balances.

Thus, the falling off in customs revenues, owing partly to decreased volume of imports and partly to the lower price level—which reduces proportionately the collections under the ad valorem tariffs common in most British areas—largely account for the series of sharp horizontal advances during the year in the import duties of British India and of New Zealand and for the marked advance in the Australian sales tax and primage duty on most imports. The extension of the dutiable list in the Malay States, and the proposal under discussion for a Malayan customs union, involving the adoption of a more general tariff for the combined area, have also been largely prompted by fiscal considerations.

In the case of most other British areas, particularly the colonies, the character of the commodities chosen for increased duties indicates, mainly, an effort to improve the trade balance and currency values by curtailing

[5] In January, 1932, a German presidential decree authorized the establishment of compensatory duties on imports from countries whose currencies were below par. Thus far, such a compensatory duty has been ordered on only one product, butter.

imports of articles of a luxury or dispensable character. While the tariff changes of the year were predominantly upward, there were some decreases, and a considerable proportion of the applications for duties to the tariff commission of the Irish Free State were turned down.

Britain abandons the gold standard and traditional limited-tariff policy.—The events in the British Empire of greatest significance in this field during 1931 were the suspension of the gold standard by England in September, and the election in October of a coalition (National) government, heavily Conservative and favorable to tariff extension. The consequent exchange depreciation of the pound sterling carried with it the currencies of most of the Dominions, of India, and of most British colonies, as well as of a number of non-British countries, either because the currencies of these areas were tied to sterling or because of the heavy trade dependence of those countries upon the English market. Pending definite readjustments of internal costs and prices to the new exchange levels, this currency depreciation has served incidentally as an additional measure of protection to producers in these areas, through the increased cost of importing foreign goods, particularly from gold-standard countries.[6]

The new National Government in England was elected on a mandate to adopt whatever measures appeared necessary—including tariffs—to improve the trade balance and assist in relieving the serious economic depression and financial dislocation. Pending the working out of a permanent program of tariffs and other controls on imports, the British Board of Trade was given authority for six months to impose duties up to 100 per cent on imports of manufactured or mainly manufactured products, in order to check abnormally large importations in anticipation of prospective tariff action; and the Minister of Agriculture was given authority to levy duties for one year on secondary agricultural products.[7] Under these au-

[6] On the other hand, the Union of South Africa, one of the British areas remaining on the gold standard, has acted to check increased importations, detrimental to local industries, from countries with depreciated currencies. Under newly enlarged provisions of the antidumping law, the South African Government ordered in December the imposition of additional duties upon a specified list of articles (principally foodstuffs, clothing, and footwear) imported from certain countries, to the extent that their currencies have depreciated more than 10 per cent from par. The countries affected by this order included the United Kingdom and most of the British Dominions, as well as Argentina and Scandinavia.

[7] On February 4, 1932, a government resolution was introduced into Parliament proposing a general tariff of 10 per cent ad valorem on all products not already dutiable excepting for certain staple foods and raw materials, beginning March 1, with such products from Empire sources to continue duty-free, at least until after the Ottawa Conference. The appointment of a tariff commission is proposed to consider additional duties on nonessential imports.

thorities, temporary duties had been ordered on several lists of manufactured goods, and on a group of fresh fruits, vegetables, and plants, the latter being particularly designed to restrict importation of seasonal imports which anticipate the home crop. The products of the British Empire were exempted from the new duties established under all of these temporary orders. Announcement has also been made of a prospective quota control on wheat imports, as a means of assuring a good market for domestic growers, with quota preferences to Empire grain.

The departure of the British Government from its traditional free-trade or low-tariff position foreshadows important developments in two directions. It gives England a basis for bargaining with European and other countries, as a means of bringing about reductions in their tariffs—an objective that England has vainly sought for several years.[8] In fact, offers for negotiations came from several continental countries immediately upon the issuance of the first set of new duties by the Board of Trade, but the British Government deferred these until a more definite tariff policy had been developed and clearer relations with other parts of the British Empire had been established. Greater inter-Empire tariff preferences constitute the second important step in prospect, and are expected to be the principal subject of discussion at the postponed Imperial Economic Conference, now planned for Ottawa in July, 1932.

Without waiting for a possible change in the attitude of the mother country toward closer trade relations between the different parts of the Empire, several of the British areas have been engaged in negotiations for bilateral tariff agreements. Canada and Australia concluded a revised trade agreement during 1931, which gives the products of each a materially improved competitive position in the market of the other. Canada and South Africa have also been negotiating, and representatives of the Canadian and of the New Zealand governments resumed discussions toward the end of the year. This followed a previous failure to reach a satisfactory arrangement, which led last June to New Zealand imposing the general duties on most Canadian imports. Australia, British Honduras, Northern Rhodesia, Southern Rhodesia, and the Fiji Islands increased the margin of preference to British suppliers in the course of their tariff changes during the past year.

Various Empire areas tighten up on imports by administrative action.—In a number of British areas, the restriction of imports during the year through increased duties was reënforced—or substituted for—by tightening

[8] The general tariff bill of February, 1932, proposes also authorizing the imposition of additional duties upon the products of countries discriminating against British goods.

up of the administration of the tariff and customs laws. This was particularly true in Canada, where the Commissioner of Customs made very active use of his authority to set arbitrary valuations upon foreign goods for customs purposes and to declare imports subject to additional or dumping duties, the latter being invoked especially during the period since the depreciation of the Canadian dollar. The New Zealand authorities were also more active in enforcing the antidumping laws. The action of the South African Government, under the antidumping law, to check certain imports from depreciated-currency countries has already been described. In November, the Irish Free State authorized its Executive Council, for a period of nine months, to impose provisional duties or restrictions on imports, when there appeared to be a likelihood of dumping or abnormal importation that would occasion industrial injury, any such action to be subject to prompt ratification by the Dail.[9]

Subsidies were given more active consideration during the year in a number of the British areas. Canada established a bounty on coal and on wheat (the latter in the form of a freight rebate), Australia reduced the earlier bounty on butter, and Kenya Colony imposed one. South Africa imposed an additional duty of 5 per cent ad valorem on most imports, to provide funds for the payment of export subsidies on its primary products, usually 10 per cent, partly for the purpose of offsetting the handicap on South African producers in selling to the depreciated-currency markets.

Latin America

Primarily dependent for their fiscal stability as well as for their basic economic prosperity upon the supplying to world markets of staple foods and raw materials, the countries of Latin America were particularly affected by the overproduction and sharp drop in prices of natural products which have marked the depression. The need for increased revenue, the effort to redress unfavorable trade balances by curtailment of imports, and toward the latter part of the year, the efforts by control of foreign exchange to maintain or improve the exchange value of the national currency—these considerations, more than protection of domestic industries, appear to have dominated the commercial policy of most of the Latin American countries during 1931, and to furnish the prime explanation for the drastic measures taken by many of them to restrict or discourage imports.

Revenue and trade balance chief objectives of the many trade control

[9] The imposition of a sliding scale duty on bacon, early in 1932, is the only action thus far taken under this authority.

changes.—The protective motive appears to have been prominent in the substantial increases in duties effected during the earlier part of the year by a few countries, notably Chile, Colombia, Cuba, and Uruguay. However, the revenue, trade balance, and financial considerations appear to have been the prime explanations for the successive increases of the Argentine tariff on wide ranges of goods (either by increase of rates or valuations, or by the 10 per cent ad valorem surtax established for one year); as well as for the series of increased duties ordered by Chile, Colombia, Costa Rica, Ecuador, Nicaragua, Paraguay, and Uruguay during the latter part of the year. Fiscal needs primarily explain also the horizontal increases in the tariff of Surinam, in the sales and luxury taxes of Cuba, and the advances by several of these countries in the percentage of the value of imports collected as consular fees.

Most of the duty changes during the year were upward, both in the countries earlier mentioned as having made general changes, and in various of the other Latin American Republics which had occasion to make limited changes. On the other hand, the changes made in Peru and El Salvador were almost all downward, as were individual modifications in other countries, most of them directed toward making more cheaply available supplies of foreign machinery or materials for agriculture or other lines of production, aimed at alleviating unemployment by fostering local enterprises.

The sense of tension and unsettlement was also evidenced in Latin America during the year in the measures vesting larger authority in connection with tariffs and other foreign trade controls in the hands of the president, ministerial boards, or national councils. Such delegation of authority took place in Argentina, Colombia, Ecuador, and Uruguay and was renewed in Mexico. In about a half dozen of the Latin American countries authority to control foreign exchange and to scrutinize the sale of exchange for import transactions was vested in either the central bank or in an exchange control committee. The trade restrictive effect of such controls has been described earlier in connection with the developments of the year in Europe, although reports do not indicate that the exchange controls in Latin America are operated with quite the severity prevailing in some of the countries of Europe.

Curtailment of imports through higher duties were in some cases enforced or replaced by restrictions on importations, either totally or conditionally. Several countries—notably Colombia, Ecuador, and Uruguay—ordered certain lists of articles regarded as dispensable completely excluded, although these drastic measures were often withdrawn or tempered before they had been in operation very long. Brazil and Chile required the purchase or the mixing of domestic alcohol in given proportions to the amount of foreign gasoline imported. Cuba required the mixture of yucca flour in all bakery products, and Peru of domestic with foreign wheat. The Brazilian Government prohibited the importation of flour for eighteen months, in connection with the large-scale exchange of coffee (about 1,250,000 bags) for wheat (25,000,000 bushels) with the United States. Brazil also prohibited the importation of certain types of industrial machinery as a means of checking overproduction in certain lines.

Colombia authorized a monopoly on matches, Costa Rica established a monopoly on gasoline and proposed such handling of the trade in flour and matches, Nicaragua established a monopoly on petroleum products and matches, and Uruguay decided upon a monopoly on alcohol and petroleum products and the making of cement for public works. The primary purpose in establishing monopolies is the increase or better collection of governmental revenue, and, as is usual in such cases, whether the monopoly be governmentally operated or by a concessionaire, importations of the commodities involved are either prohibited or limited to the monopoly administration.

In the matter of export duties and controls, it is observed that the export duties were reduced in 1931 in several countries (Brazil, Mexico) or their suspension authorized (Haiti). Bolivia was one of the parties to the international agreement for the restriction of tin exports, and Cuba led in the so-called Chadbourne agreement with other producing countries to restrict the production and exportation of sugar. On the other hand, Chile adopted a plan for paying bounties to foster exports of agricultural products and to improve local prices.

Much discussion of economic agreements, regional and overseas.—A project sponsored early in the year by Foreign Minister Planet of Chile for a conference of the Latin American states, looking to joint economic action and involving consideration of a customs union, made little progress. As the year closed, a conference was being held between representatives of Argentina, Uruguay, and Brazil for a similar purpose. The sponsors are more hopeful of results because of the more limited scope of the proposed agreements, and the more nearly common interests of these three neighboring countries.

The first of the tariff agreements arrived at in Montevideo, between Brazil and Uruguay, will, if ratified, provide for an interchange of products in border trade and try the experiment of reciprocal duty-free importation of certian commodities from each other, the list of which would be revised periodically. A similar commercial treaty between Argentina and Uruguay, reported to be under negotiation, contemplates reductions or waivers of duties by each country on selected export products of the other. An agreement for the concerted study of the control of the livestock and meat trade of the three countries is also reported to be crystallizing.

In addition to any bilateral treaties between these countries for the facilitation of trade with each other that may result from the Montevideo conference, there were indications during the year that a number of Latin American countries—notably Argentina, Brazil, Chile, Colombia, and Uruguay—are planning the negotiation of tariff treaties with various overseas countries for the prime purpose of securing or insuring favorable tariff treatment of their export staples in those markets. Brazil and Chile negotiated a number of such treaties during 1931. The basic laws of certain other Latin American countries also carry authority for differential treatment of the products of foreign countries, in accordance with the tariff treatment granted their products. Most of these republics have for years maintained only single-column tariffs, applied equally to the products of all countries.

Asia and Africa

Among the countries of Asia and Africa (excluding those forming part of the British Empire, which are separately considered), probably the outstanding events of 1931 were two—the new Chinese tariff, which for the first time was drafted with a view to fostering native industry as well as serving its old function as the principal source of governmental revenue, and the new system of governmental control of all import and export trade adopted by Persia. Because of the diversity of local economic conditions among the many areas comprising Asia and Africa, and the trade dependence of most of these areas upon the countries of Europe and America rather than upon each other, no common trend in their tariff and commercial policy is observable.

Much changing of tariffs for diverse purposes.—The revised tariff schedule introduced by China in the first part of the year effected a considerable number of reductions, principally on industrial equipment and materials, although most of the changes were upward, involving a broad range of commodities, and particularly so on goods considered luxuries. Beginning in December, the Nationalist Government ordered a flood-relief surtax of one-tenth the existing import and export duties, to be reduced to one-twentieth after July, 1932, and continued until the liquidation of the

American wheat loan. A beginning was made toward an abolition of the long-standing taxes levied at various internal points, known as "likin," by the enforcement of special excise taxes on a limited list of goods to replace these internal levies.

General tariff revisions took place also in several other areas of the Orient, each with a different character and with a different objective. Thus Siam put into operation two substantial sets of changes during the year, affecting mainly articles not consumed by the mass of the population. The action is reported as aiming primarily to help the budget situation by increased revenues and to restrict imports of nonessentials in the effort toward a favorable trade balance. Of another character was the temporary increase of practically all of the import duties into the Netherlands East Indies by one-tenth, as a purely revenue measure.

Still different was the revision of the tariff of Angola (Portuguese West Africa) as part of the economic reorganization of the colony, providing numerous increases in import duties, for the declared purpose of reducing the consumption of certain goods considered luxuries and of curtailing the imports of others obtainable from Portugal, on which a reduction of three-fifths the regular duties is granted.

Tariff changes of a more limited scope were made in a number of these countries. Persia ordered all specific duties increased by one-half. Substantial changes were made in the Syrian tariff, including a considerable number of reductions or exemptions of duty, mainly on industrial materials and chemicals. The limited duty changes in Palestine were in both directions. The Egyptian Government revised about 200 items, in the light of the year's experience with the new tariff, the motives adduced being to protect home industry and to provide additional revenues. Mozambique (Portuguese East Africa) ordered increases in the import duties on a range of commodities classed as luxuries for the declared purpose of compensating for the loss in revenues from the earlier duty concessions on raw materials and equipment, goods of Portuguese origin continuing to pay half the regular duties.

The Philippine Government adopted increased duties on cement and a number of staple foodstuffs, with authority to the Governor General to reduce them when changed conditions warrant. In Japan, a distinct movement for upward tariff revision is reported, with the tariff investigating committee expected to present its recommendations to the Diet early in 1932, although that was before the recent depreciation of the yen and the calling of a general election.

Persian foreign trade made a state monopoly.—The stringent system of control of importation by permits adopted by Persia during 1930 as a means of improving the trade balance through drastic curtailment of foreign purchases was carried further early in 1931 by declaring all foreign trade a government monopoly. The state either reserves to itself the right to import or export the particular products, or grants licenses for importations up to fixed quotas. The original provision that foreign goods be admitted only upon the importer's undertaking to export the equivalent in Persian commodities was later tightened by definitely limiting the granting of import permits only upon the presentation of export certificates.

Egypt established a sugar monopoly, and various provinces of China established or considered monopolies, principally on tobacco and on matches.

In the field of export control, the Chinese Government revised the specific taxes of the long-standing export schedule to an effective 5 per cent level, abolishing the temporary surtax of one-half the export duty. French Indo-China increased the levies on the exportation of rice and certain other staples.

International agreements for export control of tin and sugar.—The governments of the Federated Malay States, Johore, Siam, Netherlands East Indies, and Nigeria joined with Bolivia in the international agreement for restricting the exportation of tin, by quotas, for a period of two years. The Netherlands Indies joined with the other principal sugar producers in the international agreement for the restricting of sugar exports on a quota basis, under the so-called Chadbourne plan.

1932

ECONOMIC DIFFICULTIES UNDER DEEPENING DEPRESSION SHAPE COURSE OF TRADE POLICIES

Trade Barriers Increased in More Than Half of the Important Markets

With the continuation and deepening of the world depression, unusual motives and methods marked the tariffs and other measures of control of foreign trade taken by the various foreign countries during 1932. Aside from the restrictions on commerce arising from exchange controls, the year saw trade barriers increased by various means in over thirty-five of the sixty-five commercially important countries, with a general downward tendency in tariffs observed in only a very few areas.

To a degree seldom seen have the developments in this field during 1932 been dominated in many countries by urgent monetary and financial considerations, and by the pressure upon governments to maintain or regain something like a balance in their international payments, in the face of further reduction in the value and volume of goods that reduced purchasing power and increasing trade barriers abroad allowed them to sell. The necessity of meeting the interest or payments on a volume of debt, public and private, the burden of which had increased by the decline in prices, trade, and general economic activity, contributed to governmental difficulties in balancing payments and receipts.

Of a specific and immediate nature, the striking trade control measures of the past year have been increases in tariffs primarily for revenue or import curtailment rather than for protection, the widespread European recourse to quotas and other methods of import restriction, and the very wide resort in Europe and elsewhere to exchange controls. Of a long-term character, the year's outstanding developments in this field have been: England's abandonment of its traditional position and the adoption of a general tariff; the subsequent Imperial Economic Conference at Ottawa, which resulted in considerable extension of the system of tariff and other trade preferences among the areas constituting the British Empire; and the various efforts or projects for regional tariff arrangements or multilateral agreements, particularly in Europe but also in Latin America.

Of considerable significance for the course of commercial policy during the period ahead are the increased chafing under the obligation of the strict most-favored-nation principle, and the many expressions of desire to abandon or limit the scope of that principle, which now obligates a country party to such treaties to extend automatically to all her treaty countries any reduced duties or other trade advantages extended to any third country. The various Danubian plans proposed, the so-called "Ouchy Convention" and, in fact, most of the regional or multilateral agreements so much discussed during 1932, particularly in various sections of Europe, involve the establishment of tariff preferences or other trade advantages that are to be limited to the participating countries, and which the other nations are to be asked not to insist on having extended to them, on the grounds that these would be special and justifiable exceptions from the most-favored-nation or tariff-equality principle.

Efforts to Reduce Imports to Lowered Level of Exports

With circumstances apparently not yet favorable—or the practical methods not yet clear—for international coöperation to resolve the basic economic problems weighing more or less upon all nations, most of the measures taken in the control of foreign trade during 1932 had the immediate national interest of each country primarily in mind. Since the volume of exports to other countries could seldom be increased, the object of such measures was usually further to reduce the volume of imports, so as to improve the country's merchandise trade balance, and often also to reduce the pressure upon the local market of even the reduced volume of imports of foreign goods that were coming in. The fact that so many of the countries commonly regarded as debtor countries, whether on private or public account, have managed to improve their trade balance during the past year or so by curtailing the volume of imports into their territories more than their exports to other countries had been reduced, seems to suggest that import restrictions plus lowered purchasing power are painfully helping to reinforce the efforts of these debtor countries to redress their balance of international payments, although on a lower level of trade exchanges.

Current Hopes Rest Upon Coming World Economic Conference

With the factors of price drops, trade declines, debt burdens, depreciated currencies, disorganized finances, and excessive trade barriers acting and reacting upon each other, and with the tariff and other trade control measures of the earlier years of the depression likewise dominated by the considerations of economic nationalism, and in the absence of any measures promising early relief, the feeling appears to have grown that solution of the problem of trade barriers and related economic problems can come only through international consultations and concerted action on the part of the principal countries. While the actual measures of the year have been, with few exceptions, distinctly restrictive of international trade, and by devices often apparently as difficult to administer as they were to contend with, the thought of governments and commercial communities in many countries at the close of the year looked hopefully to the prospective World Economic Conference planned for the late spring or summer of 1933.

Continental Europe

Among the countries of continental Europe, selective changes in the duties on particular commodities or groups of commodities have indeed taken place during the past year, with the changes almost always upward, but such measures were not as frequent as in earlier years nor were they the significant feature of the year. The principal changes in the tariff rates took the form of horizontal increases in the cost of importing or distributing foreign goods, primarily to help the government's fiscal or budget problem, although sometimes also as an outright means of curtailing imports. The forms taken by such horizontal advances were various, ranging from the Netherlands increase of most existing duties by three tenths, to the French advance of the so-called "import tax" by 2 or 4 per cent of the value of the goods, to the extreme case of the Estonian levy of a 15 per cent ad valorem tax on all payments abroad in addition to the regular duties.

In connection with the horizontal tariff increases, there might be mentioned the French levying upon imports from selected additional countries, whose currencies had depreciated by varying amounts, a so-called "exchange compensation surtax," usually of 15 per cent ad valorem. No other European country took similar general measures against imports from depreciated-currency countries; in fact, several governments adopted or threatened counter measures to the French action.

Spread of import quota or license restrictions.—Perhaps the most distinctive feature of the year among the countries of continental Europe was the adoption of measures other than tariffs for the control of import trade. The system of quantitative limitations of imports by quotas, which had been revived in a number of countries during the preceding year, spread rapidly in 1932, both as to the number of countries resorting to it and the range of commodities so controlled.

Another form of quantitative limitation of imports employed by a large number of European countries to greater or less extent—strongly reminiscent of the postwar years—was the requirement that import licenses be procured from an official body for each transaction in specified commodities, but without advance announcements as to the total quantity that would be admitted, either as a whole or from individual countries. While varying in the extent of the country's total import trade thus controlled, so general did either the quota or the license systems of trade control become during the year that only three out of twenty-five countries on the European continent were found not to have resorted to one or both of these types of import control, namely, Bulgaria, Denmark, and Spain (disregarding the long-standing Spanish practice of alternately inviting or prohibiting wheat imports, depending upon the domestic crop).

The method of allocation of import quotas varied considerably in the different countries. Sometimes they were apportioned in accordance with the volume of goods brought in by the particular importer during earlier years; more often they were divided up into national quotas, with the total amount of a particular commodity permitted importation during the year or quarter usually declared to be determined by the relative imports from the various countries during earlier unrestricted periods.

However, this method of allocation of national quotas in proportion to earlier trade does not appear to have been very uniformly carried out. Variations in the prior-period base for different commodities have been quite common, and the amount of the quota to be allocated to a given country—or even the freedom of certain commodities from quota restrictions—has often been made a bargaining matter, and adjusted in accordance with the counterconsiderations obtainable from the government of the country of origin in favor of the merchants or the trade of the operating country. Considerable complaint was heard, from both governments and merchants in various countries, regarding the fairness of operation of the different quota and license systems, although no clear principles for the operation of such systems have yet been worked out or internationally recognized.

Exchange restrictions, often discriminatory, become dominant control.—Another type of foreign trade control prominent in Europe during 1932 arose from the financial difficulties of the governments of many countries, which became prominent in midsummer of 1931 and were aggravated during the latter months of that year by the suspension of the gold standard in England, followed as that was by most of the British Empire, by Scandinavia, many countries of Latin America, and later by Japan. In the effort to prevent depreciation in the exchange value of the country's currency or check the measure of depreciation, and to conserve gold reserves or credits accruing from exports, either for the payment of fixed foreign obligations or for insuring a means of purchase of indispensable commodities from abroad, all but seven (Belgium, Finland, France, Lithuania, the Netherlands, Poland, and Switzerland) of the countries of continental Europe had, by the end of 1932, adopted some measure of foreign exchange control.

These controls of the allotments of foreign exchange for various purposes—whether operated by the central national bank, some other specially constituted body, or by the voluntary agreements of banks—varied widely in the degree of severity with which ordinary commercial transactions were affected. In a few countries the prime effort was to prevent speculation in exchange and the transfer of capital for investment or deposit abroad, and regular foreign trade transactions were afforded the necessary exchange upon documentary proof of the importation, and subject only to the usual import duties. A majority of the European exchange-control systems, however, are reported to have operated as material additional restrictions upon importation, often to the point of rendering unimportant the height of the duty or the ability to find a buyer or obtain an import permit.

With funds derived from exports insufficient to meet earlier obligations, and also to pay for all imported commodities that might be desired, exchange control bodies usually gave priority to foodstuffs and raw materials, or such products as were essential to the export industries of the country, with many classes of manufactures often completely barred as dispensable luxuries. In addition to this commodity preference, which, however understandable, operated to curtail imports from some countries more severely than from others, direct national preferences in the allocation of exchange have also developed in many cases, that is, more severe limitation on the amount of foreign exchange for which permit is given for the purchase of a particular class of goods from one country than from another.

In a number of cases, exchange controls were either limited or concentrated upon imports from countries which themselves limited the funds made available for the payment of imports from the given country, being thus in the nature of a restriction offset, which was often resolved by a special arrangement for the clearing of credits or other facilitation of trade between the two countries. In cases of exchange controls against imports from all sources, preferential treatment in the granting of exchange, in accordance with the country whence the goods were to come, has not infrequently been admitted by the administrating authorities, who justified their action on the grounds of greater volume of purchases by one country than another of the export products of the controlling nation. Such diversion of the supplying of a country's import requirements from one source to another has been defended also on the grounds that it was necessary to bring about a closer balance of imports and exports with each trading country. A tendency has also been observed for some countries maintaining exchange control systems to use them as general bargaining weapons, by making the amount of exchange allotments conditional upon counter-considerations or advantages of various sorts, including larger import quotas for its products by the other country or the release of "blocked accounts" or funds due its citizens.

Efforts to temper restrictions by bilateral clearing agreements.—Efforts have been made to temper the full severity of the system of exchange controls and import restrictions that have been put into effect during this disturbed period. There has developed, both among the European countries and between them and overseas governments, a considerable number of clearing agreements or compensation arrangements for the direct balancing of credits derived from transactions between the two countries, or the exchange of specified volumes of particular classes of goods, sometimes approaching direct barter.

Considering the conditions under which they have been resorted to, these clearing and compensation agreements are declared to afford some immediate relief in allowing a somewhat freer flow of goods or settlement of accounts. However, toward the latter part of 1932, it was reported that many of these arrangements were proving too cumbersome and unsatisfactory and would not be renewed. The criticism has also been heard that such clearing or compensation agreements are premised upon what some regard as an unsound principle, of expecting that the volume of trade between each set of countries should approximate an annual balance, as against the long-established commercial practice whereby inequalities between the amount any one country annually sells to another and the amount it buys from that country are balanced off, in the aggregate of world commerce, by triangular or polyangular trade movements and settlements.

In the matter of bilateral commercial treaties between various pairs of countries, which has traditionally been one of the important means of adjustments of tariffs among the countries of continental Europe, the year 1932 saw unusual developments. There were few new treaties made with European or overseas countries, and those usually simple exchanges of most-favored-nation assurances.

The majority of the large number of treaty negotiations consisted rather of revisions of old agreements, and principally for the purpose, not of exchanging new concessions in duties, but rather for securing release from the treaty obligation not to increase the duties on specified lists of products. Such releases of old bound rates were not always compensated for by substitute concessions on other products, and the countries usually took advantage of the release from bound rates promptly to increase the duties.

The apparent chafing over the lack of liberty of action to change the rates of duty on commodities bound by treaties, and the desire to keep more free for the period ahead, were evidenced further in the provision embodied by France in the agreements with Italy and Germany that were revised during the year. Hereafter, each contracting government is to have the right to modify any one of the conventional rates, upon brief notice, whereupon the other government may request the immediate opening of negotiations, in order to restore the equilibrium of tariff advantages, and, failing that, receives the right to increase its bound duties to an equivalent extent.

So definitely do quotas and exchange controls appear to have been accepted as methods of trade control, at least for the relatively short term of the agreement, that promises with regard to the size of quotas on particular commodities or exchange allocations have been written into various European commercial agreements of the year as offsetting treaty concessions in duties or other matters. Revised agreements between at least two or three pairs of countries provided for reciprocal quota allotments, in the effort to attain a particular ratio in the value of the total annual trade between the two countries.

An appreciable number of commercial agreements of the past year have been for the purpose of settling reciprocal complaints, as the action of one country had aroused retaliatory response on the part of the other. The initial action provoking these disputes varied from increased import taxes, between France and Belgium; threatened import quotas, between Germany and Italy; depreciated currency surtax, between France and Portugal; supertariffs, between Germany and Poland; and maximum duties, between Germany and Canada.

Possibly the most significant long-term tendency of the year in European treaty making has been the desire, by various means, to limit the scope of the unconditional most-favored-nation principle, which now obligates a contracting country to extend automatically to all her treaty countries any reduced duties or other trade advantages extended to any third country. In at least three revisions of treaties between important European countries during the year the former general most-favored-nation promise was replaced by a promise to extend equality of treatment only with regard to limited lists of commodities, upon the insistence of the French and Spanish governments.

Moreover, in line with the agitation of several years past in favor of measures of relief to the agricultural countries of Eastern Europe, by affording their products assured and preferred outlets in the markets of the grain-importing countries of Europe, France and Germany each concluded within the last two years a series of treaties with each of several Eastern European countries in which they undertook to accord either reduced duties or refunds on all or specified quotas of grain from those eastern countries. These duty preferences were to be conditional upon the consent of other grain-producing countries having most-favored-nation rights. Some of these treaty countries have consented, others have not; this provision in the German agreement has not yet been brought into operation, although it is reported that the French provisions have been.

Of a somewhat similar character, although possibly not marked by the same large purpose, has been the still limited but growing number of cases where reduced duties are promised in treaties for fixed contingents of particular commodities from the other country, with imports above that quantity subject to the usual rates. Thus far most of these duty contingents have not been generalized to other treaty countries.

Proposed special trade arrangements to aid Danubian states.—The agitation for exceptional measures to aid the rehabilitation of Central and Eastern Europe mentioned above came to a head during September of last year at the Stresa conference among fifteen European powers. It was agreed that the four agrarian States in the Danube Basin—Hungary, Rumania, Yugoslavia, and Bulgaria—were to enjoy duty preferences on their grains in each grain-importing country represented, by a chain of preferential treaties; and recommended that a rehabilitation fund of 75 million Swiss francs annually be raised by the importing countries for distribution by the Bank for International Settlements among the Danubian countries. In return, the agrarian states pledged themselves to reduce their duties on industrial products, which reductions were to be generalized, and to mitigate the severity of exchange and other restrictions now hampering trade with those countries.

Difficulty is reported to have arisen at the last moment regarding the special Danubian fund, but the trade preferences were agreed to, to be brought into operation after approval by the League Commission on European Union and ratification by the respective countries.

North European plans for prior consultations and progressive reductions.—Aiming at the same general purpose of relieving the constrictions upon international exchanges and improving the economic condition of the participating countries, but proposing quite different methods for its accomplishment, was the so-called "Oslo Economic Convention" signed in that city at the close of 1930, by five north European countries (Belgium-Luxemburg, the Netherlands, Denmark, Norway, and Sweden), and which became effective early in 1932, upon ratification by the governments of all the signatories. Each government undertakes to notify the others before putting into effect any upward revision of its tariff, excepting emergency fiscal measures, with opportunity for negotiations before final action.

Finland requested admission as the sixth party to the Oslo group last September, and in line with the declared desire of the signatories to extend this principle of economic coöperation and consultation among themselves also to other fields, representatives of all these countries met toward the close of the year to consider a possible common attitude toward the problems to come up at the proposed World Economic Conference.

In the effort to carry multilateral agreements forward by positive measures, a convention between Belgium-Luxemburg and the Netherlands was initialed in June at Ouchy, Switzerland, providing for the reciprocal and progressive lowering of the economic barriers between the Belgo-Luxemburg customs union and the Netherlands, by the reduction of present duties by one tenth annually down to fixed low levels. It also provided that in their mutual relations, the parties would not increase duties or introduce any new measures restricting either imports or exports. The agreement was declared to be open for adherence by other nations, which could thus obtain the reciprocal favors granted under it.

Owing to the unreadiness of certain major countries having commercial treaties with Belgium and the Netherlands to recognize any concessions which the contracting countries might give each other under this Ouchy convention, as special and allowable exceptions from the most-favored-nation obligation to them, it is reported that the participating governments are holding up the parliamentary ratification necessary to bring the convention into operation.

With the various efforts of individual nations or groups of nations to relieve the depressed trade condition and general economic situation not having produced material results, expectations at the beginning of 1933, particularly among the countries of Europe, are hopefully directed toward the prospective International Conference on Monetary and Economic Questions. The conference is tentatively planned for London in late spring, and the experts designated by the leading countries were assembling in Geneva early in January to work out the agenda and preparatory material.

British Empire

The year 1932 will be remembered for two highly important developments in the British Empire in the field of commercial policy: first, the abandonment by England of its traditional free-trade or limited-tariff position for the adoption of a general import tariff, levying duties of varying amounts upon a large majority of products entering the country; and, second, the great impetus given to the movement for closer economic integration of the Empire by the preferential tariff agreements entered into at the Imperial Economic Conference held at Ottawa.

Britain adopts general tariff system, mainly on non-Empire products.—The action of the British Government in joining the protectionist ranks was particularly striking and significant in the light of the fact that Britain had long been on almost a free-trade basis, since the notable repeal of the "Corn Laws" in 1846, involving a decision to base her economic system upon fostering industrialization and depending upon the exportation of her mine and factory products to obtain the necessary foodstuffs and raw materials from wherever they could be most cheaply had.

Prior to the World War, British customs revenues were obtained from the duties on about 25 noncompetitive commodities, chiefly tea, coffee, sugar, tobacco, and spirits, which well lent themselves to revenue levies. During the war and since, various additions to the dutiable list were made, partly for protection, partly for revenue, and some for other purposes, but the great bulk of imports and range of commodities continued to enter the British market duty-free from all sources until 1932.

The present government of England was elected in the fall of 1931 on a mandate to adopt whatever measures appeared necessary—including tariffs—to improve the trade balance and assist in relieving the country's economic depression and financial difficulties. It set at once to work out a permanent program of tariffs and other controls on imports. In the meantime, the British Board of Trade and the Minister of Agriculture temporarily were given broad authority to impose high duties where regarded necessary to check abnormally large importations of industrial or secondary horticultural products, respectively. That was soon followed by the imposition, beginning March 1, 1932, of a general tariff of 10 per cent ad valorem on all products not already dutiable, excepting certain staple foods and raw materials. By the end of April, the abnormal importation duties on industrial products, as well as the provisional general 10 per cent duty, were superseded by a more carefully elaborated tariff schedule on manufactures and partly manufactured goods, ranging from 10 to 33⅓ per cent of value, with 20 per cent as the most common new rate.

This whole system of new duties was not to apply to products coming from the British colonies, and temporarily, it was also not made operative on such importations from the British Dominions, pending the outcome of the Imperial Economic Conference, which had been adjourned from London in 1930 and was to meet at Ottawa in the summer of 1932.

Ottawa Conference results in wide extension of Empire preferences.—Tariffs and trade control measures were the only subjects upon which definite agreements resulted from the Ottawa discussions. Twelve bilateral trade agreements were signed by representatives of the participating British countries on August 20, seven of them between the United Kingdom and each of the other governments (excepting the Irish Free State). The others were agreements between the Dominions, several of which had already worked out similar trade agreements during previous years.

Whatever may have been the various objectives set forth or urged in advance for the Ottawa Conference, in the direction of making a start toward an ultimate, all-round relaxation of restrictions on foreign trade, the stabilization of exchange rates within the so-called "sterling area,"[1] improvement of price levels, and so on, the agreements that issued had as their declared purpose primarily to increase the purchases from each other of many commodities now largely obtained by the various British areas from outside the Empire.

As most of these agreements have since been put into effect by appropriate action on the part of the respective governments, sometimes in modified form, a brief general statement of their essential content is now possible. In return for new or increased tariff preferences or other import facilities in the different Dominions on various groups of products of the United Kingdom, mostly manufactured goods, the British Government undertook to levy duties on foreign (non-Empire) imports of wheat, corn, copper, and linseed, which had hitherto been admitted duty-free from all sources; to increase the existing duties on foreign imports of a large range of mostly foodstuff products, all of which were to continue free from Empire sources; to control by quotas the importation of meats, and later possibly also dairy products, into the United Kingdom, primarily in the interest of the domestic producers and secondarily to afford Empire producers an increasing share of Britain's import trade; to continue the duty-free admission from the Dominions of certain products made dutiable from foreign sources under the British import duties act of 1932; and not to reduce certain specified margins of preference to Dominion over foreign products.

The inter-Dominion agreements provide for exchanges of similar increased preferences on groups of products in which the particular contracting areas saw opportunity of replacing non-British products in the others' markets with the aid of increased preferences. In an effort to make the preferential arrangements Empire-wide, the Dominions also undertook to grant preferences on certain articles of particular interest to the nonself-governing colonies and, in certain cases or under certain conditions, to extend to them most of their existing preferential rates, in return for the establishment of new or enlarged preferences on the part of the colonial areas to products that could be supplied from the United Kingdom or the Dominions.

[1] The suspension of the gold standard by England in September, 1931, with a consequent exchange depreciation of the pound sterling, carried with it the currencies of most of the rest of the Empire—with the notable exception of the Union of South Africa (until late December, 1932) and, in a partial way, that of Canada—as well as a number of non-British countries (Scandinavia, Japan, and certain countries of South America), either because the currencies of these areas were tied to sterling, or because of the heavy trade dependence of such countries upon the English or the Empire markets.

As drafted at Ottawa, all of the agreements were to continue in effect for a period of five years, excepting that with India. The measures of the various governments giving effect to these agreements did not, however, always carry any definite obligation for a given period. In fact, the English parliamentary debates on the Ottawa agreements bill brought out the definite statement that Parliament was not bound to maintain the benefits to the Empire for five years or any other period, reserving its usual right to reduce or withdraw any duty, although the current government, whose representatives had signed the agreements, declared that it would make every effort to maintain the legislation for that period.

Significance of general trade commitments at Ottawa.—The Ottawa agreements also contained a number of general qualifications or undertakings which may affect the operation of the specific preferences in an important way, and their actual operation or interpretation may materially influence the course of Empire tariffs and trade relations. In the temporary suspension of the duty on copper into England, use has already been made of the provision that the duties on wheat, copper, zinc, or lead may be removed if Empire producers are unable or unwilling to supply the full requirements of United Kingdom consumers at world prices. The mutual promise of the United Kingdom and Canada to take action to prevent the entry of any commodities from foreign countries that were likely to frustrate the benefit of the preferences by the state maintenance of prices, has already been acted upon, in the recent denunciation by the United Kingdom of the Anglo-Russian commercial treaty, preparatory to negotiating a revised agreement.

While no specific action has thus far been taken, there is much speculation as to the value of the undertakings by Canada, Australia, and New Zealand to grant tariff protection against United Kingdom products only to those local industries which are "reasonably assured of sound success," and to reëxamine existing protective duties with a view to affording United Kingdom products opportunity of reasonable competition with domestic products on the basis of relative costs of economical and efficient production, reservation being made for domestic infant industries.

By January 1, 1933, the governments of the United Kingdom, Canada, British India, Australia, New Zealand, the Union of South Africa, and Southern Rhodesia have already taken the necessary legislative or other measures to give Empire products substantially the increased tariff preferences and other advantages in their markets over foreign goods that their representatives had promised. Newfoundland is not expected to give effect to its agreement with the United Kingdom until the summer of 1933. The Irish Free State presents an exceptional situation, to be touched on later.

In addition, the British West Indies, British Honduras, British Guiana, Bermuda, Northern Rhodesia, Cyprus, Fiji, Mauritius, Federated Malay States, Non-Federated Malay States of Johore, Kedah, and Kelantan, and Sarawak have already voted the enlarged preferences undertaken by England on behalf of the colonies. The Straits Settlements and Hong Kong, whose position as transshipment points has kept them traditionally almost free ports, have adopted Empire preference in the form of a 20 per cent registration tax on automobiles from which Empire products are exempt. The governments of certain other colonies have still to act, and several of them had already put into operation increased preferences to British products earlier in 1932, in connection with general revisions of their tariffs.

As a combined result of the Ottawa agreements and autonomous action, the beginning of 1933 finds almost all important areas in the British Empire, many of which had hitherto admitted foreign goods at the same rates of duty as Empire products or had granted preferences to only a very limited extent, within the orbit of the British preferential tariff system, extending to many or most of the products of other Empire areas more favorable conditions of admission than to foreign countries generally.[2] Newfoundland (except on Jamaican products), Ceylon, Malta, and Papua appear the principal ones among the few British areas which have not introduced preferential tariffs to any degree, and the first two are understood to have the matter under consideration, while the Irish Free State and the United Kingdom have recently started to penalize rather than favor imports from each other.

Following the election of a new government in the early part of the year, radical changes were made in the Irish Free State tariff policy for the purpose of stimulating domestic industries, relieving unemployment, and providing additional revenue. During the year a series of tariff measures imposed new duties on a long list of imported goods and increased the existing duties on many others. In a few cases British Empire goods were not accorded preferential rates or lost the benefits of the preferences they formerly enjoyed. In answer to the special increases in the United Kingdom duties on animal and dairy products, arising from the Anglo-Irish dispute over the payment of land annuities, the Irish Free State imposed

[2] In a number of British colonies in Africa and in certain areas administered as mandates, the commercial "open door" is assured all nations by the terms of the original international agreements, so that Empire tariff preferences cannot well be extended to those areas.

special, new, or additional duties on a select group of commodities when imported directly or indirectly from the United Kingdom.

Preferences effected mainly by added handicaps on non-Empire goods.—It is significant that the majority of the new or increased margins of trade preference to Empire products in the various British areas have been accomplished through the imposition of additional duties or restrictions on the competitive products from non-Empire sources. Viewing the situation in perspective, therefore, and considering that the majority of the imports of the areas comprising the British Empire have hitherto been derived from outside the Empire, the tariffs and other trade control measures of the great majority of the British areas are more restrictive of international trade at the opening of 1933 than they were at the beginning of 1932. A possible important exception is Australia, which, besides reducing the duties on a number of products, removed during the year all of her import prohibitions and many of the duty surtaxes established by the party in power during 1930, although this moderation was probably largely if not wholly offset by the increase of many general duties, toward the close of the year, as a means of giving greater preferential margins to Empire goods.

The extent to which the past American trade with the United Kingdom or other British areas in the products affected by the Ottawa agreements is likely to be curtailed by diversion to competitive Empire suppliers is a matter which can be definitely determined only by experience. The measure of new advantage being created in favor of Empire products varies widely in the case of the different commodities, with even more variation in the degree to which the developed British or Empire demand for these different products of American origin can readily or fully be satisfied from Empire sources. Moreover, the course of the import trade of the British areas during the next few years is likely to be influenced by quite a number of factors and still unpredictable developments, beyond the official import preferences in favor of Empire products now being established.

In addition to the dominant motives of protection and increased Empire preference, tariff changes were made in various British areas during the past year to meet fiscal or financial situations, most often in the form of horizontal increases in the costs of bringing in or disposing of foreign goods. Thus Canada increased the special excise tax levied on imports from 1 to 3 per cent ad valorem, in addition to advancing the basic rate of the sales tax from 4 to 6 per cent. Newfoundland similarly increased its sales tax from 5 to 7½ per cent ad valorem and also imposed a surtax of 3 per cent of the duty and sales tax payable. The Union of South Africa imposed a customs tax of 7½ per cent of the value on most imports. Similar duty advances for revenue purposes, whether horizontal or selective, were reported from a number of British colonies. In the other direction were the removal of certain duty surtaxes imposed earlier in the depression by Australia, and insofar as they applied to certain of the British areas, by New Zealand.

Under the authority to fix the value for duty of any class of goods imported under conditions prejudicial to the interests of Canadian producers, the Canadian Government has been continuing the practice of setting arbitrary valuations upon imported goods for customs purposes "over true invoice value" and to declare imports subject to additional dumping duties if imported at less than that fixed price. On fruits and vegetables, the commodities mainly affected in previous years, the official valuations were usually seasonal; in extending them to industrial products of various kinds since 1930, the valuations appeared to be of indefinite term. Following the Ottawa Conference, where was stressed the desirability of avoidance of uncertainty as to the amount of charges payable on imports, Canada proposed to exempt British Empire goods from fixed values for duty in such cases.

The introduction of quota restrictions on imports of meats into England under the Ottawa agreements, toward the close of 1932, was the first important Empire use of that device, so widely used during the last few years by various countries of continental Europe. Australia had set quantity limitations on the importation of canned asparagus and sheet glass, and a license control on felt hat bodies. The Irish Free State introduced during the past year a system of licenses on imports of wheat flour, on a curtailing quota scale that contemplated independence of imports within two years. The so-called English "wheat quota act" is not a method of controlling imports by quota but rather an internal measure for improving the returns to the wheat growers from the proceeds of a tax on flour.

New British tariff made basis for bargaining with foreign countries.—With the adoption of a general tariff on imports, the United Kingdom secured a basis for bargaining with European and other countries, as a means of bringing about reduction in their tariffs—an objective that England had vainly sought for several years while on a limited tariff basis. Offers for negotiations that promptly came from various foreign countries were postponed until after the working out of a more definite tariff schedule and the completion of negotiations with the Dominions at the Ottawa Conference. In the latter months of the year, representatives from the

Scandinavian countries were invited to London for trade negotiations; representatives of South American countries were likewise reported in England; and discussions with other countries of continental Europe were expected to take place in the spring of 1933.

An official statement of the British Government indicated that offers of tariff negotiations had come to it from nineteen countries. No definite outcome of any of the negotiations had been reported by the close of 1932, although considerable speculation was reported from both Europe and South America as to the nature of possible arrangements, in view of the Ottawa agreements with the Empire and the long-time British adherence to the most-favored-nation policy toward all non-British countries.

On the side of export controls or aids, probably the most notable feature of the year in the British Empire was the continuation, at increased rates, of the subsidies established by South Africa in the fall of 1931 on the exportation of its primary products, largely for the purpose of offsetting the handicap on South African producers in selling to depreciated-currency markets, which included practically all the rest of the British Empire, as well as outside countries. The funds for this export item were derived from an additional (so-called "primage") duty of 5 per cent on most imports (removed Jan. 21, 1933). Australia increased its rate of export bounty on butter, but abolished the bounty simultaneously with an increase in the import duty on cotton yarn, while Canada did not continue the wheat bounty on this year's crop.

Partly to assist its producers in meeting the import duty recently imposed by the United Kingdom on Irish cattle, pigs, and potatoes, and partly to counteract the general drop in pork prices, the Irish Free State began to pay bounties in the fall of 1932 on exports of cattle, pigs and pork products, and potatoes. Temporary bounties were paid during the year on Irish exports of butter, eggs, poultry, and canned milk and cream, and on the manufacture of leather. Following the British imposition of special duties on certain products of the Irish Free State, the government of that state announced its intention of granting bounties, equivalent to the amount of the United Kingdom duties, on exports of many classes of goods to that country.

Early in the year the British Foreign Office announced that, after consultation with the Netherlands Government and the rubber growers, it was found impossible to frame an effective scheme for the regulation of rubber production or exportation for the East Indies.

Depreciated currencies operate as additional barrier to imports from outside.—While maintaining no license control on the amount of exchange allowed for the purchase of foreign goods, as have so many countries of continental Europe during the past year, the depreciation of the currency of almost all of the British Empire countries during 1932 enforced the various increases in the tariff rates enacted by these countries and operated as an additional barrier to the sale of many classes of products of the United States and other gold-standard countries, insofar as they had to meet the competition of suppliers in other British areas or in outside depreciated-currency countries. In the case of commodities not subject to direct competition from depreciated-currency countries, as in raw cotton, or in those of the British areas which did not object to imports of foreign goods at lower prices than prevailed in the home country, exporters in gold-standard countries have been able to overcome the exchange handicap in a measure by sharing it with their customers.

However, in most of the British Dominions, constituting a very large part of the total Empire market, efforts to reduce export prices in order to meet part of the currency disadvantage were largely prevented, in the case of goods competitive with local products, by a strict application of the antidumping laws. These are reported to have been enforced so severely as to check commercial arrangements designed to temper the handicap of exchange disparities and, in some cases, also to prevent any possible gain to foreign firms from the use of the proceeds of their sales within these countries. The United Kingdom and British India, as well as a number of colonies, have no antidumping laws, although the assessment of duties on home-market values in many of the British areas often operated partially to the same effect. Owing to the instability of the exchange rates during the year, however, prices of competitive goods from depreciated-currency countries have seldom been changed very promptly or to the extent of the depreciation of the currencies of these buying countries in the British Empire.

Canada, whose dollar had not depreciated as much as had the pound sterling or the currencies of Scandinavia and certain other countries, continued the assessment of regular duty upon imports from certain of the depreciated-currency countries upon the mint or par value of the currencies, rather than upon their current exchange rates, and applied an additional duty equal to the difference between the par value and the current exchange rate. Among the areas of the British Empire, the United Kingdom appears to be the only country for which an official valuation for dumping duty purposes was established by Canada ($4.40 Canadian). It was extended during the year to Northern Ireland and the Irish Free State, such additional or special duty being equal to the difference between $4.40 and the average value of the pound as fixed twice monthly, the value for regular duty remaining at $4.86⅔.

The Union of South Africa, which stayed on the free gold standard until the close of 1932, extended to additional countries and to a wider range of products the order issued toward the close of 1931 for the imposition of additional duties upon a specific list of articles imported from certain countries, to the extent that their currencies had depreciated more than 10 per cent from par.[8] Following departure from the gold standard and pending the formulation of new regulations, the collection of the depreciated-currency duties has been discontinued, except, it is understood, on imports from Japan.

Latin America

Reduced purchasing power prime limitation upon imports.— While the fiscal considerations continued an important motive for foreign trade control measures in Latin America during 1932, and the majority of countries there either resorted to exchange control or had limited exchange available for foreign purchases, restriction on import trade through exchange control was by no means the prime determinant of what foreign trade was possible to the same extent as among the countries of continental Europe. With foreign markets for their staple food and raw material exports continuing weak, and with the market prices for these natural products sharply depressed, reduced purchasing power was probably the most important and inherent limitation upon imports of foreign merchandise. With a few notable exceptions, where exchange control was reported severely enforced, changes in the regular import duties and related measures were the principal means of adjusting control of foreign trade in Latin America during 1932.

Four of the twenty republics south of the United States put into operation fairly general revisions of their tariffs during the past year (Cuba, Ecuador, Nicaragua, and Panama). Seven additional countries made substantial alterations in their import duties on fairly wide or important ranges of commodities, namely, Argentina, Chile, Costa Rica, Mexico, El Salvador, Uruguay, and Venezuela. Cuba and Guatemala, which are among

[8] Uruguay, Japan, and British India had certain of their products added to the list of those affected by the depreciated-currency surtax (previously applied to United Kingdom, most of the British Dominions, Scandinavia, and Argentina).

those that collect as consular fees a percentage of the value of shipments, increased that percentage, thus making a horizontal increase of 2 or 3 per cent ad valorem on all duties. Chile ordered a surtax of one-tenth of the existing duties on a broad range of goods termed luxuries. Most of the others made only small changes in their duties or on commodities small in trade volume.

While the majority of the import duty changes in Latin America during the past year were by way of increases, the cases of reductions in existing duties were numerous and often significant. Larger revenues appear to be the primary motive for most of the duty increases ordered, with protection to domestic producers often mentioned, and curtailment of the volume of imports frequently present as a prime or collateral objective. On the other hand, in a surprising number of cases existing duties were lowered, sometimes to reduce the price of staple foodstuffs but most often to facilitate the importation of equipment and materials for certain industries which it was desired to stimulate. This tendency, observed in past years, appears to have been accelerated during this period of depression as a means of making unnecessary the continued purchase of so many staple products from abroad that it is believed could be locally produced. Reductions in duty to facilitate such local production appeared among the measures taken during the year by Mexico, certain Central American countries, Brazil, Uruguay, and Chile. Argentina removed the duties on a list of foodstuffs, machinery, and other products which had been made dutiable last year.

Relative absence of quotas and similar import restrictions.—The countries of Latin America have been relatively free from quota systems and similar import restrictions that have been adopted so widely by the European countries during the past year or two. The Chilean Government was authorized to establish an import quota system, but has thus far applied it only on sugar imports. The wheat- or flour-mixing regulations prominent in Europe found their counterpart in a limited way in the requirements established by Costa Rica and Cuba during the past year for mixing domestic yucca with foreign flour and bakery products. National petroleum monopolies have been established in Chile and Costa Rica and proposed in Peru. The Chilean Government has authorized the commissariat of prices and subsistence to take control of the production and trade of the country in prime necessities, including the authority to alter import and export duties. It has also authorized the president to change duties on products found to be "in a state of overproduction." Uruguay has been considering proposals for broad governmental authority in connection with trade control, possibly involving government monopolies on the importation of certain staple products.

As a whole, the year has been characterized in Latin America by measures taken or proposed that are indicative of the tension of the situation under present unstable conditions, and of the readiness of many governments of Latin America to experiment with new methods of regulating their foreign trade, by either autonomous measures or agreements with other countries. In addition to the new authorities vested in the executive branches of the governments already mentioned, the Mexican Legislature has prolonged the authority to its president to change tariffs up or down, and has also authorized him to amend the customs law and report at the next session; Guatemala has extended the tariff-changing authority to its president for two years; and Colombia for the period until Congress reassembles. In these and other countries, the executives have been authorized not only to change tariffs in accordance with changing conditions, but particularly to take measures to meet tariff discriminations against national export products in foreign markets.

Treaty negotiations active, with tendency toward special concessions.—The year has been exceptionally active for Latin American Republics in the matter of trade negotiations with each other and with countries of Europe. In contrast to the traditional practice on the part of Latin American countries of maintaining single-column tariffs applied equally to imports from all countries and of engaging little in special commercial treaties, an increasing number of these governments are planning differential tariffs. Several have already negotiated agreements establishing two sets of rates on particular classes of goods, which are extended to some countries and not to others. Brazil has negotiated over thirty commercial agreements of the simple most-favored-nation type and of limited duration, in connection with the proposed introduction of a double tariff. Chile has made several such temporary agreements during the last two years with the United States and certain European countries, under the most-favored-nation provisions of which the Chilean duty reductions in the treaty with France have been generalized. It is notable, however, that these most-favored-nation treaties are temporary and easily terminated.

Partly induced by the agreements between England and the Dominions at the Ottawa Conference of 1932, it is reported that at least six of the Latin American governments have made approaches to the government of Great Britain for the negotiation of reciprocal tariff agreements, for the purpose of maintaining or improving the favorable tariff treatment that their export staples had hitherto enjoyed in the British market. Negotiations are understood to be under consideration also with certain countries of continental Europe, often with regard to the outlet for certain leading export products.

The readiness of a number of the Latin American Republics to grant special tariff concessions on particular products, in return for corresponding concessions on their own exports, has already been definitely expressed in certain temporary tariff agreements recently negotiated with each other, notably that between Chile and Peru, and that between Argentina and Chile, with negotiations for reciprocal favors between Argentina and Brazil reported to be in prospect. No progress has been reported on the tariff agreements worked on toward the close of last year at the tripartite economic conference between Argentina, Brazil, and Uruguay, partly owing to political difficulties during the year. However, these three countries have been conferring, with a view to a common attitude on the export disposal of their meat products, and discussions of other phases of their trade relations are in prospect.

The governments of Brazil and of at least two other South American countries have been considering plans for trade-barter agreements, possibly of an exclusive character, and at least one country has made several such agreements. With about a half dozen of these twenty countries already having tariff treaties in operation, with the governments of about an equal number possessing specific authority for the purpose, and others reported negotiating, presumably under the general treaty-making authority, the period ahead is likely to see some very active tariff negotiations and treaty agreements among each other and with overseas countries.

1933

FAILURE OF HOPES FOR COLLECTIVE ACTION PROMPTS MORE DRASTIC NATIONAL MEASURES

London Economic Conference Fails

The year 1933 saw go unfulfilled the hopes widely held at its outset for a general agreement among the nations, through the London Economic Conference, for reductions of tariffs and other trade barriers. There was indeed a brief pause in the spring for a customs truce, proposed by the United States and substantially agreed to by the countries accounting for 90 per cent of world trade, in order to afford a stable basis for the deliberations of the London conference. However, it began to crumble before the conference had barely suspended its sessions, as the nations again sought freedom of action to proceed further with purely nationalistic trade control measures that had so dominated the last few years.

Many of the foreign governments felt the need for further measures of adjustment in their foreign trade relations: some because of complaints from distressed domestic producers about the pressure from even the reduced volume of imports, either upon the market or upon prices; a few because of an intensified desire to attain greater self-sufficiency in particular commodities, especially in certain foodstuffs; and many because of the continued general strain upon their international trade balance or national financial position. Seeing little hope for early relief through material expansion of their exports, in the face of the continuation of the general depression and the cumulated trade barriers built up during the earlier years, most of these governments fell back upon the further restriction of imports by the various methods developed or recently revived, or upon the diversion of their reduced foreign purchases to selected countries on a more or less compensatory basis, in accordance with the volume of sales to those countries or the readiness of those countries to facilitate larger purchases of their export products.

General Return to National Expedients Only Worsens Situation

As a result, the level and complexity of barriers at the close of the year were, in most cases, more obstructive to the flow of trade between the nations generally than they were at its opening. The upturn in the volume of world trade during the latter months of 1933, after the continued progressive decline in the earlier part of the year, can hardly be attributed to a general easing of trade barriers and has apparently taken place in spite of them.

Continental Europe

Import quotas and exchange controls become trade bargaining weapons.—Particularly in the countries of Europe the resort to import quotas and foreign exchange restrictions became so widespread during 1933 as to be almost regarded as regular measures of foreign trade control. Moreover, starting as a temporary defensive measure, primarily to hold imports to a volume that could readily be absorbed during a depression period, and usually allocated according to the normal share of the various supplying countries, the use of quotas—and, in some cases, of exchange control—appears to have been turned by various European governments during 1930 to quite different purposes. By the end of the year they were being widely used as aggressive measures of restriction and as bargaining devices to promote exports, by withdrawing or granting quotas of permitted imports, or allocations of exchange to pay for them, in accordance with the relative balance of trade with the given country, or the offer of guaranteed or permitted purchases of national products on the part of the particular other country.

Aside from the fact that a large number of the duties of many continental countries are bound by treaties against increase for some time ahead, the tendency to resort to quotas and other direct restrictions on imports is partly explainable by the desire for measures that promised a more definitely predictable flow of trade than simple changes in duties, the effects of which are more difficult to anticipate under disturbed conditions of prices and currencies. The fact that regulation of imports by such methods is less limited by definite treaty obligations to treat all countries equally, and allows more easily of diversions of purchases of particular commodities from one country to another by the choice of base periods or other criteria, has doubtless also operated to make those methods of control attractive to some governments.

The unfavorable reaction to this program from some directions is indicated by the fact that a number of European countries gave broad authority to their governments during the year to take defensive steps against countries maintaining stringent quotas and similar restrictions against their goods, although often by the homeopathic method of authorizing the resort to like measures in retaliation.

Period marked by short-run measures to meet shifting situations.—The diffident attempts during earlier years at special arrangements between various European countries that barely skirted the most-favored-nation obligation to other countries, were followed during 1933 by bolder arrangements, frankly aimed at improving or balancing trade relations between particular pairs of countries by means that often operated to the injury of third countries, through the relative curtailment or diversion of trade from those other usual supplying sources.

In observing the succession and variety of trade control measures taken by most of the countries of continental Europe during 1933, it is difficult to escape the impression of confusion, experimentation, and instability. Most of the devices and arrangements resorted to appear to have been distinctly expedients, adopted primarily with a view to their hoped-for immediate relief for the trade or financial position of the particular country, and largely disregarding traditional methods and long-run principles, in the endeavor to meet temporary and shifting situations of an emergency character. The characteristic short term of most agreements, and the efforts of certain countries to secure release from older treaty obligations, reflect the sense of instability and the desire of governments for freedom of action as situations change.

While control upon the allocation of foreign exchange is common also in Latin America, quotas are now only slightly in use outside of continental Europe, and in a special way in England, suggesting that the nervous tension from the current disturbance to international trade is being most keenly felt by the countries of Europe. Nevertheless, the continued agitation in Europe for multilateral conventions calling for simultaneous reductions of trade barriers on the part of the contracting governments, or for regional tariff agreements designed to bring about a freer flow of trade between groups of neighboring countries, brought little concrete progress during the year, beyond a few isolated preferences here and there to certain products of particular eastern European countries.

It is too early to judge whether these exceptional devices and arrangements are likely to taper off rapidly with the passing of the present emergency conditions, or whether in some measure they are bound to be built into the permanent and continuing trade control structure of the nations.

The obvious difficulties of regulating international trade by quotas, exchange controls, and trade-balancing arrangements, without almost inevitably involving injury to third countries and risking official complaints of discrimination, raise serious question—apart from the sheer difficulties inherent in the administration of these special trade measures—as to whether they can be expected to constitute the permanent and general methods of regulating world commerce. Even the international wheat agreement, the sole agreement of the year that was distinguished by the facts that it embraced the principal wheat-exporting and importing countries and that it was designed to bring about an ultimate balance of world wheat supply with demand, is reported to be meeting with difficulties, largely because of its dependence upon quantitative limitation of production and allocation of exports.

While import duties have in many countries been superseded by other measures as the dominant methods of foreign trade control, it seems significant that, despite the considerable dissatisfaction voiced over the limitations imposed by the most-favored-nation obligation, that principle of equality of competitive opportunity for the same product from different sources has only seldom been violated during the depression in the adjustment of tariff duties between countries not politically related. Moreover, it has been observed that many governments, which have themselves been resorting to theses exceptional devices and arrangements for control of their import trade, have insisted strenuously upon their most-favored-nation rights—in quotas as well as in tariffs—when their national products met what they considered distinctly unfair or discriminatory treatment under the import control measures of other countries.

British Empire

Program for trade integration of the Empire areas spreads.—Among the areas comprising the British Empire, the year was marked by substantial further steps toward giving effect to the trade agreements resulting from the Imperial Economic Conference held at Ottawa in the summer of 1932, through the introduction of new or greater preferences to the products of each other over those of non-British areas, thus carrying forward the work of the preceding year toward closer commercial integration of the Empire. On January 1, 1933, there was brought into operation in British India for the first time a general system of tariffs preferential to the products of the Empire. Ceylon and Newfoundland similarly fell in line during the year. The program for enlarging the orbit of the British preferential system to include, in some measure, the many widely dispersed colonial areas was apparently carried forward with great thoroughness, and seemed almost completed by the end of 1933.

In the great majority of cases, with the notable exceptions of Australia and Newfoundland, the new or increased preferences granted to Empire products in the various far-flung British areas during the year were accomplished mainly by increasing the general duties, which apply to the products of non-British areas, or even establishing new general duties or restrictions on non-Empire products. As one area after another proceeded to give effect to the obligations or principles of the Ottawa agreements of 1932, the opportunities for purchases from "foreign countries" generally were progessively curtailed, and not always fully offset by replacements from competitive suppliers from within the Empire.

The consolidation of the British Empire into a closer commercial entity was advanced during the year also in other ways: by the increase on the part of the United Kingdom and many lesser areas in the precentage of Empire labor or material necessary to entitle goods to tariff preference; and by initial steps on the part of Canada, Australia, and New Zealand to reëxamine their existing protective duties with a view to affording United Kingdom products the promised "opportunity of reasonable competition" with domestic production. On the other hand, the tendency in the trade relations between the United Kingdom and the Irish Free State continued to be toward the withholding of tariff preferences or even the definite penalizing of one another's products, as a result of the controversy over the land annuities.

Import quotas and guarantees prominent in Britain's new pacts.—The substantial introduction of import quotas by the United Kingdom was a significant development of the year. Starting as a means of quantitative limitation of imports, primarily in the interest of domestic agricultural producers, quotas came to be employed also as a means of allocating imports as between Empire and non-Empire supplying countries, sometimes favoring importations from Empire areas simply by applying certain limitations only to outside countries. The fact that these quotas are tied in with the current program of domestic marketing agreements, designed to encourage the larger production of various food products within Great Britain, the scope of which is still in process of expansion, gives these measures the likelihood of longer continuation as a part of that country's trade policy than may be the case in the import quotas of most of the countries of continental Europe.

Quotas figured prominently in the series of trade agreements to the negotiation of which the United Kingdom turned vigorously in the past year, principally with a number of countries largely dependent upon the English market: Argentina, the Scandinavian, and the Baltic countries. Not only was quantitative allocation resorted to as a means of assurance to the various countries regarding the share of the British import market for particular staple farm products which they could count on supplying during the period ahead, but also as one form of requirement that Britain often made of the other country, as guaranteed that definite quantities or proportions of the particular country's imports of certain commodities—notably coal—would be derived from the United Kingdom. Even in the treaty with Germany, where England's main concession was of the more usual European type—namely, reductions in the duties on certain typical German manufactures—there was a quota assurance regarding fish, and the principal concession obtained from Germany was an increase in the minimum quota of British coal admissible into that country. In fact, a number of other countries, including two of the Dominions, had to adopt export controls on certain products in order to accommodate themselves to the British import quotas, or to introduce quantitative limitations on their incoming trade in special lines because of the market assurances that England had required.[1]

[1] Thus far, import limitation by quota has been imposed by the United Kingdom only on meats, certain fish, dairy products, and secondary cereals, although Britain's requirements for these products are so great that together they accounted for a substantial part of that country's import trade during 1932. The chief significance, however, of these quota controls, tariff bindings, purchasing agreements and similar arrangements lies not so much in their present extent as in the fact of the striking further departure of the United Kingdom from its long-established trade policies, and in its building of these novel devices both into its regulation of foodstuff imports in relation to domestic production, and into its commercial treaties with other countries.

The similar action taken by Germany during the past year, in the somewhat different form of governmental monopoly controls on imports of certain farm products, integrated with a control on the distribution and prices of similar domestic products, while important, represents less radical a departure than the British action, in view of the long-standing German policy of agrarian protectionism going back to before the war.

International agreements for export control of wheat, tea, and tin.—On the export control side the year witnessed several notable developments in the British areas. The international wheat agreement, which involved Canada and Australia, has already been mentioned. British India, in conjunction with Ceylon and the Netherlands East Indies, put into effect the tea export restriction system for five years. The governments of British Malaya and Nigeria, in conjunction with other major producers, decided upon the substantial renewal of the existing international tin restriction scheme for three years from January 1, 1934. The end of the year saw elaborate plans revived for restricting the exports of crude rubber from British Malaya, operating in conjunction with the Netherlands East Indies and French Indo-China.

Latin America

Availability of exchange still the prime trade determinant.—In the countries of Latin America, the availability of foreign exchange appeared as a more dominant control of import trade during the year—particularly in South America—than did tariffs or other more usual trade-determining factors. Even where the centralized control of foreign exchange—which has been the rule in almost all of South America and parts of Middle America for the last few years—has not been particularly severe in limiting the amounts of exchange granted for new foreign purchases, or in those countries where no control is maintained, import trade has often been limited by the sheer inadequacy of the volume of foreign exchange currently available. Owing to the still poor markets and continued low prices for their export staples, the authorities in many of the Latin American countries apparently did not have enough new foreign exchange at their disposal, from current sales abroad, to afford import merchants the necessary means of paying for very large new purchases of any but indispensable commodities, consistently with the various efforts at gradual liquidation of older obligations due to foreigners.

Perhaps the most significant long-term development of the year in the countries of South America was the quickened movement for reciprocal trade negotiations among themselves and with certain outside countries. In agreements with certain of their neighbors, the major countries of the Continent carried far the principle of facilitating the purchase of each other's products, within the limited scope that they can furnish markets for each other. They usually took the form of exchanges of substantial import duty concessions on groups of each other's distinctive products; as between

Argentina and Brazil, and between Brazil and Uruguay, there was established a considerable measure of free trade in certain products.

Contrast between British and United States trade offers to Latin America.—The agreement worked out between Argentina and the United Kingdom involving the reduction of many Argentine duties to the 1930 level and preferential exchange treatment of British creditors, in return for the funding of outstanding obligations to England and assurances regarding Argentina's share of the British market for certain products and unrestricted access in others, was a striking innovation. The invitation from the United States to a number of the countries of Latin America (Colombia, Brazil, Argentina, and Cuba) to enter into exploratory discussions, to see if a basis could be developed for reciprocal tariff agreements, marked another new trail in commercial policy on the American continent. The first result was an agreement concluded between the United States and Colombia in December, now awaiting ratification, designed to improve and stabilize trading relations between the two countries.

1934

GREAT ACTIVITY IN TRADE CONTROLS NETS LITTLE EASEMENT IN OVER-ALL RESTRICTIONS

The past year has seen much activity abroad, in the changing of tariffs, the adjustment of import quotas and exchange allotments, and in the negotiation of trade agreements between various foreign countries. Allowing for certain exceptions, however, the net outcome appears to have left the general trade control structure of the world as a whole about as restrictive as it was at the outset of the year. Particularly on the continent of Europe, the situation has, in a measure, become even more complicated because of the very developments of the year, notably in Germany. Outstanding among the developments in the opposite direction has been the easing of the restrictive effect upon foreign trade of the exchange control systems in a number of important Latin American countries.

Revival of Foreign Trade Lagging Behind Internal Recovery

The beginning of general economic recovery experienced in varying degree within many countries, during the past year or so, has thus far been accompanied by very little expansion of world trade as a whole, as measured by the aggregate quantity of distinctive or surplus products of each country that was enabled to find markets in the territories of other countries. The fact that the progressive shrinkage of foreign trade that had been going on since 1929 has been checked in the last year or so, and that some regain has taken place here and there, is encouraging. It is also noteworthy that the fluctuations in exchange rates between the currencies of the major groups of countries—the essential monetary mechanism for adjustment of all international transactions—have been kept within relatively narrower limits during 1934 than in the years immediately preceding. However, the lag between general economic recovery within most countries and the slower revival thus far of their trade with other countries appears attributable, at least in part, to the absence as yet of any material change from the spirit of intense nationalism that has become accentuated during the depression, and from the practice of tight governmental restriction of imports by various means that has characterized the trade regime of most countries during the last few years.

Despite the many conferences between various groups of countries looking to collective action of a trade-liberating character, and the attempted beginnings of such concerted efforts in a limited way, the practical results thus far from international agreements have been of little general significance. The majority of the foreign trade control measures adopted by individual countries during the past year or so have continued to be dominated by the protective and restrictive motive. Immediate relief from current local pressures has been a dominant objective, with rather little recognition that there are distinct limits to recovery through expansion of the home market only—a recognition that is essential to the rebuilding of a long-time basis for a broader flow of international trade.

Reciprocal Agreements Often Trade Diverting Instead of Enlarging

The greatest hope for removal of trade barriers has recently been attached to the only remaining method, namely, the negotiation of reciprocal agreements between pairs of individual countries. The past year has seen scores of such bilateral agreements concluded between various European and other foreign countries, but the majority of them have been trade diverting in character rather than trade enlarging. Especially on the continent of Europe, the prime aim appears too often to have been not so much to enlarge materially the volume of the country's total purchases from abroad that was to be permitted or facilitated, but rather to divert to the particular other contracting country a larger share of about the same total volume of import trade as had been permitted. Most of the European arrangements of the year consisted less of exchanges of reciprocal reductions in duties than of assurances regarding quotas of various classes of goods to be admitted from the other country or regarding the allotment of exchange to pay for them. Often they took the form of exchange clearing or trade compensation agreements, which set quantitative limits and conditions on the total volume of importations by the two countries from each other, and, in a number of cases, incidentally provided for the liquidation from the proceeds of current business of outstanding debts due nationals of the country whose normal purchases from the other exceeded its aggregate sales there.

Bilateral Balancing Idea Hampering World Trade Recovery

Moreover, in a striking proportion of instances, recent trade agreements between many foreign countries have been dominated by the idea that the value of the trade between each pair of countries should approximate an annual balance or be adjusted until it does. This conception took little account of the differences in the products that the climate, resources, developed industries, and living standards of each country enable it to supply advantageously or lead it to require from the outside, and the consequent natural inequalities in the degree to which the peoples of each country need the distinctive or surplus products of each individual other country. The ineffectiveness of agreements based on the bilateral trade-balancing principle, either in enlarging the volume of the countries' export trade or of definitely readjusting the trade balance except on a lower level, has already become apparent in the case of many of these arrangements. This has even been recognized by high officials of certain European countries.

Meanwhile, the large number of such agreements that have been negotiated, limited and temporary as they may be, have been working to weaken and disorganize rather than to strengthen the network of triangular or many-sided transactions, the operation of which over past decades has been such a vital factor in the economic development attained by the different countries, and in the building up of the huge aggregate pool of world commerce, the benefits of which flowed back to all contributing countries, irrespective of the variations in the currents between individual countries.

Until the broader considerations here indicated are given greater weight in the foreign trade policies of individual countries, as well as in the commercial arrangements between countries, it seems difficult to visualize a very substantial revival of international trade, or at least in the scope and on the scale of the predepression years.

New United States Trade Agreement Program Aims at Trade Expansion

These recent developments and trends in the tariffs and commercial policy of foreign countries give particular point to the program initiated by the government of the United States, under authority granted by Congress last June, for the negotiation of trade agreements with foreign countries involving the reciprocal reduction of tariffs and other trade barriers now unduly restricting the sale of each country's products in the market of the other. The sponsors of this program hope not only to revive the flow of international trade through a progressively growing series of reciprocal trade-liberating agreements, but also to give a distinctly new turn to commercial policy of the nations generally, toward regaining the benefits of a broader flow of international exchanges on a more sound and equitable basis, so far as that can be done consistently with reasonable protection to domestic producers. The first reciprocal trade agreement in this series, with Cuba, was brought into operation in September, and negotiations have been announced with sixteen additional countries (with seven in Europe, eight in Latin America, and with Canada), several of which are expected to be completed early in 1935.

The developments of the year in this field were quite different in character in the principal world areas and among the countries making up each group. Material changes in the duties, the usual regulators of import trade, have indeed taken place during 1934 in the majority of countries, with a number putting into effect substantial overhaulings of their tariff schedules, involving some decreases along with the more common increases in the existing rates of duty. However, one of the important features of the diverse trends in commercial policy in different parts of the world during recent years has been the varying degree to which other devices and arrangements than import duties are relied upon as the dominant controllers of the movement of foreign trade. That is best seen from a separate examination of the general trends of the year in this field in the three broad world groups of continental Europe, Latin America, and the British Empire.

Continental Europe

Quantitative controls become chief method of regulating trade.—In most countries of continental Europe direct restrictions upon the quantities of particular classes of goods that might be admitted, or upon the amount of foreign exchange made available in their payment, either as a whole or for particular countries, overshadowed import duties as the prime determinants of the movements of foreign trade, and, in some cases, made even the usual price competition a secondary matter. Several additional European countries, including the Netherlands, Italy, and Spain, have during the past year been gradually going over to the import quota method of regulating imports, or at least certain classes of them. A number of the countries that had begun to operate such quota controls in previous years expanded their scope during 1934, so as to place additional products under quantitative restriction.

Moreover, the use of quotas, resorted to at first as a temporary defensive measure, has been turned by several countries into a distinctly aggressive bargaining weapon to promote exports of natural products. The device employed has been to reduce the proportion of the global quotas which were allotted among the various countries in accordance with the share of the particular trade they supplied during some previous representative period, and to hold the balance as bargaining material, allotting these additional or "supercontingents" to this or that country in return for specific reciprocal quotas or other considerations. In order to allow greater freedom in the discretionary assignment of imports to be permitted, increasing resort has been had to placing various products under an import permit system, without allocation of national quotas or otherwise announcing in advance the conditions under which permission to import might be counted upon.

Quota bargaining frequent feature of European trade pacts.—One of the striking developments of the past year on the continent of Europe has been the increasing extent to which quantitative controls of various types have been adjusted not only through autonomous action on the part of individual governments, but also as a result of special negotiations between various pairs of countries, in the course of which reciprocal quantitative assurances figured as more important bargaining considerations than reductions or assurances regarding each other's import duties. Thus, France, Germany, the Netherlands, Poland, and Turkey, and most of the countries of Central and Eastern Europe have come to grant, increase, or withdraw quotas on the quantities of particular products permitted admission from a given country, largely in accordance with counteradvantages offered by or obtained from the other country, in the form of reduced duties, enlarged quotas, offer of guaranteed purchases of national products, release of blocked funds to its citizens, or a combination of these concessions.

The experimental and emergency nature of most of these agreements was apparent in several ways. Most of them were of relatively short duration, often covering limited or secondary categories of goods, and were subject to frequent revision, each supplementary or substitute agreement showing material shift in the commodities and quotas involved. Not infrequently the details of an arrangement were not made public, or they were left to later adjustment by consultation or mixed commissions. Moreover, many of these agreements involved a degree of particularistic control by governments upon the quantities of specified commodities which might be admitted and the countries or conditions of their importation, or of the payment that might be made for them, such as has not been witnessed since the period of extreme tension that marked the years of the World War and those immediately following.

Since these quantitative controls or other special devices for regulating import trade had not been anticipated in the days when nations wrote their long-time agreements, and there was no clear understanding that the principle of equality of treatment was intended to extend to any methods of regulating foreign trade other than import duties, many governments apparently did not feel themselves subject to any particular obligation toward producers in various countries who had come to count upon their particular markets. Indeed, one of the objectives observed in a number of the European agreements of the past year has been to establish some principles in this field to govern future relations between them, by obtaining assurance of equal consideration with any third country in the operation of these unusual and undisciplined methods of trade control, either in the form of equitable allocations of the amounts of permitted imports of products already or later subjected to restrictions, or of funds to pay for them.

Growth of centralized import controls over foods or materials.—Since the summer of 1933, there have been developing in a number of European countries systems of either governmental monopolies or other centralized controls on imports of selected classes of commodities, usually foods or raw materials. While most striking and general in the case of Germany, this system has grown during the past year also in the Netherlands, Latvia, and the United Kingdom,[1] and has been introduced, in a limited measure, also in a few other European countries, among them Italy.

In the case of farm products, these centralized controls upon imports are often being integrated with various forms of internal control upon the

[1] This is one of the exceptional respects in which the recent trade policy of the British Government has resembled that of continental Europe rather than that of the British Empire generally.

production and distribution of similar domestic products. In several countries the scheme involves the levying upon imports of additional charges, termed "monopoly fees," the proceeds from which are sometimes used to subsidize domestic producers in that line. In a few cases the monopoly or central body even prescribes the price at which the imported products are to be sold. This system of centralized control of trade—and often of prices—has been carried further during the past year in Germany than anywhere else outside of Soviet Russia, with all imports made subject to the permission of twenty-five trade control boards, with whom is lodged the discretion to issue or deny permits for various commodities in accordance with the degree of their indispensability, the amount of foreign exchange available from sales to the given country, or in accordance with other special considerations.

Financial pressures prompt efforts at bilateral trade balancing.—The concern of the majority of the governments of continental Europe during 1934 appears to have centered upon the improvement of their trade balances, and thereby also of their foreign exchange rates and general financial position. This has often been put forward as more important to them than the usual motives of protection to domestic producers from undue foreign competition, or increased governmental revenues, or even the desire to attain greater domestic self-sufficiency in particular foodstuffs or other products—which has recently been so strong an objective in certain countries. Since the prospect of early and material enlargement of the volume of sales of the country's export products in other markets did not seem very promising, in view of the still reduced level of economic activity and purchasing power all around, and the cumulative trade barriers built up during the depression years, most European governments stressed their *general* trade balance consideration in dealings with each *individual* other country. They endeavored in their bilateral agreements to hold down the volume of importations that they would allow from the other country close to the volume of sales of their products to the other country of which they could feel fairly assured, or which the other government undertook to facilitate. In fact, the party to a negotiation in whose favor the bilateral trade balance had been running often found it necessary to offer concessions in duties or enlargements of quotas to the other, in order to hold its existing market in the other country or to prevent the too severe curtailment of that market.

The advantages or assurances exchanged in the course of most of the European trade agreements of the past year did not lend themselves, by their very nature, to generalization to other countries on a most-favored-nation status with the contracting governments. In fact, it was seldom their objective to enlarge materially the volume of the country's total purchases from abroad, but rather to try to divert or redirect to particular countries and sources either the existing limited amount of total importations in various commodities, or such volume of importations as their immediate trade balance position or volume of shrunken exports appeared to permit.

Unsatisfactory operation of clearing and compensation agreements.—The numerous exchange clearing arrangements and compensation agreements entered into by most of the European countries with each other and with a number of the Latin American countries, which have been so much in the news during the year, represent an important mechanism by which many nations have been trying to give effect to this general objective of improving their total trade balance through fixing an approximate balance or a particular ratio in the volume of goods exchanged with each other country. However, these clearing and compensation agreements, which have been especially common in Central Europe—where international trade has gone back very close to a state of barter—are reported not to be working out very satisfactorily.

Aside from the administrative difficulties involved, it appears that, where an approximate balance in the trade movements between a pair of countries has been attained, it has usually been closer to the level of the lower rather than the higher previous current of trade. It seems significant that, on the continent of Europe, where for several years there has been more intense activity than anywhere else in the negotiation of special commercial agreements and trade-balancing arrangements, the aggregate foreign trade has run materially lower (in gold values) during the months of 1934 than of the preceding year, while the corresponding foreign trade movements of other parts of the world either held their own or improved in volume over previous years. It may well develop before long that bilateral balancing and compensation agreements—whatever their utility in exceptional cases or as emergency makeshifts—will be more widely recognized as ineffective, in the long run, as means of increasing the aggregate volume of a country's exports and, therefore, not to be regarded as desirable instruments of regular commercial policy.

Latin America

Unlike Europe, import duties remain prime trade control measures.—In contrast to the situation on the continent of Europe, the use of import quotas has been rare among the countries of Latin America, either in their autonomous measures or in their contractual arrangements with other countries. During the last few years the sheer shortage of foreign exchange has been an overshadowing consideration in determining the amount of new foreign purchases that could be made or paid for, even in those few areas where there has been no official centralized control of foreign exchange, which has recently been the rule in almost all of South America and parts of Middle America. However, import duties are now resuming their position as the prime regulator of imports, second in importance only to the reduced purchasing power of these countries, arising from the reduced markets and low prices for their export staples, upon which their prosperity so depends.

Better raw material prices allow freer exchange operations.—With the expansion of activity in many individual countries during 1934 and the improvement in the world price for the principal natural products of Latin America, the shortage of foreign exchange has eased up materially in many of these countries. While none of them gave up their exchange control system entirely, there has taken place in a number of important American Republics a recognition of the unofficial or free exchange market, in which funds to remit to foreign countries were made available in substantial amounts, although at a higher cost, usually ranging between 10 and 20 per cent above the official rate, and in a few cases much higher. Particularly where the spread between the open and the official rate had narrowed, opportunity was afforded for carrying on a substantial amount of new business and for liquidating some old accounts outside the official exchange control system, with prices on new business often being adapted to the higher open market rate.

Tariff revisions took place during 1934 in several countries of Latin America, although for different purposes. The Brazilian general revision included, with its increases or readjustments of the old duties, an appreciable number of material reductions on a range of foreign products, which either are not directly competitive or are regarded as necessary to the economic life of the country, with provision for selective protection to certain developing national industries, through customs facilities for raw materials or equipment needed from abroad. The Cuban revision adjusted many duties to conform to the provisions of the new reciprocal trade agreement with the United States, involving numerous reductions from previous rates and also the abolition or moderation of surcharges and consumption taxes previously imposed as emergency measures. As a step toward making the Republic of Panama a greater inter-American trade distribution center, that government decided in December upon the complete elimination of the import duties on about 600 classes of commodities, mostly consumers' goods. The loss in revenue from the prospective abolition of these duties is expected to be counterbalanced by a largely increased volume of international trade being conducted in Panama.

On the other hand, the new tariffs put into operation by Venezuela and Honduras, and that proposed by Peru, consisted mainly of materially upward revisions on substantial ranges of commodities. The new Salvadoran tariff system contemplates three scales of duties, with the intermediate and maximum scales, consisting of the previous rates plus surtaxes, to be applied to the various nontreaty countries according to the degree to which their exports to El Salvador exceed their imports from that country.

In addition to these general changes, selective modifications in import tariff rates were made in various of the Latin American countries during the year, with frequent evidence of a desire to foster domestic production of some lines largely imported hitherto, often by reducing or waiving the duties on imported industrial materials and productive equipment. As special aids to domestic producers, several of these countries provided varying measures of export subsidies on certain secondary crops, often deriving their funds from increases in customs duties.

Important differences in types of recent trade agreements.—The movement in Latin America for the negotiation of reciprocal trade agreements, among themselves and with outside countries, was carried considerably further during 1934, over twenty-five such agreements having been reported, most of them with overseas countries. Considerable diversity was observed in the types of these arrangements entered into during the past year.

At least six Latin American countries concluded agreements in which they granted reductions in their duties on lists of selected commodities, in return for the guaranty on the part of the other country either of its existing minimum duties or of assured import quotas during the period ahead for their important export products, notably coffee, nitrates, and fruits. These arrangements arose out of the general import limitation programs of the European countries involved.

Another type of agreement provided for reciprocal reductions in some duties and assurance against increase in others on selected commodities of particular interest to each of the countries, whether or not combined with quota provisions on outstanding products. This type was perhaps best exemplified during the past year by the reciprocal trade agreement entered into by Cuba with the United States, whereby, in return for concessions in the import duties into the United States for sugar, tobacco, rum, and off-season fruits and vegetables, Cuba granted increased tariff advantages on a broad range of commodities of which American producers had been the principal suppliers to that market. The Cuban-American reciprocity agreement is exceptional in that the special preferential relation between the two countries, established at the time of the independence of Cuba, continued to mark their relations. Similar agreements, contemplating concessions and bindings of existing favorable treatment on each side of selected products of which the other country has been an important supplier, are understood to be under negotiation by the United States with a number of other countries of Latin America, including Brazil, Colombia, Haiti, and those of Central America, the advantages of which will presumably be generalized to other nondiscriminating countries on a most-favored-nation status.

Contrasting in method and principle was the type of agreement exemplified by the arrangements entered into by Argentina with a series of European countries. The feature common to them all was the pledge secured by each from Argentina to provide exchange, at the favorable official rate, out of the volume of purchases of Argentine products by each of those countries, for the prompt liquidation of current purchases of merchandise from the other countries and for the transfer of blocked funds or other debts due their citizens, after deduction of a "reasonable amount" for general debt services. These will be recognized as modeled after the Anglo-Argentine agreement of the preceding year, and, as in that case, the insistence upon preferential exchange treatment being assured to merchants and creditors in those European countries was based upon the fact that these countries normally had need for larger importations of the distinctive Argentine products than Argentina did for their particular export commodities. The availability of foreign exchange in the open market, although at somewhat higher rates, tempered the restrictive effect of these agreements upon the possibility of sales in Argentina by producers in countries whose balance of trade was not favorable to Argentina.

This objective of bringing about a closer bilateral balance in the trade with each country figured in the special exchange compensation arrangement between Brazil and Chile recently, and led to the proposal by Uruguay for the creation of an Imports and Exchange Commission, charged with the fixing of import quotas by quantities and classes of goods, under a plan to pay for imports by allocating a minimum of 75 per cent of the exchange derived from exports to each country, the balance to be reserved for servicing public and private debts, and other transfer of funds. The Uruguayan plan incidentally illustrates the difficulty of keeping distinct the two systems of control. The quantitative control of *imports* of particular classes of goods allowed admission from different countries is not easily kept separate from the control of the allotment of *exchange* with which to pay for such imports, the two methods sometimes intermingling or serving one in place of the other.

Finally, in contrast to the efforts toward bilateral balancing of trade between individual pairs of countries through special arrangements regarding exchange control or quota allotments, were half a dozen agreements entered into by several countries of Latin America during the year providing simply for most-favored-nation treatment, which, in certain cases, was extended also to assurances regarding the granting of foreign exchange and allotments of quotas. Which of the quite diverse tendencies indicated by these different agreements entered into by countries of Latin America during the past year is likely to represent the dominant trend during the period ahead, it is still too early to judge.

British Empire

The control of foreign exchange, common in Europe and Latin America, has not been an important instrument of commercial policy among the areas constituting the British Empire during the depression, and, outside the United Kingdom and the Irish Free State, there have been only few instances of resort to the typically European device of import quotas. The program of the present English Government, designed to revive home agriculture by so limiting imports as to bring about larger home production and better prices to English producers of a series of important foodstuffs, has involved a growing system of quantitative restrictions on the importation of those products. Primarily, they applied to countries outside the Empire, although 1934 saw some extensions of the quotas also to Dominion products, and others are reported as prospective. Under authority granted during the past year to its Executive Council, the Irish Free State now has a limited but growing list of products subject to quantitative limitation, with large discretion to the government in granting quotas and licenses, including not only the designation of the country from which the goods are to come but the route as well.

Duties continue dominant, with Empire preferences growing.—Broadly speaking and with the exceptions noted, import duties have continued the primary controllers on import trade into most parts of the British Empire. Their restrictive effect upon the trade of the Empire areas with the nations generally was, however, intensified by the Imperial Preference movement, designed to bring about the supplying of the import needs of these areas more largely from each other, through an Empire-wide program of preferential treatment of each other's products, by lower tariffs or exemptions from other restrictions imposed on the admission of competitive non-Empire products. This movement received a great impetus through the series of agreements entered into between the various British areas at the Ottawa Conference of 1932, most of which were to run for five years, subject to amendment by consultation in the interval.

The year 1934 saw some reaction in a number of the Dominions from the upward movement in the tariff rates that had marked recent years, which had been particularly noticeable in most of the measures to give effect to the Ottawa commitments. These usually increased the duties on products from non-Empire sources while leaving unchanged, or even reducing, the British preferential rates on the same products. A feature of the downward tariff changes of the past year, however, has been the net enlargement in the margin of preference to Empire over other suppliers of most of the articles affected. In other ways also the year saw extension of the preferential movement, particularly in the further advantages for British products in this or that colonial area. On the other hand, there has been difficulty reported between the mother country and the Dominions regarding the proposed restrictions on the market for their meats and other foodstuffs in the United Kingdom, and the Irish Free State eliminated Empire preferences on many products in the course of revision of their duties.

In the British colonies, quotas were imposed during the past year on cotton and rayon piece goods, upon request of the United Kingdom, as a means of holding those markets for the Lancashire producers against the increase of outside competition, especially from Japan. These textile quotas, which appear to have been quite generally renewed also for 1935, limit the importations from various sources to the average share they supplied during the five-year period 1927–1931.

Treaty negotiations of diverse types and purposes.—The year saw considerable activity in the negotiation or discussion of trade agreements with various countries on the part of a number of the Dominions, as well as of the United Kingdom itself. There was, however, considerable diversity in the purpose and provisions of the agreements concluded. Thus, the principal Canadian agreement of the year—with France—provided for reciprocal concessions in duties and other advantages on both sides, as, in a more limited way, did the New Zealand agreement with Belgium. On the other hand, in a series of trade agreements between the United Kingdom and various countries of Europe, only one was reported to provide any reductions in existing British duties, and those largely by way of removal of retaliatory levies. In the agreement entered into by the United Kingdom with the three Baltic countries and Poland, the duty concessions given by the other countries and their purchase commitments for British coal were mainly in return for promises that the position of various of their distinctive products would be safeguarded in the British market against increase of duties or disproportionate quota restrictions.

In the United Kingdom agreements with France and the Netherlands, progress was made toward the recognition that the most-favored-nation principle required, in the field of quotas, the allotment of the full proportional share of any restricted commodity supplied by the other country during a previous representative period. Of quite a different type was the agreement which closed the controversy between British India and Japan. This provided, in addition to most-favored-nation assurances, for specific quantities of Japanese piece goods to be admitted at the lower duties in effect previous to 1932, in return for the guaranteed Japanese purchase of specified quantities of Indian raw cotton.

International agreements for export control of tin and rubber.—Two important developments of the year in the field of export control of raw materials, involving largely the British Empire, were the extension for another three years of the international agreement between the principal tin-producing areas (Malay States, Netherlands Indies, Nigeria, Bolivia, and Siam) for the quantitative control of the export of that metal; and the completion of an international agreement for controlling the export of crude rubber. This latter agreement, which is to run through 1938 and embraces the areas accounting for fully 98 per cent of world rubber production (Malaya, Netherlands Indies, Ceylon, British India, Burma, French Indo-China, North Borneo, Sarawak, and Siam), provided for basic annual export quotas for each plantation-rubber-producing territory, and for an international regulation committee, appointed by the various governments, which fixes from time to time the percentage of the basic quota which may be exported from each territory. The effects of the two agreements in advancing the world market prices of these important raw materials are signficant, but outside the scope of the present review.

For the purpose of stimulating domestic production or maintaining the volume of exports of particular products, mainly agricultural, several of the British areas adopted or extended bounties during the past year. Thus, the United Kingdom began to pay a bounty on domestic cattle production, and has undertaken to guarantee a tariff advantage, on a progressively reducing scale of rates, to gasoline produced from coal or shale for a period of ten years. The Irish Free State increased the rate of bounty on exports of pork, poultry, and dairy products, among others, and discontinued the bounty on calfskins. Australia announced a revised bounty to wheat growers and increased the bounty to cotton producers, the amounts depending upon the current market price. The Union of South Africa has given authority for the payment of bounties on the exportation of cattle, sheep, and their products, and plans to continue its export subsidies on agricultural and other natural products for one year, with a gradual decrease and disappearance in three years, excepting on meat. On the other hand, several of the Dominions have subjected to license the exportation of certain agricultural products, in order to conform to the plan desired by Great Britain for import limitation of those products into its market.

1935

DOMESTIC ECONOMIC RECOVERY BRINGS SOME RELAXATION OF FOREIGN TRADE BARRIERS

Notwithstanding recovery of varying degrees in their internal economic situation, the year 1935 was marked in most foreign countries by a substantial continuance or even accentuation of import restrictions. On the balance, these tendencies probably outweighed the notable but as yet few instances of easing of trade barriers during the past year. The result has been that foreign markets have afforded only little increased opportunity for export products as a whole. Tariffs and other obstacles to import trade became somewhat more moderate during 1935 in a number of the countries of Latin America, in certain of the British Empire areas, and in several of the smaller countries of Europe. On the other hand, the complicated system of quotas, exchange controls, and clearing agreements developed by most countries of continental Europe were continued, and in some cases even tightened, during the past year, especially in Germany and Italy.

Barring any outstanding new adverse developments during 1936, the resistance to many classes of American export products arising from foreign trade barriers may be expected to be appreciably reduced during the new year, as a result of the operation of the ten reciprocal trade agreements that had been concluded by the United States up to February 15, 1936 (eight of which were already in effect by that date), and the several additional agreements that are expected to be concluded within the next few months.[1]

Continental Europe

Many trade control changes but no clear policies or consistent programs.—The tremendous number of changes on the continent of Europe during 1935 in duties, quotas, exchange allocations, monopoly controls, and the like, and the many agreements made and unmade between governments regarding these various forms of trade regulation, render extremely difficult any attempt to appraise the complicated developments of the year in this field.

In very few of the European countries does there stand out from the year's mass of particular changes any distinct pattern or progress toward definite commercial policies. This very fact, however, may itself be a significant indication that most governments on the Continent have not yet come to clear policies or confident programs with regard to foreign trade. Responding to various and changing pressures, they appear to have been led, during the past year, to replace one measure or arrangement found unsatisfactory with another that was not greatly different, or to continue on the one hand to restrict imports through various arbitrary devices and to persist on the other hand in efforts to maintain and enlarge their exports. Tied up with financial and other considerations as trade control arrangements are at this time, this uncertainty and opportunism of policy may also explain why during the past year, many European countries, entered into such a variety of agreements, of almost as many types as the countries dealt with, and with one agreement often inherently inconsistent with the others.

Quantitative controls continue dominant.—Lacking new directives or outstanding developments of a long-time character, the events of 1935 on the continent of Europe were largely by way of continuation or working out of measures adopted or set in motion during the preceding year.[2] Quantitative controls and agreements continued during the past year as the dominant regulators of foreign trade. By the end of 1935, few countries of

[1] Such trade agreements have thus far been concluded by the United States with four countries of Europe (Belgium, Sweden, Netherlands and Indies, and Switzerland), five of Latin America (Cuba, Haiti, Brazil, Colombia, and Honduras), and with Canada. Taken together, these countries accounted for nearly 32 per cent of the total foreign trade of the United States during 1929, the last predepression year. Similar negotiations have also been announced with eight additional governments (Spain, France and colonies, Italy, Finland, and the other four Central American Republics).

[2] See survey of 1934, pp. 124–128.

continental Europe were entirely free from some form or degree of import quota, license requirements, or exchange control, or were without agreements of a compensating or clearing nature with some other countries, whether negotiated upon their own initiative or entered into under pressure from the other side. The extreme form of such regulation was reached in Germany and Italy, where practically all imports and many classes of exports are under strict, complicated, and often arbitrary license and exchange controls. However, in view of the special current objectives of these governments, including the conservation of foreign exchange and the increase of armaments, their present control systems may be regarded as exceptional.

While some few quotas have been given up, the tendency of the year in most European countries has been to continue earlier quota or license limitations on imports at about the global level of 1934, and to extend them from time to time to additional commodities. This has been more marked in some countries than in others, with exchange control upon means of payment often used interchangeably with direct limitation upon imports, or even overshadowing it. In fairness, it should be observed that quantitative limitations have at times been used to safeguard the level of imports from increasing instead of restricting them below the earlier level. There has been an increasing tendency to regulate imports by requiring a license for each transaction, without periodic announcement of definite quotas, or apportionment among the usual supplying countries or importing firms. On the other hand, the trend in a few of these countries has been toward replacing absolute quotas with tariff quotas, which provide that specified amounts of particular products are to be admitted under reduced rates of duty, with additional quantities admissible but only upon the payment of the former or even higher duties.

In at least two important countries, the Netherlands and France, an increased tendency was evident toward preferential treatment in their colonial possessions for goods originating in the mother country, and vice versa.

Along with quantitative regulation of imports, whether carried on by individual merchants or under some form of centralized or monopoly control, there have been spreading in Europe during the past year systems of import license taxes, "monopoly fees" or similar surtaxes on imported products. The rates either vary with the commodity, much as tariff schedules, as in France—indeed, sometimes exceeding the regular duties—or are assessed at a uniform ad valorem level, as in Italy. The frequent changeability in the rates of these fees, as well as in the quantities and conditions of permitted imports—even upon readiness to pay all the set duties and fees—naturally makes much of current international trading on the continent of Europe an unstable and precarious matter.

Trade pacts deal mainly with quotas, usually on exclusive balanced basis.—As in the past few years, trade agreements by European countries, mostly with each other, have been numerous, often quite limited in scope, and usually of short duration. For the most part, the agreements of the past year have continued to deal more with this new superstructure of quantitative and compensatory trade arrangements and less with import duties, the old and basic form of international trade control. In a number of cases, the agreements of the past year have indeed provided for reductions in duties and related matters, the benefits of which are still, under the traditional practice, usually generalized also to most other countries able to compete for the trade. In the great majority of important cases, however, the advantages or undertakings exchanged between a particular pair of countries have been distinctly exclusive or trade diverting in purpose, without any intention of following the old practice of affording equality of competitive opportunity to suppliers in different countries.

The beguiling idea so prominent in recent years that a country's trade and financial position would be improved and more secure if planned and adjusted to a bilateral balance with each other country has continued to play an important part also in the European trade agreements of 1935. It is by now a familiar story[8] how various European countries whose nationals happened to buy more in a particular country than they sold there took advantage of that fact to force special advantages in their favor, by insisting either that the other country should even up the trade balance by granting lower duties or increased quotas for their distinctive products, or that the surplus current exchange be used for preferential payments on debts or interest due their nationals. It was apparently not fully realized that, under the normal triangular and polyangular development of international trade, any given country was bound to have a favorable balance with some other countries, and that those others might in turn similarly press their advantage, where they could, to obtain special benefits for their trade and debts. The past year has afforded numerous instances both in Europe and elsewhere of such repercussions to this practice. Unfortunately, these reactions have operated to the injury not only

[8] See references to this tendency in chapters on 1933 and 1934.

of countries who first resorted to this practice but also of others, such as the United States, who had abstained.

Evidences of reaction against trade-constricting policies.—By 1935, the costliness of seeking extreme self-sufficiency, or of buying in the markets where you must, had been borne in on the peoples of many countries. Moreover, the ineffectiveness of most of the arrangements based on the bilateral trade-balancing principle, either in enlarging the volume of the country's total export trade or of definitely readjusting the trade balance, except on a lower and less advantageous level, has already become apparent in many of the cases. Various governments have admitted their unsatisfactory experience with "clearing agreements," in replies to a League of Nations inquiry on the subject during the past year; and the League committee of experts studying the subject concluded that, except as a most temporary expedient, such bilateral balancing arrangements were so ineffective, and involved so many grave drawbacks that the system should not be extended, and should be abolished as soon as any other arrangements could possibly be made.

It seems significant that representative business leaders from many countries, meeting this past summer at the Congress of the International Chamber of Commerce at Paris—in the heart of the Continent where these restrictive and trade-diverting devices have been most widely applied during recent years—reasserted "the essentially multiangular character of international trade," declared themselves strongly in favor of "the mitigation of existing barriers to trade," denounced the policy of national self-sufficiency as inviting "sure disaster," if generally pursued, and urged that bilateral trade agreements on substantially the old unconditional most-favored-nation basis be negotiated as rapidly as possible. A resolution along remarkably similar lines resulted from the discussions in the Annual Assembly of the League of Nations in September, in which the representatives of over fifty governments concurred that, even before the reestablishment of an international monetary standard becomes possible, "effective steps might be taken with a view to the removal of impediments to the exchange of goods, and that such a removal is indispensable if the economic recovery of which signs are now apparent is to be developed."

For the second year since the downward spiral of general world commerce had been checked, and the exports of most of the rest of the world had either improved or held their own, the aggregate value of the exports of the countries on the European continent have been running almost consistently lower during 1935 than during the same months of 1934 or 1933.

This fact may have accelerated the recognition on the Continent of the desirability of a broader exchange of products between the nations on a more liberal basis, both to help lagging domestic recovery programs through enlarged foreign outlets, and as an aid in the adjustment of financial and other international problems. However, the difficulties in the way of rapid replacement of the network of complex and arbitrary foreign trade arrangements developed during the depression, by measures and methods that are simpler and admittedly sounder in the long run, seem to be accentuated by several outside factors. Governments declare themselves deterred from taking active steps in that direction by the current uncertainties of the general political prospects and—despite the fact that there has been substantial steadiness in the exchange rates between the principal currency groups for a period of almost two years—by the still unstabilized and insecure state of international currency relations.

Beginnings toward more liberal trade controls.—In only a few of the European countries does the situation early in 1936 indicate that actual progress of a substantial character had been made during 1935 toward more liberal conditions of admission, either of foreign products as a whole or of the products of countries important in their economy. Thus, as a result of the agreements entered into during the past year, the tariffs or other import control systems of only the following countries might be regarded on the whole less restrictive than they were a year ago: Belgium (as a result of the trade agreements with the United States as well as with France, Germany, and Italy), Sweden (as a result of the agreements with France and Spain, as well as with the United States), Poland (as a result of the agreements with the United Kingdom, Canada, and Germany), Norway (principally the French agreement), the Netherlands (principally as a result of the agreement with the United States), and Switzerland (resulting from the agreement with the United States entered into early in January, 1936). Such aspirations as had developed in Europe for making a start toward breaking through the trade-constricting chain received considerable encouragement, during the past year, from the announced readiness of the United States to enter into trade agreements for the reciprocal reduction of barriers of every kind, and built on the very bases which representatives of business and spokesmen of governments had endorsed.

Among the trade-liberating agreements just listed will be noted agreements with the United States on the part of four European countries—Belgium, Sweden, the Netherlands, and Switzerland. These agreements are particularly significant for their reassertion of the unconditional most-favored-nation principle, and for the application of that principle to quantitative controls of every kind as well as to its original field of import duties. In fact, the principal concessions or assurances in the last two of these agreements have been largely in the matter of quotas, monopoly purchases, and monopoly fees.

The year 1935 also saw the termination of the long-standing tariff wars between Germany and Poland and between Czechoslovakia and Hungary, through the bringing into operation of agreements whereby these two pairs of countries granted each other most-favored-nation treatment plus reciprocal advantages on lists of products of importance to each other. In this connection might be mentioned also the settlement of a number of tariff disputes of shorter duration. These involved mainly France (in the course of which France has by now agreed to reduce to 2 per cent, as regards almost all countries, the import "turnover" taxes of 4 and 6 per cent levied for several years past), and Portugal (resulting in the removal, as regards an additional number of countries, of the discriminatory duties on goods brought in foreign ships).

Among the developments operating in the other direction was the termination during the past year of the important Franco-German commercial treaty of 1927, which, concluded after years of negotiation, had at the time been hailed as marking the commercial reconciliation of the two principal contending nations in the World War. Its obligations already weakened by successive amendments, the actual termination of the treaty last summer, and the resumption by both governments of freedom of action, was followed by the abolition of many conventional duty reductions on the part of Germany, and, on the part of France, by the curtailment of the size of the quotas on many classes of German goods.

In a number of European countries, steps have been taken during the last half of 1935 which promise progress during 1936 toward liberalization of existing trade control systems. The government of France, which had led off in the adoption of import quotas, announced that it had decreed the establishment of a committee—analogous to the British Import Advisory Board—to examine, with the assistance of technical studies and commercial inquiries, the advisability of replacing particular quotas by duties, although at somewhat higher rates. It was declared that the purpose was to give trade once more "the security which is essential to its development," and to relieve it from the inelasticity, monopolistic tendencies, and license abuses which appear inescapable under quota systems. Thus far, however, only a beginning has been made by France in implementing this program.

The government of the Netherlands, in connection with the presentation of the budget for 1936, recognized the greater injury and insecurity suffered by trade under quantitative controls than under a system of duties, and the Cabinet is understood to have under investigation the possibility of replacing some existing absolute quotas by other measures, possibly including tariff quotas. Greece has introduced a revised quota system designed to be simpler, and less changeable in its operation. The Turkish quota system has also been simplified, and, by a series of agreements, successive lists of products of special interest to the other countries have been rendered free of quota control.

War in Ethiopia prompts limitations on trading with Italy.—The new program of limitations upon trading with Italy that was being initiated toward the close of 1935 by a large number of countries over the world—whether under the League of Nations' efforts in connection with the Italo-Ethiopian conflict, or arising from the neutrality position of certain individual countries—combined with the threatened counterrestrictions on the part of Italy upon the trade of these countries, obviously has potentialities of serious derangements in international commerce. However, as 1936 opens, the program is still in too early and changeable a state to allow of its evaluation as a development in commercial policy.

British Empire

The widely scattered areas constituting the British Empire have been marked during recent years in the matter of commercial policy by their continued dependence upon import duties as the primary regulators of import trade. None of these areas have resorted to the control of exchange for the payment of current purchases and—with the exception of the growing system of general quotas in the Irish Free State, the recent foodstuff quotas in the United Kingdom, and the piece-goods quotas in the crown colonies—they have rarely applied quantitative limitations on imports. In general, therefore, the developments in this field in the British Empire can be viewed primarily in terms of the tariff duties. Two things need to be kept in mind, however: the Ottawa agreements of 1932, whereby the various British areas undertook to divert to each other, through special tariffs or other preferential measures, the purchases of their import requirements hitherto supplied from non-Empire countries; and the program to revive home agriculture initiated in the United Kingdom in 1933, which has involved limitations upon imports of a series of important food products through a system of quotas, from most of which the Empire areas have thus far been exempt.

British fostering of home agriculture and stop-loss trade agreements.—In the United Kingdom, there have been no important extensions during 1935 of this new program for the fostering of domestic production of certain foodstuffs, which now includes wheat and wheat flour, meats, eggs, and dairy products. Aside from the pressure of dissatisfaction with the program expressed at home and from certain of the Dominions, a more definite long-time food policy for the United Kingdom is expected to emerge during 1936, in connection with the renegotiation of the trade agreements with various non-Empire countries that are due to expire this coming year.[4]

The year saw numerous changes in the import duties of the United Kingdom, with the duties on certain products increased or supported by alternative specific rates, and reduced or waived on selected raw materials and semimanufactures. It is not clear whether these represent a definite line of development of the general British tariff adopted in 1932 or simply piecemeal adjustments in particular lines. A noteworthy development was the reduction of certain duties on iron and steel products, following a five-year marketing agreement between the British Iron and Steel Federation and the Continental Steel Cartel, involving limitations on imports of certain steel products into the United Kingdom, to be commercially regulated, and the division also of certain common markets on the basis of relative prior trade.

The trade agreements entered into by the United Kingdom during the past year with the Irish Free State, India, Poland, Italy, Uruguay, and Turkey were notably diverse in their provisions. The most prominent objectives appear to have been conservation of existing trade or efforts toward bilateral trade balancing. With the exception of the restoration to the Irish Free State of part of its earlier share in the cattle imports of the United Kingdom (without change in the penalty duty), in return for an undertaking to purchase all imported coal from the United Kingdom, and of the elimination of the Ottawa agreement duty on figs and fig cake in the negotiations with Turkey, none of the British agreements of the year appear to have involved any reductions of consequence in the existing duties of the United Kingdom, or any increases in the total amounts of the products under quota allowed admission.

Canada and United States exchange tariff concessions, reversing recent policies.—From the viewpoint of American exporters, undoubtedly the outstanding development of the year in the British Empire was the con-

[4] Most of the Ottawa agreements with other parts of the British Empire are due to run until 1937, although with the possibility of earlier modification of their terms by consultation.

clusion of a reciprocal trade agreement between Canada and the United States, coming into effect essentially at the beginning of 1936, whereby these two neighboring countries—which have been the second largest customers for each other's exports—reversed the policy pursued during recent years of restricting their purchases from each other. While negotiations had been initiated some time back, the signature of this trade agreement of wide scope and importance to the producers and consumers in both countries—the first such successful effort in over seventy years—culminated in November, 1935, following the return to power in Canada of the Liberal party after a campaign in which lower trade barriers, and particularly toward the United States, was a major issue.

Primarily, the arrangement provided for reciprocal duty reductions or assurances of continued favorable conditions of admission on broad ranges of distinctive export products of each, agricultural and industrial, for which the other country had been an important market in the past. In addition, the agreement was notable for the recognition by Canada, after many years of opposite practice, that American products should receive at least as favorable customs treatment as those from any other non-British areas, and for the assurance of substantial withdrawal or moderation of the elaborate arbitrary valuation system on imports, under which many Canadian duties had during recent years been increased well beyond the nominal or statutory rates of duty, and often by unpredictable amounts.

In addition to a supplementary agreement with France and a commercial convention with Poland, in the course of both of which Canada made reductions in the duties on selected products of interest to the other side, Canada entered into arrangements with Austria and five of the smaller Latin American countries, providing essentially for the exchange of most-favored-nation treatment. Action was also taken by Canada to assure the United Kingdom, Australia, New Zealand, and South Africa the benefit of the lowest duties that may be hereafter granted to any country. The clear rededication by Canada to most-favored-nation policy during the past year is noteworthy in view of the deviations from that traditional principle on the part of other countries, particularly in Europe.

The selective autonomous tariff changes made by Canada during 1935 were largely on the downward side. Exceptional was the 33⅓ per cent surtax ordered on all Japanese products in July, following the Japanese application of a 50 per cent surtax against important Canadian products, because of the Canadian insistence upon levying exchange dumping duties on Japanese products on the ground of extreme depreciation of the yen.

A truce was worked out between Canada and Japan at the end of the year by which both sides canceled their surtaxes.

Australia revises tariff downward; South Africa sets penalty duties.—The tariff action of the Australian Government during 1935 was also outstanding. Giving effect to the policy that duties should not exceed what is found "reasonable and adequate under existing conditions of exchange," that protection should be limited to goods "economically manufactured in Australia," and that account should be taken of the burden upon consumers and users, the United Australian party—governing in coalition with the Country party—brought forward during the year two series of predominantly downward revisions from the high duties and surtaxes built up during the early years of the depression, affecting a considerable range of products. These changes were made only after studies by the Tariff Board and, where changes were made in both the general rates and the British preferential rates, the previous margin of advantage to Empire suppliers usually remained unchanged. Of interest for the future is the Australian plan for an intermediate schedule of import duties (somewhat below the present general duties), to be used for tariff bargaining purposes; at present it is inoperative, pending the negotiation of trade agreements with foreign countries. There was relatively little change in the New Zealand tariffs during the year.

In the Union of South Africa, the most striking development during 1935 was the establishment of the three-column tariff, by the addition of a maximum scale of duties that may be applied to selected imports from nontreaty countries. Such maximum duties have already been proclaimed on a half dozen classes of goods when coming from five such countries, including the United States, the new duties being 5 to 10 per cent ad valorem above those applied to non-British countries generally. The report of the special commission that has been making a survey since 1934 of the tariff policy of the Union, especially as to its effect upon secondary industries and the cost of living, is expected to come up for serious consideration by the Parliament in 1936. In accordance with the original plans, the subsidies paid on certain South African exports, principally agricultural products and raw materials, were reduced during the year by approximately one-third, with the expectation of a similar reduction in 1936, and their total abolition in 1937.

In its budget for 1935–1936, the Irish Free State further developed its growing tariff by new or increased duties on a considerable number of commodities, declared primarily for the purpose of increasing revenue.

The import quotas of the preceding year were generally continued and similar restrictions established on additional products. Apparently in the effort to build up alternative markets on the Continent for Irish agricultural products—in place of the usual English market, which is still seriously curtailed—the Irish Government appears to have been led into negotiations of the European type, providing for reciprocal quota undertakings with Belgium and Spain and for a fixed trade ratio with Germany. The partial moderation during 1935 of the tariff war of several years' standing between the Irish Free State and the United Kingdom, providing larger purchases of Irish cattle in return for British coal, has already been described.

The year saw few important new developments in the comprehensive system of Empire preferences that had been built up during the recent period. The events of the year in several Empire areas suggest some reaction from the tendency toward increased duties on the products of non-Empire countries, by means of which the Ottawa agreements had been largely implemented.

Differing experiences of international export controls on rubber and tin.—In the field of raw material export controls, two of the major schemes now in operation, by agreement among the principal territories producing crude rubber and tin ore, both chiefly involve British Empire and Dutch colonial areas. The operations of the two controls during 1935, however, have been quite different.

The International Rubber Regulation Committee successively reduced the percentage of allowable exports by 5 per cent a quarter, down to 60 per cent for the fourth quarter, at which level it has been fixed for the first six months of 1936 (although subject to possible revision). Apparently because of the slowness with which surplus stocks had been reduced, despite the gradually increased restriction on new supplies, the world market price of rubber has not advanced much since the inauguration of the new control plan in June, 1934. However, the 1935 price level was much above that prevailing in 1932–1933, before the present international agreement was foreshadowed, and, with improvement in the statistical position, the price of rubber has been tending firmly upward since the closing months of 1935.

Under the tin control, on the other hand, despite four successive quarterly increases of 5 per cent in the basic export quotas for the principal producing areas, a scarcity of supplies developed in certain major markets which in October sent the London price for tin to the highest level in about seven years. This led to two further quota increases that month, up to 80 per cent of the standard tonnages. For the first quarter of 1936 the quota has been set at 90 per cent, or double that of a year ago.

Latin America

While not characteristic of the whole of Latin America, a striking development of the past year in a number of important countries in that area has been the efforts to "correct" the trade balance with those countries where their nationals have been buying more than they have been selling.

"Correcting" bilateral balances by raising duties or restricting exchange.—The methods used have been several. Thus, Cuba, Haiti, Guatemala, and Ecuador adopted the practice initiated by El Salvador during the preceding year of establishing multiple tariffs, instead of the traditional single column of rates applicable to all countries. They have begun to apply these several scales of duties—or the previous rates, plus varying surtaxes—to products from various nontreaty countries, according to the degree to which imports from those countries exceeded their purchases of national products. In order to secure the benefit of the minimum or even intermediate rates, instead of the much higher maximums, several European and other governments have entered into agreements with these Latin American countries, undertaking to purchase during the current year, say Cuban products, to the extent of at least 25 or 50 per cent of their sales in that market. In other cases, the Latin American government adopting such differential tariffs hastened to denounce certain most-favored-nation agreements with various important overseas countries in order to regain freedom of action at the earliest date. Whether because of the state of the trade balance with the United States, or because of existing treaty obligations, in no case thus far have the higher scales of these multiple tariffs been applied to the products of the United States.

In a number of other countries much the same objective was sought through the control of foreign exchange. Notably Argentina and Uruguay have attempted to regulate the volume of their trading with different countries through differential allocation of foreign exchange for the payment of purchases from different countries, or through differing readiness to make available such exchange at the "official" or lower rates. Promptness of remittance or the rates at which exchange could be obtained have been made to depend, in part, upon the relative necessity or dispensability of the particular product, but mainly upon the relative volume of exchange being created through recent or current purchases of the country's leading export products by the nationals of the other country.

Recovery in exports and prices allow some relaxation of import controls.—Although on the part of certain governments there has been this tightening of exchange control selectively toward particular countries, as a whole, the past year has seen an appreciable easement in Latin America in the volume of exchange available for payment of imports and in the freedom of its disposal.[5] This has been made possible by the measurable recovery during the past year or so in the value of the exports of practically every major country of Latin America, accompanied in some cases by improvements in the unit prices obtained by producers for their staple export products, even though at times these have been artificially aided by governmental price guarantees or export subsidies. For instance, the year 1935 saw a significant rise in the value of purchases by the United States from practically all Latin American countries, and some recovery in the value and share of the imports of most of these countries that were supplied from the United States.

This easement in the availability of exchange has been in general true of Argentina, Uruguay, Brazil, Colombia, and Ecuador. Control on payments for current imports was entirely lifted in Ecuador, and practically so in Brazil and Colombia as regards their imports from most countries. In the case of these last two, the relaxation of control was accompanied, so far as private commercial transactions are concerned, by a substantial depreciation in the external value of the currency, following closely the trend of world prices of coffee. In most of the Caribbean areas and Middle America generally, there has been no exchange control, although in certain Central American countries there has recently been considerable delay in obtaining exchange.

Readiness for concessions in trade-easing agreements.—In the matter of import duties, which, in the countries of Latin America more than in Europe, constitute the prime regulators of imports, the year 1935 has seen a few revisions or successive series of changes on varying lists of commodities. The general tendency has been upward, although, in a number of countries, more selectively than in the past. In several countries there were downward changes to allow a larger flow of imports, especially in necessities

[5] It will be recalled that foreign exchange had been under control for several years in about half of the countries of Latin America, and that, even in some of the areas where there was no official or centralized control, sheer shortage of exchange created by curtailed exports had often been an overshadowing consideration in determining the amount of new foreign purchases that could be made or paid for.

of life and in equipment for the gradual diversification of production, agricultural and industrial. To avoid an undue burden upon consumers and an increase in costs of living, there have been evidences in Mexico, Colombia, Ecuador, and certain Central American countries of a closer scrutiny of the operation of protected industries and of local requests for additional tariff increases.

This more critical attitude toward local protectionism has figured also in connection with the trade agreement negotiations, in which the year has been an exceptionally active one for Latin America. Perhaps its most notable manifestation was the satisfaction expressed by practically all the economic elements in Cuba over the operation of the reciprocal trade agreement with the United States, brought into operation in September, 1934, which involved decided curtailments of the measure of protection to domestic industries stimulated or expanded during the period of high Cuban tariffs. It has been expressed also in connection with agreements entered into with the United States by Brazil, Colombia, and several of the smaller Caribbean areas, and in the eagerness of various other governments of Latin America to enter into similar negotiations.

Especially in view of the high duties, quotas, and other restrictions which various European countries now impose on many of the staple food and raw material exports of the Latin American countries—upon which they so depend for their prosperity—some of the American Republics have apparently come to feel that it warrants the sacrifice that may be involved in the reduction of some of their duties, in order to obtain agreements that will assure continued unrestricted access to important markets on favorable terms for certain of their products, and improved conditions of admission for others, particularly when the general basis of the agreement is on liberal principles that promise further ultimate enlargement of their trade possibilities.

Stiffer attitude in pacts with countries pressing for trade balancing.—Quite in contrast has been the attitude of most Latin American countries toward those of Europe, most of which have maintained, so far as conditions would allow, the distinctively restrictive policy in their trade arrangements with the Latin American Republics. On the one hand, the year has seen a further development and adoption by additional European countries of the practice earlier referred to of seeking special advantages from those countries of Latin America where they happen to buy more than they sell. Quite a number of countries, particularly of South America, have been led during 1935 to enter into arrangements involving on their part reductions in duties, purchase undertakings, or preferential allocation of exchange, in return for noncurtailment of their previous volume of sales in those European markets, or even upon assurance of restricted but definite minimum import quotas for their coffee, nitrates, meats, or other important exports.

Perhaps the most striking development of this type, and one which has led to particular complaint from competitive suppliers in the United States and elsewhere, has been the so-called "askimark" arrangements which Germany has worked out with a number of Latin American countries since 1934. These provide that the mark proceeds from the sale of, say, coffee or nitrates, shall be available only for the purchase of at least an equivalent value of German goods, such special marks being usually available at a discount because of the lack of demand for German products to the full extent of the German purchases of Latin American products.

On the other hand, in those cases where the American countries had been buying from these particular overseas countries more than they had been selling, there was evidenced the tendency earlier referred to, to resort to the European practice of insisting on an increase in the volume of purchases which the overseas country would take or facilitate, under penalty of higher duties, less favorable exchange allocations, or other restrictions.

These efforts on the part of certain Latin American countries to enforce, when they could, a closer balance of trade with their foreign suppliers were directed during the past year not only at European countries but also at Japan, whose exporters of cotton piece goods and other products had been shipping considerable quantities since 1933, especially to the Caribbean and the north coast, while hitherto buying Latin American staples in only slight amounts.

The growing movement on the part of various of the Latin American countries for enforcing something like a balance in their trade relations with different overseas countries, through penalty duties, differential exchange allocations or rates, or the forcing of increased purchase undertakings, has the appearance of a defensive movement against the pressure which various countries of continental Europe and the United Kingdom have been exerting upon those countries from which they happened to buy more than they sold, to grant them special market openings for their products or preferential treatment in the allocation of exchange for the payment of current purchases and the clearing up of debts. It appears also to be something of a reaction against the pressure applied recently upon a number of countries of Latin America by certain European governments, which have endeavored to short-circuit the normal triangular movements of trade, through which particularly the raw material and foodstuff-producing areas of the world—notably those of the American continent—have normally been adjusting their international balances, finding their largest markets in one group of countries but buying their import requirements more from another group, with the credits created with the first group normally going to pay for their excess obligations to the second group.

Further reciprocal trade easements between South American neighbors.—Alongside of these varying attitudes toward the United States and overseas countries, there has been some further development during the year of the tendency for the countries of South America to exchange with neighboring countries reciprocal free trade or substantial concessions on selected distinctive products of each other. The outstanding developments of this character during 1935 were the enlarged reciprocal agreements signed between Argentina and Brazil, Chile and Peru, and between Brazil and Uruguay. Strangely enough, one of these countries, which did not have extended to it the concessions exchanged by one of the other pairs, claimed discrimination and took retaliatory action.

Import quotas and licenses, which had rarely been resorted to by the countries of Latin America, were introduced during the past year with regard to selected commodities or countries in a number of these areas (Bolivia, Chile, Colombia, and Peru). However, the motives and purposes appear to have been various, and thus far no Latin American country has developed a comprehensive system of quantitative limitations as a regular means of controlling import trade, as is now common in Europe. Governmentally controlled organizations for the production or distribution of gasoline and other petroleum products have been put into operation during 1935 in an additional country (Chile), and a refinery for this purpose is under construction in another (Uruguay). The purpose, however, has been not so much to restrict the quantity of imports by private traders, as to protect local consumers against excessive price, and to assure a sufficient supply under domestic control. It will be recalled that in earlier years the governments of Argentina, Bolivia, Chile, Cuba, Ecuador, and Uruguay had taken steps to control the local distribution and prices of certain necessities and raw materials in the interest of consumers.

Wide resort to subsidies and other aids to staple exports.—To aid their producers and assist the sale of their products abroad, several of the countries of Latin America have during the past year paid or authorized bounties on staple products, including: Venezuela on coffee, cacao, and livestock; Ecuador on new market openings; Peru on sugar; Uruguay on wheat and flour, and, by preferential exchange, on wool and other animal products. Argentina has recently advanced the guaranteed prices to its producers of wheat and linseed, which the government then holds for export at world market prices.

The efforts on the part of the governments of Brazil and of Colombia to maintain profitable returns to their producers of coffee, in terms of the national currencies, through allowing the external value of the currency to depreciate to a considerable extent, has been earlier noted. In several lesser instances, somewhat the same purpose was apparently sought through the abolition or suspension of the duties hitherto levied on the exportation of particular products, or by establishing systems and standards of export control to improve the quality and marketability of national products abroad.

1936

TRADE RECOVERY FAVORED BY IMPROVING CONDITIONS HELD BACK BY UNCERTAINTIES

Year Marked by Two Opposing Types of Developments

In the field of foreign trade policy, the year 1936 was marked by two discordant types of developments. On the one hand, important steps were taken by a number of countries toward a freer flow of commerce, through relaxation of trade barriers and through a more stable realignment of currencies. At the same time, certain other countries carried further their official controls on foreign trade and continued the directed diversion of purchases by their nationals to selected countries, through quantitative limitations on the movement of goods or on the exchange made available in payment for them.

As a result, United States trade can move more freely and on a more competitive basis, at the outset of 1937 than a year ago, with Canada, with certain republics of Latin America, and with a number of countries of Western Europe. On the other hand, the strenuous efforts of certain European countries to attain greater self-sufficiency, at almost any cost, have led them to increasing restriction and governmental management of their own import trade, and to a widening series of special compensation and exchange clearing agreements with other countries. Such agreements have involved especially the countries of Central Europe and of the Balkans, and, to an increasing extent, certain countries of South America. Consequently, these markets have become more difficult of access to the products of the United States, and of other countries that are trying to operate on the competitive, free-exchange basis, than they were a year ago.

German Program Extreme Example of Subsidies and Tied Sales

The extreme example of this type of program is presented by Germany, and, in view of the widespread series of special arrangements concluded by Germany with other countries, it is the most significant. Impelled by the inadequacy of foreign exchange available to cover its import needs for raw materials and certain deficit foodstuffs, after diversion of a large part of the proceeds from its exports for the purposes of its special nationalistic programs, Germany has resorted to a system of export stimulation through subsidies and aids of various types, and to insistence, in its trade arrangements with many countries, that the proceeds due them for their sales to Germany be spent exclusively for German products. Under the circumstances, the scope of normal trade by suppliers from competing sources is obviously curtailed with those other countries, as well as with Germany. To a less marked degree, something of this tendency has been noted also in the recent actions of a number of other countries.

The basic undesirability of the system of practically international barter that has been developed by certain European countries during the last few years has been admitted even by the sponsors. Moreover, the disadvantages of the related system of forced annual balancing of trade or of payments between each pair of countries, insisted upon by a number of the European powers in their dealings with the smaller countries near by and overseas, have in some cases become so evident as to bring open complaint recently, especially from a number of the Balkan countries. At the same time, efforts to bring about closer trade balances with those individual countries from whom their purchases exceeded their sales became more noticeable during the past year on the part of a number of the smaller countries. The movement has spread beyond Europe to Latin America and to Australia, these efforts being usually put forward as defensive measures against the restrictive effect upon their exports of the similar arrangements earlier insisted upon by certain of their important customers.

It is difficult to appraise the prospects of a material weakening of this restrictive bilateral trade system. However, the way back to a freer and more open basis for international trading, which almost all governments now profess to be their ultimate objective, has been made easier during the past year by three sets of developments.

Reviving Economic Activity Stimulates Freer Flow of Commerce

First, there is the appreciable progress in economic recovery in many countries. This increased activity is requiring a larger volume of foreign as well as domestic products, and is also stimulating rising prices for many lines of commodities. Price advances have been most marked in raw materials and in certain basic foodstuffs, the latter partly the result of shorter crops. This fact has operated to improve particularly the income of the non-European primary producing countries. One of the indirect effects has been the larger supply of foreign exchange accruing to certain of the South American countries, which has allowed them to furnish exchange more freely for the payment of purchases from abroad, and at more favorable rates.

Without attempting to estimate the extent of the increase in productive activity that represents demands for the nonproductive purpose of rearmament programs, or to appraise the soundness of the costly efforts in process in various countries toward greater national self-sufficiency, in certain foods or other staple products, it is obvious that the rate of economic recovery is highly uneven in different areas, and in some cases of doubtful stability.

While international trade still lags behind the rate of gain in internal activity, the impetus from the domestic recovery in the various countries has been felt in the perceptibly higher volume and value of goods moving in world trade during 1936. The increase in foreign trade has been most notable in the countries of North America, although, for the first time since the depression, the continent of Europe shared, if only moderately, in the expansion.

United States Trade Agreements Give Lead to Liberalization

In the second place, there is the definite lead to a more liberal commercial policy on the part of the nations generally that has been given by the United States, in actively pursuing its program of trade agreements, involving reciprocal reductions of excessive trade barriers and the stabilization of the conditions of trading on a broad equitable basis. In addition to the four earlier agreements, the United States brought into operation during 1936 similar trade agreements with ten governments, including the important countries of Canada, Brazil, and Colombia on the American continent, and France, Netherlands, and Switzerland on the European continent. In the case of most of these agreements which have been in operation for a sufficient period of time and under circumstances that allow a fair judgment, the trade of each of these countries with the United States, both import and export, has shown a greater increase than their trade with the world generally.

Impressed by the bold initiative on the part of the United States, and possibly also by the failure of other methods to revive their foreign trade, the spokesmen for most of the governments represented in the Assembly of the League of Nations strongly endorsed, in October, 1936, the importance of working toward the reduction of trade barriers, on an equality-of-treatment basis, insofar as financial and other considerations allowed return to more liberal trade policies. Agreements of a trade-liberating character have been concluded during the past year also by a number of other pairs of countries; and with somewhat greater frequency than during 1935 have agreements of the past year embodied the unconditional most-favored-nation clause, especially those involving countries outside the European continent.

Gold Bloc Countries Devalue and Ease Trade Controls

The third development of the past year that has opened the way to freer and more confident trading relations between nations, has been the realignment of the currencies of most of the so-called gold bloc countries of Europe (France, Netherlands, Switzerland, and Italy), bringing them again close to the predepression exchange parities with the dollar and the pound. This action brought further revaluation of the Czech crown, and currency readjustments on the part also of several of the smaller countries in Europe.

An international undertaking was entered into by the United States, Great Britain, and France at the time of the revaluation of the French franc late in September, 1936, whereby these three governments would use their exchange stabilization funds to hold to a minimum fluctuations in the exchange values of their currencies. In this they were later joined by several other European countries. That arrangement obviated the commercial uncertainties and possible competitive depreciations, or other defensive action on the part of other countries, which had unfortunately accompanied the earlier successive currency revaluations by individual countries when acting alone. In fact, it was quite generally hailed by merchants as allowing more normal international price relations, and as giving that much-desired assurance of substantial stability in the financial basis of international transactions, both of which had been lacking for the past five years. Moreover, the currency agreement was accompanied by a joint declaration that the success of the policy was "linked with the development of international trade," the participating governments attaching "the greatest importance to action being taken without delay to relax progessively the present system of quotas and exchange controls with a view to their abolition."

A beginning toward giving effect to this undertaking was promptly made, when France, the Netherlands, Switzerland, and Italy, as well as some of the smaller countries whose currencies were also revalued, announced reductions in duties, relaxations of import quotas, and other measures tending to lower their import barriers. However, these beginnings have not been carried much further since, and some have questioned whether the relaxations announced have even fully offset the increased cost of importing foreign goods into these countries resulting from their devaluations. In view of the price increases of varying degree that have been taking place since in most of the devaluing countries and, in some cases, also internal adjustments of other types, it is to be expected that some time may elapse before there will be definitely established the conditions under which goods may move into these countries under the new currency and price levels.

However, it is reported that several of the governments concerned hesitate to proceed with a program of broad demobilization of trade barriers set up during the period of currency disparities, partly because of the resistance from the domestic producers loath to lose the additional protection indirectly afforded by the emergency measures, and partly because of a desire to maintain them for the purpose of bargaining with other governments. They call attention to the fact that the exchange control countries have done little to relax their special restrictions, and, until opportunity is afforded for the devaluing countries to increase their exports materially, they do not feel warranted in allowing a much broader flow of imports. There are indications that the devaluing countries would consider themselves in a position to move more freely in the direction of this relaxation, if an effective way could be found of limiting the benefits of tariff or quota easements to countries which maintain a free commercial exchange market, and are not artificially promoting their exports, whether through direct subsidies, exchange manipulations, or other means.

Progress in Trade Liberalization Deterred by Uncertainties

In the present state of extreme economic experimentation by certain countries of Europe, of continuing although moderated financial difficulties in many countries, and of an overshadowing sense of general political uncertainty, the full and successful operation of the new forces that have been put into motion during 1936, capable of working toward the gradual revival and stability of international trade, will obviously depend upon many external factors. Considerable progress can be expected from these new constructive forces, however, in the period ahead, if international peace is maintained, if the countries that concluded these promising trade and exchange agreements during 1936 are courageous and loyal in giving effect to their undertakings, and if the countries maintaining exchange controls and related trade-restricting arrangements see their own long-time interest in taking steps that will make possible the early realization of the broad trade-liberating programs, for which so many nations are ready and for which the developments of the past year have opened the way.[1]

[1] Apart from the salient developments and tendencies of 1936 just indicated, the year's events in this field have been largely by way of continuation of the same types of measures and arrangements as have marked the tariff and trade control policies of the respective countries during the last few years. These have been fully discussed in the review for 1935. Particularly in the present period of unsettlement and opportunistic change, a detailed analysis of the many and confused events of 1936 in this field does not seem warranted.

1937

EASEMENT OF DEPRESSION TENSIONS ENCOURAGES RELAXATION OF EMERGENCY MEASURES

Year Sees Net Progress in Checking Depression-born Restrictions

Aside from those countries in which normal economic activity has been subordinated to special nationalistic objectives and a determined program of high self-sufficiency, and a number of the smaller states economically dependent upon them, the year 1937 saw in general a distinct check to the policy of restriction and diversion of international trade which had marked the depression years. An appreciable number of steps in the opposite direction—even if moderate ones—were actually taken during the year, and others were foreshadowed.

In the main, the huge and complicated structure of trade barriers and direct governmental interventions in economic life built up in so many countries since 1930—and frequently accompanied by arbitrary and discriminatory trade channelization—still persists. Import duties are still much higher in most countries than they were at the onset of the depression, and in many cases are now accompanied by additional charges under various names. Quota restrictions on the quantities which may be admitted of particular products or from particular countries, or official controls on the allotments of foreign exchange with which to pay for them—or a combination of both of them—continue to dominate the conditions of trading with most of Central, Southern, and Eastern Europe, parts of Latin America and even of Asia.

The attainment of an annual balance in the trade with each individual country, or a closer approach to such a condition, still seems a motivating principle in the trade control measures or agreements of many governments in various parts of the world. On the part of Germany, Italy, Soviet Russia, and Japan, a large measure of self-sufficiency in certain basic foodstuffs, raw materials, and even industrial equipment—at almost any cost—is among the declared objectives of those governments, as part of their special current nationalist programs. On more limited ranges of products, efforts toward greater self-supply figure also in the domestic programs of a number of lesser countries.

Japan, Germany, and Italy Move Toward Greater Restrictiveness

In fact, 1937 was marked by a number of important additional measures restrictive of international trade. Early in the year Japan instituted exchange control on imports, which was applied with increasing strictness. After the outbreak of the Sino-Japanese conflict, drastic state control of all phases of Japanese economic life was decided upon, including prohibitions on the importation of some products and limitations on the volume of others. Germany further tightened restrictions on imports in aid of its autarchy program, to the point of imposing a high duty on natural rubber with which to finance the domestic production of a synthetic substitute. As part of a general economic program very similar to that pursued by Germany, Italy insisted in most of the numerous trade agreements negotiated during the year upon bilateral balancing of new trade, mainly through reciprocal quotas, and upon an export excess for the liquidation of any frozen debts.

Following the further decline in the value of the franc during the summer, France increased the import duties on many products substantially to the level that prevailed before the horizontal reduction of duties put into effect after the devaluation of the franc in September, 1936; toward the close of 1937, numerous increases were ordered on selected products, for revenue purposes. Mexico ordered a succession of substantial increases in duties on broad ranges of foreign products; these were followed, at the close of the year, by further drastic tariff increases, which it is feared will practically prohibit importation of many classes of manufactured goods.

More Typical Are the Moves Toward Trade Barrier Moderation

On the balance, however, these measures appear to have been more than offset during 1937 by the steps which a wider range of countries have taken toward the relaxation of high and arbitrary trade barriers.

While none of the countries that have been operating import quota systems have as yet abolished them entirely, increases in the amounts of goods admitted under quota or even abolition of individual quotas have been more frequent than in preceding years. In July, Turkey went so far as to abolish all import quota restrictions and to revise the tariff downward, although limiting the new quota regime to the products of countries with which Turkey consistently had an active trade balance. These included the United States. In December, the Australian Government authorized import permits to be granted freely for broad lists of products which had been under restriction from the United States and certain other countries since early in 1936, and promised release of the remaining products as soon as study could be made as to the adequacy of the protection afforded by the existing duties.

Czechoslovakia and Portugal abolished their exchange control on payments for imports during 1937, although the former still maintains an import permit system on many classes of products. The improved market demand and higher prices prevailing for their natural products allowed various Eastern European and Latin American governments to administer their exchange controls with greater flexibility, and with more scope for trading with free-exchange countries.

In import duties—formerly the sole condition of international trading—reductions have been more frequent in many countries during 1937 than increases, contrary to the trend of recent years. While most of these reductions in duties and related charges have taken place in the course of reciprocal agreements between various pairs of governments, not infrequently during the past year have reductions been made autonomously by individual governments. These duty reductions of both types have usually been extended to most other trading countries.

"Oslo Powers" Begin Joint Action for Reducing Trade Restrictions

A particularly noteworthy development of the year was the convention entered into at The Hague, in May, by the seven countries of Northwestern Europe known as the Oslo Powers. As a modest beginning in collective action toward the gradual reduction of trade barriers, Belgium-Luxemburg and the Netherlands agreed to lift the quota restrictions on certain distinctive products of the others, and not to impose any fresh barriers upon them, while Denmark, Norway, Sweden, Finland, and Netherlands Indies were not to increase the duties or introduce new restrictions with respect to lists of products of the other signatory countries. While the agreement was hopefully left open to adherence by additional like-minded governments ready to assume similar obligations, the benefits of the immediate undertakings were extended by several of the Oslo group to a number of outside treaty countries, including the United States.

Reciprocal exchanges of most-favored-nation treatment, whether alone or in combination with other trade arrangements, were embodied more commonly during 1937 than during recent years, especially in agreements between countries not strictly committed to the bilateral balancing principle. Increasingly, also, has this obligation of equality of competitive opportunity been undertaken with regard to quotas and other forms of import control. Italy and Chile, both of which have been arranging their trade relations with various countries on special bilateral bases, undertook agreements with the United States for an exchange of unconditional most-favored-nation treatment, applying that principle to quota and exchange controls, as well as to import duties.

Proposed United Kingdom–United States Trade Negotiations Raise High Expectations

What has been widely hailed as perhaps the most important development in years, looking toward the reversal of the trade restrictive type of policy, was the simultaneous announcement by the governments of the United Kingdom and the United States, late in November, that they had agreed upon the bases for a reciprocal trade agreement. The importance naturally attached to the prospect of a trade-liberating agreement between the two countries which are the world's largest traders, and leaders also in other respects, was enhanced by the understanding that the existing preferential margins among the various parts of the British Empire, which had been widely extended under the Ottawa agreements of 1932, would now be subject to reduction by negotiation.[1] High expectations are widely entertained for these negotiations, not alone for the direct improvement of

[1] The United Kingdom is dealing also for Newfoundland and the British Colonial Empire.

trade possibilities in these two great markets for the many products of which each had been an important supplier to the other, but also for the impetus such an agreement may give to similar reciprocal agreements between other countries. Similar negotiations between certain of the British Dominions and the United States are already expected to follow.

Improvement in Demand, Prices, and Financial Stability Favorable Factors

The working out of the commercial policy developments of the past year, and the prospects for the period ahead, depend largely upon the relative strength of the conditions and forces which have been operating to encourage—and to restrict—this return to freer and more open competitive conditions of international trading.

Most important has been the marked economic recovery in almost all countries during the past two years, stimulating a larger volume of both foreign buying and selling. The resulting improved general position of most countries apparently made governments more able, and more readily disposed, to follow a more flexible attitude toward imports.

Particularly have the rising needs from the industrial countries for raw materials and foodstuffs increased the demands upon the primary-producing countries, and afforded them enlarged outlets and improved prices for their staple export products. Probably for the first time since the depression, the relative price level of most primary products rose to that of manufactured goods during early 1937, thus closing the so-called "price scissors," which for a number of years had especially depressed the position of the producers of primary products.

In fact, by early 1937 there were evidences of a considerable easement of the principal tensions which, during the early years of the depression, had prompted many governments to resort to greater import barriers and to various special arrangements that have operated to restrict and divert trade. The difficulties and fears arising from the earlier disparities in currency values, with the apprehensions concerning their effect upon relative prices and trade movements; the low prices, particularly for those natural products least capable of prompt adjustment of supplies to reduced demand; and the precarious financial position of many governments, with foreign debts and other obligations staying rigid or increasing at the very time when all sources of income were shrinking—these and various related pressures and problems of the early 'thirties had been largely removed or were well on their way to correction.

With basic internal conditions thus eased in many countries, there appears to have been a greater readiness to recognize the irksomeness as well as the costliness of the various elaborate governmental restrictions and international arrangements which, after all, appeared to have helped them little toward a definite revival of trade or prosperity.

Probably not without effect at this time also were the bold example of the United States in pressing forward with its program for reciprocal trade-liberating agreements[2] and the growing consensus of opinion of spokesmen of many governments and of business at various international gatherings on the importance of working toward reduction of trade barriers, insofar as financial and other considerations allowed a return to more liberal trade policies.

Some Doubts as to Stability of Recovery Counsel Caution

On the other hand, there are a number of situations and attitudes working in the opposite direction, or counseling caution even when the improved domestic conditions in a particular country might warrant a less restrictive control of imports.

Many doubts are expressed as to the stability and soundness of the measure of recovery that has been attained recently in domestic activity and in international trade. It is not too clear how long particular countries may continue to be good markets, as a whole or for individual commodities. Thus, there have been markedly increased importations of grains and other foodstuffs on the part of various countries during the past year, a fact which has contributed substantially to the revived prosperity and improved financial position of certain agricultural countries. These importations were facilitated by reductions or waivers of import duties on such products by at least ten governments during 1937. However, since this increased foodstuffs trade was due mainly to simultaneous crop shortages in a number of areas, it is bound to be largely transitory.

Trade Expansion Stimulated by Rearmament Regarded Dubiously

Even more striking have been the increased volumes of industrial materials and equipment that have been moving in international trade since 1936, stimulated in the case of iron and steel by reductions or sus-

[2] By the end of 1937, the United States had concluded such agreements with sixteen countries (and their colonies), which together accounted for well over a third of the total American foreign trade, and all of them were in operation. Six additional agreements are now in various stages of negotiation.

pensions of import duties on the part of a number of governments, notably the United Kingdom, Germany, and Japan. However, these increased trade demands and tariff easements are known to have been prompted, in considerable measure, by the exceptional needs of the wide-spreading rearmament programs and auxiliary purposes, as well as of the more normal revival of durable goods industries. In certain cases they even served the self-sufficiency or substitution programs of particular governments. The doubts are therefore understandable as to how long the stimulus of these activities may continue, and whether such heavy expenditures for largely unproductive purposes are not likely to be followed by a slowing down of purchasing power and of international trade.

Somewhat related are the doubts concerning the level of prices for basic commodities that is likely to prevail, after the recent subsidence of the exceptional spurt of demand between the summer of 1936 and the middle of 1937. Important factors in the explanation for the recent sharp rise in prices of primary products, and for the subsequent relapse, have been that the heavy stocks accumulated during the early years of the depression had been gradually worked off, and that supplies of most of these commodities are not readily adjustable to rapid changes in demand and price, especially during a speculative and nervous market.

In the broader financial field, while the exchange relations between the major currencies have—with one notable exception—been maintained with remarkable stability since the Tripartite Agreement of September, 1936, any long-time view of the international monetary situation is still obscured by various elements of material uncertainty.

Closed-economy Programs of Totalitarian States Cause Concern

An important restraining influence on the demobilization of "emergency" trade control measures is the fact that the totalitarian states are continuing their efforts toward more closed national economies with increased energy, and that most of such imports as are permitted into these countries are arbitrarily controlled as to source, and often subject to special compensatory trade arrangements and stringent limitations upon payments. Consequently, various of the other countries standing in close economic dependence upon these states, as markets, hesitate to venture any material relaxation of their own trade control measures. Certain countries are reported to be continuing quota systems largely for their value as bargaining material with those countries operating almost exclusively on the quota basis.

Finally, with the current intermingling of political and economic developments and objectives, the shadows of political uncertainties in various parts of the world cannot but materially influence economic initiatives in many countries.

Despite the contrary influences at work, and some tightening of foreign markets toward the end of the year, an objective observer of the trends in the commercial policies of the various foreign countries during 1937 and preceding years, in the light of the broader currents of world developments, would appear to be warranted in a moderately encouraging expectation for 1938. If, for a fair stretch ahead, the nations could feel assured of no serious further political disturbances, of substantial stability in currency values, and of measurable recovery from the recent drop in the price of many primary commodities, the readiness that intrinsically improved conditions have developed in a considerable number of countries during the recent period for a progressive relaxation of foreign trade barriers might express itself even more freely in concrete form during the next year or two.

1938

INCIPIENT TRADE LIBERALIZING MOVES CHECKED BY RECESSION AND POLITICAL TENSIONS

The incipient movement abroad toward the moderation and stabilization of tariffs and the relaxation of quotas and exchange controls that had been observed during 1937 was largely checked during 1938. This seems to have been due chiefly to the combined influences of the renewed world economic recession, which was felt in the United States from the fall of 1937 to the summer of 1938, with its depressing effect upon world prices of many commodities, as well as upon the trade and financial position of many countries, and of the spreading political tensions and apprehensions in various parts of the world during the past year. However, the developments of the year were by no means uniform; they were of great diversity and in different directions.

Distinct progress was made during 1938 by a number of countries toward more liberal conditions for foreign trade exchanges, particularly on the part of many members of the British Empire in their relations with the United States. On the other hand, in a considerable number of other countries, the year saw a distinctly tightening tendency in the measures and plans of the governments for control of their foreign trade. Moreover, political motives and pressures played an unusually large part in determining the movement of imports and exports of certain countries.

Late Upturn in American Economy Reverses Earlier Trade Slump

With the rapid upturn in American business recovery since the early summer of 1938, the influence of renewed United States demand for foreign materials and products is stimulating improved conditions also in many foreign countries—reversing the depressing effect upon other parts of the world of the recession of 1937–1938. As a consequence, the purely economic forces, that operated through the middle of 1938 to check the trend toward moderation of trade controls, became less of a compelling factor during the closing months of the past year. This trend was notably revived by the announcement, in November, of a successful conclusion of the broad trade-liberating agreement between the United States and the United Kingdom, and of the revised Canadian-American trade agreement, amplifying the scope and depth of the benefits exchanged in the agreement of three years previously. These agreements tended to give an encouraging tone again to the attitude of numerous governments toward a freer international economy.

Political Apprehensions Over German Program Create Uneasiness

However, the political apprehensions that spread in a cumulative way as the year progressed, particularly following the Czech crisis in September, influenced the attitudes of many governments in the opposite direction. The fact that the foreign trade of some countries did not decline more sharply during the past year was partly due to the continued and even increasing demands for various materials and products to serve the accelerated armament programs of many countries, large and small.

The intensified efforts of Germany during the latter months of the year to tie up various countries of Southeastern Europe and of Latin America through a variety of bilateral measures aroused widespread concern, lest they restrict further the trade possibilities in those areas for the nations operating on a competitive free-exchange basis, and the more so because in many instances these trade arrangements seemed to have distinctly political implications. Toward the end of the year, however, there were evidences of a stiffening attitude on the part of certain of the leading free-economy countries, and announcements of a number of moves and plans designed to check any undue or unfair encroachments upon their established interests in common export markets. These moves are taking various forms, including governmentally sponsored loans to aid financially weaker countries in acquiring desired equipment and supplies.

Despite the spread of German barter arrangements, analysis of the trade records finds that the relative recovery in the value of German exports from the depth of the depression has not been as great as that of either the United States or the United Kingdom. Moreover, even after the inclusion with the totalitarian states of those secondary countries whose trade might be regarded as predominantly controlled, over 70 per cent in value of all world commerce is found to be still carried on by countries operating on a predominantly open and competitive basis.

United States, United Kingdom, and France Protest Japan's Trade Violations in China

In connection with the developments in China, where Japanese control had been extended by force of arms, a protest was lodged in October, 1938, by the United States, charging Japanese violation of the "open door policy" and discrimination in various ways against American trade and interests in the areas of China under Japanese control. The Japanese reply of November, declaring that the "ideas and principles of the past" were no longer applicable in the "new order" in Eastern Asia, was rejected by the United States at the turn of the year, on the grounds that alterations in rights enjoyed by virtue of international agreements "can rightfully be made only by orderly processes of negotiation and agreement among the parties." The governments of the United Kingdom and of France have since taken a similar stand in this matter.

Moves Toward Trade Barrier Liberalizations

Outstanding among the developments during 1938 in the direction of restoring freer movement for international trade was the conclusion, in November, of the reciprocal trade agreement between the United Kingdom (which dealt also for the various nonself-governing British colonial areas) and the United States, and the simultaneous revision in amplified scope of the trade agreement of 1936 between Canada and the United States. The fact that Canada and the United States, after three years' experience under the operation of the first agreement for the reciprocal facilitation of imports from each other, found it desirable to renew and extend that agreement, was regarded as evidence of the mutually beneficial character of this type of trade arrangement.

United States agreements with United Kingdom and others important impulse to freer trade.—The importance naturally attaching to the reciprocal reduction or stabilization of many duties on the part of the United Kingdom and of the United States—which between them represent the markets for close to 30 per cent of total international trade—was considerably enhanced by the fact that these two leading world powers should jointly throw their weight in favor of this method of trade accommodation on a more open and competitive basis, and one from which other countries may also benefit insofar as they can supply the particular products dealt with in the agreement. The agreement was significant also as marking the first important instance where the countries participating in the Ottawa agreements of 1932, whereby the various parts of the British Empire undertook to give reciprocal preference to each other's products, were ready to release each other from some of those commitments in order to make it possible for each of them to enter into broader trade arrangements with non-Empire countries.

Of a similar reciprocally liberating character were the trade agreements concluded with the United States by Czechoslovakia in the spring, and Ecuador in the fall, and the tentative agreement with Turkey, initialed at Ankara in December, all on the general lines established in earlier United States trade agreements. General treaties or agreements, all providing for reciprocal most-favored-nation treatment, to be applied in the broadest sense to all trade relations, were entered into with the United States during the past year by Venezuela, Chile, Greece, Iraq, and Liberia, and a similar treaty of 1937 with Siam was brought into operation.

Also of particular interest to the United States was the removal by Australia, in May, of almost all the remaining import license restrictions maintained by that government since 1936—although in some cases the abolition of the license restriction was accompanied by an increase in the import duty. This followed the removal of Australia from the list of countries which had been denied the generalization of the reductions in the United States duties under the trade agreements program. American products had been the principal ones affected by this temporary trade-diversion policy of Australia.

Although of little direct bearing upon American products, an important development toward trade liberalization was the Anglo-Irish agreement of April, 1938, which put an end to the tariff war of several years' standing between the two countries, arising from the dispute over the payment of the Irish land annuities to Britain. The special penalty duties and restrictions maintained against each other's products were substantially abolished, and Anglo-Irish trade was placed on very much the same preference basis as that between the United Kingdom and the various British Dominions.

Unilateral tariff reductions and restriction easements encouraging.—While there were relatively few general tariff revisions on the part of foreign countries, the changes in their import duties made by different countries during 1938 on selected groups of products included an appreciable proportion of reductions, notably affecting industrial and construction materials and equipment, and in some cases foodstuffs, in the interest of lower local prices and to aid the development of diversified industries within the legislating countries. Such duty reductions were observed especially in Mexico, Venezuela, Uruguay, Finland, and Turkey, although some of the same countries imposed additional restrictions on other products during the course of the year.

Bolivia lifted in October the import prohibitions imposed on many products in 1936 and 1937, although importations of prime necessities are still subject to prior permit, with particular scrutiny as to cost and resale price. Among the few trade easements on the continent of Europe was the removal of the import permit requirements from a successive series of products by the Danish Government, which has for some years been closely regulating imports and diverting them to countries affording the largest markets for Danish products, especially to the United Kingdom and to Germany.

Moves Toward Greater Trade Restrictions

Bountiful harvests bring reversal of 1937 easings of grain trade.—During 1937, at least ten foreign governments reduced or waived import duties on grains and feeds, in order to facilitate larger importations of such products to make up for their temporary crop shortages—which incidentally contributed to the revived prosperity of certain agricultural exporting countries. These were practically all withdrawn during 1938. In fact, with the reversal of the crop situation in late 1937 and in 1938 to a condition of exceptionally bountiful harvests, the year was marked by a sharp reversal in trade policy. About a dozen countries either increased their import charges on wheat and other grains or feeds or imposed permit systems on imports or requirements for the mixing of percentages of domestic grains in milling.

Furthermore, most of the important grain-exporting countries, in the effort to dispose of large surpluses in the face of shrunken foreign import requirements, have during 1938 resorted to various forms of price guarantees to domestic growers, accompanied by vigorous efforts to export the surplus, with the governments making up the difference between the domestic and world prices. The meeting of the revived International Wheat Advisory Committee, held in London in January, 1939, represented an attempt on the part of representatives of twenty-two nations to explore the possibilities of an international wheat agreement for such control of production and marketing as will restore a better world market equilibrium and profitable returns to wheat growers.

Oslo Powers give up joint effort for trade control relaxations.—The Hague Convention of May, 1937, by which the seven countries of Northwestern Europe known as the Olso Powers attempted a beginning in collective action toward the gradual reduction and stabilization of their trade barriers, open for adherence by additional like-minded governments, was allowed to expire by joint agreement in the middle of 1938, on the grounds that "world conditions" would not permit its renewal. The contracting governments did agree to continue their general commercial coöperation under the Oslo Protocol of 1930.

In December, 1938, the Netherlands, one of the leaders in the Oslo movement, amended its Tariff Empowering Act to permit the government to use import tariffs for purposes of protection. This represents the first avowal of such a policy on behalf of the traditionally liberal Netherlands Government, although that country has been on a virtually protective basis, particularly on farm products, since the early days of the depression. No action has yet been taken under this authority.

Impelled by the further decline in the value of the franc, and her generally difficult financial position, France, by a series of decrees, increased import duties and taxes on selected groups of commodities. Imports into a number of the French colonies were likewise restricted, either by selective duty increases or quota restrictions, partly to bring about closer trade relations with France. Tariff changes on various groups of products, predominantly upward, were ordered during the year also by a number of other continental countries—although on a smaller scale than by France—notably by Norway, Sweden, Belgium, the Netherlands, Switzerland, Italy, Yugoslavia, and Greece. In a number of cases, additional products were put under quota or the amounts admitted under existing quotas were reduced. The Netherlands Indies increased its horizontal import surtax from one-quarter to one-half of the basic duties, to become effective in January, 1939.

On the American continent, the sharpest tariff changes of the year were made by Mexico, which first increased the duties markedly on a wide range of products in January, and then substantially withdrew the increases in August. However, the depreciation in the exchange value of the peso in the meantime had so increased the cost of foreign products as to lead the Mexican Government to subsidize the importation of certain articles of necessity, in connection with a domestic program of fixed maximum prices to consumers on a broad range of foods, textiles, and the like. The subsidization of these imports of essential products was in part financed by an additional duty of 12 per cent on those export products of Mexico which had yielded substantially increased profits as a result of the depreciation of the peso.

Declines in exports and prices prompt primary producers again to restrict imports.—With the fall in the export volume of their staple products, and usually also in the prices obtained for them, and the consequent deterioration of their general trade and financial position, primary producers in various parts of the world again moved to cut down the volume of foreign purchases by their nationals. Thus, Argentina and Uruguay enforced import or exchange licenses for individual transactions in many commodities, or from those particular countries with which their direct trade balance was "unfavorable." Ecuador reintroduced a general system of import permits. Honduras joined those Latin American countries maintaining three-column schedules of duties, in accordance with the trade balance with individual countries. New Zealand, at the close of the year, announced an individual license control over all import and export transactions, in the effort to rectify the sharp drop in her trade balance and currency reserves.

The efforts of the United States and of the United Kingdom to maintain the nondiscriminatory "open door" for their trade and enterprises in China have already been indicated. Largely due to the Japanese military control of the coastal areas of China, and to the restrictions they have been imposing upon the trading activities of other countries, general commerce with China is now limited and conducted only under handicaps. Such is the reported current condition, despite the introduction of a schedule of lower import duties into the Japanese-controlled northern provinces of China in January, 1938, and its extension to the central provinces in June.

Drastic state control of Japanese economy extends to foreign trade.—Trade with Japan continues subject to close restriction, as part of the drastic state control of all phases of Japanese economic life. Various changes were made during the year in the official attitude toward the admissibility of particular products, or as to the quantities of them which Japanese might purchase. These changes seem to have been largely dependent upon the relative state of Japanese supply of the materials needed in connection with the Chinese conflict, and upon the amount of foreign exchange currently available from the exports of Japanese products under the linked import-export arrangement recently instituted.

Examination of Spread of Barter Trade and the Reactions to It

Germany and Italy intensify tightly controlled compensation deals.—The effort for a close balancing of imports and exports with each trading country, which has been a particular feature of the trade policies of most countries of Central and Eastern Europe, continued along much the same lines during 1938, with some intensification. Thus, Rumania, Yugoslavia, and Turkey endeavored to make the importation of additional products subject to the compensatory export of particular domestic products. The Italian Government, which has been aiming at adjustment of its trade and financial relations with most countries on a balanced basis, began the formation of "combines" for the purpose of promoting exports in a particular line through the centralization of import permits for that general class of goods in the hands of the same trading houses. The Polish Government has for some time been trying to use the import requirements of the country as a means of promoting its exports, through a variety of complicated devices. Recently, these devices have included the offer of extra import permits—which are made more profitable by the very difficulty of obtaining them—to firms proven to have exported Polish products.

Following the expropriation of the properties of the larger oil companies in March, the Mexican Government entered into several barter arrangements, principally with Germany and Italy, providing for the shipment of Mexican crude petroleum and derivatives, to be paid for by equivalent values of European industrial products and materials.

The German annexations of Austria in March, and of the "Sudeten" areas of Czechoslovakia in October, were promptly followed by absorption of these territories into the German system of strictly controlled trade and exchange relations. Both Austria and Czechoslovakia had gradually moderated their exchange controls and were moving toward freer international trade relations.

Special concern over German deals with the Balkans and Latin America.—The visit of the German Minister of Economics to the countries of Southeastern Europe and to Turkey for trade discussions, closely following the partition of Czechoslovakia, directed special attention to certain efforts upon which the German Government had been engaged for a number of years. In order to minimize its dependence upon overseas sources of supply, Germany has been concluding barter deals and similar arrangements with the near-by countries, designed to take advantage of their food and raw material surpluses and resources, and to guide the agricultural and industrial development of these countries along lines that will furnish Germany with needed supplies for current consumption and for the general German strategic program. The extension of compensation arrangements to various of the Latin American countries has been motivated primarily by the German desire to obtain certain raw materials and foodstuffs without payment in free exchange, and to push its export outlets for certain classes of products.

The methods for conducting foreign trade developed by Germany during recent years—featured by strict designation of the country of origin of imports, and even of their price, by various types of barter arrangements involving a minimum use of foreign exchange, and by differential export subsidies and varying currency manipulations—are doubtless quite familiar by now. The past year has seen some intensification of these methods and considerably wider attention to them. Since it has not been the practice to make public many essential provisions of the special bilateral arrangements negotiated by Germany, Italy, and other controlled-economy countries in recent years, full appraisal of the additional trade arrangements entered into by them during the past year will be possible only after observation of the actual trade movements resulting from them. However, reliable reports from the other countries involved, thus far received, indicate that the arrangements of the past year have not been greatly different in character, if somewhat broader in scope, from the types of compensation arrangement that have been in operation with various countries for a number of years past.

The various "loans" or "merchandise credit" arrangements announced as having been concluded by Germany with Poland, Turkey, and some other countries, are reported to be largely variations of the familiar arrangements of recent years whereby Germany takes substantial quantities of the natural products of the smaller countries, and undertakes to pay not in cash or freely disposable exchange, but in the form of Reichsbank credits. These may then be used only for the purchase of German products, and often only of those particular types of industrial or military equipment, or other products, which Germany may find it convenient to supply.

Considerable complaint has been voiced by American exporters of severe competition in a number of markets from German products imported under the barter and subsidy arrangements. This has been confined largely to Latin America, and particularly in certain lines of goods, notably hardware, office appliances, iron and steel for construction purposes, machinery, and vehicles. Without minimizing the need for close study and effort on these particular situations, the fact that, according to official trade records, the recovery in the value of total German exports to all countries from the depth of the depression has not been as great as that of the United States or the United Kingdom—and is still not as close to predepression levels as the export trade of both the other major industrial countries—suggests that on the whole only relatively moderate results have thus far attended these exceptional German methods.

Analysis of trade results finds German relative gains quite limited.—Analysis of the recorded trade experience of over fifty important markets during the last half-dozen years finds that Germany's relative position as a source of imports has shown appreciable increase only in certain regions of the world.

Germany's place as a supplier has increased sharply during recent years in the countries of Central and Eastern Europe (including Turkey and Egypt as well as Italy in this general grouping), with the exception of Czechoslovakia, Poland, and Russia, where it had been on the decline through 1937, and the Baltic countries where the trade has been erratic. There has been a definite decline in the share of total imports obtained from Germany in all of the countries of Western and Northwestern Europe, with the possible recent exception of Portugal.

Germany has recorded marked improvement during the last few years as a supplier to the markets of Brazil, Chile, Peru, Ecuador, several of the Central American areas, and latterly also Mexico—although mainly at the expense of countries other than the United States. There have been small increases in the German share of the import trade of most of the other Latin American countries, but no significant change in the position of German goods in the important markets of Argentina, Uruguay, and Cuba.

In most of the various areas comprising the British Empire, where Germany is usually quite a secondary supplier, the experience has been one of no change or of a decline in the proportion of total imports that was supplied from Germany, with British India the only important area showing an appreciable relative increase in German imports. China appears to be the one important area in the Far East where the place of German goods had improved noticeably over the last half-dozen years.[1]

Over 70 per cent of world trade still on open competitive basis.—Moreover, despite the frequent press notices of the spread of barter deals and similar types of restrictive trade arrangements in various parts of the world during recent years, a statistical testing of the situation on the basis of the foreign trade returns for 1937 discloses that, even with the inclusion of the trade of Japan and of all China in the same category with the totalitarian states of Germany, Italy, and Russia and those secondary countries whose trade might be regarded as predominantly controlled, over 70 per cent in value of total world trade is still carried on by countries operating predominantly on an open and competitive basis.

Reports from various of the countries with which Germany and others have made these special arrangements carry frequent expressions of local dissatisfaction with the commercial results, and with the pressures and uncertainties that often accompany them. The governments of a number of countries are reported to be endeavoring to avoid the building up by their nationals of an excess of sales to Germany above the value of their purchases from that country, so as to minimize the accumulation of frozen credits at the Reichsbank or of "askimarks" in the hands of their own banks, with the consequent necessity of taking German products of a type not normally desired or in quantities beyond the current consumptive needs of their countries.

The discovery that a portion of some of the products taken under these barter arrangements has afterwards been resold by Germany in third countries for free exchange, thus interfering with the other usual markets for the original producing countries, while forcing them to take the full value of shipments to Germany in German goods, frequently upon disadvantageous terms, is accentuating the reluctance to expand such barter arrangements when any other outlet can be found.

United Kingdom and United States take steps to offset barter trade and stiffen resistance.—During the later months of 1938, there were evidences of a distinctly stiffening attitude on the part of a number of the leading

[1] Of the two principal regions where German barter competition has been concentrated, the concern of United States exporters has been mainly over the countries of Latin America, where the United States has been the supplier of about one-third of the total imports and has afforded the market for an almost equal share of their aggregate exports. The stake of the United States in the foreign trade of the countries of Southeastern Europe and of Turkey is relatively much smaller, having supplied during the past decade from 5 to 7 per cent of their total imports, and taken from 4 to 6 per cent of their aggregate exports.

countries operating on an open and competitive trade basis, to check or offset undue extension of the opposite type of trade policy. Prominent among these efforts have been those of the United Kingdom and the United States.

In May, 1938, the government of the United Kingdom extended to that of Turkey a credit of about 80 million dollars for the purchase of capital goods and military supplies. In December, a bill was introduced into the British Parliament authorizing the Export Credits Guarantee Department to expand both the scale and variety of its operations. The bill increases the total guarantee that may be outstanding at any one time from about 250 million to 375 million dollars, and allows reëxports as well as domestic goods to be covered. An initial fund of about 50 million dollars is proposed to be placed at the disposal of the Board of Trade to facilitate export transactions that are considered "in the national interest." The British Parliament and press has also been discussing plans whereby British exporting industries are to organize themselves to act as units in meeting unfair competition in common markets, with an indication that certain British industries have already been organized to present a more united and effective front to such competition.

Through the Export-Import Bank, the United States recently extended a 25 million dollar credit to China for the purchase of automotive and other equipment, and a 10 million dollar loan to a large American utility firm to support its operations in Latin America, with an additional amount advanced for this purpose by commercial banks. Negotiations are understood to have been completed for a 6 million dollar credit to Poland to finance the purchase of American cotton and copper on relatively long terms of payment. The Export-Import Bank has also been aided in the thawing of frozen credits due to American firms for goods sold in an important Latin American country, and has indicated its readiness to consider financial aid to facilitate equipment for productive enterprises in the other American countries. Plans are under consideration for technical as well as financial assistance for the development, on a satisfactory commercial scale, of noncompetitive natural products of those areas that could be used by industries or consumers in the United States.

While competition from barter-trading methods has continued to give particular concern in many Latin American markets during 1938, more promising recent commercial experiences are reported to be encouraging United States exporters in various lines to closer study of the situation and greater trade promotive efforts in these countries. Such official trade figures as are available for 1938 show that, in general, the United States maintained its important position in most of the major markets of Latin America.

The unanimous reassertion by all the American Republics, at the Lima conference of December, 1938, of their preference for trading on a more open and competitive basis, and the common resolution to work toward greater reliance upon "reasonable tariffs," rather than upon the various other forms of trade control, also improve the prospect.

1939

OUTBREAK OF WAR BRINGS WIDE RESORT TO PRECAUTIONARY CONTROLS AND DEALS

PREWAR PERIOD (BEFORE SEPTEMBER 1)

The war in Europe, which actually broke out on September 1, cast its impending shadow ahead. Especially among the countries on that continent, it influenced the trade control measures of the earlier months of 1939, as it distinctly overlaid them during the later months of the year. There were few striking events or innovations in this field during the first part of the year. With certain notable exceptions, most of the various foreign governments made only minor adjustments in the duties, quotas, or other aspects of their trade control structures built up over recent years, and occasionally entered into agreements with other governments for some modification in the regulation of their current trade. However, these efforts to proceed along established lines were in many cases accompanied by precautionary measures of various types, apparently reflecting the apprehension that the uneasy peace might not last indefinitely.

Europe

Wide adoption of precautionary trade measures against possible emergencies.—To their current programs for military preparedness, various countries, particularly of Europe, added measures of trade control designed as prudential steps toward commercial preparedness for any sudden flare-up. Thus, Belgium, France, and Switzerland were notable among the countries which modified their regulations on the conditions of private importation of various foods and fuels during the early months of 1939, with a view to building up reserve civilian stocks of daily essentials within the country. This was apart from the war reserves of many products for military use which the different governments had been accumulating for some time. Even more widespread during the same period were the measures to make the exportation of various metals, oils, and other raw materials subject to permit, so as to conserve supplies already on hand for domestic industries.

Some European governments openly announced the appointment of special bodies to develop programs for the mobilization of food supplies and the broad coördination of economic activities, in case of emergency. Moreover, the promptitude with which such programs were put into operation upon the outbreak of war, in many countries both in and out of Europe, indicated the widespread, if unannounced, advance planning of economic and trade controls for emergency use that was going on during the spring and summer of 1939.

Expressive of planning of a more long-range character was the German-Rumanian treaty concluded in March. Rumania agreed to the development of its agricultural, mining, and forestry resources and means of transportation, with German industrial and financial assistance, in the light of German import needs, and Germany agreed to take Rumania's surplus production so far as necessary to supplement Germany's own supplies. Less radical, but related in purpose, were the French agreements of about the same time with Yugoslavia and Rumania, and the British protocol with Rumania of a little later, aimed at expansion of trade relations with these countries. The French agreements provided for preferential facilities for the importation into France of increased quantities of Yugoslav food and forestry products, and of Rumanian petroleum and corn. The British agreement was marked by a purchase undertaking for Rumanian wheat, and a 25 million dollar credit for the purchase of British textiles and other products.

Early in 1939, plans were made for meetings between groups of British and German industrialists to consider governmentally supported agreements regarding operations in common export markets that would minimize undesired forms of competition, presumably through some form of international cartelization. Shortly before the scheduled meetings to discuss the feasibility of such a program, German troops occupied Czechoslovakia in March, and the British sponsors dropped the matter.

Basic trade control changes following territorial occupations.—The military occupations of Austria (in 1938), Czechoslovakia, and Memel by Germany, of Albania by Italy, and—late in the year—of Poland by Germany and Russia, were followed by a number of basic tariff and treaty adjustments. In the course of these, the former customs regimes of Austria, of the Sudeten area, and of Memel disappeared. Trade with those areas became subject to the same conditions as trade with Germany, and the existing commercial treaty commitments to them by neighboring countries were transferred to Germany. Through declaration of a customs union, Albania was incorporated into the Italian economic system. Bohemia-Moravia and Slovakia still maintain some features of the Czechoslovak tariff system, although largely under German control. Adequate information is not available as to how far the portions of Poland occupied by Germany and Russia have been assimilated into the respective trade systems of those countries.

British Empire

United Kingdom and United States arrange bulk exchange of rubber for cotton as war reserves.—Among the precautionary measures marking the prewar period was the agreement between the United Kingdom and the United States, providing for the exchange of 600,000 bales of American raw cotton for rubber of equivalent value, both commodities to be held in storage by the respective governments as reserves against a major war contingency. In late August, with war imminent, the United Kingdom made subject to license the exportation of a very extensive range of mineral, textile, oil-bearing, and other raw materials.

The other British areas proceed with more normal trade programs.—The actions taken by the other areas in the British Empire during the earlier part of 1939 were of a more normal character. On January 1, Canada brought into operation the reductions in duties and preferences undertaken in the revised trade agreement with the United States, concluded the preceding November, designed to broaden and deepen the reciprocal concessions exchanged in the original agreement of 1936. Both countries extended these concessions to the like products of other countries with which each was on a most-favored-nation status. In its annual budget in April, the Canadian Government removed from all products originating in non-Empire treaty countries the special excise tax of 3 per cent ad valorem, which had already been waived for Empire products in 1935. This went beyond the undertaking in the revised trade agreement with the United States, to remove this horizontal tax from the American products specifically figuring in that agreement.

Under a series of orders, the government of Eire increased duties on imports of various products from non-Empire sources, and at the same time established for certain of these products preferential rates in favor of the United Kingdom and Canada. This followed the Anglo-Irish trade agreement of the preceding year, which terminated the long trade war between the two governments. The South African budget in May increased the import duties on a variety of products, for the protection of local industries.

The reductions and bindings of duties and preferences undertaken by the United Kingdom in the reciprocal trade agreement concluded with the United States in November, 1938, came into effect at the beginning of 1939, except for the undertakings on behalf of the various nonself-governing British colonies, which required implementation by local action. During the early months of 1939, the British colonies made the necessary changes in their tariffs with regard to the various products on which reduced margins of preference were promised. These were effected principally by lowering the general rates hitherto applicable to American products, but in some cases by increasing the preferential duties on British products.

In the revision of its trade agreement with the United Kingdom, British India reduced its duties on the important item of British cotton piece goods, the new rates to vary with the volume of imports and the quantity of Indian raw cotton imported by the United Kingdom. This was offset by a substantial curtailment in the broad list of British products that were granted preferential customs treatment in British India under the Ottawa agreement of 1932. The United Kingdom was to continue, in the main, the earlier preferences on British Indian products.

Latin America

Early months relatively uneventful in trade controls.—In the countries of Latin America, the first eight months of 1939 were relatively uneventful in the field of commercial policy. Tariff changes were few, and included duty exemptions extended to selected machinery and industrial materials by the governments of Argentina, Uruguay, and Venezuela.

Mexico continued its unusual program of subsidizing the importation of various essential foodstuffs of which there was a domestic shortage. This had been instituted in mid-1938, following the sharp fall in the exchange value of the peso, and the disorganization in the Mexican landholding system, and is being financed from the additional tax then imposed upon Mexican export staples.

Agreements providing for reciprocal duty exemptions or reductions on selected products were worked out with Paraguay by Uruguay, and in a limited measure by Argentina. With overseas countries, a few general most-favored-nation treaties were signed, but more striking were the negotiations of Germany and Italy with Argentina for enlarged trade on a strictly balanced basis. The German agreement, completed in March, provided for the barter of additional quantities of Argentine wheat, wool, and other products, against a large order for German railway equipment, with a proviso that the Argentine products taken were to be consumed entirely in Germany.[1] In its agreement in June, Italy offered specific import quotas during 1939 for various Argentine staple farm products up to a total value of 25 million dollars, and Argentina made its imports of Italian goods dependent upon the value of Argentine exports to Italy, with a similar proviso against any resale by Italy.

Another trade-balancing agreement, of the type made familiar in recent years, was that between Venezuela and Germany, brought into effect in December, 1938, for the year following. It contemplated large takings by Germany, principally of Venezuelan coffee and cacao, with payment to be made in "askimarks," redeemable only in German goods.

Of quite a different character was the trade agreement concluded by Venezuela toward the close of the year with the United States, designed to facilitate increased private trade in both directions through reduction and stabilization of existing import controls, but involving no government assurances with regard to purchases, nor attempting to hold trade to a close bilateral balance.

Far East

Japan tightens hold on China; United States denounces treaty with Japan.—The complicated restrictions upon trading with the Japanese-controlled areas of China, arising from the permit, foreign exchange, and shipping obstacles, continued. In some respects they were reported to have been aggravated during 1939, and to have hindered particularly transactions by other than Japanese firms or organizations sponsored by the

1 When war broke out, none of the German railway equipment had been delivered, although a substantial part of the Argentine wheat had been taken. The orders for some of the equipment were later placed in the United Kingdom and United States.

Japanese Government. The United States, the United Kingdom, and France had made representations to Japan during the winter of 1938–1939, seeking removal of discriminations against the trade and interests of their nationals in the areas of China under Japanese control.

On July 26, 1939, the United States Government gave the stipulated six months' notice of its desire to terminate the most-favored-nation treaty of commerce with Japan of 1911, "with a view to better safeguarding and promoting American interests as new developments may require."[2]

WARTIME PERIOD

Europe

General move for centralized controls over all economic life.—Shortly after the outbreak of the war in Europe on September 1, many neutral governments of Europe, as well as the belligerents and most of their dominions and overseas territories, installed or authorized new systems of control over their import and export trade. These usually called for licenses for each prospective transaction, or permits for all transfers of exchange, or a combination of both. In most cases, these controls over foreign trade have been the counterpart of measures of centralized control over domestic economic activities, supplies, and prices.

Many of the European neutrals, as well as the belligerents, moved within the early weeks of the war to adopt measures of control of their economy and trade that were not resorted to during the War of 1914–1918 until several years after its outbreak. However, the rather dramatic circumstances of their invocation may have conveyed an exaggerated impression as to the extent of wartime trade control restrictions in Europe, or the severity of their operation in restricting ordinary movements of foreign trade.

Closer study of these measures, and the later commercial and official advices as to their operation, show a considerable diversity of experience. Broadly speaking, it appears that the wartime controls of Great Britain and France are operating to curtail materially the importations from the United States of many agricultural and other products which normally constitute a large part of American sales in those markets, while allowing increased importations of a range of materials and equipment more needed for the war effort.

[2] To date, January 29, 1940, no announcement has been made of any new arrangement to replace the commercial treaty which expired on January 26, nor has either government introduced any change thus far in the previous treatment of each other's trade and shipping.

The economy and trade of the third belligerent, Germany, had already been on a war basis for some time, and the opening of hostilities was accompanied by no important new measures of foreign trade control. With imports from overseas countries largely cut off by the Allied blockade, German effort has been directed rather toward measures and arrangements with accessible continental countries to stimulate increased shipments into German territory, particularly of certain raw materials and farm products.

Trade control machinery of neutrals primarily precautionary.—On the other hand, most of the new trade control measures authorized by the neutral countries of Europe have been largely precautionary, to enable the respective governments to take prompt steps in the further regulation of their foreign trade, by administrative action, as the developing wartime situation may require. There is little evidence thus far that they are intended to curtail materially the usual importations in important lines of merchandise, other than those regarded as luxuries or dispensable during a difficult period.

In fact, up to late January, 1940, quite a number of the European neutrals have not brought into operation any new general license restrictions upon imports. Among these are the Netherlands, Belgium, Switzerland, and the Scandinavian countries. Norway and Sweden have adopted informal exchange controls, but these were announced as not intended to be restrictive of bona fide commercial transactions, and Denmark extended its long-standing exchange permit system to certain additional classes of imports. Over a period of several years, Italy had built up an all-embracing import license and exchange control system, and no announcement has been made since September of any material adjustments within that system, although some changes may have been effected administratively.

Belligerents' contraband controls prime restriction on commerce with neutrals.—Shortly after the opening of hostilities, Great Britain and France established contraband controls in the effort to prevent supplies of a very broad range of products from reaching Germany from overseas, and in December announced that vessels suspected of carrying German exports would also be intercepted and searched. These and the German counter-efforts to weaken their effectiveness—by naval means and otherwise—seem more likely during the period ahead to be the limiting factor upon American sales to most of the neutral markets of Europe, rather than any import restrictions on the part of these countries themselves. The extensive list of products for which the Belgian Government has found it desirable to prohibit even the important transit privilege at its ports without specific permit, illustrates the pressure upon near-by neutrals arising out of the contraband control situation.

Destination control prime object of export-licensing systems.—License controls upon exports have been adopted—or extended in scope—more commonly than import-license systems by the countries of Europe since September. The prime purpose has been to assure adequate domestic supplies of essential products which it would be more costly and difficult to replace under wartime conditions. Secondarily, there has been the desire to control the destination of shipments, in accordance with the country's political or economic interests. In some cases the desire was frankly indicated of wishing to direct exports to countries from which necessary imports could be obtained under prevailing conditions, with evidence of a distinct preference to facilitate exports to free-exchange countries.

Excepting in the case of those products the domestic demand for which had been increased by the war needs or mobilization programs, the efforts of most governments have been not to curtail the sales abroad of commodities of which the countries normally had surpluses. For such products the effort has been rather to maintain—and if possible expand—the usual volume of exportation, so far as urgent domestic needs, the availability of transport, and the limitations set by the contraband controls and naval operations of the belligerents would permit. Need for an assured inflow of foreign exchange with which to pay for necessary imports, joined with the desire to maintain employment and income among their peoples, has led the governments of even the belligerent countries to give priority to export orders, second only to military needs, in the allocation of raw materials.

Britain and France restrict imports to conserve exchange and shipping.—Since direct American trade with Germany is largely precluded for the present, and Great Britain and France are the principal European countries using their wartime trade controls in a materially restrictive way, closer consideration of their motives and methods of operation seems warranted. Immediately upon the outbreak of war, the governments of Great Britain and France introduced broad systems of centralized controls over their domestic and foreign trade. Within the countries these included governmental requisitioning of available and arriving supplies of many commodities, the centralized organization of production and distribution in many lines, either by the government or by established trade associations operating under its supervision, and the imposition of price-control measures upon foodstuffs and various industrial materials.

To regulate their external trade relations, both Great Britain and France promptly established systems of licenses for import and export transactions, and of careful control upon the movements of foreign exchange. The declared purpose of the controls upon imports was primarily to conserve the countries' supply of foreign exchange for necessities and to save shipping space, in the light of the prospective heavy war requirements from abroad. In the administration of these controls thus far, permits for importation from foreign sources have in general not been granted for what are regarded as luxury goods, nor for those products which can be supplied in adequate volume by domestic producers or from within the British and French empires. Where importation has been permitted of products other than those considered necessities under wartime conditions, it is understood they are being admitted only in reduced volume, and that considerable discretion is often exercised by the control bodies in choosing or designating the foreign source, in accordance with particular economic and political considerations.

Close Anglo-French economic collaboration includes trade and currencies.—Thus, open general licenses were early established for the importation into the United Kingdom of certain foodstuffs and other products when coming from any part of the British Empire. Pursuant to the general aim, early decided upon, "to coordinate in the fullest possible manner the economic war effort of the two countries," open general licenses were issued by Great Britain in November for specific food products from France and its colonies, and the British Board of Trade announced that licenses for increased quantities of textiles and apparel would be granted for imports from France, while no applications would be approved to import such products from any other foreign country. As early as September, France undertook to supply Great Britain with sizable quantities of calfskins for military use, while denying licenses for exportation to other countries, even on previous contracts.

During November and early December, the British and French governments announced specific agreements toward unified programs in economic and financial matters, as well as in military affairs. These agreements, to remain in force until six months after a treaty of peace, provided for "the best use in the common interest of the resources of both countries in raw materials, means of production, tonnage, etc."; for pooling of their foreign purchase programs; for pegging the existing rate of exchange between the pound and the franc, and for the settlement of accounts in either sterling or francs.[3] Following the first of these agreements, the British Chancellor of the Exchequer was reported as declaring that permission would be granted for a large list of French products to be imported into England without special license.

Moreover, in the effort to support in an economic way certain countries of Southeastern Europe to which they had given political guarantees, and to render the Balkan areas generally less dependent upon the German market, both Great Britain and France, notably Great Britain, undertook mass buying from these countries of various staple foods and raw materials which normally were purchased principally in other countries. In this category, have been, among others, the heavy Allied purchases during recent months of tobacco and dried fruits from Turkey and Greece, Rumanian oil and grain, and Yugoslav lumber and minerals.

British and French imports of American goods selective, to conserve dollars.—A considerable number of commodities, normally shipped in substantial volume from the United States to Great Britain and France, are reported to have recently been either prohibited importation into those markets, or seriously curtailed under their license or exchange controls. Other products, while also nominally under some form of trade control, have apparently been admitted freely into these countries, in response to increased demands under war conditions. In view of the very nature of the discretionary administrative controls, which at the present time largely determine the movement of foreign trade in many foreign countries, and the shifts in attitude toward particular products or sources with changing conditions, no official position or categoric statement with regard to many of these matters is possible.[4]

The administration of the import-control policies of both Great Britain and France seems thus far to have been dominated largely by the effort to conserve their foreign exchange resources, particularly of dollar exchange,

[3] In the matter of import controls, a particular provision was embodied whereby no fresh restrictions are to be imposed during the war by either government on imports from the other country, for protective purposes or exchange reasons.

[4] Neither Great Britain nor France have published any trade figures since September that throw light upon the source and character of their imports during the war months. The export records of the United States afford a partial picture. In the aggregate, exports of American products to the United Kingdom during the last four months of 1939 varied little from the total value of such exports during the corresponding period of the preceding year; total shipments to France ran close to those of the preceding year during September through November, and rose sharply in December. The declines in the shipments of various usual lines of products to these countries, which may have been curtailed under war conditions, seem thus far to have been roughly balanced in value by the enlarged shipments of other materials and products of American origin, particularly needed by Great Britain and France in connection with the prosecution of the war.

for the purchase of products not otherwise obtainable. Apart from the considerations of wishing to favor their own empires, each other, and certain other countries for political reasons, this effort appears to have been prompted in large measure by the strong desire to avoid repeating economic and financial practices during the War of 1914–1918 that resulted in inflation of prices, wages, and currencies, with their distressing consequences, especially as they could not now count upon large foreign loans. The resort by both these governments early in the war to domestic price regulation and to controlled distribution of foodstuffs and other supplies purchasable by civilians, and the current plans for forced or stimulated public savings, seem evidences of the same anxiety.

A number of European countries, especially Belgium, Denmark, Germany, the Netherlands, and Sweden, have sought to obtain additional revenue by increasing excise or various other taxes on specified imported products, and usually also on the corresponding domestic commodities.

Neutrals negotiate to maintain normal trade against opposing pressures.—The trade agreement negotiations by European governments during the latter months of 1939 were distinctly dominated, and often dictated, by the war situation. Thus, the neutral countries of Western Europe and Scandinavia were engaged in extended negotiations with the British and French on the one side, and with Germany on the other, in the effort to work out conditions under which they could maintain as much as possible of their normal foreign trade, shipping, and transit business, under the pressures of the opposing contraband positions of the belligerents. An agreement between Italy and the United Kingdom, concluded late in October, set up a joint standing committee "to promote closer collaboration in the economic sphere," with particular regard to the circumstances imposed by the state of hostilities.

Strenuous rivalry of belligerents for products of the Balkans.—The Balkan countries were the scene of a particularly active program of trade negotiations. Germany made strenuous efforts to arrange for increased supplies of various primary products from these countries, to replace former imports from overseas sources. As earlier indicated, Great Britain and France endeavored to offer these countries attractive alternative outlets for their surplus products, and in some cases to preëmpt by mass purchases supplies of commodities particularly essential to Germany. Italy also tried through various trade negotiations to increase the importance of its place in the economy of the countries of Central and Southeastern Europe. In fact, the combined import undertakings on behalf of these four powers for certain products of at least one of these Balkan countries have been observed to amount to more than that country's total available surplus.

The Soviet Union concluded agreements with Estonia, Latvia, Lithuania, and Bulgaria, as well as with Germany, each announced as being designed to increase markedly the volume of goods to be exchanged between the contracting countries.[5]

Despite the increasing trend during the early war months toward direct governmental understandings with regard to the movement of particular commodities, it is notable that many countries of Europe with the longest experience in barter trading have recently endeavored to limit, in various ways, the extent of further undertakings that involved receiving payment through clearing accounts, in such merchandise and at such time as the other contracting party could deliver.

Turkey failed to renew the former clearing arrangement with Germany, after it expired on August 31. Under that arrangement, about half of Turkey's exports had for several years gone to Germany, under conditions that had so distorted price levels of Turkish products as to render difficult the maintenance of normal trade with other countries. Turkey has since concluded commercial and financial agreements with Great Britain and France providing, in addition to loans and credits by the Allies for various special purposes, for substantial purchase undertakings of important Turkish surplus products.

Taking advantage of the existence of alternative offers, several of the Balkan countries have recently insisted that only specified products be delivered under compensation arrangements against their raw materials and foods which the other negotiating countries particularly desired. To avoid the hazard of further frozen credits accumulating in the Reichsbank, certain countries are reported to have insisted that the volume of their commodities taken for shipment to Germany shall not exceed the volume of specified German products already delivered. Not infrequently free exchange was insisted upon as the payment for certain products or services, or for additional takings beyond the value covered by deliveries made.

The inherent limitations upon countries being able to satisfy each other's needs through strictly bilateral trade arrangements was strikingly illus-

[5] Unfortunately, essential provisions of many of the trade agreements concluded by European governments since the outbreak of war, and sometimes even their existence, are not being made public. The necessity of depending upon fragmentary and secondary sources of information as to the provisions of many recent intergovernmental trade arrangements, or upon the obviously magnified accounts issued by the contracting governments for psychological purposes, often leaves it for the later record of the actual movements of trade to reveal clearly the character or significance of the understandings.

trated by a recent incident. A particular country of Europe ran short of petroleum. The country adjoining is an important petroleum-producing country. However, there was no clearing arrangement between them, and the country needing the petroleum had no free exchange with which to pay for it, since almost all of its exports had been sold on a compensation basis. It found itself obliged, therefore, to ask a distant European country, with which it did have a clearing agreement, to obtain the desired supplies and arrange for shipment from that adjoining country against their clearing arrangements. The cost of the petroleum was then charged to the direct account of the ultimate purchaser with the distant country.

British Empire

Wartime controls advance commercial integration of sterling areas.—The trade control measures and arrangements adopted since the first of September, 1939, constitute long strides toward a closer commercial integration of the various parts of the British Empire than has probably ever existed, at least since early colonial days. This has found expression in several ways: in the character of the import controls adopted in most of the Dominions and colonies, in the special purchases or guaranteed prices by the United Kingdom of a number of the principal export staples of the Empire, and finally, in the importance attached by most of the British areas to so operating their trade control measures as to concentrate trade within the Empire.

Within this general program of Empire commercial coöperation, considerable diversity is observed in the scope and severity of operation of the trade control measures of different British areas. The regime set up by the United Kingdom, and its operation, have already been discussed in connection with the European situation. In the various Dominions distant from the theater of war, the situations were less exigent, and the measures taken varied with their special foreign trade positions and prospects. Changes in import duties have figured very little in these adjustments, the principal measures of this character being increases for revenue purposes in the levies upon certain consumers' products, such as alcoholic beverages, tobacco, tea, coffee, and in the case of the United Kingdom, also upon sugar and sugar products. The principal measures relied upon have been direct administrative control over products and transactions through licensing systems.

Dominions apply their administrative trade controls lightly.—Canada authorized in mid-September far-reaching control over imports, exports, and all transactions in foreign exchange. In operation, this system has thus far been precautionary, rather than restrictive, for the great body of transactions. Upon the normal flow of imports into Canada from the United States no restrictions have to date been applied. (It is not known how far this applies to Canadian trade with other foreign countries.) Licenses are being granted freely and promptly to regular importers from this country, and permits for the transfer of exchange in payment are being regularly granted at prescribed rates of exchange.[6] It is understood that for the present the Canadian Government intends to continue this attitude, and that the authority of the newly established foreign trade regime will be utilized to develop the information essential in formulating future plans for the control of Canada's foreign commerce and exchange.

An interesting innovation is the authority recently vested in the Canadian Wartime Prices and Trade Board—for its task of preventing undue advances in the prices of necessaries of life, and of insuring an adequate supply and equitable distribution of such commodities—to recommend that particular necessities be admitted into Canada free of duty or at such reduction of existing duties as will "give the public the benefit of reasonable competition." The first action taken under this authority has been to suspend the duties on imports of raw wool into Canada.

In September, Australia ordered a series of duty changes on a range of miscellaneous products; in December, the government declared subject to license imports from all countries except British Empire areas on a sterling basis.[7] A fourfold category of import products was established, with the products in the fourth category prohibited altogether from such sources, and certain of the other products to be permitted entry on a reduced quota basis.

New Zealand, which in May, 1939, had extended to additional products the individual license control over all foreign trade transactions, in the effort to strengthen her trade balance and sterling reserves, announced in October, 1939, that this import restriction regime was to be continued, and on a more stringent basis, during the first half of 1940. A short time was given for the filing of applications to import during that period. Preference is to be given to commodities considered essential from a national view-

[6] The recorded values of United States exports to Canada during the last four months of 1939 were consistently higher than during the corresponding periods of recent years. How much of this increase represents transit trade, or is intended for reshipment to Europe, is not known.

[7] Canada, Newfoundland, and Hong Kong are the principal Empire areas regarded as not in the sterling group for the purpose of trade control measures of this type.

point, specifically those required for defense and health purposes, and materials needed for export industries and for domestic manufacture.

The Union of South Africa created in September a National Supplies Control Board, authorized to regulate imports and exports, and to recommend the establishment of maximum prices and other internal controls on specified commodities. The only use thus far made of this authority, in connection with foreign trade, has been to require the licensing of transactions with specified European countries. The control of exchange established in September is reported to present no hindrance to transfers for normal commercial imports.

Eire instituted foreign exchange control, and designated a sole importer of wheat and corn, with government control over their distribution. No special import controls on ordinary merchandise are reported to have been adopted by British India since September.

Under the general United Kingdom war powers, most British colonies and mandates received authorization to control the foreign trade of their areas.[8] In actual practice, the use of this authority is reported to have varied considerably. Most of the British colonies have announced, in addition to supervision of foreign exchange movements, a general licensing system upon import transactions. In a few cases, licenses are understood to be freely granted for the usual purchases from abroad. In the majority of the colonies, this regime has been distinctly restrictive of imports, to the point of prohibiting certain products, and insisting that for others import licenses must be obtained before orders are placed abroad.

Moreover, only few of the colonies have applied their import controls against all sources. Some have limited them to the areas outside of the British Empire, but most often they are applied to all nonsterling areas. This places Canada in much the same category with the United States and other non-Empire areas, although in certain colonies preference is granted to applications for importation from Canada over other "nonsterling areas." Furthermore, the practice has varied in the different colonies with

[8] The situation in the French colonies differs from that in the British colonies, in that there was no similar general authorization for wartime license controls over imports, corresponding to that of France, and they have not been instituted as widely. According to present information, such import license systems are in operation mainly in the near-by areas of North Africa, that is, Algeria, Morocco, and Tunisia, and also in the mandate of Syria.

The French official exchange permit system, instituted early in September, was made automatically applicable to all parts of the French Empire, as was the French regime of official license control over the exportation of extensive categories of products, although the manner of its application was to be adapted to local conditions in each colony.

regard to exemptions from newly established controls for goods en route or orders covered by established letters of credit.

The frequency with which the import restriction systems adopted since the war in the British colonies has been limited to nonsterling areas reflects again the British concern over conserving foreign exchange. In operation, these are reported to have materially curtailed importation of American products into a number of the colonies for which the United States had normally been the principal source of supply. This has been observed particularly in certain of the British West Indies.

Almost all important areas in the British Empire have instituted license controls over exportations. These apply particularly to raw materials, often to foodstuffs, and frequently also to a wide range of other products. In most of these areas, actual prohibitions upon exportation are applied only to limited lists of specified commodities, the balance being granted individual licenses within the discretion of the authorities, or even given an open general license intended definitely to stimulate their exportation. In the case of commodities of which the areas are not themselves producers, the purpose is obviously to conserve domestic stocks. However, even in regard to domestically produced commodities for export, variation in treatment is often observed, depending upon the destination.

British purchase or price undertakings for staple Empire exports.—A very important development in this field has been the broad program initiated by the United Kingdom for either the outright purchase or the guaranteeing of price of the exportable surpluses of various natural products from the Empire. The purpose appears to be partly to stabilize the economic position of such Empire areas during the uncertain days ahead, but mainly to insure that the Empire, and particularly the United Kingdom, will have within its control adequate supplies of certain raw materials and consumers' staples.

Thus, it has been announced that the United Kingdom is to purchase, for varying periods, all of Australia's surplus supplies of wool, meat, dairy products, sugar, canned and dried fruits, and zinc, and a large percentage of that area's output of wheat, lead, and copper. Similarly, the New Zealand exportable surpluses of wool, meat, butter, and cheese are to be reserved for the United Kingdom. Without actual purchase, South Africa was guaranteed certain minimum prices for the unsold portion of its wool clip. Purchase arrangements between the United Kingdom and Canada are reported to cover, for varying periods, the entire Canadian exportable surplus of copper, lead, and zinc, and substantially increased quantities of lumber and bacon, with negotiations regarding additional commodities still pending.

The British Food Ministry is reported to have concentrated early upon securing all available sugar within the Empire, and to have negotiated for all the existing disposable balances and the current year's crop. The entire West African cocoa bean crop was recently purchased by the United Kingdom.

In the case of those products of which the underwritten supplies are in excess of the needs of the United Kingdom, or other deficit Empire areas, arrangements are being worked out for making the surplus available to the usual buyers in other countries, under conditions and prices set in London by the British Ministry of Supply, or its subordinate trade groups. The arrangements made by the American wool importers with the British Government, in the effort to maintain nearly normal supplies of various Empire wools, is a notable case in point.[9]

Latin America

The relatively lighter impact of the war in Europe upon the Latin American countries than upon other areas has not thus far led to any appreciable number of significant changes in their regimes of foreign trade controls. Their actions since September 1 in this field seem to reflect the sense of uncertainty, as to how the war may develop, what effect it may have upon the availability of the usual supplies from the major European countries, and how far the usually large purchases by European belligerents and neutrals of Latin American staples may be maintained or increased. The measures reported to have been taken thus far have been principally of two types.

Obtaining supplies and conserving stocks objects of trade control measures.—In a few of these countries, there has been some lessening of the rigidities of import control, in order to facilitate the importation from the United States and other accessible countries of products which the belligerents and adjacent countries of Europe are now less able to supply or less certain to deliver. Thus, Argentina relaxed its exchange restrictions on successive lists of products from the United States, some of which had for some time been prohibited importation. The easement took varying forms, consisting either of allocation of larger quotas of exchange for particular classes of goods, or making available exchange at the lower official rate, and

---

[9] Late in January, 1940, it was reported that the British Food Ministry was encouraging the exportation of raisins, presumably to dispose of excess supplies acquired through its heavy purchases from Australia and the Near East.

in some cases allowing importation in unlimited quantities for three to six months ahead. Venezuela reduced its import duties on certain essential foodstuffs, including wheat and flour, rice, oats, potatoes, lard, and butter, and authorized the fixing of maximum sales prices on these products. Ecuador first moderated the system requiring prior import permits before goods could be shipped from abroad, and later abolished the whole system and restored uncontrolled imports.

In the other direction were the measures taken by two of the Central American countries. Concerned over the problem of foreign exchange shortage, Costa Rica announced preferential allocation of exchange for various classes of products according to their essential character, and Nicaragua restored the system of prior import permits.

The second type of precautionary measure appears to have been prompted by fears that difficulties in obtaining replenishment of imported staples might lead to domestic shortages, and cause speculation and undue price rises. Quite a number of Latin American countries vested in either the executive or newly established bodies broad authority to control their foreign trade, particularly to restrict exports of prime necessities, in order to conserve domestic supplies, and to regulate prices.

Thus, Mexico prohibited the exportation of certain necessities, including sheep, goats, and their products, wool, beans, and corn, for the declared purpose of preventing scarcity and further increases in prices. Nicaragua also prohibited the exportation of certain foods for the same purpose. El Salvador permits the exportation of certain fibers, sugar, hides, and tobacco only under specially authorized export permits. Argentina prohibited the exportation of all fuels, metals, new or used, and jute sacking. On the other hand, Argentina abolished the basic minimum prices for wheat and linseed, which it had been guaranteeing producers for some time. On wheat, the reason given was to prevent speculation; on linseed, because world prices had consistently exceeded the guaranteed minimum.

Uruguay established an additional general tax of 5 per cent on exports of certain animal products, to replace a temporary war-profits tax imposed partly to check rising prices on prime necessities. The exportation of unworked metals and scrap, coal, and petroleum were made subject to license by that country.

Apparently, the uncertainties of the political prospects in Europe, particularly following the Munich agreement regarding Czechoslovakia in September, 1938, impelled various of the Latin American countries that were heavily committed in barter or clearing arrangements with Germany and other European countries to seek to liquidate outstanding "askimark" or similar accounts, by increased importations from those countries during 1939. The outbreak of war in September found many of these countries with heavy orders on the books for a broad range of products from the major European countries, notably from Germany. According to the best available information, however, the outstanding "askimark" or similar balances, which might have to remain largely immobile during hostilities, had in most cases been reduced to small proportions.

The principal exception was in the case of Mexico, whose bulk exports of petroleum to Germany and Italy during 1939, mainly against anticipated deliveries of various manufactured products for private and governmental purposes, had been far from covered by such deliveries, leaving substantial amounts of frozen credits. In the fall, the Mexican Government was reported to be seeking an expansion of the barter contract with Italy entered into in April, which gave Italy a virtual monopoly over the imports of rayon yarn into Mexico, against shipments to Italy of Mexican petroleum.

French and British engage for Argentine staples under tied sales.—Very few new commercial treaties or agreements have been negotiated by the countries of Latin America since the outbreak of war in Europe. Notable was the Franco-Argentine commercial arrangement of late December, reported in the Argentine press as consisting of undertakings by the French war purchasing mission for increased quantities of wool, meat, linseed, hides, and other Argentine staples, and by the Argentine Government for "the most favorable treatment possible" in exchange matters. The latter undertaking has since taken the form of regulations whereby the franc credits created are to be utilized only for payment of imports from France or for other remittances due in France. A similar arrangement is understood to be in operation between the governments of Great Britain and Argentina. Hitherto, the balances of foreign exchange accruing to Argentina from those countries with which it had favorable balances of payments were available for payment of imports from other countries.

On the other hand, the Dominican Republic suspended in December the commercial convention of 1936 with France, when that government found itself unable to continue its purchases of Dominican coffee. This resulted in the Dominican duties on a number of products from all sources being restored to the higher levels which preceded the French agreement. Reference has earlier been made to the conclusion in November of the reciprocal trade agreement between Venezuela and the United States, which had been under negotiation since the preceding year.

To check a rapid price rise in sugar after the outbreak of the war, the United States suspended the duty reduction of the 1934 trade agreement with Cuba, in connection with lifting of all quota limitations upon the amount of sugar that could come upon the American market. Toward the end of the year, a supplementary Cuban-American agreement restored the duty reduction on sugar, contingent upon the restoration of consumption quotas by the United States, which followed almost immediately.

1940

SPREAD OF THE WAR CAUSES SHARP SHIFTS IN WORLD TRADE AND CONTROLS

Increased Demands for War Supplies Offset Drop in Normal United States Exports

While the official measures of trade control by various countries, with which this review primarily deals, have during the past year been predominantly of a restrictive character, such measures have often been offset or overbalanced by the larger forces that have determined the general volume and direction of the foreign trade of various countries, notably that of the United States. In fact, the war developments which have led to most of the restrictions here discussed, and have shifted or cut off many large movements in international trade, have themselves brought on important alternative movements of large volume, though these have commonly involved different commodities and countries. In particular, they have given rise to a suddenly increased volume of foreign trade in war materials and equipment, beyond any peacetime magnitude.

Whatever the ultimate effect of the foreign trade control developments of the past year upon the movements of international commerce, when war demands and constrictions eventually taper off, the actual foreign trade experience of the United States for the year 1940 may be summarized as follows: The export trade of the United States for the past year was valued at 4 billion dollars, an increase of 27 per cent over the preceding year, and the highest value recorded since 1929. The general imports of the United States exceeded 2.6 billion, an increase of 13 per cent over 1939. The net export balance of merchandise for the year approximated 1.4 billion dollars.

Continental Europe

Spread of war and contraband controls determine trade possibilities.—The basic limitation upon foreign trade movements and controls during the past year has obviously been the spread of the conflict in Europe by successive stages, until, by the middle of June, most of continental Europe west of the Soviet Union had either been overrun or come under the domination of the German and Italian military forces, or was practically cut off from overseas communication by the war developments and by the British blockade. Under the circumstances, it seems hardly necessary to detail here the temporary measures taken during the early months of the year by the various European countries, in their endeavor to placate both sets of belligerents and at the same time maintain the flow, into and out of their territories, of goods so essential to their economic life.

It will be the task of historians of this war to trace the early efforts of the countries of Scandinavia and northern Europe, caught between the British blockade and the pressures from Germany, to guard their neutrality by apparently sincere attempts to deal evenly with both sides; of Italy, to obtain minimum supplies of essential deficit materials, such as coal from England, while maintaining the status of "a nonbelligerent"; and of the southeastern countries, not to yield so much to the economic pressures from either side as to bring the war into the Balkans. The present review of the developments of the year, as affecting the European continent and its overseas territories, will concern itself primarily with the trade control arrangements and measures after the fall of France in June.

Separate consideration will be given to the several groups of countries that find themselves at the beginning of 1941 in distinctly different relations to the results of the military, political, and territorial shifts of the past year, namely, those actually annexed, those which are occupied but nominally independent, the nonbelligerent or "neutral" countries of continental Europe, and finally the overseas territories of the occupied countries. No separate discussion will be attempted of the year's developments in Germany, Italy, or the Soviet Union in this field. The foreign trade of these countries had for some time previously already been highly centralized, in connection with their respective military preparations, and any changes in the application of their commercial policies toward other countries are best seen from an analysis of their impact upon the other countries concerned.

Areas annexed militarily usually lose customs identity.—The territorial spread of military activities resulted during the past year in the physical annexation or absorption into the customs areas of the occupying powers of a number of countries or portions of them. Such areas have thereby been bereft of independent outside trade relations, and have become subject to the same conditions of foreign trading as the absorbing country. According to the latest information available, not yet confirmed officially on all points, these changes may be listed as follows:[1]

1. March, 1940.—Albania was formally absorbed into the Italian trade system by the establishment of a "customs union."
2. March.—Part of southeastern Finland was annexed by the Soviet Union and made part of its customs territory.
3. May.—The German invasion of Belgium was followed by incorporation into the German customs area of Luxemburg, and of the districts of Eupen, Malmedy, and Moresnet.
4. May.—The German invasion of France was followed by the reported absorption of Alsace and Lorraine, later in the year.
5. June to August.—In successive partitions of Rumania, the Soviet Union took over the province of Bessarabia and northern Bukovina, and incorporated them into its customs area; the northern portion of Transylvania was ceded to Hungary, and southern Dobruja to Bulgaria.
6. August.—Political incorporation of the Baltic republics of Estonia, Latvia, and Lithuania into the Soviet Union was followed, toward the end of the year, by removal of the customs frontiers.
7. October.—After several transitional steps, Bohemia-Moravia was incorporated into the German customs area.
8. December.—Following several preliminary steps, import duties were lifted on the movement of goods between Germany and the Netherlands, in either direction.
9. Most of Poland, overrun in the fall of 1939, has been absorbed into the German and Soviet customs areas, respectively, although definite reports are lacking. The area of Central Poland temporarily set up as a separate "Government-General" was, during the year,

[1] As the result of previous military occupations, Austria had been incorporated into the German customs regime in 1938, and the Sudeten area of Czechoslovakia and Memel in 1939.

taken "under the protection" of the German authorities, although it appears still to maintain a separate customs regime and clearing accounts with other areas.

Germany directs economies and trade of "independent" occupied areas.—At first, it appeared that the areas occupied by Germany and not definitely annexed were to maintain their own import duties and taxes and general fiscal regimes, as well as carry on negotiations with the accessible countries, although subject to German supervision or approval. Denmark seemed to be in a more independent status than Norway, the Netherlands, Belgium, or occupied France. For a time, the Danish authorities at Copenhagen were reported to be making agreements directly for trade exchanges with other countries of Europe (for example, Switzerland and Yugoslavia), with payments cleared directly through their own national banks. Toward the end of the year, however, German authorities took over the direction of such negotiations with Denmark.

The Netherlands have been drawn into especially close trade relations with Germany. In October, reduction or omission of levies on imports was authorized by the German occupying officials. Shortly thereafter, the restrictions on movements of goods and of payments between Germany and the Netherlands were considerably relaxed. In December, the German duties on Netherlands goods were lifted, and the reciprocal duty-free admission of German goods into the Netherlands followed.

Such scope for autonomous trade control and independent action in negotiations as appears to have been retained by the occupied areas has been distinctly limited by the prior and overriding action of Germany, in taking over domestic products or imported stocks accumulated in the occupied areas, presumably to be covered by German goods in such quantity and variety as that country could spare, beyond the amount charged to the costs of the German forces of occupation. No published records of movements of goods between Germany and the occupied areas are available. However, the reports of sharp increases in the living costs in the occupied areas, and of rationing to the civil populations of long lists of products and materials, including commodities of which the countries normally have a surplus above domestic requirements, seem significant.

Some specific data have become available regarding the recent movements of goods between Denmark and Germany, which may be more or less representative of the situation with regard to the other occupied countries. At the time of the occupation in April, Denmark owed Germany a small amount on their clearing account. According to a published statement by the Danish Minister of Commerce, made in August, 1940, the Reich had apparently succeeded, within four months, in converting this small German credit into a huge debt on the clearing account, owed to Denmark, amounting to 800 million crowns. Part of this was accounted for by the costs of the army of occupation, but the greater part represented heavily increased shipments of goods from Denmark to Germany. It was estimated that, at this rate of accumulation, Germany's clearing debt to Denmark would reach, by the end of 1940, the equivalent of 1,500 million crowns. The amount which Germany will have borrowed from Denmark, in eight months of occupation, is roughly equivalent to the total value of the aggregate Danish exports of merchandise during 1938, the last full normal year.

An important element in trade arrangements between Germany and the occupied areas has been the change in the terms of trade, to the disadvantage of those areas, resulting from the new exchange ratios established between the respective national currencies. For the declared purpose of readjusting the relative price levels, the exchange ratio of their currencies in terms of reichsmarks was regularly lowered, and in several cases more than once. These successive cheapenings of the other countries' currencies had the immediate effect of increasing the purchasing power of German money for the products of the occupied countries, and of making German products dearer to their populations.

Progressive shrinkage of areas accessible to overseas trade.—For the countries of continental Europe not involved in the war, progressive shrinkage of areas open to overseas trade was the overshadowing development of the year. With the increased domination by Germany of the major portion of the European continent, the entrance of Italy into the war, and the extension of the British blockade so as to close off the Mediterranean as well as most of the Atlantic coast, very few European countries had any important lines of communication with overseas areas open to them by the end of 1940.[2]

[2] The British are understood to be maintaining a blockade against all shipments bound for Germany, Italy, and the areas of continental Europe occupied by them, including unoccupied France. The blockade is applied also to the dependent areas of Algeria, French Morocco, and Tunisia, and (but see below) of Syria, Madagascar, Reunion, and the French West African territories of Mauretania, Senegal, French Guinea, the Ivory Coast, and Dahomey. Exceptionally, purely medical supplies are allowed through the blockade for distribution in the occupied territories and in unoccupied France.

Under the navicert system, calling for verification of ultimate destination before shipment, the British authorities are controlling imports also into countries adjacent to those under blockade, from which such goods could reach Axis territories or the areas under their control. Specifically, the navicert system was reported to be applied in January, 1941,

The principal exceptions were: Soviet Russia, with its Asiatic frontiers, although subject to the limited facilities of the Trans-Siberian railroad; Greece and Turkey, both able to maintain some trade through eastern Mediterranean outlets, thence around the Cape of Good Hope; Spain and Portugal, which have ports open on the Atlantic, with Lisbon attaining exceptional importance as temporarily the principal port of entry for Western Europe; and Switzerland, which has thus far managed to obtain double clearance for two specially chartered ships via Genoa, and for some transshipments at Lisbon, to deliver quantities of its specialty products to the United States, partly for redistribution to other countries, and for one east-bound vessel to carry essential supplies needed by Switzerland. One other port open to the Atlantic has been Finnish Petsamo, capable of handling only a very limited volume of traffic for Finland and Sweden, even when permission of the belligerents could be secured.

Water traffic within the Mediterranean, which was quite active for some time after its closure to overseas merchant vessels, was sharply curtailed after the Italian invasion of Greece in late October. This contraction could only in small measure be offset by the limited rail transport facilities across the continent available for movement of civilian merchandise.

Neutrals centralize regulation of foreign as well as domestic transactions.—Not all of the countries of continental Europe were equally affected by the shrinkage of the area open to trade, the situation varying principally in accordance with the ease of communication possible with other than the Axis Powers, and with the degree of German economic and political influence in the particular country. In general, however, practically all the countries of Europe not already living under a controlled economy appear to have adopted, for the time, a pattern of trade control closely resembling that of a controlled economy. In their increasing economic isolation, most of these countries apparently found it necessary for the government to charge itself with close regulation and direction of the nation's whole economy, in the effort to ensure the minimum supplies necessary to its population and industries.

---

upon shipments to Portugal and Spain and their Atlantic Islands, Portuguese Guinea, Spanish Morocco, and Liberia; and to Sweden, Finland, Switzerland, Yugoslavia, Hungary, Rumania, Bulgaria, Greece, Turkey, and European Russia. Subject to the general policy of blockade referred to above, the navicert system is to a limited extent also operative in the case of French dependencies of Syria, Madagascar, Reunion, and French West Africa. The navicert system is not understood to be operative with regard to areas in the Pacific.

The degree to which navicerts are granted or refused on specific shipments is reported to vary considerably, in accordance with the country involved as well as other circumstances in the particular case.

In the field of foreign trade, almost all of these neutral countries of Europe sooner or later during the year reached the stage of a fully centralized system of government regulation of most, if not all, import and export transactions by permits. In a number of cases these were apportioned through trade syndicates or unions, whose members alone could trade in the particular products. Foreign trade control was usually closely tied in with extensive state intervention in domestic production and distribution and often with rigid price control measures, accompanying increasing lists of products rationed to civilian populations in limited quantities.

In the governmental direction of foreign trade, the usual commercial objectives and methods, in several of the countries subordinated for sometime past, were now very largely displaced. Early steps were often taken to reduce or waive the duties on articles of necessity, so as to encourage their importation wheresoever obtainable. New or increased export duties were often imposed, and an increasingly wide range of products, manufactured as well as natural, were put under export license control. In the granting of import and export permits, preferences and priorities were gradually expanded, often serving objectives more political than commercial.

Negotiations between reachable areas center on obtaining supplies.— The year was marked by considerable activity in the negotiation and renegotiation of trade and payments agreements on the part of the neutral countries of Europe. Such activity was naturally limited almost entirely to those countries reachable under the constricted situation. The agreements usually provided for definite trade turnovers, commonly in the form of assigned quotas of specific products which each was to make available, with settlement made through clearing accounts, although not necessarily on a strictly balanced basis.

The series of arrangements between the Soviet Union, Sweden, Denmark, and Finland well illustrate efforts on the part of the neutral countries of Europe to develop to the utmost alternative sources among the reachable areas for needed products now difficult to obtain from overseas. Russian commercial treaty-making activity during 1940 was particularly notable for the range of the other countries involved. These included Yugoslavia, Hungary, and Bulgaria, with whom the Soviet Union had had no trade exchanges of any consequence for years, and with the first two of whom there had not been even diplomatic relations. The trade negotiations by Switzerland with countries as far apart and as difficult of access as Finland

and Turkey constitute another illustration of the supply problems of the secluded areas.

The trade arrangements with Germany were usually the outstanding ones, and most of those were apparently dominated by the German desire to obtain increased quantities of products or stocks from the other countries, in return for such German goods as could be promised delivery, or by arrangements for the balancing of accounts by supplies from third countries.

Germany intervenes in arrangements between neutral and occupied areas.—The trade relations between the neutral and the occupied countries of Europe have tended to become increasingly tied up with trade arrangements with Germany. As earlier indicated, negotiations on behalf of the occupied areas with outside countries are being conducted under the close supervision of the occupying authorities, and Germany has required that payments for trade with the occupied areas be made through special clearing accounts in the Reichsbank at Berlin. According to reports, payments for trade between the occupied areas and Finland, Sweden, Switzerland, Italy, Yugoslavia, Bulgaria, and Greece are now required to be made through such Berlin clearing accounts—and the list is probably not complete.

This is in line with the plans much discussed in Germany during the year for developing a collective clearing system for all European trade, to center at Berlin. However, this appears to have objectives in addition to the financial convenience of clearing the accounts of various countries through a single currency. The system is reported to be operated also as a means of securing additional supplies from countries to which Germany is already heavily indebted, by utilizing the balances or absorptive ability of certain other countries through three-cornered transactions. Thus, according to a dispatch appearing in the official German foreign trade journal, a trade agreement between Sweden and Denmark provided that, during the second half of 1940, Denmark was to be furnished with Swedish goods to a value of 35 million Danish crowns, but was to make direct deliveries of Danish products to Sweden to a value of only 24 million Danish crowns. The difference between these sums was to be covered by transferring the amount to the German clearing account with Sweden. This apparently growing tendency for Germany to figure in trade agreements between various pairs of European countries is illustrated also in the reported unwillingness of certain Balkan countries to furnish foodstuffs to occupied countries of northern Europe, except on the condition that Germany supply them with certain specified needed products, on a triangular basis.

The significance of many of the trade agreements negotiated and revised between various European countries during this war year cannot be well judged from the formal announcements, which are usually optimistic as to the prospective benefits and effects, but meager as to essential provisions and details. Understandably, the official announcements may often be intended to impress outsiders rather than inform them. The usual alternative for gauging the character of commercial agreements by the trade movements under them is seldom available, since official statistics of trade have not been published by most European countries for some time.

Such evidence as is available—often from secondary and unconfirmable sources—indicates that some of the trade arrangements are amounting to much less than confidently asserted at their conclusion. It is not always clear whether this is the result of actual inability to furnish or transport the various products in their promised volumes, or of unwillingness to reduce the exporting country's own supplies too seriously, or whether the actual terms of the agreement were more modest than the public had been led to believe. Moreover, the fact that certain agreements had to be made the subject of fresh negotiation, sometimes more than once, within the past year—such as the Russo-German agreement which contemplated the exchange of huge quantities of goods—suggests that they had apparently not come up to expectations.

On the other hand, in connection with the German-Rumanian agreement of December, 1940, concluded after certain radical territorial and political changes in Rumania, and designed to intensify the general plan of the preceding year for expanding Rumanian production and developing its transportation system in accordance with Germany's economic needs, it is reported that the implementation had actually been begun even before the agreement was signed. German press comment at the time pointed out that, since political obstacles which obstructed close economic cooperation had been removed, Rumanian agricultural and industrial production could now be "coordinated with the requirements of the German market."

Germany tries to adjust arbitrarily terms of trade with other Europeans.—As in the case of the annexed and occupied territories, the trade arrangements during 1940 with most of the neutral countries of Europe, now largely dependent economically upon Germany, provided for adjustments in the price levels and terms of trade with the Reich, through increasing the value of the mark in terms of the other currencies. Following the announcement in November of negotiated increases in the premiums above the legal parity of the reichsmark that were to be paid by the banks of Yugoslavia, Bulgaria, and Hungary, in making payments through the clearing accounts, press dispatches from Berlin quoted official commentators to the following effect: "The Reich in its present dominant position as seller and buyer probably could obtain still better terms, but the Government is apprehensive of the effect which higher reichsmark rates might have on the ability of the Balkan countries to buy German goods, considering the limited buying power of their populations."

As earlier intimated, not all neutral countries of Europe were in a position which obliged them to accept such unfavorable terms in their commercial dealings with Germany. Greece and Turkey were notable among those reported to have maintained much more independent positions in their negotiations. Each had concluded trade agreements during the year with both Great Britain and Germany, and carried on a fairly active trade with both, although the volume of German-Turkish trade was much reduced. Both these countries also carried on an active trade under agreements with Italy during most of 1940; the Greek treaty was terminated by the Italian invasion in late October, and the Turkish agreement was allowed to lapse at the end of the year. Early in December, arrangements of broad scope between the British and Turkish governments were announced, which were declared to be designed "to bring about a considerable increase in trade through commercial exchanges between Turkey and the British Empire." The means provided for attaining that end were not made public.

A number of the neutral European countries made strenuous efforts to capitalize the bargaining power of their possessing products that were much desired by other European countries. In view of the limited range of sources of supply, they endeavored to ensure that they would receive certain vitally needed imports from the other countries in return for particular exports they agreed to furnish, sometimes preferring the delivery of specific imports even to free exchange. In the case of some raw materials and essential manufactures, the effort was often made to prevent any supplies from being shipped out of the country.

Trade arrangements of European overseas territories vary greatly.—After the fall of the home country, the changes in the trade connections and commercial policy of the various European colonies and territories overseas varied widely. Information with regard to the situation in some of these areas is meager, but certain differences and tendencies are quite discernible, and their present accessibility to American commerce warrants particular observation of their current trade positions and policies.

In the French Empire at least three different types of commercial orientation and policy appear to have developed since the capitulation of France in mid-June. The North African areas of Algeria, French Morocco, and Tunisia, nearest to France, and cut off by the British blockade from most of their former trading connections, appear to have continued in the same position as unoccupied France proper. In fact, except for the small turnover with France and with each other, the foreign trade of these areas during the latter part of the year has been reported as negligible.

French Indo-China, the most important French dependency (Algeria being regarded as a Department of France), stands in a somewhat intermediate position. Being cut off indefinitely from its principal markets and sources of supply in France and the Continent, and obliged to make new adjustments with the countries with which the trade lanes are open, Indo-China has been authorized by the Vichy Government to assume a large measure of customs autonomy. Under the new regime, the local government may negotiate with foreign countries for reciprocal trade arrangements, and reconstruct the duties and restrictions of the colony on a basis allowing curtailment of the preferential treatment which France and French colonial products have enjoyed. Heretofore Indo-China had been classed as an assimilated colony. As such, free trade had prevailed between it and France and most other parts of the French Empire, and the import duties and quotas, as well as the trade relations of Indo-China with other areas, were determined for the most part from Paris, and primarily in accordance with the interest of France. In its new status, the Indo-Chinese Government is participating in negotiations with Japan for a trade agreement along new lines.

Among the non-Mediterranean French areas of Africa, a definite separation has developed. French West Africa has remained under the close control of France proper, and a local proposal for relative lowering of the duties on non-French imports was vetoed by the Vichy authorities. In contrast, certain areas of French Equatorial Africa set up, at the end of August, a regime termed "Free French Africa," with full power to carry on the rule of these areas, "pending the complete liberation of the Metropolitan territory (France) and its constitution." The remaining areas of Equatorial Africa and the mandate of Cameroon later adhered to this regime, and such preferences as existed in favor of French goods were discontinued, being replaced by a single tariff now applying to imports from all sources.

Britain promises to maintain economies of Free French Africa and Belgian Congo.—In December the British Colonial Secretary announced that economic arrangements had been negotiated with the Free French colonies in Africa intended "to give general effect to the British Government's pledge to maintain the economic structure of the countries in question by buying as much of their produce as we can, and by providing in return such imports as are necessary for the life of the country." Scattered reports indicate that Tahiti and the related group of French islands in the Pacific, and the islands of New Hebrides and New Caledonia, appear also to have expressed their adherence to the Free French regime set up in Africa. New Caledonia in particular is reported to be reorienting its trade into closer relations with near-by Australia.

Some of the lesser outlying French colonies, whose financial accounts had been cleared through Paris during the early months of the war, are reported to be finding themselves with limited financial resources, and endeavoring to make the best arrangements possible with accessible areas for essential supplies and markets.

In a somewhat similar position to Free French Africa is the colony of Belgian Congo, an important source of copper and various tropical agricultural products. An economic agreement is reported to have been negotiated by a British mission, with the approval of the Belgian Colonial Minister, under which Great Britain pledged itself, as in the case of Free French Africa, to maintain the economic structure of the Belgian Congo, by the purchase of its products and by supplying its import necessities. Under an international agreement of long standing, the products of all countries have been accorded equal tariff treatment in the Belgian Congo.

Netherlands Indies treated like sterling bloc by eastern British areas.—Since the invasion of the Netherlands, the local government of the Netherlands Indies has been exercising broad powers in trade control matters, as in other respects, under the general direction of the Netherlands Government temporarily at London. After May 11 exchange restrictions on foreign payments were established, special permits were required for all imports, and a general control of exports was introduced. Additional wartime taxes were imposed on exports of rubber, tin, cinchona, and petroleum products, for which there was high demand, and agreements were negotiated with various countries regarding the conditions of obtaining supplies. By agreement with British India, the import restrictions into that country were lifted on products of the Netherlands Indies, and the area was placed on an equal basis with those constituting the sterling bloc. Australia has similarly waived its import license restrictions on goods from the Netherlands Indies. In the Netherlands West Indies, which had early been occupied by the Allied forces for the duration of the war, all foreign trade is under license, and is operated in close relation to the sterling areas.

Following the occupation of Denmark, the legislature of the joint kingdom of Iceland declared its autonomy. The British have extended their protection to the island, and its trade relations have since been directed principally toward the United Kingdom and the United States.

British Empire

Desire to maintain normal trade gives way to needs of war effort.—British sea power has allowed Great Britain and the various members of the British Empire to continue fairly active trading with all parts of the world other than the belligerent, occupied, or secluded areas of continental Europe, and the adjacent North African coast. However, under the spread and intensification of the war, the desire to maintain foreign trade in normal variety and volume had to give way progressively, during 1940, to the imperative need of utilizing all available resources at home or from abroad primarily for the war effort. The trade control measures adopted during the year by the British Empire,[3] especially by the United Kingdom and Canada, reflect the stages in the growth of this dominating purpose.

While somewhat less marked in the more distant parts of the British Empire, the same general objective stood out. Representatives of the British Dominions and colonies east of Suez conferred at Delhi in October for the purpose of organizing their combined resources, both to make the participating countries more nearly self-supporting and the better to contribute toward the Empire war program.

In the United Kingdom, the growing pressure of the war brought during the year a series of interlocking measures. These increasingly centralized the conduct or direction of foreign trade, as well as of the domestic econ-

[3] The increasing restrictions on the importation of many products into the United Kingdom and various Empire areas during 1940, here described, have led to a shift in the composition, rather than a curtailment in the total, of the trade of the United States with most parts of the British Empire. In fact, the increased purchases of wartime supplies, especially by Great Britain and Canada, have compensated—in aggregate value—for the loss of American markets on the continent of Europe.

For the first twelve months of the war, total shipments to the United Kingdom were 57 per cent higher than during the year preceding, although the character of British purchases had shifted sharply, from the normal range of American agricultural products of a broad variety, and of manufactured products for consumer use now regarded as dispensable, toward products more vital to the conduct of the war. During the latter months of 1940, nearly two-thirds of the total value of United States exports were accounted for by the British Empire, as compared with one-half or less prior to the war.

omy, in the hands of governmental agencies; imposed or extended rationing and price control over many commodities; curtailed the range of products for civilian use permitted to be imported, particularly from outside the Empire; and expanded to an unprecedented degree purchases and contracts abroad, especially in the Empire and the United States, of materials and products essential to the conduct of the war. At the same time, Great Britain sought, by its naval blockade and prior verification of the destination of shipments through the navicert system, to hold to a minimum the delivery of goods of whatever origin to Germany, Italy, and the territories under their control.[4]

Britain seeks imports, officially selected, and preferably from Empire sources.—In the control of imports into the United Kingdom, the year's changes in duties were almost all by way of reductions or exemptions, apparently to facilitate the importation from any source of desired materials or products. The determining control, however, was exercised through import-license and exchange-permit systems, the scope of which was greatly extended. First, all luxury and nonessential commodities were controlled; then, by March 18, imports of all foodstuffs were subject to license; and by June 10, prior import licenses were required for practically all remaining products. Many commodities for which licenses were at first granted in limited quantities were later cut off altogether. Purchases abroad of foodstuffs came under the control of the Ministry of Food, and supplies of major materials and manufactured goods for military purposes came increasingly under the Ministry of Supply or Air Ministry, operating in the United States largely through the British Purchasing Commission.[5]

For the declared purposes of conserving foreign exchange, particularly dollar exchange, for the purchase of military supplies, and of supporting the economic position of various classes of producers in the Dominions and colonies, the various import controls were utilized so as to concentrate purchases of particular commodities so far as possible within the British Empire, or in certain countries politically allied, principally Greece, Turkey, and Egypt. As the countries of Western Europe came under German occupation, this preference was extended also to certain of their overseas territories.

The program inaugurated shortly after the outbreak of the war, for purchase undertakings to different parts of the Empire and allied areas,

[4] Fuller statement on the current status of the British blockade and navicert system appears on p. 205, in connection with discussion of continental Europe.

[5] Early in January, 1941, all British import activities were centralized under an "Import Executive," headed by the Minister of Supply.

for large quantities or the entire exportable surplus of various natural products, was enlarged during 1940. In some cases, preëmptive purchasing was reported of products that Great Britain desired to keep from its opponents.

Pressure to curtail civilian purchases and to conserve shipping.—As the year proceeded, the scope of permitted imports, even from the Empire, was curtailed, in line with the program for concentrating domestic productive effort on necessities, minimizing any expansion of consumer purchases of nonessentials, and diverting a larger share of income to war bonds. In October, a purchase tax of 33⅓ per cent on a wide range of luxury products, and of half that on certain convenience products, was imposed on both imported and domestic products. It was frankly characterized as "a consumer's tax."

With increased sinkings of merchant vessels in the fall, the conservation of shipping space became a more prominent consideration in the motives for curtailment, rationing, or stoppage of particular imported products. In the case of bananas, colonial growers, particularly Jamaican, were compensated for their crops to the extent of a million pounds sterling, and the fruit was then discarded, for lack of ships to carry it to England.

While additional materials and equipment were made subject to export restriction during the year, to conserve essential supplies, the general effort was to keep up exports to friendly countries, as a means of maintaining employment and of building up foreign exchange holdings, especially needed in view of the huge increase in war imports. The Empire areas coöperated in this program by prohibiting or curtailing the importation of many products from nonsterling sources.

Credit balances from British imports made usable only for sterling products.—Under pressure to conserve foreign exchange, the British Government developed during the year a broad series of arrangements whereby payments for purchases from most countries were made through special sterling accounts at London, which could be drawn upon only for the purchase of goods from sterling areas or for remittances to them. Since Great Britain needed to import from various sources much more than the volume of her exports to those countries, sizable credit balances often accumulated in London, but these were not available for use by the selling countries to pay for imports from third countries. This British system of bilateral trade and exchange, while understandable under the circumstances, is reported to be operating as a material limitation upon United States trade with certain countries, particularly of Latin America, which have need for American products to a greater value than the American market has need of their products, and which require the free use of the balances due them from countries where they sell more than they buy.

Empire trade oriented to Britain's needs and restricted with others.—The general license control over imports, exports, and foreign exchange, introduced by Canada in September, 1939, was operated for a time as a precautionary rather than a restrictive measure. However, with the closer gearing into the needs of Great Britain, under the intensified tempo of the war, and the necessity for larger Canadian purchases of war supplies, mainly from the United States, the Canadian system developed during 1940 into a wartime foreign trade control of a seriously restrictive character upon many types of transactions. In June, a 10 per cent war exchange tax was imposed on all imports from non-Empire sources, and restrictive license controls were imposed upon the imports or exports of selected products during the course of the first war year. Finally, on December 2, 1940, a series of drastic measures was applied, prohibiting altogether the importation from nonsterling areas of a broad range of consumers' products regarded as dispensable, and limiting the importation of certain other products on an avowed decreasing scale. As a transition measure, three months were allowed for completing deliveries on firm prior orders.

At the same time, sizable excise taxes were established on a number of Canadian-produced articles, to prevent the expansion of domestic production of articles which were being prohibited or restricted from importation. This was in line with other domestic measures, including a sales drive for war-savings certificates, designed primarily to curtail public expenditures upon dispensables. The use of aluminum for the manufacture of household articles had already been prohibited, and a ban was placed upon production of new-model automobiles and a variety of appliances and equipment requiring the use of machine tools.

Simultaneously with the restrictions applied to nonsterling areas, Canada announced the removal or reduction of import duties on a list of products from the United Kingdom, as an aid to British payment for the increased volume of Canadian war materials.

Australia continued and enlarged the license system imposed in December, 1939, upon broad groups of imports from nonsterling areas. As the quotas to import were renewed for each quarter of 1940, the restrictions were applied to additional products. In December, further restrictions were imposed on certain softwoods—some prohibited and others to be licensed on a diminishing scale. In July, the products of the Netherlands Indies were placed on the same preferred license basis in the Australian market as those of the sterling area.

The New Zealand import restriction system, inaugurated in December, 1938, primarily to correct the foreign exchange position, was continued for each half of 1940, with some further tightening on particular products. The announcement of its continuation for the year 1941 carried some easements.

The Union of South Africa, in an exceptional position in various ways, maintained substantially its prewar trade regime, except for an exchange control system reported not to be operating restrictively, and for license controls on the importation and exportation of a few raw materials.

In late spring, British India established a license control over a considerable range of products from non-Empire sources, and a few also from the Empire, covering mainly products obtainable from sterling sources or regarded as dispensable. Toward the close of the year, a number of important additional products were placed under permit. When licenses were granted, they were on the basis of the importer's past trade, and, for several months, firm existing orders were allowed to be delivered against the new quotas. In July and early August, open licenses were announced for all imports from the Netherlands Indies and from many of the French colonies, and also for certain products from Egypt, Sudan, and Iraq. Wool, which appears to have been of special interest to American firms among the British Indian products made subject to export license, was prohibited shipment to the United States after March, but again permitted in October on a quarterly quota basis.

The government of Burma followed closely the pattern of trade control measures adopted during the year by British India. A British restriction upon the use of "the Burma Road" for the transit to China of specified war materials and transportation equipment through Burma was enforced on July 18 and lifted three months later.

As the year progressed, most of the British colonies enlarged the lists of products that could be imported from nonsterling or non-Empire areas only under license. In some cases, particularly in the West Indies and African colonies, all imports were brought under control. Many are reported to have come to the position of refusing to grant licenses for the importation from outside the Empire of much beyond essentials, or products for which substitutes could not be found at home or in some Empire area.

In a number of the British colonies seeking additional local revenues, duty surtaxes were imposed or increased on most dutiable imports. The revenue incentive figured also in the action of a larger number of colonies in increasing the duties on tobacco, alcoholic beverages, petroleum products, toilet preparations, and other products. In some of these cases, there appeared the incidental motive of the authorities of desiring to discourage expenditure upon such products.

This growing general desire to hold down optional purchases and to conserve exchange resources locally was evidenced also in the frequent extension of the import license control to products from Empire sources. In the case of curtailments on the importations of iron and steel and various types of equipment, even from Great Britain, the purpose appears to have been to carry through the express desire from London that the Empire areas hold down their calls for products needed by the United Kingdom for war purposes.

In the effort to guard their supplies of foods and other necessities, most colonies came to control by licenses or quotas the exportation of many foods and essential manufactures. These colonies devoting themselves to the production of certain tropical agricultural products, notably sugar, bananas, cocoa, and copra, turned to Great Britain for relief from the loss of European markets and low prices for their staple—sometimes sole—money crops.

Many Empire staples purchased by Britain or used as "exchange arsenals."—The year's arrangements with Australia well illustrate the continued operation of United Kingdom purchase agreements for many staple products of the Empire areas. Australia was assured a continued market for the exportable surplus of a number of minerals (lead, zinc, and copper), as well as of its principal agricultural products. The latter included wool, meats, butter, and cheese, canned and dried fruits, and sugar. The Commonwealth Government itself took over the season's crop of wheat and of apples and pears, the chief remaining farm surpluses.

In line with the general program for economic support of the various parts of the Empire, the British Government made wide purchases of various such colonial products, sometimes well beyond the ability of the Empire to consume them or the ability to spare shipping for their delivery. Similar to the purchase and discard of the year's colonial banana crop, earlier mentioned, was the destruction of part of the cocoa crop of the West African colonies, the entire supply of which was taken over by Great Britain for the second year.

Often working in connection with international control committees, those colonial areas producing raw materials that were much sought after for defense or stock purposes, notably rubber and tin, regulated the exportation of these products with particular care. Additional export duties were imposed on various raw materials in high demand, and the large dollar credits created through their increased shipment to the United States were carefully conserved by the governments of Malaya and other colonies. The use of these funds for increased purchases from the United States was discouraged, in order to conserve them for the purchase of war supplies by Great Britain.

Far East (China and Japan)[6]

Trading conditions restricted with Japan and occupied China.—In the Far East, the Sino-Japanese conflict, continuing into its third year, appeared to be the overshadowing consideration, particularly as regards the trade control measures of China, Japan, and adjacent areas. The Chinese situation was marked by some shifting in the areas of military activity and Japanese control, the extension southward of the type of trade restrictions previously imposed by the occupying authorities in the northern provinces of China, and of the blockade against coastwise shipping. The conduct of import and export trade in the occupied areas is reported to be increasingly diverted, by the operation of various trade control measures, into the hands of Japanese firms or Japanese-sponsored organizations.

Trade with Japan itself has for some time been severely restricted by the operation of the various governmental controls and by the diversion of resources to the military program. Consumption of "luxury" articles has long been banned, and many civilian necessities are closely rationed. Further steps were taken during 1940 toward concentrating the conduct of foreign trade in the hands of governmental agencies or of officially sponsored import and export combinations, into which individual firms in particular lines have been merged.[7] (Since October, Japan has published no import or export statistics.)

In order to check evasion of the domestic price control measures, by

---

[6] Important developments in other areas in the Far East have been touched upon either in the foregoing section on the British Empire, or in the section on overseas territories, beginning on p. 210.

[7] As observed also in the case of certain other parts of the world, the net effect of the developments of the past year upon the trade of the United States with the Far East has been more in the nature of a shift in the principal commodities involved, and in the local channels through which the trade was conducted, than in the total value of the trade. For the first eleven months of 1940, United States exports to Japan, as well as imports from that country, have run slightly ahead of 1939. With China as a whole, the volume of the merchandise moving, in both directions, has aggregated totals far in excess of those of the preceding year.

large-scale exports of Japanese products to China and Manchuria, export certificates began to be required in September, 1939, on such shipments of a wide range of products. In August, 1940, the Japanese Government enlarged the list of commodities for which official permission must be secured prior to shipment to the so-called yen-bloc areas. Shipments to yen-bloc areas, of course, yield Japan no foreign exchange, so much needed for outside purchases.

It is reported that, in the expectation of a more limited participation in foreign trade during the period ahead, many pivotal Japanese industries are undergoing extensive changes, in line with the policy gearing the national economy to military needs. Foreign trade control is also being directed more and more toward the contemplated "new national structure" of Japan and in the light of the prospective "Greater East Asia Co-Prosperity Sphere."

Latin America

Loss of continental European markets the dominant problem.—Though not participants in the European war, and distant from the center of its operations, the countries of Latin America have been among those feeling keenly the impact of the war upon their trade. Normally exporting the bulk of their staple products, these countries are more dependent than most upon the continued availability of foreign markets at fair prices, not only for a major part of local income, but also for the means of paying for the large volume of consumption and capital goods which need to be obtained from abroad. The progressive curtailment and final closing off of most of continental Europe, constituting in recent years nearly 30 per cent of their aggregate markets, and supplying a somewhat larger proportion of their import requirements, has naturally been a severe shock to their economies.[8]

Not all of the countries of Latin America have been equally affected. The influence of the war has been less marked in certain countries around the Gulf and the Caribbean, which normally find their major markets in the United States. On the other hand, products such as meat and wool found foreign markets better sustained in countries able to take delivery

[8] Continental Europe afforded markets for Latin American products to a value of about 500 million dollars during the last prewar year. The United States, the largest single market for Latin America as a whole, purchased not much less than all the countries of continental Europe put together. United Kingdom's purchases have amounted to about 300 million dollars annually although, in contrast to those of the United States, they have been largely concentrated in Argentina, Brazil, Chile, and Uruguay.

and pay for them, than coffee and bananas, the consumption of which has been materially restricted in many countries during wartime.

Broadly viewed, however, the disruption of European markets caused by the war has been the dominant trade problem in most countries of Latin America during the past year, and various efforts to readjust the situation constituted the mainspring of most of their trade control projects. Pending the working out of supporting or remedial measures, various countries of South America resorted to defensive measures, in the form of new or additional restrictions on imports, either through exchange control or other means, particularly during the latter months of 1940.

During the early months of the war, most of these countries still saw a fair prospect for the readjustment of their trade position. Their various raw materials were finding increased markets in the United States; the British and French were negotiating for large purchases, particularly of foods and fibers; and most of the ports of continental Europe were still accessible. However, with the closing off of most of the continental markets in the spring of the year, and with the curtailment in the actual amounts of various commodities which Great Britain alone could take, the problems of undisposable surpluses and of limited exchange resources for financing imports became acute.

Increase in replacement purchases from United States greater than in sales.—In the meantime, merchants in most countries of Latin America had turned to the United States for supplies and equipment not available from the usual sources. The result was a sharp increase during the first twelve months of the war in Latin American purchases from the United States, by 243 million dollars, which brought the total value of that trade to about 50 per cent above the preceding year. The parallel increase in United States purchases of Latin American products during the same period was substantial (147 million dollars or 31 per cent), but did not quite keep pace with the quickened flow of the merchandise movement southward.

Under ordinary circumstances, such a temporary shift in the trade balance might have been taken care of by the credits built up by the various Latin American Republics in the countries with which they had an export balance. However, under the plan early adopted by Great Britain, and for a time followed also by France, as a means of conserving foreign exchange, payment for their purchases from many important countries of South America was made into special accounts at London or Paris, which could be drawn upon only in payment for purchases from the sterling or franc areas, or for other financial settlements with them. This development of close bilateral trade arrangements with their principal active markets other than the United States, left many of the South American countries with relatively small amounts of free exchange with which to pay for their increased purchases from the United States, beyond the additional dollar exchange created by increased current sales of their products to the United States. This exchange situation constituted an outstanding obstacle to the generally desired expansion of trade between the countries of Latin America and the United States.

South American exchange shortages prompt more import restrictions.—To a degree, shortage of foreign exchange has been a chronic condition for a number of the countries of Latin America in recent years, a situation that had already led many of them to the adoption of exchange controls and other restrictions on foreign trade. Under the aggravated situation resulting from the war, three additional South American countries resorted to strict systems of priorities, among different categories of products or classes of obligations, in their allocation of available exchange—Colombia in April (tightening up the system introduced in December, 1939), Ecuador in June, and Venezuela in October. Several countries which had been exercising such control for some time, notably Argentina and Uruguay, ordered successive curtailments, with only occasional relaxations, of the exchange to be made available for imports from the United States for other than the most essential products.

Sharp increase in Brazilian purchases from the United States to replace products normally obtained elsewhere developed an import balance from this country, an unusual experience, which diminished Brazilian ability to make prompt payments. Peru, which has maintained its distinction among the countries of South America as having no formal control of foreign exchange, found it necessary to conserve exchange by increasing duties on a range of products considered luxuries or domestically replaceable, and by restricting the importation of certain cereals. Ecuador and Venezuela imposed permits on imports during the year, in connection with the enforcement of their new systems of exchange control, although the latter was clearly the determining method of regulating the course of their foreign trade. Ecuador also increased duties on an extensive list of products.

Among the ten republics of middle America, there were fewer developments in the way of material tightening of import controls during the year. Only three of them (Costa Rica, Honduras, and Nicaragua) operate an exchange control, and no serious restrictions were reported on the part of the first two of them, beyond some delay in payments. The government of Cuba controls exchange but thus far has applied no limitations upon payments for imports. None of the other countries of middle America have any formal control of foreign exchange, namely, Mexico, Guatemala, El Salvador, Panama, Haiti, and the Dominican Republic.

Arrangements with United Kingdom and United States for disposal of surpluses.—In addition to defensive measures of the type just indicated, the year saw exceptional steps and agitation for a variety of measures, designed for either immediate support or long-run improvement of the trade position of various American Republics. Efforts to dispose of unmarketable surpluses brought several developments. Arrangements with Great Britain provided for substantial British war purchases of certain staple products of a number of the South American countries. Considerably increased purchases were made by the United States during 1940, partly under special national defense arrangements, involving particularly wool, hides, manganese, copper, nitrates, and tin ore.

As the first of what its sponsors hope will prove a series of multilateral agreements for the better marketing and support of important staple products, an agreement regarding coffee, drafted by the Inter-American Financial and Economic Advisory Committee, was signed in November by representatives of fourteen coffee-producing countries of the Western Hemisphere and by the United States. It provided for a proration by quotas among the coffee-exporting countries of Latin America of the most important market for this commodity, that of the United States, with an allotment set aside for markets other than the United States as they again become available. Work is now under way on a similar agreement respecting cacao.

Local crop supports by official purchases or required mixing.—In addition, several governments bought up, or guaranteed the prices for, various major export staples. Thus, Argentina purchased the current crops of corn, wheat, and flaxseed, at fixed minimum prices, and later also of barley. The commission established by Uruguay with authority to grant premiums on exports, fixed a basic minimum price for flaxseed, and is paying a bounty to exporters to make that price effective. To help move large stocks of wool, sheepskins, and cattle hides in Uruguay, the payment of an exchange premium was ordered for a short period in June, 1940, and has since been twice renewed. The Paraguayan Government was authorized to purchase the unsold remainder of the cotton crop from growers at a fixed price, for disposal when possible. The general economic program placed before the Argentine Congress in December contemplates wider authority for governmental support of the country's crops.

Compulsory admixture of domestic with imported products was another device widely resorted to. Brazil made effective in October the plan long worked on for compulsory mixing of mandioca and other native flours with wheat flour, compelling importers to install the mixing machines. Jute and sisal products were made subject to import license, and such products domestically manufactured were required to be mixed with a portion of caroa or other domestic fiber. Paraguay put into effect measures calling for the admixture of domestic corn flour with wheat flour, and for a domestically produced carburant to be added to naphtha. Peru ordered that flour from imported wheat be mixed with a proportion of domestic rye and quinoa flour. Argentina began to require that, as a condition of obtaining exchange for imported fuel, importers obligate themselves to purchase specified amounts of domestic corn for fuel purposes.

Financial aid from United States for immediate needs and long-term development.—Among the supporting measures of immediate application was the financial aid extended by the United States Government, in response to widespread calls to help various of the other American Republics in their special problems. Such loans or credits were established by the United States during 1940 to an aggregate value of over 200 million dollars, mostly through the Export-Import Bank, in favor of the following countries of Latin America: Argentina, Brazil, Chile, Colombia, Costa Rica, Cuba, Dominican Republic, Ecuador, Panama, Peru, Uruguay, and Venezuela. The individual grants varied in amount, and were usually made either directly to the other government or its central bank, or to the local industrial or transportation enterprise concerned; in a few cases, the loan was made to the manufacturing or exporting firm in the United States interested in the sale of the equipment or other products involved. The purposes of the credits were several: to help finance essential current imports from the United States, particularly of machinery and transportation or construction equipment; to clear current accumulations of unpaid dollar drafts; to afford the means for carrying through certain internal development projects; and, in two cases, to support or stabilize the local currencies.

Among the longer-range measures, considerable discussion was heard during the year of the desirability of developing the natural resources in various countries of Latin America, of promoting more and wider industrialization, and of improving their transport facilities. In plans of this character, there was repeatedly stressed the importance of joint United States and local financial investment, and possibly also joint operation, to help ensure soundness of projects and favorable national attitudes toward such enterprises.

These developmental proposals were urged from a number of directions and with several objectives in view, including: the development of larger sources of supply in Latin America of raw materials and handicraft and other manufactured products, hitherto obtained by the United States largely from other parts of the world;[9] the increase of the general productive capacity of these countries, and ultimately of the purchasing power of their peoples for more imported as well as domestic products, and in greater variety; and the diversification of production in countries of Latin America, so as to minimize the economic shocks to which areas concentrating on a few products are subject. Groups of technical and commercial specialists were sent from the United States during the year, officially and privately, to explore also the possibilities of developing new or expanded sources of supply in the other American Republics of minerals and tropical or subtropical vegetable products, which could be made available on a dependable commercial basis, and which could find markets in the United States without directly or injuriously competing with domestic producers.

The Inter-American Development Commission, an official agency set up during the year by the Inter-American Financial and Economic Advisory Committee, has assisted in the undertaking of two experimental projects, upon the outcome of which others may depend. These are the building in Brazil of a large steel plant for the smelting and processing of local ores, and of a smaller plant for the processing of the locally grown mandioca. Branches of the Development Commission are being formed in a number of the Latin American Republics, to be composed primarily of outstanding businessmen, to propose promising new industrial enterprises for joint United States–local financing.

Trade control measures of the more usual type, also directed to the fostering of local industries, were adopted by a large number of the Latin American countries during the past year, who reduced or waived their import duties on industrial equipment and materials, either for particular types of production or for new manufacturing enterprises generally. Among the countries adopting such measures have been Costa Rica, Cuba,

[9] Argentine shipments to the United States during 1940 of sizable quantities of European-type cheeses and vermouth, not now obtainable from their original sources, illustrate this new type of imports from Latin America.

Ecuador, Mexico, Paraguay, Uruguay, and Venezuela. The general recovery program under consideration in Argentina is reported to have the encouragement of diversified industries as one of its main proposals.

Plans for intensifying economic relations of American Republics.—The general programs for closer continental solidarity among the American Republics and for coöperative measures for their common defense and welfare, toward which long strides were taken at the two conferences of their foreign ministers thus far held, at Panama in October, 1939, and at Havana in July, 1940, have had also an important economic aspect. The Havana Declaration on inter-American economics envisaged a broad program of many-sided coöperation among the American Republics in economic and financial matters. Particular emphasis was placed upon the disposal of surpluses and upon related problems, and upon the indispensability of mutual economic support against undesirable pressures from overseas. The maintenance so far as possible of the liberal and peaceful principles of international commerce was pledged.

These broad inter-American objectives have been reflected in many of the measures and proposals of the year in connection with trade controls and arrangements earlier mentioned, and are to be the subject of continuous study and elaboration by the Inter-American Financial and Economic Advisory Committee, functioning from the Pan American Union in Washington, and by related agencies in the United States and other American Republics.

In line with this general objective also, have been efforts for intensifying trade relations between the various Latin American countries themselves. Due largely to the nature of their products, the inadequate intracontinental transportation facilities, and to the early established overseas connections, the trade between them has heretofore been relatively small. In the aggregate, the twenty republics of Latin America had furnished the markets for less than 10 per cent of each other's exports. During 1938, only Argentina, Brazil, and Chile had imported more than 10 million dollars worth of goods, each, from all the other Latin American areas put together.

During the past year, substantial increases have taken place in the volume of purchases by the Latin American countries from each other. How much of this will continue when the usual sources of supply are again open is problematical. However, various steps have been initiated to provide for permanently enlarged inter-Latin American exchange of goods, principally through agreements for moderation of duties and other trade obstacles. A number of trade agreements that had been concluded during recent years between various pairs of Latin American countries were ratified during 1940, and the negotiation of additional agreements was quickened under the impulse of the war situation.

Thus, an agreement between Chile and Argentina providing for reciprocal import duty concessions on a number of products important in the trade between the two countries, which had been concluded in 1938, was ratified and brought into effect in October, 1940. The benefits of these duty concessions were generalized to various other countries. A similar agreement of 1936 between Chile and Colombia, providing for reciprocal duty concessions, was ratified by Colombia in December, 1940, and now awaits Chilean action.

In an agreement with Colombia, Argentina secured most-favored-nation treatment, in an effort to bring about a more even flow of trade. That motive figured also in a commercial treaty between Cuba and Argentina, signed in December, designed to foster larger Cuban imports of a broad range of Argentine agricultural products and larger Argentine purchases of Cuban tobacco.

A commercial treaty was concluded early in 1940 between Argentina and Brazil, now awaiting ratification, which provides for reciprocal waivers or reduction in duty on a considerable range of each other's distinctive products. In addition to a general undertaking for unconditional most-favored-nation treatment, Argentina bound itself not to follow a policy of barter or compensation agreements that would divert the flow of imports from Brazil of coffee, cacao, rice, maté, tobacco, and lumber, and Brazil undertook the same obligation concerning imports of wheat and flour from Argentina. In October, the Ministers of Finance of Argentina and Brazil agreed to recommend further steps to facilitate trade relations between the two countries, including the clearing up of existing obstacles to the full sale of certain products of each in the other's territory. A novel proposal contemplated a reciprocal guaranty for ten years of no protective duties against new products, the manufacture of which might be undertaken in either country, with similar minimizing of competition in products considered distinctive to one of the two countries.

Much was heard of the plans for a regional conference of the River Plate countries to assemble at Montevideo in late January, 1941, at which the representatives of Argentina, Brazil, Uruguay, Paraguay, and Bolivia were to consider various projects for facilitating trade between their nationals. Special measures are contemplated for economic aid to the landlocked republics of Bolivia and Paraguay, in a particularly depressed condition since the Chaco war. Considerable advance interest has been expressed also in the general American Conference of Associations of Commerce and Production, planned for Montevideo in May, 1941, which is expected to give impetus to business coöperation in inter-American trade matters.

Thus, the past year has seen the resort to an unusual variety of trade control measures affecting Latin America, and the putting forward of a still greater range of projects, for both the immediate support and the ultimate improvement of the commercial relations of the American Republics, among themselves and with outside countries. Some of them will probably prove transitory or of doubtful feasibility. Many plans are still in the exploratory stage, and in fact, by their very nature, some of the most impressive proposals are designed for a long-term improvement rather than for relief of the pressure of surpluses or of other immediate situations. Moreover, much will depend upon developments during the period ahead in the European war.

However, it is notable that, under the stress of a war emergency, the basic trade problems and possibilities of the various Latin American countries are being made the subject of more searching study than ever before, and within the framework of a heightened concept of continental interrelations. The impetus given to new ideas and bold experimentation may, in time, profoundly affect the economic development and commercial orientation, as well as the trade control programs, of the American Republics.

1941

YEAR OF COMMERCIAL DETERIORATION IS CLIMAXED BY PEARL HARBOR AND WORLD-WIDE WAR

Far East

Japanese attacks close off already shrunken Far East trade.—The Japanese attacks on the American, British, and Dutch territories in the Pacific Ocean beginning December 7, 1941, which converted the existing conflicts in Europe and in China into World War II, also broke the few remaining trade ties between the principal overseas countries and Japan and the Asiatic areas under its control.

Even before the outbreak of the war in the Pacific, however, the foreign trade of Japan and of most of China had shrunk to a fraction of its normal volume, and the main currents of their overseas commerce had practically dried up. A progressive deterioration in Far Eastern trade relations with the outside world had been taking place since shortly after the beginning of "the China Incident" in the summer of 1937. The decline proceeded slowly for a time, but culminated during 1941 in a rapid series of final constrictions, self-imposed and external. The military events of December, 1941, simply marked the formal close of the chapter.

Since October, 1937, three months after its invasion of China, Japan had been subjecting its own foreign trade to a system of license restrictions. Certain foreign products were prohibited altogether. A long list of others could be imported only under license, and a group of specified Japanese products were not to be exported without special permission. By successive expansions of these lists, and the tightening of its general exchange control, Japan had sought during the last few years increasingly to restrict the country's purchasing power for imported products to materials and equipment regarded essential to its military program and to certain of its basic industries. Many consumers' staples which were imported into Japan, or dependent upon imported materials, have been closely rationed for several years.

However, certain industrial materials which Japan wished particularly to acquire, for current use or for stock-piling, became increasingly difficult to obtain from abroad during the past year or so. This was due partly to the increased demand for the very same products for the enlarging defense programs of the British Empire and the United States, and partly to the gradual extension and tightening of the export control systems of the United States (later applied also to the Philippines), of the major British areas, of the Netherlands Indies, and of the various republics of Latin America. During the past year also Japan's principal remaining channel of trade with Europe was cut off, as will appear later.

Japan aims at self-sufficient regional economic bloc under her direction.—Meanwhile, apparently in the expectation of a more limited participation in world trade during the period ahead, many pivotal Japanese industries were undergoing consolidation and extensive readjustments which were designed, among other things, to reduce their high dependence upon foreign countries as sources of their materials and as markets for their products. The conduct of foreign trade was gradually concentrated into a limited number of governmentally controlled associations. The dominant objective was the adaptation of the Japanese economic structure to the government's military program and to its project for establishing a more self-contained regional economic bloc, to operate under Japanese direction, and expected to comprise a large part of Eastern Asia. This goal was given the name of the "Greater East Asia Co-Prosperity Sphere."

The movement of goods into and out of Manchuria and North China has for a number of years been subject to a tightening system of license and exchange restrictions, operated by quasi-military Japanese authorities. Imports were held down to indispensables and, to conserve foreign exchange, were supplied so far as possible from within "the yen bloc," the term applied to combined area of the Japanese Empire, Manchuria, and North China. Exports were strictly controlled, largely channeled to Japan, and their profits partly drawn off through arbitrary exchange rates and other official devices. The resulting hardships upon the population of the occupied or blockaded areas of China, in the form of extreme shortages of necessities and price inflation, have been matters of common newspaper report.

By discriminatory operation of the various measures of control, Western trading firms and enterprises were being progressively crowded out. The import and export trade of occupied China was increasingly diverted into the hands of certain Japanese firms or Japanese-sponsored organizations, designated by the military authorities, who are reported to regard goods moving in foreign trade as a particularly suitable source of revenue for their purposes.

In March, 1941, a revision of the Japanese customs law authorized the lowering or waiving of import duties on the products of regions "in propinquity" to Japan. No reports have thus far been received of any formal steps being taken under this authority toward the establishment of a frankly preferential trade relationship between Japan and the occupied portions of China.

Overseas trade with the unoccupied regions of China, which the Chungking authorities sought to foster, continued to be carried on in substantial volumes, both ways. The trade moved partly through the ports of Central and South China, although precariously, and increasingly through Rangoon and overland via the Burma Road, the principal entry route for Lend-Lease products from the United States, and the export channel for the metals and other "free Chinese" products bound overseas. The inland routes of trade with Russia and Siberia also continued to be used, but little is known regarding the volume of traffic moving over them.

German invasion of Russia plus British blockade cut Japan's trade routes.—The German invasion of Russia on June 22, 1941, closed the overland route for Japanese trade with Europe. The British naval blockade had made the ocean routes unsafe for over a year. It is reported that substantial quantities of tropical products and other Asiatic raw materials had been regularly procured by Japan, and shipped to Germany and other European destinations over the Trans-Siberian railroad, in return for German military equipment and other European manufactures moving eastward for disposition by Japan.

The Russo-German conflict also cut down the possible volume of Japanese trade with Russia itself, despite the new Russo-Japanese commercial agreement concluded earlier that very month, which contemplated an increased trade turnover between them in their distinctive products. Just before the outbreak of that conflict Japan had given up as a failure its strenuous negotiations with the Netherlands Indies, in the course of which it had sought assurance of being supplied with exceptional quantities of various raw materials, part of which was quite obviously for reshipment to Germany.

Early in July, 1941, Japan apparently reversed its previous policy of seeking to promote exports to outside countries for the purpose of acquiring foreign exchange with which to pay for necessary imports. Restrictions upon the exportation of all classes of commodities were authorized, and the customs clearance of all shipments to other than yen-bloc destinations was suddenly suspended. This was declared to be preparatory to working out a revised foreign trade schedule, based upon equalizing the exports to individual non-yen-bloc countries with the imports obtainable from each such country.

United States, British Empire, and Netherlands Indies apply economic sanctions to Japan.—Before the end of that month, however, the United States, the British Empire, and the Netherlands Indies ordered the freezing of all Japanese assets in their territories as an expression of protest against the further Japanese encroachment upon French Indo-China. This drastic action practically put an end to the trade of Japan, and to a large extent also of occupied China, with this important group of countries. Taken together, they had constituted the source of about three-fourths of all Japanese imports from outside the yen bloc, and of an even greater proportion of the materials essential to Japanese military and industrial operations. This appears to be the first instance of thoroughgoing application of economic sanctions upon an aggressor country, through the concerted trade control measures on the part of its major suppliers.

During the months following these credit-freezing orders and until the outbreak of the war in the Pacific in December, Japan was perforce confined in its trade relations mainly to the yen bloc. Despite the reported accumulations in Japan of substantial reserves of many foreign commodities, the cutting off of the accustomed inflow of various raw materials and other products for which the country depended upon overseas was reported to be causing considerable industrial curtailments and consumers' hardships.

Japanese program exemplified by commercial subordination of Indo-China.—The commercial agreement between Japan and French Indo-China, concluded in May, 1941, when Japan had only a limited foothold in that country, afforded an indication of the type of economic relationship which Japan would establish with areas entering even partially into its projected co-prosperity sphere. Under the agreement Indo-China undertook to reduce or abolish its existing duties on the principal products of Japan and was to receive "favorable" customs treatment for its products in Japan. More important was the undertaking by Indo-China to send Japan practically its entire surplus of rice and to authorize the shipment of at least certain specified quantities of the other foods and raw materials produced in the country. Apparently to facilitate this canalization, the Indo-Chinese Government later in the year prohibited exports from the colony to all destinations other than Japan without special license.

In return, Japan was to supply Indo-China with specified quantities of textiles and other manufactures. However, the unlikelihood of Japanese delivery of these products in sufficient volume to balance the increased quantities of Indo-Chinese products taken—which became the subject of Indo-Chinese official complaint within a few months—was apparently envisaged in the payment arrangements provided. General settlement was to be made through a clearing account, up to a certain amount, but payment for the Indo-Chinese rice, its principal product, was to be blocked for at least a year.

This trade agreement between Japan and French Indo-China closely resembles the similar arrangements set up by Germany with the various countries of continental Europe which came under its control, or had no outside alternative. Further resemblance to the German method of economic penetration of the occupied European areas, particularly in the Balkans, appears in the provisions of this agreement for the admission of Japanese commercial firms into the federation of Indo-Chinese importers and exporters, and for the participation of Japanese capital in agriculture, mining, and hydraulic concessions in that country. How much further Japanese control over the economy and trade of Indo-China was carried after the complete military occupation of the country, toward the close of the year, is not yet known.

British Empire

While British seapower permitted the members of the British Empire[1] to continue to carry on trade with practically all parts of the world

[1] The increasing wartime restrictions on the commercial importation of many products into various of the British Empire areas, here indicated, have resulted in a considerable shift in the composition of their trade with the United States, but not in a curtailment of the total volume.

In fact, there has been a decided increase in the value of the shipments from the United States during the past two years to almost all of the principal British countries, and sizable increases in the importations into the United States from a number of the Empire areas, other than the occupied and secluded countries of Europe and the adjacent African coast—at least until the outbreak of the war with Japan in December—the trade policy of Great Britain shifted during 1941 toward curtailment of volume and selectivity of markets in the matter of exports, and a radically changed program of import procurement, involving much greater dependence upon the United States as the source of its requirements.

United States Lend-Lease Act allows Britain to ease export drive.—The change in official policy amounted to a virtual suspension of the drive for increased exports enjoined upon British producers early in 1940. Large production for export markets was then declared as second in importance only to the production for war purposes. Empire markets would thus be kept supplied without drawing upon nonsterling exchange, and sales to other markets would build up the foreign exchange with which to pay for the increased volume of war materials that needed to be obtained from abroad. However, the recognition soon grew that the production of nonessential civilian commodities for shipment to the sterling areas was as undesirable as supplying them to the home population. Joined with the increasing pressure upon available shipping space, this had led even during 1940 to a selective policy in the official attitude of Great Britain toward exports.

The approval by the United States Congress in March, 1941, of the Lend-Lease Act, authorizing the President to supply necessary products to those countries whose defense he considered essential to America, without requiring current compensation, brought about a fundamental change in the export as well as the import policy of Great Britain. The ability to call upon the huge resources and productive capacity of this country "on open account," removed much of the motive for maintaining a high volume of exports to the United States and other foreign countries for the purpose of building up foreign exchange resources. In fact, it made possible the intensification of the British effort to devote all available materials, capacity, and manpower to production for war purposes, and was followed in

---

notably from Canada, Malaya, and Australia. The declines in restricted commodities have been more than offset by the mounting flow of war equipment and supplies to the British areas, and by the increased importations of strategic and other raw materials from them.

For the second war year, September, 1940–August, 1941, United States exports to the principal British countries as a group were greater than during the preceding year by 848 million dollars (or 50 per cent), and imports from them by 284 million (or 29 per cent). The shipment of Lend-Lease materials accounted for only a minor part of the increase in the exports during that period.

For detailed figures on United States foreign trade during the first two war years, see article in *Foreign Commerce Weekly* for November 22, 1941. Publication of details of United States exports and imports was suspended after September, 1941.

September, 1941, by an announced intention to restrict that country's export trade "to the irreducible minimum necessary to supply or obtain materials essential to the war effort."

A collateral objective has been the desire to avoid any unfair competition with United States exporters, in supplying common markets with materials or products of the types restricted from the United States on the grounds of short supply, or with products similar to those being supplied to Great Britain under Lend-Lease. Approval of British exports to Empire areas is now understood to be largely dependent upon the degree of essentiality of the goods to the receiving country, and in the case of the remaining neutral markets—particularly of Latin America—upon the amount of essential foodstuffs or materials which those countries can furnish in return, and for which Great Britain can arrange shipping.

Volume of goods supplied Britain under Lend-Lease far exceeds normal trade.—It has been upon British import policy that the adoption of the Lend-Lease principle by the United States in 1941 has had the most marked influence, constituting as it does the boldest and overshadowing development in the field of international economic relations since the outbreak of the war. Within less than a year, an aggregate of about 13 billions has been authorized for expenditure by the President for the benefit of countries regarded eligible for such aid.

Up to the end of November the total Lend-Lease aid rendered amounted to 1,200 million dollars, of which about 600 millions represented the value of products actually exported. With the largest part of Lend-Lease funds still in the allocation and production stages, the Lend-Lease aid actually rendered had reached a monthly total of 283 millions by November, 1941, and was steadily rising.

The major part of the Lend-Lease funds allocated during 1941 was for the account of Great Britain, and some measure of their relative magnitude is afforded by a comparison with the value of our normal exports. The Lend-Lease appropriations voted by the end of the year amounted to over three times the annual value of all merchandise exported from the United States to all countries during recent years, and to close to five times the combined exports from the United States to the entire British Empire, the Soviet Union, China, and the Netherlands Indies during the second war year, which included the heavy shipments made during that period against the cash purchases by the British and other foreign buying commissions. The value of combined imports into the United States from this group of countries during that period was equivalent to only about 13 per cent of the total Lend-Lease aid authorized during 1941.

While the bulk of the defense aid is to consist of military equipment and supplies, close to 3.5 billion dollars have been designated in the appropriation acts for "agricultural, industrial, and other commodities and articles." The amount thus earmarked for nonmilitary supplies alone under Lend-Lease is greater than the value of the total United States exports to the areas cited during the second year of the war, which included large shipments of war materials.

With the waiver of the requirement for current payment, and the legislative earmarking of substantial funds for the purpose, Great Britain has during recent months been calling for sizable quantities of certain foodstuffs, industrial materials, and manufactured products of nonmilitary character. The importation of many of these products into Great Britain had until recently been severely curtailed or prohibited from the United States.

The foodstuffs being procured for shipment to Great Britain under Lend-Lease, which constitute the greater part of the nonmilitary supplies, consist largely of high-protein products which have not normally been exported to that country or in anything like the quantities now called for. This has required the United States Department of Agriculture to set increased production goals for American farmers or processors of these products during the period ahead, goals which have in mind also provision for postwar foreign relief needs, and for a long-term program of improved nutrition for the American people.

While the various parts of the British Empire and certain allied countries are also being drawn upon heavily for the provisioning of Great Britain, the shipping shortage and the need for convoyed sailings are understood to have influenced the considerable concentration upon satisfying such British import requirements from United States and Canada, the short crossings allowing quick voyage turn-around of the ships available.

Empire areas tighten import controls in support of war program.—The various countries of the British Empire tightened their local measures of trade control during 1941 in general support of the program of Great Britain just sketched. Broadly viewed, the developments in the measures and objectives of the trade policies of the different Empire areas since the outbreak of the war in September, 1939, have followed much the same line of progression, although with appreciable variation as to intensity and timing.

The early months of the war were usually marked by the fairly general installation of exchange control and of an import-licensing system. Since conservation of foreign exchange was then the prime objective, the principal restriction took the form of curtailing the importation of a gradually expanding range of products from nonsterling or non-Empire areas, particularly luxury articles and those replaceable at home or by purchases within the Empire. Under the intensified military activity and the increased sinking of merchant vessels during 1940, the scope of permitted imports even from other Empire countries began to be curtailed into a number of these areas, in order to conserve shipping space and to reduce the civilian call upon materials better utilized for war production.

During the past year further steps were taken in various British Dominions and colonies to curtail the local consumption of many articles now regarded as dispensable, so as to make available all possible funds and productive resources for purposes related to the war. Broadening and tightening of the restrictions upon the importation of foreign products were the principal methods used. Additionally certain Empire areas sought to cut down their people's purchases of particular classes of goods, even if domestically producible, by sales taxes of sizable amounts, by limiting the quantities of metals or other materials available to their producers, and, in special cases, by prohibiting their production for civilian use.

While moving in the same direction, in general support of the wartime program of the United Kingdom, the different parts of the British Empire showed considerable variation in the character of the particular foreign trade control measures taken during 1941, especially in the Eastern areas.

Thus, Australia has been tightening its wartime restrictions on imports with each successive quarter, by expanding the list of prohibited articles and by curtailing the quotas assigned to others. For over two years this system had been distinctly limited to imports from nonsterling areas, although there had been intimations that sterling resources might also have to be conserved. In December, 1941, the Australian import restriction regime was made applicable also to several hundred classes of goods from most Empire sources and, in the majority of cases, their importation was entirely prohibited.

New Zealand, which had been restricting imports from all sources for several years, announced well in advance that its import-licensing schedule for 1942 would call for limiting allocations to 50 per cent in value of that granted for a given country during 1940 except in special cases. For a considerably increased number of items, it was indicated, license applications would be considered individually as to country of supply.

With each of the several successive extensions of the British Indian import license control during 1941, ranges of additional products from non-Empire sources came under restriction. The administration of the control system has also been reported as gradually tightening, although not uniformly at all ports. While conservation of dollar exchange for more essential uses still appears the dominant objective of the import licensing system of British India, for the first time during the past year its more drastic application was officially urged as an effective means of directly curtailing consumption.

The Union of South Africa was exceptional among the Empire areas in not ordering a general system of license control upon imports from nonsterling sources until September, 1941.

For the declared purpose of better apportionment of foreign supplies of metals, machinery, and other essential products, now increasingly difficult to obtain from the United Kingdom or the United States, the principal sources, the authorities in a number of the larger British areas are reported to be calling for the concentration of such foreign orders in the hands of government agencies. These agencies plan to place the combined orders through their official purchasing missions abroad, after clearing on their essential character with the authorities of Great Britain.

Canada and United States coördinate production programs to aid democracies.—The movement between Canada and the United States of the specialized materials and equipment which each is best able to supply, has been considerably facilitated during the past year, despite the tightening of the general export control systems of both governments. Joint committees have been set up to work out the implementation of the Hyde Park statement of April 20, in which President Roosevelt and Prime Minister Mackenzie King jointly agreed upon a general program for the most prompt and effective utilization of the resources and productive facilities of the two countries, for the purposes both of common defense and of coördinating assistance "to Great Britain and the other democracies."

To this end the Canadian Government extended the principles of its drawback law so as to waive the payment of duties and taxes, or to provide for their refund, upon imports of munitions and supplies for the fulfillment of war contracts placed by the Canadian Ministry of Munitions and Supply or on behalf of the United Kingdom or any allied government. In connection with the general Canadian price control program inaugurated on December 1, the Canadian Government has announced that it would either pay import subsidies or reduce its duties and taxes if the price of foreign products whose continued importation it regarded as essential should rise above the price ceilings set for them in the Canadian market.

British extend support undertakings for Empire staples.—The program initiated early in the war, whereby the British Government undertook to purchase, or to underwrite, the entire exportable surplus or large quantities of a wide range of primary products of the Dominions and colonies, was substantially continued during 1941. Outstanding among the developments in this field during the past year were the identical coöperative arrangements entered into for dealing with the surplus problems of Australia and New Zealand for the period of the war.

In addition to the undertakings on the part of the British Ministry of Food to purchase and pay for the produce that could be shipped, it was arranged that reserve stocks of storable foodstuffs were to be created up to agreed quantities. The financial burden of acquiring and holding these stocks is to be shared equally between the governments, and the payments are to be fixed with a view to keeping the industries operating efficiently while avoiding the creation of unmanageable surpluses. Apparently recognizing that plans for support of primary products may require agreements involving a large number of countries, it is provided that the Dominion governments are to be ready to collaborate in any discussions within the British Commonwealth or internationally to consider marketing or related problems.

The privileges of trading freely within the Empire as members of the sterling area have by the end of 1941 been extended by Great Britain to Egypt, Iraq, the Belgian Congo, the Free French areas, and Iceland. The Netherlands Indies have been accorded that status by British India, Australia, and other Eastern areas. Revised economic agreements were entered into with certain colonies of Free French Africa and with the Belgian Congo, whereby Great Britain undertook to purchase their principal crops and raw-material outputs and to furnish essential supplies for local consumption.

Latin America

A year ago, the mounting pressure of undisposable surpluses had stood out as the dominant economic problem of most of Latin America. With the fall of France in June, 1940, and the extension of the British blockade to most of the European continent, the countries of Latin America had practically lost a group of markets that used to buy their products to the amount of about 500 million dollars annually. This brought about the tightening of import restrictions by many of these countries, and stimulated the consideration of a wide range of measures affecting their trade and general economy.

Increased United States purchases and support programs avert economic crises.—During 1941, that situation was substantially relieved, mainly through the sharply increased purchases by the United States. The need for relief was intensified by the curtailment which Great Britain has had to make in the quantities of certain Latin American products which it could continue to take. The expansion of compensating markets within the American hemisphere for many—not all—of the Latin American staples and for certain secondary products, and at distinctly improved prices, resulted in the building up of sizable export balances during the year on the part of almost all of the Latin American countries. The consequent improvement in their general economic condition and prospects, and particularly in their foreign exchange position, has allowed most of them to make some relaxation in their exchange controls or other forms of restrictions upon imports.

The economic crisis that had threatened in 1940—particularly in those countries of South America which are especially dependent upon overseas markets for their prosperity—was largely averted by a combination of measures on the part of the United States, private and governmental. The expanding domestic industrial program led to greatly increased commercial purchases by United States firms of wool, copper, hides, and other Latin American staples. By special arrangements with certain Latin American countries, to be discussed later, agencies of the United States Government undertook to purchase large quantities, if not the entire output, of various nonferrous metals and other strategic and critical materials. In doing this, four purposes were in view: the needs of the defense program, for stock-piling, to preclude their reaching members of the Axis, and general relief for the economic position of the other American Republics.

Under the inter-American coffee-quota agreement of October, 1940, the United States, the principal consumer, afforded the fourteen coffee-producing countries of the Western Hemisphere assured markets, somewhat enlarged in volume, and at improved prices. At the end of the year the United States announced the purchase of the entire Cuban sugar surplus of 1942, at slightly above prevailing prices. It is to be taken in the form of raw sugar and of molasses for industrial alcohol, and the purchase is to be partly for British account.

The increased purchases of each other's products on the part of some of the Latin American countries themselves operated as an auxiliary measure of relief. This appears to have been the result both of the wartime difficulties of obtaining supplies from the usual sources and of the newly stimulated sentiment for closer hemispheric relations in many fields. Although the aggregate value of such inter-Latin American trade is still a relatively small part of the total, the recent steps in its expansion constitute a notable development.

General financial improvement allows relaxation of import controls.— The shifts in the trade of Latin America with the United States—now clearly the principal market as well as supplier—became the determining factor during 1941 in the general trade position and economic prospects for practically all of the southern republics. This applied even to those South American countries whose major trade relations had normally been with the United Kingdom and continental Europe. At the rate at which the trade had been moving up to the fall of 1941, it was estimated that, for the entire year, the total value of Latin American exports to the United States would exceed a billion dollars. The increase in purchases by the United States would thus appear to have offset in value almost the entire loss to Latin America from the practical closing off of the continent of Europe.

Sales of United States products to the other American Republics increased somewhat during 1941 over the level reached during 1940 but, for reasons to be later indicated, have not risen at the same rate as the flow during the past year of Latin American commodities northward. The result has been a striking shift in the trade balance of Latin America as a whole with the United States, from an import excess of 107 million dollars during 1940 to an export balance of about 150 million during 1941, effecting a net improvement in the Latin American merchandise balance with the United States within the year of about 250 million.

The export balance has naturally been uneven in its distribution and, in the case of certain countries, reflected some reduction in imports as well as an expansion in exports. However, there was evidence through the year that this improvement in their general trade position, joined with the influx of considerable refugee capital into certain of the countries, has afforded most Latin American Republics more ample exchange for current import needs, has given increased stability to their currencies, and in some cases allowed the building up of sizable exchange reserves against future contingencies.

As indicated, the improvement in their general foreign exchange position during 1941 enabled many of the Latin American governments to ease the official conditions of importing foreign goods. Thus, Argentina took several steps during the year, even before the conclusion of the reciprocal trade agreement with the United States in October, to furnish exchange for the importation of certain American products previously barred, to accord more favorable exchange rates in the payment for others, and generally to minimize the formalities. The Argentine system of prior exchange permits was abolished in July. Several other Latin American governments either lifted the restrictions on exchange permits for the importation of certain products, announced increased allotments for specified classes of imports from the United States, or were reported, in general, to be granting dollar exchange more freely.

From quite a number of American Republics in which considerable delays in obtaining remittances for imports had been the common experience, even when no formal control of exchange was in operation, reports during 1941 told increasingly of shorter or no delays, at least on products in the categories regarded as essential. Some of the smaller countries reorganized their control systems, under plans calling for devoting certain shares of the increased volume of exchange being currently created for the clearing up of overdue obligations. Permits for new imports were then granted according to the amounts of exchange remaining, but possession of an import permit now carries assurance that exchange will be available when due.

Where systems of exchange priorities had been earlier established, according to the purpose of the funds or the relative essentiality of the products to be imported, they were generally maintained. However, Colombia shifted many commodity classifications under its import control with a view to fostering local industries, by granting lower exchange rates on necessary foreign materials, and by making more onerous the importation of finished products competing with domestic manufactures. Venezuela was reported as intending to use its exchange control to withhold permits at the favorable official exchange rate from imports competing with local producers, however small.

Among most of the countries of South America, exchange control has, during recent years, become the dominant mechanism for foreign trade regulation, and changes in import duties or other controls have been less common or less determining of the course of trade. During the past year, however, Uruguay ordered the free admission of certain consumers' staples, up to specified amounts, and authorized the executive to reduce or remove duties on articles of prime necessity in case of scarcity or undue price advances. Paraguay reduced its duty on a wide range of products, in order to keep down retail prices of import staples.

Chile charged its Commissariat of Subsistence and Prices with direct control of the foreign trade as well as the production of certain textiles, to check the mounting prices of clothing.

A different motive for tariff changes appeared in the Peruvian 20 per cent increase in the existing import duties, except on foodstuffs, and the sliding-scale surcharge on the export duties, moving up with the rise in export prices. Additional revenue was given as the purpose; the Peruvian duties are specific in form and the exchange value of the sol had fallen. Moreover, the prices obtainable for Peruvian export products were going up. Ecuador allowed importers to use half of their import quotas for the first quarter of 1942 during November and December of 1941, and again permitted the importation of certain products previously restricted as dispensable.

United States undertakes to facilitate supplying essential import needs of Latin America.—The movement toward liberalization of import controls, which the improved foreign exchange position made possible during the year for many countries of Latin America, was partly offset by other factors. These prevented the easement being fully utilized and reflected in a generally increased volume of importations, particularly from the United Kingdom and the United States, the two principal accessible sources. Under the pressure upon shipping, and the need for devoting materials and productive capacity to its own wartime needs and those of the Empire, Great Britain has been moving toward a more limited and selective program of exports to most countries. The adoption of the Lend-Lease program by the United States in the spring of 1941 led Great Britain to concentrate the procurement of its import requirements heavily upon the United States, and to reduce the volume of its exports to Latin America, especially to the more distant republics.

The orders from Latin America directed to the United States for many manufactured products, as well as industrial materials and equipment, grew in volume as the year proceeded. The main purposes seemed to be twofold: to replace supplies previously obtained elsewhere, and to allow carrying through new industrial and construction projects stimulated by the war situation. However, the aggregate volume of these orders soon came to exceed the ability of United States producers to supply in full, owing to the mounting needs for these very classes of products for the country's own defense program, and for shipment to Great Britain and other nations resisting aggression. Concern grew in various of the southern republics that important new projects, essential national industries, and in some cases even public utilities might be slowed down or suspended because of the difficulties of obtaining necessary imported materials, equipment, or replacement parts.

However, in pursuance of its policy of maintaining the economic stability of the Western Hemisphere, the United States Government early declared its intention "to facilitate insofar as is feasible the exportation to the other American nations of at least their essential import requirements."

Interlocking hemisphere controls to prevent undesired reëxportations.—At the same time, it seemed important to ensure that the products so exported reached their desired destination and no other, and that the strategic materials and resources of the hemisphere were utilized in the continental defense. It was therefore urged by the United States that these objectives of interest to all the American Republics might best be realized by the creation of an inter-American system of export control, combining restrictions upon shipments outside of the Western Hemisphere, with the maximum of free movement within the hemisphere that is compatible with defense requirements. This situation led to a threefold program of interlocking trade control measures and arrangements between the countries of Latin America and the United States.

While varying in precise scope and form, as each country proceeded to take action in accordance with its own constitutional procedure, by the fall of 1941 all of the twenty republics of Latin America had adopted systems for restricting the reëxportation of specified lists of materials and products essential to defense, or of all products subject to control in the country of their origin, and usually also the exportation of similar products of domestic origin. In the meantime the United States had gradually extended its own system of export license control, initiated in July, 1940, until it included practically all commodities.

United States allocates scarce products on basis of joint requirements surveys.—In recognition of the parallel measures of control on the part of the other American Republics, the United States began to enlarge the list of controlled products that could be freely exported to them under "general license," which required no prior individual application or loss of time. As the industrial organization of the United States became more and more subject to rigid priorities and allocations control, however, the emphasis shifted from simple export licenses to more direct procedures. In the case of products for which the increasing demands of the United States defense program and Lend-Lease aid threatened inadequate supplies for civilian needs, organizations were established in Washington to give special consideration to the more important requirements of the Latin American countries, so as to secure for them, as far as possible, the necessary clearance on priorities as well as the export licenses.

As distinct stringencies developed toward the end of 1941 for certain products in high demand, the United States authorities recognized the need, in certain cases, for going beyond the granting of permission to export, or even of priority ratings to suppliers. Surveys were undertaken of the essential import needs of each of the other American Republics for a broad range of industrial materials and equipment as a basis for determining the specific amounts that could be allocated to them from the limited supplies. Tin plate was the subject of the first of this series of allocations. Serious shortage had developed in the southern republics, particularly for the canning of food products, and an aggregate of 218,000 metric tons was set aside in December for shipment to Latin America during the year ahead.[2]

The coöperation of the governments of the other American Republics was enlisted in these surveys of their over-all import requirements, commercial as well as official, for the essential products in short supply. Prospective importers were directed to apply to their own governments for certificates of recommendation. In a number of the Latin American countries it is contemplated that the governmental agency designated to centralize this work, and to pass upon the relative urgency of the various import orders for license purposes, may also have a hand in supervising the distribution within the particular country of what the United States authorities approve for shipment.

United States makes bulk purchase agreements for Latin American strategic products.—In urging that an inter-American system of export control be established over strategic materials, and others produced in the American Republics, that are important in national and continental defense, the United States Government declared that its appropriate agencies "stand ready to give consideration to purchasing supplies of such commodities as a regular part of its program for building up its own defense reserves and supplies." A beginning in this direction had been made during 1940 in the agreement with Bolivia, guaranteeing that the United States would

[2] This was followed, in the middle of January, by the announcement of specific allocations, for the first quarter of 1942, on 26 of the 110 commodities for which the United States plans to make definite allotments to the Latin American countries.

purchase specific quantities of certain minerals, notably tin, for which refining facilities were being built in the United States.

During 1941, the negotiations for three broad agreements of this character were concluded with Brazil, Mexico, and Peru; and discussions of similar arrangements with Argentina, Chile, and other Latin American governments were reported active at the close of the year. While the agreements varied somewhat in their specific terms, that concluded with Mexico in July illustrates the general nature of the series. That government undertook to restrict the exportation of certain of its strategic and critical materials exclusively to points within the Western Hemisphere. The United States undertook that its official agencies will buy, at the market prices current at time of purchase, any quantity of these commodities not sold to private industry in the Western Hemisphere. Included among the materials covered by the Mexican agreement were antimony, graphite, lead, mercury, tungsten, tin, zinc, and henequen.

Taken together, this series of interacting trade control measures worked out by the American Republics during the past year constituted an encouraging example of the possibilities of coöperative action on the part of independent countries for reciprocal economic support. In the voluntary action of the respective governments, and in the planning of each measure with a view to the benefit of the individual participating countries as well as in the light of the broad economic strategy for the group, this inter-American program stands out in striking contrast to the trade arrangements entered into during the same period by the countries on the continent of Europe, under the "leadership" of Germany.

Local support of undisposable surpluses and diversification of production.—As earlier indicated, the enlarged purchases by the United States of the surpluses of the various Latin American countries did not extend to all surplus products. They could hardly apply to cereals, cotton, and other commodities of which the United States was itself a surplus producer. The purchases of some of these products by the United Kingdom and, for a time by Japan, tapered off during the year, although for different reasons. However, a number of the governments of Latin America adopted or extended measures for domestic support of certain undisposable surpluses. This program was observed also during the preceding year, but was facilitated during 1941 by the more ample funds at the disposal of the respective governments from the enlarged sales of other products to the United States.

Thus, the Argentine Government bought up the bulk of the current crops of wheat and linseed at guaranteed minimum prices. The requirement enforced by Argentina the preceding year, that prospective importers of fuel must undertake to purchase specified quantities of domestic corn for burning, was continued. Brazil set fixed prices for wheat flour, and continued its requirement that millers mix Brazilian mandioca in grinding the wheat. That government also granted loans to cotton growers at fixed minimums.

The revenue derived partly from the coffee tax imposed in connection with the inter-American coffee agreement enabled the government of Colombia to buy up, and destroy or store, surpluses remaining after filling the United States quota and small sales elsewhere. Paraguay offered to buy all surplus sugar at a fixed minimum price, and Uruguay proposed to do the same for wheat.

The stimulus given to the expansion of old industries or the establishment of new lines of production has been widely noted as one of the outstanding reactions in many of the Latin American countries to the war situation. Governments have been eager to assist efforts to diversify their country's economy, and especially to expand manufacturing, in small as well as major lines. As various manufactured products from abroad, particularly staple consumers' goods, became increasingly difficult to obtain, there has naturally been an incentive for their production locally, and the high cost or absence of the usual imported products automatically afforded such enterprises the equivalent of additional tariff protection. During the past year, further measures were taken by several of these governments to foster this movement.

These measures have included the granting of duty and tax exemptions on industrial or agricultural equipment and materials from abroad, making exchange readily available for their importation, or assuring protective duties on the finished products. The use of their foreign trade control systems for this purpose by the Colombian and Venezuelan governments, has already been mentioned. In several of the larger republics, the expansion of manufacturing in a growing number of lines, notably the processing of local materials, appeared to count upon the near-by markets as well as upon the needs of the domestic population. The increasing prominence of cotton textiles among the exports of Brazil and Mexico to other American countries well illustrates this tendency. The government of Argentina sought authority to pay drawback of duties on foreign materials and products embodied in Argentine manufactures exported to other American areas.

Long-term moves for closer inter-American economic relations.—In addition to the increased current trade between the republics of Latin America and the United States, and among themselves, that is being stimulated primarily by the wartime needs and developments, the impetus given during the preceding year to the consideration of various long-term arrangements for closer inter-American economic relations gained increased momentum during 1941.

Outstanding was the trade agreement between Argentina and the United States, announced in October and brought into operation in November. It represented the successful conclusion of exceptionally difficult negotiations that had been carried on intermittently for some years.

In many respects, the agreement resembles those previously concluded between other Latin American countries and the United States, in providing for reciprocal concessions and assurances regarding duties, quotas, and other forms of import control, and on a nondiscriminatory basis. Additionally, it carries a number of special provisions and reservations, some of which may not continue long after the close of the war. Many observers regard the Argentine–United States agreement as less significant, however, for the direct commercial results to be expected during the period immediately ahead—since other forces are currently more determining of the course of trade—than for the fact that these two leading American governments have been able to work out a basis for coöperative trade relations along liberal lines, and have laid a sound foundation for their postwar commerce.

The second supplementary trade agreement between Cuba and the United States, concluded in December, 1941, broadened and deepened various tariff and other concessions in favor of the other's products provided for in the original agreement of 1934. Preliminary discussions looking to reciprocal trade agreements with the United States were carried on during the year by a number of other Latin American governments, notably Uruguay, Peru, and Mexico.

The facilities of the Export-Import Bank of the United States continued to be made available during 1941, both to assist current trade transactions with the other American Republics and for selected long-term developmental projects, notably highway construction, and thus contributed their influence upon the course of inter-American trade.

Among the Latin American countries themselves, the past year has witnessed exceptional activity in the way of intergovernmental negotiations and visits of official missions, to discuss measures for the stimulation of increased trade among them and closer economic relations in other respects. In many cases appreciable progress was reported toward the planning or actual negotiation of commercial treaties for the reduction of trade barriers, of financial or credit agreements, or of arrangements for improved transportation and transit facilities.

Without attempting to describe the many negotiations during 1941 between various sets of the Latin American countries, certain characteristics of the commercial agreements might be mentioned. The majority of those concluded or discussed were built around the traditional exchange of reductions or stabilizations of duties on selected products of particular interest to the contracting countries, and were usually accompanied by broad assurances of unconditional most-favored-nation treatment in trade control matters generally. In a number of cases, however, distinct efforts were noted to limit the benefits of concessions to neighboring countries exclusively to them, or to establish the idea that more distant countries should waive their most-favored-nation rights to the special tariff treatment or other advantages which may later be granted to adjacent countries.

Recognition of the propriety of special concessions between contiguous countries was urged particularly at the regional conference of the River Plate countries, held at Montevideo early in the year. Here interest centered upon facilitating measures of special economic aid to the landlocked republics of Bolivia and Paraguay, still in a depressed state following the Chaco war. A more ambitious proposal put forward at that conference, looking to the eventual formation of a customs union in the River Plate region, was simply recommended for study by the participating countries.

The idea spread during the year for the establishment of mixed commissions by various sets of American governments, either to supervise the operation of existing agreements or to study the possibilities of closer economic relations between them, through trade facilities, credit grants, developmental projects, or transport arrangements.

Among the inter-Latin American trade agreements of 1941, special prominence was given to that signed between Argentina and Brazil in November, implementing a proposal of the preceding year. Broadly, it was designed to afford a wider market area for the productive forces of the individual countries than their own populations afforded, starting with the nascent industries. Specifically, these two governments agreed to foster the establishment in their countries of industrial and agrarian activities which did not yet exist in either, and undertook not to impose any duties or other restrictions in their territories upon the products of these new industries for a period of ten years. Similar liberal treatment is to be given to commodities now produced in only one of the two countries, or of no great economic importance in the other. There was also envisaged the possible later application of this principle to competitive products, where existing duties can be gradually reduced without injury to the respective national economies. The agreement now awaits ratification.

Continental Europe

The trade policies and arrangements that have been operating inside Europe during 1941 are of significance for the United States mainly as an advance exemplification of the pattern of the international trading system and general economic structure which Germany would set up, if it were in permanent control of any large part of the European continent.

Since most of the European countries are now either engaged in war or under control of the Axis, and moreover are rendered practically inaccessible to overseas commerce by the British blockade, the specific changes in their trade control measures and relations during the past year are of little immediate commercial interest, except to the peoples in other parts of the Continent that are still reachable.

The present review will therefore be general in character. It will first sketch the recent developments in the progressive seclusion of the European continent, the restrictions upon trade with Europe imposed from without, and the further steps taken toward the economic absorption of certain areas by the Axis. This will be followed by an analysis of the current trade relations between Germany and the occupied countries, the nature of the principal commercial arrangements between the European countries during the past year, German pressure upon the remaining neutrals through trade agreements, the trade arrangements between Italy and the other European countries, and, finally, of the increasing centralization of European trade settlements in Berlin.

In many respects, the present conditions of trading on the Continent are of an emergency character and, in detail, largely transitory. Fundamentally, however, they appear as advance moves toward the proposed "New European Order" as envisaged by Germany.

Conquests progressively cut off continent from overseas trade.—The extension of the military control of the Axis during the year, through the Balkans and to the Aegean Sea, not only cut off Southeastern Europe from outside trade but made the eastern Mediterranean hazardous for merchant shipping. The German attack upon the Soviet Union closed off the Trans-Siberian railroad, for some time the principal channel of traffic between

Europe and the outside world. Finally, the entrance of Finland into the conflict cut off the thinner line through the Finnish port of Petsamo.

The only "neutral" countries remaining at all open to overseas trade are Sweden, Switzerland, Spain, Portugal, and Turkey. Outside trade with the first four is now narrowly limited by meager shipping facilities, even when no objection is interposed by either Great Britain or Germany, and overseas deliveries to Turkey can now be made only with difficulty or over circuitous routes.

British blockade plus all-American export license controls restrict external supplies.—The maintenance of the British naval blockade continued to restrict closely the overseas trade, in either direction, of Germany and Italy, and of the European areas under their occupation or control. Limited supplies of selected products were permitted to reach the few remaining European neutrals from across the Atlantic, regulated largely by the British navicert system, which established quarterly quotas and called for advance verification of ultimate destination.

These measures were supplemented by the increasingly strict export license systems operated by Great Britain itself, and by the various outlying countries of the British Empire. They found reinforcement in the expanding system of control upon the exportation of essential products developed since the middle of 1940 by the United States. These controls, in turn, were fortified in June, 1941, by the freezing of all United States assets of Germany and Italy, as well as of the occupied countries of Europe. The successive adoption of license controls during the year by the twenty Latin American Republics, upon the exportation of varying lists of products, operated further to tighten the external restrictions upon trade with Europe.

Since the British blockade and navicert system could not be extended so well to the areas on the Pacific Ocean, it was understood that substantial quantities of Asiatic and other materials continued to reach Germany and other European destinations from that direction, partly through the intermediation of Japan, up to the summer of 1941. There was also a movement eastward of European manufactures, for Japan and overseas destinations, although of much smaller volume than the westward flow. The German invasion of the Soviet Union in late June quickly put an end to the delivery of such supplies as that country itself had been shipping to Germany and the rest of Europe.

Further German steps toward commercial absorption of conquered areas.—Few further steps were taken during the past year in the formal process of annexation or incorporation of new territories into the customs areas of the Axis powers, such as had taken place during 1939 and 1940 with regard to Austria, Albania, parts of Czechoslovakia and Poland, certain districts of Belgium, Luxemburg, and Alsace and Lorraine. Aside from the formal setting up of the Croatian part of Yugoslavia as a separate entity, the announced developments of this character during 1941 were mostly in the nature of adjustments in basic changes earlier initiated.

Following the virtual abolition of the tariff frontier between the Netherlands and the Reich at the end of 1940, further price adjustments were ordered in the Netherlands and, on April 1, foreign exchange restrictions on transactions between the two areas were ended. However, in revised form, the former Netherlands system of foreign trade licensing control was reported to be continued in nominal operation. Later in the year, Netherlands products were further channeled toward Germany. All exports to other destinations were made subject to permit, and shortly thereafter the shipment of certain additional commodities to Germany was exempted from Netherlands export licenses.

After a series of adjustments of wages and prices in Bohemia-Moravia to the German levels, the remaining restrictions on the exportation to Germany of certain industrial products of the Protectorate were lifted on July 1. While accomplished by successive steps, the German absorption of Bohemia-Moravia is reported to have been exceptionally drastic and thoroughgoing. Its huge productive installations as well as the disposal of its products are now completely under the control of the occupying authorities.

German exploitation of occupied areas through one-sided trade transactions.—Aside from those countries or provinces annexed and incorporated into the same customs area with Germany (or Italy, in the case of Albania), it has usually been represented that the European countries occupied by the Axis Powers have been permitted to maintain their own fiscal systems and trade control arrangements.

In actual operation, however, it appears that the foreign trade of the occupied areas is being increasingly channelized toward Germany, both as market and as source of supply. Commercial transactions with all other areas are subject to the detailed directions of the occupying authorities.

German military dominance, and the fact that inter-European business is now conducted almost entirely on a compensation or clearing account basis, without the use of foreign exchange, has facilitated the process of drawing off for German use the domestic products of the other countries and the stocks of imported goods on hand. While they take the form of normal purchases for export, and often at seemingly good prices, these transactions have apparently seldom been compensated by shipments of equal value from Germany.

Such meager reports of a reliable character as have come out of Europe during the past year have told repeatedly of heavy drafts by Germany upon the products and stores of most of the other countries on the Continent, for which it gave in return largely promises of future deliveries of various materials and manufactures. Thus, the German press accounts of the prosperity brought to Rumania, as evidenced by the greatly increased record of exports, do not appear to have indicated the disparity between the value of Rumanian exports to Germany and of German return shipments to Rumania. Reports reaching Britain in the fall of 1941 indicated that the ratio was running about 4 to 1.

The mounting credit balances being built up at the Reichsbank by most of the countries of continental Europe apparently represent the formal record—so far as record is kept—of the uncompensated, and often involuntary, shipments of their goods to Germany. In the absence of published statistics of exports and imports, the unofficial reports of acute shortages in most of the European areas, even of products of which the particular country is itself usually a surplus producer, afford practical confirmation of what has been happening. The resort to bread cards in Hungary, to breadless days in Rumania, to rationing of dairy products in Switzerland, and the shortages of fish in Norwegian cities, are cases in point.

A considerable part of the recently increased trade activity on the continent of Europe has consisted of the materials and finished products moving across frontiers under Germany's program of utilizing the manufacturing facilities and trained labor of the other countries for increasing its supplies of military equipment or parts.[8]

This system of the placing out of such war contracts, or the subcontracting arranged by German manufacturers with other European factories, is reported to have extended beyond the industrialized countries of Western Europe and Scandinavia, even to the small metal and household goods plants in the Baltic countries. Apparently this exceptional movement of goods forth and back across frontiers is not subject to the usual duties or other trade controls applying to products for local consumption.

[8] A measure of the extent of this program, as affecting one of the occupied countries, is afforded by a recent report reaching England. More than a quarter of the 1,500,000 workers normally employed in Belgian industry are reported to be now working for Germany. About 200,000 of them have been sent to Germany, and an approximately equal number are working on German orders in Belgian factories.

An extreme instance of the arbitrary exercise of German authority over the economic life of an occupied area through trade control measures appeared in September of the past year, when reports were current that the population of Norway was not "collaborating" as desired. According to the Swedish press, commercial firms in Norway were advised that imports from Germany would be stopped, that machinery already ordered would not be delivered, and that licenses would be granted only in exceptional cases. This occurred at about the same time that all available metals in the country were being diverted to the expanding Norwegian arms industry, working exclusively for German account, and when all wool blankets in Norway were requisitioned for the German armed forces.

Less has been announced with regard to the trade arrangements with the Balkan countries which have come under German control during 1941. It is understood, however, that the German-Rumanian agreement of December, 1940, has been the model by which Germany has already begun to reorganize the economies of Southeastern Europe, so as to "coördinate" their agricultural and industrial production with the requirements of the German market.

The German rigid supervision of external trade of occupied areas.—Since the middle of 1940, the various secluded countries of Europe have been very active in the negotiation and renegotiation of compensation agreements with other reachable countries on the continent, in the effort to develop alternative sources for essential products now unobtainable from overseas. In these agreements, each country usually promised the delivery to the other during the next half year of fixed quantities or values of specified products, up to a set maximum value for the entire trade. In return, the other country undertook shipments of similarly designated products up to a given value—not necessarily of equal value—with payments to be made through a clearing account. So definitely had the emphasis shifted from finding markets to getting needed supplies, that negotiations between certain sets of countries were reported to have fallen through when one of the countries lacked suitable export products of interest to the other.

As earlier intimated, Germany's requirements from the occupied countries, and its trade agreements with them, took precedence over all others. Announcements were made during the year of the conclusion by Germany of revised trade agreements with Italy, Denmark, Bulgaria, and a few others, in addition to certain of the neutrals, to be later mentioned. With most of the occupied countries of Europe, however, no such revisions were reported during 1941. This has raised the supposition that the formalities of negotiating with the nominal governments of the countries under its control are coming to be dispensed with by Germany, when the periodical alterations in the schedules of reciprocal deliveries need to be worked out.[4]

Close German supervision over the negotiations for trade agreements between various pairs of European countries, whenever one of the occupied countries was involved, had been observed during the latter months of 1940. During 1941, this intervention was carried further. Several such trade agreements were reported to have been negotiated recently where German officials alone acted for the governments of the occupied countries. Moreover, it appears to be common practice now for Germany to be giving undertakings which other countries are to carry out. Thus, Germany promised, in its latest negotiations with Switzerland, that that country would get certain quantities of petroleum from Rumania; or, it arranged that Belgium and the Netherlands would get certain deliveries of timber from Finland.

German pressure on neutrals through trade, credit, and price arrangements.—Germany's effort to use its dominant position to obtain one-sided trade advantages from other European countries was apparently not confined to the occupied countries. The revised commercial agreement between Switzerland and Germany, announced at Berne in July, 1941, is reported to have carried a provision that, if "present difficult circumstances continue," the clearing balance (normally about 50 million Swiss francs) might be increased, by advances on the part of the Swiss Government to exporters to Germany, up to a total of 400 million Swiss francs by the end of the year, with a probability of further Swiss advances being required in 1942.

In a similar agreement between Germany and Sweden, concluded in September after prolonged negotiations, Sweden was required to grant Germany an advance in merchandise to the amount of 100 million crowns, to be repaid by German deliveries in 1942.

According to press accounts, the original German request was for a much larger overdraft on the clearing account. Although this was to be a nonrecurrent transaction, when the Swedish-German trade agreement for

[4] This supposition appears to be confirmed by a series of recent articles in the *Frankfurter Zeitung,* purporting to set forth the principles upon which Germany's plans for the new European order were based, which are reported as stating, in effect, that formal statutes are not considered necessary in developing European economic coöperation. The country assuming the leadership is declared to have the duty of determining the special needs and capabilities of the weaker countries, and of taking their interests into consideration.

1942 was concluded late in December, the Swedish press expressed misgivings about the new credits to which Sweden had to agree. Owing to the service due on large old Swedish investments in Germany, the normal balance of payments between the two countries called for a surplus of German exports to Sweden.

The government of Turkey, with a similar experience of German short deliveries on the previous compensation agreement, but with some alternative trade channels open to it, was able to take a firmer stand on the German requests in connection with the commercial agreement concluded in October, 1941. It is understood that it was successful in its insistence that it could not violate the existing Anglo-Turkish agreement, pledging the entire Turkish chromium output to Great Britain until January, 1943, and that no large shipments of Turkish products to Germany would be made until Germany had made delivery, to an equal value, of certain war materials and heavy equipment promised.

A striking feature of the German trade agreements of the past two years with most of the other countries on the Continent has been the lowering of the exchange value of their respective national currencies in terms of the reichsmark, and often more than once. This had the effect of increasing the purchasing power of German money for the products of the other country, and of making German products dearer to its population.

In certain negotiations during 1941 with neutral countries of Europe, German proposals for similar reductions in the general exchange ratios between the currencies were reportedly not accepted. Much the same change in the terms of trade appears to have been obtained in certain cases, however, by holding down the unit prices at which the principal products to be delivered by the other country were to be valued for the purpose of the clearing account, while the prices set upon the German products involved were materially advanced.[5]

Trade arrangements between Italy and other European countries.—Italian trade relations with the various occupied countries of Europe are governed by agreements negotiated between Italy and Germany, and the settlement of accounts between Italy and those countries is now made through the Italo-German clearing account.

[5] In a recent article in the Stockholm *Tidningen,* a notable Swedish economist declares that Sweden's standard of living had been lowered, and points out that "while export prices in 1941 remained constant at a level 40 per cent above the August, 1939, figures, import prices continued to rise. In November, 1941, import prices reached a point 160 per cent above the prewar figures." About three-quarters of Swedish foreign trade has recently been with Germany.

The revised trade agreement of February, 1941, between Germany and Italy themselves provided that, for the duration of the war, there was to be no limitation on exports from either country of materials of military importance, regardless of the state of the trade balance or of the clearing account.

Required trade settlements through Berlin presage "New European Order."—There was carried forward during 1941 the system developed during the preceding year whereby payments for intra-European trade were required by Germany to be made through accounts set up at the German Clearing Office in Berlin. This was to apply not only among the occupied countries, but also between them and a number of the continental countries then still independent.[6]

Since the value of the merchandise delivered from one country to another during a given period seldom corresponded exactly to the value of the products obtained from the second country, however, the unequalized balances in the clearing accounts at Berlin soon called for some multilateral adjustments. These adjustments appear to be arranged in accordance with the discretion of the German economic authorities.

In some cases, the clearing accounts involving a number of countries have been definitely merged. Thus, the new German-Swiss clearing agreement of 1941 was reported as expanded to cover the settlement of accounts also with Alsace, Lorraine, and Luxemburg, as well as Belgium, the Netherlands, and Norway. After the Balkans were overrun, it was officially announced that payments on new commitments between Rumania and Greece, and between Rumania and Serbia, would be cleared through the German-Rumanian clearing account in Berlin. The arrangements for the settlement of accounts between Italy and the occupied countries through the Italo-German clearing agreement have already been mentioned.

These steps to develop a "collective clearing system" for the trade of the European continent, centering at Berlin, form an essential part of the much-discussed German plan for the postwar organization of Europe. As repeatedly indicated by official German spokesmen, this plan envisages the European continent—and whatever adjacent areas can be brought under control—as an economic unit, operating under the leadership and direction

[6] While no complete data are available as to the volume of current inter-European trade, it may be indicative that, according to the semiofficial *Dienst aus Deutschland,* the aggregate value of the transactions recorded during a recent month under this centralized Berlin clearing system, in which fifteen countries are reported to be participating regularly, amounted to only 145 million marks. This is equivalent to a very small fraction of the value of the average monthly inter-European trade before the war.

of Germany. The principal industries in the various countries are to be tied in with the corresponding industries of the Reich, and each country is to adapt its economy to the production of such agricultural, mineral, and manufactured products as are called for by the economic interests of "Greater Germany." The present political helplessness of most of the other European countries, and their practical seclusion from the alternative of trade with overseas countries, are apparently allowing the German economic and technical staffs to make some headway during the war in the direction of this proposed "New European Order."

1942

AS WAR BECOMES GLOBAL NORMAL TRADE RELATIONS ECLIPSED BY EMERGENCY ARRANGEMENTS

FORCES CONTROLLING TRADE WITHIN THE AXIS AND NON-AXIS WORLDS

With the greater part of the world now actually or potentially encompassed by World War II, and with the few remaining neutrals moving uneasily in its shadow, the usual trade relations of most foreign countries, and the measures of official control over them, had by 1942 been eclipsed if not replaced by those arising out of the war situation.

The military developments of the past year have brought a number of striking changes in the accessibility of various areas to the several groups of countries—changes which have reflected their influence also upon the relations between other sets of countries. The Japanese precipitation of war in the Pacific in December, 1941, and their overrunning of Southeastern Asia during the early months of 1942, from the Philippines to the East Indies and Burma, have added that region of the world to the areas already practically closed off from general overseas trading by military operations and the naval blockades.

On the other hand, the Allied occupation of Algeria and Morocco in November, and the subsequent adherence to the Allied cause of all French Africa except Tunisia, joined with the Rommel retreat into Tunisia and the British occupation of Madagascar, have brought within Allied control and access all of the continent of Africa, outside of the currently disputed

Tunisian bridgehead. The only other non-Allied areas are the African colonies of Spain and Portugal, both of which have maintained a neutral position.

The Two Axis-dominated Regions Blockaded and Separated

From the commercial viewpoint, the developments of 1942 divided the countries of the world into two fairly distinguishable, mutually exclusive groups—"the Axis" and "the rest of the world." However, while Germany and Japan are united politically and ideologically in their hostility to much the same opposing powers, principally Britain, Russia, and the United States, they have achieved no significant connections either militarily or commercially. In fact, the Axis commercial world has come to consist of two quite isolated regions, which are almost identical with the areas within the military control of Germany on the continent of Europe and of Japan in Eastern Asia.

The spread of the war and the extension of operations of the Allied forces during the course of 1942 left the two Axis groups, at its close, almost entirely cut off from even such trade intercourse with each other, and with the outside world, as was still possible to them in December, 1941.

Trade Routes to Most Other Areas Kept Open by Allied Navies

Outside of the two Axis-controlled regions, most international trade routes have been kept substantially open by the British and American navies, despite heavy sinkings. They now allow active trading among the United States, most of the British Empire, Latin America, most of Africa, and the Near and Middle East up to Burma, including the neutral countries in these regions as well as those which have declared their belligerency.

The Soviet Union is receiving substantial supplies via three approaches: the Arctic route, although at considerable risk and loss; the Pacific-trans-Siberian route, in some measure; and the Persian Gulf route, in increasing measure, as the harbor and overland transport facilities are being improved.

Free China has been almost entirely closed off to foreign trade during the year, following the cutting off of even the limited volume of trade which had moved into the interior, although precariously, through the ports of Central and South China, and through Rangoon and the Burma Road. It is now dependent upon what can be flown in by cargo planes based on Eastern India, and such supplies as continue to be moved by the inland routes from the Soviet Union, branching off from the Turk-Sib railway.

The thin and uncertain lines of overseas trade which the neutrals on the European continent (Sweden, Switzerland, Spain, and Portugal) have striven to keep open, throw into relief the seclusion of the rest of Europe. The Allied occupation of French North Africa and the German occupation of the rest of France, late in 1942, only intensified that seclusion. While the Germans can now draw more openly upon the resources and production of hitherto unoccupied France, both France and Germany have lost access to the important supplies of foods, phosphates, and other minerals and fertilizers formerly drawn from French Africa.

Moreover, such limited supplies of rubber, tin, and other Far Eastern raw materials as Germany has been able to get from Japan via the blockade runners, in return for specially desired industrial equipment, have now had an important link cut. It is no longer possible to unload these products at West Africa, and move them overland to Mediterranean ports for the brief run to Marseilles or Genoa.

Whether the shorter Mediterranean route to the Middle East, now unsafe for either Axis or Allied commercial shipping, can become a more usable route for either side, will depend upon the military campaign in progress as the year closed.

War Demands on Commodities and Shipping Curtail Civilian Commerce

The active participation of the United States, the enlargement of the potential theater of war to almost global dimensions, and the general intensification of the war program, have called for drastic diversion of resources, manpower, and productive facilities of the belligerent Allied nations to war purposes. This has further curtailed, during the year, the volume and range of goods available for ordinary civilian use, either of their own populations or those in foreign markets, despite the strenuous drives for expansion in their volumes of production.

The supply situation has been materially aggravated by the shortage of certain raw materials hitherto largely obtained from the Far Eastern areas now under Japanese control, although, for a number of these, alternative sources or synthetic substitutes are actively being developed.

Moreover, the shortage of shipping available for the carriage of goods to or from countries outside the zones or bases of military operations has materially limited the movements of international commerce even between areas accessible to each other. This has affected also various commodities of which ample surpluses are available in the countries of their origin, such as coffee, bananas, and even petroleum, but for which cargo or tanker space cannot now be spared.

Differences Between the Axis and Allied Pooling of Resources

Upon the physical facts of shortages of essential products and of shipping, which were coming to be increasingly felt during the preceding year even among countries located on accessible world trade routes, there were superimposed during 1942 two important governmental decisions which profoundly affected the movement of commodities between the non-Axis countries. These were the huge enlargement of its Lend-Lease operations by the United States, after its active entry into the war, and the arrangements for the pooling of economic as well as military resources on the part of the British and American governments and, in some measure, also on the part of others of the United Nations. In connection with both these policies, the urgency of need of the various countries in relation to the war program, rather than capacity to make current payment, grew in prominence as the determinant in the allocations of available supplies of essential products.

International pooling of supplies and concentration of productive resources had been going on since 1940 among most of the countries of continental Europe, including not only those occupied by the Axis, but also those under its influence or without sufficient alternative outlets. However, that program differs radically, in certain vital respects, from the one that has been developing more recently among the non-Axis nations.

Such international pooling of supplies as has taken place within continental Europe during the war has been mainly under German orders or pressure, and the reciprocal exchanges of goods among the various secluded European countries has been largely dependent upon what was available after the prior German claims or arrangements had been satisfied.

Moreover, the direction of concentration of resources, including the movement of much plant equipment and manpower as well as of merchandise, has been primarily toward Germany, for the benefit of its military program or its population.

The predominantly one-way flow of this movement has been officially acknowledged, in the repeated German assurances to the peoples of other European countries that the huge balances due them on the clearing accounts at Berlin—insofar as goods transported to Germany are recognized and recorded as exports rather than as requisitions—should be regarded as "iron savings," which will be "refunded to them in goods after the war."

Among the non-Axis countries, by contrast, the Lend-Lease and pooling programs are distinctly voluntary, and represent a giving as well as a getting on the part of the United States and, in a measure, of the participating British countries. The pooling of supplies and resources envisages the needs of all the Allied nations engaged in the war, in accordance with their relative urgency. Moreover, the program for mobilizing more intensively the strategic materials and other essential products from the neutral countries, and from those not actively engaged in the war, definitely involves a counterundertaking to endeavor to supply those countries with their essential import requirements, so far as the naturally prior claims of the military programs allow.

This latter arrangement has particularly marked the trade relations of the year between the United States and Latin America, as the war developments made the southern republics increasingly dependent upon the United States, as the primary supplier of their import needs as well as the buyer of their surplus products. Canada and the United States have gone far during the year toward facilitating their reciprocal exchanges of commodities, as part of the integration of their war production programs.

The progress during 1942 toward the Allied pooling of economic resources and products; toward the adoption of the Lend-Lease principle by the United Kingdom and certain of the Dominions (Australia and New Zealand), and the expansion of Lend-Lease operations by the United States and the other participating countries; and toward the integrated consideration of the essential civilian import needs of friendly countries not actively engaged in the war, as well as of the supplies obtainable from them—together represent the most striking and significant developments of the year in the trade policies and general economic relations between the non-Axis nations. Their influence cannot but extend well beyond the actual trade movements they made possible during the past year.

Cash and Private Trade Not Displaced by Intergovernmental Shipments

Despite the huge movements of equipment and supplies between nations during the past year on intergovernmental account, for direct military use or the maintenance of the wartime civilian economy of the combatants, a very substantial volume of what corresponds to normal private foreign trading has continued to be carried on during the year.

Such coördinated private orders or bulk purchasing through governmental channels of commodities for civilian use, as has been resorted to by some British and Latin American countries, has thus far been limited, with the notable exception of the United Kingdom, to special products which constituted a small part of their total imports.

In fact, a large proportion even of the products that were exported from the United States for the account of foreign governments, other than purely military equipment—whether against cash purchase or under Lend-Lease—has continued to be procured from the usual commercial producers, although often indirectly, and to move largely through private channels at this end, and through established importing and distributing channels in the countries of destination. This has been particularly the case in dealings with the United Kingdom and the British Empire areas generally.

In the case of the United States, in particular, the amount of direct cash exports was remarkably well maintained during 1942, approximating closely the value of total United States exports during the years immediately preceding the war. Understandably, those exports have differed considerably from the normal, both in the relative importance of the various lines of goods and of the different destinations. On the whole, however, the goods shipped abroad under Lend-Lease have apparently represented mainly additions to the past value of cash exports, rather than their replacement.

The United Kingdom, and reportedly certain of the British countries, have granted exemptions from duty for the bulk of the goods imported into their territories for government use. Private trade transactions, on the other hand, with practically all countries that are open to commerce, have during the past year been subject to increased measures of governmental control at one or both ends. In fact, goods have seldom moved internationally during the recent past unless the governments regarded it as distinctly in accord with the national interest to have them move—or at least *not contrary* to that interest—and often only to specifically approved countries of destination, and even limited to approved consignees within those countries.

Trade Determined More by Controls of Exporting Than of Importing Country

Under current conditions, however, with the war needs having first call when supplies of essential goods are inadequate to all needs, and with the shortage of shipping limiting the movement of all commodities, whether scarce or ample, the decision whether a particular private transaction in international trade shall be consummated now rests, in the majority of cases, in the country of exportation rather than the country of importation. This is particularly true with regard to importations from the United States.

The judgments of the authorities of the originating country as to whether the particular goods can be spared for commercial exportation, and as to the relative availability of ships to carry them, are now the decisive considerations. Increasingly, during the past year, this situation has rendered quite secondary the duties, import licenses, or exchange controls which had been set up by most countries during the earlier years, when foreign goods were readily available and the choice was up to the buyer or his government.

Axis Intensifies Efforts for Commercial Absorption of Controlled Areas

The foregoing discussion is concerned primarily with the developments of the past year in this field among the non-Axis countries. Owing to the absence of Allied governmental or press representation in the Far East Axis zone, and the meagerness of authentic reports from the European zone, only general impressions or fragmentary accounts have been available as to the developments during 1942 in the commercial relations between the areas constituting each of the two secluded Axis regions, and in the official policies or controls that have governed such relations.

In a general way it is known that, on the continent of Europe, the past year has seen an intensification without radical change of the centripetal program developed by Germany since 1940, to govern the movement of commodities with and between the various countries under its control or influence. In the overrun Far Eastern region, the Japanese are understood to have launched a program for the commercial absorption of the products and resources of the areas under their present control, which is remarkably similar to the German method of dealing with the European areas under the control of the Reich. The character of that program had been earlier foreshadowed in the Japanese trade relations with North China and French Indo-China, even before the outbreak of the global war.

One striking difference between the contemplated Japanese-dominated regional economy and the German has already become manifest. Neither Japan itself nor the areas within its so-called "co-prosperity sphere" have the facilities to process or the ability to consume the huge volumes of the various natural products of Eastern and Southeastern Asia, upon the profitable disposal of which those countries depend for the maintenance of employment and for even minimum prosperity. Nor has Japan, now or in early prospect, the manufacturing capacity adequate to supplying, in return, the peoples secluded within this region with even their most essential import requirements.

ECONOMIC POOLING AND LEND-LEASE OPERATIONS AMONG THE ALLIES

Within a short time after the United States was thrust actively into the war in December, 1941, and the Japanese attacks upon the American, British, and Dutch territories in the Pacific converted the European and the Far Eastern wars into World War II, certain of the leading belligerent Allied governments took steps toward unifying their economic strategy, so as to facilitate the most effective use of their common resources and of those available to them in friendly countries.

Unprecedented Movements Superimposed On Traditional Trade Patterns

In effect, these constitute important new forms of international commercial policy, which, at least for the duration of the emergency, have been superimposed upon the previous pattern of the channels and policies of world trade, traditionally conceived as primarily a private commercial function.

Alongside of the continued large-scale movements of ordinary commodities among the non-Axis countries—although often restricted in volume, limited in the range of commodities, and considerably different from the normal in sources and destinations—there has grown into prominence during the past year a series of exceptional international currents of goods in support of the war programs of the various belligerent Allies. They have consisted not only of finished munitions but of materials and tools for the production and maintenance of the military equipment, and, to certain war areas, also of foodstuffs and ordinary products necessary to make up local shortages of essentials for the armed forces or for the maintenance of the population on a wartime basis, or to compensate for the unavailability of supplies from the usual sources due to shipping exigencies.

Overshadowing by the end of the year the more normal trade currents and the controls over them, these exceptional commodity movements have been largely made possible and directed by two types of governmental policy decisions, which are unprecedented in scope, in technique of operation, in basis of compensation, and in their possible significance for the future. They are:

First, the arrangements for the concentration of productive resources and for the pooling of supplies on the part of the United States and the British Empire, and in some measure, also of other friendly nations, in the light of what would best advance the common interest in the winning of the war; and

Second, the broad adoption by the United Kingdom and certain of the Dominions, and the enlargement by the United States, of what has come to be known as the Lend-Lease principle, under which the relative urgency of need of the various Allied countries, rather than their ability to make monetary repayment, is the prime determinant in the transfer among them of available supplies of essential products.

Moves for Concerted Economic Action Broadened Since Pearl Harbor

While considerable progress had been made before Pearl Harbor in the integration of the war production programs of Canada and of the United States, it was not until after the precipitation of the United States into the war that the general program was launched for the pooling of the economic as well as the military resources available to the Allied countries.

It does not appear that there has, as yet, developed a clear-cut and comprehensive organization, directly representing all of the United Nations able to participate, for mobilizing and utilizing their aggregate economic resources and products for the common cause, excepting insofar as the British and American governments may be regarded as acting for them.

In the important matter of controls over import and export trade, no appreciable progress has yet been made toward concerted programs among any large number of the Allied governments, beyond general agreement upon certain broad long-time objectives. Most of such wartime measures of a similar nature as have actually been taken by several of them for the control of their foreign trade have been, at most, roughly parallel in operation, but autonomous in origin—and so subject to unilateral alteration or withdrawal—rather than the result of international engagements having any binding character.

Insofar as there have developed agreements or joint action among Allied governments in the economic field, they have been mostly bilateral or regional in character, the majority consisting of arrangements between the United States and one of the other United Nations or friendly countries.

However, taken together, the arrangements entered into during 1942 do constitute long strides toward developing and implementing a concerted economic strategy on the part of the United Nations. These measures and organizations have already profoundly affected the conditions under which materials and products have been moving among them, and the countries accessible to them, during the past year. They will doubtless be of increasing influence during the war period; and, in modified form, some of them may continue into the period of postwar relief and reconstruction.

The one organization referred to as comprising in its membership a large number of the United Nations is the Inter-Allied Committee on Post-War Requirements, also known as the Leith-Ross Committee. It was set up in London by representatives of the European Allied governments in September, 1941, for the purpose of laying concerted plans to secure "food, raw materials, and articles of prime necessity" to be "made available for the postwar needs of countries liberated from Nazi oppression." However, it has not grown in membership, nor is it reported to have advanced much beyond the research stage.

What has been done in the way of supplying food and other materials to the peoples of North Africa, since the arrival of the Anglo-American forces, has been distinctly a joint British-American effort, operating through the North African Economic Board. However, the more comprehensive United Nations relief organization, which is to deal with the problems to be faced in areas occupied during the war and in the liberated countries after the war, is understood to be in process of formation.

Related in purpose to these organizations, actual and prospective, for furnishing relief supplies, is the agreement reached at Washington in July, 1942, by representatives of the governments of the five nations with the largest stake in the overseas trade in wheat, namely: Argentina, Australia, Canada, and the United States as the major exporting countries, and the United Kingdom as the principal importing country. It provided for the establishment of a pool of wheat to be available for intergovernmental relief in war-stricken and necessitous areas, as soon as the international situation permits. The United States, Canada, and the United Kingdom are to provide the basic relief pool of 100,000,000 bushels, with the four exporting countries to share in any additional contributions to the pool that may be necessary. While this is an emergency arrangement, it is presented as the first step toward the conclusion of a comprehensive international wheat agreement, as soon as circumstances permit its consideration by a broader body of interested countries.[1]

The Joint Canadian-American committees to coördinate the utilization of the combined resources of these neighboring countries and their war production program,[2] as well as the series of agreements for the bulk purchase by the United States of all or most of the output of certain strategic and critical materials of various countries of Latin America, had been inaugurated during the earlier years of the war, and are now fairly well known.[3]

British-American Combined Boards Act for All Friendly Nations

Of the developments of this character during 1942, easily the most important has been the series of British-American combined boards set up soon after the entrance of the United States into the war. In the scope of the resources to be mobilized and of the needs to be met, if not in their directive membership, they appear designed to comprise all of the United Nations and other accessible friendly countries. The Raw Materials Board, the Munitions Assignments Board, and the Shipping Adjustment Board were set up by President Roosevelt and Prime Minister Churchill in January, 1942. To these were added, later in the year, the Production and Resources Board and the Food Board. The statement announcing the creation of the original combined boards, whose membership was limited to Great Britain and the United States, indicated that their members would confer with representatives of Russia, China, and such others of the United Nations as necessary to attain common purposes and to provide for the most effective utilization of the joint resources of the United Nations.

While the fields of their concern are indicated from their names, a number of notable differences are observed in the functions of these various

---

[1] The draft convention prepared for this purpose goes well beyond most earlier international agreements for stabilizing the markets for particular commodities, in that it contemplates provisions for production controls, maximum and minimum prices, and reserve buffer stocks, as well as for the allocation of export quotas among the principal surplus-producing countries. Moreover, its sponsors envisage the scheme as a pattern for the handling of other staple commodities, and claim it would promote more efficient world production of wheat and the liberalization of international trade barriers.

[2] The "Hyde Park Agreement" for the coördinated utilization of the resources and productive facilities of the United States and Canada, mentioned in the preceding chapter, has since Pearl Harbor been actively implemented along several lines.

[3] A full account of the detailed working out of the United States arrangements for the bulk purchase or underwriting of various Latin American commodities, briefly mentioned in the preceding chapter, will be found in an article by the author in *Foreign Commerce Weekly* for May 1, 1943.

boards and in the manner of their actual operations. Thus far, little has been made known officially regarding the working of most of these combined boards, so that only certain general observations are now possible.

The Munitions Assignments Board envisions the entire munitions resources of Great Britain and the United States as a common pool. The coördinate boards promptly formed in Washington and in London operate, under the direction of the Combined Anglo-American Chiefs of Staff, in advising on all assignments among the United Nations, both in quantity and priority, of the finished munitions available from the respective countries, "in accordance with strategic needs." A similar committee has been set up in Australia, and another is being formed in India. Canadian surplus production has been allocated either by a committee at Ottawa, or by one of the two main boards, in Washington and in London. The production of the munitions within each of the countries is planned and controlled by its own military and war production authorities.

The Combined Shipping Adjustment Board, similarly, is based upon the principle that the shipping resources of Great Britain and the United States are "deemed to be pooled." The joint boards set up in Washington and London have the task of coördinating the operations of the merchant shipping owned or controlled by the two countries. The actual movements and allocations of the ships are directed by the United States War Shipping Administration and the British Ministry of War Transport, respectively.

The Combined Raw Materials Board is primarily a planning and coördinating organization, although possessing also certain operating functions. The report issued by this body allows a more concrete characterization of its operations. It was created because of the recognition that "a planned and expeditious utilization of the raw-materials resources of the United Nations is necessary in the prosecution of the war." As the board has described its task, "it must maintain an over-all view of the raw-materials position for the United Nations, and on the basis of this over-all picture it must determine what combined action is necessary to ensure the maximum supply, and most effective distribution and use, of strategic materials throughout the United Nations." It does not absorb the functions of the two governments responsible for the control of the raw-material resources available to them, relying on the operating agencies of the British and American governments to implement its decisions.

The Raw Materials Board has been allocating among the United Nations the supply of those scarce raw materials available to the United States and the United Kingdom, including emergency shifts from one country to another to meet temporary shortages that cannot be solved nationally. The board has also been helping to coördinate the search for, and development of, new sources of supply throughout the accessible world, maintaining close contact with the various United States or United Kingdom raw-materials missions. In order to bring out greater supplies while avoiding competitive bidding, and to provide long-term contracts at fair prices, the purchase outside their home territories of all supplies of certain commodities has been concentrated in single agencies of one government or the other. For example, all procurement of crude rubber in Latin America and Liberia is being made by the agencies of the United States Government, while the rubber available from the rest of Africa and Ceylon is being purchased by the British Ministry of Supply.

In dealing with each of the strategic materials that are its concern, the Combined Raw Materials Board reports that it generally finds it essential to recommend simultaneous action in many fields, by various agencies and in different parts of the world. The series of programs for meeting the tin shortage situation after the Japanese occupation of the East Indies is illustrative of the scope of such tasks, and of the importance of integrating what is done in a particular area with what is done in others. The board is also active in promoting the pooling of the technical experience of the United States, the United Kingdom, and other countries in the conservation of critical materials in war production, and in the elimination of dispensable civilian uses.

The Combined Food Board is charged, in the field of foods, food materials, and the equipment for their production, with functions which are approximately similar to those of the Combined Raw Materials Board. Such information as is available regarding its actual operations indicates that they are developing along lines roughly parallel to those of the Raw Materials Board. Canada is also represented on the various committees of the Food Board in Washington, and the other British Dominions and Colonies are in contact with the board through the London Food Committee.

The Combined Production and Resources Board was established later in the year, "to complete the organization needed for the most effective use of the combined resources of North America (United States and Canada) and the United Kingdom for the prosecution of the war." The functions of the board are "to combine the production programs of the United States and the United Kingdom and Canada into a single integrated program, adjusted to the strategic requirements of the war... and to all relevant production factors; ... to take account of the need for maximum utilization of the productive resources available to the United States, the British Commonwealth of Nations, and the United Nations, the need to reduce demands on shipping to a minimum, and the essential needs of the civilian populations"; and, "in close collaboration with the Combined Chiefs of Staff, assure the continuous adjustment of the combined production program to meet changing military requirements ..."

The countries which are in a position to make the principal contributions of supplies toward the common war effort, the United States, Great Britain, and in particular cases the Dominions, have thus far constituted the membership of these combined boards and of their committees. In the matter of procurement, these governments have undertaken the task of mobilizing the aggregate supplies, actual and potential, of essential materials and foodstuffs from sources even outside their own territories. This includes large purchases and developmental programs in Latin America, the British Empire, and such other areas as are accessible. In their allocations of the aggregate munitions, foods, materials, and other products thus made available, however, the directing governments of these combined boards are taking into account the needs of all the various United Nations and friendly countries, in accordance with their relative urgency and the availability of shipping.

Physical limitations, particularly of transport, have thus far prevented the resources of Russia and of China from becoming available in connection with this program in any sizable volume.

Joint Plans for Supplying Needs of Special Areas and for Preclusive Buying

While unlike the British-American combined boards in certain respects, there have been developing during the past year or so a number of other important new types of arrangements to govern international movements of commodities. From the viewpoint of American foreign trade, the most outstanding of these is the coöperative plan initiated during the past year between the United States and certain countries of Latin America: first, for ascertaining the total requirements of those countries for various essential products desired from the United States; and second, for dovetailing the import control system of the individual importing countries in Latin America with the United States systems of priority allocations of scarce commodities, export licensing, and allocation of shipping space.[4]

[4] An analysis of the situation out of which that unusual inter-American arrangement arose, and of the manner of its operation, will be found in an article in *Foreign Commerce Weekly* for April 24, 1943.

Similar in purpose have been the special arrangements between the United States and the United Kingdom for coördinating their respective export programs, with a view to satisfying the civilian requirements of certain areas, for which those two countries are now the principal sources, in the light of the best use of the limited supplies of goods and of shipping space available. The Anglo-American Caribbean Commission (centering at Washington) and the Middle East Supply Center (operating from Cairo, with a policy committee functioning also in London) represent specific applications to particular areas of the general plans being developed, through Anglo-American collaboration, for the ascertainment of the requirements and the allocation of supplies for the essential needs of particular regions of responsibility.

A different type of concerted Anglo-American economic action which developed during the past year has been in connection with certain activities of the United States Board of Economic Warfare and of the British Ministry of Economic Warfare. They have included: the coördination of the American export-licensing system with the British navicert system, in the control of shipments to the neutral countries of Europe and adjacent areas through the naval blockade, with the American and British representatives having an equal voice in the decisions of the Blockade Committee; and the closer integration of the preclusive buying activities on the part of the agencies of the two governments, of essential raw materials available in countries accessible to Germany.

Suspension of Usual Duties and Controls on Products for Official Use

In order to implement this general program of economic pooling of commodities essential to their war programs, three of the leading United Nations have taken steps to facilitate their actual movement by a substantial waiver of the duties and other controls otherwise applying to commercial shipments of the same products.

Thus, by a Treasury Order issued late in 1941, the United Kingdom granted exemption from import duties for a broad range of goods which are imported wholly or mainly for official use, whether the goods are consumed directly by the government, or whether they first pass into commercial channels with their end products being bought by the government. In making the announcement, the Chancellor of the Exchequer pointed out that: "The exemptions in question are unconnected with tariff policy, and are designed as a wartime measure to save the labor involved in the collection of the duties from Government departments. They are made possible by the fact that all imports are now subject to rigorous control."

Goods shipped under Lend-Lease from the United States require no export licenses similar to those now generally applicable to most products shipped out of the country. Moreover, the procurement of all products for Lend-Lease purposes, and of the materials embodied in them, are facilitated under special arrangements for obtaining for them allocations and priorities when otherwise required, and their forwarding is facilitated by the joint operations of the War Shipping Administration and of the British Ministry of War Transport.

In addition, the United States Government has moved during the past year to facilitate the importation into the United States of materials of foreign origin that are considered strategic or critical. An Executive Order of May 30, issued under the First War Powers Act, extended to various departments and agencies of the United States Government the authority, hitherto limited to the Secretary of the Navy, to make emergency purchases of war materials abroad, and to have them admitted into the United States free of duty.

Beginning in the latter months of 1941, Canada took administrative steps to waive the payment of duties and taxes, or to provide for their refund, upon imports needed in the fulfillment of war contracts placed in that country by the Canadian Ministry of Munitions and Supplies, or on behalf of the United Kingdom or any Allied government. This was carried further during 1942 and, by Order-in-Council of September 9, statutory authority was obtained for the remission or refund of duties and taxes on importations for war contracts or services for the Allied governments, on the broadest possible basis.

While the experiments in international economic collaboration for common ends, just described, have been resorted to under the pressing necessities of war, they are bound to influence the attitudes of governments toward similar coöperation after the war. If these experiences prove encouraging, they cannot fail to furnish a body of global information, and a technique and habit of concerted action that would be invaluable in any future endeavors in that direction.

In a statement accompanying the recent report to the President on the first year's operations of the Combined Raw Materials Board, William L. Batt, Vice-Chairman of the United States War Production Board, and American member of the Combined Board, declared:

> When the war ends, there will be a scramble by all nations for avail-

able supplies in order to restore their economies to a peacetime basis as speedily as possible.

Experience after the first World War has shown that such a scramble can result in complete demoralization of supply, price, and other factors in a peacetime economy.

It is impossible to see how such a situation can be met unless through some form of combined machinery. Existence of the Combined Raw Materials Board might contribute substantially to the solution of this important post-war problem.

Spread of Lend-Lease Principle Among the Allied Nations

The Lend-Lease idea was initiated by the United States early in 1941, when the ability of Great Britain to pay in dollars for the huge quantities of munitions and supplies needed to continue the war was rapidly diminishing. Since then, this principle of sharing the one country's production and supplies with other countries engaged in the common struggle, without regard to their ability to make monetary repayment, has been adopted also by other United Nations. In a measure, a return flow of reciprocal aid to the United States from the beneficiaries of its program had begun during 1941, especially from the United Kingdom. During 1942, however, this was broadened considerably, and the Lend-Lease principle came to be manifested not only in the increased volume and variety of supplies and services furnished to the United States as reciprocal aid, but also between certain of the other Allied countries themselves.

While the United States was still a nonbelligerent, the Act of Congress of March 11, 1941, authorized the President to make available to any country whose defense he deemed "vital to the defense of the United States" any essential article, information, or service. "The terms and conditions upon which any such foreign government receives any aid" so authorized "shall be those which the President deems satisfactory, and the benefit to the United States may be payment or repayment in kind or property, or any other direct or indirect benefit which the President deems satisfactory." The breadth of the basis to be applied in evaluating the contributions of the respective United Nations in the common war effort was indicated from the statement in the President's Lend-Lease report to Congress of June 11, 1942, that: "If each country devotes roughly the same fraction of its national production to the war, then the financial burden of war is distributed equally among the United Nations in accordance with their ability to pay."

Operation of United States Lend-Lease program: volume, composition, and destinations.—Up to the end of 1942, the cumulative value of Lend-Lease aid rendered by the United States was 8¼ billion dollars. The value of the aid has been mounting at a rapidly accelerating rate. Fully 7 billion dollars of that total represented aid rendered during 1942, four-fifths consisting of goods transferred and one-fifth of various services rendered.[5] These services have been mainly in connection with shipping and supply activities, and have consisted of the rental and charter of ships, the development and operation of air ferry routes and supply bases abroad, the construction of special facilities in the United States for the production of Lend-Lease equipment, and the repairing of Allied warships and merchant vessels in the United States. All but about 10 per cent of the goods transferred to the governments of Lend-Lease countries are reported to have been sent abroad. Military items amounted during 1942 to well over half of Lend-Lease exports, and have been comprising an increasing proportion of the total value of goods so supplied.

While forty-four nations have thus far been declared eligible for Lend-Lease aid, the bulk of the goods furnished by the United States under this program has been sent to the United Kingdom (49 per cent for the period through 1942); to the Middle and Far East, including Australia, New Zealand, and the African areas (30 per cent); and to Russia (19 per cent). The relative distribution to the different areas has varied from time to time, principally in accordance with the shifting war pressures and the limitations of transport facilities.

By the beginning of 1943, Russia was becoming the major beneficiary of American Lend-Lease in certain important arms and in foodstuffs, passing even the United Kingdom in this respect. The United States Lend-Lease Administrator has recently declared that: "Since the inception of the Soviet aid program in October, 1941, we have transferred to the Soviet Union supplies, including food, which cost more than one billion and a quarter dollars."

Transportation difficulties are reported to have kept Lend-Lease shipments to China comparatively small. During 1941, Lend-Lease aid to China was devoted principally to improving transport conditions over the Burma Road, "resulting in more than doubling monthly tonnage carried

[5] The recorded value of all exports from the United States during 1942, as recently announced by the Department of Commerce, was 7.8 billion dollars. Of this, total cash exports amounted to an aggregate value of 3.2 billions; with 4.6 billion representing the value of shipments recorded by the customs as going out during the year under Lend-Lease. Planes and ships moving abroad under their own power are not included in these customs records—nor do they include the great quantities of food and other supplies and equipment sent to American forces abroad.

over that route," and to building a new railroad from Burma to China, to facilitate the delivery of the increased quantities of supplies that were planned to follow. Since the closing off of the ports of Central and South China, and the loss of Burma, air transport across the Himalayas based upon Eastern India has been the only direct means of bringing Lend-Lease supplies into Free China. Plans are reported for increasing these shipments considerably, over the air route and by other means. Lend-Lease goods shipped to China since the beginning of the program have consisted mainly of planes, trucks, ammunition, gasoline, and medical supplies.

Lend-lease shipments to Latin America have been confined to limited quantities of military supplies.

Lend-Lease operations by United Kingdom, Canada, and other United Nations.—Part of the munitions and supplies sent to the United Kingdom by the United States under Lend-Lease has been forwarded to Russia, Egypt, India, and other areas. In addition, Great Britain has sent a major part of its own production of war supplies to these fronts. Under an agreement concluded in the middle of 1942, Great Britain undertook to deliver to Russia military supplies of Empire manufacture free of charge, subject only to the return to the British Government, after the termination of hostilities, of such of these articles available as Great Britain desires to recover. Military supplies of United States origin that are reshipped to Russia by the British Government, whether obtained by purchase or under Lend-Lease, are to be supplied on the same terms as they have been received by Great Britain. The United Kingdom is providing equipment, under Lend-Lease, for the forces of many of the governments-in-exile fighting with the British armies. Great Britain has also been furnishing supplies and pay, as well as munitions, to Chinese troops operating in Burma and India, on a Lend-Lease basis.

Canada has not been a direct beneficiary of Lend-Lease aid from the United States. The shipments to Canada described as Lend-Lease materials have been mostly either for reshipment, or embodiment in products ultimately exported, to Great Britain or other United Nations. Trade between Canada and the United States is on a cash basis, and, up to the close of 1942, the movements of war materials between the two countries were reported to have been almost evenly balanced.

In March, 1942, the Canadian Parliament approved an outright gift to the government of Great Britain of one billion dollars Canadian, to be used toward defraying British expenditures in Canada for war purposes, including the purchase of any commodities or supplies "essential to the conduct of the war and the maintenance of the people of the United Kingdom." The figure set was judged to represent the maximum necessary to meet the requirements for about a year's operations, and to provide "sufficient funds to take care of Britain's dollar deficit until sometime early in 1943." That fund has now been exhausted.

Early in February, 1943, the Canadian Government requested its Parliament to sanction the establishment of a Canadian Mutual Aid Plan. A billion dollars is to be appropriated by which to make available, to any of the other United Nations, Canada's wartime surplus production of munitions, materials, and foodstuffs, beyond its own requirements. Australia, New Zealand, Russia, and China, as well as the United Kingdom, are specifically named among the contemplated direct recipients of these Canadian war supplies, to be assigned by a Canadian Allocation Board.[6]

The Governor-in-Council is to set the terms of such allocations, and may require such reciprocal action, or any direct or indirect benefit, as he deems appropriate. Concerning reciprocal benefits to Canada, the Canadian Minister of Finance has stated that: "In some cases, it may be possible to arrange for the return after the war of the equipment or vehicles which Canada provides under this new program. In still other cases, the nation receiving the war supplies from Canada may be able to provide it with some other form of postwar benefit." However, the proposed law stresses that "it shall be good and sufficient consideration for transferring war supplies to other United Nations, that such supplies are to be used in the joint and effective prosecution of the war."

Increasing reciprocal Lend-Lease to aid United States forces abroad.— An element of increasing importance during the past year has been the reciprocal aid which the Allied nations have been furnishing to American forces abroad, in the form of equipment, food, supplies, and local facilities of various types, when that is found to be the most expeditious use in the common cause of available resources and shipping space. These are being furnished under the reciprocal Lend-Lease agreements concluded during the year with the United Kingdom (which dealt also for the Colonial Empire), with Australia, New Zealand, the French National Committee, and

[6] The Canadian Minister of Munitions and Supplies announced, in November, 1942, that 70 per cent of the Dominion's total war production was going to the United Nations; 50 per cent of it was being sent to Great Britain, either for its own purposes or those of Russia, and 20 per cent was going to Pacific areas on behalf of the United States. Direct shipments to Russia from Canada had already totaled more than one hundred million dollars, the most important item being tanks. This represents total exports from Canada, and not simply that shipped under the first billion-dollar credit to Great Britain, described above.

with Belgium. Most of the reciprocal Lend-Lease aid received by the United States has been provided to its forces outside the country.

Specifically, the United States has been receiving reciprocal aid in various forms from the United Kingdom in the British Isles, in the British Colonies throughout the world, and in India, Egypt, the Middle East, North Africa, and Iceland. The maintenance and operations of American troops in the South and Southwest Pacific areas have been with the aid of substantial Lend-Lease supplies from Australia and New Zealand, especially of foodstuffs. Fighting France is furnishing supplies, facilities, and services to American forces in New Caledonia and Equatorial Africa as reciprocal aid, and the Belgian Government is supplying similar aid in the Belgian Congo. Limited amounts of reciprocal aid have also been extended by the Union of South Africa, mainly in the form of ship repairs, and by the Chinese Government, in the transfer of the "Flying Tiger" planes originally purchased from the United States.

No precise figures are available as to the aggregate value of the reciprocal Lend-Lease aid being afforded to the United States by the other Allied nations. In fact, the Lend-Lease Administrator has declared in his recent testimony before a congressional committee that: "There never has been and there never will be developed a standard of values by which we can measure lives lost against the cost of airplanes and guns." However, the measurable volume of reciprocal aid furnished to American forces abroad is reported to have already reached large proportions, and is expected to increase in volume as American forces move overseas to the fighting fronts.

Bearing of Mutual Aid arrangements on postwar trade policy.—From the viewpoint of the future, perhaps the most significant development of the year in connection with the Lend-Lease arrangements has been the series of Mutual Aid Agreements concluded by the United States under the Lend-Lease Act of March, 1941, with the United Kingdom, China, the Soviet Union, and with seven of the other United Nations, viz., Belgium, Poland, the Netherlands, Greece, Czechoslovakia, Norway, and Yugoslavia. In addition, Australia and New Zealand have adhered to the provisions of the Master Agreement with the United Kingdom, and Canada has accepted the essential principles in this regard in an exchange of notes with the United States. These documents all carry pledges on the part of all the contracting governments to coöperate after the war, in a program of collaboration designed to promote more liberal conditions for international trading, and a more prosperous and expanding world economy.

Specifically, Article VII of the Master Agreement with the United Kingdom, concluded on February 23, 1942, which appears in identical terms also in all such subsequent agreements, provides that:

> In the final determination of the benefits to be provided to the United States of America by the Government of the United Kingdom in return for aid furnished under the Act of Congress of March 11, 1941, the terms and conditions thereof shall be such as not to burden commerce between the two countries, but to promote mutually advantageous economic relations between them and the betterment of world-wide economic relations.[7] To that end, they shall include provision for agreed action by the United States of America and the United Kingdom, open to participation by all other countries of like mind, directed to the expansion, by appropriate international and domestic measures, of production, employment, and the exchange and consumption of goods, which are the material foundations of the liberty and welfare of all peoples; to the elimination of all forms of discriminatory treatment in international commerce, and to the reduction of tariffs and other trade barriers; and, in general, to the attainment of all the economic objectives set forth in the Joint Declaration made on August 12, 1941, by the President of the United States of America and the Prime Minister of the United Kingdom.
>
> At an early convenient date, conversations shall be begun between the two Governments with a view to determining, in the light of governing economic conditions, the best means of attaining the above-stated objectives by their own agreed action and of seeking the agreed action of other like-minded Governments.

The Joint Declaration of August, 1941, referred to in these agreements is what has come to be known as the Atlantic Charter, which set forth the following broad international objectives for the post-war period in the economic field:

> Fourth, they will endeavor, with due respect for their existing obligations, to further the enjoyment by all States, great or small, victor or vanquished, of access, on equal terms, to the trade and to the raw materials of the world which are needed for their economic prosperity;
>
> Fifth, they desire to bring about the fullest collaboration between all nations in the economic field with the object of securing, for all, improved labor standards, economic advancement and social security.

[7] Of similar tenor is the provision in the new Canadian Mutual Aid Plan, that the conditions under which Canadian war supplies are made available to the other United Nations "should not be such as to burden post-war commerce, or lead to the imposition of trade restrictions, or otherwise prejudice a just and enduring peace."

1943

TRADE CONDITIONS WORSEN IN AXIS REGIONS WHILE IMPROVING AMONG ALLIES

COMMERCIAL SHIFTS RESULTING FROM MILITARY DEVELOPMENTS

The Allies' military offensives during the past year have tightened further the commercial seclusion of the two Axis-controlled groups of countries in Europe and in the Far East, and have increased the difficulties of trading within these regions. On the other hand, while the areas accessible to the commerce of the non-Axis nations have thus far been only slightly enlarged by the military campaigns, the Allied military progress of the past year has reopened shorter and more direct routes between important regions, and has rendered much more secure some of the sea lanes that had been open to the Allied and friendly nations at its beginning.

The map on page 282 sketches roughly the two secluded Axis regions, and the shifts in the areas within their commercial reach during the past year.

Access to Mediterranean Basin Curtailed for Axis; Enlarged for Allies

The forced withdrawal of the Axis armies during the past year from their last foothold in North Africa, and progressively from Sicily and southern Italy, has done more than deny Germany access to the products and markets of these liberated areas themselves. It has practically closed

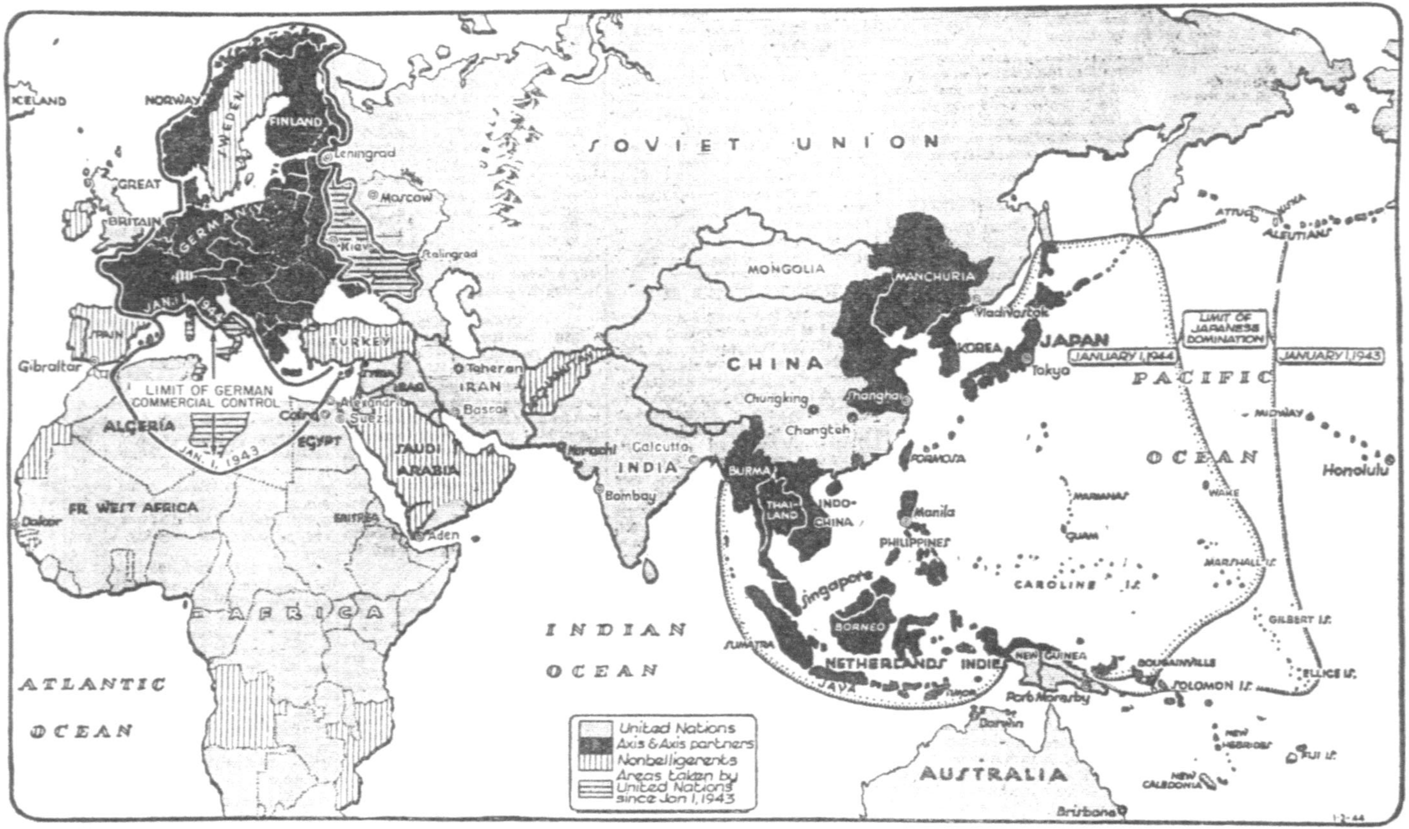

Shifts During 1943 in Areas Within Commercial Reach of the Axis and Allied Nations

off German-dominated Europe from open commercial intercourse with the rest of the Mediterranean basin. The only exceptions are Spain and Turkey, and with them trade is now largely limited to what can be moved overland.

Similarly, the regaining of the wide belt in Eastern Europe by the Russian forces has not alone restored most of the Ukraine and the adjacent territory to Russian use. It has removed the concern felt at the beginning of the year, lest the Germans' hold upon the Black Sea and the Caucasus might be extended to give them access to the supplies of petroleum and other valuable materials from that region and from the Asiatic countries beyond.

The reopening of the Mediterranean by the Allies' military progress in that region during the past year has not only given them access to the liberated areas of North Africa and Italy. It has restored the use of the shorter, direct route between the North Atlantic and the Middle East. By allowing quicker turn-arounds than had been possible by the Cape of Good Hope route, this has resulted in the delivery of greatly increased quantities of munitions and supplies to the countries of the Middle East and, across the rapidly improved ports, highways, and railroads of Iran, to the Soviet Union.

Commercially, it has also made possible an appreciable revival of a two-way exchange of ordinary commodities with certain areas around the Mediterranean. Possibly the most striking instance was the plan reported in November, 1943, for the resumption of shipments of citrus fruits from Palestine to England, for the first time since the Italian entrance into the war in 1940 practically closed the Mediterranean to normal commerce. These shipments were to be made under governmental auspices, by arrangements between the British Food Ministry and the Palestine marketing authorities.

In return for the general merchandise being supplied to the French African peoples by the United States and the United Kingdom, through their joint North African Economic Board, sizable countershipments of phosphates and other minerals from those areas have already been resumed. The continuation of military activities in the Mediterranean has not thus far allowed the restoration of commercial transactions with North Africa and the adjacent Italian areas from official to direct private channels, although the official directing agencies have expressed their hope that this may not be long deferred.

Smaller Shifts in Pacific Region, Also to Allies' Advantage

While the Japanese have been forced back from sizable reaches of the Pacific Ocean, the land areas recaptured from Japan during 1943—the Aleutian Islands, the Gilberts, the Solomons, and portions of New Guinea and of adjacent islands—are not in themselves of much commercial significance. Their possession by the Allies has commercial importance, however, in shortening and rendering more secure the sea lanes between the United States and Australia and the Southwest Pacific generally.

Moreover, the heavy Allied sinking of Japanese merchant vessels during the past year, even within the contracting perimeter of the Japanese-dominated area, has been curtailing their ability to utilize the resources of their newly acquired southern possessions as well as to deliver goods to them in return.

TRADE TRENDS OUTSIDE THE AXIS REGIONS

General Features of Current Limitations on Civilian Trade

Among the Allies and the nations friendly to them, the progress of the war, and its insatiable demands for ships, equipment, and supplies, have been the prime determinants during 1943 of what was possible and what was allowable in the way of shipments of goods between them. These extraordinary forces have not only been overriding the free choices of merchants; they have also rendered quite subordinate the tariffs and other usual foreign trade controls of individual governments, and the normal trade-negotiation activities between governments. As such, they have become the primary influences upon the commercial policies of governments and upon the consequent pattern of foreign trade.

The course of the war has, necessarily, been determining the basic accessibility of the various regions and countries of the world to each other. Next in importance only to the military operations themselves have been the developments in the respective war-production programs to support them, and the changes in the transport facilities available for ordinary commerce, after satisfying prior military demands and taking account of war losses and replacements. Consequently, the official controls and facilities designed to govern the movements of goods between countries have either been adapted to the furtherance of the war-production and delivery programs, or have had to operate within the framework that they set and the limitations they imposed.

The high degree of official control over both exports and imports now reached in practically all countries is probably unprecedented in modern times. Moreover, the controls of individual governments have, during the war, become increasingly tied in with arrangements and decisions of an intergovernmental character. Under the circumstances, the commercial considerations and channels normally involved in transactions between peoples in different countries now have free play only insofar as they serve—or at least are not inconsistent with—the national interests of their respective countries. These national interests, in turn, need to be viewed by individual governments in the light of their interdependence with the interests of other friendly governments.

Despite these limitations, the volumes of goods to meet ordinary civilian needs that were exchanged during the past year, at least between most of the Allied and neutral countries, came to a surprisingly large percentage of the foreign trade that they normally carried on during the prewar years. Of course, these wartime trade movements have differed considerably from the prewar, in the relative importance both of the various classes of goods and of the different sources and destinations. The fact, however, that these countries have been able to maintain so large a part of their normal volume of commercial exchanges, in the face of the war and alongside of the huge shipments of military supplies, seem significant as well as gratifying.

Moreover, despite the degree of governmental and intergovernmental intervention in the direction of international trade, and the large amounts of bulk purchasing by or through official agencies, the major part of the goods moving between the non-Axis countries—other than military equipment—appears to have continued to be actually channeled through private trading firms, both in the countries of origin and of destination.

Improvements in Allied Shipping Allows Freer Flow of Many Products

The mounting output of the Allies' shipbuilding during 1943, joined with the 60 per cent reduction in sinkings by the increasing success of their operations against Axis submarines, had by the latter months of the year considerably eased the shortage of merchant shipping in the non-Axis world. This had for over a year been the basic limitation, upon both the delivery of goods to many countries and upon the bringing of essential products from them.

The easement from the availability of more ships was in addition to the increased effectiveness of existing shipping, arising from the shorter and safer sea routes made possible by the Allied military progress during 1943, earlier mentioned. In fact, not the least commercial advantage to the Allied and neutral nations from the reopening of the Mediterranean has been the release of more ships for use on other trade routes. The abatement in the risks of sea transport of merchandise also reduced its costs, which was reflected in the series of marked reductions, during 1943, in the surcharges on ocean freight rates and in the war risk insurance premiums to various major trading regions.

The marked improvement in the Allied shipping position has recently been making possible not only a substantial step-up in the flow of military supplies to the various war fronts and bases, but also a fuller and freer movement among the Allied and friendly countries of their enlarged aggregate outputs of all classes of goods, including civilian supplies as well as materials for war purposes.

The latter months of 1943 have witnessed the transport from distant places to the principal Allied countries of increasing quantities of various types of commodities, both essential and secondary—some of which had been undeliverable the preceding year because more urgent needs absorbed the ships available. Thus, the termination of coffee rationing in the United States at the end of July, the more ample supplies of sugar, tea, and cocoa, and the recent reappearance in the markets of bananas—all reflect the easement in shipping as well as the improved safety of the Atlantic and other sea lanes.

Among the more essential commodities, it has been possible to build up increased reserves in the United States, for example, of vegetable oils from Latin America, cork from North Africa, burlap from India, and of wool from Australia and elsewhere. This has been carried to a point where governmental agencies are now able to release their stocks of such materials more freely to private industry, to be processed for civilian use.

In the other direction, the prior demands of their war production programs still limit what the United States, Great Britain, Canada, and other Allied workshops can spare in many lines for commercial shipment overseas. The more comfortable shipping situation of recent months has, however, been allowing somewhat better satisfaction of the civilian import requirements of each other, of friendly nations, and of the areas for which certain Allied governments have assumed special responsibility.

Expansion of United States–Canadian Output Allows More Goods for Civilian Trade

The cumulative result of the war-stimulated expansion of facilities and output in most of the countries outside the Axis-dominated regions, which the easement in shipping helped make more freely available to each other, has been an enormous increase during 1943 in the quantities of goods that moved among them. Naturally, the great bulk of the goods has consisted of material and equipment shipped for use in the respective war-production programs of the major Allies, and to support the vigorous military offensives by their forces on the various fronts. In fact, the attainment by the Allied nations of the ability to outproduce the Axis nations, and to deliver the matériel on the fighting fronts, promises to be the decisive determinant in the ultimate outcome of World War II.

No definite measure of the volume of military supplies shipped out of their territories by the Allied countries during the war may ever be available.[1] It is known, however, that the magnitude of such shipments during 1943 was several times that of the ordinary goods that moved between countries during the most prosperous of peace years, and quite dwarfed the volume of the commercial shipments for civilian use that continued to move during the year. Despite these hugely enlarged shipments for war purposes, the indications are that normal commerical trade among the Allied and friendly countries has, as a whole, been maintained at levels not much different from those of the preceding year. Apparently, the licensing governments and intergovernmental allocating agencies were able to make the enlarged volumes of output, attained during the year in most of these countries, serve both civilian and military needs.

For the United States in particular, there were evidences during the latter months of 1943 that various classes of products, including metals and other recently scarce commodities, were becoming more freely available for civilian use and commercial exportation. This trend was assisted by the fact that the construction of most of the facilities for war production and training approached completion, and that the rate of output of finished articles in some lines passed the peak volume required by the military program, or was "cut back" to adjust to shifts in war-production plans. This easier supply situation—while not general, and declared subject to

[1] A number of the principal Allied countries have suspended the publication of their records of foreign trade; only the United States makes a clear distinction between exports under Lend-Lease and for cash; and no countries make known the volume of the supplies sent to their own armed forces abroad or for their overseas bases of operation.

possible tightening up later in 1944—has already been reflected in a material relaxation of the official controls that had been developed to regulate exportations from the United States, particularly to the countries of Latin America.

The United States and Canada are the two principal belligerent Allied countries "located away from the fighting theaters of war," and have been in a position to spare sizable portions of their increased production in various lines for the other Allied and friendly peoples. They differ markedly in this respect from the Soviet Union and China, which require all they can produce for the support of the war on their own soil, and less markedly from the United Kingdom or Australia, which need to retain most of their enlarged output of goods for their own forces and those of their Allies stationed in their territories, and to maintain their populations in a state of war. The over-all records of American and Canadian foreign trade may therefore be regarded as generally indicative of the trend during 1943 compared with the years immediately preceding.

TRADE TRENDS WITHIN THE AXIS REGIONS

While the accounts of commercial developments on the continent of Europe that became available during the past year have often been indirect and fragmentary, they build into a fairly consistent pattern. They indicate that 1943 was marked by increasing deterioration of supplies and growing difficulties of commerce among the countries under the domination or influence of Germany, and a rising disinclination—although not always successfully maintained—to make their goods available on Germany's terms.

Basically, no radical changes appear to have taken place in the structure of official trade controls or in the general conditions governing the exchanges of goods over most of the European continent, which had been imposed by Germany as her sway spread during the early years of the war.[2] The recent changes have been mainly in the scope of their application and in the manner of their current operation.

Conditions of Trading for the German-controlled Territories

Certain of the conquered territories have been successively annexed to Germany, and are now treated commercially as integral parts of the German customs area. In addition to Austria, they include Luxemburg, Alsace and Lorraine, and portions of Czechoslovakia, of Poland, and of

[2] These were analyzed rather fully in the chapters covering 1941 and 1942.

Belgium. Those countries of Europe which are regarded by Germany as "occupied areas" have also, for some time now, lost effective control of the right to determine the conditions under which goods enter or leave their territories. Their trade and financial arrangements for 1943 with other countries, including the European neutrals, were usually concluded for them "upon German initiative."

The German aim has been to have payment for all comercial transactions within Europe cleared through the "multilateral clearing system" set up at Berlin. The neutral countries of Europe, however, in their relations with each other and often also with occupied countries, have preferred to settle their obligations through bilateral clearing accounts or other direct arrangements. Moreover, a certain amount of inter-European trading is being conducted on the basis of private compensation, even among the satellite and occupied countries, subject to some German supervision. Reports during the past year also indicated that small but increasing volumes of goods are being delivered, especially in the Balkans, only against free exchange or gold, partly outside of contracts.

Germany's requirements from the occupied countries, and its trade agreements with them, have for several years been taking precedence over their arrangements for trade exchanges with all other countries. In December, 1942, the German import duties were officially abolished on the entry of most classes of goods from the occupied areas (except those of the Soviet Union), partly for the declared purpose of improving "the economic equalization of European countries." German export duties on shipments to those countries were also declared lifted, although those had applied to only a few products.

Shortages of Supplies Plus Bombing Damage to Plants and Transport

With the approaching exhaustion of the large reserve stocks of various commodities accumulated by Germany before the outbreak of the war, and of the supplies of foodstuffs and other commodities requisitioned from the occupied countries during the early years of the war, the Allied blockade reduced the exchanges of goods within Axis-controlled Europe during 1943 very largely to those currently produced within the Continent.

However, the Allied bombings of many production centers in Germany and the German-held areas which have marked the past year, joined with the battering of various European ports, and the frequent disruption of overland transportation facilities by air raid and sabotage, have been appreciably curtailing the volumes of many classes of goods that could be turned out, and materially reducing the quantities that could be moved among the countries of continental Europe.

This has been evidenced repeatedly in the reports of drastic reductions in the trade turnover between many pairs of European countries, especially during the second half of the year, from the volumes anticipated in the agreements as originally concluded. Thus, in April, 1943, the German export quotas for certain consumption goods to Hungary were canceled, "because their production had been suddenly suspended."

The growing difficulties of commerce within Axis Europe were even more apparent from the reports of the negotiations during 1943 for new agreements to govern trade exchanges between various pairs of countries, for the balance of the year or for 1944. The volumes of trade anticipated under the new agreements were often frankly announced as considerably less than that of the preceding period.

One such agreement concluded between two important European countries was described as based upon that of the preceding year, "with certain adjustments to the present capacities of the suppliers and the existing transport difficulties." In a revision of its trade agreement with Germany during 1943, Sweden was reported as having abolished for certain commodities the earlier system of fixed quotas, and provided that those products were to be exported to the extent determined by domestic supplies, and by the necessity of having exports to barter with other countries.

Mounting Complaints Over Uncompensated Exports to Germany

The declining military prospects of Germany have apparently increased the expressed reluctance of those continental countries which retain any measure of independent action to continue furnishing goods on Germany's terms and prices. They have become less willing to accept in return for their products increased credit balances in their clearing accounts at the Reichsbank, or promises of deliveries of desired goods after the war. The neutrals have, however, been more successful than the satellite countries in maintaining this position during the past year. Hungary, Rumania, and Bulgaria were each reported to have had to grant new clearing advances to Germany, against elaborate German undertakings for future shipments of industrial equipment and armaments.

When necessary, the Germans have shown a high degree of flexibility in the diversion of the supplies available to them. In the aggregate, however, it appears to have become recognized that Germany will not be able to offset its takings from the dependent countries by the supplying of equivalent goods during the war, even after the earlier measures for reduction of the exchange value of their national currencies, and the recent repatriation of much of their old German-held state securities in part payment of the clearing debts, notably in the case of Hungary. To allay the uneasiness in Rumania over the large clearing debt, Germany is reported to have sent that country a sizable amount of gold last spring.

The recognition that German repayment for much of the goods now being supplied by other European countries can take place only after the war was again expressed quite frankly in the recent address by Dr. Walter Funk before the annual meeting of the Reichsbank on February 9, 1944: "During last year Germany's clearing debt again increased toward some of our foreign-trade partners.... Germany's foreign creditors should ponder the fact that their claims in reichsmarks have stable value and... that the immensely increased productive strength of the Reich is a safe guarantor for the repayment of a claim in kind after the end of the war...."

As President of the German Reichsbank, Dr. Funk had earlier expressed concern over the vicious circle which he saw developing in a number of European countries, from their uncompensated exports and mounting clearing balances against Germany. He pointed out that the consequent shortages of goods in those countries were having inflationary tendencies, resulting in increases in local wages and prices. These, in turn, advanced the prices of their export products to Germany, compelling the delivery of a greater quantity of German goods in order to pay for the same quantity of imports, to the point where the increased cost of imports endangered the internal level of prices in Germany.

Stiffening Attitude of Neutrals Against Further Credits to Germany

Particularly striking have been the stiffening attitudes against German commercial demands evidenced by most of the neutral countries of Europe during the past year. Thus, Sweden refused to renew for 1943 the system of extending sizable trade credits to Germany, as had been done in preceding years. In the subsequent negotiations for the trade agreement to cover 1944, the Swedish Government maintained its refusal to the point of insisting that the major part of the official export credits outstanding be liquidated during the coming year. Germany has undertaken to supply to Sweden during 1944 a value of exports greater by 250 million crowns (about 60 million dollars) than that of the Swedish goods to be sent to Germany during the same period, with the understanding that Swedish export quotas could be cut if German shipments during the year should fall below the figures set. Moreover, German increases in prices were balanced by corresponding increases in the prices of certain Swedish products.

The large credit granted by Switzerland to Germany under the old trade agreement was reported to have been covered by orders by the beginning of 1943, although a considerable part of the orders under it had not yet been actually shipped. The negotiations for the renewal of the agreement broke down in January, reportedly over differences regarding the terms for the exchange of goods during 1943, with each side endeavoring to reduce its exports. The former regime was continued de facto, but the volume of goods supplied to each other was much reduced during the year. A provisional arrangement is reported to have been reached toward its close, which provided for the progressive elimination of the German arrears which had lately accumulated.

Spain likewise seemed intent upon reducing substantially its credit balance in the clearing account with Germany. While ready to see sizable quantities of a broad range of the country's surplus products disposed of in the German market, to the point of helping finance their sale, the Spanish Government appeared concerned most about getting goods of equivalent value in return. During most of the past year, it is reported to have been regulating the current trade exchanges with Germany closely, holding back export licenses when the desired German products were not forthcoming in the volumes promised.

For some months, the sought reduction in the clearing overdraft appeared to be in process, partly through a marked increase in the shipments of German goods to Spain. Toward the close of the year, however, a settlement of the debt to Germany incurred during the Spanish Civil War was concluded for 400 million pesetas (about 40 million dollars). This appeared to be, in effect, a replenishment of the German supply of pesetas, against which larger quantities of Spanish products could be obtained without increasing the old clearing debt.

The position earlier taken by the government and merchants of Turkey, that the goods from Germany or German-held territories promised under trade agreements must be delivered at the Turkish frontier before the release of the compensating Turkish raw materials and agricultural products, has been maintained.

A similar insistence appears to have developed during the past year on the part of the Portuguese authorities. Since the Germans failed to deliver the contracted amount of iron and steel products under the trade agreement of the preceding year, the Portuguese are reported to have taken the position, in the negotiations for the 1943 agreement, that consignments to Germany of the much-desired wolfram ore would be released only against actual deliveries of German iron and steel products, on a pro rata basis.

Limited Outside Trade Contacts of European Neutrals

By means of a limited number of vessels based on Göteborg, which were granted "safe conduct" through the war zones by both sides, Sweden had for several years managed to maintain a precarious exchange of essential products with various countries of the Western Hemisphere, principally with South America. In actions attributed to the stiffening attitude of the Swedish Government on several matters, the Germans suspended their assurance for this service twice during 1943, and thus for several months cut off Sweden's chief outside trade channel. Agreement for the resumption of this Göteborg traffic during 1944 was finally concluded in early January, and it is reported that the range of these safe-conduct vessels was enlarged, to allow Sweden to obtain fruits and vegetables from Spain and fish from Iceland.

Despite Switzerland's land-locked location and the double scrutiny of the Allied and Axis blockade controls, the Swiss had striven to keep up a fair exchange of goods with American and other outside countries, by overland transit arrangements and a small war-acquired Swiss merchant fleet. Since the outlet through Genoa was cut off in September, 1943, and the overland connections became limited to Marseilles and the more distant Iberian ports, Swiss overseas trade is reported to have declined.

Of the other neutral countries on the European continent, the geographic position of Spain and Portugal has allowed them to maintain actively a number of outside trade currents, with South America as well as with the United Kingdom and the United States.

Sinkings Cut Down German-Japanese Exchanges of Scarce Products

Until the Bay of Biscay incident in late December, 1943, involving the sinking of a blockade runner from the Far East and several of her convoying German destroyers, and the sinking in the South Atlantic shortly thereafter of three German ships that were carrying vital raw materials from Japanese-held ports, little had been heard during the year about clandestine exchanges of scarce products between Germany and Japan, which had not been uncommon through 1942. It is known, however, that strenuous efforts had continued during the past year to carry through the German-Japanese agreement for compensation deals, of critical raw materials from the Far East against machine tools and technical equipment and data from Europe.

The actual deliveries are understood to have been small. According to the British Minister of Economic Warfare, the Germans lost 75 per cent of their blockade runners to the Far East last season. The improved Allied sea and air surveillance of the ocean routes, and their rising success in sinking the ships engaged in this traffic are reported to be holding down the efforts to effect commodity exchanges between the two Axis-controlled regions.

Japan Unable to Utilize Products or Supply Needs of "Southern Regions"

Economic reports from the Far East during 1943 have been meager, and often of doubtful reliability. Only general observations are therefore warranted as to the developments of the past year regarding the movements of goods, or the general economic relations, between Japan and its controlled territories, especially the countries and islands of Southeast Asia acquired during the winter and spring of 1941–1942, or among these southern areas themselves.

It had early become clear that, while the Japanese economic program for exploiting the resources of the new territories under Japan's control closely resembled that of Germany on the continent of Europe, there were important differences. Japan could not furnish sufficient markets for the full volumes of many of the natural products upon the disposal of which Southeast Asia depends for its livelihood; nor, under wartime conditions, did it have the shipping or the manufacturing capacity adequate to supplying, with even their *most essential* import requirements, the huge populations secluded within that region. The reported developments during 1943 indicate little progress in overcoming these deficiencies.

Only in sharply limited categories has Japan been at all replacing the normal world markets for the products of Southeast Asia. Petroleum and a few other critical minerals (including manganese, bauxite, nickel, and chromium), rice, salt, and certain woods appear to be the principal commodities of that region upon which Japan is concentrating. The huge quantities of rubber and tin produced in those areas, normally the chief sources of supply for the entire world, are much beyond the ability of Japan to utilize or dispose of. Even in the case of rice, it is reported that the Burmese export surplus of 3 million tons crowds its warehouses, undisposable, while Japan and other Eastern peoples are reported short of supplies of their basic foodstuff. The Japanese are being told that the obtainment of petroleum and other war materials from these distant areas must take precedence even over rice.

Japan's current trade with its new possessions appears to be far from a balanced two-way exchange of merchandise, and the indications are that the Japaneses do not expect, during the war, to balance off with goods of equivalent value the increased quantities of raw materials they are obtaining from "the southern regions," as they are commonly referred to in Japanese broadcasts.

Difficulties of transport, accentuated by the heavy sinkings of Japanese cargo ships during 1943, afford the major explanation. Japan lacks overland rail connection with the southeastern mainland, and the inadequacy of Japanese merchant shipping for frequent intercourse with those distant areas and the outspread islands has been recognized as Japan's crucial economic weakness. Even though Japan is able to stock-pile raw materials locally—as at Saigon, where warehouses have been continually enlarged to care for these surpluses—the lack of shipping prevents their utilization in Japan proper, or their effective distribution throughout the occupied areas.

Second in importance to the limitations of shipping is the question as to the quantity of manufactured goods which the Japanese are able or willing to spare for the peoples in the newly acquired territories. The observed facts in Japan's recent trade relations with Indo-China, the nearest of the southern areas, are illustrative.

The Japanese–Indo-China commercial agreement for 1943 signed in January provided in great detail for the quantities of grains, notably rice, and of various minerals that were to be supplied by Indo-China to Japan during the year. The discussions regarding the return exports from Japan, however, continued for seven months before agreement was announced, and what is recorded was a general assurance that the Japanese would spare all they could.[3] It is reported that, for 1942, the tonnage of supplies promised to Indo-China from Japan amounted to about one-fifth of Indo-Chinese normal imports, when that country was open to world commerce, and that less than half of the amount promised was actually delivered.

[3] On January 27, 1944, an official Tokyo broadcast announced the renewal of this arrangement for the new year in these terms: "The Indochina-Japan trade agreement to export and supply rice to Japan from Indochina was completed on January 5."

Southern Reports of Economic Distress, Forced Loans, and Crop Diversions

The combined effects of the closing off of their usual world markets, of the shortage of shipping, and of the meagerness of supplies from Japan, are evidenced in reports such as these, coming during the past year from various directions: the rotting of rice in Burma while neighboring Malaya has an acute food shortage; the scarcity of the simplest consumers' goods in most of the newly acquired Japanese territories; the general curtailment of production, except in those products specially fostered to make up a Japanese deficiency; and the drop in market prices, to the point where tin was reported as selling for less than half the 1941 price, and rubber for a cent a pound.

Speaking of conditions in Java, Kazuo Aoki, head of the new Ministry of Greater East Asia, is reported to have declared in May, 1943: "Needless to say, the living conditions of a great many people have been curtailed to a great extent, and the surplus power has been extended to the military. . . . The people must put up with the living conditions as much as possible, and contribute toward the consummation of the sacred war."

Some indication of the extent of the contribution expected was afforded by the proposal of the Japanese Finance Minister to raise 3.3 billion yen (about 800 million dollars) by public borrowing in the occupied areas during the budget year 1943–1944. Obviously, the principal form in which such an amount could be transferred to Japan—huge as it is in relation to the level of income of the populations concerned—would be as commodities of their production for which no early compensation was to be expected.

The measure was described as "the first step toward the establishing of a common financial system for Greater East Asia," and the Japanese Finance Minister declared that the races within that area "should, in accordance with their power, bear the military expenditures necessary for the prosecution of the war." It was later reported that the budget also contemplated the raising in the occupied areas of an additional 1.6 billion yen (400 million dollars) during 1943–1944, through the sale or lease of materials seized during the military operations, as well as through general mobilization of their financial resources by "voluntary" contributions, war bond drives, and other measures.

"Closer economic cooperation on the basis of reciprocity" was one of the five basic principles set forth in the Joint Declaration issued at the close of the Greater East Asia Conference held at Tokyo in November, 1943. Whatever the plans for the future may be, however, what has been happening during the past year indicates that the newly acquired territories are now apparently being treated primarily as sources of raw materials, to be drawn upon by the war industries and for stock-piling in Japan and the earlier-conquered northern territories. Little progress appears thus far to have been made toward the development of these areas in themselves, or toward their integration into the general commercial structure of the promised "Greater East Asia Co-Prosperity Sphere."

The forced conversion of sugar lands in the Philippines and of rice fields on the Asiatic mainland to the growing of cotton, a notable Japanese deficit, is well known. In addition, the production of certain staple surplus commodities of these areas, such as coffee, tea, and rubber in the case of Java, were reported during 1943 to have been ordered drastically curtailed, as being in excess of the Japanese purchase program. Plantations which can be uprooted are being diverted to the growing of grain and other locally deficient crops.

For the wartime at least, the Japanese aim appears to be to encourage greater local self-supply on the part of these southern areas, in foodstuffs and in simple manufactured goods, so as to reduce the demands upon Japan for goods and for ships to carry them. The Japanese administrators are also trying to foster an increased measure of interregional commercial intercourse among the peoples of Southeast Asia. Encouragement is being given to the interchange of local surpluses among them, and to the building of small wooden ships for their transport. It is declared to be the Japanese desire that imports and exports between pairs of countries should balance, however, and transactions are reported to be carried on largely by barter, through officially sponsored agencies.

Plan for Self-Sufficient "Inner Zone" of Japan and Near-by Areas

The commercial consolidation that is going on in the Far East is rather between Japan and the near-by earlier-conquered areas, forming a compact "Inner Zone," consisting of Japan Proper, Korea, Manchuria, North China, and Formosa. It is among these areas that some freer movement of goods is encouraged by the Japanese authorities, coincident with the exploitation of their natural resources essential to the heavy industries and armament production, and the expansion of the basic processing capacity already developed there. It is understood, however, that even to the northern areas the supplies of ordinary consumers' goods have been small, and that the shipments to them from Japan have consisted mostly of supplies for the military forces, and of machinery and equipment essential to the local production and transport of war materials for Japan's use.

The aim is obviously to develop the most complete strategic self-sufficiency possible within this "Inner Zone," while the areas comprising the "Outer Zone" (Central China and the southern regions) are to serve as sources of supply of deficit or supplementary materials, with their military occupation affording a protection in depth for the heart of the contemplated Japanese economic system. In fact, it is reported that the development of synthetic oil plants, the utilization of aluminum shale, and the extraction of iron ore from poor deposits have been intensively promoted in the northern territories, during this very period since Japan has had within its control the natural and richer deposits of petroleum, bauxite, and iron ore of the southern regions. The shortage of cargo tonnage for the long hauls, serious as that is, hardly appears to be the full explanation.

These reports lend confirmation to the belief that the varying patterns of economic development and commercial facilitation—with the Inner and Outer zones of the present Japanese possessions—are motivated not alone by present shortages of transport or supplies. They suggest also recognition of the contingency that future Allied military operations in the Far East may cut off Japan from access to some of the southern areas, and leave the country dependent upon its own resources, stocks, and productive capacity, and upon those of the near-by continental areas.

1944

PROSPECT OF WAR'S END BRINGS PLANS FOR MORE NORMAL TRADING CONDITIONS

COMMERCIAL SHIFTS RESULTING FROM MILITARY DEVELOPMENTS

The progress of Allied arms during 1944 has shrunk the area of Japanese domination in the Pacific, and cut off Germany from access to the resources of large parts of the European continent. However, the continuation of military operations, the highly disordered state of the recovered territories, joined with the poor conditions of transport, have thus far kept most of the liberated areas from resuming any appreciable foreign trade, at least through private channels.

Progress toward the resumption of normal commerce has advanced further with certain colonial territories in Africa and outlying islands than with the continent of Europe. Such goods for civilian use as have thus far been supplied to the recovered areas of Europe have been handled through military or other governmental agencies, primarily for relief purposes. Only a small beginning had been possible, by the end of 1944, toward reviving overseas exports from these European countries. The present limitations upon private trading and the prospects for its resumption vary with the individual areas.

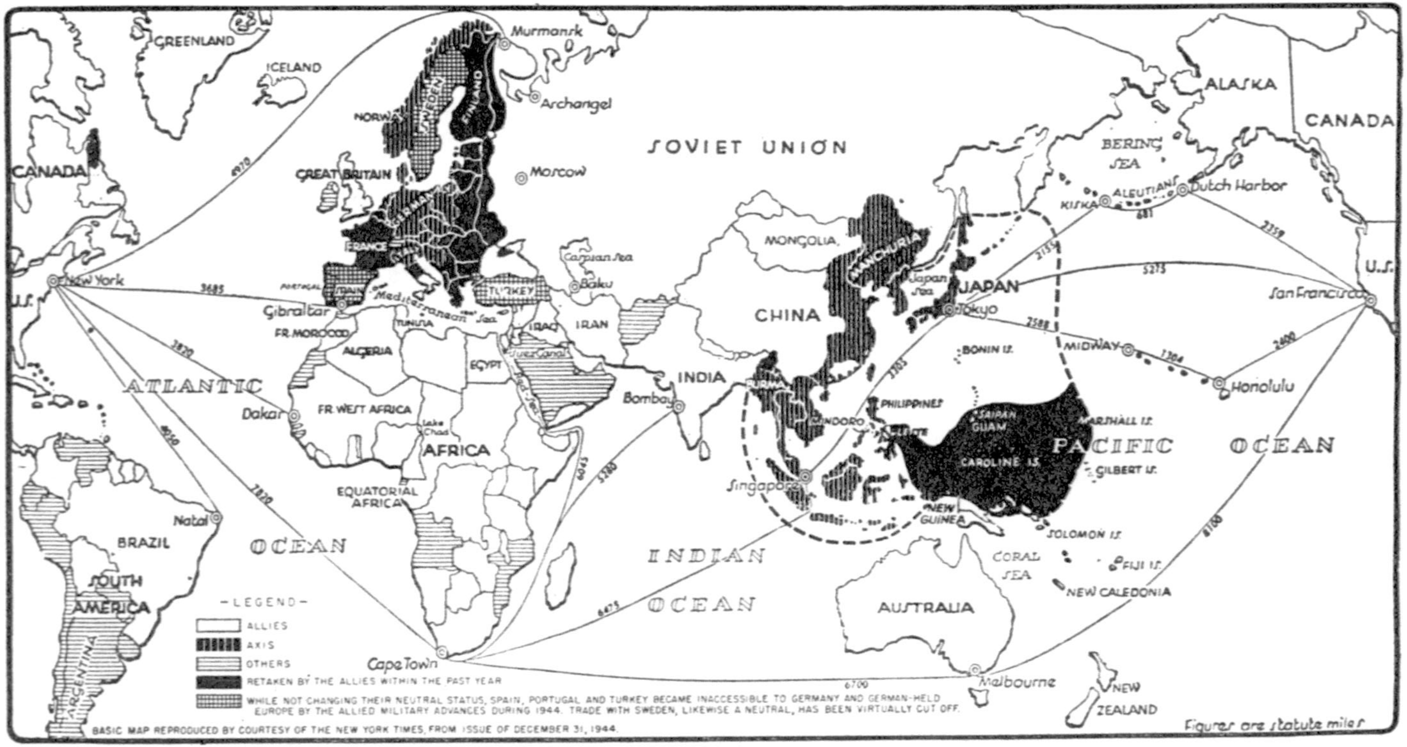

Shifts During 1944 in Areas Within Commercial Reach of the Axis and Allied Nations

Sharp Shrinkage in European Areas Within Trade Reach of Axis

The two Axis regions, in Europe and in the Far East, had been cut off from open trading with each other for some time by the Allied naval blockade, broken only by occasional blockade runners. With the reconquest of France during the latter half of 1944, the Germans lost the Bay of Biscay ports, which had served as the base for such blockade running as had been maintained during the last few years. This has practically put an end to such little help as the Germans and Japanese could extend to each other in the way of supplying strategic materials or equipment.

With the general progress of the Allied forces during the past year, Germany has successively lost access to its markets, and—what is more important—its sources of supply, in most of its former allied and occupied countries of continental Europe. The combined Allied pressures from three directions had, by the end of 1944, cut off Germany from France and Belgium in the West; about half of Italy in the South; and in the East, from the balance of the occupied Russian territories, the Baltics, and Finland; from much of Poland, Hungary, and Yugoslavia; and from all of Rumania, Bulgaria, and Greece. Beyond such farm products, raw materials, and machinery as the Germans had confiscated before their retreat and carried from those areas into their own country, they can now draw upon, or trade with, only a minor part of the Europe that lay beyond their 1939 territorial borders.

In a radio appeal for intensified food production in Germany in November, 1944, Food Minister Backe declared that "now we have to rely almost entirely on ourselves in food production. The help which we got in the past from territories outside Germany is no longer avaliable." While this somewhat overstated the actual situation, it may well constitute the sober expectation of the German Government as to the situation that its people are soon to face.

Neutrals Begin to Divert Their Trade Toward the Allies

The trade of Germany and of its allied and occupied countries with the neutral countries of Europe, which was still very active at the beginning of 1944, had shrunk greatly by the close of the year. Allied reoccupation of France virtually severed communications with Spain and Portugal, which had been the sources of certain products quite important to the German military effort. The minerals, fibers, and tobacco of Turkey were lost, even before the fall of Bulgaria, when the Turkish Government terminated commercial relations with Germany early in August, thus putting an end to what had been a fairly active movement of goods with all of Axis Europe.

Although commerical relations between them have not been formally broken, the important trade exchanges between the German-dominated countries and Sweden, the source of large quantities of iron ore and lumber, are described by Swedish sources as having virtually ended in the fall of 1944. Such limited supplies of Swedish products as German ships can still bring, have to take circuitous and dangerous routes. Sweden's sole link with the outer world, namely, the series of specified ships granted safe-conduct from both belligerents, is reported as continuing. This has allowed Sweden to maintain a fair-sized trade with a number of South American and other overseas countries, and has afforded it supplies of many commodities important to its national economy.

The Stockholm press has recently announced a few beginnings in the resumption of Swedish trade with the Allied countries. Certain machinery and other goods ordered by Russia before the outbreak of German hostilities in 1941, which had been stored at Stockholm, are now being transported to Leningrad by the use of Finnish vessels. Some British lumber contracts concluded in 1940, which had been halted by the subsequent blockade, have recently been renegotiated, with payment to be made even if undeliverable at once. Sweden is already providing Finland and Norway with considerable supplies of food and clothing, on a relief basis, and with some other products on credit.

The only neutral country with which German trade has continued on anything like the basis which prevailed during the earlier war years is Switzerland, due mainly to the physical location of that country. However, in the periodic renewal of their trade arrangements with Germany during 1944, the Swiss insisted upon exports to that country being currently adjusted to the volume of desired products coming from Germany, and upon the curtailment of supplies in certain lines of production which had been expanded for the German market during the war.

In the Far East, the progressive closing in upon the outer ring of Japanese-held islands during 1944, combined with the continued sinkings of Japanese vessels, further restricted Japan's access to its occupied territories in Southeast Asia, curtailed as that had already become. The Allied progress during the past year in regaining control over large expanses of the Pacific has thus far carried with it little commercial advantage, beyond ensuring safer lines of communications with Australia and New Zealand.

Efforts Toward Resumption of Trading with Liberated Areas

In the Pacific.—The Philippine island of Leyte is the only area in the Pacific recovered during the past year with which an appreciable current of merchandise movements with the United States has yet begun. Special interest has centered upon the resumption of such supplies of hemp for cordage and of copra for soapmaking as could be obtained from the Philippines. Understandably, at this stage, any merchandise supplies to or from the recovered Pacific areas are incidental to the military operations, and are handled through governmental channels.

Considerable progress in the restoration of the productivity and commerce of New Guinea, begun soon after its substantial recovery in 1943, was reported during the past year by Australia, to whom part of the island had been assigned after World War I as a mandated territory. The special New Guinea Production Control Board, formed, among other purposes, to promote and control the production of the primary products of the regained territory, reported early in 1944 that the majority of the rubber and copra plantations either had been restored to their owners or were being operated by the board. Production of both of these major crops was declared to be approaching prewar figures, with appreciable quantities of rubber already delivered to the mainland.

In Africa and other colonial areas.—With the outlying colonies and dependencies of the European countries, and especially with their African territories, greater progress has been made in the return to normal trading arrangements than with the European countries themselves. Trade with French West Africa and with Equatorial Africa (and the Cameroons) is already in process of substantial restoration to private channels. Commodities shipped to and from French North Africa have thus far been handled on a government-to-government basis. However, this situation was studied on the ground last fall by a special economic mission from the United States, composed of commercial as well as governmental representatives, and arrangements are being worked out with the French to facilitate the progressive resumption of direct commercial trading with their North African dependencies.

Private trade has already been restored in many or most categories of goods with the French West Indies and French Guiana, with St. Pierre and Miquelon, and with Madagascar and Reunion. American trade with the French Pacific island of New Caledonia has remained on a private basis throughout the war. The same has been true of the Belgian Congo, except for items of military supply and for direct use by the government, which have been handled by the Belgian Congo Purchasing Mission.

In Western Europe (Italy, France, Belgium, and the Netherlands).—Continuation of some military activities in most of the sections of Europe which have been detached from Axis control, combined with the few good harbors available and the badly disrupted state of internal transport, has prevented, up to January, 1945, any resumption of private trading with those areas. Limited commercial communication by mail has been resumed, beginning in the fall of 1944 with the accessible parts of Italy and of France, and followed later with Belgium and the recovered portions of the Netherlands.

Under present inter-Allied arrangements, the military authorities are to handle, for a period of approximately six months after occupation, such supplies as can be furnished to the areas liberated by the United States and British armies, and such surplus export products as can be made available from those areas. Thereafter, or as soon as they cease to be zones of military operations, the task of supplying the import requirements of the liberated areas is turned over to the civil governments of those areas and, where they are not able to pay for them, to the United Nations Relief and Rehabilitation Administration. Products which continue to be in over-all short supply remain, for all these areas, subject to allocation by the British-American Combined Boards, upon the recommendations of UNRRA. The exportation of such goods as the liberated territories can furnish for foreign markets become subject, after the period of military control, to the regulations of the local governments.

To the liberated portions of *Italy,* such goods as it has thus far been possible to deliver, principally food supplies, have moved through military channels, with some participation of the UNRRA organization in early prospect. The primary limiting factors are transport and various conditions connected with military operations.

Some importations of Italian merchandise into the United States have arrived recently, and larger shipments are contemplated. Thus far, they have consisted of certain strategic materials, some wine, essential oils, and a few other Italian specialties. These goods are bought by the Allied Commission in Italy and consigned to the United States Commercial Company as its agent. The strategic materials are distributed as directed by the War Production Board and the War Food Administration, and the other goods among American importers for sale in the open market, the United States Commercial Company utilizing private trade channels to the fullest practicable extent in distributing the supplies. The funds obtained from the sale of these goods are to be made available in the United States for the use of the Italian Government.

The Provisional Government of *France* announced, on September 29, 1944, that all importations and exportations are to be subject to the prior obtaining of an official license. French officials are reported to have no objection in principle to some private imports being permitted, under governmental license, as soon as conditions allow. Under the disturbed conditions which prevailed to the end of 1944, however, and the inadequacy of ocean shipping and internal transport, the possibility of delivering anything besides army supplies in France has been limited to the primary essentials for the maintenance of the French population.

The basic French order of September 29, earlier cited, specifies that, "in principle, no imports or exports can for the moment be effected by sea route for the account of private parties." For the time being, the French Supply Mission in Washington is the sole purchasing agent in the United States for such supplies of necessary commodities as can be obtained and shipped.

If the French officials who arrived in the United States late in December succeed in effecting arrangements for the procurement and shipment of any appreciable part of their announced program of imports desired for France during the first six months of 1945, that would amount to a sizable resumption of American exports to France, although the sole buyer would be the French Supply Mission. While a very broad range of commodities have been mentioned, there have been indications that, for the period ahead, prior consideration for shipment to France would be accorded to the raw materials, fuel, and machinery necessary to rehabilitate French industry and transport.

The prospect for the resumption of direct trading connections with private French importers still appears to be somewhat remote. When conditions do allow such resumption, the trade will be favored by the temporary suspension of import duties into France which the Provisional Government has ordered for all but certain specified categories of goods.

With regard to exports, the French officials favor the early resumption of private overseas trade, under license, although the lack of many of the usual exportable surpluses in that country, joined with the problems of pricing and foreign exchange, are declared likely to operate against any sizable volume of outbound trade from developing for some time. However, plans are reported under consideration for the early resumption of the commercial exportation from France of a wide range of French specialty products, with the quantities to be dependent largely upon what French exporters are able to assemble and deliver at the ports for the ships returning to the United States promptly after having discharged their eastbound cargoes.

The French Colonial Supply Mission in New York has been purchasing some commodities in bulk for certain of the colonies, in accordance with their schedules of import requirements as consolidated from the local commercial requests. As earlier noted, trade has been restored to direct private channels with various of the French dependencies in many classes of consumers' goods.

Moreover, the Foreign Economic Administration has declared that both the French Supply Mission and the Colonial Mission are expected to deal increasingly with private interests in the United States, instead of with the United States Government. In the past, many of their purchases in the United States had been effected through the Lend-Lease procurement channels, on a cash reimbursable basis. The Foreign Economic Administration has also recently announced that, for similar commodities and where the end-use is comparable, no preference or higher priority will be given to export license applications from foreign purchasing missions than to applicants from the trade.

While *Belgium* had been liberated in the fall, and the government-in-exile returned to Brussels, toward the end of the year, eastern Belgium was again overrun in a German counterattack. Antwerp, the port most essential to the delivery of foreign supplies to Belgium in any volume, did not become usable by the Allies until late November, after the enemy forts dominating the Scheldt River from the Dutch side had been overcome. At best, Belgium, as well as Luxemburg and the recovered portions of the Netherlands, are still in the early relief stages, and the resumption of private trade with them is obviously some time off.

An important step for the future has already been taken, however, in the agreement for a temporary customs union of Belgium and Luxemburg (already united economically for some time) with the *Netherlands,* which was concluded in September, 1944, by the governments-in-exile at London. Planned to become effective as soon as the respective governments are reinstalled in their territories, the agreement proposes the immediate abolition of duties on all trade movements between the constituent areas, and the establishment of a common scale of duties on imports from other countries. Coördination of other forms of commercial regulation is also provided, pending the long-term economic union which they propose to work out. The joint tariff schedule, already published, is on a simplified ad valorem basis, with a level of duties generally lower than those previously in effect. Moreover, essential food supplies, as well as materials and equipment for the reëstablishment of production, are to be temporarily admitted into the joint area free of duty.

As a practical matter, this combined liberalized tariff may not operate as the prime determinant of the import trade of these countries for some time. Import-licensing systems, special taxes, and other controls upon imports are contemplated in the agreement as continuing, and it has been intimated that the governments may be the sole importers and exporters for a period following liberation.

The Belgo-Luxemburg-Netherlands Customs Union is notable, however, as representing the first concrete instance of the formation of larger economic units on the European continent, designed to facilitate trade with outside countries as well as with each other, of the type which has been projected for various groups of European countries during the war. This agreement for commercial unification is a sequel to the Monetary Convention concluded between the same three states in the preceding October.

In Eastern Europe.—The liberated territories in Eastern Europe are understood to be still under military control, and nothing definite is yet known as to the prospects for the resumption of outside trade with them.

STEPS TOWARD RELAXATION OF WARTIME EXPORT CONTROLS

In the non-Axis world, the scope for commercial trade broadened appreciably during 1944, and its prospects brightened as the result of a combination of developments, including a beginning in the relaxation of wartime export controls. The general scale earlier set for Allied production of military supplies reached its peak in the first part of the year, and the supply as well as the safety of shipping had improved. The gratifying progress of the military campaigns on all fronts, until the December setback in Europe, further encouraged some of the Allied governments in their planning as to how soon and to what degree facilities and materials could be released for reconversion to serve civilian purposes. Prominent among the claimants for easement from the wartime restrictions upon civilian supply were the exporters and producers for foreign markets.

For several years, the normal operations of commercial exporters had understandably been curtailed and channeled in various ways, as required by the overriding needs for goods and ships for each country's own military operations and those of its Allies, and for the assistance of the populations in the active war zones. Foreign traders naturally have pressed for the earliest possible release, not only from the wartime restrictions upon the volume of their operations, but also from the complicated and time-consuming official procedures in connection with foreign transactions. For some time these have usually involved governmental controls and often licenses in both the countries of exportation and importation and, in many cases, additional arrangements were required for their integration with one another.

The governments of the United States and of the United Kingdom have announced their endeavor to ensure, to the extent practicable, that the exporters of neither country receive undue competitive advantage as a result of the war. However, the precise timing and the degree of easement of wartime economic controls upon commercial exportations might be expected to differ in the various countries, in accordance with their relative supply situation in basic materials, and with the degree to which their manpower and facilities have had to be diverted to war purposes. Thus, until the changed prospect in December for an early end to the war in Europe, conditions in the United States promised to allow an earlier and somewhat larger margin of materials and facilities to be released for civilian uses, both domestically and for foreign markets, than in the case of the United Kingdom and of most other countries.

Even in the United States, however, the actual developments in this field during 1944 have been more in the nature of simplification of existing wartime procedures, and in some cases their elimination, rather than any large-scale release of supplies for uncontrolled disposal. Some materials and products were indeed made more freely available during 1944 for civilian use, both at home and for export, but the supplies of a great many commodities are still limited, and they have continued under control. In view of the interest of commercial concerns in the procedural as well as the supply changes, a brief analysis of the principal developments of the past year in the three principal Allied exporting countries seems worth while.

Procedures Simplified on United States Exports to Large Part of World

Beginning early in 1944, the export control authorities of the United States progressively rolled back the "decentralization" procedure, which had been instituted in March, 1943, to govern exports to the other

American Republics. Adopted originally in order to allow the governments of those other republics a voice in determining the relative essentiality of the various purposes for which the limited supplies and shipping available for their countries might be allocated, the need for arrangements involving the complicated procedures called for by this program had become less urgent.

Specifically, the former general requirement that import recommendations be obtained from the "country agency" of each of the other American governments for most commodities, before export licenses could be issued in the United States, was successively curtailed and, by January, 1945, applied only to a limited "positive" list of commodities. Certain commodities were put on general license, or were in other ways relieved from the requirement for obtaining individual licenses for each transaction, or for each consignee in the same market.

Similarly, the "program license" procedure, which had governed the exports of supplies to most of the British Empire, the Soviet Union, the Middle East, and to the French, Belgian, and Dutch possessions, was discontinued on October 1. That relieved exporters from the necessity of obtaining a "release certificate" from the foreign purchasing missions, established here by those countries, as a condition of securing an export license from the United States authorities for transactions with this broad range of areas. It did not affect the need for obtaining an import license from the government of the country of destination, where that is required. On the contrary, as in the trade relations with Latin America, when the controls at the exporting end are relaxed, those in the countries of importation tend to become more determining.

At various times during the past year, steps also were taken to facilitate, or to restore to normal private channels, the flow of trade in certain lines of exports to Turkey, the Middle East, and to various of the French and Belgian colonies.

For a considerable part of the war period, the supplying of the essential import requirements of certain countries has been programmed through a series of United Kingdom and United States "Combined Area Committees," which also designated the source of supply. An important step toward the return to normal trading with those areas was taken in the fall of 1944, when the United States authorities adopted the principle that, for commodities in long supply, the choice of the importer in the foreign countries as to the country from which he prefers a given item to be supplied should govern, subject to the availability of shipping and the special considerations present where Lend-Lease funds are involved.

At the close of 1944, steps were taken toward freeing trade with the Middle East from the centralized control which had been exercised for several years by the Middle East Supply Center, operating from Cairo under Anglo-American direction. That had been established in 1941, after the closing of the Mediterranean to the Allied shipping rendered the supplying of the essential civilian import requirements of this region an exceptionally difficult problem. With respect to most products, other than those regarded in general short supply or which present special tonnage considerations, the government of each of the countries in the Middle East—from Egypt to Iran—are now to license and control their own importations directly. They are, however, subject to the limitations upon supplies at source and upon the total shipping tonnage available for the region, and must make their own arrangements regarding dollar exchange for purchases to be made in the United States.

United States Discourages Foreign Bulk Buying Through Purchasing Missions

The attitude of the United States administrators toward governmental bulk buying, which had been found the most expedient method in certain cases during the war, but which appears to be preferred by some foreign governments as the continuing method of purchase, has recently been materially clarified. The Foreign Economic Administration announced in December that, where similar commodities are involved and the end-use is comparable, no preference is given and no higher priorities assigned to applications for export licenses submitted by foreign purchasing missions than to applications submitted directly by the trade.

In an instruction released at the end of September, President Roosevelt has already directed that, after the defeat of Germany, the foreign Economic Administration "should relax controls over exports to the fullest extent compatible with our continuing war objectives, . . . with a view to encouraging private trade without interfering with the successful prosecution of the war against Japan." Such action depends, of course, upon the degree of relaxation over strategic commodities and others in short supply which the War Production Board feels warranted in authorizing. Moreover, it has been officially stressed in this connection that the amount of shipping which can be spared from military needs would continue to be a limiting factor upon the volume of commercial exports from the United States at any given time, as would be the current needs for domestic civilian use, and the changing demands for relief and rehabilitation purposes abroad.

A renewed tightness in the commercial shipping situation did develop toward the end of 1944, attributed to the intensification of the war both in the East and in the West, and to the long turnabouts in European ports, still inadequate in number and unloading facilities. Moreover, there were official indications early in 1945 that, in view of the likelihood of a longer war in Europe, all past supply programs of the Allied countries would need to be reviewed. How far this is likely to affect the continued relaxation and simplification of foreign trade controls begun during 1944 is still uncertain.

Revival of British Exports Planned but Controls Only Slightly Eased

In a statement to the House of Commons on November 16, regarding the prospect for the relaxation of the various British wartime economic controls, Prime Minister Churchill cited the restoration of the country's export trade as one of the prime purposes for which "after the defeat of Germany it will be possible and necessary to turn over an increasing part of our resources to civilian production." In a subsequent parliamentary debate on the subject, however, the Minister of Production was emphatic that, for Britain to start now "to resume exports in a substantial way," would mean delay in victory and greater loss of lives.

Up to the close of 1944, only minor relaxations in the British export-licensing controls or procedures had been authorized. Under two orders of the Board of Trade, in March and in November, permission was granted for the exportation of limited lists of secondary commodities,[1] without license, to all countries other than those with which trade is entirely prohibited. As late as April, however, British export license control was extended to include a number of additional minor manufactures. In November, the Board of Trade removed a number of areas from the list of destinations for which *all* exports from the United Kingdom had for some time been subject to licensing. These comprised most of Africa (except North Africa), the French and British possessions in the Pacific, and the French colonies in the Western Hemisphere.

An early indication of the desire of the British Government to allow the gradual revival of British exports in lines largely cut off during the war appeared in the announcement that, beginning in October, British woolen mills could resume the production of fabrics and blankets for the United States and for the countries of Latin America, if they could execute such

[1] Mainly pharmaceutical and toilet preparations, wax polishes, furs and specified manufactures, certain chemicals, typewriter ribbons on spools, and certain glassware and optical instruments.

orders without interfering with prior obligations. Allocations were granted at the rate of about half of the basic exports for those areas, and the sale of raw wool for that purpose was authorized. This trade had been banned for sixteen months, during which export allocations of woolen manufactures had been restricted mainly to Empire countries and to certain overseas territories of friendly European countries.

The first material moderation of the British wartime restrictions on exports was planned for the beginning of 1945. Revised arrangements regarding supplies under Lend-Lease were announced simultaneously in Washington and London on November 30, which contemplated substantial reductions in the Lend-Lease assistance to be needed by the United Kingdom in the period following the defeat of Germany. To some degree, such Lend-Lease aid was to be reduced even before the defeat of Germany, and this in turn affected the operation of the controls upon exports from the United Kingdom.

After January 1, 1945, certain manufactured goods and certain raw and semifabricated materials, notably iron and steel, were no longer to be provided by the United States to the United Kingdom under Lend-Lease. From the British point of view this will have the effect, as Prime Minister Churchill announced in Parliament, that they will "then be free to export a wide range of goods made from those materials." He was referring to freedom from the limitations of the so-called "White Paper" of September, 1941, in which the British Government had undertaken that articles received under Lend-Lease from the United States, or similar to items so received, would not be exported commercially from the United Kingdom without prior agreement of the two governments. There has been no change in the principle of the "White Paper," and its limitations continue to apply to materials or products which are received from the United States under Lend-Lease, and to all articles in short supply obtained from the United States.

While the prospect for a revival of British exports during the coming year in products made from materials no longer in the Lend-Lease category has been widely hailed in public discussions in the United Kingdom, the chairman of the Board of Trade has warned against early expectations of any "large turn-over of capacity and labor to the export trade."

Canada Waives Export Permits for Many Products, but Guardedly

Early in December, 1944, Canada lifted the requirement of a permit for exportation from nearly 200 commodities, when shipped to British Empire countries or to the United States. The products affected ranged from furs and pig iron to machine tools and cosmetics, and the Minister of Trade and Commerce explained that the measure was in line with the official policy "to relax export permit restrictions as soon as a firm trend toward progressive improvement in the general supply situation became evident."[2] The Canadian administering officials have indicated, however, that it was not intended to allow "excessive diversion of goods from the home market" and that, if by substantial increase in the exports of a commodity a short supply domestically should develop, they will recommend the reinstatement of export control. Exporters were also warned to assure themselves, before making shipment, that the importer was in possession of a valid import license from his government, where that was necessary.

Small but Definite Increase in Commercial Trade Among Non-Axis Countries

The United States, the United Kingdom, and Canada have been the three principal countries upon which the non-Axis world has come to depend as general sources of supply during the war. Only in part are the statistics on the foreign trade of these countries for 1944 yet available, by which to judge how far their relaxation of export restrictions and simplification of procedures during the past year, joined with the easement in supplies and shipping, had resulted in actual increases in their merchandise exports, and to which destinations. What is now available, however, is fairly indicative.

For the United States, the preliminary returns indicate an increase in the cash exports during 1944 over the preceding year of close to 400 million dollars. This appears to have been accomplished concurrently with an increase of over a billion dollars in the value of goods shipped abroad during the year under Lend-Lease. The major part of the increase in cash exports during the year was to Latin America. While varying with the individual countries, such exports from the United States to Latin America as a whole were about one-third higher in value than during 1943.

Canadian exports increased during 1944 by nearly 500 million dollars over the preceding year, to a record total. Since the amount which Canada could send to its Allies during the year under Mutual Aid, the Canadian equivalent for Lend-Lease, was limited by the 1944 budget to a value some-

[2] Some of the products thus exempted are not produced in Canada in appreciable surplus. Their removal from export permit control, like their original placement there, was to parallel the United States export controls, in view of the close wartime coördination of the economies of the two countries.

what less than in 1943, the increase in total exports presumably measures roughly the enlargement of Canadian cash exports. For the United Kingdom, no trade figures have been made known for 1944.

In varying degree for different classes of products, the somewhat advanced prices over the preceding year account for part of the higher values recorded for the foreign trade of the past year. All things considered, however, the statement seems warranted that, in addition to continued large international movements of goods under Lend-Lease and Mutual Aid programs, the year 1944 was marked by a small but definite increase in the volume of total commercial trade among the non-Axis countries, with particularly sizable increases on the part of most countries in the Western Hemisphere.

REACTIONS OF IMPORTING COUNTRIES TO PROSPECTIVE SUPPLY EASEMENTS

In the non-Axis world, diverse changes in import controls of various countries which have marked the past year have been the expressions partly of a sense of relief from the stringencies of recent years, and partly of a sense of caution over what may be ahead. These new or modified import-control measures were prompted in some cases by the changes in their own economic and financial positions but, principally, they appear to have been in response to the actual or prospective freer availability of supplies from other non-Axis countries.

Many countries have given evidence of welcoming the prospect of obtaining supplies from abroad more readily and with less burdensome procedures, and some have already begun to simplify their wartime methods of control over the placement of foreign orders and over the importation of goods into their territories. A number of governments, however, particularly in Latin America, have adopted measures during the past year which appear designed to be more restrictive of future imports, although most of these may simply reflect the desire to keep a firmer rein over the flow and make-up of their country's imports during the unsettled period ahead. In a few cases, the new measures apparently look to the postwar rather than the transitional period.

Tested by the extent to which they influenced actual trade movements, most of the changes of the past year in the field of import controls are seen as still in their potential stage. The continuing huge demands of the war have allowed only moderate amounts of additional supplies of certain goods to be released for exportation from the principal supplying countries. In consequence, neither the relaxation of the former trade restrictions, nor the potentially restrictive new import controls, have yet had very wide scope or occasion for their application.

Some commercial concern has been expressed, however, over early indications of the possible continuance beyond the emergency of certain of the measures for regulating foreign trade resorted to during the war. This concern has been mainly over the restrictive possibilities of the import-licensing systems recently adopted or elaborated by many governments, the implications of certain wartime changes in the British and French empire trade preferences, and the apparent inclination of some governments to carry over bulk buying or other forms of governmental centralization of imports into the postwar period.

The current trends in this field are best seen by examining the principal changes during the past year in the import controls of the different parts of the British Empire and of the various countries of Latin America—the two groups of countries which together have constituted the markets for the bulk of the commercial exports of the United States during the war. None of the governments of the liberated areas of Europe are yet in a position to formulate definite programs for the conduct or the control of their foreign trade after the military and relief stages will have passed.

Canada, India, and Australia Relax Restrictions on Nonsterling Goods

Effective August 1, 1944, the Canadian Government lifted the general license restrictions or prohibitions upon the importation from the United States and other nonsterling countries of a long list of products, considered of secondary essentiality, which had been in effect since the War Exchange Conservation Act of 1940. The greatly improved foreign exchange position of Canada was cited as the reason for terminating this emergency measure, which the Minister of Finance recognized as regrettably discriminatory, and which "would not, in normal circumstances, be compatible with our Trade Agreement with the United States."

It was officially recognized, however, that the Canadian price ceiling may not make it profitable to import some of the items on which the restrictions had been lifted, and that the supply situation in the United States or other foreign sources may in any case limit possible importations. Moreover, many of the products affected continued liable to import restrictions of a less formal character, within the discretion of the various commodity controllers, but with the difference that such restrictions would apply to imports from all countries, including those in the sterling area. Such trade reports as are now available indicate that, while importations into Canada from the United States and elsewhere have been resumed in a considerable number of minor items, no important lines have thus far shown any sizably increased importations.

In October, the government of British India announced a liberalization of its import control policy in certain directions, with the object of ensuring increased supplies of essential consumption goods for its civilian population, and of checking the rise of prices. The Chief Controller of Imports declared that the Indian quota system was intended to save foreign exchange and shipping space and not to serve as a protective measure; and, now that shipping space was easier, the general policy would be to issue licenses for the importation of consumers' goods, provided foreign suppliers would accept firm orders. The classes of goods for which increased imports are reported to have been arranged include: medical stores, paper, textiles, apparel, stationery, sewing machines, typewriters, and paints.

In July, 1944, Australia announced a relaxation of import restrictions on certain products from nonsterling countries. Some of them, chiefly replacement parts for various classes of machinery and apparatus, are now admitted without limit as to quantities; others may now be imported, but on a quota basis. The importation of many classes of goods from nonsterling countries through commercial channels had been severely restricted into Australia since December, 1939, for the declared purpose of conserving foreign exchange, principally dollars, for the most essential wartime requirements. The Australian exchange position had recently eased appreciably, and the Minister for Trade and Customs declared that these relaxations might be regarded as a first installment, with further steps depending upon the war situation, but that no general removal of import restrictions is possible at the present time.

Of related significance is the recently reported tendency for the Australian Government gradually to curtail bulk buying abroad through its purchasing missions, a practice which had been especially prominent in its commerce with the United States during the last few years. Doubt has been expressed, however, whether any substantial increase in over-all commercial importations into Australia is to be expected until the conclusion of the war in the Pacific.

The situation in New Zealand seems quite different. In announcing the import-licensing schedule for 1945, which embodied no material changes from the prevailing situation, the Minister of Customs made this declaration: "All will appreciate that the increased calls which will be made on our overseas funds in the immediate post-war period, particularly for essential requirements of industry in the form of raw materials and replacements and additions to plant, leave no alternative but to conserve those funds, and in the meantime, therefore, no general relaxation of the limitation applied to imports of certain classes of goods will be expected."

In December, 1944, Bermuda canceled the import embargo established in 1942 on a long list of products from all sources, and on specified articles from nonsterling sources. The principal limitation upon the quantities imported is to be the over-all dollar allocations to importers.

This action on the part of Bermuda seems, however, to have been exceptional among the British colonies and dependencies. There has been no indication that any broad instructions have yet been issued from London for the early relaxation of the exchange control and import-licensing systems which were instituted generally in those areas early in the war. Applied originally to selected importations from nonsterling or non-Empire countries, as a measure to conserve foreign exchange, these controls came to apply to a broad range of products and, for some time now, licenses have seldom been granted for such importations by the local administrators, unless the goods were considered very essential, and could not be replaced from within the sterling area or the British Empire.

Diverse Reactions Among Latin American Countries

At least three different types of reactions were discernible during 1944 among the countries of Latin America to the prospective freer availability of foreign products, and especially to the progressive rollback of the decentralization procedure for licensing exports from the United States, which had come to be by far their predominant source of import supply.

In all of the other American Republics, the function of screening the many applications for foreign orders, and of selecting those to be recommended for favorable action by the export-licensing authorities of the United States, lost its former high importance. The local body hitherto charged with this task either was reorganized on a revised basis, or had its reduced function merged with those of some other body having general supervision over the country's foreign trade and exchange matters. Commercial interests concerned with imported goods generally hailed the relief thus afforded from the complicated procedures and delays naturally involved in getting clearance for a transaction from governments in two countries.

Not in all cases, however, has the relaxation in the export control or procedure on the part of the United States been followed by a corresponding discontinuance of the direct official control over import transactions which, in many of the Latin American countries, had been installed only to make possible the functioning of the joint "decentralization" program. In fact, a number of the countries announced new import control plans, which appeared designed either to restrict enlarged imports, at least in selected lines, or to keep a close administrative check over foreign orders and the use of the country's foreign exchange resources. In certain instances, the new measures apparently were intended to extend beyond the emergency period, and reflect rather the long-term plans of the governments for the development of the economies of their countries, involving some changed attitudes toward the importation of particular classes of goods.

Brief characterization seems worth-while of the principal reactions of these different types among the countries of Latin America during the past year.

Some loosen import controls to reduce living costs.—With the improvement of the United States supply situation in various lines early in 1944, a concerted movement developed among manufacturing interests in Chile to secure protection for the local plants started during the war, by opposing the renewed admission of competitive foreign merchandise. The Chilean National Foreign Trade Council— the "country agency" under the decentralization plan—announced in April that, as a tentative policy, it would grant licenses for the importation of articles now more freely obtainable, in order to reduce the cost of living, until the respective domestic industries demonstrated that national production of such articles was satisfactory with regard to quality, quantity, and price. A public protest against this policy from the Confederation of Production and Commerce to the President of Chile was rejected by him as "not justified." Later in the year, the council was reorganized for the purpose of simplifying the complicated procedures of importation, which it was claimed had impeded desirable transactions.

A related indication of the preparatory Chilean readjustment from wartime expedients was afforded by the presidential direction to the semiofficial Fomento (Development) Corporation in September, in connection with the appointment of a new head for that organization, that it liquidate its trading operations, "so that the activities of the corporation should be devoted exclusively to the promotion of production." The corporation had been criticized locally for having gone beyond its original purpose, and for having established subsidiary corporations to engage in import trade in competition with established private concerns.

The proposed inauguration of a general import-licensing system on the part of the Peruvian Government met with so much commercial opposition that the requirement actually established, in August, simply called for importers to send to the Minister of Finance every fifteen days a complete list of all import orders by commodity, amount, and country of origin. This was declared to be intended to operate as a mild system of observation over prospective imports, in order to detect unduly large orders for luxuries and dispensable products which might involve a heavy drain upon the country's foreign exchange resources.[8]

In Venezuela, the pressure to reduce the exceptionally high cost of living prompted the issue of two sets of sharp duty reductions on selected products during 1944, including trucks and automobile parts and some household equipment, but mainly machinery and materials useful in stimulating industrial development. Reductions of the duties on foods have been widely urged but not yet decided upon. The exceptionally large revenues being received by the Venezuelan Government from the petroleum industry and from the new income tax are credited with allowing it to forego some revenues from duties on imports.

In February, the Nicaraguan Government required the obtaining of prior permits for the importation from the United States and Canada of merchandise not under the decentralization control, and for all imports from other countries. This was withdrawn at the middle of the year, to comply with the rollback of the export control from the United States, although exchange allotments were retained. To check the rising cost of living, the subject of current complaint in many of the Latin American Republics, the Nicaraguan Government is reported to have arranged for the purchase of low-priced cotton textiles valued at a million dollars from Mexican mills to be sold to the public at cost. To the same end, a project is reported under study to lower the country's duties on various articles of prime necessity.

At the beginning of 1944, Costa Rica put into effect reductions in the import duties on agricultural implements, cotton fabrics, and certain other products, for the declared purpose of assisting the country's working

[8] Late in January, 1945, the Peruvian Government installed a comprehensive import and exchange control system. While the types of transactions which are to be discouraged seem the same as those formerly announced, previously approved permits are now to be required for all importations. The primary objective appears to be the building up of the government's reserve fund of foreign exchange.

classes by lowering the cost of essential articles. On the other hand, a specified list of products regarded as luxuries were made subject to a surcharge upon the existing duties to provide funds toward the payment of the government's share of social security benefits.

To facilitate local food production in Guatemala, exemption from all import duties and taxes was authorized in April for agricultural implements and tractors.

Others adopt measures potentially restrictive but lightly applied.—In a number of the countries of Latin America, the reaction to the immediate improvement in the supply situation, and more especially to the prospect of the later general reopening of international trade, has been to apply an independent import permit system or to take other measures which lend themselves to several interpretations. They may be simply prudent safeguards for their national economies during the readjustment period ahead, considering the high dependence of all these countries upon their external trade; or they may be intended to be distinctly restrictive of increased importations, at least of certain classes of goods. Much will depend upon how they are administered in practice when world commerce reopens in a broad way. As earlier noted, there has thus far been only a moderate increase in the actual quantities or range of products freely available from abroad, and most of these new import controls have as yet been only lightly applied.

The governments of Colombia and of Ecuador are among those which have continued their independent licensing of import transactions, even in cases where that was no longer necessary in order to obtain licenses for the exportation of the particular products from the United States. Their import control agencies were reorganized during the past year, and directed to scrutinize applications for import permits from the standpoint of their "economic convenience" and the tendencies of local prices, as well as that of the state of the country's exchange availabilities. There were indications that the present intention was to place restrictions principally upon the importations of articles of a luxury character, the authorities declaring their desire to minimize control on the importations of other commodities into their markets as rapidly as possible.

Coincident with the prospective modification of the decentralization plan by the United States, the Venezuelan Government introduced in the fall of 1943 a new import control system, requiring a prior permit for all imports from all countries except for a limited list of unrestricted products. Despite official assurances that the permit system would be administered flexibly, widespread opposition in Venezuelan business circles led during the past year to appreciable relaxation of the plan. In June, 1944, and again in November, the categories of articles not requiring import permits were considerably enlarged. These are understood to have represented a compromise between the Venezuelan industrial elements desiring licensing control over virtually all imports, and the importers and the press which have been strongly urging the greatest possible relaxation of all restrictions on foreign trade.

The official explanation given in Venezuela for the maintenance of this import permit system is worth noting, as being fairly typical of that given in a number of foreign countries for the new import controls introduced. It is declared necessary: (1) to protect the national economy from sudden changes in the international markets which are likely to occur as the end of the war approaches; (2) to control the relative essentiality of imports permitted so long as the shipping situation remains uncertain; and (3) to protect and promote national industry. In addition, a number of governments have been stressing their concern over making the best use of the foreign exchange reserves accumulated during the war.

What may be simply a precautionary measure was that taken by Bolivia during the past year, by which all banks agreed to increase the amount of deposit required as a guaranty for opening letters of credit in connection with import transactions from a former uniform 25 per cent to an ascending scale, ranging up to 40 per cent, varying with the essentiality of the product. The sale of foreign exchange for imports into Bolivia is now restricted by periodic directions from the Minister of Finance to the banks, fixing the amount of dollars or pounds sterling which they may sell for the various authorized imports during the following month.

One of the declared purposes of the Bolivian Government's exchange policy is to reduce speculative overbuying of foreign merchandise and the duplication of orders. Some evidences of this tendency have recently appeared in a number of the Latin American countries, giving rise to concern lest the domestic market become overstocked with foreign goods, and importers find themselves unable to meet payments or to market their high-priced imports.

The import controls introduced during the past year by Brazil and Mexico appear potentially more restrictive. All branches of the Bank of Brazil were instructed in April to make a prior review of each exchange application for importations, in order to determine how essential was the proposed transaction. While the government is being urged to use its control over imports to protect local industries started or expanded during the war, the official attitude is that the large exchange balances built up in recent years need to be controlled primarily with a view to their use for the foreign goods considered most important to the economy of Brazil. There is a strong feeling that the large present foreign balances will not suffice for all imports that will be desired after the war, and that they should be retained as a reserve for rehabilitating the transportation facilities of the country, bringing in industrial machinery for the equipment of factories and, in general, for fostering the long-range development of the country.[4]

Following the rescinding of the substantial increases in the Mexican import duties on an unlimited range of products, which were planned for the middle of January, 1944, an executive decree was issued in May empowering the Ministry of Finance to formulate lists of articles the importation of which is to be restricted, and to permit the importations of such products only under a prior license. So far as known, the only classes of goods made subject to import license under this decree during 1944 were lard, hides and skins, and common salt; and no announcement has been made as to the general criteria which are to guide the administrative application of this broad authority. Some fears have been expressed in Mexico lest the market be flooded by imports as the war approaches termination, which might exhaust the present large dollar and gold reserves upon nonessential commodities, and also injure war-born or expanded Mexican industries.

At the close of 1944, a Mexican executive decree ordered substantial increases in the duties on a limited range of products, and the levying of new duties on several items hitherto admitted duty-free, effective in thirty days. The action appears intended to protect certain branches of Mexican industry developed during the war, and partly as a revenue measure. None of the products included in the United States–Mexican Trade Agreement of 1942 were affected by this decree.

[4] On January 25, 1945, an executive order was promulgated at Rio de Janeiro requiring prior import licenses for the importation into Brazil of specified classes of goods contracted for from that date. The products specified are: precious and semiprecious stones; glass and glass products; refractory materials; ceramic manufactures; a list of nonmetallic materials and their manufactures; mineral ores in general; ferro-alloys; semimanufactures and manufactures of iron and steel, and of nonferrous metals and alloys, including precious; steel-mill manufactures; and machinery, equipment, utensils and instruments in general, and parts and accessories (except agricultural).

The order stated that this requirement was to be operative "as long as the effects of the war continued," but stressed that it was not attempting "to protect uneconomic industries, which can only subsist at the cost of permanent official favors and to the prejudice of Brazilian consumers."

Several set import conditions designed to advance industrialization.— Suggestive of preliminary planning for the period after the war were the measures taken during the past year by several of the American Republics. Primarily, these measures seem part of the general programs now under active consideration by many governments, in Latin America and elsewhere, for promoting by various means greater industrialization and diversification. Incidentally, however, they sometimes involve plans for reducing the cost of importing productive equipment or, on the other hand, for limiting the possibilities for the renewed sale in their markets of certain products formerly imported.

Thus, in April, Cuba authorized a three-year duty exemption for imports of machinery and accessories from the United States for the establishment of new industries. Primarily intended for industries not manufacturing articles already produced in Cuba, duty exemption is possible also for machinery to be used in existing industries, if they are producing less than 30 per cent of the quantity needed for the consumption of the country. This privilege is accompanied by a provision for price regulation of the products of new industries, in the general interest.

In May, 1944, the Chilean Government promulgated the conditions under which customs privileges are to be granted for the entry of machinery for new industries, for which general authorization had earlier been vested in the president. This exemption was to be granted only on future importations for new plants to manufacture products from domestic raw materials which met certain conditions. The new industries must (1) not be already established in the country, or (2) meet domestic needs which cannot be filled by plants already established, or (3) produce or transform domestic copper, iron, or steel of national origin. The President of Chile is to decide as to the most suitable project in each case, and to determine the zone in which the new industries shall be established. An interesting condition set upon these exemptions is that the charges normally applying may be collected when the president determines that the recorded profits of the industry permit their payment.

Argentina also authorized or extended import duty exemptions on various products to aid domestic industrialization projects. A number of other countries of Latin America, notably Brazil, have for some time carried on their statute books authority for selective duty exemptions or reductions on the importation of designated types of industrial equipment.

Of wider potential significance was the Argentine executive decree issued in June, and presented as designed to develop and protect national industries. Three methods are contemplated: (1) additional import duties, for the encouragement of new industries or protection of existing industries against "dumping"; (2) import quotas and, if necessary, prohibitions on imports; and (3) subsidies. The original authority is intended not to exceed a period of five years. The practical significance of this decree can be judged only by the way it may be implemented.

Concern Over Indefinite Continuation of Wartime Expedients

Potentially arbitrary use of broad import license systems.—The spread of import license systems to additional foreign countries during the past year or so, notably in Latin America, and the extension of foreign exchange controls, which many of them have operated in some form since the 1930's, may represent simply transitional or precautionary measures or may have more disquieting implications. They have the potentialities, if continued beyond the emergency period as purely unilateral measures, of developing into means of materially restricting imports after the most urgent wartime shortages have been made up, or of encouraging uneconomic self-sufficiency through shielding new industries and old against the competition of renewed imports from the old-established sources.

Those possibilities are enhanced by the fact that the terms of the authority of most import-permit or exchange-licensing systems are quite broad, and seldom are any definite criteria announced for their application. Their practical operation would apparently depend largely upon the discretion of the administering officials, since there is usually no provision requiring prior legislative approval of the application of such import restrictions to particular products or sources.

Fear of British and French preferential licensing continuing.—Somewhat similar concern has been expressed with regard to the possible continuation into the postwar period of the preferential licensing systems which, since early in the war, have been superimposed upon the prewar duty preferences among the various parts of the British Empire, or at least those in the sterling pool, as emergency measures to reserve their foreign exchange resources, principally of dollars, for the most essential wartime requirements. As earlier noted, Canada, British India, and to a limited extent Australia and Bermuda, appear to be the only British areas which have taken action thus far, as their exchange situations eased, to relax the license restrictions earlier imposed, under which orders could not be placed in nonsterling countries for many classes of goods if they were at all obtainable from sterling or Empire sources.

If these preferential license restrictions of the various British countries, plus the prewar tariff preferences, continue on anything like their present basis into the postwar period, they are capable of constituting strong instruments for reserving Empire commerical markets more exclusively than ever for other Empire countries, and for affording hidden protection to war-stimulated local industries by holding down the resumption of lower-cost importations from the United States or other nonsterling countries. In the aggregate, such a prolonged carry-over of wartime expedients may seriously obstruct the full-bodied restoration and expansion of international trade, which is generally recognized as essential to the recovery and prosperity of all peoples.

Within the French Empire, where a trade preferential system existed before the war second only to that in the British Empire, a number of steps taken during the past year or so, under the exigencies of the war, may prove of material importance later on. Noteworthy have been: the large degree of local tariff autonomy which the French Committee for National Liberation has promised Indo-China, upon liberation; the suspension of the schedule of import surtaxes on goods of non-French origin into French West Africa; and, on the other hand, the declarations of French spokesmen that closer integration will be sought after the war between France and its colonies.

Concern over official bulk buying becoming regular import method.—Bulk buying of certain basic commodities, or other centralized handling of imports in particular lines through governmental agencies, is another type of exceptional trade arrangement that has been widely resorted to by various countries under the exigencies of the war, and which some countries have already shown signs of desiring to continue in a measure beyond the war.

The possibility that a number of the countries of continental Europe may concentrate their postwar foreign trade in governmental hands, which has emerged in the preliminary expressions of attitude on the part of certain of their spokesmen, has received a good deal of public attention during the past year. It seems still too early, however, to judge how far such tendencies are likely to be translated into concrete measures when the countries involved have been fully liberated, and when the new responsible governments develop the general economic programs for their countries, of which the control of foreign trade is but one aspect. Nor does it seem warranted to assume that temporary expedients, which may be resorted to during the greatly disordered conditions faced directly following the war, will necessarily continue as the regular methods of controlling their imports and exports after the transitional period is over.

More definite significance would seem to attach to the bulk-purchasing arrangements which certain of the noninvaded countries are considering. During the latter half of 1944, the government of the United Kingdom announced the conclusion of long-term contracts with those of New Zealand and of Australia for the bulk purchase of the entire exportable surpluses of meats and dairy products of those countries. These arrangements run from two to four years, or as far as 1948. Their provisions regarding guaranteed prices, and payment irrespective of deliveries, resemble less normal peacetime commercial arrangements, than those which were typical of the procurement contracts and economic support arrangements resorted to by various of the belligerent countries under the exceptional conditions of the early war period.

Somewhat similar arrangements were negotiated in May with Canada, for the British purchase during the next two years of specified quantities of meat and cheese, greatly exceeding the prewar shipments. The British Ministry of Food has indicated that extension of bulk-purchasing arrangements to Argentina and other South American countries is also contemplated.

In announcing the arrangements with Australia and New Zealand in September, the Minister of Food declared that the government was making them "as part of its policy for safeguarding food supplies for the United Kingdom for the next few years." Nevertheless, there has been considerable discussion recently in British publications and commercial circles of the danger of bulk buying being retained as the regular method of satisfying the country's import requirements in primary products. The concern expressed has been on the grounds of the undesirable principles of commercial policy such a program would perpetuate, as well as over the unnecessary replacement of governmental operations for competitive importations by private trading firms.

United States Curtails Bulk Procurement and Centralized Control of Imports

In the case of the United States, on the other hand, there has been begun during the past year a tapering off of the official bulk procurement of certain imports, and a relaxation of the centralized governmental control upon the importation and distribution of many foreign commodities, which were earlier found necessary to the war production program.

Many of the procurement and bulk-purchase contracts entered into by the United States Government with the various countries of Latin America during the last few years—both to obtain greater supplies of strategic materials for war needs, and to support particular surplus crops vital to the economies of those countries but temporarily not marketable—either expired during 1944 or are due to expire within the next year or so. The scope of these procurement activities of the United States is being curtailed, and the directive interest for certain of the foreign developmental programs, notably for natural rubber and cinchona, is being shifted to the governments of the other countries concerned. Such procurement contracts as have been made, or renewed, during the past year by the United States governmental agencies have been on a smaller scale, for shorter terms, or on a more flexible basis than those concluded earlier in the war.

In his published letter of September 29 regarding the responsibilities of the Foreign Economic Administration after the defeat of Germany, the President has directed that, in view of the curtailment which is then to be made in our war production, plans should be worked out for "an appropriate cut in the foreign procurement program for strategic and critical materials needed in the prosecution of the war. The adjustment to this reduced program should be made in such a way as to prevent undue and unnecessary financial losses to American taxpayers, to best preserve our foreign relations, and to strengthen the foundation for a high level of international trade in the future."

During the course of the past year, the War Production Board has relaxed its import controls over a number of strategic materials, removing completely the previous restrictions upon private importations for certain commodities, and again permitting for others free commercial distribution after arrival in this country. As nonstrategic materials are becoming available in liberated countries, study is made of the usual channels of trade through which such commodities had been imported in the past, and the Foreign Economic Administration consults with an advisory committee of importers of the commodity with regard to the best methods of handling the particular products.

Imports into the United States have been running consistently higher in value during the past year than in 1943, with the present indications that the total for 1944 exceeded that for the preceding year by over 500 million dollars. Most of this increase has come from the other countries of the Western Hemisphere, which have been the source for fully two-thirds of United States imports during the last few years.

1945

WAR'S END BRINGS ONLY LIMITED PROGRESS TOWARD DEMOBILIZATION OF CONTROLS

GENERAL SURVEY OF POSTWAR READJUSTMENTS AND PROSPECTS

By the end of 1945 only limited progress had been made, except by the United States and a few foreign countries, toward demobilization of the wartime controls and restrictions upon foreign trade. Resumption of trade with the areas formerly under Axis control has thus far been slow and uneven. Nor had much progress been made toward harmonizing the diverse commercial programs of the individual countries on the basis of common principles, in a concerted effort to facilitate the general revival and expansion of international trading. However, the prospect for greater progress in this field during 1946 was considerably improved by a number of developments late in 1945. These comprised the conclusion of the Anglo-American financial negotiations; the proposal by the United States, with British support, for an international conference on trade and employment within the coming year; and the completion of the necessary ratifications for setting up the Bretton Woods monetary and financial organizations.

The termination of the war in 1945 put an end to the forced commercial seclusion of most of Europe and of the Far East, and to the arbitrary diversion of the production and trade of those regions to the purposes of Germany and Japan. It also made no longer necessary many of the wartime trade restrictions that had been resorted to by the United Nations in order to meet the overriding military demands upon the available supplies, funds, and shipping. Considering the drastic changes in the economic and financial position of so many countries wrought during the war, however, and the widely disorganized conditions left in its wake, a rapid or general return to prewar trade relations could hardly have been expected.

Progress Toward Return to Normal Uneven in the Different Regions

The *United States, Canada, the Union of South Africa,* and a few other countries located outside the zones of active conflict had, by the end of 1945, removed most of their various wartime restrictions upon foreign trade. Although usually continuing their price controls, these governments have gone far toward clearing the way for their nationals to resume the exportation and importation of most commodities under something like the prewar pattern, insofar as the conditions set by other countries permitted.

In a positive way, the substantial enlargement during the year of the loanable funds of the Export-Import Bank of the United States and the new export credit facilities of Canada made it possible for those two governments to finance, on credit, the continued flow to their Allies of certain civilian goods which before the end of the war had been planned for shipment under the Lend-Lease or Mutual Aid programs, and also the supplying to various of the war-ravaged countries of Europe of their unusually large import requirements for replenishment and reconstruction, beyond current ability to offset with their export goods or with cash. Sweden and Switzerland also facilitated the postwar restoration of international commerce through the extension of substantial official credits.

Most countries, however, have felt that the particular economic and financial position in which they found themselves did not allow them to restore equally unrestricted conditions for foreign trading, at least not until they could make many domestic readjustments in various fields and, in some cases, conclude financial arrangements with supplying countries. The changes in the measures for foreign trade control actually made during 1945 varied considerably, therefore, in the different regions or groups of countries, in the light of their special circumstances and immediate objectives.

With the passing of the joint emergency controls on imports which the *Latin American* countries had adopted to conform to the export controls of the United States, their principal wartime supplier, many of these governments have been replacing them with stronger local controls upon the volume and character of their country's imports. By the end of 1945, Mexico and all but two of the countries of South America were requiring import permits for each transaction in all or broad ranges of goods. Their principal concerns appear to be, to see that their foreign exchange reserves and earnings are used primarily for the importation of essentials, especially productive equipment, and to shield certain war-developed local industries from severe foreign competition. However, both the newer import permit systems in Latin America and the older exchange controls were restrictively applied during 1945 only to a limited extent, and thus far appear to be largely precautionary measures.

Such relaxations of their wartime controls as most members of the *British Empire* have made during 1945—with the exception of Canada and South Africa, earlier noted—have been confined mainly to trade within the Empire, and with the few non-British members of the sterling area. The dominant consideration in their continuing—and sometimes even tightening—the existing restrictions upon trade with outside countries has been their inadequate holdings of nonsterling exchange, especially of dollars. The future trading possibilities of the entire sterling area with outside countries, notably with the United States, were involved in the Anglo-American financial negotiations held at Washington in the fall, to be later discussed.

On the European continent, the four *former neutral countries* had managed to continue commercial dealings both with the German-dominated areas and, irregularly, also with the outside world. The termination of the war apparently required no radical changes in their official controls over the foreign trade operations of their nationals. Sweden and Switzerland were exceptionally active during 1945 in reorienting and enlarging the range of their trade relations. Their governments assisted through the negotiation of agreements with various European countries, for each to grant permits freely for the exportation of specified products to the other, and often with provision for official credits to cover temporary excesses in shipments to those other countries above what goods could now be obtained from them in return.

Among the former secluded areas of Europe, only the countries of *Western Europe* and *Scandinavia* made any substantial progress during 1945 toward the general resumption of trade, either with other European or with overseas countries. The bulk of their importations during the past year, especially from the United States, has been arranged through purchasing missions or other centralized agencies of their governments, if not actually carried through by them. All these governments have stressed, however, that this arrangement is to be regarded as distinctly transitional.

Thus far, overseas trade even with liberated countries of Western Europe and Scandinavia has been more or less a one-sided movement, of goods shipped to them. The revival of sizable exports from them in most of their accustomed lines has to await the restoration of their domestic production to a point where they have much to spare for shipment abroad, and often also the deflation of their trade-inhibiting price levels and exchange rates.

Some beginnings have been made by a few of these liberated countries toward authorizing direct foreign importations on the part of their commercial firms. That is still quite limited as to the products covered, and official permission is required for each transaction, which needs to be sufficiently essential to the general import program of the country to warrant allocation of funds out of their inadequate exchange holdings or foreign credits. Gradual improvement in their internal economies, readjustment of exchange rates, and the currently active negotiation of foreign loans or credits, together, should facilitate progress during the period ahead, both as to the total volume of the foreign trade of these countries and as to the degree of direct participation in it of private commercial firms.

In the matter of resumption of foreign trade and the methods of its control, Italy and Greece are in the same general position as Western Europe.

The state of political as well as economic unsettlement of most of the countries of *Eastern Europe*—comprising, in general, all east of Germany—the disrupted state of their transport, and the meager foreign exchange at their disposal, render more remote their resumption of any substantial imports from Western European or overseas countries, beyond the relief shipments supplied by UNRRA (United Nations Relief and Rehabilitation Administration). The extensive experimentation with state control of domestic industries that is going on in almost all of these countries, the close reorientation of the economies of several of them with that of the Soviet Union and, in the case of the former German satellites, the heavy deliveries to the invaded eastern areas called for under the reparations account, operate further to limit their early resumption of sizable trade with outside countries. There has as yet been little indication from most of the governments of Eastern Europe as to how much scope they contemplate for private trading.[1]

[1] In their present stage of military occupation and basic reorganization by the Allies, both Germany and Japan are as yet outside the scope of possible normal trade relations or policies.

In many of the formerly secluded areas of the *Far East,* the process of liberation from enemy control was going on through most of 1945. The present prospect is that governmental agencies or officially designated commercial organizations will handle the external trade of many of these areas during the initial period of its resumption, with private transactions to be gradually restored, under governmental license. The greatest progress toward the restoration of normal trading has been made in the case of the Philippines. The recent lifting of centralized wartime controls by China, over most imports and some exports, is expected to facilitate trade resumption there, as soon as physical and financial limitations allow.

Prospects for More Normal Trade Policies and Collective Action in 1946

Looking ahead, the prospect for greater progress during 1946 toward more normal foreign trade relations and policies, and toward more concerted action on the part of the nations in their commercial programs, was considerably brightened by a series of developments during the closing months of 1945.

Bretton Woods agreements promise wide collaboration in financial relations.—The early setting up of the International Monetary Fund and the International Bank for Reconstruction and Development was assured late in December, with their ratification by the great majority of the countries which had participated in the Bretton Woods Conference of the preceding year. Essentially, the Bretton Woods agreements make provision for the orderly adjustment of the exchange values of the various national currencies, for the tiding over of particular countries experiencing temporary exchange difficulties, and for long-term loans, under international auspices, for the reconstruction and productive development of the various member countries requiring them. Much is expected from this first venture in the broad economic collaboration of the nations toward the revival of their commercial and financial relations on a stable and liberal basis.

These two financial institutions are expected to facilitate the transition from war to peace in international trade and finance in a number of ways. The operations of the International Monetary Fund are designed to minimize a repetition of the sudden and arbitrary exchange depreciations by countries acting alone, which made many long-term international transactions hazardous for a long period after the last war. Its program is calculated to promote substantial stability in the monetary relations of nations, combined with such flexibility as many be necessary to effect the adjustments called for in many countries after so disruptive a war. The provision for financial accommodation to countries experiencing temporary exchange shortages for current transactions is intended to make it easier for countries maintaining restrictive exchange controls to relax them, and ultimately to eliminate them, and to make it less necessary for countries having difficulty in their balance of payments to resort to measures which would reduce or divert international trade.

In addition to such loan or credit arrangements as may be worked out between individual countries, the International Bank is designed to assist in the reconstruction and development of the member countries through long-term financing of productive projects. Because of the international guaranty it can offer, the bank is expected to stimulate the revived flow of private capital into foreign loans and investments, and to supplement that with direct loans out of its own governmentally subscribed funds or others available to it. It aims to promote the long-range balanced growth of world commerce by encouraging international investment in the productive resources and facilities of the less-developed countries.

United States loan to Britain expected to hasten trade liberalization.— More limited in the scope of the participants, but promising to make possible the reopening of trade on a freer and more competitive basis with a considerable range of countries, were the Anglo-American discussions that were concluded in Washington early in December. Highly significant understandings in the field of commercial policy accompanied the two financial arrangements: definitive settlement of all Lend-Lease obligations and war claims between the two countries, and the extension by the United States to the United Kingdom of a line of credit for new purchases—together aggregating 4.4 billion dollars—at moderate rates of interest, and repayable in a flexible manner over a long term of years.

Through affording the United Kingdom the means for financing its exceptionally large import needs during the transition period, the way was opened for several important trade-liberating measures. Exchange restrictions upon payments for current imports into the United Kingdom from the United States are to be lifted promptly upon the coming into effect of the credit arrangement. Within a year, any quantitative restrictions maintained on imports of particular products into the United Kingdom are to be applied without discrimination against the products of the United States, and such sterling funds as may then be available to any of the Empire or other areas for current use are to be freely convertible for purchases in dollar countries or elsewhere.

High hopes for program of collective action on tariffs and trade principles.—Finally, a program was launched for the early simultaneous negotiation of agreements for reductions of tariffs and trade preferences between the United States and a group of important trading countries, including all the British Empire countries.

No less important, from a broader view, was the concurrence of the British and American governments in a set of basic principles and policies concerning the reduction of trade barriers and related matters, the general acceptance of which is expected to bring about a revival and enlargement of the trade of all countries, on a more liberal, multilateral, and nondiscriminatory basis. These proposals were promptly placed before the community of nations by the United States, as the basis for an international conference on trade and employment, now contemplated tentatively for the latter part of 1946. The broad program there proposed in the field of commercial policy, and the Bretton Woods agreements in the monetary and investment fields about to come into operation, were designed to supplement and reënforce each other, in promoting the restoration and expansion of the trade, employment, and general prosperity of all participating countries.

READJUSTMENT MEASURES BY UNITED STATES, BRITISH EMPIRE, AND LATIN AMERICA

Wartime Joint Controls Taper Off as Supply Situation Improves

Early in December, 1945, the governments of the United States, the United Kingdom, and Canada announced that the Combined Raw Materials Board and the Combined Production and Resources Board would be discontinued at the close of the year. This brought to an end most of the concerted programs under British-American auspices which had been in operation since 1942, for the joint procurement of essential commodities and products in short world supply, and for their allocation among the Allies and friendly neutrals on the most equitable basis, and in such a way as to be of maximum use to the war effort. Certain important joint controls are, however, to continue for a period ahead.

A limited number of industrial materials and products that are still in critically short world supply continue subject to joint international control by a series of five special commodity committees, the membership of which has been enlarged to include the major producing and consuming countries of each. These committees are for rubber; tin; hides, skins, and leather; textiles; and coal. In general, their function is to keep under review the world position in their respective commodities, and to recommend to the appropriate agencies of the individual governments such international allocation of the exportable surpluses as would avoid inequitable distribution of the limited supplies and abnormal price fluctuations.

The Combined Food Board is to continue in operation into 1946, to look after the equitable distribution of the various agricultural staples of which current supplies still fall short of aggregate world demand, increased as that has been by the needs of the liberated countries.

The Middle East Supply Center, which had been operated at Cairo during most of the war period, was dissolved on November 1. First as a British then as an Anglo-American enterprise, it had for several years exercised strict control over importations into the countries of that region—extending from the central Mediterranean east to Iran and south to Ethiopia—in the effort to keep them supplied with essential foreign goods in accordance with the most economical use of the goods, tonnage, and exchange avaliable for civilian use. Several hundred import commodities were thus freed from all control except that imposed by the local governments, with British and American official assistance continuing for certain goods in short supply. Some relaxation of the operations of the Middle East Supply Center had been made at the beginning of 1945.

United States

Controls on civilian production and commerce promptly relaxed.—The United States was in a position to adjust itself most promptly to the end of the war, in the way of relaxing its emergency restrictions upon civilian production and upon foreign trade. Official control over the use of manpower was lifted promptly after VJ-day. Even before then, the War Production Board began releasing for general use, including exportation, various materials and products that had been under its control. By the fall of 1945, that process had progressed so far that the board itself was abolished, and such controls as it was desirable to continue were transferred to the new Civilian Production Administration, with a shift of emphasis to reconversion to peacetime production.

The system of export licensing inaugurated in 1940 was progressively relaxed during 1945, through placing increasing categories of goods under general license and broadening the range of foreign areas to which shipments could be freely made. By September, as more and more commodities became freely available for civilian use, about 75 per cent of the products formerly subject to export license in the United States had been decontrolled. In fact, the former procedure, under which all commodities were regarded as subject to some form of control unless specifically exempt, was reversed, and a short "Positive List" was established, numbering several hundred classes of goods, which alone continued subject to individual license or specific allocation. Occasional subtractions from, or additions to, this "Positive List" were made during the closing months of the year.

The maintenance of such restrictions on exports from the United States as are continued is declared to be guided by two broad objectives: first, to assure that the domestic market has its fair share of the supply of goods still short, and, second, to assure a fair share to foreign countries and equitable distribution among them.

After several partial expansions as to markets, the United States licensing authorities announced early in 1946 that they were prepared to consider applications to export licensable commodities to all countries with which private trade was suspended during the war, except to Germany and Japan. The declared purpose was to permit the widest resumption of full commercial trade, as promptly and insofar as physical limitations and the authorities of the other countries concerned will permit.

Similarly, the procurement and distribution of all but a limited number of the imported commodities hitherto controlled by the United States Government were progressively permitted to go back to private commercial channels. By January 1, 1946, only 14 categories of industrial materials were still under direct official import control. In addition, a considerable but reduced list of food imports continued subject to public purchase or license control, with a number of them planned to be released before long.

End of Lend-Lease followed by large credits for foreign rehabilitation.— The termination of Lend-Lease shortly after the surrender of Japan in August marked the most important transition of 1945 from wartime trade conditions. For several years, close to four-fifths of the total value of all goods sent from the United States to foreign countries had been procured, financed, and shipped abroad under this unique arrangement. These Lend-Lease and commercial shipments together came to several times the prewar exports. The relative urgency of the needs of the various Allies, and the most expeditious way of meeting them, were the determining criteria under the Lend-Lease program in the allocation of products available, rather than the current ability to repay in goods or services.

As a transitional aid, the procurement facilities of the United States Government were offered to the other Allies on a reimbursable basis for sixty days after VJ-day, to allow them time to work out their own commercial arrangements for continuing the flow of such nonmilitary supplies from the United States as they still desired. Thereafter, foreign purchases in the United States were to be made directly from private firms, although the current programs of the countries of continental Europe called for the procurement to be effected, for the time being, mostly through their official purchasing missions, whether on their own account or for private importers in their countries.

To minimize any sudden postwar drop, both in the flow of supplies to the other countries concerned and in the foreign outlets for the American producers who had expanded their operations during the war, several financial arrangements have been employed.

Of the goods already in inventory or contracted for under Lend-Lease for the account of the various Allied governments of Europe as of VJ-day, substantial portions are being delivered to them against payment to be made under special thirty-year credit terms, which had earlier been worked out for "long-life goods" supplied under certain Lend-Lease agreements. The Export-Import Bank dealt with the financing of goods requisitioned under Lend-Lease programs but not yet contracted for as of VJ-day, and also with the new purchases, by the Lend-Lease and other countries, of broad ranges of American products urgently desired under their rehabilitation programs, in amounts beyond their immediate ability to offset with their export products or with cash.

The United States Congress voted in July an increase in the loanable funds of the Export-Import Bank of 2.8 billion dollars, making a total of 3½ billion. By the end of 1945, credit arrangements for the above purposes had been concluded by the Export-Import Bank with a number of foreign countries, mostly of Western Europe, for commitments aggregating over a billion dollars, and others were in process of negotiation.[2] In view of certain unique features of the British situation, including the concomitant understandings with the United States regarding commercial-policy measures and exchange arrangements, the proposed line of credit to the United Kingdom is regarded as a special case. It now awaits specific congressional approval.

[2] The credits of varying amounts authorized by the Export-Import Bank during the second half of 1945 under its enlarged funds were allocated as follows: continental Europe (France, Belgium, Netherlands, Denmark, Norway, and for purchase of raw cotton by various European countries), total of 920 million dollars; Latin America (Brazil, Chile, Mexico, Peru, and Ecuador), total of 106 million; Asia (Saudi Arabia and Turkey), total of 8 million; and for miscellaneous purposes, 6 million. The grand total of commitments came to 1 billion, 40 million dollars.

To facilitate financial settlement for international transactions, the United States Treasury issued a general license toward the close of the year permitting the ready transfer, to all countries except the former enemy states and the neutrals, of the funds created by their current sales to the United States. Beginnings had earlier been made toward the release of the foreign funds frozen in the United States during the war, by the negotiation of separate arrangements with the governments of individual countries, subject mainly to safeguards against the use of the funds for the benefit of ex-enemy nationals.

British Empire

Canada relaxes most export and import controls and extends foreign credits.—The wartime economy of Canada had been operated in especially close coördination with that of the United States, and the demobilization of its emergency controls upon materials and productive facilities is being effected along lines parallel to those applied in the United States. In the matter of controls upon foreign trade, Canada as well as the United States had begun to make partial relaxations even before the end of the war, with the progressive easement of the emergency pressures upon supplies and, in the case of Canada, also upon foreign exchange.

As far back as August, 1944, Canada repealed that part of the War Exchange Conservation Act of 1940 which had prohibited or restricted importation from the United States and other nonsterling countries of a long list of products considered of secondary essentiality. A considerable proportion of those products, however, continued subject to import permit regulation, incidental to the operations of the various commodity controls set up to regulate the general Canadian distribution and use of commodities in short supply. These are applicable to any imports of the particular products, from all countries, including those in the sterling area. During 1945, successive reductions were made in the categories of goods subject to any form of import control. By the end of the year, they numbered under 200.

Moreover, in October, Canada abolished the 10 per cent war exchange tax, which had been imposed since 1940 upon imports from non-Empire sources in addition to the regular duties, for the purpose of conserving supplies of dollars for essential war materials by shifting importations to sterling sources. Several selected groups of products had been exempted earlier in the year. In proposing its repeal, the Canadian Minister of Finance declared that such a discriminatory tax could not be justified under conditions of normal trade. It was recognized, however, that the continuation of wartime price ceilings would constitute a check upon the availability to Canadian purchase of various foreign commodities, even when relieved of the license restriction and of the 10 per cent surcharge.

On the export side, Canada had in December, 1944, lifted the requirement of an official permit from about 200 commodities, when shipped to British Empire countries or to the United States, as improvement in the supply situation became evident. A number of these exemptions from export permit were withdrawn in 1945, but the general movement during the year was distinctly toward relaxation. Since June, 1945, all products except those specifically listed have been exempt from export control when shipped to destinations within the Western Hemisphere as well as to other parts of the British Empire.

Shipments of Canadian goods to the United Kingdom and to others of the Allied countries under Mutual Aid—the Canadian counterpart of Lend-Lease—were terminated shortly after VJ-day, as in the case of the United States. In order to maintain the enlarged volume of Canadian exports on a commercial basis, and to assist countries whose rehabilitation needs for Canadian products exceeded their current ability to pay, the Canadian Government concluded loan arrangements with a number of the European governments during 1945, under its new Export Credits Insurance Act. (These countries were: Belgium, Netherlands and Netherlands Indies, Norway, Czechoslovakia, and the Soviet Union.)

In December, the Canadian Parliament approved an increase in the loanable funds for this purpose from 100 million to 750 million dollars and negotiations for its use are reported in progress. In addition, the extension of a large trade credit to the United Kingdom, to cover its exceptional needs during the transition period, has been under informal discussion in Canada for some time.

Exchange shortage forces sterling areas to restrict dollar imports.—Such relaxations of the wartime restrictions on imports as have been made by the various parts of the British Empire other than Canada—which is not a member of the sterling area—have been confined mainly to the products from other sterling countries.[3] Their inadequate supply of dollars, especially American dollars, has been the dominant consideration in the recent trade control measures of this important group of countries.

[3] The sterling area now comprises the British Empire (exclusive of Canada and Newfoundland) and all British mandates or protectorates, and also Egypt, the Anglo-Egyptian Sudan, Iraq, Iceland, and the Faroe Islands.

The Union of South Africa is in an exceptional position with regard to foreign exchange, owing to its large production of gold. Shortly after the surrender of Japan, the South African Government abolished the necessity for import permits or certificates of essentiality for all goods that could be exported from the United States under general license. Importations from the sterling areas had already been exempt. In placing the United States, Canada, and other countries whose trade is conducted on a dollar basis upon the same footing, it was felt that the Union Government took an important step toward the general reopening of its postwar foreign trade. Incidentally, this action dispelled the fear earlier expressed in that country that the wartime import license system might be continued as a means of protecting local industries developed during the war.

For the other sterling-area countries, the exceptional volume of their import needs from the dollar countries for replenishment and rehabilitation far exceeded their combined dollar reserves, which had been pooled during the war, or the amount of dollar exchange that they could earn through current sales to those countries. The United Kingdom itself, in diverting its resources drastically to the prosecution of the war, had not only been forced to curtail sharply the volume of its commercial exports. It had also liquidated a large portion of its foreign investments, and lost a substantial part of its merchant shipping and other foreign service facilities. The income from these sources had normally been counted on to pay for a large part of Britain's huge import requirements. However, before its exports can now be rebuilt, the United Kingdom requires large replenishments of raw materials and equipment from abroad, which are obtainable mainly from the dollar countries.

On the import side, the necessity for retrenchment came home to the British people most forcefully after the surrender of Japan in August and, with it, the cessation of the considerable shipments of supplies, needed for the maintenance of the civilian population as well as for military purposes, that had been coming from the United States under Lend-Lease and from Canada under Mutual Aid. It had been expected that postwar commercial imports into the United Kingdom from all sources would need to be restricted during the reconversion period, on a selective commodity basis. This now became inescapable, and it was particularly stressed that, until the stringency of North American currencies was relieved, all importations from both the United States and Canada would be cut down to what was absolutely vital, especially for domestic reconstruction. While the amelioration of this situation was one of the purposes of the Anglo-American negotiations held at Washington in the fall, the relaxation of the British exchange restrictions which the extension of the American credit is to make possible awaits the approval of that credit by the United States Congress.

Most of the other countries of the British Empire and of the sterling area now have the bulk of their foreign exchange reserves in the form of sterling balances to their credit at London, which are not convertible for use outside the sterling countries without special permission. These had cumulated during the war years to the huge total of about 14 billion dollars, as a result of the great increase in the quantities of goods and services which these countries had furnished to the United Kingdom for the prosecution of the war, and of the sharp reduction in the quantities of exports to them with which that could be offset from the war-shrunken British civilian economy.

It became clear that the United Kingdom would be unable, for some time, to furnish any large quantities of goods to the other members of the sterling area against their accumulated sterling credits. In fact, the United Kingdom would itself require a very large excess of imports of food, raw materials, and equipment during a transition period of several years, to meet even the present austere level of daily consumption, and to give its industries the means for resuming volume production of civilian goods for any purpose. This combination of circumstances produced great uncertainty during most of 1945 regarding the future trading possibilities of the entire sterling area with outside countries, notably with the United States. It heightened the general concern over the outcome of the Anglo-American financial negotiations held at Washington from September until December, and constituted the dominant explanation for the trade control measures of most of the sterling-area countries during 1945, especially as affecting trade with the United States.

Thus, when the Australian Government exempted more than 100 items from the requirement of an import license in September, only a few of the relaxations applied to the products of countries other than the sterling group. The Australian Minister for Trade and Customs frankly declared that the lack of resources in nonsterling funds compelled the retention of a greater degree of restriction on imports from such countries.

The revised import license schedule of New Zealand for 1946, announced in November, provided for substantially increased imports to be permitted from the United Kingdom, but further restricted imports from nonsterling areas. The Minister of Customs declared that the policy of obtaining New Zealand import requirements from the United Kingdom to the maximum of its ability to supply would be continued and that, in view of the uncertainty regarding imports from nonsterling sources, it had not been generally possible to provide allocations for such imports in the meantime. This applied to the products of Canada as well as of the United States.

The government of India announced in August that, in view of the improved supply situation in the United Kingdom for certain steel items, licenses for such imports would be issued more freely, and that import applications for them would be approved more readily also for other sterling countries. In one respect, the former British Indian restrictive policy was liberalized also toward imports from the United States. Indian firms having prewar trade connections with the United States suppliers of goods considered essential for the requirements of British India can now obtain licenses for such goods even when they are otherwise obtainable from sterling-area countries, although not to the full extent of prewar importations. An open general license had been issued earlier in the year for a wide range of consumers' goods from the United Kingdom, which was extended to additional products in October, but such imports from other countries remained subject to individual license.

With some local variations, the principal type of change in the trade control practices of the British West Indies and of the British colonies and territories in Africa was the curtailment of centralized bulk purchasing through control boards, and the gradual reëstablishment for most commodities of direct importation through regular commercial channels. In certain colonies, bulking of import orders virtually ceased. However, various colonial administrators stressed that, since the wartime considerations of short supplies, shipping, and exchange still prevailed, preference in import licensing would be given to foods and other essentials and that import orders from nonsterling areas would continue subject to license restrictions, and limited to essential goods not obtainable from sterling countries. An official declaration of import policy in Jamaica included the additional provision, that imports from Canada would be licensed on a par with the sterling areas in the ordering of essential categories of goods.

United Kingdom gives priority to exports at cost of domestic austerity.—Shortly after the surrender of Germany in May, 1945, the government of the United Kingdom released for civilian purposes most productive facilities and materials, and reduced materially the list of goods requiring licenses for exportation. It also announced that, in the allocation of materials in short supply, definite priority would be given to production for foreign markets. The British public was asked to forego an immediately higher standard of consumption than the wartime "austerity" level, in order to ensure a better and more stable level of comfort in the future, when the country had once more regained its ability to pay for needed imports.

Latin America

Trend to firmer import controls after United States relaxes export control.—Among the countries of Latin America, the end of the war brought few drastic changes in the matter of controls over foreign trade. However, a number of these governments took steps during 1945 to put themselves in a position to control directly the volume and character of their countries' imports during the readjustment period, either by installing import permit systems or by tightening up former import permit or exchange control requirements. Thus far, these appear to have been applied only lightly, except on distinct luxury goods, although they do indicate a growing precautionary attitude on the part of many Latin American governments against possible injury to their economies from an uncontrolled revival of imports. Their principal concerns appear to be, to see that their foreign exchange reserves and earnings are used primarily for what they consider essential imports, and to shield certain war-developed local industries from what they regard as undue foreign competition.

Most governments of Latin America had begun to adjust their import controls to the prospective easement in foreign supplies even before the end of the war, prompted by the tapering off during 1944 of the "decentralization" procedure for operating the United States export-licensing system. With the general relaxation of the United States export control during 1945, and the progressive reduction in the categories of products requiring individual licenses, the special wartime organizations which had been set up in each of the countries of Latin America, to determine priorities among the various prospective purchasers from the United States through "import recommendations," either were abolished or had their functions merged with other governmental agencies.

Several of the Central American and Caribbean countries abolished practically all their wartime controls upon foreign trade transactions in the fall of 1945, excepting on the importation of the commodities still subject to export control or allocation in the United States. On the part of Mexico and most of the governments of South America, however, the reaction to the easement of controls and of supplies in the United States and elsewhere has been to build up a firmer control over individual transactions at the importing end.

With the exception of Peru, which first introduced exchange control in early 1945, all the countries of South America and three of Central America have for years maintained some degree of official control over foreign exchange transactions. Since they required exporters to turn over part or all of the exchange earned by foreign sales to a central control agency in return for local currency, the governments were in a position to set the conditions and the rates under which such exchange was to be made available in payment for imports. Indeed, the method of allocating foreign exchange for imports in accordance with the categories of essentiality assigned to the goods in question, which is followed by several Latin American countries (notably Nicaragua, Colombia, Bolivia, and Paraguay), constitutes in effect a qualitative control upon imports.

During the past year or two, however, there has been a distinct trend toward exercising direct official supervision over the character of the purchases from abroad, through requiring import permits on prospective orders, whether for all or for selected classes of products. In a number of countries, moreover, the allocation of funds for foreign purchases is being tied more closely to the current exchange availabilities.

Brazil, Bolivia, and Peru inaugurated import permit systems during 1945. In Brazil, permits were required for a substantial list of important products;[4] in the two other countries, for *all* commodities. Mexico, which had started such a requirement in 1944, applicable to a few special products, has extended it during recent months to broader ranges of commodities. Colombia again enforced its import permit system in 1945, with fixed limits to the shares of the exchange currently earned to be available for goods in different categories of essentiality. Nicaragua, while relieving most goods from the necessity of import permits, required prior deposit of the value of proposed orders, and set up flexible categories of essentiality, with small scope for imports of what the authorities might consider luxuries.

On the other hand, Venezuela, which had introduced an import permit requirement on most commodities in the fall of 1943, cut that down to a much shortened list in September, 1945, and for those authorized definite annual import quotas. Paraguay gave up its import permit requirement, but tightened its foreign exchange control, with the availability and rate of exchange dependent upon how essential and immediately needed were the proposed imports.

At the end of the year, eight of the Latin American Republics were

[4] Early in January, 1946, the Brazilian Government suspended its prior import permit system, with the expectation that when reissued it will be on a reduced scale.

operating import permit systems on a broad scale. These were: Mexico, and all the countries of South America except Argentina, Paraguay, and Venezuela. Argentina, Venezuela, and several of the smaller Caribbean and Central American countries require specific import authorization only for products subject to export control in the supplying country. Nicaragua has since October, 1945, required an advance deposit to the full value of the proposed import order, and Colombia had earlier in the year increased the percentage to be deposited for all but a group of preferred import products. The majority of these countries do not now require separate exchange permits; the import license, if granted, usually entitles the merchant to purchase the necessary foreign exchange for remittance.

Direct import controls, lightly applied, have several purposes.—In their avowed objectives for operating both forms of import control, the governments usually stress their desire to hold down importations of luxuries or other dispensable products, and to prevent speculative orders for foreign goods beyond the market's essential needs. Each expresses concern that its country's wartime accumulations or current earnings of foreign exchange would otherwise prove inadequate to pay for the large anticipated importations of producers' goods and of other equipment essential to its economic development, especially through industrialization. While the intention to protect "uneconomic industries" is often disavowed, the shielding of local industries started or expanded during the war, against the competition of more freely available foreign products, appears to have been figuring in the operation of several of the import control systems of Latin America during the past year. This purpose has been explicitly announced by the Minister of Finance of Mexico.

Since these licensing systems usually operate through unpublished administrative decisions upon a succession of individual applications, it is not known to what extent desired importations into the various countries using them have actually been curtailed during 1945. The indirect indications are that they have been only lightly applied in most cases. Considering that practically all of the Latin American countries have during the war built up large exchange balances in the United States, and some of them also in the United Kingdom, that large pent-up demands exist for foreign goods of many kinds, and that the actual increases in the available supplies from abroad have been rather moderate up to now, that is understandable. In fact, many of these governments recognize that their domestic inflationary tendencies can be checked only by improving the supply situation and that, in the case of many products, this can be done only by larger importations. The experience of the past year, however, may not be indicative of the potentially restrictive use of these import control systems of Latin America after the replenishment period.

There were only a few instances in Latin America during the past year of marked increases in the import duties on particular products which appeared to have a clear protective purpose. Probably most notable were: the action of Brazil in sharply advancing its duties on wool and woolen goods, and the several Mexican measures increasing its tariffs on a range of goods—in January, on a miscellaneous group of locally produced commodities, mainly chemicals, and in August, on various manufactures of iron and steel. The long list of goods on which the former Mexican duties were doubled at the turn of the year was apparently selected to cover mainly articles used only by the upper-income group of the country.

On the other hand, there were an appreciable number of tariff reductions ordered during 1945, although not of broad scope. These were usually motivated by the desire either to reduce the delivered cost of foreign equipment for local industries and utilities, or to encourage the importation of staple necessities of which local supplies were short and prices high. In the latter type of case, the reduction or remission of duty was usually indicated as temporary and often limited to specified quantities.

Foreign bulk purchase contracts for strategic materials taper off.—Most of the wartime arrangements with the United States and other outside countries for the bulk supply of various minerals and other products from Latin America, which had been temporarily required in exceptional quantities for the Allied war production programs, were tapered off or not renewed upon expiration during the past year. The uncertain prospect during the period ahead, as to foreign markets and prices for some of their major export staples, has been an additional long-term consideration in the current commercial policy of various Latin American governments. The desire to avoid possible later difficulties in financing developmental projects requiring heavy imports, and in maintaining a favorable balance of payments, essential to currency stability and to the servicing of their foreign debts, has been among the reasons given by some for operating import permit systems and for generally guarding their foreign exchange position.

The majority of the Latin American countries still require some form of official authorization for the exportation of many classes of goods, although substantial curtailments in the lists of products subject to export control were made by several of them during the year. With the passing of the wartime objectives—of keeping essential materials from reaching Axis destinations, and of reserving the surpluses of certain commodities for which the United States or the United Kingdom had contracted in bulk—the chief current purpose of such controls appears to be to prevent undue drain upon supplies of goods needed for the local economy, especially articles of prime necessity to consumers. So far as we know, these export controls have had no seriously restrictive effect upon the availability to United States importers of the staple commodities normally obtained from Latin America.

In August, 1945, the Argentina Government announced that, since the prospects for the marketing of the country's exportable grain surpluses and price conditions in the international market were satisfactory, government marketing of wheat, linseed, and corn would no longer be necessary. For several years, it had been the policy of Argentina, primarily as a farm-relief measure, to purchase these crops from the producers at fixed prices, adjusted periodically, and to handle their sale through a governmental export monopoly.

This change, it was indicated, would not interfere with fulfilling Argentina's commitment to the United States to furnish linseed and other oilseeds and their products in return for petroleum fuel oil of equivalent heat value. The agreement for that exchange had been concluded in June of 1945, whereby the United States Commerical Company was the sole buyer of these edible oils on behalf of the United Nations, under direction from the Combined Food Board, with the supplies obtained to be shipped principally to the liberated countries of Europe.

EFFORTS TOWARD TRADE RESUMPTION WITH FORMER SECLUDED AREAS

The termination of the war in 1945 ended the forced commercial seclusion of most of continental Europe and of the Far East. Except for the limited overseas trade maintained by the European neutrals, the two former Axis-controlled regions—in Europe and in the Pacific—had for several years been practically cut off from commercial intercourse with the outside world, and were even isolated from each other, with the general production and trade within each region largely directed to the purposes of Germany or of Japan. Although the Allied victories have made those former secluded areas again safely accessible, their actual resumption of general world commerce has been beset by many difficulties and problems. Appreciable progress was made during 1945 only by certain countries of Western Europe and Scandinavia and by the Philippines. Trade recovery has been markedly uneven among the different countries or groups of countries released from Axis domination, in accordance with their special circumstances and limitations.

Former European Neutrals

Operating without special controls, seek broader trade range.—From the viewpoint of the recent developments in foreign trade relations and policies, the countries of continental Europe fall into at least three groupings: the former neutrals, the other countries of Western Europe and Scandinavia, and the countries of Eastern Europe, comprising roughly all east and southeast of Germany, except Italy and Greece.

None of the four countries of continental Europe which had remained neutral during the war—Sweden, Switzerland, Spain, and Portugal—made any important changes in its trade control measures during the past year. Within the limitations imposed by the blockades of the contending powers and by the tides of the war itself, these countries had managed to continue commercial dealings both with German-dominated Europe and, irregularly, also with the outside world. Their wartime trade had often been subject to intergovernmental arrangements and close supervision, but the actual transactions continued to be conducted almost exclusively by their private merchants. Having changed little during the war, the trade control measures of the former neutrals apparently required no radical alterations after its close.

As the wartime limitations were removed, the nationals of these countries were free to seek an enlargement of the range of their trade with other European and with overseas countries. This was especially important to them because their trade with Germany and certain of the former German-controlled areas, which had been quite substantial during most of the war period, was no longer possible. The principal hindrances to the resumption of general trade by the former neutral countries were not the official restrictions of their governments, but rather the physical shortages of the products they desired from other countries and the inadequate transport facilities available. In the case of Spain, an additional handicap was the limited foreign exchange now accruing from exports, after the decline of its unusually profitable wartime sales, especially those made under the preclusive purchase contracts.

In none of these four countries has any general program been introduced for concentrating foreign trade transactions in the hands of governmental agencies, as has been the case in many of the former belligerent countries.

Sweden and Switzerland assist liberated areas with goods and credits.—Sweden and Switzerland have been exceptionally active in the negotiation of new arrangements for merchandise exchanges with other countries, especially with the liberated countries of Europe. In these agreements, commonly for periods of six months, the contracting governments undertake to facilitate the delivery of specified classes of goods, up to indicated quantities, by granting the necessary export licenses. Settlement is to be made through clearing accounts and, while a balanced value of trade exchanges is usually aimed at, provision is frequently made for reciprocal credits to cover overdrafts up to specified amounts. In such cases, the Swedish or Swiss exporters are paid by their governments out of a general line of credit to the other country. Sweden embodied definite credit offers in its agreements with quite a number of countries, including Norway, Denmark, Belgium, the Netherlands, Czechoclovakia, Poland, and the United Kingdom.[5] Switzerland undertook to extend similar trade credits to Belgium, the Netherlands, France, Italy, and Czechoslovakia.

Special official arrangements for broadening the trade relations of the former neutrals with overseas countries seldom appeared necessary, since commercial transactions continued to be carried through mainly by private firms and the means for financing them were usually ample at both ends. Thus, recent Swedish exchange of notes with Argentina regarding their future trade consisted essentially of promises to facilitate whatever purchases of each other's goods their merchants might be able to arrange, by issuing the necessary export and import licenses. The arrangement specified no definite quantities even for the products indicated as specially desired, and no time limit was set.

In the trade agreement between themselves concluded by Sweden and Switzerland late in 1945, both governments stressed that they were anxious for the fewest restrictions on either commodity exchanges or modes of settlement, and that they would support any endeavor to restore multilateralism in the international movement of goods and of payment for them.

Western Europe

Under prevailing disorganization, imports arranged by governments.—Commercial interest in the possible resumption of trade connections with the countries of Europe that had been engaged in the war has

[5] The Swedish-British arrangement is somewhat different from the others. It contemplates a sizable excess of British imports over deliveries, with Sweden in turn authorized to use its sterling holdings to finance imports obtainable from any country in the sterling area.

focused during the past year mainly upon France, Belgium, and the Netherlands in the west, Norway and Denmark in the north, and Italy and Greece in the Mediterranean. For the present discussion, these countries may roughly be referred to as Western Europe, to distinguish them from the former belligerent countries of Europe located east of Germany, where trade conditions and prospects are usually quite different.[6]

Even those European governments most eager to see their countries' foreign trade move back toward normal were handicapped by the disorganized conditions left in the wake of the war—the destruction of productive facilities, the exhaustion of supplies, the disruption of transport and distribution channels, the scrambled ownership in industry, the inadequacy of foreign exchange assets, the internal financial confusion, and often also the unsettled status of the governmental regime itself. These conditions were not equally serious in all these countries but, in practically all that had been directly involved in the war, a large measure of governmental control and even direct official intervention in foreign trade arrangements seemed unavoidable, at least for a time.

Each government feels that its immediate responsibility for its country's economic rehabilitation includes planning for its essential import requirements, and direct supervision over the utilization of the limited amounts of foreign supplies, shipping, and exchange that are available, to ensure that the most vital needs of the nation are given priority. This attitude seems general, even in those European countries whose long-term plans do not contemplate governmental control of particular industries or sectors of the domestic economy.

Most of these European countries made some beginning during 1945 toward the resumption of foreign trade through commercial channels. By the end of the year, however, the private importations were still limited, and were confined mainly to trade with the other continental countries and, to a certain extent, with the United Kingdom.

Their trade with the United States and most other overseas countries has been slower in getting reëstablished, owing to difficulties of transport and unsettled financial relations. The bulk of the overseas importations into these countries of Western Europe during 1945 was arranged by purchasing missions or other centralized officially sponsored agencies. That situation appears likely to continue for at least some months ahead, although in many cases to a decreasing degree.

[6] In the matter of receiving relief goods from UNRRA, Greece and, to a smaller extent, Italy have been in much the same position as most countries of Eastern Europe. In their trade relations and commercial-policy tendencies, however, both Italy and Greece are most closely associated with the Western countries.

The exportation of many classes of goods from the principal potential overseas sources of supply continued to be officially controlled, and financial arrangements often needed to be negotiated with the supplying countries in relation to an over-all schedule of desired imports. These were additional considerations prompting practically all the governments of Western Europe to operate through official purchasing missions as an aid to effective foreign procurement, even setting them up in certain cases where they did not previously exist. The official spokesmen for all of these seven countries have declared it their firm intention to move toward the restoration of their import trade to normal commercial channels, in most if not all lines, as improved conditions make governmental intervention less necessary, and as the arrangements for financing private trade are worked out with individual foreign countries.

Insofar as private importations are permitted, a govermental import permit and the authorization of foreign exchange is necessary for each transaction, which usually needs to be regarded as essential to the over-all import program of the country.

Revival of exports hampered by shortages and commercial derangement.—The revival of these countries' exports of their familiar prewar products has lagged behind that of imports, at least so far as overseas countries are concerned. Official trade restrictions have seldom been the obstacle. The authorities are eager to see an increase in exports, especially to dollar countries, since the proceeds from such sales increase the countries' purchasing power for imports from them. In fact, in several European countries, the bulk of the revived output of certain specialty products is being reserved for export markets.

The basic obstacles to their resumption of exports in volume lie elsewhere. Only in the case of a few products have these countries as yet developed sizable surpluses for export. Supplies of fuel, materials, and of various accessories to production are notably short. Commercial assembly arrangements are still in process of reorganization, and internal transport facilities are still inadequate. Internal price levels have usually risen sharply and, particularly at the exchange rates prevailing during 1945, foreign buyers too often found prices of the export products too high even when supplies were available.

As these limiting conditions are relieved, however, the prospect for the restoration to private channels of the actual conduct of exportations from this group of countries seems even better than in the case of imports. None of these countries, with the temporary exception of Italy, has concentrated the disposal of its export staples in the hands of official agencies, as they usually have done in the procurement of many import products. In some cases, a closer organization of the local producers controlling the bulk of a given export product has been taking place but, so far as known, these are commercial organizations without governmental participation.

It is to be expected, of course, that exports from these countries will be subject to governmental license for some time, both to prevent undue depletion of domestic supplies of particular products, and to maintain official control over the disposition of the country's foreign exchange earnings.

Import duties often suspended to reduce cost of essential supplies.— Very few permanent changes in their import duties have been made by the former belligerent countries of Europe since the close of the war. Since import transactions are now either arranged by the government or dependent primarily upon whether an official license can be obtained, and the principal current considerations are where each country can obtain the various essential products of which it is short, and how it can pay for them, the customs duties on imports are playing a subordinate role for the present. In fact, the collection of import duties on many or most classes of goods has been temporarily suspended by a number of the continental countries—notably France, Belgium, and Czechoslovakia—in order that their nationals might secure essential supplies from abroad at the lowest cost.

Changes in the official levies on imports have figured in an important way during 1945 only in a few countries, where the domestic prices had gone so far out of line with world market prices that a program of official price adjustment of both imports and exports was regarded necessary. Thus, beginning in April, 1945, importers of most products into France were required to pay an import surcharge, varying with the commodity. This was designed to bring delivered prices of the foreign goods close to those in the domestic market, and to have the difference between the import price and that prevailing locally accrue to the government rather than to the merchant. Out of these revenues, exporters of French products were paid varying premiums, in order to make their selling prices attractive to foreign buyers under the prevailing official exchange rates.

A somewhat similar price equalization system was also operated in 1945 by the governments of Belgium and Greece, and has been officially proposed for Italy. Provision for such systems has been written into a number of the trade agreements concluded by various pairs of European countries during the past year. Presumably, the need for such price equalizations would be removed or reduced, if it should be regarded desirable to scale down the foreign value of the country's currency to conform more closely to its actual international purchasing power. Thus, shortly after the devaluation of the French franc in December, the application of the French price equalization system on foreign transactions was suspended.

Trade negotiations center on exchanges of goods each desires.—The liberated countries of Western Europe and Scandinavia have been very active during the past year in negotiating official agreements with each other, and with other countries of continental Europe, to regulate the resumption of trade between their territories. These have been distinctly transitional, usually for short periods, and have not attempted to embody changes in the structure of the tariffs or of other basic foreign trade controls.

Roughly conforming to a pattern, their principal feature is the list of goods which each country is especially desirous of obtaining, and the delivery of which the other government agrees to facilitate through the granting of export licenses, usually up to specified quantities for each class of goods. An estimated total is commonly set for the aggregate value of the trade in each direction during the period, and payments are to be made through clearing accounts in the respective national banks. While aiming at a balanced value for their bilateral exchanges, some provision is commonly embodied for reciprocal credits to cover overdrafts, although usually quite limited as to amount.[7]

Several common objectives have been observed in most of the trade negotiations of the countries of Western Europe and Scandinavia during the past year. There appears to be a general desire to avoid wide resort to the crude and restrictive international barter or compensation deals, which were so common in Europe during the period right after World War I, and have recently reappeared in certain parts of Eastern Europe. Limiting the amount of goods that could be exported to the other country is apparently intended both to minimize the risk of an excessive drain upon the local supplies, and to avoid building up large involuntary foreign credits if the other country proves unable to offset its current receipts with goods and services of equivalent value.

Perhaps the most striking characteristic of these recent inter-European trade agreements is the reversal of the usual objectives in such negotiations.

---

[7] Reference is made elsewhere to the instances where various of the liberated European countries have been extended definite lines of credit in advance, to assist them in financing their rehabilitation imports—notably on the part of the United States, Canada, Sweden, and Switzerland.

The current emphasis is upon the goods which each country desires to obtain from the other, instead of the prewar stress upon more favorable opportunities for the sale of its distinctive export products in the territory of the other. The present situation obviously reflects the temporary widespread shortages of many classes of goods, and will doubtless pass with improvement in the general state of supplies.

Because they have been subject to some misunderstanding, as well as for their intrinsic importance, special mention should be made of the series of monetary agreements, of similar pattern, which the United Kingdom has been negotiating with various European countries. By the end of 1945, these had come to include Scandinavia, most of Western Europe, and Czechoslovakia. These agreements fixed the rate of exchange between the pound sterling and the other currency, in certain cases setting a value for the currency of the continental country appreciably below its existing level, and then provided that the central bank of each country will buy the currency of the other at that rate, with some allowance for overdrafts in case the commercial transactions between the two countries did not quite strike a balance. In certain of the British agreements, notably with Sweden and Norway, no limit was set to the amount of uncleared balances in the other's currency which each undertook to hold.

These British monetary agreements concerned only new trading transactions, with outstanding obligations left for separate treatment. However, to allow the broadest scope for the resumption of new trade exchanges, the sterling acquired by the other country from exports to the United Kingdom may be used to buy goods anywhere within the sterling area, and the foreign currency acquired by the United Kingdom may be used anywhere within the domain of the other country, including overseas colonies. While bilateral in form, these agreements regularly provide that their terms would be reviewed in case either government adhered to a general international monetary agreement, toward which they are regarded as partial steps.

United States helps revive trade by unfreezing funds and extending credits.—The former belligerent countries of Western Europe (using the term in the sense earlier indicated) have been looking to the United States as a most important potential source of needed imports. The United States, on its part, took a number of steps during 1945 to facilitate the revival of trade with Europe.

The American export-licensing authorities progressively relaxed their control during the year, both as to scope of products and range of countries. By January, 1946, individual export licenses or allocations were required only for a limited "positive" list of products still in short supply in the United States. For those licensable products, applications were being considered for export transactions to all European countries except Germany, insofar as physical limitations and the governments of the countries of destination permitted.

As conditions of supply and shipping improved, means of payment came to stand out as the principal problem. Since there was no early prospect of the European countries reviving their exports to the United States even to the prewar volumes, their ability to buy the exceptionally large volume of American goods they now desired for replenishment and reconstruction depended upon finding means of paying for them. Payment had to come mainly either out of such foreign exchange reserves as they had, especially the funds frozen in the United States during the war, or out of new dollar loans or credits.

During 1945, the United States Treasury began the negotiation of arrangements with individual European countries for the release of their foreign funds, under suitable safeguards. In December, it lifted official control over the transfer to all countries of Europe, except Germany and the former neutrals, of the funds created by their current exports to the United States. Moreover, agreements were concluded during the latter months of 1945, or were under negotiation at the year's close, with many of the liberated countries of Western Europe, under which the United States Government is to extend to them credits of varying amounts to cover the financing of two classes of transactions: supplies requisitioned during the operation of the Lend-Lease program but not delivered until after the close of the war, and purchases in the United States made thereafter in the open market. Some additional credits were arranged with private American banks.

Most buying in United States handled or coördinated by official agencies.—The great bulk of the purchases made in the United States during 1945 by almost all of the countries of continental Europe were effected through their official purchasing missions. Sometimes these missions acted for centralized buying agencies of their governments, and sometimes as coördinators and expediters of orders previously negotiated directly with American suppliers by the private foreign importers.

As official understandings were reached with the governments of individual liberated countries of Europe—notably with France, Denmark, Norway, and Greece—to the effect that they were prepared to issue import permits for direct transactions by their private importers in certain classes of goods, the United States authorities announced that they would issue licenses to exporters upon orders approved by the governments of the countries of destination, if the products still required individual licenses. As indicated, this action was later broadened by an announcement of general readiness on the part of the United States to consider license applications for shipments to all countries with which private trade was suspended during the war, except Germany and Japan, in order to permit the resumption of full foreign commercial relations as promptly as other circumstances will permit.

When conditions within the respective countries allow, and satisfactory intergovernmental arrangements regarding unfreezing of funds and new credits can be worked out, it is anticipated that additional European countries will authorize their private traders to resume direct commercial transactions with American exporters during 1946, if only to a limited degree at the outset, and that the range of products now open to private trade will in time be enlarged. As an interim measure, a number of the Western European purchasing missions in the United States are reportedly allowing preliminary direct negotiations between buyers and sellers, with considerable latitude in specifying particular American makes and brands even when the orders are placed through the mission. In the case of one of the Scandinavian countries, the purchasing mission in the United States is accompanied by representatives of local industrial and trade associations, who consummate purchases on behalf of individual member firms within the broad framework of essentiality and fund allocations determined by the governmental authorities.

Eastern Europe

Imports from the West mainly relief supplies.—The general reestablishment of foreign trading on the part of the countries of Eastern Europe—comprising broadly all located east and southeast of Germany except Italy and Greece—was much less advanced by the end of 1945 than that of the other continental countries.[8] Beyond the relief goods being supplied by UNRRA and certain private organizations, few large-scale or regular currents of commercial imports from Western European or overseas countries appear as yet to have been reëstablished, or to be likely very soon. Several circumstances seem to have contributed to this situation.

[8] Germany is as yet outside the scope of normal trade relations or policies, since it is still in the stage of military occupation and basic reorganization by the Allied powers, and such limited goods as are sent into, or out of, that country are under their control. The Soviet Union announced no changes during 1945 in the structure or policy of its long-standing government monopoly of foreign trade.

Impoverished and disorganized, oriented to Russia, trade resumption meager.—Disruption of productive facilities and of transport, meagerness of foreign exchange assets and general monetary deterioration, and, indeed, general political as well as economic disorganization, have been much greater in nearly all of these countries of Eastern Europe than elsewhere on the Continent. The early resumption of sizable trade with the Western countries is especially limited by the fact that the economies of most of the countries of Eastern Europe are being closely oriented with that of the Soviet Union. The bulk of their trade movements reported thus far have been with that country, mainly eastward. In the case of the former German satellites, the heavy deliveries on reparations account to the Soviet Union and other invaded Eastern countries further restrict the volume of goods which could be offered, from their reduced production, against imports from Western countries. For few have the exchange reserves, or have yet acquired the credits, to finance any substantial imports beyond what they can currently pay for with their exports.

A number of trade agreements were concluded during the year between various pairs of Eastern European countries, and a few between Eastern and Western countries, for the exchange of selected products up to specified quantities. Sometimes, settlement was to be made through clearing accounts, not infrequently in terms of some outside stable currency, such as Swiss francs; sometimes, the goods were exchanged directly through compensation arrangements or private barter deals. While some of these agreements have as yet stimulated very little trade, limited movements of goods between these countries are reported to have begun during 1945, so far as cross-border transport facilities allowed.

All foreign transactions in Eastern Europe are regularly subject to official approval and, in the present low state of supplies and of foreign exchange, the granting of export licenses is largely dependent upon what can be obtained from the other country in return for the limited amounts of domestic goods that can now be spared for export. Priority is given to foreign products urgently needed for essential consumption or reconstruction.

From the meager information thus far received, it appears that only Czechoslovakia and, to a smaller extent, Finland and Poland had managed to arrange, by the end of 1945, for any appreciable trade exchanges with countries outside of Eastern Europe. In the case of Czechoslovakia and Finland, this has been assisted by some extensions of credit on the part of the other governments concerned.

Governmental control of economies dims prospect for private foreign trade.—Extensive experimentation is going on in nearly all of these countries with the nationalization or state control of certain local industries or particular sectors of the economy, sometimes centering upon the heavy industries and sometimes upon all plants of a given size. Even those Eastern European governments which profess a basic belief in private enterprise claim that, in view of the "scrambling" of industrial ownership during the period of German domination, de-Nazification of certain branches of industry and finance can be accomplished only through their control by the government. They declare that theirs will be a decidedly mixed economy, at least for a transitional period.

With variations in scope and degree, it now appears likely that the structure of domestic production and distribution of most countries of Eastern Europe during the period ahead will be largely governmentally controlled, in some cases approaching the Soviet pattern. The "economic collaboration" agreements concluded during the past year by the Soviet Union with Rumania, Bulgaria, and Hungary provide for large-scale Soviet participation in the development and operation of their industries and natural resources. On the other hand, certain of the Eastern European governments have shown a distinct unwillingness to accept Soviet proposals either for the handling of their foreign trade as a joint monopoly or for the joint operation of their industries.

As yet, there has been little definite indication from most of the governments of Eastern Europe as to how much scope they contemplate allowing for private foreign trading. Whatever degree of governmental control of their domestic economies may be adopted by these various countries as a continuing program, however, there appears to be no warrant to assume that it would necessarily extend to the conduct of their foreign trade with countries which operate on a predominantly private-enterprise basis. Thus, the exchange of goods between Finland and the Soviet Union during the past year is reported to have been carried through entirely on a barter basis. At the same time, the limited trade revived between Finland and the United Kingdom was being conducted in many products through normal commercial channels.

When the Czechoslovak program for nationalization of certain industries was announced, it was observed that there was to be no general nationalization of commerce, the trade in motion pictures apparently being considered as an exception on cultural grounds. In fact, the new regulations regarding the control of imports and exports by Czech firms, issued in December, 1945, followed closely the prewar licensing practices of that country.

For at least certain of these countries, there is not precluded the possibility that—outside of a limited number of consumers' staples or products which continue in prolonged short supply—such trade as is resumed with the Western countries may be handled either by private commercial firms under license, within the framework of a broad official program, or by industrial or commercial associations which are governmentally regulated but privately operated. Appreciable variation may be anticipated in this respect as between the different countries of Eastern Europe. Witness the fact that the Czechoslovak Government has been seeking the renegotiation of its commercial treaties with a broad range of outside countries, and is stressing its desire for the renewed trading relations to be on a most-favored-nation basis. The assurance of competitive opportunity can have little practical meaning unless a sizable volume of foreign trade with the Western countries is contemplated, and through commercial channels.

United States eases reëstablishment of commercial channels with Eastern Europe.—With a few notable exceptions, the prewar volume of the United States trade with the countries here referred to as Eastern Europe was relatively small.[9] However, in the closing months of 1945, the United States authorities announced that, for those products still requiring individual licenses for exportation, applications for shipment to most of the countries of Eastern Europe would be given consideration, when based upon firm approved orders from the countries of destination. It was recognized that, for the present, trade with these areas would necessarily be restricted, because of the difficulties of obtaining clearance from the appropriate authorities in those countries, and the lack of adequate transport facilities. Nevertheless, the United States apparently desired to make known its readiness to aid in reëstablishing commercial channels with the countries of Eastern Europe, in the interest of facilitating the restoration of private trade with those areas as promptly as circumstances permitted.

Far East

Liberation incomplete; abnormal conditions hold back trade resumption.—In many of the formerly secluded areas of the Far East, the process of liberation from Japanese control was still going on through

[9] Total United States exports to this group of countries during 1936–1938 averaged 61 million dollars or less than 1 per cent of all sales to continental Europe. Total United States prewar imports from these countries averaged 79 million dollars or 1.5 per cent of all purchases from continental Europe. Only with Czechoslovakia, Poland, and Finland did United States trade before the war, in either direction, amount to 10 million dollars a year.

most of 1945, and reoccupation by the former authorities had in some regions not yet been fully accomplished at its close. Even where the local military and political situations presented little difficulty, the resumption of general overseas commerce has been held back by a combination of factors—the economic disorganization, if not destruction, left in the wake of the long Japanese occupation; the poor condition of harbors and inadequacy of interior transport; the confused state of prices and currencies, and the uncertain foreign exchange prospect; and the secondary but practical need for the reëstablishment of responsible commercial channels and banking facilities.

Among the major areas of the Far East, the greatest progress during the past year toward the restoration of external trade, and increasingly through normal commercial channels, was made in the Philippine Islands, the earliest liberated. In China, the relaxation of the wartime license system on imports and the resumption of regular commercial shipping to Shanghai in the fall of 1945 were promising, but the restoration of active commercial relations even with that region is still greatly hindered by the continued strict control on exports and the highly abnormal exchange situation.

In the colonial areas of Southeast Asia, the general prospect appears to be that governmental agencies or officially authorized commercial groups will handle the external trade of several of those territories during the initial period of its resumption, with individual private transactions restored gradually, under governmental license. In most of these colonies, the resumption of anything like normal foreign commerce must apparently await the provision of food and other minimum supplies for the neglected native populations, and the rehabilitation of the local facilities for the production of their export staples, after the stripping, diversion, and neglect under Japanese rule.

Japan itself and certain of its former colonies are as yet outside the scope of normal trade relations or policies. They are still in the stage of military occupation and basic reorganization by the Allied powers, and such limited amounts of goods as are sent into, or out of, those areas are under special Allied arrangements.

Only Philippines and China able to begin restoration of overseas commerce.—Since the resumption of foreign trade in the Far East has been most advanced in the case of the *Philippines,* the steps in this reëstablishment may be worth noting. Up to September 1, 1945, the United States military authorities looked after the rehabilitation needs of the islands as they reoccupied particular areas, distributing both relief and purchasable commodities. Licensing of commercial exports from the United States had been authorized, within limitations, as early as May. Beginning in September, the Foreign Economic Administration was charged with the responsibility of providing the Philippines with essential civilian goods until such time as normal trade could be completely reëstablished. At the same time, it undertook to arrange for the procurement of Philippine staple export commodities, particularly copra and fibers, and to assist the Commonwealth Government in reëstablishing private trade with the United States.

Commercial imports were at first limited to categories essential to the Philippine economy, as established monthly by collaboration between Philippine and American authorities. To the extent that private trade could not meet the minimum import requirements of the program set up, the Foreign Economic Administration undertook to supply the deficiencies through the facilities of the United States Commercial Company. Shipping to the islands was resumed by private services in November. As private traders steadily increased their shipments of civilian goods through commercial channels, the United States Commercial Company has been curtailing its participation. By the end of 1945, conditions had sufficiently improved so that it no longer was necessary to require American exporters to obtain "registry numbers" from Manila to cover their individual shipments.

During the war, all Chinese cash purchases in the United States, whether for private or governmental account, were handled through the Universal Trading Corporation at New York, a Chinese governmental agency. Most of the important products exported from *China* were handled by official monopolies, with some opportunity for private transactions under license. Within the physical limitations of the situation and the unsettled condition of prices and exchange, the government of China took certain steps shortly after the surrender of Japan which promised an early resumption of overseas commerce and, in considerable measure, through private channels, but relatively little actual progress had been made by the end of 1945.

In October, the Chinese Ministry of Finance announced the elimination of the wartime requirement of import permits for all but certain special products. The reorganized Chinese Supply Commission, which formerly handled Lend-Lease arrangements, was to have direction of procurement in the United States only of governmental purchases. Beginning in November, ships of various flags were scheduled for regular sailings to the Far East, serving Manila, Hong Kong, and Shanghai. By the close of 1945, foreign banks were reopening and prewar commercial houses were being reëstablished.

The actual resumption of importations even into the Shanghai area has thus far been small, however. Foreign exchange at the low official rate is sold only for the importation of commodities which the authorities consider essential. Since very little free exchange is available in the open market, even at the very much higher rates, there has been almost no scope for other than the import transactions approved as "essential." The marked shortage of foreign exchange in relation to the volume of imports desired for replenishment and reconstruction limits the possible extent of all Chinese imports, until arrangements can be made for sizable foreign credits. The need for such credits has long been under discussion in China.

In November, the purchase and sale of certain Chinese products which had been handled during the war mainly as official export monopolies were reported restored to commercial channels. A number of important Chinese exports continued in official hands, however, and, varying only in degree for different commodities, the sale abroad of most leading products is subject to license and the surrender of the foreign exchange earned thereby. In addition to the unresolved question as to the exchange value of Chinese currencies, the resumption of volume exportations from China is further handicapped by the difficulties of transporting goods from the interior to the ports and, in some cases, by the unsettled legal status of enterprises taken over from Japanese control.

In November, the military administration of *Hong Kong*, the British-controlled island off the south coast of China, announced that the colony was open to normal trading except for a few commodities in short world supply, the importation and distribution of which would be controlled by the government. For the time being, a system of import licensing is to be maintained. It is planned to grant such licenses generously except for luxury goods. Facilities for the granting of foreign exchange for purchases outside the sterling area were being arranged, but that would be available only for imports approved as essential to the rehabilitation of the colony.

Rehabilitation of economies of Southeast Asia in governmental hands.—At the end of August, 1945, the French Government announced the creation of a Supply Center for *Indo-China* which was to purchase all food and other essential goods for the Indo-Chinese population immediately after liberation, arrange for their transport, and sell them to designated local firms. In the United States, the French Colonial Agency was to act for the Indo-Chinese Supply Center.

Under the new program proposed by the French Government for its overseas possessions after the war, Indo-China has been promised a large measure of autonomy in customs matters, as in various other respects.

For some time back, the Netherlands Government at London had been developing a master relief plan for the population of the *Netherlands Indies,* under which large-scale purchases were to be made of food, textiles, and equipment for the rehabilitation of the various export industries, to be ready for delivery immediately after liberation. To bridge the period between government buying and distribution and the time when both imports and exports could be returned to normal private channels, governmentally sponsored joint commercial organizations were planned for the handling of both imports and exports, with the firms formerly engaged in the business, both in the Indies and abroad, sharing in proportion to their relative prewar operations.

In view of the disturbed political situation, the military authorities have recently announced that the Netherlands Indies Government Export-Import Department would serve as sole agents for buying and selling in the islands for some considerable time. It is declared that the present situation would not permit of any private trading for several months, and that the entry of commercial men of whatever nationality was not feasible until the political situation is stabilized.

No information is yet available as to the system set up in *Siam* for the regulation of postwar commerce, nor as to the arrangements under which foreign importers or exporters may resume trading relations with that country.

By special agreement concluded at the close of 1945 between the United Kingdom and Siam, which had been at war with Britain, the surplus rice stocks of Siam are to be made available for shipment to Malaya and other near-by food-deficit British areas.

Under the system recently installed in *Burma,* the government is to make initial procurement of certain essential commodities. No other goods may be imported except under license and, in general, licenses will be entertained only from previously established importers, on the basis of orders definitely accepted by a supplier. Import priority is to be given to essential commodities.

The reoccupation of *British Malaya* had not progressed sufficiently during 1945 to allow an active resumption of its overseas commerce. Late in December, 1945, the British military administration at Singapore announced that the general emergency program for the control of imports and exports, which had been introduced in Malaya as in other British colonies in 1940, would be enforced from January 1, 1946. Under that ordinance, the local authorities have broad powers to regulate foreign trade in their discretion, and imports of most products from countries outside the sterling area are to be restricted, on exchange grounds, to those highly essential and not obtainable from sterling countries.

Since the economy of Malaya is primarily dependent upon rubber and tin, the British Government has visualized as its first task here the rehabilitation of those industries and the provision of food and other basic necessities for the population. While the government has undertaken to supply the essential needs of the small rubber growers in order that they might resume production, the rehabilitation of the rubber estates (of over 100 acres) is being carried out by a governmentally supported Malayan Estate Owners Company. The estate owners were to combine into groups of 100,000 acres or more, in order to participate equitably in the allocation of the labor, materials, and equipment available. In the case of tin, a committee from the industry, in association with representatives of the British Ministry of Supply, has gone to Malaya to survey the properties and equipment and to prepare plans for their rehabilitation. Meanwhile, the British Government has placed substantial orders for mine equipment.

At the outset, the British Ministry of Supply is to act as buyer of all rubber and tin which become available from Malaya. The allocation of such supplies is to be made by the international commodity committees for these products, which had been set up by the former Combined Raw Materials Board. Malaya is the only rubber-producing area of Southeast Asia from which any but token shipments were received during 1945, and a standard price of 20¼ cents per pound has recently been set by the governments participating in the Combined Rubber Committee. Only two small shipments of tin from Asia have been received since the close of the war. The supplies to become available from British Malaya, as well as from the Netherlands Indies, are to be allocated by the International Tin Committee among the normal consuming countries, as in the case of natural rubber.

1946

ACUTE NEEDS OF RECENTLY WAR-INVOLVED AREAS ARE THE DOMINANT TRADE FORCES

PRINCIPAL TRADE PROBLEMS AND EFFORTS TO DEAL WITH THEM

Insofar as trade policies determined the movements of goods between countries during 1946, the official decisions as to how much of particular commodities should be exported and where they should go were, on the whole, more influential than were the duties or other official conditions of admission set by the governments of the importing countries. Of greater influence than either export or import controls, however, have been the acute needs of the war-involved areas for the immediate necessities of life and for products essential to the rehabilitation of their economies, and the unprecedented pent-up demand everywhere for goods that had not been freely available for a number of years.

Shortage of Goods and Inability to Pay Are the Chief Limitations

Two factors, in the main, limited the huge volume of international trade needed to meet these exceptional demands: the general world shortages of many essential commodities, especially foodstuffs and coal, and often also of the means for transporting them; and the limited ability of many countries to buy such foreign goods as were obtainable. Most of the changes during 1946 in the trade control measures of individual countries, and of the many special commercial arrangements worked out between various sets of countries, seemed largely prompted by these limitations inherent in the disordered postwar situation. In the case of particular countries, certain special motives have been figuring prominently in the regulation of their foreign trade, namely, to hold down imports which compete strongly with similar domestic products; to advance the government's control over the country's economic structure and development; to give special attention to the current trade with particular other countries; or, in certain regions, to promote closer long-term economic relations. During the past year, however, these have usually been subordinate to the above overriding considerations.

The general improvement during the course of the year in the conditions of world supply of various commodities, along with the progress toward rehabilitation in a number of countries, especially in Western Europe, allowed the relaxation during 1946 of some of the trade controls in operation at its start by various international bodies and individual governments. However, the return of many countries to more normal world trade relations depends in large measure upon the various political settlements yet to be worked out and to be brought into effective operation. Moreover, most of the countries which had been directly involved in the war are still suffering from the general disorganization of their internal economies.

Varying only in degree, the possibility of these countries resuming foreign commerce in anything like the usual volume and manner is still distinctly limited by many factors, including: their low level of production—itself partly the result of inadequate supplies of imported raw materials and fuel, the disordered domestic commercial channels, and the unstable state of internal prices and currency values. Even many countries that were outside the active war zones are still in the process of adjustment to the shocks to their economies resulting from the conflict, in the way of dislocation of old industries, stimulations to new developments, and changes in their financial position. Under the circumstances, the major conditions which limited the movements of goods between countries during 1946, and chiefly dictated the year's changes in trade control measures, might on the whole be expected to continue well into 1947.

While war-inherited conditions and short-range pressures are thus still dominating the current foreign trade measures of most countries, certain preparatory steps taken during 1946, upon the initiative of the United States, have prepared the way for a series of international consultations and negotiations during 1947 which may set the pattern for world trade for the period ahead. This year should show how far the important trading countries are ready to agree upon a concerted long-term program for liberal foreign trade policies, as relaxation in the pressures of the postwar transition period allows them more freedom of action.

Credit and Relief Offered Meet Financial Needs Only Partly

The financial considerations controlling international commerce have been of a highly unusual character. Among the countries of Europe and the Far East that had suffered destruction and impoverishment by the war, inadequacy of export goods or of other means with which to pay for the large volume of immediate import needs was to be expected. In addition, certain countries possessing foreign exchange resources had them largely in the form of balances in other countries, which were not freely convertible for use in third countries where particular products desired might be more available. This has been especially true of most of the British Empire areas and of certain others for whom the United Kingdom has been the major market. Moreover, a number of governments of Europe and of Latin America which had usable financial reserves felt impelled to be selective in the importations permitted. They have been particularly restricting purchases of various consumers' goods, chiefly to reserve their funds for foreign products considered more essential to the economy of the country.

On the other hand, a major aid to the resumption of purchasing by many countries with inadequate financial resources were the credits extended them for this purpose, mainly by the United States, Canada, Sweden, Switzerland, and, to a lesser extent, by certain other European countries, and by Argentina and Brazil. A substantial part of the imports during the past year into the countries of Western and Northern Europe that had been engaged in the war was made possible by the various forms of credit extended them during 1946 or earlier. The greater part of the immediate import needs of the war-ravaged countries of Eastern and Southern Europe and a sizable part of the import needs of China were met by relief shipments, mainly through UNRRA, and by transfers on credit of war surpluses located in those regions.

Governmental Trade Controls Important Mainly on the Export Side

Governmental trade controls, insofar as they were decisive regulators of the movements of commerce during the past year, were for most countries exceptionally important on the export side. These took several forms: international allocating bodies, principally the successors to the wartime Combined Food Board and Combined Raw Materials Board; agreements between various pairs of countries as to the goods for which they would facilitate shipment to each other; and the export-licensing controls of individual governments. The international allocating bodies endeavored to provide for the most equitable distribution among the nations of the limited supplies of the particular commodities under their control. The export controls of individual governments were usually guided by the desire to prevent undue drain upon supplies needed by their own peoples, and to hold down domestic price advances. Frequently, such controls were used to assist in obtaining needed products from abroad, by making the permitted exports to a particular country dependent upon what that country could furnish in return.

Very few governments made major changes in their import duties during the year, although a number of tariff revisions are in preparation. In some cases, these are being held up until the prospect as to price levels and the general trend of postwar trade policies becomes clearer. Insofar as governments could exercise choice as to the character, volume, or source of the goods imported into their territories, the principal controls used have been import license or exchange permit systems.

Only a few countries relaxed during 1946 the administrative import controls they had in operation at the opening of the year, and some countries even tightened them or introduced new regulatory measures. China was prominent among those which extended rather than relaxed their import controls, although in some measure that tendency was evidenced also in a number of countries of Europe and Latin America. These actions are largely attributable to the fact earlier mentioned, that most countries had yet achieved only a moderate degree of economic readjustment to postwar conditions. Particularly on the part of the countries of Europe that had been involved in the war, strict licensing control of most imports continued the rule, in order to make the best use of their limited financial resources in the face of unusually large import needs.

Most Purchasing Missions Giving Way to Controlled Private Trade

In general, the extent of direct governmental intervention into import or export transactions of the types developed during or immediately after the war was reduced during the past year. Exceptions to this general trend are Argentina and most of the countries of Eastern Europe,[1] which are moving toward a high degree of governmental control of their entire economies, with foreign transactions either reserved to official agencies or conducted under their close direction. Most official purchasing missions, so prominent a year ago, especially in the overseas trade of Western Europe, were either winding up or had sharply curtailed the scope of their operations by the end of 1946. Broadly speaking, trade arrangements for the great majority of products are progressively being returned to private importers or groups of them, although still subject to governmental licenses for many individual transactions or for the transfer of funds in settlement of them. As an exception to the general rule, however, even certain countries of Western Europe apparently intend to retain governmental purchasing—or at least close official direction of private purchasing—of selected basic import commodities for some time to come, and in some cases also of certain foreign equipment for reconstruction or modernization.

Most of the large-scale intergovernmental procurement arrangements entered into during the war have been terminated or are tapering off. However, official bulk-purchase contracts of a peacetime character, covering large parts of the importing country's needs of selected basic foods or industrial materials, were a prominent feature of the 1946 trade programs of a number of countries, notably the United Kingdom. These recent bulk-purchase agreements appear to have several common characteristics.

Although broadly arranged for between governments, the actual transactions are in most cases to be consummated by private traders. Moreover, while some governments have declared a definite preference for centralized bulk procurement of certain staple import commodities, the majority of the contracts actually entered into during the year seemed temporary arrangements, and prompted largely by the uncertain prospects as to supplies or markets and as to the stability of prices during the transitional period. In only few cases do the initial terms run beyond a year or two, and even within that period the arrangements are often subject to modification in the light of the conditions under which supplies of the particular commodities become available from other countries.

[1] Throughout this chapter, the term "Eastern Europe" is used as a short means of referring to the following group of countries: Poland, Czechoslovakia, Hungary, Yugoslavia, Albania, Rumania, and Bulgaria. The term "Western Europe" is understood to include Scandinavia.

Bilateral Supply Agreements Make Possible Limited Trade Resumption

A striking feature of the past year has been the exceptionally large number of agreements between various pairs of governments regarding commercial transactions between their nationals. These agreements typically include lists of products the shipment of which each government is to permit or facilitate, up to a specified quantity or value, through the operation of its particular export-control system. Permission to import them into the country of destination seems commonly assumed. Settlement is usually through clearing accounts set up in the respective national banks, in order to minimize uncovered balances and to require the least transfers of currencies or gold. Barter deals have seldom figured except in the arrangements with certain countries of Eastern Europe. Only rarely have these arrangements provided for the governments themselves to supply or buy the products involved.

Such agreements have been most common among the countries of continental Europe and certain of the Latin American Republics.[2] In the inter-European agreements, a rough annual balance in the value of the goods exchanged is usually aimed at, with only limited overdraft permitted, except in those few cases where definite lines of credit are extended by the more prosperous country.

Usually negotiated for not more than a year, the great majority of the many recent arrangements of this type appear to be makeshifts, and do not necessarily imply a fixed program or preference for bilateralism as against open competitive trading. Typically, what each country is primarily seeking is assurance of supplies of particular needed commodities from the other, with the least drain upon its own products or hazard of excess exports becoming frozen credits.

In most instances, these temporary arrangements to make possible a controlled if limited resumption of trade between the particular pair of countries are understandable. They afford a means of carrying on the most essential exchanges of goods until greater freedom of choice in foreign trading is made possible for these countries, through more ample availability of goods to buy and to sell, through the accumulation of exchange reserves, and through the expected assistance of the International Monetary

[2] For dealing with countries like the United States, whose currencies are convertible and which do not feel obliged to operate on the bilateral balancing basis, no country able to pay for its purchases need necessarily have a formal trade agreement regarding reciprocal supplies, as is now the practice among European and certain other countries.

Fund in facilitating the normal multilateral settlement of trade balances. Only a few of the bilateral agreements concluded during the past year carried evidence of definite intention on the part of the contracting countries to give special preference to each other's needs or products, without regard to the possible limitation upon the reasonable access of third countries to their goods or markets.

Limited Exchanges with Occupied Areas Handled by Governmental Bodies

Thus far, such shipments as have been made into or out of Germany and Japan have either been carried through by the respective occupying authorities or arranged by them. In addition to the imports of supplies necessary to maintain the prescribed minimum living standards, the occupying governments have arranged to ship in certain raw materials for local processing, with the advances paid for from the exports of the manufactured products. In order to offset the costs of these official imports, and to resume the supplying of the distinctive peacetime products of Germany and of Japan to the countries which had come to depend upon them, the occupying authorities began during 1946 to encourage local production for export and to find foreign markets for it.

The major part of the export products that have become available to the United States authorities have been disposed of in near-by countries under intergovernmental arrangements, against goods or dollars, although actual deliveries may be made to private merchants. The goods in which American buyers have expressed interest have thus far been handled through the United States Commercial Company as emergency intermediary. From Japan, the principal product shipped to the United States has been raw silk, and, since that is duty-free, no customs problem has been involved. From Germany, the early shipments have been cleared through the customs by the United States Commercial Company.

The early resumption of private trade between the United States and the occupied countries has been announced as the definite official objective. However, the opening up of direct purchases by American importers of dutiable products from either Japan or Germany waits upon the settling of a number of problems. Among them is the working out of a satisfactory basis for their customs valuation, since no established home market values yet exist in either country. This and other difficulties arising from the lack of a commercial exchange value for the mark and the yen have been temporarily avoided by pricing mainly in dollars.

An economic merger of the British and American zones of Germany begins in 1947, with the way left open for the Russians and the French to join. This merger is expected to afford a broader basis for foreign trading, as well as to facilitate interzonal exchanges and, within a few years, to make possible a self-supporting German economy.

Prospects for Concerted Action Toward Liberal Trade Policies

Despite the current confused and constricted international trade situation, the very facts of the continuing general economic unsettlement and of the need for resorting to awkward improvisations in trade policies—at a time when nations feel so keenly their dependence upon each other—appeared to improve the prospect for the long term. They seemed to make many governments more responsive than they were before the war to the idea of acting jointly, in devising means for promoting the recovery and trade expansion of each through international consultation and reciprocal accommodation.

Setting up of exchange parities a step toward currency stability.—Following the ratification by forty governments of the Bretton Woods agreements, the first step toward broad international collaboration in the financial field, the International Monetary Fund and the International Bank completed their organization during 1946 and prepared for early operations. The International Fund, in announcing in December its acceptance of the existing exchange rates of thirty countries as their initial postwar parities, from which no material changes may be made without prior consultation, took the first concrete step toward world currency stability. This fixed the basis also upon which the fund is to begin performing, in March, 1947, its authorized function of assisting member countries in temporary exchange difficulties, by making available to them limited quantities of particular foreign currencies needed for freer import operations, and thus gradually facilitating the shift back from restrictive bilateral settlements to multilateral trading.

On the essential companion program in the trade field, encouraging progress was made in the fall of 1946 by the Preparatory Committee for an International Conference on Trade and Employment, which was convened at London by the Economic and Social Council of the United Nations. Working on the technical level, the representatives of eighteen important trading countries reached broad agreement upon plans for the formation of an International Trade Organization, upon a tentative draft of a charter of standard principles of liberal commercial conduct, and upon a concrete program for their early implementation.

Large goals set for prospective international trade conference.—The broad objective of the program is the general expansion of the production, exchange, and consumption of goods. It is sought to achieve this mainly through reduction of trade barriers and discriminations in world commerce, and of unduly restrictive trade practices of private or public origin; under certain circumstances, through intergovernmental arrangements regarding the marketing of selected primary commodities; and through concerted action to assist the programs of member countries for high employment and economic development, under safeguards to minimize the possibility of measures in the interest of one country operating to the injury of others.

The full International Conference on Trade and Employment, at which this comprehensive program is to be placed before the nations generally, is now planned for the latter part of 1947. Before that is convened, a testing out of its feasibility is to take place in April at Geneva. In conjunction with the perfection of the draft charter for an International Trade Organization at that meeting, the same eighteen governments are preparing to negotiate consolidated trade agreements for the reciprocal reduction of the barriers to trade with one another, in order to give practical effect among themselves to one of the main objectives of the charter, as the basis and pattern for a world program.

The prospective developments during 1947 should therefore be highly significant, in showing how far the important trading countries of the world can find it possible to agree upon common operating principles and reciprocal undertakings toward these large objectives of acknowledged desirability. The London meeting of last fall has indicated that the chief difficulties will probably come from the necessity of reconciling the obligations involved in such a program with two factors: first, the need felt by many of the war-ravaged countries for an extended transition period, before they would be ready to give up the arbitrary and often discriminatory trade controls and practices which they now consider necessary; and second, the strong desire on the part of various underdeveloped countries for sufficient freedom to restrict imports when that is found necessary to support their programs for diversification and, especially, industrialization.

The working out of methods for satisfactory commercial intercourse with those countries resorting largely to state trading in some form constitutes another of the difficult problems to be faced this coming year. In view of the distinctly minor place in the aggregate volume of world trade of the commerce of the countries which operate predominantly on a state-trading basis, the formation of an International Trade Organization embracing the principal trading countries is not dependent upon their immediate adherence. Earnest effort is being directed to the solution of this problem, however, in order to obtain the broadest possible participation of the nations in the prospective concerted program for freer and fuller world trade, in the interest of greater general prosperity and durable peace.

SALIENT DEVELOPMENTS IN CONTROLS ON EXPORTS

Joint International Controls Terminating Except on Farm Products

A series of international allocating bodies known as Combined Commodity Committees had been set up in December, 1945, as successors to the British-American Combined Boards on Raw Materials and on Resources and Production of wartime origin, to supervise the distribution of selected nonagricultural products then still in short world supply. Most of them had terminated operations by the close of 1946. Tin is the only such commodity which continues subject to broad international allocation into 1947. Shortage of coal is mainly a European problem, with the European Coal Organization continuing to make recommendations regarding allocation of the supplies being made available from the United States and other overseas countries as well as from continental sources.

In agricultural commodities, where critical shortages continued over large parts of Europe and Asia, the former Combined Food Board was replaced in mid-1946 by an International Emergency Food Council with broadened membership. That body continued to keep under review the allocation of most of the available exportable surpluses of much the same classes of farm products and fertilizer as its predecessor. Only minor changes in the scope of its activities were made during 1946, or are known to be contemplated for early introduction.[8]

Operations of UNRRA to End Early in 1947

Upon the decision of the major contributors to the United Nations Relief and Rehabilitation Administration, the operations of that

[8] For a number of commodities of minor export importance, however, allocation recommendations were discontinued during the latter months of the year. These included argols, tartaric acid, dairy products, dried fruit, spices, vitamins, phosphate rock, most seeds, and certain kinds of canned fish. Some additional commodities of secondary trade importance are likely to be dropped during the early months of 1947.

agency are not to be extended beyond the end of 1946 for Europe and the end of March, 1947, for the Far East, as earlier planned. In view of the delayed deliveries occasioned by strikes, however, the time limit for shipments under earlier approved contracts was extended three months in each case. After the passing of UNRRA, relief supplies to war-ravaged countries not in a position to pay for them are to be arranged for directly between each pair of governments. The prospective programs of the various supplying countries are to be coördinated by exchange of information through the United Nations Secretariat, following a preliminary general survey of foreign relief needs during 1947.

United States and Most British Areas Relax Export Controls as Supplies Improve

The United States and most of the major British countries progressively removed or relaxed their export license controls over many classes of products during the course of 1946, as their domestic supply situations improved. (The special situation in India will be dealt with later.) The United Kingdom definitely limited the immediate availability to its own population of the enlarged output in many lines of goods, in order the sooner to rebuild its war-shrunken export markets. In that way, it is sought to assure a stable level of British comfort in the future, through the nation's improved ability to pay for needed imports from current earnings.

Latin America Widens Export Controls on Foods and Materials

In many countries of Latin America, license controls were widely imposed or extended during 1946 over the exportation of important ranges of commodities, notably foodstuffs and basic materials. Export quotas were frequently set up, and for some commodities outward shipments were entirely suspended for a time. Most of these measures appeared to be distinctly temporary, usually prompted by the desire to prevent an undue outflow of products needed domestically, and to check the inflationary price trends which have been experienced by the majority of these countries since the war. In certain cases, export controls were officially used as means of negotiating with other Latin American and a few European countries, in return for supplies of specific products especially desired from those countries or for certain financial settlements.

Argentina, Brazil, Chile, and Mexico were conspicuous among the Latin American countries resorting to export restrictions. Argentina, which took long strides during the year toward official control of its economy in various respects, reserved to official agencies the sole right to market or license the exports of many staple products of the country, with the sale of grains and meats confined to intergovernmental arrangements.

Western Europe Uses Export Controls in Bargaining for Supplies

In general, the countries of continental Europe continued to control by license the exportation of most classes of products, with a few of the Western European countries finding it possible during 1946 to ease their restrictions somewhat. In the countries of Eastern Europe, with the notable exceptions of Czechoslovakia and Poland, very limited progress has thus far been made toward production above local needs and shipments required for reparations. The large calls made upon what was available, for shipment to the Soviet Union under barter or other arrangements, allowed only small exportations elsewhere during 1946, and very little has been sent to Western European or overseas countries.

The controls upon exports by the various European governments served both to ensure minimum supplies for their own populations and, especially in their relations with other European countries, as a means of allocating what could be spared for export in accordance with the goods which the particular other country promised to supply. Mention has already been made of the general effort among the European countries, during this period of short supplies and inconvertible currencies, to aim at an annual bilateral balance in their trade exchanges, except in those few cases where special credits were granted to cover an anticipated export balance.

Special Situations in India and China

Among the major countries of Asia, India was notable for its elaborate export controls over many important staple commodities, for at least parts of the year. With the successive dissolution of the international allocating bodies on nonagricultural products, an increasing number of Indian export commodities came under local control. Commerce flowed through private channels but subject to strict licensing, and shipments for various destinations were often regulated by quotas, set in certain cases by intergovernmental negotiations. In addition to its concern over the reëstablishment of normal foreign markets for its jute, hides, and other staple exports, through proportionate allocation of the currently short supplies, the government of India is placing great stress on the prior claims of its domestic processing industries upon these essential materials, so as to encourage their exportation in the manufactured instead of the raw state.

Various important Chinese export products continued in official hands, while those that had been released to commercial channels toward the close of 1945 remained subject to close exchange controls. Hampered by the continuing military activities and generally disordered internal economic conditions, notably the high abnormal course of prices and of exchange values, the resumption of exports from China was retarded in 1946. The aggregate value of goods shipped out of the country during the year was reported as less than one-fifth of the goods imported.

Efforts in Southeast Asia to Shift Trade Out of Governmental Hands

In most of the war-affected areas of Southeast Asia reopened to general commerce, strong efforts were made during the past year to resume exportations in volume of the staple primary products formerly furnished by them to world markets. Rapid resumption was hindered by the slow progress toward political stability and rehabilitation of normal economic life, and by inadequate transportation facilities. As a rule, the initial programs for exportation from these areas have been centralized in the hands of governmental agencies or under their close control, although the early return of the trade to prewar commercial channels is generally contemplated.

In the Philippines, the return of most commodities to private trade had already been accomplished in the fall of 1945. In the Netherlands Indies, private exportation has been permitted since October, 1946, of products not under international allocation, except in the case of Java and Sumatra, the political status of which was still in process of settlement at the close of 1946.

Exports from French Indo-China were still governmentally handled at the end of the year, with large accumulations of rubber moving out, although political conditions in certain regions continued unsettled. Private trade channels have been reopened in Siam, subject to exchange control and often export licenses. The major export commodities of that country continued subject to allocation by international agencies through 1946. Private exportations from Burma and British Malaya have been resumed, under close license and exchange control.

SALIENT DEVELOPMENTS IN CONTROLS ON IMPORTS

United States Ends Most Administrative Controls and Official Procurement

As already indicated, license systems and exchange controls, rather than customs duties, were the principal means through which the majority of governments endeavored to regulate the current imports during 1946.

The United States was among the notable exceptions. By the end of the year the improving general supply situation had allowed it to remove most of the administrative import controls carried over from the war period, and to return to private channels all but a few of the commodities which had been procured from abroad through governmental agencies during the emergency period. This movement was accelerated by the termination of various international allocating bodies during the year, and by the pressures for the removal of United States price controls in the fall.[4]

Exchange Shortage of Sterling Area Holds Back Outside Purchases

The United Kingdom and most of the other British countries carried further during 1946 the liberalization of the wartime controls upon importations of goods from each other. Thus far, however, they have relaxed only moderately their restrictions upon the admission of many products from nonsterling countries. Since the early days of the war, importations from such sources have been licensed only for the most essential products that were not otherwise obtainable.[5] The inadequate supply of foreign currencies at the disposal of the sterling group of countries, particularly of dollars, in comparison with the exceptional volume of their postwar import needs from nonsterling countries, continued to operate

[4] As of January, 1947, it was understood that the United States is to continue exclusive official procurement abroad only of rubber, tin, certain hard fibers, and sugar (including molasses and alcohol). In addition, nonexclusive public purchases are planned of Latin American cinchona and Chinese antimony. If special circumstances require it, some other short commodities may be officially purchased, mainly to supplement what is imported through commercial channels. Shipments to complete old contracts, especially of certain minerals, are also to continue into 1947.

This statement concerns only importations for civilian resale, and does not include official purchases for strategic stock-piling, which were authorized by Congress in 1946.

[5] Canada, which is not a member of the sterling area, and the Union of South Africa, exceptional because of its large production of gold, had removed most of their wartime import controls during the latter months of 1945.

as the primary limitation upon such trade during 1946, as it had during the preceding year.

Important easement of that general situation is due in July, 1947, under the provisions of the loan to Britain that was approved by the United States Congress in July, 1946. Within a year of its coming into effect, such sterling funds as may then be available to any of the Empire or other areas for current use were to be freely convertible for purchases in dollar countries or elsewhere.

As a partial transition measure, the United Kingdom arranged during 1946 with Canada, the United States, and several other nonsterling countries for a controlled system of token imports of an expanding list of products. These are mainly consumers' items which formerly had an established market in the United Kingdom, but which had been prohibited admission during the war as dispensable. The producers of these products were permitted reëntry up to 20 per cent of the value of their prewar shipments, in order not to lose their acceptance in the market as well as to afford British consumers limited quantities of such articles of convenience.

On the other hand, the expansion during the year of the program of the British Government for entering into bulk-purchase contracts for certain foreign foods, fibers, and minerals, earlier noted, has occasioned some concern in other countries. Thus far, these contracts have been limited mainly to various other British areas, and to staple commodities for which the United Kingdom had been their principal market in the past. A notable exception was the four-year agreement with Argentina to underwrite the bulk of that country's meat surplus, partly for resale.

Latin America Eager for Imports but Concerned over Exchange Reserves

While not applied quite as generally or as broadly as in other regions, exchange control or the requirement of prior import permits for selected products, or both, continued through 1946 as important regulators of the flow of imports into the majority of the countries of Latin America, and especially those of South America. Few important changes in their operations were effected during the year. Such alterations in their import tariffs as were made consisted mainly of reductions or temporary suspensions of duties on basic necessities, notably foods. In a few instances, import subsidies were resorted to, in order to attract foreign supplies and to hold down retail prices.

The current attitude toward imports in many Latin American countries appears to be dominated by two strong motivations, sometimes in conflict. Almost everywhere there is pressure for increased imports, to meet the large local demands for various products that have been scarce for several years, and to check domestic price inflation and popular unrest. At the same time, there is a pronounced desire to conserve and channelize the use of the country's exchange resources.

Chile, Peru, and several of the Central American Republics found their supply of foreign exchange, especially of dollars, actually insufficient during the latter months of 1946 to cover even importations considered essential. However, a number of the Latin American countries with sizable reserves and current earnings of foreign exchange were likewise intent, during the past year, upon limiting the exchange allocations or import permits granted for certain classes of products, particularly consumers' goods. The declared aim was to reserve the country's buying power primarily for the importation of products considered more essential to the rebuilding and development of its economy, such as productive and transport equipment, as they become obtainable. However, there was also frequent evidence of a desire to minimize competition from renewed imports to war-developed local industries.

Several of the larger Latin American countries endeavored to resume trade relations with various countries of continental Europe, and concluded agreements for the reciprocal facilitation of exports to each other. In view of the limited supplies of goods which most European countries could as yet furnish, in return for the large quantities of foods and raw materials they desired, several of the more prosperous Latin American governments undertook to supply goods to certain of them on official credit (for example, Argentina to Spain and Denmark, and Brazil to Czechoslovakia and Finland).

Argentina's food surpluses, at a time of shortages among various other countries of South America, have recently enabled it to conclude a series of advantageous trade agreements with a number of them. The agreement with Chile of December, 1946, contempates official Argentine investment in Chilean enterprises, to increase the output of certain commodities for which Argentina is to have a preferential right of purchase.

Beyond Basic Needs, Western European Imports Moving Into Private Hands

As earlier mentioned, most of the official European purchasing missions, which had handled so large a part of the immediate postwar imports of those countries from overseas, had considerably curtailed their operations by the close of 1946. In nearly all of the war-affected countries of Western Europe, successive classes of products were returned during the year to direct commercial importation by private firms or groups of them, after the governments had provided for the most urgent rehabilitation imports, and had arranged for means of financing that part of their import program which could not be offset by the prospective export surplus from the recovering domestic production. Mention has earlier been made of the intention of some of these countries to continue governmental or centralized purchasing of certain foreign products for some time.

Until their reviving exports come into closer balance with the value of their import needs, most of these countries must continue to depend for a considerable portion of their imports upon credits of various types granted them by other governments, or which they may obtain through the International Monetary Fund, the International Bank, or from private financial institutions. Under the circumstances, foreign exchange availabilities are carefully husbanded, and proposed import transactions must be considered essential to the country's general import program to be granted the import license or exchange permit usually required.

Eastern European Trade Closely Controlled and Oriented Toward Russia

It became increasingly clear during the past year that the programs of the present governments of Eastern Europe called for a high degree of state control of their foreign trade, as well as of their domestic economies, with the importation of certain commodities often reserved exclusively to official bodies, as in the completely state-controlled system of Soviet Russia. Appreciable differences are observed among them, however, in the form and extent of the governmental control, and in the amount of leeway permitted individual enterprises in their foreign transactions.

Varying only in degree, Soviet Russia was apparently the principal source of such imports as most of the countries of Eastern Europe received during 1946 of other than relief goods, although not quite to the extent to which it has been the predominant destination of their exports since the close of the war. Czechoslovakia has been the principal exception to this experience. These governments have endeavored to promote trade exchanges secondarily with others in the Soviet sphere, typically on a barter basis, although thus far usually with quite limited results.

The countries of Eastern Europe seldom started with any significant foreign exchange reserves, and have as yet been able to obtain little foreign credit. Since most of the goods available for export are being pledged to Russia or some other Eastern European country, and on a basis that seldom yields usable foreign exchange, the prospects for obtaining commercial imports from Western Europe or overseas countries have thus far been distinctly limited. The notable exceptions have been: Czechoslovakia, with its variety of distinctive consumers' products well known in the West, and Poland, with its surplus of coal, from new and old territories. Only these two appear to have made any substantial progress during 1946 toward revival of imports from countries other than Russia and Eastern Europe, and that usually on a clearing basis.

Relief shipments have constituted the major part of the goods thus far brought into these territories from Western sources, chiefly through the United Nations Relief and Rehabilitation Administration. More than 90 per cent of these shipments has been supplied by the United States, Canada, and the United Kingdom.

China Still Disordered; Other Asian Trade Moving Into Private Channels

Relaxations in the Indian import license requirements during 1946 applied principally to purchases from other sterling countries, as was the case in most other countries in the sterling area, where the inadequate amounts of the shared supply of foreign exchange was a major trade curb. However, goods from other sources also shared in the distinct easement upon imports into India, especially in the latter months of the year.

In China, the continued disordered internal conditions, the highly unstable exchange situation, and the slow recovery of exports, combined to make importing a lucrative but difficult and precarious business. After two sharp currency devaluations, a drastic revision of the Chinese foreign trade regulations in November subjected all commercial transactions to a strict system of prior import licenses, as well as exchange control. Importation of certain classes of goods was made subject to quotas, to be commercially allocated among the licensed importers; the admission of other commodities was "temporarily" suspended; and the list of prohibited imports was lengthened.

In the Philippines, importation as well as exportation of practically all classes of merchandise had reverted to the usual commercial channels by the close of 1945.

In the Netherlands Indies, the governmental agency which handled all imports during the relief period released certain categories of goods to private traders in late summer, and set early 1947 for the general liquidation of its control. However, centralized control of imports of a bulk nature, especially foods and textiles, will probably continue for some time. Moreover, the Exchange Control Bureau is to exercise supervision over imports generally, to ensure utilization of the limited exchange for the most essential purposes.

Because of the shortage of goods and of exchange, importation into French Indo-China is still in governmental hands. As a rule, purchases abroad are made through the official supply agency at Paris, on the basis of the recommendations of syndicates of local importers, and the effort is made to place orders in France before seeking elsewhere. In Siam, private trade channels have been reopened, but all imports are subject to import license and exchange permit, with priority dependent upon the relative essentiality of the goods.

In near-by British Malaya, the government ceased the procurement of all general imports after August, 1946, as private trade channels were rehabilitated. Transactions are subject to license, which was reported to be granted freely only for imports from sterling areas. In Burma, likewise, importations are privately conducted, under license and exchange control, with the trade plan up to late 1946 calling for the filling of the country's import requirements as fully as possible from sources within the sterling area.

1947

INCREASED IMPORTATIONS BEYOND EARNINGS BRING RENEWED TIGHTENING OF CONTROLS

Slow European Recovery and Overbuying Cause Wide Restrictive Reaction

International trade during 1947 was marked by the apparent paradox of abnormally high imports into most foreign countries over the greater part of the year, combined with a spreading tide of new official restrictions on the importation of products regarded as not entirely essential. In many countries, these restrictions apply especially to purchases from countries where payment needs to be made in dollars.

[The following basic facts regarding the state of world trade are presented as background for this analysis of current trade policy trends.

The data now available on the imports and exports of the principal countries for 1947 indicate that, as a whole, world commerce attained a substantially higher value during the past year than in 1946. After allowing for price rises, it is estimated that the total volume of goods moving in international trade during the first half of 1947 was at an annual rate of between 10 and 20 per cent greater than in 1946, although there was some decline from that level during the later months of the year. The volume of world commerce would appear to have risen during 1947 to slightly above the prewar level, and, because of the higher prices, the value of the trade last year was greatly above that of the prewar period.

The exports and imports of individual countries since the war have been considerably different from the prewar pattern, in size, composition, and direction. The trade of the countries of the Western Hemisphere and of several of the European neutrals has been well above their prewar height, while that of most of the war-disrupted countries of Europe and Asia is still markedly below prewar.

On the basis of the record for the first eleven months of 1947, United States merchandise exports for the year are estimated at 14½ billion dollars, an all-time high, and United States imports at 5½ billion. The United States has recently had a marked surplus of exports over imports with most foreign countries, and especially with the countries of Europe. During the prewar period of 1936 to 1938, when prices were substantially lower, United States exports averaged about 3 billion a year and imports about 2½ billion.]

To a considerable extent, this situation was brought on by the disappointing slowness in European economic recovery and financial stabilization, which was aggravated by the severe weather, crop failures, and work stoppages of the past year. The continued unsettled conditions in various parts of the world, and the retarded resumption of trade with Germany, Eastern Europe, and the Far East, were also contributing factors. In quite a number of countries, however, particularly in the Western Hemisphere, the exceptional volume of their imports since the war has itself been partly responsible for the restrictive reaction. The high rate at which their peoples had been buying foreign commodities of various types since the war, well beyond the value of their current exports, could hardly have continued indefinitely. The consequent drain upon the exchange resources of those countries aroused their governments' concern, and led to the adoption of stricter import controls, as financial safeguards.

Some signs of new difficulties had appeared in a few scattered countries during the spring of 1947, but the wide resort of governments to the restriction or closer scrutiny of imports of various classes of goods considered dispensable did not assume the proportions of a general movement until about midyear. It spread with especial rapidity after the British attempt, beginning in July, to make other countries' holdings of the sterling proceeds from current transactions again convertible into dollars. The unexpectedly heavy run on the British dollar holdings that ensued, and the forced suspension of sterling convertibility in little over a month, came as a general shock.

It brought widespread realization that the disruption of the economies and of the commercial potentialities of many countries by the war had been greater than estimated, and that the expectations of an early return to more normal conditions of international trading had been overoptimistic. In quick reaction to this realization, many governments took steps to protect their own financial positions by closer regulation of their foreign trade.

During the early months of the year, indeed, a number of governments even in Europe had felt warranted in relaxing somewhat the licensing controls over their foreign commerce which have been the rule in so many countries since the war. By the close of 1947, however, new or tightened controls upon imports had been brought into operation in the great majority of foreign countries, in both the Western and Eastern hemispheres.

Summary of Salient Developments in the Different Regions

Particularly drastic were the new restrictions on the importation of goods of secondary essentiality which have come to prevail in all the countries of Western and Northern Europe except Switzerland, and in practically the entire British Empire except the Union of South Africa. The sharp curtailments of the further purchases of many classes of foreign products ordered by the United Kingdom, France, and Canada in the fall of 1947 were probably the most publicized, but they formed only part of a long series of such actions during the past year, varying mainly in their severity. They apply especially to purchases from dollar countries.

Moreover, most of the European and British countries have become anxious to attain a closer balance in the annual value of their exchanges of merchandise with their various trading partners. Many of these governments have indicated their intention of favoring the importation of particular products from those sources where there would be involved least drain upon their foreign exchange, and of directing their exports more to those markets where payment can be had in "hard" currency, which is usable for purchases anywhere. To improve their over-all balance of international payments, a number of these governments are also working on various means for bringing about an increase in the volume of their countries' exports, often at the cost of restricting the quantities of certain national products made available to their own people.

Several of the Latin American Republics which had developed extensive trade relations with the countries of Europe, especially with the United Kingdom, felt keenly this deterioration in the European commercial potentialities. For the majority of the countries of Latin America, however, the trade difficulties that developed during the year came chiefly as the result of their own heavy excess of imports over exports since the close of the war.

By the latter months of 1947, all but certain of the Caribbean and Central American countries had in operation tighter controls over their imports than at the beginning of the year. Mexico and several of the South American countries have brought into effect wide increases in their import duties, partly for the protection of local producers. Chiefly, however, the new measures have taken the form of close selectivity as to which classes of foreign products were to be licensed for admission, or which were to be entitled to the means for payment promptly or at favorable rates of exchange.

In the countries of Eastern Europe, foreign trade has since the war been subject to a high degree of governmental direction, and in some cases to direct government buying and selling. During the past year, they were exceptionally active in the negotiation of agreements designed to bring about a closer orientation of their trade relations, over the long run, both toward the Soviet Union and toward each other. It was observed, however, that those Eastern European countries which had already rebuilt active commercial relations with the Western countries took steps during 1947 to intensify them, and that most of the others sought to negotiate agreements with the countries of Western Europe for exchanges of the distinctive products which each was able to supply now or in the near future.

The year saw little abatement of the highly unsettled conditions in a number of important areas of the Far East, notably China and the Netherlands Indies, which have held back the full resumption of foreign trading with them. The setting up of the Dominions of India and Pakistan has thus far not altered the former system of trade regulation, although, as in the sterling areas generally, control of imports was again tightened here, and also in Burma and Malaya. The Philippine Republic continued exceptional, in its absence of import restrictions and in the return of practically all foreign trade to private channels.

A substantial beginning was made during the past year toward the limited resumption of private trade with Germany and Japan, under license from the local officials, within the conditions set by the occupying military governments. Further steps are under consideration to facilitate the flow to world markets of the products for which their countries had been important sources of supply, and at the same time to increase their ability to pay for their own imports, so as to hasten the restoration of the German and Japanese economies to a self-supporting basis.

Prime Aim of Restrictions to Readjust Buying Programs to Ability to Pay

The recent adoption of import curbs by so many countries has seldom reflected changed attitudes by the peoples of those countries about the desirability of obtaining imported goods. Nor has it usually indicated a voluntary shift in governmental policy toward greater economic self-sufficiency. In most of the Latin American countries and several of the European neutrals, reports do indicate that the postwar satisfaction of the deferred demand for many consumers' goods has been pretty well completed. In various lines of merchandise, a number of those markets are understood to be even overstocked. That condition is still very remote in most countries outside the Western Hemisphere, however, and in almost all countries the demand for equipment and materials for restoring and expanding local production and transport continues strong, often exceeding the supplies likely to become available for some time. In fact, several governments have expressed regret when announcing that some investment projects would have to be postponed or contracted because they required large outlays for imported capital goods, which they did not feel the country could now afford.

The prime motive of most governments which have recently tightened up on imports has been to readjust their countries' general buying programs to their reduced ability to pay for all the foreign goods desired, with the proceeds from current exports and with other means now available. In only a few countries, notably in Latin America, has the desire to foster local production of similar goods appeared as a primary motive in their recent restrictions upon the importation of particular foreign products. The temporary curbs on imports for conservation of exchange may have an incidental protective effect, but its importance would depend upon how long and how steadily the restrictions are kept in effect. It has been observed that the make-up of the restricted lists and of the categories of varying priority is subject to frequent change.

The size of the gap between the total imports and total exports of individual countries has varied considerably. Under the unusual postwar conditions, however, that alone has often not been the measure of a country's problem in carrying on its foreign trade. The strain upon the foreign exchange resources of many countries has been intensified by the commercial and financial difficulties of other countries with which they had important trading relations; for practically none of the war-ravaged countries has yet regained the level of production that allows a sufficient exportable surplus to pay for its current import needs. Moreover, with the notable exception of the Philippine Republic, they have not yet reached that stage of financial stability that would make their currencies freely convertible into other moneys.

As a result, a country that has shipped goods to one of the war-disrupted countries to a greater value than that of the goods it has received from that country in return finds that it is holding, for that much of its exports, either an intentional credit that is not payable for some time, or a balance in a foreign currency that is not readily acceptable elsewhere. In either case, it has to that extent reduced its ability to settle for its own import balances from third countries, or to make new purchases where desired goods are obtainable.

Canada constitutes a striking instance of this character. The value of its over-all exports since the war has consistently been exceeding that of its imports. But so large a part of its shipments to European countries has been on credit, or has yielded only balances in inconvertible currencies, that the Canadian Government has had to keep drawing heavily upon its usable reserves to help pay for its traditional import balance from the United States, and finally found itself obliged, late in 1947, to resort to drastic restrictions on its imports.

It is partly to minimize strains of this character that a number of European and British countries are now trying to direct more of their exports to particular markets, which either are in a position to supply in return goods of the types particularly desired, or which can pay in dollars or other "hard" currency that is usable for purchases anywhere. Conversely, they are trying to shift the source of imports, wherever possible, either to those countries which can be paid in the same currency, as in the case of the sterling areas, or from which additional goods can be obtained against earlier export balances to them, without calling for further outlays of foreign exchange. When taking such action, the governments have often been at pains to disavow any intentional policy of discrimination against the goods or markets of particular countries, and to point to the compulsions upon them arising from the differing state of their trade balances with the various countries, and of their holdings of the other countries' currencies.

The tightened import controls of the past year have usually been put forward as temporary measures to meet an emergency. However, unless bold and concerted action is taken before long to offset the lagging progress toward economic recovery and stability, especially on the part of the war-disrupted countries of Europe, the conditions which prompted the recent wide resort to new trade restrictive measures may well call for most of them to continue in operation for some time to come, even in some of the countries outside of Europe. In fact, at the opening of 1948, the governments of a number of countries were contemplating further restraints upon their imports, through increased duties, quantitative restrictions, or other means.[1]

Is Dollar Shortage or Production Shortage Prime Cause of Trade Imbalances?

Inasmuch as the present trade difficulties and restrictions of most countries arise mainly from financial limitations, especially in their relations with the major countries of the Western Hemisphere, the situation has been rather superficially described as one of "dollar shortage." As sometimes used, that term appears to imply a failure on the part of the supplying countries to conduct their affairs so that prospective customers have command of sufficient dollars to make the desired purchases. Actually, total importations into the United States and Canada, the two principal "dollar countries," have been running well above the prewar rate, even when allowance is made for price rises. Significantly, however, the volumes of goods that have been obtainable from the Eastern Hemisphere countries, especially those of Europe, have been considerably below the prewar rate.

The fundamental difficulty in the present world trade situation has arisen primarily from the serious imbalance between the different countries, following the war, in their relative productivity and financial resources. Particularly striking has been the unprecedented demand upon the productive capacity of certain countries of the Western Hemisphere, where the measure of purchasing ability is expressed in terms of dollars (United States or Canadian) or in currencies readily convertible into dollars (for example, Cuban pesos). The so-called dollar shortage being complained

[1] While the new import restrictions recently introduced by the various countries are cutting down the volume of new orders being placed abroad, their practical effects in curtailing the actual movements of goods are often not apparent until some months after their issue. This is due to the fact that large quantities of goods are usually en route or covered by firm prior order or import permit at the time, and that exemption or special consideration is commonly granted for such goods.

of by many countries is thus seen rather as an indication of the insufficiency of their own production available for export, plus other means of payment, in relation to their current import needs. It is consequently the result, rather than the cause, of their inability to pay for all their desired imports from the "dollar countries," which happen to be those in the best position to supply them.

This imbalance in current resources has been accentuated by the fact that the import requirements of so many countries for replenishment and rehabilitation after the war have been abnormally high. In the case of most of the war-disrupted countries of Europe and Asia, the difficulty of meeting their exceptionally large need for commodities of many kinds has been rendered more acute by the disappointingly slow recovery in local production, especially of food, and in the general stabilization of their domestic economies. The exports of those countries during 1947 were still running considerably below imports, and their other prewar sources of foreign income were greatly reduced.

Moreover, despite the cuts that have been made since the war in the external value of the currencies of various of the countries of continental Europe and of the Far East, considerable uncertainty is still felt as to the ultimate exchange value of many of them, especially in the case of those countries whose political position is unsettled or whose domestic economy is still far out of balance. Consequently, other countries, when unable to obtain from these countries equivalent return for their exports in goods particularly desired, have been anxious to avoid accumulating credit balances in currencies of doubtful stability or which are blocked from use elsewhere. Various countries in Europe and the Western Hemisphere have, in fact, not only been requiring the settlement of all trade balances at the end of stated periods in dollars or other "hard" currencies, but have been insisting upon partial payments in dollars for some of the essential commodities they supply.

Shrinkage in Means of Covering Trade Deficits Forces Drain on Reserves

The difficulty of many countries in maintaining the volume of their imports has been increased by the fact that the alternative means which have been available to them during earlier postwar years for covering their trade deficits had shrunken considerably by the latter part of 1947. Shipping, foreign investments, tourists' expenditures, and other prewar sources of alternative foreign income, which used to be so important to various European countries in balancing their international accounts, have recently been yielding only a fraction of their former amounts.

The governmental credits in various forms that had been extended by certain of the more prosperous countries during 1945 and 1946, especially to the former belligerent countries of Europe, and which had made possible a substantial part of the importations of those countries since the close of the war, had to be drawn on in increasing volume in 1947. Thus, whereas 20 per cent of the total United States exports of goods and services during 1946 were financed through credits, by the second quarter of 1947 foreign countries on the average had to draw upon credits to cover fully one-third of their purchases from the United States, and for certain individual countries the proportion was very much higher. It is not surprising that, by the latter months of 1947, most foreign countries found their unused credits approaching exhaustion.

The quantities of goods going abroad as relief supplies and gift shipments and as other unilateral transfers, which had accounted for another 20 per cent of United States exports in the preceding year, represented a much smaller proportion of United States exports in 1947, after the tapering off of UNRRA. A large part of the recent unilateral transfers have consisted of deliveries of basic essentials to the occupied areas. The United States foreign relief program of 1947, which was the principal successor to UNRRA, was confined to Austria, Greece, Italy, and Trieste. The emergency relief program for France, Italy, and Austria, approved by congress in December, is intended to cover the shipment to those countries of the minimum requirements of food, fuel, and similar essentials for the next few months, pending the working out of longer-range plans.

Most countries which had reserves of gold and foreign exchange, or which had accumulated them during the war, have since been drawing upon them at an increasing rate to cover their current trade deficits. The foreign sales of gold to the United States and net drawings on official dollar balances during the first half of 1947 came to more than the amount for all of 1946. By late 1947, the principal countries known to be holding such reserves over the minimum needed to back their currencies or to finance their current flow of international trade were reduced to: Switzerland, Portugal, and Turkey; South Africa; the Philippine Republic; and Cuba, Venezuela, Uruguay, and Argentina.

A number of foreign countries have resorted during the past year to requiring their citizens and enterprises to register their foreign-held balances and other assets, and to place them at the disposal of their governments, in return for the equivalent in domestic currency. The proceeds of such liquidations of foreign assets as are known to have taken place have apparently relieved the balance-of-payments position of those countries in only small measure.

The funds for reconstruction and development projects and to tide governments over temporary deficits in their balance of payments, which the International Bank and the International Monetary Fund, respectively, have felt warranted in advancing during 1947, have helped importantly in particular situations. The number of countries involved, however, has thus far been small.

In addition to the United States, a number of other governments have extended substantial trade credits since the war, in support of their own exports and to help other countries to obtain needed imports for which they were not yet able to pay. Most notable in this regard have been Canada, Sweden, Switzerland, Belgium, Argentina, and Brazil. By late 1947, however, almost all of these leading governments found themselves overextended, and made it known that they were not in a position to grant any further trade credits. In fact, they had become concerned over the inadequacy of their reduced exchange reserves to cover their own current import needs.

Normal Trade with War-disrupted Areas Awaits Aid in Rehabilitation

It has become clear that, before a wide restoration of more normal trading and payment arrangements can be expected, especially on the part of most countries of Europe and Asia, considerable progress would have to be made in their rehabilitation. The volume of their production and of their exports would need to be increased, their current needs for food and other essentials more fully satisfied from domestic sources, the values of their currencies stabilized, and, in general, favorable conditions restored for the freer exchanges of goods and settlement of balances with other countries. The past year has witnessed a good deal of earnest planning and courageous effort in these directions on the part of various countries. Particularly notable for the degree of planned coöperative utilization of joint resources toward common recovery was the program developed by the sixteen countries of Western Europe which conferred at Paris during the summer of 1947, under stimulus from the United States.

Increasingly, however, opinion has grown that the action which the United States would be prepared to undertake would be the decisive factor in the progress of the general recovery program, especially in tiding over certain war-disrupted countries until their own recuperative efforts, individually and jointly, have had time to work out and to bring results, and in assisting them to rebuild and expand their productive and trading capacities. During that recovery period, the ability of certain of those countries to maintain their importations at high level, even of the more essential types of products, and to avoid resort to greater discrimination against American commerce, will apparently depend largely upon the magnitude of the shipments to them which the United States may furnish or finance beyond their current ability to pay.

Marshall Plan Proposes Reinforcing European Efforts Toward Recovery

If the Marshall Plan—under congressional consideration at time of writing—should be substantially adopted, considerable quantities of goods would be supplied during the next few years, under loans or other special arrangements, to the countries of Europe that are ready to participate in the coöperative program for European recovery. Insofar as the United States, by goods and funds, thus reinforces the program for self-help and reciprocal assistance on the part of European countries agreed to at the Paris Conference of 1947, and as those countries progress toward economic recovery and general stability, the basic pressures causing the recent spread of restrictive and arbitrary trade controls will have been relieved in the region where they have been most acute.

Considering that the countries involved in the European Recovery Program have normally accounted for nearly one-half of world trade, as they regain their ability to pay their own way, and in currencies acceptable for purchases anywhere, the present trade difficulties in other regions should also be eased. In fact, since it is contemplated that an appreciable portion of the commodities to be furnished, especially of those in short supply, shall be procured wherever obtainable outside the United States, other countries in the Western Hemisphere and elsewhere would be benefiting directly from the very initiation of this program, in the way of both larger markets and a more ample supply of dollars. Moreover, as the participating European countries are helped to increase their productivity, more goods would be becoming available for export markets. Thus, countries outside of Europe could be gainers in two ways: they would have additional sources of supply for their import requirements, and would not need to send so much of their export products to Europe on credit or against unusable currencies.

The events of the past year have demonstrated vividly how deterioration in the trade and financial position of one group of countries can create difficulties for various other countries with which they have important commercial relations. Conversely, if the European Recovery Program is even substantially successful, it should be bringing about conditions favorable to the relaxation of restrictions on international trade and payments also on the part of countries in other regions.

Geneva Agreements for Tariff Concessions Significant for the Future

Despite the present preoccupation of most countries with their immediate foreign trade difficulties and their recent resort to increasingly restrictive measures, the past year saw marked evidence of a widespread recognition that it was desirable to work out long-term principles and programs, to be ready when relaxation of the current transitional pressures allows governments greater freedom of choice in their trade policies.

Representatives of twenty-three countries participated in the simultaneous negotiations held at Geneva in the summer of 1947 for the reduction of trade barriers in all forms. Eighteen of them also agreed upon a draft charter for an International Trade Organization, through which the member countries are to coöperate in bringing into general operation a detailed code of international conduct that is designed to promote trade expansion and economic development on a mutually advantageous basis. At the full International Conference on Trade and Employment, convened by the United Nations at Havana toward the close of the year, the Geneva group was joined by forty additional countries, for the purpose of perfecting and adopting a definitive charter for the ITO in a form that would command wide adherence.

The first step taken thus far toward implementing this broad program has been the bringing into provisional operation in January, 1948, on the part of nine countries, which together used to account for over half of all world trade, of the duty concessions to each other worked out at Geneva and also the easements with regard to other forms of trade control to the extent that their existing legislation allows. These countries are: Australia, Belgium-Netherlands-Luxemburg (Benelux Customs Union), Canada, Cuba, France, United Kingdom, and the United States. However, all of these countries except the United States and Cuba are now restricting the importation of many classes of goods, in order to bring their purchases into closer balance with their current ability to pay. Indeed, in recognition of the abnormal conditions in international trade now widely prevailing, the Geneva Agreement on Tariffs and Trade provides that, under certain circumstances, the obligation upon governments to avoid resort to quantitative restriction on imports or to apply them without discrimination may not be fully binding until March, 1952.

On the other hand, in the case of many of the commodities on which the reductions in American duties have been made, few foreign countries are yet in a position to increase substantially the volume of their exports to the United States. Moreover, the official exchange rates of a number of countries, especially of continental Europe, have come to overvalue their currencies, and the prices at which their products would now need to be sold in the United States are often reported as too high to induce volume purchases, even at the reduced duties. For the immediate future, therefore, the increase in international trade as a result of the new concessions in tariffs and preferences by these nine countries is not likely to be of large proportions.

Some time may elapse before any important number of additional countries conclude similar reciprocal trade agreements or make effective those negotiated at Geneva, and before the various governments signatory to the ITO Charter complete the necessary ratifications to make that binding. Even allowing for the postponed practical effect and for some defections, however, the steps taken are highly significant. For the first time in history, the nations normally accounting for the great bulk of world commerce have looked beyond their immediate limitations, and have agreed upon common principles and practices to govern their trade relations over the long run, and these are distinctly more liberal and expansive in character than have been the actual trade practices of many of them for some time past.

The very existence of the Geneva trade agreements, and the wide acceptance in principle of the ITO Charter, with the prospect of each participating country ultimately sharing in the benefits from the concessions and undertakings by each of the many other participants, can have appreciable influence upon the general trend of postwar trade policies. They might well serve both as restraints upon the adoption during the emergency period of extreme measures which might later be difficult to change, and as setting the general direction and pattern toward which governments might be prompted gradually to adjust the methods of regulating their foreign trade, as they work out of the present abnormal conditions and regain the ability to choose among alternative courses of action.

Western Europe

Nearly all the countries of Western Europe[2] experienced more or less of a setback during 1947 in their efforts to regain a balanced foreign trade position, and found it necessary to resort to new restrictions on imports and to other measures calculated to mitigate the situation, if not to correct it.

This reaction did not become widespread until the latter half of 1947. The year started with fair prospects, and, during the early months, several governments felt warranted in relaxing somewhat the direct official control of both imports and exports which has marked the trade regime of the former belligerent countries, and to some extent also of the neutrals, since the end of the war. Thus, by April, Belgium had freed from prior license requirements more than half of its imports as well as most of its exports. The list of French products exportable without license was expanded by successive steps in the spring until it included the majority of that country's exports. In June, Switzerland relieved certain classes of goods from special import permits. The official purchasing agencies of several Western European countries, whose activities had been so prominent a feature of the immediate postwar period, saw further curtailment in their scope and functions, with actual foreign-trading operations reverting to a greater extent to private hands.

The commercial operations of the private European importers and exporters continued, however, to be subject to more or less close official regulation. As a rule, most foreign transactions still required governmental sanction, with approval dependent upon their fitting into the country's over-all import or export program for the period, or upon the current status of the import priorities or export allocations for the various classes of commodities.

Approval of particular foreign transactions has often been dependent also upon where the goods were to come from or to go to; for the trade of most European countries, with each other and with some overseas, has

[2] The term "Western Europe" is used roughly to cover all the countries of Europe except Soviet Russia and those commonly regarded as in the Russian sphere of influence. The year's developments in that group of countries are discussed later in this chapter, under the heading of "Eastern Europe." The relative commercial importance of the two groups is roughly indicated by the fact that the countries here grouped as "Western Europe" used to account for seven-eighths of the foreign trade of all Europe, and "Eastern Europe" about one-eighth.

Germany is to be dealt with separately, in the section on "Trading with the Occupied Ex-Enemy Countries."

since the war been regulated by bilateral agreements. Under these agreements, each of the contracting governments has usually undertaken to facilitate by its licensing systems the exportation of particular classes of goods which the other desired to have imported, up to specified quantities or values, with the country of destination giving corresponding assurance that those goods would be admitted. Unless special provision was made in advance for trade credits or overdrafts, it has commonly been expected that the values of the goods moving in each direction during the course of a year would approximately equal each other, and that outstanding balances would be settled in gold or convertible currencies. Until very recently, the agreements of the United Kingdom with the continental countries have differed from this standard pattern by providing, in most cases, only for the over-all payments arrangements.

Principal causes of European trade difficulties.—In large part, the importations into the war-ravaged countries of Western Europe since the close of the war from a number of important sources, notably the United States, Canada, Switzerland, and Sweden, have been made possible by credit arrangements of various types, mostly intergovernmental. It was expected that, for a time, the former belligerent countries would need to obtain from abroad exceptional quantities of commodities of all kinds, for replenishment and rehabilitation, in amounts well beyond the value of the goods they could as yet export in return.

By the middle of 1947, however, most of these credits had been used up, and the heavy drafts made since the war upon their official reserves of gold and foreign exchange, to help cover the current import excess, could not be continued much further without risk to their necessary minimum balances. The income earned abroad from shipping, foreign investments, and other sources, upon which United Kingdom and several other Western European countries used to count to pay for a considerable part of their merchandise imports, now came to a fraction of the former amounts.

Meanwhile, it was becoming evident that the wartime disruption of the industrial and financial structures of most of the countries of Western Europe had been greater than estimated, and that the restoration of the normal functioning of their economies would be slower than anticipated. Additional setbacks during 1946 and 1947 were caused by the severe weather, crop failures, and work stoppages in various of the European countries. Consequently, the rate of recovery in their production of essential foods and industrial commodities was proving disappointing.

In addition to the above handicaps on the revival of their foreign trade, there were several retarding factors of an external nature. Many of the bilateral trade agreements between particular pairs of European countries were not working out satisfactorily. The political status of Germany continued unsettled, and the meager progress toward its economic rehabilitation under the divided control by the occupying powers held back the resumption of its former position, as an important supplier of coal and industrial products to many other countries of Europe as well as a market for their distinctive products. Similar in its effect was the shrinkage in the normal flow westward of foodstuffs and other export staples from the Danubian countries, and of the return supplies of the manufactures from the Western countries.

The continued unsettled conditions in various areas of the Far East, and the slow resumption of their usual supplies of important raw materials to the Western countries, constituted another retarding influence upon the recovery of Europe. An important indirect effect of these conditions has been an intensified general European demand for substitute supplies from the United States and other Western Hemisphere countries, and often at greatly increased transportation costs.

As the combined result of these various unfavorable circumstances, few of the Western European countries have yet made sufficient progress toward the rebuilding of their exports to be able to pay for more than part of the large volume of imports they continue to require. With the shrinkage during the past year in the available foreign credits and other alternative means of bridging the gap, vigorous measures to readjust their foreign trade arrangements seemed inescapable. Restriction of imports has usually been the first recourse.

General resort to restricting imports of less essential goods.—Probably the most publicized were the drastic actions of the governments of the United Kingdom and France in the summer and fall of 1947, in suspending the imports of certain classes of goods altogether and in sharply curtailing others. Actually, all of the countries of Western Europe, with the exception of Switzerland, apparently found themselves impelled, at some time during the past year, to take more or less stern measures to reduce the drain upon their dwindling external financial resources resulting from the continuing gap between their imports and exports.

Since a very large part of the trade of the countries of Western Europe has been with each other, one country's action in denying itself the importation of particular foreign products often operates to cut down the exports of other countries in that region, and consequently their purchasing power for imports. The cumulative effect of a succession of such import restrictions by a number of these countries is obviously a further contraction of their over-all trade potentialities.

Typically, efforts to correct the trade balance took the form of suspension or curtailment of imports of various classes of goods considered dispensable, in order to reserve the limited foreign exchange for more essential foods, fuel, raw materials, and capital equipment. In a number of important countries, the imports of these more essential classes of goods also had to be cut down in volume. In certain extreme cases, even the imports of industrial equipment were ordered curtailed for projects regarded as postponable. The governments of Britain and of Norway were notable for frankly telling their people that continued or even increased austerity in their standard of living would have to be accepted for some time ahead.

This pressure of a continuing high call for imports well beyond ability to pay for them was not limited to the countries that had suffered directly from the war. Indeed, one of the first European countries to introduce new import restrictions in 1947 was Sweden, a neutral. That country had built up a substantial foreign exchange reserve during the war, but found that it was being too rapidly depleted by the heavy importations of many foreign products denied its people for a number of years. This was particularly striking because the Swedish Government had not felt it necessary after the close of the war to subject most imports to licensing, had made large import commitments in various bilateral agreements, and had, moreover, extended sizable credits to a number of the less prosperous European countries.

Imports of dollar goods especially limited to essentials.—Since many of the commodities most needed were obtainable mainly from the Western Hemisphere, restrictions on dispensable importations were often applied with particular severity to purchases from the "dollar countries," in order to conserve the limited dollar resources for the more essential products. For the same reason, various of these European governments announced their intention of directing their countries' exports, through the official licensing controls or through coöperative arrangements with the respective industries, to those markets where they could earn most, either in the form of foreign products particularly needed, or in terms of dollars or other "hard" currency that is usable for purchases anywhere.

Drive to increase exports handicapped by overvalued currencies.—As another means of improving their balance of payments, a number of the

Western European countries have been making strenuous efforts to increase the total volume of national exports. This has sometimes been done even at the cost of denying to domestic consumers a large part of the output of certain distinctive national products for which ready markets can be found abroad. In the United Kingdom, definite quantities are being set up as export targets for various industries. In support of this export drive, several of these governments have announced their intention to divert manpower and to give priority in various ways to their exporting industries, or to particular firms capable of rapid increase in their exports, especially in the allocation of controlled raw materials, domestic as well as imported.

A number of European countries have, during the past year, encountered considerable price resistance from foreign buyers interested in their export products. Usually, the domestic prices in such a country have undergone sharp advances over prewar, and the disparity between the official exchange rate for its currency and that prevailing in the open market has been quite marked. Italy is the only country of Western Europe which reduced the official exchange rate of its currency during 1947 to conform closely to the open market rate, in order to stimulate larger foreign sales of its export products. Similar action is reported under consideration by several of the other countries, although the timing may in some cases wait upon the attainment of a stronger position for the currency in the home market.

Despite operating difficulties, bilaterally balanced agreements continued.—The persistent shortage of goods for export and the inconvertibility of most Western European currencies left little alternative to the continuation of the bilateral trade and payment agreements, earlier described, which have regulated the trade relations among most European countries since the war. A considerable number of them, however, had to be revised during 1947; some because they had proved unsatisfactory in actual operation, and others because of the new urgencies upon various governments to readjust their general foreign trade program.

In some instances, the trade exchanges under the earlier agreements were sufficiently satisfactory to encourage an appreciable enlargement of the lists of commodities and of the quantities to be licensed to each other during the new agreement period, usually a year. In a good many cases, however, this has not been the experience. Despite the usual aim at an approximately equivalent value in the movement of goods in each direction, the actual record for 1946 showed that the trade balances of the countries of Western Europe which could not be settled currently through merchandise movements amounted to over 20 per cent of the total trade among them. Between some pairs of countries, the gap was much more marked. In fact, several governments have admitted that, in order to see some return for their export surplus to particular countries, they had to sanction the importation of various nonessential products to a value well beyond what they had originally felt they could afford.

In the course of some renegotiations during the past year, an export balance on the part of one of the trading partners was insisted upon, in order to reduce the trade debt incurred during the preceding period. On the other hand, while the countries usually tried to find a balance in their trade exchanges on the higher rather than the lower level, the Netherlands was among those which, knowing their own shortage of exportable surpluses, chose to reduce their imports from certain other countries during the new agreement period rather than incur new debts.

With increasing frequency there was apparent resistance to accepting luxury products, and insistence upon the offsetting supplies being made up of goods which the receiving country considered essential to its economy. In fact, undertakings to approve the exportation of certain products from one country were frequently made contingent upon the receipt of certain specified products from the other.

Very few of the new intra-European trade agreements of the past year provided for the extension of additional credits, or for as sizable overdrafts as had the earlier ones. Spokesmen for the former lending countries have generally come to the position that hereafter their bilateral agreements will have to be self-liquidating. The principal exception to this attitude was the series of long-term agreements concluded with Poland by a number of Western European governments, in which they undertook to facilitate substantial overshipments to Poland during the period immediately ahead, chiefly of industrial equipment, to be compensated by Polish deliveries of coal over a number of years on an increasing scale.

It was against this background of general deterioration in their foreign-trading position and tightening of trade controls, that spokesmen for sixteen countries of Western Europe came together at Paris in July, 1947, to confer on the situation. As earlier stated, the purpose was to work out a coördinated program to advance their common recovery, by energetic national and joint measures, that would give sufficient promise of restoring their economies to a self-sustaining basis within a few years, so as to warrant the assistance which Secretary of State Marshall had indicated the United States might extend.

Benelux and other Western European customs union projects.—During this abnormal period when quantitative restrictions and exchange controls are the determining regulators of the foreign trade of the European countries, such modifications of their import duties as are taking place are of more importance for the long term than for the immediate future. However, the coördinated revision of the import tariff systems of Belgium, the Netherlands, and Luxemburg that was completed during 1947 was of exceptional importance. It was the first step toward the long-planned Benelux Customs Union. From the beginning of 1948, import duties on each other's products are waived entirely, and a common tariff schedule applies uniformly at the frontiers of the three countries upon the goods from all outside sources (except insofar as some of them continue temporarily suspended). This step is preparatory to their prospective full economic union, under which the quantitative restrictions and other present taxes and controls of the constituent countries are to be replaced by completely unrestricted trade among them, and the general economic life of the composite area is to be closely harmonized.

In connection with the Paris conference of the Western European countries, earlier mentioned, studies have been initiated into the possibility of their attaining a closer economic integration through a similar unification of the customs systems of that entire group of countries, or of particular members of it. However, it was recognized that, even if further European customs unions were found feasible, they could not be completed and brought into operation for quite a number of years.

Eastern Europe

Among the countries of Eastern Europe, the past year has been marked by the launching of ambitious plans for the long-term orientation of their economies more closely toward Soviet Russia and toward each other, through a network of trade agreements. At the same time, there was continued activity on the part of the countries in the Russian sphere in the negotiation of trade arrangements with various Western European countries, to facilitate the exchanges of needed commodities which each could now or in the near future supply.

In the matter of trade policy, the countries of Eastern Europe are broadly distinguished from those of Western Europe by the higher degree of governmental direction of their foreign trade, as part of the general movement in that region, since the war, toward centralized state control of their entire economies. Official decisions regulate more closely here than elsewhere the details of foreign transactions, even when conducted by private firms, as well as the broad programing of the commodities to be imported and exported. In a number of the Eastern countries, the foreign trade program is more or less subordinated to a long-range plan for general economic development.

Appreciable differences are observed among the various countries, however, in the extent to which the conduct of commerce is concentrated in official or state-controlled agencies or participated in by individual enterprisers, and in the amount of leeway left to private firms where they are permitted to operate. Thus, in Poland, Yugoslavia, and Bulgaria, foreign trade is conducted mainly through a series of state agencies or controlled combines, with only small scope for private enterprises, whose operations are usually directed by one of the state-controlled bodies. On the other hand, the Czechoslovak situation is characterized by semiautonomous nationalized corporations that are expected to operate on a profit basis. Here, and in Finland, an appreciable measure of foreign trade is understood to be conducted by private firms, especially in dealings with the Western countries.

Refusing Marshall Plan, Russia makes long-run agreements with satellites.—Shortly after the decision of the Soviet Union, early in July, 1947, not to participate in the proposed coöperative program for European recovery known as "The Marshall Plan," and the parallel action of each of the countries in the Soviet sphere, there were announced in rapid succession a series of bilateral trade agreements of a broad character between Soviet Russia and Czechoslovakia, Yugoslavia, Poland, and Bulgaria. More limited agreements have been entered into with Hungary, Rumania, and Finland. While scheduled deliveries were usually set up only for the year ahead, the major Russian agreements called for the later negotiation of arrangements for larger exchanges of goods over longer periods, designed to advance the economic development programs of the respective countries. In several instances, it is contemplated that Russia would furnish certain industrial equipment on credit.

From such facts as were made public, the exchanges of goods between the Soviet Union and the other countries of Eastern Europe scheduled for the immediate future are in most cases relatively limited, with the large-scale deliveries apparently regarded as long-range goals. The data available with regard to actual trade movements during 1947 indicate a falling off, from the preceding year, in the relative importance of the Soviet Union in both the exports and the imports of most of the other Eastern European countries.

In their relations among themselves, the various countries in the Soviet sphere had been active throughout the past year in the negotiation of agreements regarding the commodities to be obtained from each other. Outstanding among these arrangements of 1947 were the bilateral agreements worked out by Czechoslovakia, Poland, and Yugoslavia with each other. They contemplate considerably increased exchanges of goods between each pair of countries, and the continuous coöperation of allied branches of their respective economies. These agreements are usually planned to run for five years, with specific schedules of commodity exchanges to be worked out each year. In general, Czechoslovakia, as the principal industrialized country in this region, is counted upon for capital goods and light manufactures to meet the needs of other Eastern countries, in return for the foodstuffs and raw materials which these countries can supply.

Albania was economically merged with Yugoslavia at the opening of 1947, when the Yugoslav tariff and currency system was extended to the joint area. A much-publicized meeting of representatives of Yugoslavia and Bulgaria, held at Bled in August, wound up with the announcement of a goal of economic unity for the South Slavs. This envisages an eventual customs union between the two countries, with steps toward the coördination of their economic plans to be worked out in the meantime.

Satellies seek pacts also with the West and increase trade with them.— Despite these many arrangements with each other, the need of the countries of Eastern Europe for many materials and products obtainable mainly from outside countries led to persistent efforts during the past year to find means for enlarging trade relations with them, principally with the Western European countries (including Germany), which had been their chief sources of supply as well as markets before the war. The data now available regarding the commerce of the countries in the Soviet sphere of influence during 1947 indicate that the value of their total foreign trade was substantially larger than in 1946, and that, for the group as a whole, the proportion of their exports shipped to the Western European countries the preceding year was maintained or somewhat increased during 1947, and the share of their imports supplied from those Western countries appreciably increased.

Czechoslovakia, with its diversified consumer products, Poland with its coal, and Finland with its forest products, were able to make substantial arrangements with many of the Western countries for sizable quantities of raw materials and equipment in exchange for the commodities they could furnish, and to some extent, even to obtain some advance shipments on credit. Particularly notable is the series of long-term agreements concluded by Poland with a number of countries of Western Europe, earlier mentioned. In exchange for coal deliveries in increasing scale over the later years of the period, Poland was assured facilitation of large shipments of industrial equipment and materials for use in its economic rehabilitation, from France, Switzerland, Sweden, Norway, and the Netherlands. The latter is to aid in the rebuilding of Polish shipping.

The other countries of Eastern Europe have had less goods to offer for export to the Western countries, especially in view of their reduced production of basic foodstuffs, and the large proportions of their output pledged for shipment to the Soviet Union under various arrangements. Their shipments of goods to and from the Soviet Union, apart from reparations, and the exchanges among themselves, have been mainly on a compensatory basis which has seldom netted them any foreign exchange usable for purchases elsewhere. With small reserves of gold or freely convertible exchange, and little credits obtainable, they could offer only limited quantities of their exportable products in return for the commodities urgently needed from the West. Yugoslavia and Hungary, in particular, have made earnest efforts recently to negotiate agreements with various Western countries for balanced exchanges of merchandise, but reportedly with small practical results thus far.

The principal new Soviet trade arrangement with a Western nation during 1947 was that concluded with the United Kingdom in December. It called for the early Russian supply of a quantity of coarse grain for livestock, in return for the British agreement to facilitate the placing of orders in the United Kingdom by Soviet importing organizations for various types of mechanical equipment. Later negotiation is contemplated of a broader accord for the long-term exchange of goods, on the basis of balanced trade between the two countries. In a number of earlier Soviet trade agreements with Western European countries, revised annual schedules of reciprocal exports for 1948 were arranged for.

While private barter still figured in the trade arrangements among some countries of Eastern Europe, there appears to be a definite shift to the general compensation or clearing method of payment. Private barter was usually objected to by the Western European countries, and a number of the agreements with them allowed such transactions only under special authorization. Several of the countries of Western Europe attached special importance to the problem arising from the nationalization of properties in Eastern Europe which had belonged to their citizens, to the extent that a number of the arrangements regarding reciprocal trade exchanges were made contingent upon the settlement of those compensation claims.

Trading with the Occupied Ex-Enemy Countries

A substantial beginning was made during 1947 toward the limited resumption of private trade with Germany and Japan, and steps are under consideration for vesting in the local officials greater control over their country's foreign trade, under the general supervision of the occupying authorities.

Private trade with Germany being resumed, mainly in exports.—An economic merger of the British and American zones of Germany came into effect in January, with the way left open for the French and Russians to join. The aim was to make the merged area more self-sustaining and to reduce occupation costs, by facilitating foreign trading as well as interzonal exchanges. In March, the restrictions of the Trading-with-the-Enemy Act were lifted so as to allow the resumption of private trade between United States and German nationals. German suppliers were permitted to negotiate preliminary contracts with foreign firms, subject to local approval, with the export price approved by the Joint Export-Import Agency.

Pending adjustment of the German internal price system and the working out of a commercial exchange rate for the mark, export prices have been based in general on world market prices for the various products, and to American firms prices are quoted in dollars. Payment is made to the Military Authorities, and is required to be in dollars or in other currencies that are usable in obtaining essential imports. The German seller receives payment in reichsmarks.

Under present circumstances, primary emphasis is being placed on German exports. Bulk imports for the general economy of the Combined Area are still handled centrally by the Joint Import-Export Agency. However, German firms are now permitted, under certain conditions, to procure on their own behalf materials and supplies necessary to the production of specified export goods. Plans are under consideration for the financing of commodity advances to German firms on a self-liquidating basis, repayable out of the resulting production. The objective is to make fuller utilization of German labor and manufacturing facilities and to increase the volume of exports, in order to help cover the cost of food and other essential imports for the maintenance of the population.

Somewhat different arrangements for private trading transactions are in operation in the French and Russian zones of Germany, where the occupying authorities exercise closer official control over the conduct of foreign business.

During the past year, the foreign trading agencies of the Military Authorities in the respective zones have negotiated agreements to regulate the trade exchanges with a considerable number of areas. These have included the other occupied zones of Germany as well as many of the countries of continental Europe, Eastern as well as Western, which used to depend to such an important degree upon Germany both as a supplier and as a market. The arrangements usually called for the goods obtained from Germany to be offset by specified products of the other country considered essential to the German economy in its present stage, with balances settled periodically by dollars or other funds usable for imports.

Beginning of private trade with Japan, curtailing official operations.—Broadly, the developments during 1947 toward the resumption of foreign trading with Japan, and especially through private trade channels, followed the same general pattern as indicated for Germany, although initiated somewhat later in the year. On August 15, Japan was opened to the visits of foreign private traders, and an expanding volume of business is reported to have been consummated since September 1 with a wide range of countries. The arrangements for the negotiation of contracts, pricing, and payments are substantially the same as developed for Germany. As there, the prime interest is to encourage export transactions in local products now available or which can be produced for foreign sale, and import transactions in foreign raw materials needed in Japan to further the approved production program. Similarly, plans are being worked on for financing the importation of commodity advances to Japanese processors on a self-liquidating basis.

As private trading with Germany and Japan is resumed and gradually broadened, the scope of governmental trading operations is contracting. The United States Commercial Company, which has served as an emergency intermediary in reopening trade with the occupied areas, terminated its purchases at the close of 1947. Certain of its Japanese merchandising programs are to be taken over by representatives of the occupying authorities, however, and commercial transactions with both Germany and Japan on the part of a number of foreign countries are to continue temporarily to be arranged through their centralized purchasing agencies.

For both Japan and the Anglo-American Zone of Germany, exports are still running far below the value of current imports, and large expenditures by the occupying powers continue necessary to cover the cost of the indispensable supplies being shipped into those areas. To reopen the American market for their dutiable products on a predictable basis, during this period of abnormal price and exchange conditions in the occupied areas, arrangements were worked out during 1947 whereby the dollar export value of German and Japanese goods at time of shipment would be recognized by the United States Customs as the basis for assessment of import duties. Germany and Japan are also to be extended the benefit of the reduced United States duties provided for in the Geneva Tariff and Trade Agreement which came into operation in January, 1948.

British Empire

The British balance-of-payments crisis in the summer of 1947 and its repercussions constituted one of the most significant developments of the year in the field of international trade. It was not only followed by a wave of restrictions on imports into all of the closely related parts of the British Empire, but also had widespread influence upon many outside countries.

Drain upon sterling-area dollar resources causes financial crisis.—When its shrinking dollar resources forced the United Kingdom to tighten up on its imports, first by moderate restriction upon certain products in June and then by more drastic curbs in August and September, the United States and a number of other major suppliers were directly affected by the curtailment of the important British market for various of their staple exports. Of only secondary importance was the fact that various countries of the Western Hemisphere and of Europe could no longer count upon obtaining as many dollars as the United Kingdom had been making available to them, in payment for certain of the products they supplied and in settlement of current balances. Thus, the effect of the British crisis in reducing numerous other countries' prospects, both for export sales and for income in freely usable currencies, led various of them, in turn, to announce curtailments in the volume of foreign goods which they felt they could afford to import during the period ahead, especially from the "dollar" countries.

The drain upon the British exchange resources which brought on the drastic import restrictions during 1947 was only partly due to the large volume of foreign products that had been imported into the United Kingdom, beyond the ability of that country to cover with its current exports and reduced foreign income from other sources. The drawings upon the

British dollar and gold reserves, as well as upon the credit from the United States, have been used also to pay for a considerable part of the import requirements of most of the countries in the sterling area. Moreover, British dollar holdings have been spent not only in the United States, but also for purchases and in settlement of balances in other countries requiring American dollars to help pay for their own imports. These include Canada and various countries of Latin America and, to a smaller extent, of continental Europe.

Under the Anglo-American Financial Agreement of 1946, sterling funds available to any country for current use were to be made freely convertible, beginning mid-July, 1947, for purchases in dollar countries or elsewhere. Many countries were looking forward to this as an important step toward the return to multilateral settlement of international balances. To prevent undue drain, the United Kingdom negotiated in advance a series of arrangements with a number of countries defining the accounts to be transferable. However, with the currencies of the other former European belligerents still inconvertible, the eagerness of various countries to obtain dollars for their sterling holdings soon proved so much greater than had been expected, that the British Government was forced to suspend the general conversion offer, with the United States' assent, on August 20.

As corrective, British countries cut imports, notably of dollar goods.—The earlier British expectation of paying for a much larger part of its imports during 1947 with increased exports had met a number of unexpected setbacks, including an extremely severe winter, a poor harvest, and the slow rate of recovery on the European continent. By October, 1947, the combined effect of all the unfavorable developments brought British dollar availabilities to so low a point, with little prospect of early improvement, that the government was impelled to announce further stern measures for correcting the country's balance of payments. They included: savings on all imports by producing more at home; substituting nondollar for dollar sources of supply as far as possible; pressing for expansion of exports even at the cost of greater domestic austerity and, by coöperation with the industries involved, directing them toward "hard-currency" countries. The principal direct economy in dollars was to be effected by further curtailment of importations from the United States of foods and raw materials, the temporary stoppage of all tobacco purchases, and by rigid licensing of manufactured goods, including machinery.

Consultation with other governments in the sterling area was held in London in October, to consider what reductions in "hard-currency" expenditures were possible, and what assistance could be given in other ways to strengthening the gold and dollar reserves of the sterling area. Most of the British Dominions and colonies took steps promptly to readjust their import programs to further these general aims.

While the precise action of the individual British governments has varied, the measures taken by Australia are roughly illustrative. Certain categories of foreign goods were banned altogether, and others were to be permitted in reduced quantities from the "dollar areas," comprising the United States, Canada, and most of the Western Hemisphere countries. Outstanding licenses for most products were required to be returned for review, with only the most necessary expected to be approved under the new stricter criteria of essentiality. In December, 1947, still further cuts in imports were announced, effective at the beginning of 1948.

The Union of South Africa, with its large production of gold, had for some time been following a course independent from the rest of the sterling area, and did not regard it necessary in 1947 to curtail imports from dollar areas. Its assistance in the financial difficulties of the United Kingdom took the form of a three-year loan of 320 million dollars in gold.

Unusable European balances force Canada to cut dollar imports.—Canada, which is not a member of the sterling area, found itself in much the same position as those countries. For while Canada continued to export heavily to the United Kingdom and Western Europe, a large part of those shipments has been on credit or has yielded only balances in inconvertible currencies. As a result, they have not afforded the funds with which Canada has traditionally covered its normal excess of imports from the United States. Moreover, Canadians had recently been making exceptionally large purchases of American goods, as wartime shortages and restrictions were eased. The combined effect was so heavy a drain upon Canadian reserves of United States dollars as to lead to a series of drastic import restrictions in mid-November, comparable only to those of the United Kingdom itself.

The importation of some products into Canada was completely prohibited; a long list of others was placed under quota; and certain capital goods, mainly industrial machinery, were to be dealt with on a selective basis, favoring particularly the importation of new productive facilities for export. The quota system is reported as designed to reduce imports to about one-half the current rate from the so-called "scheduled" countries, mainly the United States and other Western Hemisphere countries, while allowing for material increases in the imports of the same commodities from other countries.

The trade exchanges within the British Empire itself are apparently also due for some contraction. The United Kingdom and several other British countries have taken the position that under present conditions they just cannot afford to import certain products in the normal quantities, if at all. In the colonial territories, the new import control orders often stressed the interdependence of the United Kingdom and the colonies, and the need for restoring the financial position of that joint monetary group by holding to a bare minimum of essentials the imports from all other countries, including the British Dominions. Moreover, colonial administrators have been urged by London to restrict imports into their territories also of certain United Kingdom products, which can be sold for dollars or for hard currency, or which are in short supply and can be used in trade negotiations in order to obtain essential supplies.

Latin America

Since the close of the war, importers in most countries of Latin America appeared to have been animated by the desire to order from abroad the many classes of goods that had been difficult to obtain for a number of years, and to get them as soon as possible while local demand and prices were high. Practically all of these countries had accumulated considerable reserves of foreign exchange, from the greater sales of their products to the major belligerents than those countries had been able to supply in return. As a result, they found themselves in a favorable position to finance the purchase of foreign goods freely as they again became available.

Heavy buying surge drains war-accumulated exchange reserves.—Until 1947, the attitude of most of these governments apparently favored ample importations, several even declaring them to be desirable as a means of meeting local shortages and checking price inflation. While many of the Latin American Republics had been operating exchange controls for some years, and several had since the war introduced import permit systems on a limited scale, these controls had appeared largely precautionary and did not, in most cases, constitute material restrictions on imports.

The recent demand in these countries for various classes of imported consumers' goods had been heightened by the fact that the domestic price level had in many cases risen more sharply than in the United States, their chief source of supply, and that certain elements in their population now enjoyed much higher incomes than before the war. Combined with the eagerness to obtain from abroad materials and equipment for the maintenance of productive and transportation facilities and for their expansion, this consumers' buying surge had by early 1947 resulted in an unprecedented volume of importations into most of the Latin American countries. The consequent drain upon the countries' foreign exchange resources caused the governments increasing concern. Deliveries on earlier orders were particularly heavy during the spring of 1947, with many ports and customhouses reported congested and merchants unable to obtain the funds to clear the shipments.

In a few cases, lagging domestic exports or other causes contributed to the deterioration of the country's balance of payments, but the conditions just described were fairly representative. They brought a succession of measures by most of these governments during 1947 to regulate the volume and character of imports by more selective controls. By the end of the year, some such action had been taken by all the countries of South America, and also by Mexico and several of the Central American Republics.

General resort to selective import license and exchange priorities.—The form of the restriction has varied with the different countries. A number of Latin American governments have made the obtaining of a prior import license obligatory for broader ranges of commodities, with several of them now requiring such licenses for all imports. In certain countries, the future imports of particular products were definitely curtailed, and in a few cases suspended. Most commonly, the tightening up was effected through the operation of the country's exchange control, under which goods are classified in various categories of priority in accordance with their relative essentiality.

The two principal objectives of these measures have been: to hold import authorizations in line with the estimated amount of current foreign exchange earnings, and to allocate the available funds among the various classes of expenditures so as to favor the importation of basic necessities and of goods required for reëquipping and expanding local production. From a number of these countries, it was reported that the demand for imports of capital goods alone could exhaust the earnings from current exports, and that some ambitious programs for industrial expansion previously planned would have to be curtailed.

Mexico, Argentina, and Chile announced during the past year the complete import suspension of certain classes of products regarded as luxuries or dispensable. More often such goods have not been entirely excluded but, since they lack preferential status, it has been made clear that payment for them would have to await the availability of foreign exchange, or be delayed for specified periods. In several countries, the importer of goods listed as nonessential has been officially required to pay more for the exchange remittances, or permitted to settle for them only with exchange bought in the open or auction market at higher rates. In the case of Ecuador, the adoption of such a system of differential exchange rates for different classes of goods followed a recommendation of the International Monetary Fund. To hold down speculative orders, several governments have required the deposit of a given proportion of the value of the shipment when granting the import permit.

Usually the restrictions were announced against importations of particular commodities without distinction as to the country of origin. The relative availability of the different foreign currencies has sometimes, however, been a factor in their practical application. Argentina announced in September that exchange permits would be more freely granted for importations from contiguous countries and from certain countries of Europe, because a surplus of the currencies of those countries had accumulated as a result of large export balances. Concern has been expressed in a number of the other Latin American countries over the adverse balance of trade that had been developing with the "hard-currency" countries, while a large part of the current receipts was in pounds sterling or other currencies not readily convertible.

It is important to note that most of the Latin American governments did not tighten up their import controls until the volume of incoming merchandise had gone far above prewar levels, and that greater selectivity of imports rather than drastic restriction was often the prime objective. The new control measures are intended to favor the admission of certain classes of goods over others, but the total importations that may be licensed under them during the period ahead may still be well above prewar, although below the abnormally high level of 1946–1947.

More protection for local producers through tariffs and license restrictions.—While the need to conserve or budget foreign exchange has been the primary reason given for the recent widespread tightening of controls on imports among the Latin American Republics, local pressure for increased protection to various industries established or expanded since the outbreak of the war found strong expression in a number of these countries. Tariff increases on broad ranges of commodities were ordered during the year by several countries, notably Mexico, Peru, and Chile. The declared purpose was partly protection, and partly to compensate for the fact that, with the advance in price levels, the effectiveness of fixed specific duties had been reduced. Broad revision of import duties, tending upward, is reported under consideration in Brazil and a number of other Latin American countries.

The curtailment of particular imports for exchange-conservation reasons is, in some cases, incidentally affording additional protection to local producers of similar goods. In fact, the availability of similar domestic products has been cited in several countries, notably in Argentina and Chile, as a criterion in the choice of the foreign commodities to be restricted. How important this indirect effect may prove will depend upon how long and how steadily the restrictions are maintained. There have been frequent changes during the past year in the make-up of the different priority categories which govern the granting of import licenses and exchange allocations. One South American government, finding its exchange position improved toward the close of 1947, announced that it would enlarge import quotas for the next few months.

Efforts to increase exchange receipts by official assistance to exports.— As another means of improving their balance-of-payments position, several countries of Latin America have sought to increase their exchange receipts by official fostering of exports. Exportation of various classes of goods prohibited by Brazil during the preceding year, for local supply and inflationary reasons, was again permitted under license during 1947. Uruguay authorized preferential exchange rates to assist the sale of certain export products. Effective January, 1948, Mexico abolished the 12 per cent "aforo" tax which had been levied on its staple exports since 1938, and revised the regular export duty schedule downward, with many products now entirelv exempt.

Argentina continued its system of controlling the local market and the exportation of various staple commodities, so as to capitalize upon the high current demand for them abroad, using a share of the profits for financing its industrial development program. A number of products were removed during 1947 from the list of those reserved for disposal abroad through the Argentine Trade Promotion Institute, although the official export monopoly over grain is still maintained.

A number of trade agreements were concluded during the past year or so among South American countries, which were featured by reciprocal assurances of preferred consideration in the export allocation of certain essential products not freely available in world markets. The principal commodities sought through these agreements have been: grain from Argentina, cotton textiles from Brazil, and nitrates from Chile.

Argentina negotiated agreements during 1947 with France, Italy, and Czechoslovakia, which involved granting those countries revolving credits to spur the resumption of trade. These agreements are to run through 1951, and contemplate an export surplus of Argentine agricultural products during the early part of the period, up to specified amounts, which is to be compensated for later by manufactured products from those European countries.

Argentina has been proposing to a number of other South American countries arrangements calling for closer trade relations, and involving the extension of credits to the other countries for designated developmental and public-works projects. Such an agreement with Bolivia was ratified late in 1947, and now awaits implementation. The principal agreement of this type, that concluded with Chile late in 1946, has not yet been ratified.

Far East[8]

India and Pakistan, now independent, develop separate trade regimes.—The large inflow of goods which followed the relaxation of the Indian import license restrictions begun in the summer of 1946 aroused the government's concern early in 1947, lest its foreign exchange prove inadequate for imports of needed food and capital goods. This led to a progressive restriction of new business, from sterling as well as from other sources, and to the calling in of outstanding licenses for selective revalidation. Varying degrees of liberality regarding the period of delivery on orders covered by licenses were applied to different classes of goods for the second half of 1947, with several hundred commodities suspended and others limited by quota.

The new Dominions of India and Pakistan, inaugurated in August, 1947, concurred in a "stand-still agreement" providing that, at least through March, 1948, free trade would be continued between them, each would apply in its area the tariff rates and import controls in effect on the date of independence, and would honor the prior import licenses issued.

The new commodity schedules announced by India in December, to govern the issue of import licenses for the first half of 1948, were marked by a return to the distinction between dollar and nondollar sources of supply, although a somewhat more liberal attitude was indicated toward the importation of certain products previously prohibited. Acting independently regarding imports into its own areas, the government of Pakistan likewise announced early in January, 1948, that its revised license lists

[8] The progress during 1947 toward the resumption of private trade with Japan was discussed under "Trading with the Occupied Ex-Enemy Countries," p. 408.

would accord more favorable treatment to certain imports from sterling than from nonsterling countries.

During the immediate postwar period, the exportation of many classes of Indian raw materials had been restricted, in the interest of the local processors. During the past year, the export license controls have been liberalized; and raw wool and certain categories of hides and skins have been among those commodities again allowed to be freely exported.

In the effort to have imports covered more fully by current earnings of foreign exchange, both Dominions have recently announced steps to assist the expansion of exports from their territories. A controversy has recently developed between them regarding the division of the important revenue from the export tax on raw jute, which is grown mainly in Pakistan and shipped overseas chiefly from Indian ports, and a tax on raw jute is now levied at the land frontier between the two Dominions.

Chinese trade corrective efforts hampered by civil war and yuan depreciation.—The successive efforts of the Chinese Government during 1947 to regularize the country's foreign trade, and to place it on a stronger and more balanced basis, were largely negated by the continuing civil war, the generally disordered internal economic conditions, and by the intensified depreciation of the national currency. The value of Chinese exports has continued during 1947 to run at a fraction of that of the country's imports. The very frequency of changes in the trade regulations, the difficulties in their administrative application, and the constant possibility of new exchange adjustments, increased the uncertainty and speculative character of foreign commercial transactions.

Perhaps the most sweeping trade control change was made in August, when exporters were permitted to sell their foreign exchange at the open market rate, then more than triple the official rate which had previously been insisted upon. At the same time, importers were required to purchase their exchange in most cases at the open-market rate; the more favorable official exchange was to be made available only for certain basic necessities, to keep down delivered prices. In addition to putting the country's foreign trade on a more realistic basis, it was hoped that the volume of essential imports would be increased, by merchants utilizing private foreign exchange holdings or remittances, without straining the official reserves. However, the widening spread between the official "open market" and the "black market" rates has held down the volume of exportations, in anticipation of higher prices, while administrative difficulties retarded the hoped-for increase of imports.

The current regulations provide definite allocations of foreign exchange only for capital goods, apportioned among the different regions of the country. Most industrial materials and certain other staple imports are admitted under quota, and the official effort is to direct such imports to users rather than dealers. Other products are licensed for importation only from time to time.

No important modification in the *Philippine* trade control situation took place during 1947. The agreement between the United States and the new republic for transitional tariff and quota arrangements over a period of twenty-eight years was officially proclaimed at the beginning of the year, but that made no immediate change in the Philippine duty treatment of United States products.

The Philippine Republic is conspicuous among the war-devastated countries for its convertible currency, its absence of import restrictions, and for the fact that both imports and exports of practically all classes of merchandise have for some time been back in normal commerical channels. It has built up a large dollar reserve, mainly from the various war settlements and credits by the United States; this is available for the importations of both consumers' goods and capital equipment for reconstruction.

Many Netherlands Indies exports and some imports revert to private hands.—Imports into the Netherlands Indies have been held down by the shortage of exchange, due to the limited amount of regular exportations which it has been possible to effect under the disputed control between the Netherlands and the Indonesian Republic over Java and Sumatra, the chief producing areas. To improve the exchange position, the Netherlands authorities announced in August a special arrangement to facilitate the exportation of stocks of plantation products through a Central Sales Organization, leaving the question of ownership to be settled later. It appears, however, that progress toward making the important raw materials of the Netherlands Indies fully available to world markets awaits a satisfactory solution of the political problem.

In the areas fully under Dutch control, NIGIEO, the temporary official trading agency, had toward the close of 1946 returned to private hands the exportation of all commodities except rubber, tin, and copra, which were then under international allocation. It had begun a corresponding release of imports and, in the early months of 1947, extended the range of goods to be privately handled. It was planned to terminate all official purchasing activities before the end of the year, but apparently that was not found possible. The Netherlands authorities continue to program such limited commercial imports as funds allow, assigning the carrying through of most transactions to private firms, on the basis of their relative prewar turnover.

Indo-China and Siam ease trade barriers; Burma tightens them.—The new autonomous tariff for Indo-China brought into operation at the beginning of 1947 carried substantial reductions in duties, especially on products essential to the country's rehabilitation. The new tariff levies the same duties on goods of all origins, and is applicable throughout the Indo-Chinese Federation, although certain areas are still politically unsettled. Prior to the war, French products had been admitted free or at considerably lower rates than others.

All importations require prior purchase authorizations, which are granted only for the essential products included in the general Plan of Importation. While importers' requests for foreign credits need no longer be referred to Paris, they are to be authorized only if similar French goods are not obtainable or would be subject to unreasonable delay in delivery.

Siamese license controls over foreign trade were liberalized early in 1947. During the year merchants were granted increased discretion in the use of their export proceeds for the purchase of imports. However, the earnings from the exports of rice and cement, and part of the proceeds from rubber, tin, and teak—products which together furnish the bulk of the Siamese income—are still required to be turned over to the Foreign Exchange Pool. From this governmental share of the exchange, allocations are granted only for the importation of products regarded as first essentials.

Burma, which became officially independent of the British Empire in January, 1948, increased its duties on a wide range of products in June, 1947, to help balance its budget. Licenses and exchange controls are, however, the principal regulators of its foreign trade. In October, severe restrictions were imposed on imports from all sources, with licenses assured only for products listed as highly essential. The declared purpose was to ensure a favorable trade balance and a stable rupee, with assurance given of easement as soon as possible.

1948

SUBSTANTIAL IMPROVEMENT FAILS TO MATERIALIZE AND THE MARSHALL PLAN IS LAUNCHED

The basic conditions which led to the widespread tightening up on imports by so many countries in 1947 have not yet materially improved. Still unable to pay for the exceptionally large volume of foreign products wanted by their peoples, most countries continued through 1948 the sharply restrictive import controls resorted to during the latter months of 1947. In fact, a number of countries introduced new restrictions or tightened existing controls during the past year, notably the Union of South Africa, Sweden, Argentina, and Mexico. Canada and the British West Indies stand almost alone in announcing for 1949 some relaxation in the drastic restrictions previously imposed.

Since most countries are still finding it exceptionally difficult to pay for all the goods they would like to procure from the United States and the other dollar areas, their recent import controls, especially those of Western Europe and the British Commonwealth, have been applied with particular severity to certain classes of purchases from the dollar areas. On the other hand, with the currencies of the majority of the other countries still not freely convertible, most countries of Europe and several of South America have been making strenuous efforts to avoid export surpluses to those countries where there cannot be obtained, in return, desired products of equivalent value.

Certain developments during 1948, however, carry a measure of promise for the long-term improvement of the economic position and of the trade control programs of many of the countries involved. The three chief developments are:

1. The United States undertaking to bolster the economies of the countries of Western Europe during the next four years, while they work out more basic recuperative programs through self-help and mutual aid;

2. The effect of the new trade control measures of Canada and of certain countries of Latin America, in checking the deterioration of their financial position, and in readjusting their import programs for the period ahead to a pattern more nearly in line with their financial limitations; and

3. The broad range of tariff concessions put into provisional application by twenty-two of the twenty-three countries which had participated in the simultaneous trade negotiations at Geneva in 1947, even though in most cases the benefits will not be fully realized until conditions allow the relaxation of the import license and exchange regulations, now dominant.

United States Marshall Plan Aid Materially Alleviates World Dollar Shortage

The new grants and loans extended by the United States to the countries of Western Europe under the Marshall Plan are alleviating considerably the dollar shortage of the directly participating countries. In varying degree, they have also been easing the financial position of Canada and certain other areas where the European countries have been procuring various products authorized under this program. But for this action by the United States, the curtailment of foreign markets that was experienced during the past year by producers of many classes of goods of a less essential character would have been more severe, and would probably have extended also to various essential products which the importing countries could not have paid for.

Even with this financial assistance from the United States, however, and with appreciable increase in the volumes of goods which the European and other countries could offer for export, most foreign countries were not able to maintain their purchases on the scale of 1947. This was particularly true of purchases from "dollar countries"—by which is usually meant the United States and the other Western Hemisphere countries—upon which much of the rest of the world had since the war come to depend heavily for import supplies. As a result, many countries have tried to concentrate their limited resources for purchases from the dollar countries upon the products which they consider most essential, and which are not readily procurable elsewhere.

One of the striking characteristics of international trade during the past year has been the pressure felt by so many countries to divert imports away from the United States or other "hard-currency" countries to those where they could more readily pay for them. The members of the sterling area have sought, when possible, to buy from those countries with which settlements could be made in pounds sterling. The countries of Europe have tried to satisfy their import needs through the operation of the clearing arrangements built into most of their postwar trade agreements with each other and with some overseas areas; these agreements are designed roughly to balance off goods against goods with the least use of cash.

Inconvertibility and Unreal Exchange Rates Hinder Freer Goods Exchanges

The international trade situation is complicated by the fact that most countries still suffer from the postwar dislocation and imbalance of their internal economies, and from uneven degrees of inflation in their domestic price levels. A limited number of countries have by now restored fair balance in their internal monetary structure and, through increased ability to cover necessary imports with exports and services, have regained considerable external strength and prestige for their currencies—a few even partial convertibility. Viewed broadly, however, the currencies of the majority of countries—including nearly all of those which were directly involved in the war—still have no dependable market value and no wide acceptance outside each country's own boundaries.

The consequent limitation upon multilateral settlement of uneven trade balances between pairs of individual countries is holding back the potential trade expansion which the reviving production of many countries might otherwise allow. However understandable the difficulties in the way of correcting the situation, and the reasons for postponing rectifying adjustments, so long as unreal exchange ratios between the currencies of different countries continue, they hinder progress toward the fuller interaction between their economies which is essential to the restoration of freer and more normal international exchanges of goods.

As the monetary situation stood, however, since most countries had used up the greater part of their reserves of gold and hard currencies in settling for their import surpluses during the earlier postwar years, and were now finding their sources of new foreign exchange income other than exports badly shrunken, many countries made a determined effort this past year to achieve a close balancing of their current trade with each country whose currency was not freely convertible. They want to avoid the necessity either for holding sizable bank balances in unusable currencies as payment for their export surpluses, or for covering import surpluses from their limited holdings of hard currency or gold.

Easement of the means of settlement for intra-European trade balances has been one of the major tasks undertaken during the past year in connection with the European Recovery Program.

Partial or Selective Depreciation Widely Tried as Trade Balance Corrective

France and Mexico were the principal countries which tried to reduce the gap in their balance of payments during 1948 by substantially devaluing their currencies and allowing them to approximate their market value. By such action, they hoped among other things to stimulate larger movements of exports and of tourists, and to discourage certain classes of imports. (The short-lived revaluation of the Chinese yuan, and the setting of a uniform conversion rate for the German mark, were currency adjustments of a rather special character.)

Quite a number of countries have been trying to deal with their unbalanced trade positions by what amounts to partial and selective depreciation of the external values of their currencies. The principal method has been the use of multiple rates of exchange in the settlement for different categories of imports and often also of certain exports. Direct resort to multiple rates of exchange of varying scope has been most common in South America. In fact, the majority of South American countries now carry on much of their foreign trade on other than the basic official exchange rates. Spain, Greece, and several of the Eastern European countries have resorted to devices of similar effect, in the form of "price equalization" schemes, exchange certificates, or other arrangements by which the exportation of certain classes of goods are rendered more profitable, usually out of funds raised by surcharges upon certain imports.

Giving Production for Export Priority Over Domestic Needs Another Device

Stimulating the expansion of exports through external depreciation of the country's currency, general or selective, has been only one of the methods used to reduce trade deficits. Better harvests and increased industrial production during the past year enabled a number of countries, particularly of Europe, to reduce their recent heavy dependence upon imports for certain commodities, and to enlarge the range and quantities of their products available for export. Special attention to the requirements of foreign tourists has already yielded several of these countries rewarding increases in foreign exchange usable for imports.

A number of the European countries have been definitely favoring those domestic industries which are capable of enlarging the output of goods in demand in world markets, by giving them preference in licenses for importation of equipment, allocation of controlled raw materials, access to credit facilities, and the diversion of local manpower. The United Kingdom has been outstanding in denying to domestic consumers much of the reviving and enlarged production in various lines, in order to channel more to foreign markets, especially where there can be obtained in return either needed import products or "hard currency" that is usable anywhere.

Summary of Salient Developments in the Principal Regions

Western Europe.—The shrinkage of foreign exchange resources with which to cover their continuing import deficits was most acute among the countries of Western Europe,[1] as their gold and dollar reserves dwindled, and the earlier credits and other special resources approached exhaustion. Even with the grants and loans made available by the United States under the Marshall Plan, the participating European countries have found it necessary to carry on their procurement quite selectively. In planning their import programs for the next few years so as to put themselves progressively on a more self-sustaining basis, these countries have set it down as a guiding principle that commodities are not to be purchased from dollar areas if they can be obtained elsewhere.

To reduce the recent excessive dependence upon imports from the Western Hemisphere, these European countries have been applying a particularly strict standard of essentiality during the past year in determining the classes of goods they would authorize from dollar areas. They have been seeking to satisfy their import requirements more largely from each other and from their colonies or associated territories overseas. Prospective importers were often frankly advised by European trade control authorities to try to fill their needs through utilizing the trade balances which were already built up, or were in prospect, under their bilateral agreements with other European countries. Under these agreements, each country promises to facilitate delivery to the other in the course of the year of

[1] In view of the exceptional importance of the developments of the year in Western Europe, they are made the subject of a more detailed analysis later in this chapter.

certain listed products, the aggregate values of which are expected to balance by the end of the period.

Many of the bilateral agreements between Western European countries that were revised during 1948 contemplated appreciably broader exchanges of goods. However, the increased concern of these countries over the holding of unusable balances in inconvertible currencies, when their trading partners could not supply desired goods of fully equivalent value, frequently led to scheduling reduced shipments for the next period. In a surprising number of cases, this concern has led to virtual suspension of trade between particular pairs of countries for months at a time, until some new basis for balanced trading could be devised.

In many of these revised European bilateral agreements, each country promised to admit specified quantities of the other's distinctive products that were recognized as "nonessential," but which had traditionally figured in the trade exchanges between their nationals. This arrangement was apparently forced by the growing recognition that the simultaneous efforts of numerous countries during the recent past to curtail the importations of less essential products were reacting badly, by cutting down the export potentiality for some important products of each of them in the markets of the others. At the same time, countries which were in a favorable position to supply essential products or those readily marketable tried to utilize that advantage in their trade negotiations, to secure whatever assurance the other could give regarding countershipments of the products which they particularly wanted.

It was in the effort to break into this trend toward tightening bilateralism in the trade relations of the Western European countries that an Intra-European Payments Plan was put into effect in the fall of the year. Under this plan, varying parts of the grants-in-aid from the United States to the ERP countries were designated to pay for certain portions of the goods they expected to sell to the various other participating countries, beyond what those countries could offset with their own exports. These special funds or "drawing accounts" in the currencies of the European creditor countries, upon which the European debtor countries were authorized to draw to finance their import deficits, are expected to make possible the equivalent of an additional 500 million dollars of intra-European trade during the current fiscal year. The sponsors hope that this assistance from the United States may stimulate the Marshall Plan countries to grant each other larger credit margins on their own account, and gradually to return to the multilateral settlement of uneven trade balances between individual pairs of countries.

Eastern Europe.—The tendency for close official control over all foreign trade, and for its concentration in a limited number of governmentally supervised organizations, which had been growing since the war in nearly all the countries within the Soviet sphere of influence, apparently came to a head during 1948. Poland, Czechoslovakia, Hungary, Rumania, and Yugoslavia each brought into operation last year a number of state trading companies, and granted them monopolies in particular groups of commodities.

The series of broad agreements for the long-term orientation of the economies of the countries of Eastern Europe toward the Soviet Union and toward each other, through increased exchanges of goods and technical assistance, that was announced in 1947 after their refusal to participate in the Marshall Plan, was expanded during 1948 into a fairly comprehensive network. So far, however, there have been no evidences of any composite plan for the general economic collaboration of the countries which are parties to this series of bilateral arrangements, beyond a general agreement in January, 1949, between Russia and five of the other countries for the periodic exchange of economic experience and for mutual assistance in technical and commodity matters.

Indeed, in only few instances has there been much evidence of activity toward the implementation of the long-term projects for the coördination of the economic programs of various neighboring countries in this region. The firmly scheduled lists of products which the various Eastern European countries undertook this past year to supply or license to each other have, so far as is known, usually been moderate in volume, and quite generally called for a close balance in the value of the goods currently moving in each direction.

While carrying on these negotiations with each other, the countries of Eastern Europe did not abate their efforts during 1948 to work out trade arrangements with the countries of Western Europe—their principal traditional markets and sources of supply—to obtain highly desired equipment and other goods that were not available within Eastern Europe, in return for what they could furnish the West, mainly foods, fuels, and other natural products. While East-West trade in Europe is still well below the prewar level, such data as are available for 1948 indicate a continuing moderately upward trend in the share of Western European imports derived from Eastern Europe.

Following political difficulties within the Soviet bloc in the summer of 1948, and curtailment of the scheduled deliveries of products to Yugoslavia by several of the other Eastern European countries, Yugoslavia decided to divert its important surpluses of minerals and other natural products for sale to the West in order to obtain there the capital equipment desired.

Several of the Western European countries whose nationals had large investments in properties in Eastern Europe that had been expropriated since the war had been insisting upon the recognition of those claims before entering into any broad agreements regarding exchanges of goods. During the past year, Czechoslovakia, Poland, and Yugoslavia each came to agreement with various of the Western European countries upon the bases of settlement for such nationalized properties, usually to be paid for out of future export surpluses to those countries.

British Commonwealth.—While the goods supplied to the United Kingdom under the Marshall Plan averted the extreme application of the import program announced in the fall of 1947, prohibiting American foodstuffs and reducing purchases of cotton and tobacco, the general British program for holding down to the most essential commodities the importations which need to be paid for in dollars continued dominant. Australia, New Zealand, and the various British colonies staunchly supported, in the administration of their local import controls, the central objective of minimizing the drafts upon the dollar resources of the sterling area.

These sterling countries allowed unrestricted admission for most classes of goods originating in each other's territories; while importers of goods from the United States, Canada, and other dollar countries received licenses only for essential products, or for equipment not procurable at home or from nondollar sources. The net result was a considerable cut in their huge 1947 import deficit with the dollar areas. So far as these former imports from dollar sources were replaced, they were procured mainly from other sterling areas and the European countries.

The Union of South Africa, whose gold production and exchange reserves had allowed it to lift import restrictions directly after the war, found its resources heavily drained by the uncontrolled buying abroad which ensued. Late in 1948, it reimposed a sweeping regime of import restrictions, prohibiting certain products from all areas, and rationing importers from nonsterling countries to half the value of their 1947 purchases.

Canada continued with little change until late in 1948 the program of drastic restriction on a broad range of imports from the United States and other Western Hemisphere countries, which had been resorted to in November, 1947. The reason then given was that the large import balance from these areas could no longer be met in the traditional way, by the proceeds from export surpluses to the United Kingdom and Europe, whose currencies were now largely inconvertible. Canada sought during 1948 to reduce its unusable sterling balance by facilitating increased importations from the United Kingdom, through duty suspensions and other means.

The United Kingdom, at the same time, scaled down its purchase programs for various foods and other natural products of Canada, in order to minimize building up further dollar obligations to Canada. The recent agreement under which Poland is to supply the United Kingdom over the next five years with large quantities of foodstuffs and timber on a rising scale, in return for industrial materials and equipment, is a case in point. It exemplifies both the trend to divert British purchases to nondollar areas and the effort to broaden the exchanges of goods between Eastern and Western Europe.

The sharp curtailment of Canada's imports from the United States during 1948, together with the marked enlargement of its sales in the American market, and the European purchases in Canada financed under the Marshall Plan, combined to improve the Canadian exchange reserve position sufficiently to warrant some relaxation toward the close of the year in the degree of import austerity earlier imposed. Importation of fresh fruits and vegetables was again permitted and, beginning in January, 1949, many foods and consumer conveniences were taken off the restricted list and various manufactured goods formerly banned were placed on a quota basis.

Also effective for 1949 is the United Kingdom release to its Caribbean colonies of a limited amount of dollar currency to be used for the importation of certain goods formerly excluded as nonessentials, in order to keep marketing channels open for usual suppliers in Canada, the United States, and other nonsterling countries.

Latin America.—As in other regions, the tighter and more selective controls upon imports brought into operation during 1947 by all but one of the countries of South America, and by Mexico and several of the Central American Republics, were continued substantially through 1948. In fact, several of the Latin American countries resorted to further tightening of their import controls during the past year. Only Cuba, Venezuela, and certain of the smaller Caribbean republics continued free of both exchange control and broad import restrictions.

The most drastic new action was that ordered by Argentina, which found itself heavily overbought and unable to cover even its outstanding dollar commitments. Brazil resorted to the requirement of prior licenses for most imports and exports, and authorized letters of credit only for the most essential commodities. Similar concern over their dwindling exchange resources led several other Latin American countries, including Colombia, Peru, Bolivia, Mexico, and Costa Rica, to take further action to reduce the importation of various categories of goods regarded as dispensable. Several methods were used: direct curtailment of licenses or exchange allocations; increase of the delivered cost through higher charges or unfavorable exchange rates; and withholding assurance as to when the exchange necessary for remittance would be available. Mexico resorted to outright devaluation of the peso, as well as substantial upward revision of its import duties.

In a number of the southern republics, however, the recent developments in the matter of trade controls may have a salutary effect for the longer run. In addition to checking the deterioration in the country's exchange position, they have in several instances been accompanied by a budgeting of the country's total anticipated foreign exchange income, and by a closer coördination between the new import orders authorized and the funds that would be available to pay for them. In those cases, there is an improved prospect for more dependable commercial remittances during the period ahead. Brazil, Chile, and Colombia are notable among the countries which have been limiting the amount of foreign exchange to be made available for new imports, in order to carry through definite programs for clearing up the accumulation of remittances past due for goods earlier imported.

During the past year, the governments of several of the major South American countries became particularly anxious over the inadequacy of their dollar earnings and reserves, apart from the general concern over their diminishing foreign exchange resources. They held down authorizations for new purchases from the United States or other hard-currency countries, and used their import controls to favor the shifting of such purchases to those European countries where they had favorable balances from earlier shipments on credit, or with which they had clearing agreements under which the trade exchanges were to approximate a balance without requiring cash settlements.

The gradual recovery of production in Europe has made it easier for Latin American countries to find alternative sources of supply for various manufactures in those countries, and to reduce the earlier high dependence upon the United States for their procurement. Increasingly, however, the over-all trade relations of several of the major countries of South America with those of Europe came to be characterized by efforts to enforce a strict balancing of the current trade exchanges, along the lines observed among the European countries themselves. They apparently want to be assured of obtaining equivalent supplies of needed products from Europe in return for their own exports, and to avoid further shipments on credit or for unusable currencies.

Asia.—India and *Pakistan,* now independent countries, both permitted purchases from soft-currency countries much more freely than from hard-currency countries, with important classes of goods from the dollar areas subject to an over-all monetary ceiling. As their general foreign exchange position improved in the course of the year, they progressively relaxed their import-licensing restrictions, but least for the dollar countries. Pakistan, which had a more favorable trade balance with the dollar areas, and is less able than India to replace imported goods with domestic substitutes, maintained a more liberal attitude toward imports from dollar sources, and at midyear expanded the range of such products which would be considered for admission. Both countries are pursuing a policy of encouraging exports, and especially to hard-currency countries.

India and Pakistan have been trying to reduce the hampering effects of the import duties and export controls which, since March, 1948, have been applying to trade movements between them. The transit of each other's products across their territories is permitted, and efforts have been made to work out arrangements for facilitating supplies of their distinctive products to each other.

China made several attempts during 1948 to put the country's foreign trade on a more stable and realistic basis, including the reintroduction of "linked trading" to encourage exports, and the effort to stabilize the yuan on a gold basis and to call in the peoples' holdings of gold and foreign currencies. In practice, however, none proved very successful, in the face of the continuing inflation in connection with the conduct of the civil war, and the rapidly deteriorating general economic situation. The rapid advances of the Northern armies into Central China, toward the end of the year, rendered the conduct of foreign trade with China precarious and the conditions of its future regulation highly uncertain.

After several years of trade unhampered by licenses or exchange controls, the *Philippine Republic* put into operation at the close of 1948 an import control law. The importations of articles classed as "luxury and nonessential" are to be reduced to specified percentages of the trade during the preceding fiscal year. The declared purposes are to conserve dollar resources for goods more essential to the development of the country, to protect local industries, and to provide a definite share for new importers in the handling of the controlled lines.

Despite the continued unsettled political situation in Java and Sumatra, the year saw appreciable recovery in the quantities of the leading products of *Indonesia* available for export, stimulated in part by imported incentive goods. While the actual conduct of importation as well as exportation has practically reverted to private firms, all foreign transactions are subject to close supervision by the Netherlands authorities and to a considerable measure of official direction.

The bodies now entrusted with recommending the general planning and allocation of the imports into Indonesia represent predominantly the old-established trading houses. Such houses receive preferential consideration in the allotment of imports, in accordance with their prewar shares in the trade, although a margin is provided for qualified newcomers. On the export side, special agencies control the movement of copra, quinine, mineral ores, and produce of undetermined ownership.

The occupied areas.—Several steps were taken during 1948 to facilitate the conduct of private trade with *Japan* and *Western Germany,* and to broaden the scope and scale of their commercial exchanges with their normal prewar trading partners. The aim is again to make available to world markets the large quantities of essential civilian commodities formerly produced by Japan and Germany, in return for the foreign materials and products they need and, at the same time, to reduce the costs to the occupying powers of supplying necessary imports, by making those areas more self-supporting.

Export contracts may now be executed directly between Japanese sellers and private foreign buyers, although they are still subject to approval by the Japanese and Occupation authorities, for consistency with the price ceilings and general export program. All imports into Japan continue subject to the consent of the Occupation authorities, and are understood still to consist mainly of basic necessities and raw materials for industrial operations.

The joint arrangement concluded by Japan with five sterling-area countries—United Kingdom and colonies, Australia, India, New Zealand, and South Africa—contemplates for the fiscal year 1948–1949 a considerable increase in the volume of trade between Japan and this group of countries, which have been traditional markets for Japanese textiles and other products and important sources of Japan's necessary raw materials. Agreements were also concluded during 1948 with a number of other countries, of Southeast Asia and of Europe, for the exchange of goods between them on the familiar open-account basis, with any net balance to be settled in dollars.

Since December, 1948, it has been possible to make export contracts for most commodities from the British and American zones of Germany directly with the suppliers, within the framework of certain general regulations. Earlier in the year, the import procedure was modified so as to allow increasing participation by German firms in the actual procurement of certain scheduled imports. Many of the purchases for the Bizonal Area are still being handled by the Joint Export-Import Agency.

The most important recent stimulus to the German economy was the revaluation of the mark in May, and the adoption by the Military Authorities of a uniform conversion rate of 30 cents for import and export transactions in most commodities.

With the additional arrangements concluded by the Bizonal authorities during 1948, trade agreements are now in operation with all but three countries of Europe, and are under negotiation with several countries of South America. These agreements, under which the volume of German exports has increased substantially, typically provide for the products of which each country is to facilitate delivery to the other, and are planned so that movements of goods in both directions shall approximately offset each other in aggregate annual value.

Under agreements reached late in 1948, the French-occupied Zone of Germany is to be merged economically with the joint British-American zones early in 1949. The conditions of foreign trading developed for the Bizonal Area are to be progressively applied to the whole of Western Germany.

The trade agreement between the British-American and Soviet zones of Germany for 1948 called for an enlarged exchange of goods, on a balanced basis, to a value 50 per cent higher than during the preceding year. However, these interzonal trade movements were cut off after the attempted Russian blockade of Berlin from the West.

Western Europe the Scene of Exceptional Developments in Trade Relations

Marshall Plan aid part of larger program for recovery and collaboration.—The substantial American assistance under the Marshall Plan has unquestionably been the most important influence of the past year upon the trade and the economies of the countries of Western Europe. That influence has extended beyond the immediate benefits from the foods, materials, and equipment supplied or financed by the United States. Those deliveries were part of a larger program, designed to support the efforts of the individual participating countries for increased production and general reconstruction, and to stimulate them to take measures for closer collaboration and reciprocal accommodation. Indirectly, the influence of the program has extended in varying degree to other countries, in and out of Europe, with which the direct participants had important trade relations.

The United States assistance, in alleviating the dollar shortage of the countries of Western Europe under the Marshall Plan, has also been serving to temper the more extreme restrictions upon imports which their deteriorated external financial position might otherwise have required. It is bolstering the purchasing power of these countries for foreign products, during the working out of the more basic recuperative measures for increased output and interchange of goods—measures which are expected to make them progressively less dependent upon extraordinary outside aid.

Still unable to afford all imports desired, selective restrictions continued.—Basically, however, there was little change during 1948 in the pattern of more selective import controls, to which all the countries of Western Europe except Switzerland had resorted by the close of 1947, in order to make the best use of their shrunken buying power for foreign goods. In fact, these controls have in many cases been applied with more calculated rigidity than in previous years, even in relations with other European countries. Sweden, Norway, and Portugal tried to adjust themselves in 1948 to some curtailment in the over-all volume of foreign goods which they could afford.

Under present conditions, the foreign trade of nearly all the countries of Western Europe is carried on under more or less close official regulation. As a rule, individual import transactions are subject to the procurement of an official license or an exchange allocation, or both, and most exports are likewise subject to official control. Most of these governments are now regulating their countries' foreign purchases in accordance with rather detailed import programs, which are periodically revised. These programs are closely correlated with such supplies as their trading partners under various bilateral agreements have promised to facilitate in return for their exports, plus what can be paid for with the dollars or other acceptable foreign income anticipated for the period ahead.

Spokesmen for these governments justify the continuation and even accentuation of stringent import controls during 1948 on the ground that there has thus far been only small progress toward removal of the conditions responsible for the general tightening up in latter 1947. Even with the better harvests and increasing industrial output of the past year, few of the countries of Western Europe have as yet been able to spare a sufficient volume of goods—beyond what they feel they need to devote to current use and to domestic replenishment and rebuilding—to pay for all of the exceptionally large quantities of foreign products they still want.

Moreover, the income from shipping, foreign investments, and other "invisible exports," with which Western Europe as a whole used to pay for about one-fourth of its merchandise imports before the war, has seriously shrunken. The substantial trade credits extended during the earlier postwar period by a number of the more prosperous European countries as well as by several from the Western Hemisphere, to help the war-ravaged countries obtain needed imports for which they were not yet able to pay, have been almost exhausted. Finally, the reserves of gold, dollars, and other convertible assets accumulated over the years by the countries of Western Europe had, by 1948, been heavily drawn down.

Dollar resources reserved for essentials; other purchases diverted elsewhere.—Being unable, under these circumstances, to support continued importations on the 1947 scale, many countries of Western Europe tried to manage their import programs for 1948 so as to hold down further trade deficits, by restricting the new purchases of various products that were not entirely essential. Since the total amount of goods they desired from the United States and Canada by far exceeded in value that of the goods and services they could supply them in return, the curtailment of the range of imports from those countries was particularly marked.

The expenditure of dollars upon many classes of consumers' goods was severely restricted, especially if they could be obtained with other currencies. Most of the European governments felt it necessary to reserve their limited dollar income primarily to cover the countries' most essential requirements for food, fuel, raw materials, and productive equipment. Indeed, the degree of enforced import austerity faced by several European governments at the outset of 1948 caused them concern over its possible adverse domestic effects, through declines in production and employment in industries dependent upon foreign supplies which they could not then afford.

The United States Interim-Aid Program of December, 1947, made possible the maintenance of essential shipments of food, fuel, and fertilizer to France, Italy, and Austria during the early months of 1948, pending consideration by the Congress of the longer-term European Recovery Program. That program made available about 5 billion dollars—under grant or loan—to cover the cost of the supplies to the participating countries which the United States was prepared to furnish or finance during the first year or so. Nevertheless, they were not able to maintain as broad and ample a purchasing program for American products as during the preceding year.

The greater part of the cut made by the Western European countries in their import deficit during 1948 was effected through curtailment of imports from the United States and, to a smaller extent, from Canada. Commercial firms in those countries were at times advised by their import control authorities to try to satisfy their needs for particular foreign products from other European countries and their colonies or associated overseas territories, where payment in dollars was not required.

Insistence on bilateral balance retards intra-European trade recovery.—Next to the Western Hemisphere, the countries of Europe as a whole have been one another's principal source of supply. In fact, before the war, about half of all Western European imports were derived from within Europe, and about four-fifths of that amount came from within Western Europe. As late as the first half of 1948, however, the countries of Western Europe as a whole were supplying barely a third of one another's imports. This failure of intra-European trade to return to its high prewar level has been one of the important elements in the slowness of general European recovery, and in the exceptionally heavy dependence of Europe since the war upon supplies from the Western Hemisphere.

As earlier noted, few of the European countries, even with reviving production, are as yet able to cover their full import needs with what they can offer in return. Moreover, the development of their full potential foreign trade has been hindered by the fact that, while the currencies of several of the European countries have regained considerable strength and even limited convertibility, not one of the European countries that were directly involved in the war yet has a currency with a dependable market value, or one which is fully acceptable outside its own boundaries.

Under the circumstances, commerce between most pairs of European countries is still carried on within the limitations of the bilateral agreements which have been regulating their trade relations since the close of the war. Typically, these carry lists of desired products which each country undertakes to license or otherwise facilitate to the other. The amounts due for individual transactions are offset, in the special account maintained in the Central Bank or other "clearing" institution, against what is due for shipments in the opposite direction, with only the net balances calling for settlement at periodic intervals in gold or transferable currency, beyond the limited reciprocal overdrafts commonly provided for. Except in those cases where credits had definitely been extended by one of the trading partners, the aim in these bilateral agreements has usually been that the aggregate value of the goods moving in each direction should approach a rough balance in the course of the year, so as to call for the least settlement in gold or currencies.

In the renegotiations of their bilateral agreements during 1948, many pairs of Western European governments tried to provide for appreciable increases over the preceding year in the volume of the trade between them. To some extent, this reflected an increased output of domestic products available for export by both contracting countries. Quite often, however, the prospective increases were only on one side, and the purpose of providing for such increase in exports was to offset an import balance that had developed under the previous agreement, or to pay off credits extended during the earlier postwar period. Beyond limited overdrafts to cover temporarily uneven movements of goods between them during the course of the year, it was rare for any new credits to be extended by one European country to another in connection with their trade arrangements of 1948.

On the contrary, the most striking characteristic of the trade agreements negotiated or revised during 1948 by the Western European countries has been the widespread insistence that current trade exchanges be held more closely to a balance. Lacking sufficient acceptable foreign exchange to buy where they wanted, they tried to get the most out of their bilateral trade arrangements which, as earlier indicated, did not necessarily call for immediate payment in foreign currency. Desired products available in one of the countries with which such clearing arrangements were in force could often be obtained by payment in the importer's currency, since the amount due the other country could be balanced off against goods already exported to that market, or in prospect under the schedule of reciprocal supplies usually provided by the agreement. An intensified concern was evidenced by practically all of these countries, both to get the utmost advantage out of such goods as their countries could supply, in the form of countershipments of needed goods, and to avoid any further accumulations of "favorable" trade balances which would yield only unusable currencies.

Trade often scaled down to avoid gold payments or unusable credits.— Norway, the Netherlands, and France were among the countries that sometimes chose to reduce the volume of goods which they asked the other contracting government to authorize for exportation to them, in order to keep within their limited prospective ability to pay in goods or services. The British export drive ran into difficulties with several countries of continental Europe, because they could not meet the increased amount of goods which Britain was able and ready to supply with corresponding increases in their own export products. Adjustments had to be negotiated during the course of the year; the highest level of trade exchanges was usually sought, but on a balanced basis, which would require neither country to hold unusable trade credits or to deliver gold or dollars in settlement.

In a surprising number of instances during 1948, trade between various pairs of European countries was virtually suspended, often for months at a time, because of the inability of one of the countries to pay for its import surplus from the other with either acceptable goods or usable currencies. France, which had as yet made little progress in cutting down its sizable trade deficit, frequently found itself in this predicament. In several instances, when trade was resumed, it was based on a sharp scaling down of the commodities originally scheduled to be licensed for export by the surplus country—although sometimes with the hopeful provision for restoration of the original quotas if the deficit country's deliveries should exceed the expected amounts.

Switzerland, Belgium, and Portugal were notable among those which were able to maintain or regain a strong position in their own over-all balance of international payments, but found themselves restricted in their trade potentialities by the weaker financial position of their neighbors. Because these stronger countries could not get paid for part of the goods they sold to the weaker European countries, they were less able to pay for all their desired imports from dollar countries. At the same time, the markets for some of their important national products, such as Swiss watches, Belgian tapestries, or Portuguese wines, were being curtailed because other countries of Europe felt they could not now afford to allow the importation of such products in normal quantities.

Resistance to "nonessentials" reacts against each country's exports.—Indeed, the cumulative effect of the decisions of so many countries during the past year or so to cut down on the admission of various foreign products regarded as not entirely essential was in the nature of a boomerang, since the result was a curtailment of old-established markets for some of each country's own export products. The United Kingdom and several of the continental countries recognized this situation and, in renegotiating their bilateral agreements during 1948, undertook to admit moderate quantities of certain of each other's normal trade goods of a nonessential character, in order to ensure for some of their own traditional industries adequate market outlets and continued high employment.

On the whole, however, the effort to hold down importations of a luxury or semiluxury character has continued, and the countries which could offer essential or readily marketable products for export had an advantage in their trade bargaining. For instance, Sweden was reported as insisting that exports of wood pulp to Italy would be made only in return for certain Italian products, notably textiles; on the other hand, France was reported willing to receive more fish from Norway if it could obtain also increased quantities of forest products. The strong general demand for coal enabled Poland to obtain promises from several of the Western European countries that part of its coal deliveries would be paid for in dollars or other freely transferable currencies.

Artificial exchange rates cause trade distortion and irregular deals.—The disparity between the official exchange rates of their currencies and what they bring in the open market varies considerably for the different European countries. Taken together with the varying degrees of price inflation within the individual countries, this situation has been restricting the recovery of intra-European trade, distorting the normal pattern of exchanges, and often forcing unusual makeshift arrangements.

Italy, for instance, which had allowed the lira to find its level close to the open-market rate during the preceding year, found itself in 1948 a creditor in relation to practically all the countries with which trade settlements were made through clearing arrangements. When paid for at the current official exchange parities, the products of those other countries now proved too expensive to allow Italian imports to increase as rapidly as its exports. An appreciable part of the recent trade of Italy and of a number of other European countries has therefore been carried on through so-called "reciprocity deals," resembling barter. Crude as it is, this method apparently affords the necessary flexibility in adjusting the relative prices for the particular products of the two countries involved, without getting tangled in unreal exchange partities.

France experimented during 1948 with the revaluation of the franc, on a partly controlled basis. This was largely prompted by the high prices resulting from the marked domestic inflation and the distinctly unreal previous exchange rate. Austria exemplified another type of solution when producers found that the official exchange rate of their country's currency handicapped the sale of their traditional export products. It is reported that export transactions were sometimes concluded outside official channels, with the foreign exchange proceeds not made available to the Central Bank.

The difficulties of dealing on the basis of official exchange values of the Spanish peseta and of the Greek drachma led to much of the trade of those countries during the past year being conducted on unusual bases: differential exchange rates in settling for different classes of commodities; "exchange certificates" for sale in the open market; or other arrangements which amounted to the payment of premiums on certain exports out of surcharges levied on certain imports.

Secondary importance of import duty revisions and suspensions.—With the trade of the European countries now so largely determined by direct controls and by special arrangements with other countries, the height of the import duties has been of relatively less concern than usual. Few important tariff revisions were made effective during the year. The principal changes were those duty reductions or bindings brought into operation by the United Kingdom, the Benelux countries (Belgium, Netherlands, and Luxemburg), France, Norway, and Czechoslovakia, in pursuance of the General Agreement on Tariffs and Trade concluded by twenty-three nations at Geneva in the fall of 1947.

The new schedule of import duties introduced jointly by the Benelux countries in January, 1948, was in large part immediately suspended, in order not to handicap necessary importations for the period ahead. Many of these duties are to continue suspended through 1949. The duties of the new French tariff, which was likewise inaugurated in January of 1948, were similarly suspended for the time being. During the course of 1948, however, the new French duties were put into force on several successive lists of products. For customs purposes, the territory of the Saar has during the past year been merged with that of France.

Special arrangements to loosen up intra-European trade and payments.—Among the major aims of the European Recovery Program are: to strengthen the economies of the participating countries through widening of the markets for their products in one another's territories, and to reduce their excessive recent dependence upon the Western Hemisphere for imported supplies.

The need for special effort to this end became more acute during 1948. The European countries with deficits in their trade relations with other European countries found themselves less able to finance them, and those with export surpluses were less able or ready to advance new credits. At the same time, the fact that most European countries were still not in a position to make their currencies convertible, prevented the restoration of the traditional prewar mechanism for the multilateral clearing of uneven trade balances between particular pairs of countries. The net result has been, as earlier noted, that Western European countries have increasingly insisted upon a stricter bilateral balancing of their current trade exchanges with each other. To loosen and possibly reverse this trade-constricting trend, two methods to ease the payments difficulty were introduced in connection with the first year's operation of the European Recovery Program.

Under the first or "offshore purchase" method, supplemental allotments were made by the United States to the European debtor countries, on the basis of their prospective import deficits with each of the other participating countries, to finance purchases of needed recovery products available from other countries within the group. These dollars were officially described as doing "double duty." The debtor countries were enabled to buy from their neighbors additional goods beyond what their own resources permitted; and the selling countries, in turn, could use those dollars to finance their own necessary imports from the Western Hemisphere. Close to 9 per cent of all the goods supplied to the European countries under the sponsorship of the Economic Cooperation Administration came from within the participating countries themselves.

This method was replaced in October, 1948, by an Intra-European Payments Plan, put forward by the central organization of the ERP countries as a more effective way of accomplishing the same objective, particularly because it encourages the broader financing of their trade with one another in local currency rather than in dollars. Under this plan, agreed portions of the dollar aid allotted by the United States to the respective ERP countries were made conditional upon their setting up special accounts of equivalent value in their own currencies, equal to the anticipated surplus of exports over imports in their trade with the other participating countries, estimated a year in advance. The debtor countries can draw upon these accounts to finance those trade deficits with their European creditors.[2]

While most of the countries are to grant as well as to receive such "draw-

[2] While for simplicity the plan is here described in terms of trade surpluses or deficits, it actually takes account also of other elements in the current balance of payments between particular pairs of countries, including various services to their nationals, and the often rather substantial item of tourists' expenditures and earnings of foreign workers.

ing rights," the two countries that are scheduled to supply the greatest net surpluses of goods to the others under the plan during 1948–1949 are the United Kingdom (representing the sterling area) and Belgium. The principal net deficit countries are France and, to a much smaller extent, the Netherlands, Austria, and Greece. To make the payments plan flexible, and to render the "drawing rights" as effective as dollars in inducing advantageous trading, debtors may under certain circumstances ask to have portions of them transferred to another creditor country.

In the aggregate, this new plan is expected to make possible during the fiscal year 1948–1949 a net additional volume of trade and services between the participating European countries of over half a billion dollars. The plan is not regarded as in itself a solution for the intra-European payments problem, but rather as an important aid while the more fundamental causes are being dealt with. The basic solution appears to depend upon the progress in the concurrent economic recuperation of the participating countries that is achieved over the next four years, particularly as expressed in: expansion of individual production, coöperation in the joint utilization of resources, greater stabilization of their domestic financial structures, better balance in their international accounts, and more ready international acceptance of their currencies.

The Economic Commission for Europe and the Organization for European Economic Cooperation (the central organization of the ERP countries) are studying various methods for making the present system of bilateral trade more flexible, as an approach toward a multilateral system. The sponsors of the Intra-European Payments Plan are hopeful that its help, particularly in removing the immediate necessity for the strict bilateral balancing of their current accounts, will stimulate the participating countries to greater reciprocal accommodation in their trade policies, including, when necessary, the extension of credits to each other on their own responsibility. How far any such payments plan will bring about an inherent relaxation of the present constricting bilateral structure of intra-European trade, however, beyond the extent of the funds for clearing uneven trade balances provided by the United States, may not be known for some time.

1949

FIRST BROAD EFFORTS TO "LOOSEN UP THE LOG JAM" OF TRADE AND CURRENCIES

While only very limited progress has been made thus far, the past year has seen the first efforts on a broad scale to loosen up the log jam of governmental controls upon the normal flow of goods in international trade and upon payment for them, which have been building up in most countries since the war.

Summary of Salient Developments in the Different Regions

Of a preparatory character was the action of all the sterling areas except Pakistan, and of all the Western European countries but Switzerland, following the British example in September, 1949, in readjusting downward the unrealistic official exchange values of their currencies in terms of the dollar. The prime object was to rectify their competitive position pricewise, so as to be better able to take active steps to reduce their continued large trade imbalance with the dollar countries.

In Western Europe, each country participating in the European Recovery Program had made a beginning, by the turn of the year, in relaxing its quantitative restrictions on selected products from most of the others. The object is to break through the prevailing system of delimited bilateral supply agreements, which have come to constrict the potential expansion of trade within Western Europe, in order that the region as a whole may make more rapid recovery and move forward toward a more self-supporting position.

In Latin America, Mexico and Peru made sharp general cuts in the official exchange rates for their currencies, while Argentina, Uruguay, Paraguay, and Chile devalued their currencies by varying amounts for transactions in different categories of commodities. The majority of the Latin American Republics maintain either prior license or exchange restrictions on imports, and most of these tightened their restrictions on particular classes of goods during 1949. However, quite a number of these countries instituted arrangements for clearing off the accumulation of unpaid foreign commercial debts, and for preventing a repetition of their recent experience when more foreign goods were being admitted than could be paid for from current earnings.

In the major Asiatic areas, the political developments during 1949 were especially important, making the conditions of access to their markets and supplies for the period ahead distinctly precarious in the case of China, somewhat difficult in the case of India and Pakistan because of their current estrangement, but more favorable for Indonesia and Japan. In the two principal areas occupied by the Allies, West Germany and Japan, the greater part of the trade has recently been returned to private channels under the control of the newly reorganized local governments, with the procedures for doing business greatly simplified.

Only among the countries of Western Europe are there any major changes now under consideration in the matter of their international trade relations. The current ferment of ideas and proposals in that region is expected to produce some more advanced program during 1950. Still far from definite in detail, or even certain of general acceptance, they all look to the further liberalization of quota restrictions on each other's trade, and at least partial intertransferability of European currencies. The immediate aim is to encourage greater intra-European trade by facilitating the settlement of uneven trade balances between particular pairs of these countries through a multilateral clearing arrangement. This is to be made possible by a combination of wider credit accommodation among themselves, and of some assistance from the United States in the liquidation of net trade deficits of individual countries with the group, from the funds granted for the continuation of the general European Recovery Program.

Basic Structure of Foreign Trade Controls Unchanged and Even Tightened

Apart from the above steps, most of which were taken too late in 1949 for their effects to be yet clearly visible, there have been few basic changes in the structure of restrictive trade controls which since the war have come into use by the great majority of foreign countries, to a degree and complexity unprecedented in modern times. In fact, the past year brought a distinct tightening in the foreign trade measures of a number of countries. Perhaps most notable, from the viewpoint of North American exporters, were the decisions of the Union of South Africa and of the Philippine Republic to adopt new curbs on imports generally, and of the sterling-area countries to curtail further by 25 per cent their total expenditures for purchases from the dollar areas, even from Canada.

Viewing the present situation broadly, out of eighty-five foreign countries and colonies—comprising most of the trading world—the governments of all but eight now either require an official license to be obtained as a condition of importation of many if not all products, or control the granting of the foreign exchange necessary in settlement for foreign purchases, or do both. An appreciable number of countries prohibit altogether the importation of certain classes of goods. As will appear from the following brief summary, the majority of foreign countries now operate to some degree both import-license and exchange restrictions, and the issue of an import license does not always carry with it the assurance of foreign exchange in payment.

Current Status of Foreign Import License and Exchange Control Systems

The countries marked † (below) require import licenses for only limited lists of products. In those marked *, the granting of new import licenses is understood to carry with it the right to foreign exchange in payment.

COUNTRIES OPERATING IMPORT LICENSES AND EXCHANGE RESTRICTIONS—

Continental Europe and associated overseas territories: Austria, Belgium-Luxemburg,* Belgian Congo,* Bulgaria, Czechoslovakia,* Denmark,* Finland,* France,* French Indo-China,* French Overseas Territories,* Germany,* Greece,* Hungary, Iceland, Italy,* Morocco (French* and Spanish*), Netherlands,* Indonesia,* N. W. I. and Surinam,* Norway,* Poland, Portugal, Portuguese Colonies, Rumania, Spain,* Spanish Colonies,* Sweden,* Turkey, U.S.S.R.,* Yugoslavia.*

British Commonwealth: Australia,* Canada,* Ceylon, India,* Ireland,† New Zealand,* Pakistan,* Union of South Africa,* United Kingdom,* British Colonies and Dependencies* (except Hong Kong).

Latin America: Argentina, Bolivia, Brazil, Chile, Colombia,* Ecuador,* Paraguay,* Uruguay.*

Other areas: Anglo-Egyptian Sudan, Aden, Burma, China, Egypt, Iran, Iraq, Israel,* Japan,* Jordan, Korea, Philippines,†* Syria and Lebanon.

COUNTRIES REQUIRING PRIOR IMPORT LICENSES BUT HAVING NO SEPARATE EXCHANGE RESTRICTIONS—

Europe: Switzerland.†

British Commonwealth: Hong Kong.†

Latin America: Venezuela,† Nicaragua.*

Other areas: Saudi Arabia,† Thailand.†

COUNTRIES RESTRICTING EXCHANGE BUT REQUIRING NO PRIOR IMPORT LICENSES—

Latin America: Costa Rica, Honduras.

Other areas: Ethiopia.

COUNTRIES APPLYING NO EXCHANGE RESTRICTIONS BUT PROHIBITING ENTIRELY IMPORTATION OF MANY CLASSES OF GOODS—

Latin America: Mexico, Peru.

COUNTRIES NOT OPERATING IMPORT LICENSES, PROHIBITIONS, OR EXCHANGE RESTRICTIONS—

Latin America: Cuba, Dominican Republic, El Salvador, Guatemala, Haiti, Panama.

Other areas: Liberia, Tangier International Zone.

The prime reason for this continued wide prevalence of direct trade controls is that few foreign countries are yet in a financial position to pay, at least in acceptable currencies, for the exceptionally large volume of products which their people want to import. Only second in importance is the fact that the currencies of the majority of countries are still not freely convertible. As a result, even those countries whose over-all balance of international payments may be quite satisfactory, and who hold funds in various foreign currencies earned from their surplus of exports to certain countries, often find themselves unable to pay for balances due particular third countries with which they would normally have an import surplus.

Moreover, from a commercial viewpoint, it is still true that adequate supplies of many important commodities are obtainable mainly from the countries of the Western Hemisphere which deal in dollars, principally the United States. The consequent inability of most countries to pay for all their needs from the dollar countries, with what goods and services they are currently furnishing the nationals of those countries, is what has created the central problem in world trade today. From its symptoms, this is often superficially referred to as "the dollar shortage."

Influence of Domestic Inflationary Pressures on Excessive Import Demand

The need of foreign products for postwar replenishment and most urgent rehabilitation has been fairly well satisfied by now in most countries, at least outside of Eastern Europe and the politically disturbed areas of Southern Asia and the Far East. However, the demand for imports has in many cases been kept high largely by domestic inflationary pressures. These have been partly induced by more or less controllable factors, such as enlarged governmental expenditures beyond current revenues, extensive programs for local development (official and private), and even speculative ventures in merchandise or real estate. The resulting increase in the amounts of money in local circulation, when not accompanied by corresponding addition to the supply of commodities or services, has been intensifying the demand for goods, forcing up prices, and making the obtainment of foreign products especially attractive.

Alongside their effort to restrict the supplies of incoming goods to what the country can afford to pay for currently, a number of foreign countries are prudently trying to reduce the volume of import demand. This is being sought through a variety of measures, including programs of consumer austerity, tightening up on credit for expansionist ventures, curtailment of governmental expenditures, and various methods for holding down overambitious or postponable local investment projects. Some governments are trying to curtail especially those projects which do not hold early promise of increasing the supply of goods which can replace those otherwise obtained from abroad, or of increasing the volume of exportable commodities.

United States Financial Aid to Europe and Japan a Bolster to General World Trade

As in the preceding year, the funds made available by the United States, under the Marshall Plan and the civilian-supply program for the occupied areas, helped directly to sustain the purchasing power for imports into most countries of Western Europe and into Japan. Indirectly, this has benefited not only suppliers of goods in the United States, but also those in various other countries from which procurement of supplies under these funds have been authorized. About one-third of the goods paid for from the grants and loans extended by the United States have been the products of countries other than the United States—principally Canada, Latin America, and the Marshall Plan countries themselves, thus indirectly supporting their exports and bolstering their general economies. To the extent of the grants and loans thus extended by the United States, which amounted to more than 5 billion dollars during 1949, there has been averted the curtailment of the over-all volume of international trade which might have taken place under the full application of the restrictive trade controls in operation in most foreign countries.

Since the demand in most countries for the products of the Western Hemisphere continued much greater than the dollars they could currently earn or draw from their shrunken reserves, nearly all members of the sterling area, many countries of Europe, and several of South America applied their import controls during the past year with special severity to trade with the dollar areas. With increased frequency, these countries have been denying licenses for the purchase of certain products from the United States and other dollar areas, while granting them quite freely for other countries, where they could more readily pay for such imports, even though at greater cost. The justification has been that it was necessary to apportion their limited dollar availabilities mainly for the products from the dollar areas most essential to their economies and not obtainable elsewhere.

While the markets in these countries have thus been curtailed for American producers of various consumers' products or other goods regarded as nonessential, thus far the over-all effect of the foreign import controls upon United States trade has usually been selective as among commodities, rather than restrictive of the total. Some countries have improved their holdings of gold and dollars during the year, and others have drawn down their limited reserves somewhat. In the aggregate, however, the nations of the world as a whole purchased American goods and services in 1949 fully up to the value of the proceeds from the goods and services they currently furnished the United States, plus the amount of the grants and loans abroad extended by the United States during the year.

Protectionist Element in Import Restrictions, Emergency or Otherwise

Most governments which have resorted to import license and exchange restrictions since the war justify their action on the ground indicated, namely, that during this highly disturbed period, their balance-of-payments position forces them to be sparing in the use of their limited foreign exchange earnings or reserves. They feel obliged to utilize them for the products most essential to the economy of their country, and to buy foreign goods where obtainable with the least drain upon their free funds. Although such programs have often involved violation of existing commitments to other countries, and discrimination in preferential import licensing according to source, they have usually been tolerated as emergency measures of temporary duration.

Indications have been multiplying during the past year, however, that the incidental temporary shields against competition accompanying such restrictions for balance-of-payment purposes are often coming to be regarded as vested rights. The efforts of the Western European countries to bring about the generally desired concerted relaxation of import quota restrictions, even among themselves, have been meeting considerable resistance from domestic producing interests, which have for several years enjoyed exceptional protection from competition for what now may clearly appear to be overexpanded or uneconomic operations.

When selecting the products that were to be restricted of importation or to be given the least favorable terms of payment, for the ostensible purpose of conserving foreign exchange, some governments of Latin America often appeared to be influenced not only by the relative essentiality of particular products, but also by the desire to afford additional protection or stimulation to domestic production in those lines, beyond that provided by the import duties.

In fact, the protective motive has appeared as a primary consideration in an appreciable number of restrictive measures adopted during 1949 by several of the Latin American governments, although it has figured also in the trade measures of governments elsewhere, if not so clearly or so frequently. Thus, Colombia, Venezuela, and Guatemala now make the granting of a license for certain foreign commodities conditional upon the prior purchase of similar products of domestic origin, sometimes prescribing the percentage that must be drawn from domestic sources. These restrictions do not seem related to any general balance-of-payments problem.

This tendency toward the unwarranted use of import restrictions for protective purposes is among the subjects to be considered at the meeting of the contracting parties to the General Agreement on Tariffs and Trade which is to open at Geneva in late February.

Western Europe

Despite recovery, high demand for dollar goods keeps restrictions on.—The overshadowing current problem in the trade relations of the countries of Western Europe arises from the fact that, while most of them succeeded during the past year in regaining and in some cases even surpassing their prewar volume of production, their import deficit with the dollar countries of the Western Hemisphere continued very large and even worsened during some parts of the year.

The rising ratio between the total exports of the Western European countries during 1949 and their total imports reflected a gratifying improvement in their internal economic condition and over-all balance of international payments. The increase in their exports, however, went almost entirely to other European countries and to overseas nondollar countries. In the face of their continued exceptional demand for the products of the Western Hemisphere, their failure to regain even their prewar share in supplying the import requirements of the dollar countries gave cause for apprehension.

As a corollary to the trade problem, Western European leaders have become concerned over the insufficient attention being given to promoting coördination of investments and production in the various countries participating in the European Recovery Program, "in order to avoid wasteful duplication on the one hand, and inadequate development of facilities on the other."[1] While the difficulties of officially directing the course of private capital investments are recognized, the problem is regarded as closely related to that of liberalization of trade among the Marshall Plan countries, on which active efforts are already under way, as later detailed. Progress along both lines is considered essential, not only to make the best

[1] This and other quoted passages in this section that carry no other attribution are from the "Second Report of the Organization for European Economic Cooperation," Paris, January 30, 1950.

use of the special resources and capacities of the various member countries, in the interest of the group as a whole, but also for the promotion of "a pattern of production that by earning or saving dollars will contribute to the final solution of the dollar problem."

While the dollar deficit of the Marshall Plan countries has been progressively reduced since 1947, the size of the remaining task is still large, and the attainment of even an approach to a close balance in the trade and payments between the Western European countries and the dollar area by 1952 is recognized as an extremely difficult task. It is in recognition of this fact that such strong calls are being heard for extraordinary efforts on the part of the member countries along several related lines during the second half of the ERP period, in order that, as American aid tapers off, Western Europe may be getting progressively into a better balanced position, and on a level enabling it to carry on thereafter without general financial crises or lowering of the standard of living.

Despite the bolster currently afforded by ERP aid, the inability of most Western European countries to pay for all they desired from the United States with what goods, services, and funds they could furnish directly in return, without further drain upon their shrunken reserves, has been prompting them to apply their import controls with especial severity to proposed purchases from the United States. During the past year they continued—and often even intensified—their efforts to hold down importation from the United States of various types of consumers' goods and others considered less essential, in order to reserve their limited dollar resources for the more indispensable supplies and equipment from that source.

The fact that the currencies of most foreign countries are still not freely convertible into dollars has prevented the use in the dollar markets of such credit balances in "soft currencies" as any of the Western European countries may have acquired through export surpluses to particular other markets. When possible, therefore, purchases were diverted to those countries where payment could be made either from such holdings of their particular currencies, or by the goods being exported under their many bilateral trade agreements with each other or with certain countries of South America which aim at a roughly balanced movement of goods that requires the least money settlement.

With one notable exception, the countries of Western Europe made no general changes during 1949 in their earlier restrictions on the importation of goods from the United States and other dollar areas. That exception was the United Kingdom, which announced its intention in June of cutting imports from dollar sources, chiefly the United States and Canada, by a further 25 per cent. (Because of its special bearing upon the trade controls of the other sterling areas, however, that action will be better touched upon in the later section on the British Commonwealth.)

Trade still limited by bilateralism and resistance to "nonessentials."—Intra-European trade continued to be carried on predominantly under the bilateral supply agreements earlier referred to, which had become typical of the commercial relations of Western European countries since the period of extreme shortages both of goods and of funds following the close of the war. Under these agreements, the contracting pair of countries generally undertake to grant licenses for the exportation and importation of agreed lists of products, and otherwise to facilitate their movement. Each shipper is paid in his own currency out of a "clearing account," but the lists and quantities of products to be facilitated have usually been built with the idea that the aggregate values of the goods moving between the two countries during a given period should approximate a balance or a particular ratio, with a limited "swing credit" usually provided for temporary overdrafts.

Many of the revisions during 1949 of these intra-European bilateral agreements, which usually run for a year, authorized the movement of enlarged lists of goods or increased commodity quotas during the new periods. In most cases, however, trade was still confined to such delimited exchanges, and the negotiations often continued to be marked by efforts to hold down the quantities which each country would agree to admit of various customary export products of the other which are now regarded as "nonessential."

Switzerland and Belgium are the only countries of Western Europe which have felt that they had a sufficiently strong over-all trade position to warrant them reducing their requirements for prior import licenses to limited lists of goods. Most other European countries, however, in dealing with these two hard-currency countries, were watchful to avoid developing large import balances from those sources, lest that cause them to lose gold or foreign exchange reserves in settlement.

After the three joint occupying authorities of the Western zones turned over to the new Federal Republic of Germany the authority to arrange its external trade relations directly, in the fall of 1949, the government of that country tried to be guided by liberal trade principles. In its particularly important trade agreement with France, the new government carried forward the program initiated by the Trizone authorities in the agreements concluded during the year with a number of other European countries. In these, the classes of goods still subject to import quotas into West Germany were reduced to limited "negative lists," in return for corresponding liberalizations of varying degree by the other contracting governments. The operation of this advanced program is being watched with interest.

Devaluation by Britain and Western Europe a step to reduce dollar deficits.—The latter months of 1949 were marked by earnest discussion of many plans for dealing with the twofold problem facing most countries of Western Europe, namely, how to reduce their trade deficits with the dollar countries, and how to open the way for larger trade exchanges with one another and their associated overseas territories, and for a generally freer interaction of their economies.

The effort to narrow the dollar gap took the form principally of seeking means for increasing the sale of their products in the dollar areas, and especially in the United States, although the trade programs projected by various of the Western European countries contemplate also further reductions in their imports from the dollar countries over the next few years, as American aid tapers off.

The devaluation of their currencies in terms of the dollar, initiated by Britain in September and soon followed by all the countries of Western Europe but Switzerland,[2] was a preparatory step in that direction. This step was expected to reduce the overly high export prices that had developed under the inflationary conditions which, varying only in degree, had characterized the domestic economies of nearly all of these countries since the war. Along with the more realistic realignment of the exchange values of their currencies, private commercial programs were initiated in the various Western European countries for more organized and intensive marketing of their respective export products in the United States and Canada, often with special assistance or inducements from their governments.

Move to loosen intra-European trade by gradual lifting of import quotas.—On the second part of the problem, the ERP countries gave joint consideration to various means for breaking through existing trade barriers, and the other national policies of the individual countries which were restricting the potential enlargement of markets for their expanding pro-

[2] Turkey, not physically part of Western Europe although a member of the ERP group, also did not devalue its currency in September, 1949. It had devalued the lira three years previously, and felt that its present export and price programs did not make further devaluation advisable at this time.

duction in one another's territory, and were obstructing the fuller measure of general economic coöperation envisaged in the Marshall Plan as essential to the recovery and sound reconstruction of Western Europe.

On the most immediate problem of bringing about a freer flow of trade among themselves, the chief concerns of most governments involved appeared to be two. How can such a program be carried out without increasing external trade debts and further reducing the country's financial reserves? By what means can we minimize the domestic economic disturbance, in the way of dislocation of local production and employment, that is likely to follow any sudden widening of competition with more effective producers in other parts of Europe?

The impetus to action was reënforced by the urging of Mr. Paul Hoffman, administrator of the ERP, that it was indispensable for the participating countries to get bold measures for concerted action into operation soon, while the support of United States funds was available to help cover the risks, in order to get into a position to carry on without extraordinary outside assistance after the Marshall Plan period.

As the first concrete step in that direction, the Council of the Organization for European Economic Cooperation—the organization of Ministers of the countries participating in the ERP—called upon the member governments to act simultaneously, by the end of the year, in freeing the products of the others from quotas or similar import restrictions to the extent of at least 50 per cent of past trade, in each of three categories: food and feed, raw materials, and manufactures. Some of the original submissions did not quite satisfy the OEEC Central Group, set up to evaluate the measures taken, and were returned for revision. By the turn of the year, however, each member country had put into effect quota eliminations which were accepted as covering approximately one-half of its past private imports from the others, although sometimes with important qualifications.[8]

[8] The criticisms expressed by the OEEC supervisory group on various of the lists submitted are worth noting, as illustrating the difficulties in the way of any rapid and uniform action toward trade liberalization on the part of a large number of countries with different interests and relations to each other.

It was doubted whether some of the programs would result in much actual enlargement of intra-European trade, when the lists were made up largely of those products which the country was already admitting freely in its own interest, while many of the competitive products remained restricted. Moreover, usually no change was offered with regard to imports effected directly by governments, which in some cases accounted for a sizable portion of the total; and at least one country maintained exchange control on the items freed of quota limitations. Finally, the benefits of the relaxations were in several cases withheld from certain of the economically stronger countries of Western Europe (particularly Belgium and Switzerland, less frequently, West Germany).

Early in 1950, the council tentatively agreed upon a series of future steps: (a) a reciprocal increase of liberalization to at least 60 per cent of imports on private account as soon as a satisfactory payments plan comes into force, which provides for the multilateral transfer of the currencies of member countries; (b) examination after midyear of possible further progress during 1950 toward 75 per cent liberalization, subject to progress being made in suppressing "practices that may prejudice free competition among European countries," which was understood to refer particularly to dual pricing and dumping; and (c) "in any event, quotas still existing after December 31, 1950, would have to be justified."

Decision on proposed intra-European currency clearing plan postponed.—In order to encourage the relaxation of quantitative restrictions, without aggravating the problem of settling for still larger uneven trade balances between particular pairs of countries, several plans were put forward in December, 1949, for the establishment of a European Payments Union, to replace the earlier arrangements for that purpose which had not proved entirely satisfactory.

Essentially, the various drafts have had the same general objective: to allow the clearing of trade balances of the individual countries with the ERP countries as a group, rather than bilaterally, by providing for the freer transferability of their currencies in the settlement of current accounts, with the maximum possible freedom also of invisible transactions (travel, interest payments, transportation costs, and so on). The net payment deficits of individual countries in relation to the group as a whole would be covered, under detailed arrangements still to be determined, by wider mutual accommodation among the member countries and by a pool of European currencies and of dollar funds, the latter allocated for the purpose out of the total amount advanced by the United States for the general European Recovery Program.[4]

The plans usually also contemplate inducements for individual countries to make such modifications of their internal economic policies, or of their exchange rates, as may be necessary to bring about a sounder adjustment of their over-all debtor or creditor positions. Many of the countries consider it essential to carry the program far enough to check the observed tendency toward undue or uneconomic expansion of production in par-

[4] In presenting the appropriation request to Congress for the third year of the ERP, in February, 1950, the Administrator stated that it is the plan "to withhold at the start from allocations to individual countries not less than 600 million dollars from the aggregate 1950–1951 appropriation, which will be available to encourage the aggressive pursuit of a program of liberalized trade and payments," part of which will be used to support a proposed European Payments Plan.

ticular lines, under the investment programs projected in individual Western European countries, and to eliminate governmental measures resulting in different prices for export than for domestic sales. The goal is to secure for all participating countries, "to the fullest extent possible, the advantage of a large competitive market with increased specialization of production."

Thus far, it has not been found possible to harmonize the different views among the governments involved, as to the degree to which the new Payments Union would supersede existing arrangements, the scope of its functions and authority, and various collateral questions. Under the circumstances, the council of the OEEC voted, at its meeting on February 1, 1950, to postpone decision on this project pending further study and negotiation.

Little progress on plans for trade liberalization among smaller groups.— In addition to plans designed to make possible the comprehensive participation of all the ERP countries, various arrangements are under discussion whereby smaller groups of Western European countries might carry further among themselves the freeing of trade movements and of currency transfers.

Most prominent have been those groupings which, from the initials of their participants, have come to be known as FINEBEL (France, Italy, Netherlands, Belgium, and Luxemburg) and UNISCAN (United Kingdom and Scandinavia). The general Payments Union and these special groupings are regarded by some as possible intermediate steps toward a more general trade or economic integration of all Western Europe. An early beginning in that direction has been strongly urged, although it is recognized as obviously a long-term objective.

Among the various plans considered during the past few years looking to a full customs union of certain smaller groups of European countries, or possibly an even fuller merger of their economies, 1949 saw progress only on the part of the Benelux countries (Belgium, the Netherlands, and Luxemburg), and that was limited to the further partial lifting of quota restrictions among them, and continued unification of excise taxes.

The Nordic Committee for Economic Cooperation found that it was not feasible at present to realize a customs union among the Scandinavian countries. The treaty calling for the working out of a customs union between France and Italy, signed in March, 1949, has not yet been ratified by either parliament.

The study group set up by the ERP countries in 1947, to develop the basis for a possible comprehensive European Customs Union, made progress during 1949 toward common ground on a number of technical aspects that would be important in any such broad merger of European economies as might later be found feasible.

Eastern Europe

Such changes in the measures for the control of their foreign trade as the countries of Eastern Europe made during 1949 have been in the direction of the more complete vesting in one or more governmental monopoly organizations of authority for the regulation, if not the actual conduct, of all import and export transactions. Also in the Soviet Zone of Germany, it is reported, foreign firms must now contract directly with the official trading organizations.

No perceptible difference after Soviet bloc sets up Economic Council.— No significant developments were reported during the year under the plan announced in January, 1949, for the formation of a Council for Mutual Economic Aid, between the Soviet Union and five of the countries in the Soviet sphere, for the declared purpose of periodic exchange of economic experience and mutual assistance on technical and commodity matters. Under the Czechoslovak-Polish five-year agreement for larger trade exchanges and for continuous coöperation in their industrial programs, which had been earlier concluded in 1947, the past year saw progress in the exchange of technical aid and in plans for the joint use of the Polish-held port of Stettin.

The trade arrangements which the countries of Eastern Europe are known to have concluded or revised during 1949, with one another and with the Soviet Union, appeared to follow the established pattern of simply providing for the reciprocal supply of specified quantities of various goods during a given period, generally a year. Higher levels of trade exchanges were commonly projected for the new periods, but the trade values in both directions were usually expected to approximate a close balance. Exceptional in this respect were the reported deliveries by Russia to Poland of industrial equipment under a ten-year credit, in accordance with the agreement concluded in 1948, designed to advance particularly the development of certain heavy industries in the former German territory of Upper Silesia which has recently been "recovered" by Poland.

Yugoslavia turns West for trade after Soviet bloc suspends relations.— The relations of the other Eastern European countries with Yugoslavia constituted a notable exception. Practically all of them have by now sharply curtailed—if not totally suspended—trade relations with that country, following the example of Russia, after political difficulties had developed in 1948 between Yugoslavia and the Cominform. To replace the canceled deliveries from the other Eastern European countries, Yugoslavia has been making arrangements with a number of the Western countries for obtaining the products most essential to its economic program. These are being purchased partly on credit but mainly from the proceeds of the sale of its various raw materials, which Yugoslavia is now in a position to dispose of more freely by reason of its release from its former Eastern commitments.

Limitation on goods to offer prevents larger exchanges with the West.—At the same time that they were trying to intensify economic relations with each other, Yugoslavia excepted, the countries in the Soviet sphere have been making active efforts to expand their trade with the Western European countries, and now apparently with official Russian approval. Czechoslovakia and Poland have been perhaps the most outspoken of the group, in making known their need for a variety of raw materials and industrial equipment not obtainable in Eastern Europe, and their desire for larger consumer markets in the West.

The heavy commitments by the countries in the Soviet sphere for shipments to Russia and to one another have constituted decided limitations upon the possible volume of their outside trade. In the absence of credits, their purchases from the Western countries were usually limited closely to what could be paid for with the proceeds of their current exports to such individual countries. In one known instance, the Soviet Union reportedly promised to extend a loan in gold and free currency, of unknown size, so that Czechoslovakia could finance its necessary imports of industrial raw materials from the West.

In addition to annual renewals of the agreements earlier entered into between various Western European countries and those in the East, usually providing for the reciprocal facilitation to each other of supplies of particular commodities of roughly equivalent total value, a number of East-West agreements of special importance were concluded during 1949. Perhaps most notable were the agreements negotiated by the United Kingdom with Poland, and with Yugoslavia, for extensive interchanges of essential commodities over a period of five years. The revised agreement between West Germany and Czechoslovakia provided for a several-fold increase in the year ahead over the recent movement of goods between them; and an agreement concluded late in 1949 between Western and Eastern Germany envisaged a sizable exchange of their distinctive products between the two areas over the next twelve months.

Most of the Eastern European countries have suspended publication of their detailed trade returns. Such records as are available from other sources, however, indicate the following: a substantial increase during 1949 over the preceding year in the exports from Western European countries to Eastern Europe; a somewhat less marked increase in their imports from countries in the Soviet sphere; and a decline in Western purchases from the Soviet Union. In a measure, this represented the completion of deliveries under earlier agreements on orders requiring long periods of production, and balanced off a reverse movement observed during 1948, when the shipments from Eastern Europe to the Western countries exceeded appreciably the value of the products obtained from them.

It has been estimated that, after allowing for price changes during the past decade, the recent improved level of East-West trade—including West Germany with Western Europe and the Soviet Zone with Eastern Europe, but excluding intra-German trade—still represents less than half of the volume of goods that used to be exchanged between the two regions before the war. If Germany were entirely excluded from the calculations, the recovery of East-West trade among the other countries concerned is estimated to have reached fully 75 per cent of its 1938 level, although the very important role which prewar Germany played in the trade of Eastern Europe before the war renders any calculation without Germany rather unreal.

Representatives of twenty-four European governments from both regions and of the United States, who met at Geneva in February, 1949, under the auspices of the United Nations Economic Commission for Europe, agreed to explore the possibilities of a collective approach to expanded trade between Eastern and Western Europe, and the Secretariat was charged with developing the groundwork by inquiries to the individual governments. At a later meeting in May, the Secretariat reported that it had found it possible to draw up fairly accurate lists of the things the Western countries needed from the East, according to their long-term import programs, but that it had not been able to obtain sufficient information about Eastern import programs or plans for future production for export.

No agreed definite procedure had yet been developed, by the beginning of 1950, for effecting the necessary exchange of information upon which the desired multilateral East-West trade negotiations could be based.

British Commonwealth

The past year saw a considerable enlargement in the volume of British production, and the devoting of a large proportion of that output to foreign markets, at the cost of continued domestic austerity. The result was an appreciable improvement in the general balance-of-payments position of the United Kingdom. The increased volume of exports went chiefly to the nondollar countries, however, especially to the various parts of the British Commonwealth and to other countries in the sterling area. Established commercial connections, absence of payment problems, and often eagerness of buyers when the purchase of similar products from dollar areas was not being authorized, were among the considerations which apparently made those markets more attractive to British producers.

Aggravated dollar deficit prompts further import cut and devaluation.— The dollar deficit of the sterling countries as a group was aggravated during the fore part of the year, following a temporary falling off in United States purchases of materials from the sterling countries, at the very time that they were increasing their imports from North America. The external financial crisis thus precipitated brought into sharp relief the large continuing imbalance between the sterling and the dollar areas. This led to a decision in June by nearly all of the countries in the sterling area to curtail importations from the dollar areas, mainly the United States and Canada, by a further 25 per cent for a period of at least a year. Some of the British colonies tightened up even more.

The obvious inadequacy of that step alone, the apparent withholding of foreign orders in the expectation of a currency change, and, to a less extent, concern over the frequency of indirect transactions financed in open markets through so-called "cheap sterling"—all contributed to the announcement by the British Government in September of a 30 per cent devaluation of the pound in terms of the dollar. This was promptly followed by similar action on the part of all the sterling-area countries except Pakistan, and by a 9 per cent cut in the Canadian dollar. The great importance of this group of countries in world trade soon forced most of the countries of Western Europe and several overseas areas also to devalue their currencies, by the same or different amounts.

Drive to increase dollar sales, partly by diversion from sterling markets.— The sharp devaluation of sterling was a preparatory step, calculated to facilitate reduction of the trade deficit with the dollar countries: on the export side, through larger sales as a result of price reductions or through higher dollar earnings; and on the import side, through further discouragement of imports from dollar sources as a result of their increased cost. It gave impetus to the various other means under consideration for dealing with the intrinsic problem of increasing the sale of British goods in North American markets.

Since most export products of the overseas sterling countries that could find a market in North America are basic raw materials, the demand for which moves primarily with the level of industrial activity, their sales are not very expansible by promotive effort. The problem therefore seemed to narrow largely to one of building up larger dollar markets for the manufactured products of the United Kingdom. To this end, programs were launched by various British trade groups for more organized and thorough marketing campaigns in the United States and Canada, and the British Government offered incentives in the way of financial guaranties to cover losses in market surveys, sales-promotion programs, and the maintenance of inventories in those countries.

Among the internal measures put forward that were directed to the same end have been: the cutting back of capital expenditures, both at home and abroad; improved production arrangements to increase per capita output and reduce costs of products; and preferential official allocations of raw materials and other productive facilities to where they could increase the flow of goods to North American markets.

In the present state of full utilization of manpower and productive capacity in the United Kingdom, increasing the sale of British products in dollar markets amounts largely to diversion of shipments from sterling areas. This fact was apparently in mind when the Chancellor of the Exchequer announced that the United Kingdom could not afford further foreign loans or credits, nor the release of sterling balances accumulated during the war, to the same extent as before. A good part of the British merchandise recently exported to certain markets, especially to various countries in the sterling area, has constituted a paying off in goods of the war debt to those countries, without their being offset by equivalent supplies of goods to the United Kingdom. It has now been declared necessary to have a larger part of British exports sent to countries where they can earn dollars or other currencies acceptable in payment for the large volumes of imports needed from those sources.

Following devaluation and the initiation of the other measures cited, the volume of exports from Great Britain and from certain of the Dominions was stimulated during the last quarter of 1949, although unevenly and partly in a nonrepeating manner. The deterioration of the United Kingdom's dollar trading position was arrested, as was the drain upon its gold and dollar reserves to cover import balances with Belgium and some other European countries. The full, long-term effects of the currency devaluations and of the recent pattern of movements in world commerce may not be clear for some time, however, until a whole chain of adjustments has been completed.

Most sterling areas follow British action on currency and import cuts.—As indicated, nearly all of the sterling-area governments followed the action of the United Kingdom, in devaluing their currencies and in realigning their import programs to effect the requested further curtailment of imports requiring payment in dollars. Australia and New Zealand, which had already reduced their deficit in trade with the United States and Canada through the earlier application of very selective import controls, were reported as finding it difficult to cut their dollar imports further, in view of the need of their economies for capital goods obtainable mainly from dollar countries. In fact, Australia had to get an advance from the International Monetary Fund to meet purchase commitments given before the new dollar curtailment.

New Zealand provided no basic allocation under its 1950 licensing schedule for purchases from the United States, Canada, Belgium, or Switzerland, the last two being also regarded as "scarce currency" countries. Each application is to be given consideration in relation to actual requirements. All New Zealand importers were requested to hold such purchases during the first half of the year to the minimum, in order to reduce calls upon the joint sterling-area dollar fund at London.

The Union of South Africa had earlier in 1949 introduced an exceptionally sharp reduction in licensable imports from sterling as well as dollar sources, following a period of very heavy foreign purchases, with a resulting sharp decline in the country's foreign exchange reserves. Owing to its large production of gold, the devaluation of sterling has since somewhat improved South Africa's position.

The various British colonies, while following the same general program indicated from London, sometimes carried the restrictions on imports from dollar sources even further. After some total suspensions, several of them are now holding the authorization of dollar imports to very limited ranges of essential products not elsewhere obtainable.

Canada became concerned over the effect upon its future export trade of the sharp devaluation by the countries in the sterling area, and of their general decision further to curtail imports from dollar sources. Canadian dependence upon foreign trade is much greater than that of the United States, and Canada's trade has been highly concentrated upon the British and other Commonwealth markets, with which until now it had on the whole been well maintained. The immediate situation was tempered by the fact that the United States found it possible to finance during the past year, under the European Recovery Program, a large part of the wheat and other Canadian products planned for shipment to the United Kingdom.

As a result, partly of this aid and partly of the enforced earlier contraction of its imports from the United States since late 1947, Canada increased it hard-currency reserves during 1949. This allowed it again to permit the importation of fresh fruits and vegetables from the United States, and to lift the new restrictions on certain iron and steel products after enforcing them for only a few months. Further relaxation of Canadian restrictions on a range of important products supplied mainly by the United States was announced early in 1950, to go into effect in April and July.

After the union of Newfoundland with Canada in April, 1949, duties were lifted between the two areas, and outside trade with Newfoundland became subject to the tariff of Canada and its more restrictive system of import control. As a transitional measure, the intention was announced of giving special consideration for a time to the former dependence of Newfoundland upon the United States for certain essential supplies, although the year's trade record showed a distinct falling off.

Bulk-purchase program curtailed for materials, continued for foods.— The program initiated by the United Kingdom during the war, for long-term official purchase agreements with the different British Dominions and colonies, especially for wheat, meat, and other foodstuffs and certain raw materials, has been altered during the past year in several respects. As world scarcities were relieved, various raw materials were returned to private channels. On the other hand, the United Kingdom made a fifteen-year agreement with Australia to take the meat to be produced under a new project for expansion of cattle raising in that Dominion. Meanwhile, a new five-year agreement was negotiated with Argentina for supplies of meat to the British market, to be balanced off in value by the supply of petroleum and other products desired by Argentina.

Measures were carried forward during the year in various British colonies, especially in Africa, to organize local producers in bodies designed to deal with the United Kingdom Government as sole or main buyer of their principal export products. That government now purchases, or arranges for the purchase of, about half of Britain's imports, chiefly in the line of foodstuffs.

Latin America

Prevalence of direct import controls and bilateral-balancing agreements.—While some degree of direct control over their imports, beyond requiring the payment of specified duties, had been exercised in a fluctuating way by a number of the countries of Latin America before World War II, since the middle of 1947 most of the twenty southern republics have come to require an official license as a condition of importation of many if not all products, or to control the remittance of foreign exchange in payment for imports, or both. The governments involved have declared themselves obliged to resort to such direct methods of controlling the imports into their territories, in order to check the drain upon their exchange reserves built up during the recent war—a drain that has resulted from the exceptionally heavy demand of their peoples for various foreign products during the past few years, to a value far beyond what the country was currently earning from its exports.

Even after the understandably large deferred demand for foreign products right after the war, for necessary replenishment and rehabilitation, had been fairly well satisfied, the demand for imported commodities of different kinds has been kept high in most Latin American countries by domestic inflationary pressures. Taken together, the exceptional volume of expenditures by governments, and of private capital investments of various types, and the speculative ventures in merchandise or real estate—which in varying degree have marked the economies of most of these countries during the past few years—have usually increased sharply the amounts of money in circulation, without creating a corresponding increase in purchasable goods or services. The results have been sharp upward movements in their general domestic price levels and in the income of certain classes—much sharper than in the United States, their principal foreign source of supply—and a consequent accentuated desire for the purchase of foreign products and equipment.

During the past year, Mexico, Nicaragua, and Costa Rica in North America, and most of the countries of South America, have operated their systems of import licenses or exchange control more stringently, or at least more selectively. The object has been to curtail directly, or to discourage by increased cost, the importation into their markets of particular classes of foreign goods which they consider noτ very essential or which were replaceable with domestic products.

Only Cuba, Venezuela, and certain of the smaller Caribbean republics have been in a sufficienly strong balance-of-payments position to continue free of both exchange control and broadly applied import license systems, although even Venezuela and Guatemala have recently introduced quantitative restrictions on the importation of a number of selected products that are also produced within those countries.

In Argentina, Brazil, Chile, and Peru, the import control systems have been applied with especial severity to various commodities from dollar sources. Those governments justify such action on the ground that their dollar availabilities are very limited, and that they can more readily finance the purchase of similar goods from Great Britain or some other European country. Although the prices of the European goods might be higher, they are able to obtain them more easily, either against the otherwise unusable balances in a particular country's currency which they had to their credit from previous sales there, or against the goods planned for exportation to the given country under their current bilateral trade agreement.

The fact is that the inconvertibility of most European currencies has led a number of South American countries to the practice that has been common among the European countries themselves since the war, of entering into agreements with various of those countries to facilitate the movement of specified products to each other, but on a balanced basis. The general aim is that the aggregate value of the goods moving in each direction shall approximate an annual balance, so as to minimize the foreign exchange problems in settling for surpluses on either side.

The 1949 revision of the Anglo-Argentine agreement—which aims even more than its predecessors at a close balance between the value of the meat and other Argentine commodities supplied to Britain and that of the fuel and other products expected to be obtained by Argentina from British sources—was a striking illustration of that trend. That arrangement has superseded what before the war was one of the historic triangles in international trade, whereby Argentina regularly used part of the proceeds from its normally large export surpluses to the United Kingdom to cover its normally large import surpluses from the United States.

While the existence of such bilateral-balancing agreements has been cited by various South American governments as justifying their diverting the importation of many products from established dollar sources to European suppliers, complaint has been heard during the past year that these agreements are not working out satisfactorily from the viewpoint of the contracting Latin American countries themselves. It has often meant shipping products on credit, and then trying to get payment in such goods as were available from those countries where they had credit balances or clearing agreements. In a number of cases, the unsatisfactory operation of these bilateral agreements has led to further curtailing of shipments under them or even suspending of shipments for periods.

Brazil and Mexico are the principal Latin American countries that experimented during the past year in outright barter deals, official or private, with soft-currency countries. They had the double object of avoiding the exchange problem involved in paying for the imports sought, and of helping dispose of certain secondary export products of their own. The volume of goods moving under such arrangements has not been very large.

Frequency of exchange manipulations to curb imports and aid exports.—As part of broad programs to redress the balance of their payments and to stabilize their general economies, Mexico and Peru decided during 1949 upon sharp general devaluations of their currencies below the previous official par value. Each adopted a single rate of exchange that was close to the free market value of its currency and which, with the support of certain internal anti-inflationary measures, it felt it could maintain without resorting to foreign exchange restrictions. While still prohibiting the importation of a sizable range of products from other than sterling sources, Peru took particularly bold action in allowing exporters full use of their foreign exchange proceeds, and in doing away with exchange permits for all goods permitted to be imported.

Argentina, Uruguay, and Chile, without going to a single rate of exchange, devalued their currencies by varying amounts for transactions in different categories of commodities, and in the case of Argentina the rate is variable also according to the other country involved. In fact, the majority of the Latin American countries using exchange control have, to some degree, been operating multiple-exchange-rate systems for transactions involving different classes of commodities.

During the past year, most of these countries resorted in some measure to what might be described as further selective depreciation. In order to tighten their import restrictions, either they required that the exchange for remittance abroad in payment for the less essential foreign commodities be bought at rates higher than the official or previously prevailing rates, or they shifted more products into the categories subject to those unfavorable exchange rates.

The general currency depreciations effected during the past year by various Latin American countries had as one of their purposes the stimulation of foreign demand for their export products, by thus reducing the prices in terms of foreign currencies. A number of other American Republics sought the same objective through other means. Either they offered more than the official rate of exchange for the foreign currencies earned by particular export products, or they reduced the percentage of such funds which exporters are required to turn over for local currency at the official parity, allowing them to retain a larger percentage for disposal in the higher free exchange market. Mexico reinforced the stimulus to its exports from its currency depreciation by reducing the rate of the export surtaxes collected on many commodities since the peso was unpegged in August, 1948.

Foreign exchange budgeting helps clear up debts and regulate imports.—As means of stabilizing the general balance-of-payments position of various Latin American countries and improving their commercial credit abroad, the practice has been growing among them during the past year of setting up a budget for current foreign exchange earnings, and a regular method of allocations to the various demands upon those earnings. This practice is designed to clear off progressively the volume of unpaid foreign commercial debts, and to hold the volume of the newly authorized importations close to the foreseeable foreign exchange income with which to pay for it, in the currency needed for payment, even if that means further limiting the range or quantities of the products importable from abroad.

The arrangements for diverting definite portions or amounts out of current earnings for the gradual settlement of unpaid past importations appear already to be showing results. Colombia cleared up its commercial backlog by the fall of 1949; Brazil is reported approaching a cleanup by the middle of 1950; and Nicaragua and several other smaller countries are making progress in that direction. Argentina, with the heaviest debt accumulation, decided last May to set aside 20 per cent (later raised to 30 per cent) of its current dollar earnings to be applied to the gradual payment of its outstanding commercial obligations over the next few years.

The very severity with which the import controls of certain countries have been applied during the past year or two, particularly in South America, has served in a number of cases to improve the trading prospects with them for the longer run. It has not only helped to clear off their debt backlog, but is bringing about a better over-all balance between the imports and exports of those countries, and is putting them into a better position to pay promptly for those goods that are permitted importation.

As the result of these tightenings of trade controls, exports from the United States to Latin America are now made up to a greater extent than formerly of the more essential types of products. In total value, however, they are still running at a level several times that of prewar, although well below that of the early postwar replenishment period. An increasing number of the other American Republics which normally maintained a favorable balance in their trade with the United States are regaining that prewar relation. The over-all gap between Latin American imports and exports with the United States had considerably narrowed by the end of 1949.

Sharp shifts in prices of export staples reflected in trade controls.—The dominant influence of the trend in commodity prices upon trade controls and general economic policies, when a country depends upon a limited number of export products for its earnings of foreign exchange, was again strikingly illustrated during the past year in Latin America.

The drop in the market price for copper reduced the foreign exchange income of Chile so far below the amount anticipated as to lead to a tightening of the country's import restrictions, and to greater efforts to divert purchases to countries where payment would involve least drain upon free funds. The decline in the price of tin which, similarly, made more difficult the balance-of-payments problem of Bolivia, prompted that government to tighten up its exchange control on imports and to offer exchange concessions for increased mineral production for export.

On the other hand, the sharp rise in the market price for coffee since late in 1949 is helping Brazil, Colombia, and several of the smaller coffee-producing countries to clear off old debts, to replenish their reserves, and generally to improve their market position for the period ahead.

Major Asiatic Areas

Exceptional influence of political developments on trade potentials.—In many of the countries of Asia which played important roles in international commerce before the war, and where conditions have since continued highly abnormal, the political developments during 1949 may have a decided influence upon the facility for trading with them during the period ahead.

One need only recall the prominence in the general news of the past year of these events in Asia: on the *trade restrictive side,* the spread of communist control over continental China; the continued civil warfare in French Indo-China; the internal disturbances in Burma; and the disputes between India and Pakistan on both political and economic issues—and on the *favorable* side, the settlement of the political difficulties in the former Netherlands Indies by setting up an independent Republic of the United States of Indonesia, as an equal partner in a Netherlands Indonesian Union; and the transfer from SCAP to the Japanese Government of the authority to regulate the foreign trade of that country.

The expanding military control of the Chinese communists during the year, which by the end of 1949 had come to embrace most of continental China, has already cut off important lines of commerce with the Western world, and has rendered the conditions of access to the supplies and markets of that vast area difficult and unpredictable.

The basic system of license and exchange control formerly in operation under the Nationalist Government was taken over and tightened up by the communist authorities. The most distinctive commercial development in Communist China, however, has been the program for concentrating both the domestic and external trade in most commodities in the hands of huge state-controlled trading organizations.

All of Manchuria's foreign trade is now reported handled through such monopolistic organizations, and a considerable part of the external commerce with Northern and Central China is conducted under their control, with the area of foreign trade left to the private merchant becoming more and more limited. The tendency toward such channeling appears to be spreading southward, as the consolidation of political control proceeds.

Owing to the Nationalist blockade and the mining of the approaches to Shanghai and the ports south as far as Indo-China, access to those regions has become highly precarious. As a result, Hong Kong, the British Crown Colony off the coast of South China, which had traditionally been important as a trade entrepôt for much of Southeast Asia, has developed even greater prominence in recent months as a focal point for conducting trade with a large part of China.

Japanese yen stabilized and private trade conditions simplified.—In April, 1949, a single basic foreign exchange rate of 360 yen to the dollar was established, to replace the widely ranging multiple exchange rates which had prevailed. This eased the way for the reorganization and simplification of the whole system for control of the country's foreign trade, and for transferring its regulation to the Japanese Government, under the general supervision of the Occupying Authorities.

Since December 1, Japanese exporters have been able to negotiate directly with foreign buyers on all terms of the contract, and export licenses have been required only for special types of transactions and certain designated commodities. All but a very small part of the export trade has been returned to private commercial channels, and arrangements for business transactions have been greatly simplified. Floor prices were abolished in the fall, but safeguards were provided against dumping or unfair competition. Export subsidies were also withdrawn during the year.

Imports are programed quarterly in accordance with the availability of foreign exchange currently earned by Japanese exports, and lists of commodities approved for importation are published from time to time. Beginning January, 1950, such imports into Japan are being handled on a private basis. Those import commodities which are purchased under United States appropriations continue to be handled on the governmental level; they now account for something less than half of the total importations.

Depleted Philippine reserves, from overbuying, forces drastic import cuts.—With the tapering off of the sizable funds that had been flowing from the United States to the Philippine Republic, for war-damage claims, army pay, and related purposes, the new government found that the large excess of imports during the last few years, beyond what was warranted by current earnings from exports, had seriously depleted the country's foreign exchange reserve. This prompted a series of steps, during the latter months of 1949, for the declared purpose of curtailing drastically the importation of luxuries and articles considered nonessential, especially consumers' goods, so that the funds available could be used for the importation of capital goods for the rehabilitation of the country.

In November, the Central Bank imposed a selective curb on credits for the importations of nonessentials. In December, the list of commodities formerly subject to license control was considerably expanded, and the import quotas previously authorized were drastically reduced. Shortly thereafter, all foreign exchange transactions were subjected to license. By these measures, Philippine officials hope to reduce the country's imports by 200 million dollars annually, thus bringing the value of imports to about the level of the country's current exports.

Indonesian independence promising for trade but dollar imports restricted.—The amicable settlement toward the close of 1949 of the political difficulties between the Netherlands and the former Netherlands Indies, and the emergence of the Republic of the United States of Indonesia, are expected to bring about more stable conditions generally within these islands. That should facilitate recovery toward prewar level in the quantities available for exportation of the various raw materials for which this region had long been an important source. With the cessation of civil strife, the anticipated greater availability of imported consumers' goods for the native population is expected to serve as incentive to help step up output, and to bring down prices of Indonesian export products closer to world levels.

In March, 1949, the former practice of allocating licenses among the importers primarily on the basis of their prewar share of the trade in the specific product was discontinued, at least with regard to imports from soft-currency countries—with such trade now reported open to all bona fide importers. The "historic rights" system of allocation was reported as still figuring in connection with the limited volume of imports authorized from dollar areas, principally the United States, Canada, and Japan. Owing to its limited dollar income, even with the allocation from the Netherlands of certain ERP funds, the government severely restricted buying in dollar markets during 1949, preferring to license imports from soft-currency areas when obtainable on equal terms.

The new authorities are understood to be continuing the general system of licenses and exchange control developed under the previous regime for regulation of the country's foreign trade.

Political and currency differences cause India-Pakistan trade impasse.— The commercial situation of both India and Pakistan has been overshadowed by the political difficulties between these two new countries in carrying through the partition of the subcontinent they jointly occupy, especially over the issue of Kashmir. During the past year, that has been complicated by new economic difficulties, arising from the fact that India devalued its currency in September along with other countries in the sterling area, while Pakistan chose to maintain the former official exchange value of its rupee.

A new Indo-Pakistan agreement was concluded in June, 1949, for the reciprocal supply of certain essential commodities and without restriction by exchange control between them. The provisions and spirit of those negotiations held out the prospect of tempering the effect of the import duties and export controls which, since March, 1948, have been hampering the normal movement of goods between their highly interdependent economies. However, this broke down almost completely after their divergent currency action and the consequent spread between their price levels, and the insistence of each government upon continuing trade only on the basis of its own valuation of the rupee. Between export embargoes and import boycotts, legal commerce between India and Pakistan is reported almost at a standstill.

Both countries have recently been trying to break away from their former close dependence upon the supplies and markets of the other. India has sought to satisfy its needs for raw cotton and for wheat from overseas sources, including the United States, and is planning the expansion of jute growing. On its part, Pakistan is trying to develop the direct exportation and some local processing of its raw jute, to shift some jute acreage to rice, and to orient its source of supplies of various commodities to outside countries.

The trade impasse between India and Pakistan is creating difficult problems also for other countries, in obtaining their accustomed supplies of various important products from this region. Most notably, the local problem of getting continued supplies for the operation of the burlap and cotton mills of India, which have long depended for their raw materials upon the region now under Pakistan, has become a problem also for the outside countries that had been the regular buyers of the products of those mills.

India announces wider range of imports; Pakistan tightens controls.— Both India and Pakistan undertook to carry out the general agreement of the sterling countries, last June, to curtail further by 25 per cent their over-all importations from dollar countries. Beyond that, however, they have recently followed somewhat different programs in their commercial relations with outside countries, through varying operation of their import-licensing controls.

India improved its balance-of-payments position as the year went on, as the combined result of several factors: the severe curtailment of imports from both sterling and dollar sources under the restrictive controls in operation during much of 1949; the increase in the value of its exports; and the sizable advances from the International Monetary Fund and loans from the World Bank. This allowed the Indian Government to announce, for 1950, the resumption of imports of various commodities that had for some time been prohibited, and the freer admission of various other products of an essential character. The division of the expected trade increase between dollar and soft-currency areas is not yet known, although a reduced over-all allocation for hard-currency imports has been indicated.

Pakistan, after a period of more liberal admission of foreign products than India, decided in the fall of 1949 to tighten its quantitative control of imports. It suspended for a time the open general license under which most products from the soft-currency areas had been admitted quite freely, and limited licenses for most imports from hard-currency countries by definite monetary ceilings, with luxury goods closely restricted. The total allocation of foreign exchange for commercial imports for the first half of 1950 is to be substantially the same as during the preceding period, but with distinct concentration of such funds for the purchase of productive equipment and essential manufactured goods.

Both India and Pakistan carried further during the year their programs for the selective removal of restrictions and taxes on the exportation of many of their staple products, in order to improve their trade balances and general financial positions.

1950

TRADE APPROACHES NORMALIZATION UNTIL KOREA BRINGS SCRAMBLE FOR SUPPLIES

The year 1950 brought the most marked improvement since World War II in the economic strength and balance-of-payments position of most countries of the noncommunist world and, generally speaking, goods have seldom moved between countries in larger volume or with higher profitability. Yet, paradoxically, this general commercial improvement was due partly to the worsening of the international political situation, and that fact is exerting a strong influence upon the current trend in the foreign trade policies of the nations.

A considerable number of governments made appreciable relaxations of varying scope in the operation of their import controls during 1950. This tendency to allow foreign goods to come in more freely became particularly marked during the latter months of the year, when the emergency situation stimulated a general eagerness for acquiring stocks of various foreign products. That, however, soon brought a tightening of export controls on the part of some of the most important suppliers to international markets.

In fact, after foreign traders have for some years come to regard the complex structures of governmental import controls as the prime limitation upon their activities, their concern appears to be shifting. During recent months, commercial opinion has been growing both in the United States and abroad that, for manufactured products as well as raw materials, the state of supplies and the strictness of the controls in the principal exporting countries might become more decisive for the course of trade during the period ahead than the conditions of admission into the importing countries.

Toward the close of the year, pressures became insistent from various directions for setting up some form of international machinery for dealing with the developing world shortages in raw materials, to increase their availability and to provide for their equitable distribution and effective use among the free nations.

Recuperative Forces Checked by Emergency Pressures After Midyear

The general trends in world commerce during the first six months of 1950 were, in important respects, markedly different from those of the remainder of the year.

Encouraged by their progressive recovery over the recent past in production, monetary stability, and trade balance, a number of governments had already made a beginning during the first half of 1950 toward liberalizing their license and exchange restrictions, which have been the dominant methods of import control in most countries since World War II. The most pronounced steps were those taken by the countries of Western Europe to facilitate their trade exchanges with each other. Moderate relaxations in their general import restrictions were put into effect by Canada and by several of the South American governments.

Since the middle of the year, however, the world trade situation has been dominated by the emergency developments arising out of the invasion of southern Korea, namely, the rearmament plans of the North Atlantic Treaty Organization countries and others, the wide moves for increased purchases of essential foreign materials, and the immediate sharp rises in the prices of many primary commodities. These have come to overshadow the more normal recuperative forces in determining much of the course of international trading, and also the character of the new official measures being taken for its regulation.

In a matter of a few months, these new developments have already influenced the course of commercial policy in several significant respects. A considerable number of governments in various parts of the world, especially in the Western Hemisphere, have been prompted to take bolder steps toward relaxing the operation of their import control systems, although certain important countries—notably most members of the sterling area—

have been holding back out of caution, especially from easing their curbs on imports from dollar sources. At the same time, the practice is spreading for governments to impose or extend restrictions of various types upon the exportation of their national products, or to levy high export duties on certain of their natural products currently enjoying high demand.[1]

A possible new turn to the course of trade policy was projected toward the close of 1950, when pressure grew from several directions for the adoption of joint—or coördinated—action to regulate the distribution and prices of raw materials, especially those essential to the rearmament effort. Intensive consultations on this subject have been going on among various groups of governments. The only definite step thus far has been procedural. Under joint Anglo-Franco-American auspices, the principal countries producing and consuming certain basic products have been invited to participate in a series of standing international commodity groups, centered in Washington. These commodity groups are to consider and recommend, to the countries of the free world, the specific coöperative actions best calculated to increase the production and availability of particular materials in short supply, and to assure their most effective distribution and use.

Continuation of Easy Trading and High Level of Exchanges Uncertain

As 1951 opened, the peoples of most countries outside the communist orbit are freer to purchase foreign goods than they have been for several years past—although often not yet as freely from dollar as from nondollar sources—and they are more able to pay for them. They look forward to a continuation of the recent high level of international trade, even though it may be subject to more official regulation and materially altered in pattern. The unpredictable state of international trade under present conditions is illustrated by such strange recent developments as these: United States firms importing sizable quantities from Europe of so staple an American export product as steel sheets, and paying premium prices for them; and European countries again bidding for millions of tons of American coal to be carried across the Atlantic at high cost, and with some of the coal reported as destined for the United Kingdom!

The changes currently being made by many countries in their measures of foreign trade control, however, do not always correspond fully to the recent changes in their general trade and financial positions, owing to the

[1] The varying trends in the different world regions, and the principal countries which have recently been resorting to these different types of trade control changes, will be cited later on.

feeling of uncertainty as to developments ahead in the economic as well as the political relations of the nations. Just as the recently intensified demand in many countries for larger supplies of various foreign products largely represents anticipation of probable future needs, so the current attitudes of many governments toward making changes in their existing controls on foreign trade seem largely provisional and precautionary. More immediately, they reflect uncertainty as to the prospect for the availability of supplies from abroad and as to the trend of prices of international commodities. For the longer range, concern is being voiced in many countries over the unpredictable consequences for their trade and financial position of the full working out of the forces set in motion by the rearmament programs of the NATO countries, and by the widespread efforts of countries generally to build up quickly stocks of foreign products essential to their regular economies.

Even if the spread of international hostilities can be averted—and the concerted rearmament efforts of the NATO countries are intended to serve as a strong deterrent against that spread—the trade control measures of many countries during the period ahead may depend, to a large extent, upon the course of various economic developments which cannot yet be clearly anticipated. As things looked at the close of January, 1951, the principal elements of doubt include:

1. Magnitude and relative timing of the newly enlarged programs for the purchase of foreign products by the various countries;

2. Extent to which the principal countries supplying essential products may be able to increase their output, or may tighten their export controls over available supplies; and, closely related to that, the extent to which it may be possible to influence the commodity controls of individual countries by coöperative international consultation;

3. Important changes in the balance-of-payments position of certain countries that may result from the new currents of import demand, from the possible drop in exports forced by diversion of productive resources to rearmament, and from the changes taking place in their terms of trade (i.e., the relative prices of their principal imports and exports);

4. Extent to which individual countries may have to revive governmental controls of various types, in the effort to safeguard recently attained improvements in financial stability and general economic balance against the newly intensified inflationary pressures; and, finally,

5. Extent to which additional controls upon a particular country's external trade may be called for, either because of controls on its internal econ-

omy, or in order to dovetail national measures into such international controls or programs as the nations may jointly decide upon in their common interest.

Sharp Reduction of Dollar Gap by Combination of Factors Eases World Trade

An outstanding development of the past year or so that is having an important influence upon the trends in commercial policy is the substantial easing of the world shortage of dollars, which had been a dominant problem in international trade almost since the close of World War II. A brief sketch of the background situation, and of the various forces which have recently been working toward the readjustment of the postwar imbalance in international commerce, should help to bring out the significance of this marked narrowing of the dollar gap.

Measured by the difference between the value of the goods and services obtained by the various foreign countries from the United States—the principal dollar country—and their ability to pay for them with the goods and services they could furnish in return, the "dollar gap" of the world as a whole in relation to the United States had amounted for the year 1949 to about 6¾ billion dollars. Deficit countries covered this discrepancy in small part by drawing upon their shrunken reserves of gold and dollars, but the greater part of the deficits of many countries was financed by grants from the United States under the ERP and similar programs, and by loans advanced by the United States and the International Bank. (Incidentally, it must be remembered that the benefits from this economic aid ramified to many countries other than the direct recipients.)

Despite that bolster, the majority of the countries had found it necessary during 1949 to hold down their peoples' purchases of foreign products by continuing strict selective curbs upon imports, and certain important countries even tightened them, notably the sterling area countries, certain Latin American Republics, and the Philippines. In many cases, these curbs were applied with particular severity to purchases from dollar sources, especially of products obtainable elsewhere with the countries' own or with soft (nonconvertible) currencies. The widespread devaluation of most nondollar currencies to more realistic levels, precipitated in the fall of 1949, improved in varying degree the competitive export position of those countries pricewise, and also curtailed the demand of their peoples for imports from dollar sources, through the higher costs in local currencies that were now involved.

Operating in the same direction, from the viewpoint of the dollar-gap problem, was the increased value of importations into the United States which started late in 1949 and extended into 1950. This reflected partly the upturn in American business activity, and partly the marked upward trend in the prices of a few bulk import commodities, notably coffee and cacao. The conjuncture of the rising value of imports, at the very time that exports from the United States to most foreign countries were sharply declining from their extraordinary recent height, had appreciably narrowed the world dollar gap as early as mid-1950.

The outbreak of hostilities in Korea in late June introduced new forces into the trend of international trade. The threatened worsening of the general international prospect aroused the United States and the other members of the North Atlantic Treaty Organization to plan the rebuilding of their defensive strength, and stimulated a wide movement to acquire larger supplies of foreign products. Demand centered at first upon essential raw materials for the enlarged industrial production that was now anticipated and for stock-piling, commercial and military.

Influence of larger United States purchases at high prices and of decline in exports.—This intensified demand from American and other sources for various staple commodities—in aggregate quantities well beyond the supplies currently available or readily producible—soon sent the prices for them in prime markets to phenomenal heights. Largely due to these higher prices, the value of importations into the United States rose with increasing sharpness beginning July, and during two months even exceeded the value of exports.

For the year 1950 as a whole, the value of imports into the United States came to a record total of almost 9 billion dollars, or within less than 1½ billion of the reduced value of total exports during the same period. The resulting sharp decline in the United States export balance within a year—amounting to more than 4 billion dollars in merchandise values, without counting the appreciable net reductions in the invisible items—contributed greatly to the improvement in the balance-of-payments and financial position of a good many foreign countries. Many of them have been able to convert import deficits with the dollar areas into export surpluses, and nearly all countries operating on an open trading basis have benefited by some reduction in their dollar import deficit.

It is important to note, of course, that the greater part of this near-closure of the dollar gap resulted less from the increased value of importations into the United States than from the decline in foreign purchases of American goods from their abnormal height during the earlier postwar years. Mention has already been made of certain reasons for this decline—the tightening of import restriction on the part of certain countries, and the weaker competitive position of certain American products in overseas markets after the currency devaluations. To these should be added the reduction in the amount of aid granted to the countries of Western Europe in 1950 under the tapering-off of the Marshall Plan. Moreover, certain foreign developments of a recuperative character also played their part in the marked decline in United States exports from mid-1949 until the last quarter of 1950.

The abnormally large import requirements of many foreign countries of goods from the United States for replenishment and reconstruction, which had dominated the early postwar period, had progressively been satisfied. Concurrently, the cumulative progress abroad in the expansion of production, especially in Western Europe under the stimulus of the European Recovery Program, was enabling many foreign countries to satisfy their own needs more fully from at home, and to build back their former markets in neighboring and overseas areas. The appearance of increased quantities of distinctive European products in Latin American markets during the past year, and the intensified price competition abroad reported by American exporters in various lines, were reflections of the postwar return toward a more normal international trade pattern.

Whatever the relative importance of the various contributing forces, the combination of marked reductions in the new dollar liabilities of many foreign countries and increases in their dollar income has, since late 1949, brought a noticeable buoyancy into their whole financial and commercial attitudes. Most of them have been able to rebuild substantially their reserves of gold and dollars, which had been heavily drawn down during the earlier postwar years. A considerable number of governments have felt they could now afford to relax appreciably the restriction on imports that had been resorted to during the earlier period of stringency.

Uneven Narrowing of Dollar Gap Reflected in Degree of Trade Easement

The benefits from the narrowing of the dollar gap have been quite uneven for different countries, however, and this is being reflected in their trade control attitudes.

The outlying countries of the sterling area (that is, exclusive of the United Kingdom), Latin America, and Canada are the principal sources of supply for the products figuring prominently in the current commodity buying boom. Those countries have been benefiting more than others from the increased purchases for American account. As a result, the outer sterling area countries, as a group, have been able to effect a shift during the past year from a previous import excess with the United States to an export surplus of fair proportions. Similarly, Latin America as a whole shifted back to an export surplus with the United States, its normal prewar relation. Canadian-American trade, usually marked by a sizable export surplus on the part of the United States, came close to a balance during 1950.

The Western European countries operating under the Marshall Plan succeeded in cutting down their direct dollar deficit, but not so markedly, and that was less the result of the increases in their sales to the United States than of the reductions in their purchases of American goods. Certain of the Western European countries are participating in the benefits from the much-increased dollar income of the overseas primary-producing countries which share the same currency pool, although it places them under obligations to those overseas areas in the form of larger sterling or franc balances. Thus, the increased dollar earnings of the outer sterling areas—notably from the larger sales to the United States, and at higher prices, of rubber and tin from Malaya, and of wool from the southern British Dominions—reinforced the gains made by the United Kingdom from its own expanded production and improved trade balance. In fact, by the close of 1950, the United Kingdom was able to get along without further Marshall Plan aid, and the extension of new grants was then suspended.

There have been indications that many governments are impressed with the uncertainty as to how long the developments responsible for the recent narrowing of the dollar gap may continue to be dominant. Much of the early advantage from the foreign devaluations of 1949 in encouraging United States imports from nondollar countries has, for various products, already been offset by price advances. More important is the concern felt over the possibility that the new forces in international commerce generated by the Korean situation—the full effects of which may not be felt for some time—might again result in their import requirements increasing faster than their ability to increase their exports, with a consequent worsening of their trade and financial balance, especially in relation to the United States. These uncertainties may be reflected in the degree of boldness or caution displayed by various governments in their measures of foreign trade control during the period ahead.

Since licensing systems or exchange controls have in the great majority of countries been the decisive consideration in determining the volume and source of much of their imports for several years past, the changes in their operation of these controls made during 1950 merit special attention. While the predominant trend was—and still is—toward relaxation, some very important countries made no material changes, and the moderations put into effect by the different countries have varied considerably in both scope and degree. Brief characterizations of the important actions or attitudes in this regard taken by the principal countries therefore seem desirable.

Canada abolishes all import restrictions; South Africa moderates them.— Canada continued to rebuild its foreign exchange reserves, aided in part by a heavy flow of investment funds from the United States, but mainly as the result of the substantially increased sales in the United States market during the past year or so of its staple export products, especially forest products (wood pulp, newsprint, and sawmill products) and metals (iron ore, aluminum, lead, nickel, and zinc). In fact, during several months of 1950, there was a fair prospect of Canada reaching a balance in the value of its trade with the United States for the year as a whole, in place of the usual import excess, but that was not quite attained. The much improved financial position of the country allowed the Canadian Government to withdraw progressively during 1950 most of its remaining license restrictions on imports from hard-currency countries, which had been resorted to in September, 1947, as an exchange conservation measure, and to abolish them entirely from the beginning of 1951.

The Union of South Africa, which went through a period of overbuying after World War II, had found it necessary by the end of 1948 to impose an exceptionally tight clamp on the importation of all but the most essential products, especially from dollar sources. For 1951, a moderate measure of relaxation has been announced. Larger aggregate imports are contemplated, conditioned upon the amount of foreign capital inflow as well as current earnings, and appreciably freer competition between hard- and soft-currency sources of supply is to be allowed under a revised licensing system.

Most sterling areas do not feel warranted in easing dollar-goods curbs.— The United Kingdom and most other members of the sterling area have improved their financial position greatly since mid-1949, as the combined result mainly of the several factors earlier mentioned—the additional cut of 25 per cent in dollar imports agreed upon by the group in June, 1949, the devaluation of the pound in September of that year, and the recently enlarged American purchases of various industrial raw materials at high prices. The expanded volume of British manufactured output, assisted in some cases by the lower delivered prices made possible by the devaluation, allowed a considerable increase in the volume of exports from the United Kingdom itself, to the dollar areas as well as to continental Europe. In the American and Canadian markets, enlarged sales of various distinctive British products were stimulated by intensive merchandising campaigns.

Although many classes of imports from soft-currency areas were freed from license restrictions during 1950, none of these members of the sterling area, which follow parallel policies, has apparently yet felt warranted in making any material change in its particularly severe restrictions on expenditures for dollar goods. To the urgings of various countries on this subject, and to the report of the International Monetary Fund that the dollar position of the United Kingdom, Australia, New Zealand, Ceylon, and Southern Rhodesia had reached the point where a beginning of progressive relaxation in their import restrictions against dollar goods was possible, the immediate reaction has been that the present improvement in their dollar situation might be largely the result of temporary factors.[2] The increases in the quantities admissible under the token import plans of the United Kingdom and of the British West Indies, which were announced late in the year, have been regarded as fairly minor and limited easements.

South Americans substantially relax import controls after midyear.— During the first half of 1950, most of the countries of Latin America continued—and in some cases tightened—the application of their selective import controls, and several of the smaller republics (Bolivia, Paraguay, Ecuador, Costa Rica, and Nicaragua) found it necessary to continue them through most of the year. During the latter months of the year, however, the cumulative improvement in their balance-of-payments position allowed the major countries of South America to order substantial relaxation of their import controls. These have taken the form of waiving the requirement of prior licenses for some products, expanding the scope of licensable commodities, or granting import licenses and exchange allotments with greater liberality.

Their improved trade position had been the combined result mainly of two factors: (1) their curtailment of imports since 1947, through rigid

[2] One exception developed in January, 1951, when Ceylon announced that licenses would be issued for a range of specified products from the United States, Canada, and other dollar countries, which formerly were restricted. This followed a new arrangement with the United Kingdom whereby Ceylon is to retain a certain portion of its dollar earnings.

restrictions as to the kinds and amounts of licensable imports, and through increasing the delivered costs of various products by various means; and (2) the increased income from the recent upsurge in the demand and prices of many of their staple export products, notably tropical foods, wool, and minerals, especially since the outbreak of the Korean conflict.

A considerable number of the Latin American governments took measures of several types during 1950 that had the effect of increasing the cost to their people in local currency of various classes of imported products, as will be detailed later. On balance, however, the developments of the past year or so have distinctly improved the prospect for large sales opportunities during 1951 in the majority of the South American markets, notably Brazil, Chile, Colombia, Peru, and Uruguay, and, to a lesser extent, Argentina. Of special interest to United States exporters is the fact that their larger dollar holdings and current income have allowed several of the South American governments to relax the especially severe restrictions on the importation of certain products from dollar countries, which had been imposed in preceding years when dollars were relatively more scarce.

Recent banking reports reveal an exceptional record of promptness in remittances for current transactions from most of the Latin American markets. Moreover, there was further progress during 1950 in the clearing up of accumulated debts, for goods previously imported, under the exchange budget systems recently introduced by a number of the Latin American countries.

In fact, in their eagerness to see built up within their territories supplies of various products in which shortages or export restrictions are feared because of the uncertainties in the international political situation, the governments of several South American countries have lately been extending the validity period for licenses already issued or granting licenses beyond the amounts set in their original exchange budgets, either for future importations or for immediate shipments under arrangements for gradual reimbursement over a period of time. This latter type of development obviously involves the hazard of building up new payment arrears, although the recently replenished exchange holdings of most of these countries may postpone that contingency for some time to come.

Most of the countries of Middle America have not found it necessary to resort to either exchange control or general licensing of imports. The exceptions are the exchange controls in Costa Rica and Nicaragua, and the spreading use of import licenses by Mexico. The most important changes in this region during the past year concerned Mexico.

Despite the recent strengthening of the Mexican economy, and the handicaps on imports from the 1949 devaluation of the peso and the successive additions to the lists of products prohibited or restricted, the continued high demand for foreign products, especially for the various industrialization projects, again brought about in 1950 an excess of imports. The termination of the reciprocal trade agreement with the United States at the close of the year, under pressure from Mexican industries seeking higher protection, was promptly followed by a broad upward revision of the Mexican import tariff. The complete prohibition on a wide range of luxury products, ordered in mid-1947 as an exchange conservation measure, was simultaneously lifted but replaced by higher duties and licensing controls.

Intra-European trade enlarged by quota liftings and payment clearances.—Among the countries of Western Europe participating in the Marshall Plan, 1950 brought appreciable progress in the movement to facilitate their trade with each other and with their dependent overseas territories, but apparently little change in the existing restrictions on importations from dollar sources.

The ministers of the ERP countries composing the Council of the OEEC have for some time been promoting a program for the progressive liberalization of intra-European trade. By the beginning of 1950, each member country had eliminated the quota restrictions covering approximately one-half of its past private imports from the others, although often with important exceptions. A further increase of that reciprocal liberalization, to at least 60 per cent of such imports, was agreed upon early in the year, to take place as soon as a more satisfactory plan for settlement of balances could be devised. Both came into effect about midyear. In October, negotiations were undertaken to bring about a liberalization to the extent of 75 per cent of intra-European trade by February of 1951, and so far as possible to work toward a common list of the products that are to move among them without restriction.

This whole program is still subject to a number of important qualifications, but that the governments concerned had the courage to go as far as they have recently, has been largely due to the setting up this past year of what is known as the European Payments Union. This arrangement provides for the multilateral settlement of the net trade balances of each country with the group as a whole, which allows them to break away from the necessity for close balancing of the trade with each individual country. The net monthly trade balances are primarily covered either by wider reciprocal accommodation among the member countries up to certain limits, or by the transfer of gold or dollars beyond the prescribed credit limit. The temporary structural deficits of particular weaker countries, and the stability of the whole program, are supported by a sizable dollar pool authorized for the purpose by the United States Congress when voting the funds for the general European Recovery Program.

Such records as are available for the early months under this multilateral payment system indicate a general upward trend in the volume of intra-European trade, and a marked tendency toward buying or selling in the most advantageous market, rather than where the state of the bilateral balance of trade with particular countries dictated. The first difficult test in the operation of the European Payments Union, in the case of the large import balance developed by Western Germany, apparently has been met by a combination of corrective measures within that country plus some external accommodation, without reversing the general trade liberalization program either of that country or of its creditors.

The intra-European trade liberalization program contemplates that its benefits shall be fully extended in 1951 to all ERP countries, including several[3] whose economically stronger position had previously led the others to deny them the benefits of the 1949 quota relaxations. The weak financial position of Norway, Denmark, and Austria may excuse them from carrying their import liberalization to the extent of the general 75 per cent goal, and a number of the European countries have made their participation in that next step conditional upon certain other developments. The further action of several European governments in this regard is to depend upon the success of the Torquay collective trade negotiations, expected to be concluded in April, 1951, on reducing the high duties of certain other member countries, which they claim are now nullifying the value of the quota liftings.

Western Europe still confines dollar purchases to more essential products.—With regard to imports payable in dollars, no significant changes from their previous position, of restricting licenses to the more essential products not readily obtainable with soft currencies, are known to have been made by the Western European countries during 1950. The extent of the decline in United States exports to ERP countries and their dependent overseas areas during 1950, as compared with the preceding year, was greater than the amount by which United States economic aid under the Marshall Plan was reduced for the year. Obviously, this marked change has

[3] Principally Belgium and Switzerland, and, less frequently, Western Germany.

been partly the result of the general recuperative forces, earlier cited, that have recently been shaping the trade pattern of Western Europe.

Under the marked recovery and expansion of production in Western Europe, the needs of these countries for basic foodstuffs, fuel, and various other products, formerly procurable mainly from the United States, could now be satisfied from within their own territories or those of their neighbors. Moreover, the progressive intra-European quota liberalization, bolstered by the improved arrangement for the multilateral settlement of trade balances, has meant that importations of many products from each other can now be more freely arranged and more readily paid for.

Varying attitudes observed in Near East and Africa.—Greece and Turkey acted in October to free from quota restrictions the importation of many products from the ERP countries. The continued shortage of hard currencies in those and other countries of the Near East, however, led them to continue their rigid limitations upon imports from the dollar areas for most of 1950. Israel, Syria, Iraq, and Iran even tightened their import controls generally, especially on luxury goods and competitive products. Toward the end of the year, however, the fear of future shortages of essential products led the governments of a number of Near Eastern countries to move in the opposite direction. Egypt went so far as to consider several official plans for stock-piling essential items, and Iraq offered to facilitate the acquisition of necessary imports by extending official credit.

The general trends in the commercial policies of the Western European countries were reflected also in their colonies and dependent overseas territories in Africa. The administrators of the British, French, and Portuguese territories in Africa continued in 1950 the basic policy of conserving exchange by holding down to the very essentials allocations for purchases from hard-currency areas. This policy has been automatically enforced during the past year by the increased landed cost of dollar goods, following the devaluation of most nondollar currencies. At the same time, the licensing controls on purchases from sterling and other soft-currency sources, especially of Western Europe, were distinctly liberalized.

Several exceptions to these general trends were observed. The trade controls of the Belgian Congo continued to be applied liberally to the importation of staple commodities from dollar sources, reflecting the stronger financial position of the Belgian franc area. The import controls of French Morocco were applied less rigidly to American trade during 1950, following extension of the "free list" (of products importable without requiring release of official exchange) and the procedural improvements under the agreement with the United States at the close of 1949. Importations into the Spanish African territories, on the other hand, continued to be closely restricted to those products not obtainable from Spain.

India-Pakistan trade still blocked; overseas imports liberalized.—In view of the close economic interdependence developed during the long period of their previous union, the trade impasse since September, 1949, between the two countries into which the Indian subcontinent is now divided has continued to hinder their own economic adjustment and to force a distinctly new orientation in their trade relations with the rest of the world. When the trade agreement hopefully concluded in April, 1950, for the facilitation of shipments of Pakistan jute in return for Indian textiles and other manufactures expired after a few months and was not renewed, regular trade between the two fell off sharply. There has been no progress toward a settlement of the exchange rate divergence which caused the deadlock.

Each country has been seeking to make itself more self-sufficient in a number of major products normally derived from the other, and to develop alternative markets and sources of supply by arrangements with overseas countries. By curtailment of imports, through strict licensing and the devaluation of the rupee, and by an increase in export earnings, India in 1950 reversed its large trade deficits of earlier years. On purchases from dollar countries, however, the license restrictions were only slightly relaxed for the second half of the year, although the import policy announced for 1951 contemplates the purchase of certain essential consumers' goods in addition to capital equipment.

The import license policy of Pakistan affecting hard-currency areas was distinctly liberalized during 1950. After midyear, many products were admitted without restriction from dollar areas, notably chemicals and machinery. The agreement with the United Kingdom regarding the dollars to be made available to Pakistan against its sterling balances promises further enlargement of such trade opportunities. Many classes of goods from sterling and other soft-currency sources have been admitted into both India and Pakistan under general open licenses for some time.

The new taxes and other conditions imposed by both countries in the fall of 1950 on the exportation of various textile materials will be touched upon later, in the section on export controls.

Chinese buying from the West active despite state-controlled trading.—Under the general communist objective of a planned economy under close governmental domination, the operation of the network of huge state-controlled trading organizations in most important commodities was extended during 1950 to all of continental China. Some areas of activity in both domestic and foreign trade were still reserved for private firms, but with the mixed system operating under direction of the state companies, on fixed prices and profit margins.

The series of Sino-Soviet agreements signed in February, 1950, provided, among other things, for a Russian five-year credit to Communist China of 300 million dollars to cover deliveries of productive equipment and supplies, which are to be repaid over a ten-year period in Chinese raw materials and dollars. Despite the efforts to orient Communist China commercially toward Russia and its European satellites, however, the great bulk of China's foreign trade continued to be carried on with the West until late in 1950. In fact, for several months after the outbreak of hostilities in Korea, the Chinese Government carried on an intensive buying drive, centered at Hong Kong, to acquire stocks of many Western products, through private firms as well as directly.

Security restrictions imposed by United States and others on exports to China.—Following action by the United States authorities in July to prevent shipment of strategic materials to continental China, the entry of Chinese communist troops into the Korean conflict in November led the United States to require specific authorization for all goods destined for continental China, Hong Kong, and Macao, to forbid American ships from calling at any port under the control of Communist China, and also to freeze Chinese assets in the United States. The Peiping authorities reacted in December by ordering an embargo on Chinese exports to the United States and Japan, suspending transactions in dollars, and freezing United States assets in China. A number of other countries are also tightening exports to China on security grounds. Incidentally, commerce with Hong Kong, which had enjoyed an excellent trade during 1950 as a two-way entrepôt for the neighboring mainland areas, has dropped sharply.

Greater part of trade with Japan returns to private channels.—The program that was begun at the close of 1949, to shift Japanese import trade to private channels in all commodities except those still purchased under United States appropriations, was carried further during 1950. The expansion of Japan's external income, accelerated by the buying boom generated by the Korean conflict, placed larger amounts of foreign exchange at the disposal of the Japanese authorities who now regulate most of the country's foreign trade. This allowed them to program a correspondingly larger volume of licensable imports. Moreover, the licensing system was simplified and liberalized to the point where, by the end of 1950, licenses for well over a hundred commodities were available on an "automatic approval" basis.

All but a small part of Japan's export trade had been returned to private commercial channels by the end of 1949, and exporters have since been able to negotiate directly with foreign buyers, subject to the obtainment of export licenses only in special cases. In authorizing the Japanese to establish commercial branches abroad, and to open governmental trade promotion offices in several countries, important steps were taken to re-establish the country as a normal member of the international trading community.

Further drastic cuts in Philippine imports to restore balance of payments.—The year 1950 saw further drastic steps toward curtailment of imports into the Republic of the Philippines. These accentuated the measures taken late in 1949 to check the depletion of the country's foreign exchange reserves which had resulted from several years of heavy importations beyond current earnings. In May, all imports were made subject to license, and quotas were established which cut allowed purchases below past imports by 40 per cent to 90 per cent, depending upon relative essentiality. Following a period of confusion and business slump, administration of the controls improved somewhat, and by the close of 1950 the heavy Philippine adverse balance of trade had been materially reduced and rebuilding of reserves had begun.

This measure of financial readjustment was apparently accomplished only at the cost of scarcities of essential supplies, a sharp rise in living costs, and serious dislocations of established commercial channels. The requirement to reserve for new Filipino firms large and progressive portions of the import licenses for a broad range of products met strong objections. An economic mission from the United States, which was invited to survey the general economic situation, recommended in October a number of important fiscal and administrative reforms, as essential to effective utilization of the economic aid which it is proposed that the United States extend to help stabilize the Philippine economy. A number of corrective measures were reported in process at Manila early in 1951.

Indonesian exchange measures stimulate exports and restrict imports.—Early in its first year of independence, with many political problems still unsolved, the Indonesian Government adopted drastic measures designed to deal with a series of related problems in its economic rehabilitation. These problems included the low level of exports, inadequate exchange reserves, and shortage of imported goods, especially consumers' goods. It established in March, 1950, a system of "foreign exchange certificates," which were issued to exporters as supplements to their basic proceeds to the extent of one-half the value of their shipments. Importers were required to buy these certificates at twice their face value when applying for exchange permits. With all foreign commercial transactions requiring licenses, this certificate scheme amounted to a 100 per cent premium to exporters and a 200 per cent increase in the cost of importing all but the basic necessities. To help check the inflationary effect, the nominal value of the currency in circulation was cut by half, with holders given long-term government bonds for the balance.

These extraordinary financial measures, plus the intensified world demand for raw materials after midyear, resulted in larger production and exports of Indonesian staple products at higher prices, a great improvement in the country's foreign exchange position, and a reduced volume of imports, although the new price level of many products is now reported to be in line with the former "free" market prices. To reduce prices by increasing the supply of foreign commodities in the local market, and to mitigate the difficulties experienced by importers in financing purchases under the prevailing foreign exchange certificate system, the Indonesian Government began in June to place various essential products on its "free list," which removed any limitation on the quantity imported and assured prompt exchange allocation. In the allocation of foreign exchange, definite priority still prevails for essential consumers' goods and commodities to facilitate production.

Tariff Revisions and Other Changes in Costs of Imports

Secondary importance of duty changes during period of direct controls.—Inasmuch as trading with so many foreign countries since World War II has depended primarily upon whether a license could be obtained for the importation of the particular purchase, and on how promptly the foreign exchange would be available for remittance, the precise amount of duty to be paid at the customs has often appeared of secondary consequence. This probably explains why so few countries have put through general revisions of their import tariff schedules during the past five years, despite the great changes in conditions of international competition and relative prices since the war.

In fact, several important countries of Europe had for a time suspended the application of the duties on a large part of their imports, in order to facilitate the postwar replenishment of domestic supplies and to hold down the ultimate cost to consumers. Various countries, particularly of Latin America, have frequently resorted during the past few years to temporary suspension of duties on basic necessities so as to check the rising cost of living.

A number of countries overhauled their import tariff schedules in order to establish a modernized basis for the collective negotiations for the reciprocal concessions in duties, which have been conducted under United Nations auspices since 1947. Italy and Germany put forward new tariffs during 1950, largely for the purpose of these international negotiations. Similar action had been taken earlier by France, Czechoslovakia, Belgium-Luxemburg, and the Netherlands, although the action of this last group was required also by their formation of the Benelux tariff union.

Significance of third round of simultaneous tariff negotiations at Torquay.—In September, 1950, there opened at Torquay, England, the third round in this program for the simultaneous reciprocal reduction or stabilization of import duties. The basic General Agreement on Tariffs and Trade (GATT) was originally concluded at Geneva in 1947 among twenty-three countries, and amplified at Annecy in 1949, when nine additional countries became contracting parties. In the negotiations at Torquay, which are expected to be concluded by April, 1951, there are participating the thirty-two present contracting parties and the seven additional governments which have expressed interest in acceding to the agreement. In the aggregate, these countries have accounted for more than three-quarters of total world trade.

As the improvement in their trade and financial positions is allowing countries to order some relaxation, if not liftings, of the license and exchange restrictions resorted to during the emergency period, the import duties are resuming their normal importance. In the case of the countries participating in the GATT, the cumulative effect of this series of collective tariff negotiations is expected ultimately to allow trade with those countries to be facilitated by the more moderate underlying level of customs duties thus worked out. Canada is a case in point. Complete lifting of the Canadian import license restrictions, beginning with 1951, brings into full effect the recently negotiated reductions and bindings on the importations of many commodities into that country.

Several unilateral tariff revisions in Latin America, mostly upward.—During the past year a number of countries, particularly in Latin America, have also made what amounts to unilateral tariff revisions. Argentina,

Colombia, and Mexico brought into operation more or less comprehensive revisions of their tariffs, while Chile and Ecuador accomplished much the same thing through imposing differential surcharges upon the basic duties for many classes of goods. These unilateral revisions differed essentially from those resulting from the collective trade negotiations under GATT in that their changes have been mostly upward. Their objectives have usually been twofold: (1) to restore their tariffs, predominantly specific in form, to the level effective before the marked rise in prices and depreciation of currencies since the war, and (2) to increase the measure of protection accorded to new or developing domestic ventures for production of products formerly obtained largely from abroad.

Portugal and Egypt put into operation broad revisions of their import duty schedules during 1950, while Israel and Syria made numerous selective tariff changes. These recent revisions, general or partial, have typically consisted of reducing or waiving duties on primary products and increasing them on luxury goods or goods competitive with domestic production. French West Africa restored its preferential tariff regime in December, when it reimposed the import duty schedule applicable to goods from non-French countries that had been suspended since 1943.

Cost of imports into many countries increased by exchange manipulations.—In effect, the cost of imported products to the peoples of many countries—in Latin America, Europe, and elsewhere—has been increased during the recent past by other means than straight increases in the tariff schedules. Much the same effect has been accomplished through alterations in the exchange rates of their currencies in terms of gold or dollars (whether brought about by governmental action or by operation of market forces), and by use of multiple exchange rate systems for the payment of imports, with frequent shifting of products among the different categories.

Quite a number of the Latin American countries increased the cost of importation to their people of various products during the year through several types of measures:

> Revising the multiple exchange systems for payment of imports (notably Argentina, Paraguay, Bolivia, Chile, Ecuador, and Costa Rica). This amounted to further currency devaluations for selected categories of goods, and often involved shifts of specific products into categories subject to less favorable exchange rates.
>
> Authorizing admission of certain less essential products only on condition that no call upon the official foreign exchange holdings would be made. Such importations were required to be effected either

(1) under barter or "compensation" transactions against stipulated slowmoving export products (notably Bolivia, Brazil, and Ecuador); or (2) by the purchase of what exchange might be available at premium rates in the open market (notably Chile, Colombia, and Costa Rica), which is often supplied largely by the exchange certificates issued against the proceeds of certain exports for free disposal by the holder.

Prescribing increases in customs duties or surcharges payable on particular products (Argentina, Chile, Colombia, Ecuador, and Mexico).

The improved general financial position of these countries, however, and the more liberal administration of their import-licensing systems appear, in most cases, to have more than offset the increased costs of imports.

Outside of Latin America, this type of measure has been less frequent. Among the European countries, Austria and Spain are notable for having increased the cost of importation of various categories of foreign products during the past year by substantial changes in their multiple exchange rate systems. In Asia, the most striking development of this character in 1950 was the 50 per cent cut in the value of the Indonesian guilder, accompanied by a sharp increase in the cost of importations resulting from the establishment of a "foreign exchange certificate" system, earlier described.

Tighter Export Controls and Higher Export Taxes

Up to the middle of 1950, the tendency of most governments, as domestic supplies increased, had been toward gradual relaxation on the restrictions on exports that were resorted to widely during the period of marked shortages following World War II. Those countries which operate exchange controls have been maintaining a general check on export transactions, in order (1) to ensure that all, or the prescribed portions, of the proceeds from foreign sales were actually turned over to the banking authorities, and (2) to prevent unauthorized capital movements through overvaluation of export shipments. Such export control, however, has been supervisory rather than restrictive.

In scattered instances, limitations were placed on exportation of particular raw materials for the purpose of favoring local processors by assuring them ample supplies at moderate prices. In some cases, also, governments attempted to guide the flow of certain of the country's distinctive exports to particular markets where they would bring in dollars rather than soft currencies. By and large, however, most countries which maintained export controls of an economic character as late as June, 1950, did so for two general purposes: (1) to prevent undue draining off of supplies of such selected essential products as were not overample in relation to domestic needs, especially if they had been imported and paid for with hard currency; or (2) to meet their commitments under existing bilateral supply agreements, in which they had undertaken to facilitate the shipment to the other country of particular commodities up to specified quantities.

Controls on exports tighten again as unusual demand for goods mounts.—The intensified demand in international markets after the outbreak of the conflict in Korea at the end of June, especially demand for strategic materials and other primary products, brought the prospect of renewed shortages developing in many commodities that had recently come into normal supply. To the increased efforts of the United States and certain other countries to acquire emergency quantities of foreign raw materials was soon added the attempt, on the part of the nationals of many countries, to build up commercial stocks of many kinds of foreign products, in anticipation of their becoming difficult to obtain or higher in price. Since the possibility of rapidly enlarging the volume of supplies was in most cases quite limited, the sharply concentrated demands and competitive bidding apparently soon brought about the very situation which the buyers wanted to avoid.

Since the middle of 1950, countries have tended to tighten up their export controls by extending the range of products for which individual licenses are required, and by more intensive scrutiny of applications as to quantities, destinations, and often prices. Such action has been taken not only by countries that are the primary sources of supply of certain important raw materials (notably the United States, Canada, the outlying sterling areas, and certain Latin American Republics), but also by many of the principal producers of various classes of manufactured products (notably in North America and Western Europe). The primary objectives have commonly been: (1) to ensure the retention of sufficient supplies for domestic consumption or processing without undue price rises; and (2) to provide for some equitable allocation of the products now in exceptionally high demand, either in accordance with established trade patterns or to fulfill obligations under reciprocal supply agreements.

In the case of a number of important raw materials with limited sources of supply, the governments of the exporting countries have sometimes refused to license individual transactions when the prices in the sales contract were below officially fixed minimum prices or lower than the market prices prevailing at the time of shipment. Among the outstanding actions of this character during recent months have been those of Spain on olive oil, India on burlap, Pakistan on wool and cotton, and Argentina on wool.

Increasing destinational control of exports on security grounds.—While most of these new or tightened export restrictions have been general in their application, there has been an accelerated effort on the part of an increasing number of countries to operate their export controls with distinct selectivity of destination, in accordance with considerations of national security. The object is to prevent or limit shipments of commodities of strategic or other potential military value to countries with possible aggressive intentions.[4] Certain countries which are themselves importers of such products are taking or considering parallel action to restrict their transshipment, or the shipment of similar domestic products, to the undesirable destinations. The recent tendency to apply or tighten export controls on grounds of national security has been most pronounced on the part of the United States, Canada, and Western European countries, Japan, and the Philippines.

Price rises of primary products prompt imposition of high export taxes.—The extraordinary upward movement in the market prices for various primary commodities which has been developing since late 1949, starting with coffee and cacao and spreading to various industrial materials after mid-1950, has led the governments of many countries to increase sharply the taxes upon their exportation or to impose high taxes where none were levied before. Among outstanding instances of particularly high or new export duties ordered during 1950 (several not put into effect until January, 1951) were: India on burlap; both India and Pakistan on raw cotton and wool; British Malaya on natural rubber; Egypt and the Sudan on raw cotton; Sweden and Norway on wood pulp and newsprint; and various Latin American countries on coffee and cacao. The export taxes on many minerals, in Latin America and elsewhere, were already on a sliding-scale basis, and they went up automatically as market prices rose.

The declared objectives underlying imposition of these high export taxes have varied. Aside from the normal interest in ensuring sufficient supplies for domestic needs, some governments have desired to keep the inflated

[4] The most extreme action of this character was that taken by the United States after the invasion of Korea by Chinese forces, when it in effect cut off the shipment of goods for Communist China or the transport of such goods on American vessels, and limited exports to such transshipment points at Hong Kong and Macao to strictly local needs.

export prices from unduly sending up domestic prices.[5] A related objective has been that of checking the general inflationary effect of the sudden and marked increase in the nation's purchasing power, especially where the economy of the country is largely dependent upon a few products.[6] As a prudent consideration, some governments plan to use the income from the high taxes to build up a reserve fund to sustain the particular industry during possible depressed periods later. Perhaps the most common purpose has been to divert to governmental revenue a considerable portion of the windfall increase in national income from the country's staple export commodities.

International action urged for equitable allocation of scarce products.—In addition to the unilateral action of particular countries to regulate the exportation of certain products by license or tax, reference has been made to the increasing pressure, particularly from the countries of Western Europe, for early and vigorous international action in this field. It is urged that, along with efforts to bring about increased production of certain basic commodities, collective action is necessary to ensure equitable allocation of materials in potential scarcity and to check sharp price rises and fluctuations. Coördinated planning of stock-pile purchases on the part of the principal importing countries is regarded in some quarters as the minimum need.

Various plans are known to have been put forward and discussed among governments, but the only action taken thus far has been the previously mentioned step initiated in January, 1951, under Anglo-Franco-American auspices. Specifically, it proposed the creation of a number of standing international commodity groups, representing the producing and consuming countries throughout the free world that have a substantial interest in the commodities concerned. Wide participation in them was invited. These specialized commodity groups would consider and recommend to governments the specific action which should be taken in their respective fields in order to expand production, increase availabilities, conserve supplies, and assure the most effective distribution and utilization of supplies.

On the other hand, a number of important countries producing primary products have indicated that, in consideration for their concurrence in any international understanding regarding raw materials, the major industrial

[5] An unusual means of meeting such a situation was recently adopted by Australia. In view of the sharp rise in the export price for its raw wool, the country is paying subsidies to domestic woolen manufacturers, in order to keep down clothing prices to its public.

[6] In New Zealand, wool growers have worked out a scheme with the government under which one-third of their income from the current season's wool is being "frozen" for an indefinite period.

countries should reciprocate with some assurances regarding allocations to them of essential manufactured products, the supply of which might become short and be subject to export control.

Trading With and Within the Soviet Sphere

Communist countries less responsive to general world trade currents.—The foreign commerce of the smaller communist countries of Eastern Europe, like that of Russia, has come to be conducted almost entirely through state-trading agencies, and the commercial policies of all these countries are being used as instruments in their over-all economic and political programs. They have therefore been less responsive than have the open-trading countries to the general developments of the year in the field of international trade and trade controls. Two exceptions to this observation should be noted. Poland has continued to use the surplus from its large coal production as an important bargaining point in trade negotiations with various countries of Western Europe, which now need larger imports of coal. Russia participated very actively in the generally intensified efforts, after the outbreak of hostilities in Korea, to acquire large stocks of certain foreign raw materials, especially rubber and wool.

Beyond the general encouragement of bilateral agreements between various pairs of Eastern European countries for increased trade exchanges, technical collaboration, and so forth, there was little evidence of activity during 1950 on the part of the Council for Economic Mutual Assistance (CEMA). This agency had been set up early in 1949 by Russia and five of the countries in the Soviet sphere, as an offset to the Marshall Plan inaugurated in Western Europe the preceding year. According to the official communiqué, its declared purpose was to organize broader economic coöperation within the group, mainly in the form of mutual assistance in technical and commodity matters, with decisions to be made "only upon the consent of the country concerned." However, with the notable exception of the 1947 Czechoslovak-Polish five-year agreement for continuous coöperation in their industrial programs, which antedated the CEMA plan, the economic programs of the respective Eastern European countries appear to have been developed individually. Such coördinated economic planning for the region as a whole as has been evident during the recent past has stemmed mainly from Moscow.

Russia presses satellites to intensify trade within the Soviet bloc.—The strong influence of the Russian Government was directed during 1950 toward reducing the commercial intercourse of the satellite states with the outside world and toward intensifying their intraorbit relations. The ambitious productive expansion programs announced by the various satellite countries seem primarily oriented toward meeting Russian import requirements, and secondarily toward their own needs or those of the other members of the group. In their current trade with the West, the prime objective of these countries appears to be to concentrate their limited purchasing power upon raw materials and certain types of production equipment, especially those in which the Soviet Union is deficient.

Despite the consequent effort to reduce their dependence upon the West for supplies and markets for the long-term, however, various of the countries in the Soviet sphere have expressed their interest in continuing trade with the West where that can be done on the basis of immediate mutual economic advantage. One of the principal handicaps upon their ability to obtain more goods from the West has been the limited amount of marketable products left for export to the outside countries, after fulfilling their heavy prior commitments to Russia and other communist states.

Poor results of efforts for larger East-West trade commitments.—This was illustrated during the past year at the much-publicized conference arranged by the United Nations' Economic Commission for Europe (ECE) to promote long-term commitments for wider East-West trade, by starting with grains, which various Western European countries had indicated they were ready to buy from the East. The net offering from the East was limited mainly to rye and coarse grains, in surprisingly small amounts. The outcome was an understanding that five of the smaller Western European countries would negotiate bilaterally with individual Eastern European countries regarding reciprocal purchases to meet their particular needs.

In view of the difficulties of obtaining commitments from the Western countries regarding supplies of equipment and other products particularly desired, and then of getting any necessary export licenses, the recent aim of Russia and other countries in the Soviet sphere apparently has been to acquire, in return for their goods, convertible currencies usable in purchasing desired products in the open market anywhere. During the past year, their interest appears to have been mainly in procuring large supplies of industrial raw materials, particularly from the sterling countries and various dependent overseas territories of Western Europe.

In this connection, Russia has increasingly assumed the role of intermediary trader for the various countries in the Soviet sphere. A substantial part of the goods shipped from Russia to the United States and to the markets of Western Europe during 1950 consisted of merchandise of non-

Russian origin, ranging from East German potash and Bulgarian tobacco to Chinese bristles. Conversely, the Russian state-trading agencies have regularly been buying a broad range of products from various countries in Western Europe and overseas for resale in Eastern Europe.

Soviet bloc tries to tie in trade of East Germany and Communist China.—The series of trade agreements of similar pattern concluded by Eastern Germany during 1950, first with Russia and then with practically all of the other countries of Eastern Europe, in each case providing for much enlarged exchanges of specified products during the period ahead, have generally been regarded as significant steps in the political and economic integration of Eastern Germany into the Soviet sphere. Efforts have also been initiated, through trade agreements and otherwise, to tie in Communist China with the Eastern European bloc, with a view to drawing upon its export surpluses and to replacing, so far as possible, its import requirements formerly satisfied by the West.[7]

The revaluations of the Russian ruble and the Polish zloty during the past year have been regarded by most outside observers as measures primarily for internal price adjustments and for the redistribution of wealth. Since neither currency is traded in on the international exchanges, their nominal revaluations have had little significance for outside commercial transactions.

Yugoslavia, which controls its imports and exports through state-trading agencies on the communist pattern, has continued to orient its commerce toward the Western countries, ever since the political difficulties of 1948 led Russia and the other members of the COMINFORM to curtail sharply all intercourse with that country. Yugoslavia's extraordinary need for imported food after the disastrous drought of 1950 is being met by assistance from the West, notably by the United States.

[7] The Sino-Soviet Trade Agreement of 1950 was described earlier in connection with the year's trade developments affecting China, p. 487.

1951

SUBSIDENCE OF POST-KOREAN TRADE BOOM BRINGS PRICE DROPS AND RENEWED IMPORT CURBS

Since the outbreak of the Korean conflict in mid-1950, the course of international trade and the measures adopted by governments for its regulation have been strongly influenced by the new economic forces set in motion by the general apprehension over the possible spread of war, and by the decision of the North Atlantic Treaty Organization countries quickly to rebuild their military strength.

HIGHLIGHTS OF THE TWO PHASES IN POST-KOREAN TRADE DEVELOPMENTS

The outstanding developments of this period have been the general upsurge in demand for imports and the consequent marked rise in prices, both of them accentuated by speculative purchases prompted by fear of later shortages. This has been especially true of raw materials. The increased demand for them developed sooner than for manufactured products, and the rise in their prices was more immediate and sharper.

Early Upsurge in Demand and Prices for Materials Checked in 1951

This increase in demand and in prices for internationally traded commodities that has been stimulated by the Korean situation has already gone through two phases. The first, covering roughly the period from the middle of 1950 to the spring of 1951, was marked by intense competitive bidding for stocks of raw materials, by governments as well as private firms, and by very sharp rises in the price obtained for them. The increased demand for manufactured products and equipment did not develop until somewhat later, and the rise in their prices has been much more gradual and moderate.

The second phase, corresponding roughly to the period since the spring of 1951, has been marked by a distinct slowing down in the volume of purchases of many basic materials, and a consequent decline in their prices from the earlier peaks although, in general, both demand and price for most primary commodities continued well above pre-Korean level for most of the year. This subsidence of demand was partly an expression of resistance by governments and merchants to what they considered excessive prices, notably for rubber, tin, wool, and wood pulp, and partly the reaction to heavy inventory accumulations during the months immediately after the Korean outbreak. The second phase has been characterized also by a broadly increased demand for machinery and other capital goods, which was fairly well sustained through the year, and for wide ranges of consumers' goods, with which many markets became overloaded by fall.

Differing Impact on Primary-producing and on Industrial Countries

To the countries of Asia, Latin America, and the overseas sterling area whose principal exports are primary products, especially raw materials, the international trade developments since Korea have usually brought distinct gains, even after the recession from the initial high demand and prices, although often at the cost of increased domestic inflation. For the industrial countries of Western Europe and North America, the greater rise in prices for their raw material imports than for their typical manufactured exports, combined with the need for greatly increased quantities of imported raw materials for their industrial expansion in support of the rearmament programs, often created distinct problems. By the closing months of 1951, these problems had developed into acute crises in the cases of France, and of the United Kingdom (and with Britain, many of the other sterling-currency countries).

Moreover, the very sharpness of the upward and the downward shifts in international demand and prices since mid-1950 has made the process of adjustment to the changes more difficult. In fact, by the later months of 1951, many of the primary-producing as well as industrial countries found that their high rates of importations were draining off their recently replenished foreign exchange reserves, and creating badly unbalanced trade relations with particular groups of countries. In the effort to check or rectify these developments, a considerable number of governments have recently reverted to closer regulation of their foreign trade.

A number of governments have announced their intention to work toward regaining balance in their trade exchanges on a high level, through greater domestic austerity and increased exports. Most often, however, the immediate corrective measure has been taking the form of a temporary restriction of new importations to the level of the country's current foreign income, either as a whole or with particular currency areas.

While the intensity and the duration of these new measures of trade adjustment may vary considerably with different countries, this recent turn toward renewed restrictiveness may be ushering in a third phase in the post-Korean trade shifts. If any large number of governments should act more prudently during the period ahead, and continue the efforts to keep a better balance in their countries' trade and other external financial relationships, an incidental result may be more moderate fluctuations in the general demand and prices for major internationally traded products.

Desire for Increased Imports Prompts Most Countries to Loosen Controls

Looking back over the recorded trade experience of 1951, however, the working out of the new trade forces is seen to have brought about, for the greater part of the year, a tendency for the loosening of import restrictions by the majority of the countries of the free world, although that was less marked among the European countries than elsewhere. In many cases, they also stimulated official participation in stock-piling, as well as extensive private buying to meet future needs in broad ranges of foreign products. Some governments were impelled to encourage imports as one means of restraining inflation, through having the quantities of goods available to the public more nearly commensurate with the increased purchasing power in its hands.

Fortunately, the improved foreign exchange position which so many countries had recently achieved allowed them to pay for larger imports. As the trade returns show, the volume of imports into the majority of the countries of the free world increased substantially in 1951, and ran high through most of the year. The experiences of several of the major countries of Europe and a few of South America were exceptional in this regard.

They ran into balance-of-payments difficulties by the fall of 1951, and their rate of importations was curtailed during the latter months of the year.

A particularly important exception was the United States, whose increased buying of foreign materials reached high levels very soon after the Korean outbreak, but which decreased in volume as early as the spring of 1951. This decrease was partly in resistance to the extremely high prices asked for certain commodities, as earlier mentioned. In part also, there was a natural subsidence of demand, owing to the fact that both official and commercial stock piles of many products had already been built up to substantial levels during previous months. Moreover, the abatement of civilian purchasing in the United States after the scare buying immediately following the Korean outbreak prompted manufacturers to more conservative inventory policies. Naturally, any sizable reduction in the level of purchases by so important a consumer of the world's raw materials as the United States was not without its effect upon the trade and income of various other countries. An appreciable pickup in the volume of United States buying of a number of basic foreign materials is expected for 1952.

Import Relaxations by Primary Producers Substantial; Moderate Elsewhere

The form and extent of the import relaxations authorized by the various governments during 1951 differed considerably, but they usually involved wide ranges of essential products and often also some less essential ones. At the outset of the year, Canada terminated its import-licensing system, which had been progressively cut back in scope during the last few years as the country's foreign exchange position improved.[1] Several Latin American and Asiatic countries went far during 1951 toward permitting practically unrestricted importation of increased quantities of various products considered essential, and in some cases extended the privilege to consumers' goods of only semiessential character.

Most of the primary-producing countries, in both the Eastern and the Western Hemispheres, have benefited substantially from the commodity boom, in several ways.[2] As a result, the great majority of them felt prompted

[1] The import controls recently imposed by Canada upon a number of scarce commodities are supervisory in character, and intended to ensure their end-use for approved purposes. In the case of butter, the import control is a corollary to the domestic price-support program.

[2] The special aspects of the 1951 trade experience of the principal groups of primary-producing countries and of the industrial countries, including the restrictive reactions of late 1951 and early 1952, will be dealt with in later sections of this chapter.

to relax their import license or exchange controls so as to admit a wider range of foreign goods and larger quantities of them. Most often these relaxations were extended, at least in some measure, also to goods from the United States and other hard-currency sources. Various of these countries had previously restricted "dollar imports" more severely than others, on grounds of the inadequacy of their hard-money resources for more than essentials. As will be later indicated, however, a considerable number of them found it necessary before 1951 was over to withdraw some of these import liberalizations.

In the industrial countries of Western Europe, to whom the new trade developments often brought problems as well as advantages, the import relaxations that were made during 1951 were distinctly more moderate than in the primary-producing countries. They consisted almost entirely of further lifting of quota limitations upon the admission of varying lists of products from other member countries of the Organization for European Economic Cooperation. The products of the affiliated overseas territories of the other Western European countries, and of some other soft-currency areas, often shared in the wider market opportunities opened up by these trade liberalization measures, but seldom have their benefits been extended to similar goods from the United States or other dollar countries.

With regard to import restrictions generally, there has frequently been observed a reluctance to give up arrangements to which both official and commercial circles have become accustomed over a number of years, with the incidental protective or fiscal advantages they often involve. Moreover, many governments apparently feel that, even when their balance of payments becomes favorable, the uncertainties of the world situation warrant them only in loosening the harness of import controls but not yet in removing it.

At the same time, the political apprehensions and economic pressures during 1951 stimulated, on the part of many countries, a progressive extension of license and other controls over the exportation of particular products from their territories. In addition to general limitations on quantities or prices, governments often applied systems of country allocations or other means of destination control. As will be later detailed, these controls were often premised upon considerations of national security as well as of shortages of supplies.

Heavy Imports Beyond Current Earnings Bring Restrictive Reaction

Toward the close of 1951, a considerable number of countries found they had been buying foreign products far in excess of their current income, even with the recently increased yield from their exports and the aid of such foreign loans as they were able to obtain. Those countries which largely depend for their income upon the exports of wool, tin, rubber, and certain other raw materials experienced a distinct drop in their general purchasing power when the market boom in those commodities began to subside in the spring of 1951. Before the year was over, many governments decided that the consequent drain upon their foreign exchange reserves required some tightening up on the importation of certain classes of goods, at least for the first half of 1952.

In certain countries the foreign exchange deficit that has developed recently appears as only one aspect of a more deep-seated maladjustment. This maladjustment usually involves a generally overextended economy and severe domestic inflationary pressures, which it is recognized requires for its rectification much more than temporary curtailment of imports. In the majority of the countries which have recently taken such action, however, the renewed import restrictions seemed temporary corrective measures—to be operative only until the current pressures upon the country's balance of payments could be relieved—rather than basic changes in the government's general trade policy objectives.

Exporters of products which have recently become restricted of admission into formerly important markets should find it rewarding to watch the month-to-month developments in the general financial position of those countries, especially as important new capital inflows develop, as their new crops come on the market, as marked changes take place in the prices of their principal exports, and as old debts are paid off.

Post-Korean Developments Create Acute Situation for Britain and France

Among the countries of Western Europe undertaking enlarged rearmament programs, the prospective increased economic strain from providing for the necessarily enlarged volume of imports caused appreciable concern during the year. This was especially true because, as earlier mentioned, the prices of their raw-material imports had increased more than those of the manufactured products they had for export. However, the majority of these countries apparently managed to adjust fairly well to the new situation in the course of the year, with appreciable trade imbalances developing mainly in their relations with the other Western European countries. During the latter months, they were assisted in this by lower prices for many of their essential import commodities.

By the end of 1951, most of the Western European countries were reported as being in no worse—and often better—over-all trade and financial position than at its outset, with two important exceptions: France and the United Kingdom (including various of the countries associated with Britain in the sterling currency area).

The opening months of 1952 are witnessing earnest high-level consideration of means for dealing with the worsened economic position of those countries. As so far developed, solution for their current problems is being sought through a combination of several types of action on their part, including some alterations in their foreign trade programs, plus such aid as the United States may be able to extend under the Mutual Security Program. The corrective measures to be taken by those countries themselves usually contemplate greater austerity in imports and the stimulation of increased exports, as well as increased production in certain lines and further restraints upon domestic consumption and credit.

The market prospects in the major sterling areas and in France during the period ahead, for products other than prime essentials, would appear to depend largely upon two things—the vigor and success of these internal corrective measures, and the plans now being worked out regarding the apportionment of part of the American Mutual Security funds among the participating countries, in the form of direct economic aid and of materials for local defense-supporting production.

Despite Inward Facing of Soviet Bloc, Wider Outside Trade Invited

The Soviet bloc countries of Eastern Europe appeared to move in a separate economic orbit. During most of 1951 they made strenuous efforts to channel their trade increasingly toward each other, and particularly toward the requirements of the Soviet Union, although the latter months of the year saw some reconsideration of that objective. Their governmentally planned trade exchanges were to be sharply stepped up, to serve their programs for greatly accelerated industrial expansion, especially in heavy industry, centering around that of Russia. The manufacturing facilities of the Eastern Zone of Germany and the raw materials of

Communist China were increasingly integrated into the trade system of Russia and its Eastern European satellites.

The volume of trade exchanges between the East and the West was further diminished during 1951. This was the joint result of the shortage of goods for export in the communist-controlled countries, and of the restrictions placed by many countries of the free world upon the shipment to the Soviet bloc of strategic materials and of industrial equipment of potential military use. Toward the close of the year, wide overtures were being made by the Soviet bloc for more direct commercial transactions with various primary-producing countries overseas, and for a general expansion of trade with the non-Soviet world.

Strong Demand for Materials and Equipment Brings Wide Controls on Exports

After the outbreak of the Korean conflict in mid-1950, the suddenly increased world demand for foreign commodities, especially for industrial materials and capital equipment, led many of the principal countries producing surpluses of those classes of products to bring them under export license, or to expand the scope of such license control as they had in operation. The primary purpose was usually to ensure that the quantities being retained in the country would be sufficient for local needs, including contemplated industrial expansion, and to prevent excessive foreign demand from advancing domestic prices unduly. To these was often added the consideration of destination control, either to meet obligations in reciprocal supply agreements or, in general, to effect an equitable sharing of scarce commodities with friendly nations.

Concern was expressed early in 1951, especially by certain countries of Latin America and the Far East, about the continued availability of foreign materials and equipment for their basic industries and development projects. This concern was caused by the intensified demands for the defense expansion programs of the United States and other NATO countries and by the spread of export controls. There was also some fear that if development projects requiring heavy imports were postponed until after the rearmament period, prices might have so advanced that their funds would then have a much smaller purchasing power.

Prospective supply shortages overestimated; consumers' goods ample.—As it turned out, the early fears in certain countries that raw material shortages would force serious curtailments of their productive operations proved exaggerated. More moderate expansion in defense production than first anticipated, some slowdown in governmental stock-piling programs, and a general decline of the intense early commercial demand as prices softened, helped to relieve these fears. On the supply side, the situation was reinforced by increased production of various commodities, the reassuring prospects of more orderly distribution of scarce raw materials after the establishment of the International Materials Conference, and the greater readiness of supplying countries to give consideration to the essential import requirements of their normal customers.

For somewhat similar reasons, serious shortages of capital goods developed in only a limited number of important lines, and the concern was oftener over inability to get prompt deliveries because of heavy prior commitments on producers' books than over restrictions arising from official export controls. The trade records for 1951 show that, contrary to widely held expectations, United States exports of most classes of machinery, vehicles, and other capital goods to the underdeveloped countries have actually increased appreciably since the acceleration of defense program activities. The leading Western European countries and Japan, likewise, recorded varying degrees of increase over the preceding year in the volumes of engineering products they exported.

Earlier anxieties over obtaining supplies, from the United States in particular, were somewhat relieved by the program worked out during 1951 to achieve equitable allocation of goods in particularly short supply, in accordance with the relative essentiality of their intended end-uses, both at home and abroad, and in the light of studies of the various friendly countries' requirements for the different purposes. This program is being carried to the point of endeavoring to provide special official assistance in the procurement of some particularly scarce materials and equipment when needed for foreign operations or projects of high priority.

Supplies of foreign consumers' goods were generally obtainable by the nonindustrialized countries in ample quantities, either from the United States or increasingly from the expanding production of Western Europe. In fact, in many of these countries the measures taken by governments to enable merchants to stock up on such foreign products, both because of the uncertainties of the international situation and to help check domestic inflationary pressures, resulted, by the latter months of the year, in the saturation of local markets with imported consumers' goods.

In many countries of Latin America and in some of Asia, this tendency to accumulate inventories led before the year-end to a double reaction. Importers who had their funds tied up in unsold merchandise found it difficult to take over newly arrived goods; and long delays in remittances, notably from certain countries of South America, have again become a common subject of trade complaint. At the same time, the depletion of their newly replenished exchange reserves by the wave of heavy imports has—as earlier indicated—led many governments, especially of primary-producing countries, to try to check that drain by reimposing some degree of restriction on further foreign purchases, at least temporarily.

Increasing curbs on strategic shipments or diversions to Soviet bloc.—During the course of 1951, an increasing number of governments adopted control measures designed to restrict the shipment from their territories to the Soviet bloc, or the unauthorized diversion to that group of countries, of strategic materials and other products capable of increasing their military potential.

The United States, Canada, and Japan have developed the strictest security controls upon the shipment of products of this character to the Soviet bloc countries of Eastern Europe. Similar controls have been adopted during the past year by the leading trading countries of Western Europe and their dependent overseas territories. The West German system of security controls upon shipments eastward has been tightened up during the past year and is reported to be operating with increased effectiveness.

Most Latin American countries are not shipping products of a primary strategic character to the Soviet bloc. The Near Eastern areas produce very few commodities of this nature. The countries of both South and Southeast Asia either do not produce, or reportedly do not ship to Eastern Europe, most of the products considered to possess strategic significance, excepting rubber and tin, in which several of these areas are continuing trade relations with the Soviet bloc.

The embargo on the shipment of goods of a strategic character to Communist China, initiated in May by most members of the United Nations and by a number of other countries, was an emphatic expression of this general attitude. This collective action had been preceded, in late 1950, by strict limitations on shipments to Communist China on the part of the United States and certain other countries.

Purposes and Effects of High Export Taxes on Primary Products

Governments of primary-producing countries began in 1950 to impose, or to increase, export taxes on their staple products enjoying unusually good prices. This movement continued into 1951. The size of the export tax was usually substantial and frequently changed in accordance with the state of the market. In a considerable number of instances the export tax was put on a sliding-scale basis, so that it would move automatically with changes in price. Export duties have normally been on a sliding-scale basis for certain minerals and other natural products subject to considerable price fluctuation.

The purpose of these new or increased export taxes continued to be mainly twofold, namely, to divert to the governmental revenue part of the windfall earnings from the country's staple products, and to check the inflationary effect upon the country's general economy of the suddenly increased national income. The latter purpose was often also served by using part of the new income to subsidize the maintenance of low retail prices on common necessities. In a few cases, an important objective has been to build up a reserve fund from the temporary high earnings from the country's leading exports, to help stabilize the situation during possible future lean years.

The additional official revenue from these new or increased export taxes, which the high market prices for various raw materials have stimulated, is having the incidental effect of enabling the governments to balance their budgets more comfortably, and to build up fiscal reserves for local improvements or other purposes. In a number of these areas, however, complaint is being voiced that the height to which the export duties have been raised is reducing the sales volume of certain of the country's basic export products. In some countries, concern is being expressed that the consequent shift by traditional buyers to alternative sources of supply—or to the use of substitute materials—may result in some permanent loss of foreign markets.[3]

International Collaboration in Allocating Raw Materials Steadies Markets

A commercial policy development of the past year with interesting possibilities has been the establishment at Washington of a series of standing commodity committees, which together compose the International Materials Conference. Their function is to look into the adequacy and best utilization of the supplies of basic raw materials available to the free world, and to develop recommendations for action by the interested nations regarding the commodities that present the most urgent problems.

Organized in February, 1951, under Anglo-Franco-American auspices,

[3] Since the above was written, the Government of India has cut in half its high export duty on burlap, declaring that move to be "necessary in order to enable the industry to improve its competitive position in the world markets."

with the principal producers and consumers of the particular commodities among the free nations invited to participate, the International Materials Conference now has twenty-eight countries represented on its various commodity committees. Provision has been made for hearing the views of nonmembers and for securing the estimates of their production and requirements.

By the end of 1951, international allocations had been brought into effect by voluntary agreement for seven especially scarce materials—copper, zinc, nickel, cobalt, tungsten, molybdenum, and sulfur—and emergency allocations had been made for newsprint to a total of eighteen countries. In order to maintain so far as possible the normal patterns of trade, the allocations for these commodities to individual countries are set in the form of total amounts, without attempting to indicate or limit a particular country's sources of supply.

In the case of the commodities for which allocations are adopted, the committees generally make recommendations regarding the elimination of nonessential consumption and the use of substitute materials. Many countries have introduced direct measures of control over the uses of these commodities. The member countries of the Organization for European Economic Cooperation (OEEC) have adopted standard lists of prohibited end-uses for copper, and, in principle, also for zinc and nickel. A considerable number of countries in various parts of the world individually control the uses of cobalt, molybdenum, tungsten, and sulfur, as well as the three earlier mentioned.

In some countries which maintain strict controls upon the movement of such commodities into or out of their territories, this selective licensing tends to form a type of end-use control. In view of the prospect that supplies of at least six of the controlled commodities are not likely to overtake demand for the next few years, small allocations or none at all are being made for stock-piling purposes, and strong encouragement is being given to the use of alternative materials or industrial processes.

The committees of the IMC also have under constant review the supply and requirement situations for a number of other important raw materials, including lead, manganese, cotton and cotton linters, wool, and pulp and paper. Whether any recommendations are to be made to the nations regarding these commodities, either for the allocation of the aggregate free-world supply or for other measures to be taken, apparently will depend upon developments in the demand-supply situation of the particular materials and upon the attitudes of their principal producers and consumers.

After one year's operation, these efforts of the free nations to deal with their common problems in scarce basic materials by international coöperation, while limited in scope and authority, appear already to have had a steadying effect on the general raw-materials situation. They have helped to dispel some of the extreme apprehensions earlier expressed by various countries regarding scarcities and, combined with the more prudent recent buying on the part of governments and merchants, they have tended to reduce the earlier intense competitive bidding for supplies and the sharp fluctuations in market prices.

POST-KOREAN TRADE EXPERIENCE OF PRINCIPAL PRIMARY-PRODUCING COUNTRIES

As earlier indicated, the outbreak of the Korean conflict in mid-1950 stimulated a general upsurge of demand for many imported products and a marked upturn in prices, first for raw materials and later for manufactured goods. From the point of view of the foreign trader, the most immediate effect of these new developments was a shift from the problem of finding markets to that of seeking supplies.

The questions of whether particular goods would be admitted under the import controls of the country of destination, and whether necessary foreign exchange could be readily obtained, were still important considerations. But with increasing frequency the dominant questions were: how readily adequate quantities of goods could be obtained at the usual sources of supply and, if they were subject to export control, whether the necessary license or allocation would be granted.

This intense concern over supplies moderated somewhat after the spring of 1951, when the second phase of the post-Korean developments set in. This was marked by a subsidence of the initial strong demand and high prices, especially for basic commodities, and by adoption on the part of various producing countries of measures designed to increase the supplies of goods, and to effect a more equitable distribution of them among the free nations. In fact, as earlier indicated, the exceptionally heavy volume of imports into most countries during the greater part of 1951 led many merchants before the year was over to buy more conservatively, and prompted many governments to take steps to check the drain upon their newly replenished financial reserves.

More Conservative Buying Plus Revived Controls Bring Stabilizing Period

This diminished eagerness for imported products on the part of many buyers, and the reversion to more restrictive governmental import controls—which date roughly from the closing months of 1951—may be ushering in for 1952 a third phase in the post-Korean trade developments. This phase shows signs of a leveling off of demand and prices, and a recognition on the part of competitive suppliers that greater selling efforts are necessary.

As most countries had by 1950 reached the strongest economic and financial position attained since World War II, the great majority were able to finance an increased volume of imports during the greater part of 1951, and to adjust to the new trade movements and price shifts without having to resort to radical changes in the structure of their trade controls. Before the end of the year, certain countries did run into difficulties which required drastic action, often including the partial reimposition of trade restrictions which have earlier been lifted in order to liberalize trade. With a few important exceptions to be later noted, however, the resilience and adaptability of most countries apparently were equal to the new strains, with only temporary restrictive adjustments.

Such adjustments to the successive post-Korean trade shifts as were found necessary have usually been effected without much formal modification of the existing trade control structures, except when revision of import duties or export taxes required legislative approval. This flexibility has been possible because, in most countries, official decisions with regard to imports and exports now rest with the licensing or exchange authorities. From their nature, these methods of regulating trade allow considerable loosening and tightening of their scope and severity by discretionary administrative decisions, as changing circumstances require.

As indicated earlier in this chapter, the general impetus to stock up on foreign products and the uneven movements of prices since Korea have affected the economies and the trade controls of various countries quite differently. The chief determining considerations appeared to be the nature of the leading export and import products of the particular country, and in many cases the size of the rearmament program it was undertaking.

Primary Producers in Net Improved Position Even After Boom Subsides

To most of the countries whose principal exports are natural products, especially industrial raw materials, the new developments since Korea appeared to have brought net improvements in their international trading and financial positions, although often at the cost of intensifying domestic inflationary pressures. During the latter months of 1950 and much of 1951, the market demand for their staple exports usually increased the income of the commercial community, allowed more imported products to be made available to the general population, and strengthened the foreign exchange position of the country as a whole.[4]

Moreover, as the prices of raw materials rose sooner and more sharply than those of finished products, and stayed relatively higher for at least the better part of a year, these countries benefited additionally from the marked improvement in their "terms of trade," since the proceeds from a given quantity of their exports could now buy larger quantities of foreign manufactures.

This situation stimulated the purchase from abroad of a wide range of products, not only for immediate use but also in anticipation of later shortages and higher prices. The governments of the majority of these countries apparently felt that unexpected increase in their foreign exchange receipts warranted some relaxation in the operation of their import license or exchange control systems. A considerable number even encouraged the import of larger quantities of foreign consumers' goods than usual. Moreover, many felt this was an excellent opportunity to obtain foreign machinery and materials to reëquip existing industries and utilities, and to launch long-cherished economic development projects.

The aggregate result of these various new trade impulses was that, through the greater part of 1951, most of the primary-producing countries in Asia, Latin America, and the overseas sterling area increased their imports substantially, and often to a value well above their current export earnings. Not all of them, however, had enough foreign exchange reserves, or received a sufficient supplementary inflow of new foreign capital, to sustain so heavy a volume of imports. As the year advanced, financing this

[4] The present discussion deals primarily with the influence of recent trade forces upon the trend of import demand in various groups of countries and upon their official measures of import control. The concurrent developments in controls upon exports, and the related problem of supply availabilities, were discussed in the first part of this chapter.

import surplus became a problem for many of these countries, especially after moderating demand and lower prices for various of their export staples reduced their current earnings from the earlier high levels.

The governments of numerous producing countries felt it necessary, during the latter months of the year or at its close, to tighten up on the volume and range of allowable imports, at least for the first half of 1952. Most often this was done by placing some commodities back under individual license, through more selective approval of licenses, and through contraction of bank credit. In some cases the governments have applied the restored restrictions more rigidly to purchases from some sources than others. Such selective restrictions reflect mainly the size of the particular country's holdings of dollars, pounds, or other currencies, in relation to its anticipated import needs from the various currency areas for certain indispensable products, such as food, fuel, or essential industrial materials.

Special Features of Recent Experiences of Primary-producing Countries

The special features in the trade experience of the different groups of primary-producing countries during the past year or so—as expressed first in the relaxation of controls and an upsurge of imports, and later often in some restrictive reaction—deserve separate examination.

South and Southeast Asia.—Probably the most pronounced changes in the volume and profitability of trade resulting from the immediate post-Korean developments occurred in the countries of South and Southeast Asia, comprising the regions from India to the Philippines. As prime suppliers to world markets of many of the basic raw materials, they especially felt the increased demand for such commodities, for expanded industrial production and stock-piling in the manufacturing countries of North America and Europe. The greatly increased income which these countries of Asia consequently enjoyed for about a year—at least until the spring of 1951, when raw-material prices began to recede from their earlier peaks—enabled them to pay for wide ranges of imported consumers' goods, some heretofore beyond the reach of their peoples, and to undertake domestic projects requiring foreign equipment. Progress on these local developmental projects was often stimulated by the technical assistance, and, in some cases by financial aid, extended them from abroad.

The majority of the governments of these countries facilitated in varying degrees the acquisition of desired foreign products, either by waiving import restrictions on lists of articles regarded essential or by licensing more liberally.[5] In certain instances, also, import duties were reduced on selected products, and licenses were granted to anyone who could get a firm foreign offer without regard to his past participation in the particular trade.

Most countries of South and Southeast Asia had previously not been maintaining as severe restrictions against purchases in hard-currency countries as had been found in some other countries. The enlarged dollar earnings at their disposal, and often the difficulties in getting early delivery of supplies of various desired products from other sources, led to a distinct increase in the volume and range of purchases from the United States. The sterling countries, as well as the others in this region, broadened in varying degree the range of products that could be imported more freely from most hard-currency countries. These countries, however, still maintained definite restrictions on such purchases when the goods were obtainable from other sterling areas, or secondarily from soft-currency countries. Ceylon carried this form of liberalization furthest during the past year, and India and Pakistan to a moderate extent.

By the close of 1951, a number of the countries in this region had materially drawn down the foreign exchange reserves earlier built up, and several developed appreciable deficits in their current balance of trade, especially with the dollar areas. The Philippine Republic is the only one in this group, however, which resorted to a substantial curtailment of new purchase authorizations for 1952 when, after a period of heavy importations, it was realized that the sizable trade surplus accumulated during the early months of 1951 would be converted to a deficit by its close.

The replacement of the general Indonesian foreign exchange certificate system by graded export taxes limited to "strong" products, which was ordered early in February, 1952, in an effort to improve the foreign sales of the country's products, was accompanied by some tightening up on imports. Although the increased imports of essential foreign goods are still to be encouraged, the import of luxury and semiluxury goods is to be discouraged. Moreover, to check depletion of the country's dollar reserves, the new Indonesian exchange system is designed to stimulate larger exports for United States and Canadian dollars, while making imports requiring payment in dollars relatively more costly.

Latin America.—The Latin American countries producing minerals,

[5] Two exceptional situations might be noted. Thailand, at one extreme, had not found it necessary for a number of years past to impose any import restrictions for balance-of-payments reasons. Indo-China, on the other hand, continued to be dominated by military operations, and did not find it possible to share in the trade liberalizations of varying degree accomplished by other countries in this region.

textile fibers, coffee, and cacao, likewise benefited from the recent increased demand, and especially from the higher prices, for these staple exports. The governments of most of them therefore felt warranted in relaxing their import restrictions in various ways. In their eagerness to see their replenished foreign exchange assets converted into goods, several of them definitely helped to build up stocks within their territories. They often authorized the placement of foreign orders for delivery over long periods of time, and issued licenses in amounts well exceeding the rate of earnings from current exports. Moreover, many felt this was an excellent opportunity to obtain foreign machinery and materials to improve existing facilities, or to carry through long-desired local developmental projects.

The relaxation in the import control system of Peru, and to a lesser extent of Colombia, amounted to the virtual restoration of unrestricted trade in a great many lines. Concurrently, however, Colombia prohibited entirely the importation of various products regarded as luxuries or nonessential, and Peru levied new or higher taxes on them. The general attitude in Latin America toward less essential goods was still usually cautious. A number of these countries operating multiple-exchange systems made the freer admission of such categories of goods conditional upon the importers undertaking to pay for them at more expensive rates of exchange, or with funds obtained in the free market without drawing upon the official reserves.

Previously, a number of the South American countries had been refusing licenses for certain products for purchases in dollars, while granting them for goods payable in other currencies. In view of the recently increased dollar receipts from sales to the United States, most of these discriminations disappeared in the course of the import liberalization moves made during 1951. In a few markets, there was a reaction later in the year, and licensing for the purchase of certain products in dollar countries again became more restricted. This was notably so in Chile, which had made exceptionally heavy importations from the United States during the first half of the year.

An appreciable number of Latin American countries found it necessary toward the end of 1951 to restrict the importation of many products which they had earlier been eager to obtain from abroad. Such has been the recent experience of Argentina, Uruguay, Bolivia, Ecuador, and, to a lesser extent, of Brazil and Colombia. Even Mexico and Venezuela, which have been able to get along since World War II without exchange controls or general import license systems, have recently asked their banks to help hold down the volume of importation through restrictions upon commercial credit.

Overseas sterling area.—Almost all overseas members of the sterling area,[6] in addition to those in Asia, mentioned earlier, shared substantially in the increased foreign income and prosperity that has come to the raw-material producing countries generally since the latter months of 1950, even though the volume of sales and the prices for certain of their leading export commodities did not continue at their earlier high level. For most of 1951, they likewise shared the general eagerness to use their improved purchasing power to get larger supplies of foreign consumers' goods, as one means of holding down domestic inflationary pressures, and, in a number of these countries, to acquire materials and equipment for their expanding production and development programs.

License restrictions had been somewhat eased in a number of these countries during the latter months of 1950, but those were moderate and confined mainly to imports from soft-currency countries. Subsequently, most of the overseas sterling countries apparently overcame their hesitation to use their replenished exchange reserves, and during 1951 they effected appreciable relaxations of their import controls. By a succession of administrative steps, most of the independent Commonwealth countries, and various of the dependent and related sterling-area countries, increased during the year the range of goods that could be admitted without individual license, and also broadened the range of countries from which such purchases were authorized.

By the fall of 1951, individual licenses were no longer required for the great majority of private importations into most of the overseas sterling countries from almost any soft-currency country, including most members of the European Payments Union and their affiliated overseas territories. The license controls continued to be maintained principally for purchases from hard-currency sources, and, in the main, licenses continued to be granted only for essential products and equipment not readily obtainable elsewhere. Their recently enlarged dollar earnings from sales to the Western Hemisphere made it possible during 1951 for the various sterling countries to replenish the stocks of such essential goods, which they had

[6] The sterling-currency area now comprises all of the self-governing Commonwealth countries except Canada (namely, the United Kingdom, Australia, New Zealand, Union of South Africa, Southern Rhodesia, India, Pakistan, and Ceylon); the various British colonies and dependent areas; and Ireland, Iceland, Libya, Jordan, Iraq, and Burma. Certain of these countries have already been covered in the earlier discussion of the experience of the countries of South and Southeast Asia.

bought sparingly during the immediately preceding years, when their dollar resources were exceptionally limited.

In several of these sterling areas, however, there was an appreciable increase also in the range of products authorized for importation from the United States, Canada, and other hard-currency countries. The Union of South Africa and the Gold Coast, like Ceylon, probably moved further than the others in the range of products made admissible from the dollar countries.

Over-all, much larger quantities of goods were actually bought during 1951 by the overseas sterling countries from the dollar countries of the Western Hemisphere, as well as from Western Europe and its overseas territories. In part, this was attributed to the inability to obtain from the United Kingdom the increased quantities of various products desired, and especially the materials and equipment sought by certain of the sterling countries to carry forward important expansion or development. In the instances of Australia and South Africa, part of the increase in the capital goods type of imports was financed by International Bank loans or by private capital investments from abroad.

As a combined result of their sharply increased expenditures for imported products, and of the recession in the prices and sales of many of their prime exports that developed in the spring, these sterling countries as a group found themselves by the closing months of 1951 in a deficit position in relation to all outside countries, whether of hard- or soft-currency areas. Individually, several of these countries earned more than they spent during the past year. As members of the sterling area, however, the purchasing ability of each of them in outside markets depends primarily upon the state of the aggregate foreign exchange and gold reserves at London of the sterling area as a whole (with the exception of South Africa and Ceylon, which have made special arrangements in this regard).

As is detailed later in the discussion concerning the United Kingdom, the joint program to rebuild the sterling area's over-all strength recently agreed upon by the various member governments contemplates some curtailment in the range and quantity of imports during 1952 into most of the sterling countries, although not necessarily to the same extent.

Near East.—Although most exports from the countries of the Near East are primary products, few are among the industrial materials that have enjoyed sharply increased market prices since Korea. Insofar as their foreign exchange resources allowed, however, and—with two notable exceptions—the countries in this region responded to the situation in much the same way as other nonmanufacturing countries.

Merchants sought to stock up on foreign products which they feared might later be more difficult or more costly to obtain. Most of the governments were willing and financially able to facilitate larger importations by relaxing their import controls, at least on the more essential products. In a number of instances, merchants were assisted further by extensions of credit, or the governments themselves made direct foreign purchases of certain popular necessities, in order to assure ample supplies on hand and to stabilize local prices. In the course of compensation or barter transactions, often resorted to in order to help dispose of particular Near Eastern export surpluses, such as Egyptian cotton, the imports arranged for in return sometimes included articles of a more-or-less luxury character for which no official exchange for payment was otherwise obtainable.

The experiences of Iran and of Israel were exceptional, but for quite different reasons. Iran, which normally counts on a large export surplus, suffered loss of revenue after British operation of the Anglo-Iranian oil properties ceased in the autumn of 1951, and it was subsequently denied access to its sterling balances in London. That government then found it necessary to withdraw its earlier waiver of import quotas on a broad range of products, essential and nonessential. It has recently cut back the value of authorized imports to the proceeds from current exports.

In the case of Israel, the gap between its current foreign exchange income (including gifts and credits from abroad) and the costs of even the essential productive equipment and consumers' goods required from abroad widened greatly during the year. This was attributed chiefly to the cost of settling and maintaining large numbers of immigrants. In October, drastic austerity curbs were placed on the importation of all but foods and other absolute essentials.

The proposals for closer economic coöperation among the Arab or Moslem states, which have been put forward by various commercial and official conferences in this region, have yet to be translated into concrete programs. Early in February, 1952, however, Syria and Lebanon, which prior to 1950 had been joined in a customs union, signed an economic accord which promises special facilities for each other's products and traders.

POST-KOREAN TRADE EXPERIENCE OF WEST EUROPEAN INDUSTRIAL COUNTRIES

Increased Rearmament Imports and Poor "Terms of Trade" Create Problems

To many of the industrial countries of Western Europe the new developments in international trade and prices since Korea have brought special problems. The sharper rise in the prices of raw materials, their principal imports, than of manufactured goods, their chief exports, turned the "terms of trade" against them. The consequent necessity for sending abroad much larger volumes of their export products to obtain the same amount of their typical imports was an additional strain upon their economies, and in certain cases threatened to upset their balance of international payments.[7] As the chief requirements of the United States from abroad are likewise primary products, this country also felt the increased cost of many of its imports—although to lesser degree than the countries of Western Europe, in view of the much greater extent to which its needs are met at home.

During the course of 1951, the world prices of many primary commodities receded from their earlier peaks. The most notable instances were rubber, tin, wool, copra, cotton, and hides. At the same time, prices of manufactured goods advanced moderately. The disadvantage of the Western industrial countries pricewise was thus appreciably reduced, but was not entirely overcome.

The ten Western European members of the North Atlantic Treaty Organization (NATO)[8] faced the need for increasing substantially the volume of their countries' goods to be offered for sale abroad. Higher exports were needed to pay for the enlarged volume of imported materials and equipment for the rearmament program, in addition to the supplies necessary for the maintenance of their basic economies. Moreover, most of these countries have to make some diversion of men and resources to defense production. Insofar as that could not be compensated for by increased over-all production, there was the risk that any appreciable reduc-

[7] Among the noncommunist countries of Europe, Belgium, Norway, Sweden, and Finland are the only ones for which the terms of trade have turned decidedly favorable since Korea. In the case of Belgium, that was mainly because of its heavy recent exports of steel at advanced prices; in the case of the others, because of their large exports of lumber and paper materials, likewise at high prices. All four finished the year in a stronger over-all balance-of-payments position than at its outset.

[8] Greece and Turkey did not join NATO until early in 1952.

tion in the quantities of goods available for civilian use would intensify domestic inflation.

An additional cause for concern was the inability of the coal-producing countries of Europe to expand their output in line with the increased fuel needs for the general European industrial expansion. An unexpectedly large part of the current dollar income of a number of these countries had to be spent to buy and transport coal from the United States. There was also some apprehension over the possible shortage of certain other essential industrial materials. As the year progressed, however, the supply situation in most raw materials turned out to be appreciably less serious than at first anticipated, for reasons indicated earlier in this chapter.

Intra-European Trade Increases Under Import Quota Liberalization

While these long-range concerns were looming in the background, the countries of Western Europe carried on a very active foreign trade during 1951, both among themselves and with the rest of the world. Among the member countries of the Organization for European Economic Cooperation (OEEC) and their affiliated overseas territories, increased purchases were facilitated by the progress made during 1951 in the OEEC program earlier initiated for the progressive removal of quantitive restrictions on intra-European imports. Early in 1951, the majority of the OEEC countries extended the removal of restrictions to items accounting for as much as 75 per cent of their 1948 private imports from the group as a whole, and in the spring they further agreed upon a common list of certain specified products which were to move freely among them.

In view of the structural weakness of their economies, Austria and Greece were exempted from this general undertaking. A number of other member countries whose balance-of-payments position was not yet strong enough were authorized temporarily to liberalize imports to less than the 75 per cent level. Western Germany was permitted to withdraw its quota liberalizations for most of 1951, in order to restore a better balance in its intra-European trade after an earlier period of overbuying.

By the end of the year, most of these countries—Germany especially—had improved their trade position sufficiently to be able to announce an increase in the extent of their unrestricted imports from the other OEEC countries for 1952. On the other hand, the United Kingdom and France found it necessary to withdraw their earlier "free listing" of many classes of goods, at least for the time being. As these shifts bear primarily upon the trade prospects for 1952, they will be dealt with later in this discussion.

National Trade Deficits or Surpluses Strain European Payments Union

The progress toward broader and freer intra-European trading effected during the past two years has been made possible by the fact that the uncovered balances in the trade between any two member countries or currency zones could now be largely cleared off multilaterally through the European Payments Union. That plan provides that net surpluses or deficits are to be cleared, up to specified limits, by credit accommodation and gold transfers on the part of the member governments.

The first strain upon this EPU arrangement, arising from German overbuying from other members in 1950, was successfully met during 1951 by the combination of a slowdown in German imports and certain measures of temporary accommodation on the part of the other countries. However, a number of new situations of sharp imbalances developed during the year, which will call for special measures of correction in 1952. Programs are already under way that are designed to bring about a generally better balance in the trade relations among the Western European countries during the year ahead.[9]

The sizable import deficits which the United Kingdom and France developed during the latter months of 1951 presented special problems, both because of the magnitude of the imports required by their national economies and because of the major importance of their foreign trade positions to the largely uncorrected internal inflationary situations in those countries. As one of their first corrective measures, both these governments have recently suspended their earlier quota liberalizations on the importation of the products of the other EPU members, and are again subjecting them currently to strict licensing of individual transactions.

[9] Western Germany, the Netherlands, Denmark, and Norway, which started the year with appreciable deficits in their trade with the EPU countries as a group, managed to reduce them substantially, and were consistently recording export surpluses during the latter months of 1951. These readjustments were usually effected by a combination of two broad classes of measures: internally, through increased production, some restraints on domestic consumption, and contraction of credit for commercial transactions and investments not considered urgent; and externally, by the stimulation of larger exports, and sometimes by a temporary reduction of expenditures upon imports, in which they were aided by the recession in the prices of many imported materials, as earlier noted.

The exports to the other Western European countries during 1951 from Belgium, Switzerland, and Italy, and to a lesser extent from Sweden and Portugal, were well beyond the value of the goods they were able to obtain from them in return. In order to rectify the situation, the countries with large EPU surpluses adopted during the closing months of 1951 various short-run measures designed to facilitate much larger imports from the other member countries and, in several instances, also to limit for a time the volume of further exports to them.

Since the British and French situations involved not only the other members of the EPU, however, but also their financial relations with the dollar countries, their problems assumed a broader character.

Larger Essential Purchases from Dollar Sources Again Widen Dollar Gap

The Western European countries took no important formal steps in 1951 toward admitting more freely from the dollar countries the classes of goods for which licensing from those sources had been restricted for some time. In several instances, commodities in general short supply were pronounced welcome from any source. Broadly, however, the greatly increased importations from the United States and other dollar areas by most of the Western European countries during 1951 appeared to have been caused mainly by larger purchases of much the same classes of materials and productive equipment as they had previously admitted—usually products not obtainable elsewhere in adequate quantities. The renewed heavy requirements for American coal, earlier mentioned, added further to their dollar expenditures for imports.

These Western European purchases from the dollar sources were primarily for the needs of both their civilian economies and the special industrial expansion contemplated in connection with rearmament. To some extent also, efforts were made to rebuild the inventories of certain basic materials, which had been reduced to low levels during the preceding year or so. The state of raw material supplies in the United Kingdom, for example, was reported at the close of 1951 to be distinctly better for many essential commodities than at its outset. When the British Government announced in November that further strategic stock-piling would be slowed down, as one of the first trade-balance correctives, it was indicated that necessary stocks of the more bulky commodities had already been restored.

It is not entirely surprising therefore that the progress made by most of the Western European countries between 1948 and 1950 toward balance in their trade and payments relations with the dollar countries was checked during 1951, with a number of the European countries again developing sizable dollar deficits by the end of the year.

Bearing of Mutual Security Program Upon Trade Programs and Controls

The administrators of the Mutual Security Program have recently decided to allocate sizable amounts from that general fund to pay for European purchases of materials and supplies for use by the importing countries in connection with local military production, and in the manufacture of defense equipment for use by other NATO countries. These allocations of Mutual Security funds, which are capable of being implemented largely through private commercial transactions, are in addition to the finished military items to be supplied by the United States and to the expenditures for American military installations within the territories of the Western European countries.

The outcome of the high-level consultations now in progress with regard to the financial arrangements among the NATO countries for carrying through the joint rearmament program will necessarily have an important bearing upon the import programs, and upon the trade controls, of a number of the Western European countries and of their related overseas areas for the period ahead. Those decisions are bound to affect their balance-of-payments positions and consequently their capacity to import, especially from the dollar countries.

Proposed European Curtailments and Diversions of Dollar Purchases

The proposed curtailments in dollar imports for 1952 thus far announced by various European countries and their overseas affiliates seem in most cases distinctly provisional in character, and subject to considerable modification in the course of the year ahead. A brief statement of the principal declared intentions in this matter may, however, be of some indicative value.

In September, 1951, Belgium announced its intention to screen very closely its imports from the United States and Canada, and to grant licenses only for those products that were essential and that could not be obtained within the EPU area. This was one of the measures resorted to by Belgium in an attempt to reduce its increasing export surplus with the EPU.[10] Portugal, in a similar creditor position, has also taken action recently to stimulate its imports from Western Europe, to the extent of authorizing complete license liberalization for all goods from EPU countries for an experimental three-month period.

Italy is likewise endeavoring to reduce its export surplus with the other European countries by waiving quantitative restrictions on virtually all products from the EPU monetary area for an indefinite period, and by

[10] The United States and Canada have formally protested against this restriction of dollar imports, contending that it is not warranted by the Belgian economic position, and is a violation of Belgium's obligations under the GATT. They are now seeking, through the means afforded by GATT, to obtain a removal of the restriction.

temporarily reducing its duties on most products. These duty reductions apply to imports from all sources.

In November, France proposed to cut its dollar import program drastically. The proposal was withdrawn after a brief slowdown period in licensing, upon American assurance regarding the amount of dollar aid planned for France in support of the common defense effort. Although declaring itself desirous of avoiding possible curtailments below the recent level, the French Government has indicated that its policy toward dollar imports would be subject to frequent reëxamination.

At the turn of the year, Sweden announced that, in view of the state of its dollar reserves, its import plan for 1952 would call for a cutback in authorized dollar purchases of other than essentials, although upward revision was possible in the event of higher dollar earnings from its pulp and paper exports than anticipated.

Sterling Area Over-all Trade Deficit and Plans for Its Correction

In January, 1952, a conference of the Commonwealth Finance Ministers was called in London to consider joint action in dealing with the new crisis of the whole sterling area, arising from the fact that the 1951 deficit in its trade balance had seriously depleted the central foreign exchange reserves of the group. This crisis could not well be met by diverting purchases to nondollar countries, since the sterling area as a whole was in deficit with soft- as well as hard-currency areas. Nor could it be resolved satisfactorily by increased diversion of British purchases to the sterling area, since the United Kingdom had reduced to small proportions its trade and payments surplus with the overseas sterling countries, and has not recently been able to offer sufficient quantities of goods of the types desired by the other sterling countries.

At the close of the Conference, the Commonwealth Finance Ministers announced that their objective was to bring the position of the sterling area as a whole into balance with the rest of the world by the end of 1952. It was agreed that immediate corrective action would be undertaken in the United Kingdom and in each of the other countries, the methods to vary according to individual circumstances.

It was recognized that the underlying problems required for their solution positive measures of a long-term character designed to combat inflation and ensure soundness in the internal economy of the respective countries, to increase export earning power, and to utilize outside borrowing for productive development. As an immediate measure, however, it was indicated that some steps might be necessary to reduce imports, at least temporarily, so that each country might live within its available means.

Import Cuts by Most Sterling Countries a Short-run Measure

The measures for curtailment of imports into the United Kingdom announced in November, 1951, applied mainly to certain consumers' products from other Western European countries, most of which had been freed from quota limitations only within the last year or so. Dollar purchases were specified only in the second series of import cuts, announced in Parliament late in January, 1952. These cuts included tobacco and coal specifically, and later possibly motion picture films. British purchases from dollar sources had for some time been confined mainly to essential materials and equipment.

The precise steps to be taken by the various other members of the sterling area in the trade field to achieve the agreed general objective are only just being announced as this article goes to press. Prior to the London Conference, there had been indications that Australia, the Union of South Africa, and Southern Rhodesia would find it necessary to curtail importations during 1952 below recent levels, and that India and New Zealand contemplated an import program for 1952 very similar to that prevailing during the latter half of 1951.

By late March, 1952, Australia, New Zealand, Union of South Africa, Southern Rhodesia, and Ireland had announced cuts of varying depths in their import programs for the stretch ahead. Australia and New Zealand have gone so far as to call in for reconsideration all import licenses already issued for purchases from the United States and certain other nonsterling countries, with some exceptions, mainly orders already shipped or covered by an irrevocable letter of credit. The import license restrictions proposed by Australia, and to a less extent by South Africa, are to apply to goods from all sources, including other sterling countries. Singapore and the Malay Federation have announced that total dollar imports would be maintained at 1951 levels, but individual licensing of consumer durable goods from all sources is being restored, with quotas set well below 1951 levels.

As earlier suggested, most programs of import curtailment recently announced are experimental, and are likely to be materially modified in the light of developments during the period ahead.

1952–1953

LOOKING AHEAD IN WORLD TRADE POLICIES

SHORT-TERM TRENDS

Reviewing the situation in the summer of 1953,[1] it appears that the character and objectives of the measures which dominated the trade control programs of the principal countries at the beginning of 1952—as sketched in the preceding chapter—are still substantially the same. It will be recalled that there was then discernible in the making a "third phase in the post-Korean trade shifts." That phase, now more definitely recognizable, might be characterized as one of cautious readjustment on the part of many countries in their efforts to reach a sustainable balance in their foreign economic relations. This readjustment was made necessary by the sharp rise in the demand and in the prices of commodities that followed the invasion of South Korea in mid-1950, and the equally sharp decline in both that started within the year, and all that those disturbances did to their foreign trade and finances.[2]

[1] This chapter has been freshly prepared, to round off the volume, and is to be regarded as presenting the purely personal estimations of the author as a student of the field.

[2] A limited number of countries—notably the United States, Canada, certain countries of Middle America, and Switzerland—have been in a sufficiently strong position to absorb the shocks to their balance-of-payments position from the disturbances to world trade that have marked the last few years, without resorting to drastic import restrictions, as most other countries have. The discussion in this section on short-term trends therefore does not apply to them.

Settling Down to an Indefinite Period of Uneasy Peace

The early fear that the outbreak in Korea would soon again plunge the world into a general war has largely subsided, and with it has passed the scramble of 1950–1951 to acquire stocks of foreign products, especially raw materials, at almost any cost. Most peoples and their governments seem to have adjusted themselves to the prospect of an indefinite period of uneasy peace, with only limited areas of open conflict. Subject to such prudential measures as the various governments regard necessary in view of possible new moves on the part of the Soviet bloc—which in the case of the North Atlantic Treaty Organization countries is taking the form of jointly rebuilding their defensive strength—the nations of the free world apparently mean to push forward toward their respective long-term economic objectives. This attitude is reflected in their foreign trade and trade control programs.

Efforts to Adjust Trade Balances, Mainly by Curbing Imports

The prime consideration in the reversion of so many governments since the latter months of 1951 toward stricter control of imports has been the current state of their balance of payments and of their foreign exchange reserves. This pressure to retrench after a period of foreign expenditures beyond current earnings, has been widely felt—in the sterling areas, in a few countries of continental Europe, notably France, and in many of the primary producing countries of South America and Eastern Asia.

Enlarged earnings through increased sales abroad could be attained only slowly, even with the specially favorable exchange rates or exchange retention privileges that some governments extended to their exporters. Aside from the special efforts in certain countries to deal with exceptional unemployment situations, notably in textiles, the early corrective measures have therefore been mainly in the way of restrictions on demand. There was some tightening upon domestic expenditures, principally through firmer fiscal and credit policies, but the most common recourse has been to restricting the classes of foreign goods for which import licenses or exchange permits would be granted, either from all sources or from the currency areas with which the particular country was most out of balance.

The trade complaints from exporters here and abroad during the course of 1952, that many foreign markets for their products had suddenly shrunk, were confirmed by the trade records available at its close. They show that most of the improvement in their trade and financial balances which various countries achieved during the year was accomplished through reducing the volume of their foreign trade, by cutting back their imports toward the level of their exports.

Factors Favoring and Retarding Greater Stability in Trade Controls

The efforts of most countries toward external readjustment have been favored during the past year or so by several factors: the good harvests in most regions; the increasing effectiveness of the measures taken to repress domestic inflation; the improved state of world supplies of most commodities that had threatened to become short; a generally moderated international demand for goods for stocking, owing partly to large inventories on hand from earlier heavy purchases; and the return to greater stability in market prices even though at a lower level. In fact, assuming no unforeseen major developments in the world situation, the general trend for the period immediately ahead appears to be toward relatively greater steadiness in the movements of world trade than during the recent past, and less violent changes in the measures of governments for regulating them.

As might be expected, of course, there are some important exceptions to these general observations. Certain countries in Western Europe are still finding it difficult to fit into their overextended economies the adjustments required by the rearmament program of the NATO countries. This has called for increased imports that have to be covered in some way, and for some, the diversion to defense production of certain of the very facilities needed to turn out the industrial equipment and the products that can most readily earn foreign exchange for them in export markets. To an appreciable extent, this problem has been eased for the industrial countries by the improvement in their terms of trade, as a result of the marked recession in the prices of most raw materials from their inflated levels of 1950–1951. Conversely, however, for a number of the primary producing countries whose economies depend upon the profitable disposal of these very materials, the sharp shrinkage in the earnings from their export staples has been retarding their return to a balanced trade position. Consequently, there has also been retarded their readiness to relax the import restrictions reverted to after the period of overbuying stimulated by the post-Korean price inflation.

Little Trade Relaxation Except Among Western European Countries

Even among countries which have succeeded in working back during the past year toward a more balanced position in their international trade and payments, however, only a few have yet felt warranted in doing much toward relaxing the restrictions which they had imposed on the down-swing. The principal easements that have taken place have been in the trade of the countries of Western Europe with each other (and usually including also the overseas areas operating in the same currencies). As regards imports payable in dollars, the funds available to these countries continue to be reserved mainly for the purchase of the most essential products or those not obtainable elsewhere. For the procurement of other products, preference is usually given to purchases from within the same or another soft-currency area. Rather than to broaden the range or volume of goods admissible from dollar sources, most countries of Europe and elsewhere which have recently improved their holdings of gold and dollars apparently prefer to rebuild their slim reserves to a higher level, so as to be in a better position to withstand possible renewal of wide fluctuations in their balance of payments.

In view of the prominence given to the recent European trade difficulties, a special word as to developments there seems warranted. It will be recalled that, as a means of minimizing the constricting effect upon intra-European trade of the inconvertibility of most currencies, and the consequent tendency to hold exports to a given country down to the level of the goods currently obtainable from it in return, a European Payments Union had been set up in 1950 with American backing. Through that agency, bilateral debits and credits arising from current trade exchanges between the members are cleared off, so that only the net balance of each with the group as a whole requires settlement. With the notable exception of France, the large deficits and surpluses within the EPU which particular countries had developed by the latter part of 1951, largely as a result of the abnormal post-Korean trade developments, had been substantially reduced by early 1953. This has made possible the partial withdrawal of some of the restrictions on intra-European trade reimposed in 1951–1952, and on the part of certain countries even some enlargement in the degree of trade liberalization announced for 1953, as measured by the percentage of imports from the others in the group to be free from quota limitations.

Export Controls on Short Supply Grounds Being Relaxed

The general changes in supply and demand earlier indicated are having their definite effect also upon the measures of control upon exports. There has been considerable relaxation during the past year or so of the export licensing and rationing arrangements that were installed or tightened during the year following the Korean outbreak, on those products of which the visible supplies seemed unequal to the prospective aggregate demands. In the export controls now maintained, the objective has largely shifted away from conserving supplies. The prime objectives now are to ensure the desired distribution among various destinations, as promised under reciprocal supply agreements or in accordance with past trade, and to curtail the shipment or transshipment to areas under Soviet domination of products capable of increasing the military potential of those countries.

Significant in this connection has been the experience of the group of standing committees constituting the International Materials Conference, which had been set up in Washington early in 1951, upon the wide insistence that international coöperation was necessary to study the free world supply and requirements of scarce raw materials and to recommend programs for their obtainment and best allocation and utilization. By the spring of 1953, it was found that the need for their assistance was almost over. Supplies of most of the commodities with which they had dealt had become sufficient for any reasonable demand.

Post-Korean Resort to High Export Taxes Being Reversed

It will be recalled that as soon as the Korean boom sent up market prices, many of the primary producing countries had imposed, or sharply increased, taxes on the exportation of the staple products of which they are important suppliers to world markets. The purpose was usually to divert part of the windfall gains to governmental use, to check the domestic inflation engendered, or to build up stabilization funds to support the particular exporting industries during the inevitable lean years. As more ample supplies and more prudent buying have been bringing the world prices of these basic materials down toward their pre-Korean level, most of the exporting countries have been sharply reducing these extra levies, and in some cases abolishing them, in order to make their products again competitive and readily salable in world markets. Those countries which insisted too long upon not allowing certain of their important export commodities to go abroad below certain fixed minimum prices have, almost without exception, lost heavily during the down-swing since 1951, and usually have had to allow world market prices again to govern.

To sum up the trends of the past year or so, the various shifts in their controls upon imports and exports to which so many countries have resorted since the latter months of 1951 are seen to be helping them to readjust gradually to the most recent disturbances to their external trading relations arising out of the Korean conflict. Most of them have come closer to a balance in their foreign trade, although at a lower level, and some have even improved the state of their foreign exchange reserves. It is becoming clear, however, that these short-run correctives—most often restrictive in character—are but palliatives for recurring bad symptoms, and that the basic problem needs to be faced, if the recurrence of trade and financial crises is to be averted.

The basic problem of many countries, most competent observers agree, is not how to rectify any sharp imbalance in their external financial position that may develop from time to time, but how to achieve a sufficiently substantial structural balance to be able to withstand the inevitable fluctuations in markets and prices without having to resort to drastic measures. Ordinarily that problem has been a concern mainly of the primary producing countries, and especially those dependent upon the export disposal of a very limited number of products. Since World War II that has been a chronic problem also for most countries of Western Europe, for reasons brought out in earlier chapters, and particularly in their relations with the United States and other dollar countries.

Currency Convertibility Depends on Balance-of-Payments Stability

Whatever the current differences of opinion as to the best method and rate of approach to the goal, there seems to be general agreement upon the desirability of moving toward convertibility of the major trading currencies as soon as practicable. At the least, it is hoped that before very long currently earned funds in any one of those currencies can be freely converted into any of the other currencies or into gold. In fact, that is generally regarded as indispensable to the reëstablishment of a multilateral trading system that can operate with the minimum of arbitrary restrictions and discriminations.

It is not yet as widely recognized, however, that a genuine return to the general convertibility of the major currencies—to be sustainable without arbitrary restrictions or hazard of recurrent crises—can be effected only to the degree that progress is made toward the attainment of closer and more stable conditions of balance in the international payments position of at least the commercially more important countries. The means to that end are not simple or easy to apply, and appear to call for a combination of more fundamental and long-term concurrent courses of action by many governments, acting—if possible—in accordance with some coördinated or widely agreed-upon program. That raises the question as to what trends are now visible with regard to such a prospect for the longer term. To the consideration of that question we now turn.

LONGER-TERM PROSPECTS

Recognitions of Responsibility Improve Prospect for Correction

The prospect that the nations with a persistent deficit in their external trade and payments will, during the period ahead, devote more attention to fundamental long-term correctives for that situation has been improved by the sobering influence of the hard experiences so many of them have had during the last half dozen years. Recent months have brought from a number of directions certain recognitions that seem vital to the solution of this basic problem, namely, that the extraordinarily high import demands of many countries since the close of World War II have in a measure amounted to their trying to live far beyond their means, and that the excesses and weaknesses of their domestic economies have had a large measure of responsibility for their international trade difficulties and for the recurrent crises in their external financial positions.

Relative Responsibilities of Creditor and Debtor Countries

There has been no relaxation of the insistence from many directions that creditor nations and those with consistent export surpluses should facilitate the admission of more foreign goods into their territories, and should undertake long-term programs of substantial foreign investments, particularly in expanding production in the less developed countries, as contributions in their own interest toward more stable and expanding free world markets.

At the same time, however, there has been growing the recognition that even the most generous action along these lines on the part of the creditor countries can only partly relieve the situation, and cannot bring about the complete and basic solution. Governments are becoming more ready to admit that the so-called "dollar shortage" or "foreign exchange shortage"—for most often it is an *over-all* shortage—which has so commonly in recent years been given as an explanation for the trade deficits of various countries, and as justification for their import restrictions and discriminations, represents in large measure production shortages on their part. Their output of exportable products has not been sufficiently large in volume, or competitive in price, to earn for them the foreign exchange required to pay for the large volume of imports they desired. Insofar as that was responsible for the situation, it obviously calls also for substantial adjustments in their internal economic and technological programs.

External Deficits a Reflection of Overspending and Overexpansion

The realization that external deficit often reflects internal overspending has come to make governments more ready to admit that neither they nor their nationals can continue to make heavy purchases of foreign equipment and materials for as ambitious expansion or developmental programs as they had planned, and frankly to announce that they cannot allow as large a part of their current foreign earnings to be spent for nonessential consumer goods as in earlier postwar years.

Understandably, restraints upon the demand for foreign products through official import restrictions have usually been turned to first during recent years when balance-of-payments difficulties developed, as promising quick if not lasting relief. Less often have governments felt themselves in a strong enough position to apply firm curbs upon domestic consumption and less essential expansion programs. The programs more recently blocked out by quite a number of countries in various parts of the world, however, seem based upon the recognition that the solution of their external economic problems calls also for vigorous internal measures with several ends in view: to restrain demand generally, and to increase the supplies of goods that are salable abroad or that can cut down the volume of need for imported products.

Importance to External Balance of Internal Economic Measures

The countries of Western Europe that have made the most substantial progress during the last few years toward equilibrium in their international payments have been those that have given most attention to building greater internal economic strength, by repression of inflation and by fostering increased production of exportable products at competitive prices. Among the Latin American governments, Argentina and Mexico have been most outspoken in their recent announcements that the earlier extensive drives for rapid industrial expansion are to be slowed down. The official support for economic development is now to be directed more largely to the increased and more effective production of the agricultural products upon which the economy of their countries primarily depend, for foreign earnings as well as for domestic sustenance.

Commonwealth Economic Plan Exemplifies New Line of Approach

The communiqué issued at the close of the Commonwealth Economic Conference at London in December, 1952, merits special attention in this connection because of the breadth of its analysis and outlook. By a combination of internal measures and international coöperation, it is aimed to increase the economic strength of the Commonwealth countries, and to enable the sterling area to achieve a stable balance of payments with the minimum of trade and financial restrictions, so that it can play its part in the general expansion of world production and trade. The discussion of the desirable internal measures to that end contains a number of significant recognitions. In agreeing to persevere in their efforts to curb inflation, the conferees recognized that inflationary conditions tend to frustrate sound development, stimulate excessive imports, and divert to internal use goods otherwise available for export. When stressing the importance of planning "to produce and supply under competitive conditions an expanding flow of exports," it is recognized that in the past the development of basic essentials had sometimes been "impeded by other developments of a less sound and permanent kind."

For the success of the Commonwealth plan, the coöperation of other countries is declared essential in several ways, notably two. Foreign investment capital is needed for the furtherance of the developmental programs of the Commonwealth countries, and they pledged a reduction of the obstacles to its movement. In the matter of trade policy, international agreement is to be sought "on the adoption of policies, by debtor and creditor countries, which will restore balance in the world economy on the lines of 'trade not aid' and will, by progressive stages and within reasonable time, create an effective multilateral trade and payments system covering the widest possible area." However, the London conferees declared that, though they have no intention of seeking the creation of a discriminatory trade bloc, their present level of reserves is still too low to warrant any substantial relaxation of the restrictions on imports from outside the sterling area.

Gap in World Payments Hitherto Bridged by Unusual Means

During the earlier postwar years, the gap in world payments was largely bridged by unusual means: at first, by the goods supplied to other war-ravaged countries against credits by the United States, Canada, Switzerland, and others, and then by the economic aid granted them by the United States under the Marshall Plan. In addition to covering current consumption needs in certain classes of goods, this aid has helped the recovery and expansion of the Western European countries, by fostering enlarged facilities and output and, to a certain extent, also higher productivity. Moreover, through enabling these countries to pay for the procurement of essential products from a range of outside countries, the program turned into a general support of world trade, with the benefits extending to many areas outside of Europe.

In a measure, the world payments situation has also been relieved by the various depreciations of currency values, general or selective, notably the series started by Britain in September, 1949; and more recently, following the Korean outbreak, by the heavy United States purchases of basic commodities at high prices from the overseas sterling areas and the primary producing countries of Latin America and of Asia.

For the period immediately ahead, the expenditures abroad by the United States for "off-shore" procurement and for various military and defense-supporting purposes, toward which the American foreign aid program has now shifted, may temporarily further ease the current payments problem of many countries, while programs of a more basic corrective character are being worked out. That appreciable progress in that direction has already been made is evidenced by the substantial shrinkage of the over-all "dollar gap" from its formidable size during the early postwar years, and conversely, by the strengthened internal and external financial position of various countries in Europe and elsewhere.

Present Balance Precarious and Dependent on Continued Restrictionism

It cannot be overlooked, however, that the maintenance of the improvement in their balance-of-payments position that many countries have recently achieved still depends upon the continuation of a considerable amount of trade restrictionism and discrimination, especially against purchases from dollar countries. Moreover, its precarious character was strikingly illustrated by the renewed financial crises experienced by so many countries from the post-Korean trade fluctuations, and by their hasty retreats to renewed restrictionism. The feeling appears to be growing that there cannot much longer be delayed the more intensive application of basic corrective measures of the types earlier cited, which so many governments have recognized as essential. In varying degree, the recognition also seems to be spreading that the successful effectuation of such long-term programs will require, during the period ahead, a high degree of coöperation on the part of the major countries of the free world in their economic programs and policies. Particularly is this regarded essential in the field of commercial policy.

Trade Policy Goals Call for More Basic Measures and Joint Programs

Repeated urgings have recently been heard of the desirability of a fresh joint examination by the North Atlantic Treaty Organization countries—which comprise the United States and Canada together with twelve countries of Europe—of the broad framework of their economic and financial relations, as a corollary to their program for building joint strength against possible further Communist aggression. In view of the key position of the United States in any such new program, intensive discussions were held at Washington in March and April, 1953, with representatives of the United Kingdom, and of the Western European countries as a group, on "measures for creating the economic and financial conditions under which the countries of the free world may be better able to earn their own living by their own industry." These discussions were intended to be exploratory, and no formal commitments were expected at this stage.

At the close of the Anglo-American talks, the two governments announced their agreement that the essential elements of a workable and productive economic system within the free world should include: (a) sound internal policies, by debtor as well as creditor countries; (b) freer trade and currencies, including the eventual convertibility of currencies and removal of payments restrictions, and the relaxation of trade restrictions and discriminations; (c) creation of conditions favorable to international investment in the development of the resources of the free world; and (d) the use of international institutions to promote these policies. The discussions with the general Western European group brought announcement of an agreement upon broad common objectives similar to those made known at the close of the United States–United Kingdom talks, and upon the desirability of furthering them "by continuing efforts and close co-operation on both sides of the Atlantic."

Together, the countries composing the NATO and their overseas affiliates account for the great bulk of world resources and trade, and a concerted program of action on their part could largely determine the dominant character of international economic relations for the period ahead. However, it appears that some time may elapse before definite programs and concrete measures are formulated whereby these countries, individually and jointly, are to move toward their agreed objectives.[3] In view of this situation, and the still greater uncertainties as to the measures which may be taken by important countries in other regions of the world under the pressures of the next few years, only the most general observations now seem warranted as to the likely direction of foreign trade policies in the coming years.

Inward Orientation of Soviet Bloc Unpromising of Trade Expansion

From the countries under Soviet influence, of course, little is expected in the way of early movement toward more liberal trade controls and expansion of world commerce. Those countries have gone over to rigid state control, if not operation, of their foreign trade as of their domestic economies, and that makes changes in their commercial policies largely dependent upon shifts in the political objectives of the governments. Moreover, even more important than the restrictions now imposed by many countries of the free world upon the shipment to the Soviet bloc of materials and equipment with possible military potential, is the very limited range and amounts of products that these countries can furnish in payment for the goods they desire from outside the Soviet bloc. For, if reports from various directions are to be believed, the economies of these countries are being progressively reorganized and reoriented toward supplying the needs of the others within the group, and particularly the needs of the Soviet Union itself.

[3] Any new trade programs on the part of the NATO countries wait upon the position which the new Administration of the United States—the pivotal country in the group—is prepared to take upon the various aspects of its foreign economic relations. Definite decisions on these matters on the part of Washington, however, are being held in abeyance until the Congress shall have acted upon the recommendations of the bipartisan Commission on Foreign Economic Policy it has recently authorized. President Eisenhower had requested the establishment of such a body, to make a thorough reëxamination of the whole field, with a view to determining how far existing legislation and regulations stemming from it "can be modified or improved so as to achieve the highest possible levels of international trade without subjecting parts of our economy to sudden or serious strains." This Commission, completed late in August, 1953, is to report early next March, with the expectation of congressional action being taken upon its recommendations during the 1954 session.

Short of a radical change in the political relations between East and West, the general character of their present trade relations are unlikely to be substantially changed soon, unless some of the satellites should be able to break away from Soviet political domination, as did Yugoslavia. If they should then follow their own interests, it would probably mean reverting to a considerable extent toward the prewar pattern of their economic relations, which had been predominantly with Western Europe.

Recent Import Curbs by Free World Nations Probably a Temporary Regression

Concern has been expressed, however, over the recent tightening of trade controls also by many countries in various parts of the free world—the sterling area, South America, and even continental Europe. The question is asked whether this indicates that a definite reversal is under way from even the moderate application of more liberal principles toward which many countries of the free world appeared to be moving for several years, as their postwar recuperation proceeded.

Despite the uncertainties earlier indicated, there seems good reason to believe that—unless the world political situation should change materially, or a widespread economic recession develops—the recent tightening of trade controls will represent for most countries only a temporary divergence from their movement toward the objectives to which they have declared their adherence. It is more than likely that the disturbances arising out of the Korean conflict will be found to have only checked, but not reversed, their progress toward economic recuperation and financial balance. And as the readjustment is worked out, there should come a resumption of gradual progress toward relaxation of the various forms of restrictive and discriminatory controls, in the interest of the benefits they expect from a fuller and freer international exchange of goods.

Inconsistencies and Domestic Political Pressures May Require Tolerance

This is not to say that there may not continue to be a call for tolerance toward the actions of some governments that are inconsistent with their professed principles and even with some contractual commitments. That may be particularly true in the case of farm products. Political as well as economic considerations appear to place many governments in a position of having to provide a specially sheltered economic regime in support of their major agricultural producers.

Indeed, for some time to come, measures of foreign trade control normally frowned upon may at times have to be accepted as inescapable expressions of the concept that has grown in recent years, that neither the domestic nor the international objectives of nations should have complete dominance over the other. Alongside of the heightened recognition of the economic interdependence of nations born of the depression and the war years, governments have also become more concerned about shielding the domestic economy from too sharp shifts in the country's foreign trade, and many now feel a greater responsibility for fostering economic development or for maintaining high employment and income for their people. Practical adjustments will in some cases have to be worked out to harmonize such domestic pressures with an acceptable international trade policy.

Such deviations from the general trend toward more liberal conditions for international trading as may develop, and such compromise adjustments between domestic pressures and external obligations as may be resorted to, are most likely to occur in the economically under-developed countries, or in those only recently established as independent governments. Various of these countries appear to be going through a period of experimentation with unusual trade and financial arrangements, and in some cases with over-ambitious plans for rapid national development.

Further Spread of State Trading in Free-economy Countries Unlikely

Concern has often been expressed over the possible spread of direct governmental participation in foreign trade. To varying extents, this was resorted to widely by quite a number of countries during the period immediately after the close of World War II. Outside of the communist countries, however, and a few others with exceptionally centralized governmental controls of the economy, the high point of such governmental intervention in foreign trade appears to have been passed some time ago. The unsatisfactory experience under most of those experiments in the political handling of commercial transactions, as well as the strong pressure in democratic countries for allowing private enterprise the prime place in the conduct of economic affairs, are unlikely soon again to prompt wide resort to state foreign trading in most Western countries. Significant confirmation of this is afforded by the succession of steps taken by Great Britain during the recent past, in returning to private foreign traders the actual importation of various bulk foodstuffs and raw materials which for some years had been the exclusive province of the government, even when there is a general intergovernmental agreement regarding the over-all purchase and supply of the particular commodity.

Progress Toward Customs Unions or International Commodity Agreements Difficult

Various types of collective arrangements in the field of trade relations have been urged in recent years. Most prominent have been the projects for the lifting of national barriers to the unrestricted movement of goods between two or more neighboring countries, or for an agreement among the principal exporting and importing countries of a particular commodity, designed to ensure greater certainty of markets and supplies, and to limit the range of its price fluctuations.

The most advanced examples of these types of arrangements are: the customs union formed since World War II by Belgium, the Netherlands, and Luxemburg (BE-NE-LUX), which it is planned to expand into a full economic union; and the International Wheat Agreement, all but one of whose members participating in the Washington meeting of 1953 agreed upon its renewal for a second period under somewhat modified terms. Projects are now in varying stages of promotion or development for similar customs-free arrangements between various pairs or groups of countries, in Europe, Latin America, and the British overseas territories, and for broad international commodity agreements involving various basic products, agricultural and mineral.

While there is usually wide concurrence in the desirability of the advantages that could be derived from such collective trade arrangements when they are first proposed, their full costs and implications are seldom recognized at that stage. The usual history of prolonged and repeated negotiations in an effort to develop a generally acceptable practical plan for the establishment of such an arrangement, and the past record of very few successful outcomes, attest to the difficulties inherent in attempts to obtain agreement upon the mutual concessions necessary in order to harmonize the conflicting interests of the different countries involved. Even in the case of the Benelux customs union, for which the predisposing conditions were exceptionally favorable, the problems of adjusting the divergent national levels of prices, wages and taxes, and of reconciling the general economic and financial policies of the respective governments, have retarded the attainment of full freedom of trade within the enlarged area and the progress toward the full economic union contemplated.

Greater Likelihood of Progress Through Concerted than Collective Action

Although the seriousness of the difficulties involved can easily be exaggerated, experience indicates that they are sufficiently real to warrant only moderate optimism regarding the likelihood of many of the negotiations for such collective agreements being successfully concluded, or of rapid progress toward their implementation if concluded. Greater progress toward the objectives of such collective projects is probably to be looked for from concurrent action by a number of countries, acting independently, but as part of concerted programs of the type for which so many governments have recently expressed their desire.

In Europe in particular, many see interesting possibilities in the way of future concerted action on the part of the countries that have been coöperating in the Organization for European Economic Cooperation and the European Payments Union, even after the termination of the European Recovery Program in connection with which those organizations were originally established. This does not imply that they necessarily share the optimism of those who anticipate a general economic integration of Western Europe. Within a possibly more limited area, some observers also anticipate a gradual extension into other phases of their economic relations of the new concept of joint European action exemplified in the "Schuman Plan" for pooling the coal and steel industries of six countries—France, Western Germany, Italy, Belgium, the Netherlands, and Luxemburg—into a single market, within which these products are ultimately to move freely without duty or restriction.

It is expected to take a number of years to work out all the steps necessary for harmonizing the presently differing conditions in these industries of the member countries. However, the fact that by May, 1953, a single market has actually been inaugurated for the coal and steel of these countries, and that a sovereign High Authority has been vested with the supranational direction of so vital a part of the economy of Western Europe, represents remarkable progress in the realization of what a few years ago was only a bold dream. Only time will tell whether this warrants the high optimism of those who believe that this program, once entered upon, will inevitably lead to the extension of the coöperation of the participating countries into other fields of common interest. It should not be overlooked, of course, that the creation of this Western European Coal and Steel Community had working in its favor certain special considerations, notably, pressures for political rapprochement between the constituent countries and the common interest in the most effective joint defense program.

Aside from the possibility of developments in the way of collective or concerted action in their economic relations on the part of limited groups of countries, along the lines just discussed, the general course of international trade and trade policy during the years ahead will presumably be determined chiefly by the autonomous action of important countries or groups of them. The question therefore arises as to the directions in which they seem to be moving in this field.

GATT System of Multilateral Trade Engagements a Definite Advance

On the part of most of the thirty-odd nations which are participants in the General Agreement on Tariffs and Trade—countries which together have accounted for about 80 per cent of world trade—there seems little ground for expecting any wide or long-term retreat from the general program which they have accepted in principle. This novel arrangement in commercial policy developed since the close of World War II has certain features that represent distinct advances in dealing with the age-old problem of the trade relations between nations. It will be recalled that the GATT consists essentially of two parts: the specific agreements for the reduction or stabilization of tariff rates and preferences; and the collective code of principles by which the contracting governments have undertaken to regulate their foreign trade in other respects, as soon as specified limiting conditions allow.

The shift from the traditional bilateral trade agreements to simultaneous negotiations by each country with each of a large number of other countries, which together usually account for the major part of its trade, and with the understanding that the resulting duty reductions or bindings are then generalized to all contracting parties, is regarded by many observers as constituting a historic forward step, in broadening the concept and pattern of international trade arrangements.

New Standards for Official Trade Practices Growing in Prestige

The general provisions accompanying the specific tariff schedules, prescribing the proper governmental conduct in other aspects of foreign trade regulation, have come to be recognized as setting up a new standard of international morality in this hitherto largely unregulated field. They have already come to operate as an appreciable restraint upon individual governments from putting into effect, unilaterally, irregular measures that may have harmful effects upon the trade of others. In those few cases where action inconsistent with their commitments under the GATT have become domestically inescapable, the growing respect for these new standards of international trade conduct has been evidenced by the fact that the member governments have recognized the need to offer justification before world opinion, at the periodic meeting of the contracting parties, and to accept an offsetting withdrawal of advantages to which their own trade would otherwise be entitled.

Some governments have at times felt irked by particular limitations upon their freedom of action resulting from their undertakings under the GATT. Although members can withdraw from the agreement upon relatively short notice, however, no important trading country has yet taken such a step, and only to a minor extent have governments taken advantage of the provision for being relieved of their obligation to maintain particular tariffs rates. The first important test came in the United Kingdom during the past year, when there was strong agitation for abandoning the GATT program in favor of an intensified preferential trade system within the Commonwealth. The decision at the earlier mentioned London Conference of December, 1952, not to abandon the GATT program, seems significant.

Serious Retreat by GATT Nations from Liberal Trade Goals Unlikely

From some directions question has been raised as to the soundness of expecting the GATT in its present form to continue as a satisfactory framework of operations for the long term, and various modifications have been proposed. Provision exists for changes in the Agreement at periodic intervals, the next occurring at the end of 1953, and some alterations in particular provisions of the agreement will doubtless be found desirable in the light of experience and changing conditions over the years. Basically, however, the majority of the important trading countries apparently believe that it is to their own long-run interest to move concurrently—as their special limiting conditions allow—toward a more liberal and less discriminatory regime in their trade relations with other countries, on a reciprocal basis, for the general benefit to be derived from an expanding world production and the most advantageous exchange of goods.

In fine, the period ahead may see some further postponements of goals in the field of international trade relations, such as happened to the earlier expectation that the period of transitional adjustment after World War II would be substantially over by early 1952, and even some limited deviations or temporary retreats from liberalized regimes once entered upon. On balance, however, the next decade is more than likely to see net progress in the direction of the more liberal standards and the more accommodating attitudes which the majority of the important trading countries of the free world have set up as their common guide and goal.

www.ingramcontent.com/pod-product-compliance
Ingram Content Group UK Ltd.
Pitfield, Milton Keynes, MK11 3LW, UK
UKHW040234290926
15471UKWH00002B/180

9 780520 34934